BRIDGES TO RECOVERY

ADDICTION, FAMILY THERAPY, AND MULTICULTURAL TREATMENT

Edited by
Jo-Ann Krestan

THE FREE PRESS

NEW YORK   LONDON   SYDNEY   SINGAPORE

*f*P

THE FREE PRESS
A Division of Simon & Schuster, Inc.
1230 Avenue of the Americas
New York, NY 10020

Book design by Ellen R. Sasahara

Manufactured in the United States of America

10 9 8 7 6 5 4 3 2

LIBRARY OF CONGRESS CATALOGING-IN-PUBLICATION DATA
Bridges to recovery : addiction, family therapy, and multicultural treatment/
edited by Jo-Ann Krestan.
p.   cm.
Includes bibliographical references and index.
1. Minorities—Alcohol use—United States—Prevention.
2. Minorities—Substance use—United States—Prevention.
3. Alcoholics—Rehabilitation—United States.
4. Addicts—Rehabilitation—United States.
5. Alcoholism—Treatment—United States.
6. Substance abuse—Treatment—United States.
7. Alcoholism counseling—United States.
8. Drug abuse counseling—United States.
9. Cross-cultural counseling—United States.
10. Family psychotherapy—United States.
I. Krestan, Jo-Ann.
HV5199.5.B75   2000
362.29'089'00973—dc21   99-049370

ISBN 0-684-84649-7

To Dad

1907–1998

Pravda Vítězí

Contents

About the Contributors

Moises Barón, PhD, Director, Counseling Center and adjunct faculty, School of Education, University of San Diego, California

Amy Bibb, MSW, Family Institute of New Jersey and private practice in Metuchen and Red Bank, New Jersey

Laura Chakrin Cable, MSW, LICSW, Co-Director of the Family Institute of Providence and private practice in Providence, Rhode Island

Georges J. Casimir, MD, Chief, Outpatient Mental Health Services, Kingsbrook Jewish Medical Center, Brooklyn, and Associate Professor of Psychiatry, SUNY Health Science Center, Brooklyn, New York

Peter Chang, PhD, Associate Professor, California School of Professional Psychology and private practice in Oakland, California

Don Coyhis, Director and Founder, White Bison, Inc., Colorado Springs, Colorado

Jeffrey Ellias-Frankel, PhD, Colts Neck Consulting Group, Colts Neck, New Jersey

Miguel Hernandez, MSW, Program Coordinator, Roberto Clemente Center and faculty, Ackerman Institute for Family Therapy, New York, New York

Jacqueline Hudak, MEd, Director, Family Therapy Associates of Monmouth County and faculty, Family Institute of New Jersey, Metuchen, New Jersey

Jo-Ann Krestan, MA, LMFT, LSAC, Visiting Faculty, Family Institute of New Jersey, Metuchen, New Jersey, and consultant, Surry, Maine and Castle Valley, Utah.

Alan Oberman, MSW, CADC, CCGC, Catholic Charities and Colts Neck Consulting Group, Colts Neck, New Jersey

Deniece J. Reid, MSW, LCSW, MATS, CDA, Director of Pastoral Counseling, The Cathedral/Second Baptist Church, Perth Amboy, New Jersey

Richard Simonelli, writer and advocate, Native American issues; Director, Mountain Sage Publishing, Boulder, Colorado

Kelly Ward, LCSW, CADC, Assistant Professor, Department of Social Work, Monmouth University and Colts Neck Consulting Group, Colts Neck, New Jersey

ACKNOWLEDGMENTS

I WANT TO ACKNOWLEDGE the following experts in the fields of cultural diversity, addiction, and family systems for so generously sharing their time and their ideas with me at one point or another in the process of conceptualizing and editing *Bridges to Recovery*. I spoke briefly with some of them, and badgered others for hours on the phone. Some of them may have little idea of how critical their own ideas, support, writing, and teaching have been to this project.

Monica McGoldrick
Celia Jaes Falicov
Dan Barmetler
Peter Bell
Sandra Coleman
Elaine Pinderhughes
Fernando Colon
Nydia Garcia-Preto
Michael Elkin
Rhea Almeida

My thanks go to my Aunt Dorothy, who has always been there.

To my editor, Philip Rappaport, and my agent, Ellen Geiger, for their belief in this project. To Celia Knight, whose sensitivity and commitment to the copyediting process was extraordinary.

To the staff and friends of White Bison: to Richard Simonelli for an ongoing dialogue that I hope will continue; to Maggie, whose support at a critical time might have saved my border collie's life; to Bea Ferrigno, who participated as needed; and to Lili, without whose intervention I might never have met the others.

To Molly Layton for continuing to tell me I had a "rising spirit" during the worst of times. To Lois Braverman for her friendship, her clear mind, and her wisdom.

To Carol Lacy, *compadre*, gadfly, and devil's advocate—the friend who always wants the best for me—for her encouragement, editorial skills, clear thinking, and tireless work on the manuscript. She brought her full heart and mind to this project, and I could never have done it without her. She also made me laugh from Maine to Mexico.

To the contributors—Deniece, Miguel, Moises, Peter, Jeff, Alan, Kelly, Amy, Georges, Laura, Don, and Jackie—from the bottom of my heart for accepting this challenge and seeing it through.

INTRODUCTION

THIS BOOK REALLY BEGAN in the early nineties, on an icy, rain-soaked January day. I had been invited to the Roberto Clemente Guidance Center, in New York City, to teach a seminar on the family systems model of treatment first elaborated in *The Responsibility Trap* (Bepko and Krestan, 1985). This model included three sets of contructs central to the understanding and treatment of addiction in family systems: over- and underresponsibility; pride, shame, and power; and the role of alcohol as a mediator of gender role constriction.

I met Miguel Hernandez that day. I was excited by his creativity; his passion for helping people. I was also struck by the creativity of the Guidance Center's multicultural group of clinicians in applying these ideas to largely poor, ethnic minority, immigrant families. Our ideas on gender and addiction signified fairly innovative scrutiny of the interfaces between the family system, the addictive system, and the larger social system as they are embedded in gender role socialization. However, what I came away with on that cold January day was a recognition of the degree to which our ideas were culture bound as well as gender bound. For instance, I had long been fascinated by Bateson's view of power in his essay on the epistemology of alcoholism, yet it had never before occurred to me that power, in the sense of "power over," might not be universally valued, which is the case in the Native American Indian culture. At the conference I listened to African American clinicians discuss overresponsibility partially as a function of the differing work potentials for African American women and men, and I recalled a conversation I had had the previous year in Santa Fe when a Navajo clinician told me that overresponsibility was not as problematic in her Nation as in the Anglo culture, because the centrality of women is overt, not covert.

After the conference, I scribbled notes for a project that would translate the ideas in *The Responsibility Trap* into more culturally relevant terms.

I spent the next few years more absorbed with other professional issues, other projects, but each time Monica McGoldrick published a work on eth-

1

nicity, or Celia Falicov wrote or talked on systemic views of culture, or the American Family Therapy Academy, where I was privileged to serve as a board member for three years, struggled with diversity, the impulse to develop my idea of a project on multiculturalism and addiction reappeared.

So here we are: *Bridges to Recovery: Addiction, Family Therapy, and Multicultural Treatment.*

Since my presentation at Clemente, there has been an explosion of writing on multiculturalism, addiction, and family systems thinking. All of us are embedded in diverse ecological contexts. *Workforce 2000,* a report by the Hudson Institute, tells us that the population of the United States is changing at a quickening rate; it claims that women, immigrants, and non-Whites will constitute more than five-sixths of the additions to the workforce between now and the year 2000. The 1990 Census Bureau statistics tell us that minorities will be the numerical majority in the United States population by the year 2056. As we enter the new millennium, health experts tell us, substance abuse remains one of the largest and most costly health care problems in America.[1] Moreover, our most basic concepts are changing: family systems thinking has been redefining the very idea of family.

Multicultural competence and the acknowledgment of class, gender, and sexual diversity are critically relevant dimensions of effective treatment in the fields of addiction and marriage and family therapy in the diverse postmodern world in which we live, teach, and practice. This book offers a framework that will help practitioners elicit and understand the specific ecological story that is needed to adequately treat addictive families. It describes those characteristics of different ethnic groups that are relevant to addiction, characteristics mediated by such relevant sociological variables as gender, class, and generation.

---

1. Although prevalence studies by the National Institute of Drug Abuse, the National Institute of Mental Health, and the Drug Abuse Warning Network are not without problems in data collection, they still show that alcohol is America's drug of choice. There has been some overall decline in alcohol consumption since 1981, but it is estimated that there are nineteen million problem drinkers and some eight million alcoholics. The use of marijuana, although still the most common illicit drug, is declining. Heroin use appears to be becoming popular again. As use of certain substances declines, use of other substances increases. Patterns of use differ in different population subgroups. Hispanics, except for Mexican Americans, seem to have a greater prevalence of alcohol problems than does the general adult population. Native Americans, although using about the same amount of alcohol as the general adult population probably use more marijuana, and inhalants. Urban ghetto populations, of all ethnic groups, shifted from heroin to cocaine in the eighties, and there are many studies of drug use by inner-city minorities that expose the relationship of drug abuse and crime. See "Epidemiology of Alcohol and Drug Abuse," in *Substance Abuse: A Comprehensive Textbook,* 2nd. ed., ed. J. H. Lowinson, P. Ruiz, R. B. Millman, and J. G. Langrod (Baltimore: Williams & Wilkins, 1992), pp. 23–25.

Addiction treatment and family therapy have in some ways grown up together. Both professions have seen tremendous growth and change since the mid-sixties. Family therapy has spawned several different theoretical and clinical models for optimal family functioning. Addiction treatment has expanded from the treatment of alcoholism and heroin addiction to include treatment for polydrug addiction, chemical dependency, and other addictions, such as addiction to sex, food, gambling, and spending.

Addiction treatment and family therapy have also influenced one another. Today substance abuse treatment and what we have come to call the "recovery movement" have broadened to include community support and residential treatment for the families of addicts, for codependents (see, for example, Krestan, 1990), and for adult children of alcoholics. The term *dysfunctional family* refers to at least sixty different maladies, all with related family problems. Addiction recovery books and articles make frequent reference to and have popularized many of the concepts in family therapy. Claudia Black, Sharon Wegscheider-Cruz, Janet Woititz, and Timmen Cermak were among the first addiction specialists to look at family roles, family rules, and the intergenerational effects of substance abuse. The PBS series *Focus on Family*, with John Bradshaw, was one of the most successful television series in recent years. Unfortunately, however, the addiction recovery movement has presented family therapy ideas in a highly hybridized and often inaccurate way in order to make them more palatable for popular consumption.

Family therapists did not write extensively on alcohol and drug addiction and the recovery movement until the mid-eighties. Steinglass, Bennett, Wolin, and Reiss formulated the concept of the alcoholic family. Coleman, Stanton, and Todd introduced creative ideas on the relationship of drug abuse to loss. Berenson, in his articles and teaching, opened a dialogue on spirituality. Elkin analyzed the relationship between power and addiction. Treadway, tirelessly teaching around the world, raised consciousness about alcoholism. Bepko and Krestan, in *The Responsibility Trap: A Blueprint for Treating the Alcoholic Family*, provided the first substantive clinical bridge between family systems approaches to addiction, the twelve-step programs, and the recovery movement. *The Responsibility Trap* also introduced the idea of addressing gender differences in socialization as a major emphasis in treatment. Bepko and Krestan's treatment model has been clinically useful with all types of substance abuse, including eating disorders and the noningestive addictions, such as gambling.

The family therapy profession has attempted to make theory and treatment of addiction and families relevant to issues of class, gender, and ethnicity. Minuchin's work paved the way for a school of family therapy that dealt with class. The feminist critique of family therapy began with Hare-Mustin's classic article "A Feminist Approach to Family Therapy." McGoldrick, Giordano, and Pearce's *Ethnicity and Family Therapy* (released in 1996 in a second edition) pioneered family therapy's consideration of cultural variables, as did Falicov's many articles. Only in the past few years, however, has family therapy as a whole dealt with issues of cultural diversity. Despite these initial efforts to bring theory and practice into the postmodern world, family therapy professionals still need a ready resource that will help them successfully treat the diverse families that come to them in crisis. The substance abuse literature is beginning to address issues of class, culture, "race," and sexual orientation. *Feminism and Addiction* (Bepko, 1991) was the first serious attempt to make the family treatment of substance abuse relevant to women.

Research and writing on multiculturalism and diversity have also increased dramatically. However, studies of ethnic and "racial" variation have gone in and out of favor and fashion with the changing political climate.

This book is a first of its kind. My hope is that we will move forward in integrating family therapy with addiction treatment and that this book will be a resource that will increase cross-cultural and interdisciplinary collaboration and spark further research. In writing our chapters, my contributors and I faced a number of challenges, including the following:

- A growing belief that the very categories we were using—not just gender but "race" and class as well—were social constructions. (Although I felt stuck with the language of categories, I feel so strongly about the social construction of the concept of "race," while recognizing its political utility, that the word *race* is frequently used in quotes in this introduction.)
- A recognition of the tremendous heterogeneity within cultural groupings.
- Concern over issues of inclusion and exclusion. (For example, who are the African Americans? The descendants of slaves? The Caribbean Islanders? The Muslims? The Baptists?)
- Problems with terminology. (Is it Native American or American Indian or Native American Indian? Latino or Hispanic? Lippard, 1990, an art writer and activist, says, "Three kinds of naming operate culturally through both word and image" [p. 19]. The three kinds of naming are "self-naming, . . . the supposedly neutral label imposed from outside, which may include implicitly negative stereotyping and is often insepara-

ble from the third, explicit racist namecalling" [p. 20]. The authors of the chapters in this book have named in different ways, for different reasons.)
- Concern for consistency between chapters. (Should the chapters be "Krestanized," or should the editor's role be to edit only for clarity while keeping the diverse voices and styles of the contributors?)

So here we are: A diversity of styles and voices won out. I have insisted on little, only that the contributors write what they truly believe. I have encouraged speculation and opinion, reasoning that this is not a work tied to empirical research (although research is extensively reviewed and cited) but a clinical work—in some cases from a somewhat anthropological and historical perspective. Several of the contributors have also made extensive use of personal interviews and communications in supplementing their other data.

ORGANIZATION AND CONTENT OF THIS BOOK

PART ONE: PERSPECTIVES

THE FIRST CHAPTER, on power and shame, explores the dominant treatment paradigm for alcoholism by deconstructing ideas of power as they have evolved from the Western Eurocentric ideas that spurred the initial colonization of the North American continent. In this chapter I introduce the concept of "values of origin" to capsulize the belief systems of different groups as they relate to addiction and recovery. Values of origin encompass not only beliefs about family, spirituality, power, and external and internal loci of control but also beliefs about alcohol and other drugs. Gender practices, spiritual belief systems, and choice of rural versus urban living also relate to values of origin. It is my belief that the concept of values of origin, if operationalized, might yield yet another lens through which we can view individuals, families, and groups instead of resorting to our socially constructed categories.

In the cross-cultural literature on alcohol studies, cultures and nations have long been classified by their attitudes toward drinking, that is, by whether they are abstinent, ambivalent, or temperate. They have also been compared on measures such as per capita alcohol consumption, alcohol and drug policies, annual deaths by cirrhosis per 100,000, epidemiology of alcohol dependence, and the social consequences of alcohol and drug addiction. They have been categorized by beverage preference (that is, as wine-, beer-, and spirit-drinking cultures) and by reasons for drinking and using drugs (that is, whether utilitarian, celebratory, ritualistic, or spiritual). They have been compared on demographics, notably social class, gender, religious denomination, and age. (Heath, 1995; Ninth Special Report to the U.S. Congress, 1997). Values of origin (Krestan) are key in determining a family's "ecological niche" (Falicov, 1995) with respect to addiction.

Cable starts her chapter on adult children of alcoholics (ACOA) by writing, "Once upon a time North American children learned to read with Dick and Jane. The White, Christian, blond-haired children lived with their mother, father, cat, and dog in a clean house on a tree-lined street." Placing the ACOA movement in historical context, Cable applies Falicov's multidimensional comparative approach to an exploration of the research literature and to the self-help traditions within the ACOA movement. Enunciating various themes as organizing principles for the material, she challenges the "tyranny of normality," celebrates resilience, and relates postmodernism to the clinical treatment of adult children of alcoholics.

PART TWO: ETHNIC ECOLOGIES

PART TWO OF THIS BOOK integrates what we know about ecological contexts, addiction, and family systems in ways that are immediately useful for clinicians.

Most of the contributors struggled with the need for a dialectical process between an ethnic-focus approach and Falicov's multidimensional comparative approach (Falicov, 1995). Ellias-Frankel, Oberman, and Ward quote an old joke: "Two Jews meet and there are three opinions." Rather than holding three opinions, they speak in terms of "ethnic themes" that do not "determine a particular response but rather [pose] an overt or covert question to which members of the group may have dissimilar responses." Dispelling the myth that Jews don't drink or have other addiction problems, they insist, "The most important fact to grasp about Jewish addiction is that it exists and is significantly underdiagnosed and undertreated."

Chang explores major commonalities among Asian Americans and Pacific Islanders while integrating highly particular and useful information about a wide range of groups. The compassionate depth of his work is reflected in discussions of the Asian historical background, especially migration and loss, and his analysis of families, relationships, gender roles, communication, harmony, and addictions. His clinical explications are extremely specific and practical. His thoughtful explorations of values and the poignancy of his depiction of the migrant's experiences of loneliness and loss stayed with me from my first reading of his first draft.

Hudak uses an ethnic-focus approach to groups of European origin. It is interesting that when I decided to treat European groups as an ethnic category, we found that there was more anthropological than clinical literature available. This presents new questions about assumptions inherent in a dominant discourse that was largely formed by the early settlers from European countries (see chapter 1). The richness of Hudak's case studies teaches us much about treatment and compensates for the lack of literature. The anthropological information that is available suggests that these individual groups do in fact have significant ecological differences that impact on addiction patterns and treatment.

Reid, a social worker, trained family therapist, pastoral counselor, and Baptist preacher, writes on African Americans with an immediacy that joins expression with commitment. According to Knox (1985), "the organized church is by far the most profound instrument available to Blacks when it comes to coping with the multiplicity of problems that beset their lives" (p. 35), and, as Harrison Pipes (1997) says, "undoubtedly, the old-time Black preacher is the Black leader today; it is to him that the great majority of Blacks in this country look for guidance" (p. 64).

Reid's chapter, which reflects her pastoral calling, is consistent with Pipes' formulation of old-time religion: it uses words familiar to her audience; a narrative voice meant for listening more than reading; a figurative style with heavy use of metaphor, often drawn from the Bible; and rhythmical, sometimes elliptical, sentences. It appeals to emotion as much as to reason.

In the chapter by Hernandez and in the one by Bibb and Casimir, our attention is directed to how U.S. foreign policy and the international drug trade closely affect addiction among Puerto Rican and West Indian immigrants, respectively. Since I do not believe we ever speak apart from context, I have no difficulty with material that some readers may consider highly politicized. As Almeida, Woods, Messineo, and Font (1998) point out, family theory has too frequently considered the systems in the "interior" of family life while neglecting the larger social systems. Even feminist theory, while introducing an analysis of power inequities, has paid insufficient attention to multiple levels of oppression. Hernandez' approach directly deconstructs addiction in the Puerto Rican population as a multilevel systemic phenomenon that is often rooted in racism, classism, and oppression. I believe that there is a place in clinical work for the acceptance and encouragement of linear rage, as well as for systemic responsibility.

Clinically, Hernandez, true to the creativity that first struck me, applies Stivers' (1976) idea of a group adopting a dominant group's stereotype when he writes, "The central theme I try to discuss is how by losing control and becoming addicted the client has fallen into the trap of acting out the stereotyped view that the dominant group has about Puerto Ricans. I tell my clients that every time they lose control, they become another number in the statistics that proves to 'them' that Puerto Ricans are 'spiks who don't do nothing but get high'. Talking about the impact that poverty, migration, and ethnic minority reality have on our lives is done to contextualize addiction within a sociopolitical context."

Bibb and Casimir state in the opening to their chapter, "Holding individuals personally accountable must be balanced with knowledge of the powerful social, geographic, and economic forces that created and now maintain the flow of alcohol and drugs abroad and in North America. It is important to attend not only to the psychological and clinical dilemmas that substance abusers face but also to their social and community context. Addiction is extremely personal and yet extremely global." Their discussion of addiction and West Indians includes specific clinical issues, suggestions for needed research agendas, and comments on the international drug trade.

Baron meets the challenge of writing about the enormous complexity of our largest immigrant group, the Mexican Americans. This group is burdened by heavy substance abuse. Baron focuses on a way of assessing a particular family at a particular moment in time. He synthesizes several models (notably those of Falicov, Sue and Sue, and Jones) in a methodology that pays particular attention to acculturation, ethnic identity development, and worldview. He also offers an extremely comprehensive review of the literature. Of the enigmatic character of the Mexican, the late Octavio Paz (1985) wrote, "It is revealing that our intimacy never flowers in a natural way, only when incited by fiestas, alcohol or death" (p. 70) and "There is nothing so joyous as a Mexican fiesta, but there is also nothing so sorrowful. Fiesta night is also a night of mourning" (p. 53).

"Mitakuye Oyasin" (Lakota for "All Our Relations")

Don Coyhis, director of White Bison, is a man I wanted to connect with for several years. I knew that Don, following a vision quest, had exchanged his corporate life for a path of bringing substance abuse recovery to his own people. In a series of "coincidences" involving a stranger in Las Cruces, New Mexico, I finally did track Don down. After much discussion he and his staff, notably Richard Simonelli, shared a series of Don's talks, originally given in the oral tradition of Don's people and transcribed by Richard. The addiction recovery program for Native Americans described in chapter 3 represents a unique blend of the wisdom of the medicine wheel and a twelve-step approach to sobriety. One of the beauties of White Bison's approach to the "red road of sobriety" is its ability to transcend the heterogeneity of Indian nations and traditions by synthesizing symbols and rituals that are common to all.

FUTURE DIRECTIONS

SEVERAL ECOLOGICAL CONTEXTS deserve more exploration in relationship to addiction recovery in the twenty-first century:

1. THE ROLE OF GENDER

It is a consistent finding across every group that the most prevalent risk factor for addiction, other than having an alcoholic parent, is gender—that is, being male. The Ninth Special Report to the U.S. Congress on Alcohol and Health (1997) concludes, "Studies confirm that women drink less and report fewer alcohol-related problems than men do" (p. 27). Heath (1995), an anthropologist, concurs: "One measure of status that is recognized everywhere is gender (what many consider to be the sociocultural implications of the biological category of sex differentiation) . . . men drink more, and more often, than do women. (This is almost a cultural universal with only two peculiar instances—both small migrant groups in novel settings—known where the opposite holds)" (p. 337). The Ninth Special Report also concludes that future research on women and alcohol use should pay particular attention to "childhood and adult violent victimizations, depression, sexual experience, and the influence of husbands' or partners' drinking" (p. 28). It seems significant that these factors, which are predictors of women's drinking, have as much to do with the women's relationship to men as to the women themselves.

2. THE ROLE OF SPIRITUAL/RELIGIOUS BELIEF SYSTEMS

It is a consistent finding that religious belief systems are often predictors of drinking behavior, and yet little attention has been paid to religion as a demographic variable since Cahalan, Cisisn, and Crossley did the original research in 1969. Alcoholism is often considered a disease of the mind, body, and spirit; Chappel (1997) and Royce (1995) consider it a spiritual disease.

There appears to be considerable cultural resistance to this idea. Relatively little research has been done on the relationship between alcoholism recovery and spirituality despite studies that identify spiritual healing as a major contributor to the overall health of individuals (Benson, 1976; Borysenko, 1988; Michaud, 1998; Ornish, 1995).

3. ADOLESCENCE

Adolescence in different groups (particularly Latino), with its potential for engendering cross-generational conflict, its heavily researched risk factors, and its vulnerability both to addiction and to early intervention deserves a book of its own. The literature on risk and protection factors in adolescence is extensive. As a start I recommend Jose Szapocznik's work on prevention of alcohol and drug abuse among Latino youth, particularly his work on multicultural effectiveness training.

4. THE RURAL CONTEXT

An excellent resource, published by the National Institute of Drug Abuse, is *Rural Substance Abuse: State of Knowledge and Issues* (1997), which decisively dispels the myth of rural insulation from drug problems. Although one quarter of Americans live in rural areas and although among some groups (for example, African Americans) there seems to be increasing migration to rural areas from urban areas, rural America has rarely been the focus of concern about substance use and abuse. The tremendous economic downturns in rural areas create special vulnerabilities to psychosocial problems and addiction, and since the agricultural community is moving more toward hiring single, male migrant workers, instead of families, we might expect alcohol and drug use within the migrant populations to escalate.

5. GROUPS OF EUROPEAN ORIGIN

We have not talked about Franco-American concentrations in New England, the legacy of high suicide rates in the Nordic countries and their relationship to alcoholism in Nordic populations in the upper Midwest, the role of vodka as a medium of exchange in a crumbling Russian economy and our increasing population of Russian immigrants.

As Lippard (1990) says, "We have not yet developed a theory of multiplicity that is neither assimilative nor separative—one that is, above all, relational" (p. 21).

What we have done is to begin.

Jo-Ann Krestan
November 1998
Surry, Maine
and
Castle Valley, Utah

REFERENCES

Almeida, R., Woods, R., Messineo, T., & Font, R. (1998). The Cultural Context Model: An Overview. In M. McGoldrick (Ed.), *Re-Visioning Family Therapy*. New York: Guilford Press.

Bateson, G. (1972). *Steps to an Ecology of Mind*. New York: Chandler.

Benson, H. (1976). *The Relaxation Response*. New York: Avon Books.

Bepko, C. (1991). *Feminism and Addiction*. New York: Haworth Press.

Bepko, C., with Krestan, J. (1985). *The Responsibility Trap: A Blueprint for Treating the Alcoholic Family*. New York: The Free Press.

Black, C., (1987). *It Will Never Happen to Me*. New York: Ballantine Books. (Originally printed 1981, Denver: M.A.C.).

Borysenko, J. (1988). *Minding the Body, Mending the Mind*. New York: Bantam.

Cahalan, D., Cisisn, I. H., & Crossley, H. M. (1969). *American Drinking Practices: A National Study of Drinking Behavior and Attitudes*. New Brunswick, NJ: Rutgers Center of Alcohol Studies. New Haven, CT: College & University Press.

Chappel, J. N. (1997) Spirituality and Addiction Psychiatry. In N. S. Miller (Ed.), *Principles and Practice of Addictions in Psychiatry* (pp. 416–421). Philadelphia: Saunders.

Coleman, S. B. (1985). *Failures in Family Therapy*. New York: Guilford Press.

Elkin, M. (1990). *Families under the Influence: Changing Alcoholic Patterns*. New York: W. W. Norton.

Falicov, C. J. (1995). Training to Think Culturally: A Multidimensional Comparative Framework. *Family Process, 34*, 181–193.

Hare-Mustin, R. T. (1978). A Feminist Approach to Family Therapy. *Family Process, 17*, 181–193.

Hudak, J., Krestan, J., & Bepko, C. (1999). Alcohol Problems and the Family Life Cycle. In B. Carter and M. McGoldrick (Eds.), *The Expanded Family Life Cycle: Individual, Family, and Social Perspectives* (3rd ed., pp. 455–469). Boston: Allyn and Bacon.

Inclan, J. & Hernandez, M. (1992). Cross-Cultural Perspectives and Codependence: The Case of Poor Hispanics. *American Journal of Orthopsychiatry, 62*(2), 245–255.

Knox, D. H. (1985). Spirituality: A Tool in the Assessment and Treatment of Black Alcoholics and Their Families. In F. L. Brisbane and M. Womble (Eds.), *Treatment of Black Alcoholics* in *Alcoholism Treatment Quarterly, 2*(3 and 4), 31–44. New York: Haworth Press.

Lippard, L. R. (1990). *Mixed Blessings: New Art in a Multicultural America*. New York: Pantheon Books.

McGoldrick, M. (Ed.) (1998). *Re-visioning Family Therapy: Race, Culture and Gender in Clinical Practice*. New York: Guilford Press.

Michaud, E. (1998, December). Do You Have the Miracle Healer in You? *Prevention* magazine, pp. 107–113.

Middelton-Moz J. & Dwinell, L. (1986). After the Tears: Working Through Grief, Loss, and Depression with Adult Children of Alcoholics. In R. J. Ackerman (Ed.), *Growing in the Shadow: Children of Alcoholics*. Pompano Beach, FL: Health Communications.

Ornish, D. (1995). *Dr. Dean Ornish's Program for Reversing Heart Disease*. New York: Ivy Books.

Paz, O. (1985). *The Labyrinth of Solitude*. New York: Grove Press.

Pipes, H. (1997) "Old-Time Religion: Benches Can't Say "Amen." In H. P. McAdoo, *Black Families* (3rd ed.). Thousand Oaks, CA: Sage.

Roberston, E. B., Sloboda, Z., Boyd, G. M., Beatty, L. & Kozel, N. (1997). "Rural Substance Abuse: State of Knowledge and Issues." Monograph No. 168, NIAAA, U.S. Dept of Health and Human Services, National Institutes of Health, Rockville, MD.

Royce, J. E. (1995). Effects of Alcoholism and Recovery on Spirituality. *Journal of Chemical Dependency Treatment*, 5(2), 19–37.

Steinglass, P. (1987). *Alcoholic Family*. New York: Basic Books.

Stivers, R. (1976). *A Hair of the Dog: Irish Drinking and American Stereotype*. University Park, PA, and London: Pennsylvania State University Press.

Szapocznik, J. (Ed.) (1994). *A Hispanic/Latino Family Approach to Substance Abuse Prevention*. Rockville, MD: Center for Substance Abuse Prevention.

Szapocznik, J., & Kurtines, W. (1989). *Breakthroughs in Family Therapy with Drug Abusing Problem Youth*. New York: Springer.

Treadway, D. C. (1989). *Before It's Too Late: Working with Substance Abuse in the Family*. New York: W. W. Norton.

Woititz, J. G. (1990). *Adult Children of Alcoholics* (Rev. ed.). Deerfield Beach, FL. (Originally published 1983).

Wolin, S. (1992). *The Resilient Self: How Survivors of Troubled Families Rise Above Adversity*. New York: Villard Books.

BRIDGES TO
RECOVERY

CHAPTER ONE

ADDICTION, POWER, AND POWERLESSNESS

Jo-Ann Krestan

THE ECOLOGY OF ADDICTION in a multicultural society requires us, as family therapists and addiction counselors, to re-examine two core ideas that have historically guided our treatment of addiction in the United States: power and powerlessness. Pride, false pride, and shame are closely related concepts and must also be viewed in a multicultural context.

Power and powerlessness are concepts laden with multiple meanings. Understanding the ecology of addiction as it relates to a particular individual or group requires us to first think about these concepts in a generic way and to then particularize them to the individual or group. The founders of Alcoholics Anonymous and family systems thinkers like Gregory Bateson based their beliefs about the nature of addiction on the Western European view, which is primarily "power over." I will address the concept of "power over" at some length, because traditional addiction treatment in the United States, often wedded to a twelve-step approach, evolved from this Western European view. It is in the context of this view that addicts are asked to embrace the idea of powerlessness over their addiction. Only then, we tell them, can they regain power over their life. The first step in recovery in Alcoholics Anonymous, the dominant paradigm for most addiction treatment in the United States, occurs when addicts recite, "[We] admitted we were powerless over alcohol, that our lives have become unmanageable." This admission of powerlessness that AA insists on is key to the shift in the addict's belief system and crucial to dismantling what Karen Horney (1937) calls "neurotic pride." In his concept of the symmetrical structure of "alcoholic pride" Gregory Bateson (1972) too recognized the necessity for addicts to shift their stance from one that asserts domination over the self, others, and the environment to one that accepts the reality of limitation, a concept that is foreign to our Western culture.

It is necessary to broaden our thinking about what it means to have

15

power or to be powerless and examine what it is about these prevailing views of power that can set the stage for addiction.

KINDS OF POWER

IN HER BOOK *Understanding Race, Ethnicity, and Power*, Pinderhughes (1989) wrote:

> People experience the presence or absence of power in many areas of life. For power is a systemic phenomenon, a key factor in functioning. . . . Internal power is manifest in the individual's sense of mastery or competence. The power relationships between people determine whether their interactions are characterized by dominance-subordination or equality. These styles of interaction are, in turn, affected by the status and roles assigned within the group or the larger society. (P. 110)

There are four related kinds of power:

Individual
Interpersonal
Socio/Cultural
Spiritual

Let us first deconstruct these kinds of power and posit how addicts think of each of them. I believe that addicts, in their addiction, identify with the dominant discourse of "power over" and that they must learn to view this discourse as "power to" if they are to recover from their addictions.

INDIVIDUAL POWER

Individual "power to" is synonymous with empowerment and includes feelings of self-control, subjectivity, and the ability to define one's own life. It is the power to choose. For example, although we have no say about the family of origin we are born to, we can learn to make choices about family relationships that empower rather than victimize us. For the addict, "power to" is the power to surrender, a paradox I examine later in this chapter.

Individual "power over" may extend to total control of one's feelings or to the illusion of total control over one's life. Gender-linked messages about the control of feelings, such as the suppression of male vulnerability or of female anger, teach people that they have individual power over their feelings, thereby constricting normal emotional behavior. Individual "power over" denies the need to act in a context with others. Those who insist on having this kind of power will have difficulty submitting to authority. Any absence of control is viewed by them as *being* controlled and therefore out of control. For example, being a member of the crew on a sailboat rather than the captain may be experienced as being powerless, rather than simply as being a team player. The individual who must have "power over" will have difficulty relinquishing control when cooperation is needed. For example, the addict says, "I can control my habit. I have power over my addiction."

INTERPERSONAL POWER

Interpersonal "power to" is the power to be heard in a group, perhaps to become the leader. It is the power to make choices and take positions about what one will or will not do, rather than just react to situations in relationships. For the addict, "power to" means the ability to leave bar friends and go to an AA meeting. It empowers addicts to exercise a healthy choice, such as to amend their relationships in sobriety.

However, interpersonal "power to" can lead to "power over." One's power to enlist in a cause may become institutionalized leadership, a legitimized form of "power over." Although "power over" may start benignly, it is vulnerable to becoming a power over others that denies equality and becomes exploitative, unjust, and even violent. There can be no "power over" without relative inequality (Sebastian, 1992). Our institutionalized "power over" that emanated from the Eurocentric subjugation of what became these United States is White, male, Protestant, and heterosexual.

The addict, desperate to hold on to "power over," says, "I will overpower your efforts to control my chemical use. *I* will control *you*." The addict's expression of "power over" might be annoying manipulative behavior or actual physical coercion.

Culture, like power, is a systemic rather than a static process. Falicov (conversation with author, 1998) points out that it is a dialogical process, with certain cultural attributes being highlighted in interaction with others.

SOCIOCULTURAL POWER

Sociocultural power is group power. For a group, "power to" may mean a centralized position (rather than marginalization), access to resources, or political power. That is, "power to" is the right to define the rules, control the discourse, select the language. For the addict, sociocultural "power to" means becoming part of a reference group that values sobriety.

Sociocultural "power over" is power that privileges certain groups at the expense of others, as demonstrated by race and class discrimination. A group that exerts "power over" creates inequality among groups. For example, immigrants come to the United States to find the "good life" portrayed in the media, but their success often depends on which race or class they belong to. It is clear that success and power in the United States are synonymous with material comfort. Immigrants of color are frequently denied access to the better-paying jobs. These people may be highly skilled, well-educated individuals who were relatively well compensated for their work in their country of origin. It is a shock for them to come in search of the "good life" only to experience a profound loss of status inflicted by a more powerful sociocultural group (Espiritu, 1997).

The original European colonists decimated the American Indians and warred with the Mexicans who once were in possession of much greater territory; their descendants interned the Japanese during World War II, despised the first Catholic Irish and Italian immigrants, and were, in general, intolerant of difference. Those addicts whose sociocultural reference group has "power over" feel more powerful than do those whose group lacks such power. This encourages the illusion in the former that they have power over their addiction.

SPIRITUAL POWER

Spiritual power comes from how we think about our relationship with the world around us. This larger picture includes self and others, spirit (in AA terms, "Higher Power"), the natural world, destiny or fate, the meaning of death. Spiritual "power to" is the ability to transform the self. It gives us courage and compassion when we meet our existential edges. spiritual "power to" is the power of Gandhi and the Dalai Lama. For the addict, it is the ability to, in the face of powerlessness, find the spiritual strength to exert power to obtain a whole, healthy, sober life.

Spiritual "power over" stems from the belief that one has a direct line to God, a relationship that ultimately privileges one to have power over others. Such a belief may be inflicted by a leader, doctrines of the church, laws of state, or cultural expectations. Spiritual "power over" is demonstrated by our efforts to control the natural world with technology. As I write this, there is a summit in Kyoto to address a result of power over nature—global warming. The U.S. Army Corps of Engineers has dammed rivers and flooded whole towns, overgrazing has decimated vast grasslands, and altering the landscape has caused houses on hillsides in California to slide into mud. The Eurocentric values held by the early colonists in this country encouraged them to subdue the wilderness, tame the rivers, and conquer indigenous peoples. Man's persistent efforts to control nature are demonstrated everywhere.

For the addict, spiritual "power over" is invincibility, perfection. The addict says, "I am my own Higher Power. No God has power over me. I am the master of my fate. I can control my own destiny."

Whatever their "values of origin" on power, addicts entering the treatment system in the United States will be exposed to the hegemony of the twelve-step approach to recovery. This approach has created widespread belief that recovery begins with admission of powerlessness over a drug, but what powerlessness means to each of us is intimately tied to our ideas about power. We must understand the sometimes equivocal uses of power in our dominant discourse.

POWER AND THE DOMINANT DISCOURSE

A DOMINANT DISCOURSE is the central story of a culture as it arises from assumptions about what is normative. It is sustained by language. Discourses are not equally privileged. According to Hare-Mustin (1994), "The dominant discourse is the one that supports and reflects the prevailing ideology of those in power" (p. 20).

The dominant discourse on power in the United States is "power over" as opposed to "power to." Hayton (1994) asserts that it evolved from European beliefs and traditions that came with the colonization of North America.

The traditions that Europeans brought to America were:
- an attitude of moral superiority,
- a belief that the universe was created to serve the needs of man,
- an intellectual and religious intolerance,
- advanced military equipment, and
- a natural inclination to be violent toward one another. (P. 105)

These beliefs and traditions became the framework for the dominant discourse on power, by those in power, in the United States today.

LANGUAGE AND INDUCTION INTO THE DOMINANT DISCOURSE

LANGUAGE CONSTRUCTS REALITY in ways that marginalize or centralize, because of the assumptions of power inherent in the dominant discourse. Social lines are often constructed between sexual orientations, races, classes, and genders. In the United States these lines translate to institutionalized "power over." Although we have supposedly shunned the assimilationist ideology of the melting pot, we still attempt to induct newcomers into our values.

RACE

We use the word *race* as though it were an objective reality instead of a social construction. Race is historically a biological term referring to physical characteristics of different peoples. However, as Zack (1995) points out, "There are no genetic markers for race. . . . The ordinary concept of race has dialectically ridden on an assumption of racial purity that has been used to racialize dominated groups as it suited dominant interests" (p. xvi). Pinder-hughes (1989) concurs: "Over time, race has acquired a social meaning in which these biological differences, via the mechanism of stereotyping, have become markers for status assignment within the social system . . . a status assignment based on skin color" (p. 71).

Historically, the dominant discourse on race in the United States placed "Whiteness" at the center, largely unexamined. Racism was studied for years in terms of its effects on Black identity rather than its effects on White identity; that is, the dominant discourse has portrayed racism as a problem for people of color rather than as a problem for all. Fine, Weiss, Powell, and Wong (1997) point out that "White standpoints, privileged standpoints, are still generally taken as the benign norm or, in some cases, the oppressive standard—either way escaping serious scrutiny" (p. viii). McIntosh (1998) examines the context that defines a White person's experience:

> As a White person, without even consciously defining myself as White, there are dozens of ways in which my skin color privileges me in everyday life, and I may barely realize them.
> - When I am told about our national heritage or about "civilization," I am shown that people of my color made it what it is.
> - I can remain oblivious to the language and customs of persons of color who constitute the world's majority without feeling in my culture any penalty for such oblivion.

- I can easily buy posters, postcards, picture books, greeting cards, dolls, toys, and children's magazines featuring people of my race. (P. 149)

It is Whites, however, who are most often unconscious of race. People of color are always conscious of it. Toni Morrison (1997) says, "I have never lived, nor has any of us, in a world in which race did not matter" (p. 3).

GENDER

Language creates gender as dichotomous: heterosexual or homosexual; male or female. The centrality of White male heterosexuality is at the center of our discourse on gender. Building on McIntosh's work, Crowfoot and Chesler (1996) built their own list of White male privileges and behaviors, which often remain just below our level of consciousness. Here are two examples:

- We [White males] feel and act freer than others to deviate from group ground rules, expectations, and "appropriate" group behavior (e.g., sitting outside a circle, coming late to a meeting, announcing alternative pressing tasks, etc.)
- We can afford to limit our efforts to talk with, seek out, and work with women and people of color to those with whom we agree or feel comfortable. (Pp. 210–211)

Although other cultures value power differently in some spheres, male heterosexual power is almost universally valued:

Our response to the idea of power cannot be separated from what women have known about power, not only from being powerless but from watching the powerful. As we explore the issue of power, we necessarily use language and concepts which contain the assumptions of a destructively power-using, power-seeking culture, and these are reflected in the choices we see for ourselves. (Goodrich, 1991a, p. 4)

The powerful who are being watched by Goodrich's women are those who enlist in the White, male, heterosexual Euro-American worldview of who has power and why. The women are watching, and so are the indigenous peoples in the United States, who have historically been overpowered, enslaved or colonized, and the immigrants, who have been pressured to assimilate, acculturate, abide by, and even emulate this Euro-American dominant discourse about power. When people from other cultures move to this country, they are expected to conform to the dominant discourse. Part of the acculturation process includes the gradual acquisition of views about what power is and who has it. Those who acquire these views of "power over" may soon despair of having it.

The results of women's socialization are pathologized. The inflammatory Moynihan Report in the 1960s pathologized female heads of household among African Americans, shifting, many scholars feel, the responsibility for Black poverty to the Black family rather than to the institutionalized structures of oppression. In the 1980s, the addiction recovery movement used language to define a whole syndrome, namely, codependency (Beattie, 1987); the idea subtly reconstructed women's experience (Krestan and Bepko, 1990).

It is significant that the universal risk factor for alcoholism, across all cultures, is gender. That is, men are more at risk for addiction than women. Women are at risk for addiction primarily consequent to their relationships with men.

SEXUAL ORIENTATION

Sexual orientation is another example of how the lens of the dominant discourse distorts our vision and privileges one group at the expense of another while allegedly creating static categories between people.

The lyrics of a song in *Kiss of the Spider Woman* (Ebb, McNally, & Kander, 1992), a musical that depicts two men, a political rebel and a gay drug addict, sharing a jail cell, express the divisiveness between categories of sexual orientation. Valentin, the Marxist revolutionary, angrily sings to Molina, the homosexual: *You're making me sick, that prissy whine. Watch me now, I draw the line. So you stick to your side, and I'll stick to mine. Never, ever cross this line!* The dominant discourse on individual sexual preference has drawn lines, and the assumptions both creating and deriving from those lines serve to perpetuate the discourse on sexual preference as clear, divisive, and necessary.

CLASS

The dominant discourse on class in America is that anyone with enough will can achieve the upward mobility of the American dream. Those who share this attitude about achieving "success" insidiously punish those who don't acquire, or aspire to acquire, it. People of color, women, the less educated, those for whom English is a second language, the differently abled—all are frequently prevented from acquiring "success" and are then shamed or held back because they are not "successful." McGoldrick and Giordano (1996) state, "Class increasingly organizes the United States in very insidious ways, including structuring the relationships among ethnic groups" (p. 16).

Of the relationships between class and other demographics, Kliman (1998) writes as follows:

> Class involves multiple relationships to economic and other social structures: race, ethnicity, religion, gender, sexuality, physical and mental well-being, and geography. It also involves relationships between classes. One's economic and social circumstances exist in relation to those of others. (Pp. 50–51)
>
> Definitions of class shift with context . . . as economic And other forms of domination operate together. (P. 51)

The media creates and promotes the language and images that support a dominant discourse on class.

The Broadway musical *Miss Saigon* depicts a seventeen-year-old Vietnamese orphan girl who falls in love with an American GI during the fall of Saigon in the Vietnam War. (This production created a huge controversy about casting when it was originally cast with mixed-race actors.) The "Engineer" is first her pimp and later her hope when he sees that her mixed race child, Tam, can be their ticket to America. This fictional love story accurately depicts how people from other cultures frequently view living in the United States. The pimp sings:

> *What's that I smell in the air,*
> *the American dream?*
> *Sweet as a new millionaire,*
> *the American dream!*
> *Luck by the tail! How can you fail?*
> *And best of all, it's for sale!*
> *The American Dream! (Boublil, Maltby, & Schönberg, 1990)*

The American dream the Engineer sings about promises a life of freedom, freedom to own land, start a business. The American dream includes the promise that if you work hard enough, you can, with a little luck, succeed in the United States. It is the promise that has lured immigrants since the discovery of America. Hayton (1994) claims that the first people to come were "dissenters, misfits, criminals, adventurers, indentured servants, and other risk-takers . . . [they had] the characteristics that helped the settlers survive in the wilderness, and these are the characteristics that stimulated invention and creativity and accounted for material progress throughout American history" (p. 105). People come to America to find material wealth and freedom from a repressive government.

DIFFERENCES AMONG DIFFERENCES

One difficulty with understanding difference is the human predilection to promote personal differences as so unique that no one else can understand them. Kliman and others demonstrate that it is the intersections between class, race, gender, and other demographics that construct "hierarchies" of oppression and shape family life. Almeida's (1994) hierarchy of oppression is created by demographics that describe collective consciousness and the external experience of self-power. Shame, in contrast, is the internalized experience. For example, a White, middle-class lesbian who is not "out" may be externally located higher up on the hierarchy of oppression. Her internalized experience, however, may place her somewhere else. Although one may claim that one's oppression is worse than another's, no one totally knows another's shame. In the United States, African Americans as a group are more oppressed externally than are Jews. However, a Jew may be more oppressed or internally feel more shame than an African American.

Whether one tells Polish jokes or queer jokes, language creates difference, and the resulting relationships of equal or unequal power. The perceived right to use language to make a joke at the expense of another illustrates an attitude of "power over."

VALUES OF ORIGIN IN WESTERN CULTURE

IN DESCRIBING HER concept of ecological niche, Falicov (1995) writes, "Multiple contexts and the borderlands that result from the overlapping of contexts call to mind ecological spaces where access is allowed or denied, locations of partial perspectives where views and values are shaped and where power or powerlessness are experienced" (pp. 377–378).

Whatever ecological niche describes a particular family at a particular point in time, it is the values that extend across the parameters of that niche, that are, in my view, most relevant as risk or protection factors for addiction.

I am indebted to a friend (Lacy, personal communication, Feb. 12, 1997) for first using the phrase *values of origin* to signify the range of values that relate to the other ecologies as class, religion, and education, among others, but that derive from one's country of birth or ancestry.

In the United States the values of origin derive from European colonization and prize "power over" in all spheres: individual, interpersonal, sociocultural, and spiritual. These values of origin assume superiority. The induction of immigrants into this dominant discourse is so thorough that it disrupts the original values of immigrant groups. In general, "power over" is a Western value. It is maintained by those in power to protect their power. The dominant discourse on values in the United States today promotes competition, individuality, mastery, youth, health, ability, and material success. It allows one person, or a few, to exert all four kinds of power.

A notable example of this is one man, Bill Gates, CEO of Microsoft, who allegedly has said, "There won't be anything we won't say to people to try and convince them that our way is the way to go."[*]

Gates, who is, according to *USA Today* (Mar. 4, 1998, p. 1), "... the nation's richest, most powerful businessman," is also the first business leader to defend himself before Congress. Gates was testifying in response to charges from his business rivals that Microsoft competes unfairly. The Senate is investigating whether to create new anti-trust legislation. Microsoft is "accused by competitors of ruthlessness. It is generally getting a public image as a greedy company out to control the world (p. 2A)."

The natural way these power holders think about their world was created and is supported by our country's dominant discourse. Those who have "power over" may not be conscious of their position, because it is their context, their difference, that predominates. It is only natural that the corrective context for recovery from attitudes dominated by Eurocentric idealization of "power over"—of excess and exploitation—and from the addictions they spawn is one of "power with."

---

[*]The Loony Bin (1998), Bill Gates Quotes . . . , Retrieved May 7, 1998, from World Wide Web. Address: http://loonies.net800.co.uk/1998.05-07/0009.html

VALUES OF ORIGIN IN OTHER CULTURES

OTHER CULTURES, compared to our Euro-American culture, have a very different discourse on power. For example, American Indians do not believe in power over the natural world. They strive for harmony with the environment and with nature. "A traditional Indian lives in harmony with the forces of life." (Simonelli, personal correspondence, January 15, 1998). As Coyhis puts it in chapter 3, "Indians look at it differently: you work with nature or the situation you are in; you understand that everything is interconnected. One of our values is to 'share the deer.' This value is the opposite of control; it's about sharing, it's about flow, it's about balance, and it's about rhythm."

Hispanic cultures view competition very differently from Euro-American culture. "White middle-class Americans stress individualism and actually value the individual in terms of his ability to compete for higher social and economic status. The Hispanic culture values those inner qualities that constitute the uniqueness of the person and his goodness in himself. To the Hispanic, family (familism) is more important than the individual" (Ho, 1987, p. 125).

Spirituality and religion are central to African Americans. Pinderhughes, Knox, McAddoo, and Boyd-Franklin emphasize the role of spirituality in the lives of African American clients and their families. Concepts of alcoholism among Whites, Blacks and Hispanics in the United States show widespread support for the concept of alcoholism as a disease, independent of ethnicity (Caetano, 1989). However, Blacks and Hispanics are more likely to think that alcoholism results from a violation of spiritual values and that addiction represents moral weakness. "Hispanics value the spirit and soul as much more important than the body and worldly materialism. A Hispanic person tends to think in terms of transcendent qualities such as justice, loyalty, or love. He is not preoccupied with mastering the world" (Ho, 1987, p. 127).

Spirituality is also central to the many different Indian nations in this country. Although belief systems vary widely among the more than five hundred federally recognized tribes, there are commonalities. These include a desire for harmony, a belief in the unseen world, and a belief in the interconnectedness of all life (Fleming and Manson, 1990).

Asian American and Pacific Islander communities have their own view of spirituality, one that is based on a history influenced by Confucianism and Buddhism. The tenets of their belief system include moderation in behavior, self-discipline, and harmony in relationships, derived from mutual loyalty and respect (Ho, 1987).

Interestingly, one of the most significant predictors of addiction—religious affiliation—is less studied than other demographic variables. Yet religious proscriptions regarding drinking, gambling, and other potential addictions are often highly correlated with drinking patterns.

The dominant discourse in the United States overtly prescribes equality for men and women, but covert power relationships between men and women are far from equal. African Americans are more likely than Whites to practice interpersonal gender equality. In her review of the literature on power relationships between Black spouses of varying social classes, Boyd-Franklin (1989) concludes that Black families appear to be more egalitarian than White couples. However, a high incidence of domestic violence suggests that this claim may represent more of an ideal than a reality.

Other countries with majority White populations also have different values of origin on some parameters as compared to the dominant discourse in the United States. The *United Nations Development Report* (1994) states:

> Traditionally, women in Europe have enjoyed greater equality with men than have women in any other region. For example, Sweden, Norway, Finland, Denmark and France top all other countries in having women's health, education and income levels approach those of men. . . . Today, however, the gaps between men and women in Eastern Europe and the Commonwealth of Independent States are widening as a result of recent changes that have taken place in these countries . . . i.e., the rapid transfer from centrally-controlled to market economies.

POWER AND ADDICTION

THE DOMINANT DISCOURSE on "power over" in the United States creates a context in which those with this power inevitably fear losing it and those without it experience shame for not having it. Fear and shame are extremely uncomfortable feelings. Most of us spend our lives trying to avoid them. They are the demons that make our knowledge and acceptance of human limitation so painful.

Pinderhughes (1989) has noted a paradox in relation to power and vulnerability: "Paradoxically then, power can create greater vulnerability to powerlessness. . . . Those in positions of power can also develop a tendency to deny their own personal pain and ignore their experiences of powerlessness" (pp. 122–123).

Different ecological contexts have different levels of significance in the evolution of, an individual's addiction and in his or her recovery from it. Different ecological contexts also produce differing experiences of power and powerlessness in people, experiences that may seemingly contradict one another. Someone with a strongly developed sense of spiritual "power to" may sustain relative powerlessness in the socio-cultural arena without feeling powerless, and one whose sense of power is diminished interpersonally within the family may invoke race, class, or heterosexual privilege in order to feel powerful. Almeida (1994) suggests that there are hierarchies of oppression, but a person seemingly high on the objective hierarchy (e.g., being male) may still feel oppressed if he is low on another (e.g., class) in a context where gender is less important than class.

Understanding addiction requires us to recognize power and powerlessness on all levels and in all their complexities. I have worked with clinicians who believed that "objective" powerlessness causes addiction and that recovery from addiction is irrelevant to those who are socially oppressed; these clinicians claim that their clients have "nothing to get clean and sober for." I have also worked with clinicians who failed to realize the ravages of addiction in families who appear to be powerful (e.g., White, materially successful, and well educated). Power can make one peculiarly vulnerable to feelings of powerlessness, and power comes with a high price (e.g., the price of power that is attached to male privilege).

Celia Falicov stresses the interactional nature of power and how supposed power forms a culture all its own (Falicov, personal communication, 1998). For example, White physicians in a setting where they are expected to help those who are culturally different often experience powerlessness.

If it were only the powerlessness of the oppressed that leads to addiction, we would expect higher than average rates of drinking and addiction in marginalized groups. However, most studies indicate that African Americans drink less than Whites and that Hispanics in the United States have rates of drinking that are lower than the national average. It seems that, with very few exceptions, acculturation to dominant White values produces more addiction problems. In many groups, adolescents, who acculturate more readily, have higher rates of drinking and drug use than adults.

Feelings of powerlessness are significant stressors in the development of addiction, whether or not those feelings are tied to actual powerlessness. The founders of Alcoholics Anonymous—two White, heterosexual men (one a Wall Street broker and the other a physician)—understandably based their beliefs about addiction and its relationship to power on the Western view of "power over." The program they founded provides a set of beliefs designed to be an antidote for this kind of power.

Addicts take false pride in an idealized image of self as "illimitable." They experience limitation as powerlessness (Bepko and Krestan, 1985). Since limitation is the human condition, the necessary and inevitable outcome for those who hold any belief system that insists on absolute power or control is intense shame. Addicts and cultures addicted to "power over" do not tolerate limitation easily. They both thrive on the denial of human limitation. Yet the intoxication of feeling invincible is necessarily compromised by reality.

Addiction can seem like a near-perfect defense against reality for a while, a seemingly effective denial of limitation. Heroin can anesthetize the despair of powerlessness. Cocaine can create an illusion of invincibility. Alcohol can do both. Gambling's illusion of limitlessness can be exciting. Addiction becomes a means of overcoming feelings of powerlessness and, temporarily at least, eliminating fear and shame.

At first, addiction feels like power over feelings, others, circumstances. Then it overpowers the addict. The addict gradually loses all feelings of power; fear and shame replace them. At that point, the addict's only defense against the feelings of fear, shame, and powerlessness is to increase the consumption of alcohol or drugs in an effort to retrieve the feelings of power. The greater the effort addicts make to have power over their addiction, the more the substance overpowers them. Ultimately and paradoxically, the addiction renders them totally powerless. Reduced to powerlessness, addicts lie to themselves about their need for the addiction. They must sustain this lie with more addictive behavior.

VICIOUS CYCLES

ADDICTION IS A specialized example of power gone awry. Indeed, "power over" can never be sustained. When one's power is threatened, one must exert more energy to acquire and maintain it. Similarly, addiction to alcohol or other drugs requires more alcohol or drugs to sustain the same level of euphoria, or freedom from discomfort. Addiction and "power over" create a vicious cycle in which the individual first insists on absolute "power over" and then recognizes and fears limitation or powerlessness.

For example, the alcoholic with false pride in his heart and a drink in his hand asserts that he is master of his fate and captain of his soul. He will not hear the word *no* to himself. He cannot recognize his own weakness or limitations and cannot say, "I can't do this. I'm too tired, I'm too frightened. I don't know how."

In the film *Clean and Sober*, Michael Keaton plays a White, middle-class addict. While in a rehab center, he is told that he cannot make a phone call to his broker. Nonetheless, he uses his counselor's phone without permission to make the call. He is, after all, master of the universe. He is like the alcoholic described in the early alcoholism literature as "his majesty, the Baby" (Tiebout, 1954). When the counselor, who is Black, again tells Keaton that he cannot use the phone, Keaton rages at him, cursing him and mocking the amount of money he makes. Rendered powerless, Keaton reacts to his fear with rage-filled racism in an attempt to invoke power over the counselor. Pinderhughes (1989), in her understanding of power in all its complexity, would interpret this scene as portraying Keaton's use of the "stance, 'better than' to manage anxiety" (p. 120).

Anyone who works with addiction recognizes this scene, recognizes the rage of the powerless asserting power. In *Clean and Sober* the addict is one-down, with respect to the counselor. However, in the larger social context the counselor's skin color places *him* one-down with respect to the addict's privileged Whiteness. The struggle feels symmetrical to the character Keaton plays as he shouts that he is equal, or even one-up. Denial of his powerlessness manifests as a need to feel power over someone else. Shamed by his powerlessness over addiction, the addict tries to shame the other by resorting to classism and racism in an attempt to bolster his false pride in his superiority and independence.

Singer, Valentin, Baer, and Jia (1992) deconstructed the case of Juan, an alcoholic Puerto Rican immigrant, by placing his "disease" of alcohol dependence within the socioeconomic, sociocultural, and political contexts of his life. Citing research data on unemployment and alcohol consumption and on the sense of powerlessness as a correlate to drinking, they presented Juan as someone who, deprived of economic power, drank to assert his masculinity in other culturally prescribed ways. They cited other researchers who concluded that "increased drinking and rising rates of problem drinking were products of the consequent sense of worthlessness and failure in men geared to defining masculinity in terms of being *un buen proveedor* (Canino and Canino, in Singer et al., 1992, pp. 537–538).

Machismo is widely assumed to be integrally related to Latino definitions of masculinity. However, stereotypical *machismo* neglects broader meanings in favor of constricted negative ones. Bacigalupe (in press) discusses the distortion of the idea of *machismo*: "*Machismo* ideology spreads the belief that men are violent because they are 'crazy, alcoholic, uneducated, poor, or from under-developed countries.'" These expressions narrow the scope of the problem, so it is perceived as an issue that affects only some individuals and not others, thus making unequal gender arrangements invisible. When *machismo* is used to explain power dynamics, the original meaning of the term is distorted. Traditionally, *machismo* was utilized as a label to name the efforts that men make at being in charge of the well-being of their family. When *addiction* results from a failure at being *un buen proveedor*, it also prevents the man from being employable.—a vicious cycle.

In cultures where drinking is defined as a male prerogative, or a badge of masculinity, drinking and using drugs are ways to assert masculinity when other avenues of power are closed. This is as true in dominant cultures as in marginalized cultures. I am not aware of any culture that sanctions women's drinking more than men's. For many years I practiced family and marital therapy in an affluent suburb of Manhattan. Among my clients were men who held seats on the stock exchange. Following the market correction in 1987 called Black Monday, the number of marriages affected by addiction escalated sharply. (I also saw an increase in related problems, such as spouse abuse. I shall never forget one woman who, having gone to her doctor after being beaten by her alcoholic husband, also a physician, was told that she suffered from "husbanditis." I told her I guessed that meant "inflammation of the husband.")

Even where providing is not an issue, as for immigrant men who are well off, drinking is associated with status. Almeida (personal communication, 1998) points out that for affluent Asian Indian men "it's even more about their definition of capitalism and making it in the White world. If they drink Dewar's and make deals they have made it." In these examples the vicious cycle goes like this:

1. He feels/has power and is afraid of losing it. He is ashamed of his fear, or He feels powerless and is ashamed of his powerlessness: He engages in addictive behavior, i.e., drinking, drug abuse, violence, competitiveness: he gains illusory control over the fear and shame.

2. The control begins to slip, and he is more frightened, more ashamed.

3. He tries harder to regain control and power, but it now takes more of the drug, the drink, the power, to achieve the same effect.

4. He finally becomes totally powerless to stop the addiction.

5. Admitting powerlessness creates more fear and shame. He is again caught in the addiction.

THE PRIDE CYCLE: REPLACING "POWER OVER" WITH "POWER TO"

BATESON (1972) VIEWED interactions as either symmetrical or complementary. Initially, addicts assert a symmetrical relationship with their drug, insisting that they are "equal to" it, that they can control themselves and it. As they become increasingly out of control, their relationship to the drug becomes complementary. The drug is one-up, and they are one-down. The struggle of addicts to continually prove mastery over their addiction is isomorphic with the dominant discourse of "power over" in the United States. Either power or addiction, when out of control, eventually establishes a complementary interaction wherein the greater the power of one side, the greater the powerlessness of the other. Alcoholics Anonymous provides a context for recovery from addiction that acknowledges the need to break the reciprocal cycle of power and powerlessness of the addiction. In breaking the denial of their powerlessness over the drug and the denial of their need for others, and in breaking the myth of self power when they feel temporarily powerful, addicts are restored to empowerment, or "power to." Bepko and Krestan have called this context of recovery the restoration of a "correct complementarity" with the world; it is an acknowledgment of *Mitakuye Oyasin*, which is Lakota for "all my relations" or interconnectedness.

The top of the pride cycle in Figure 1-1 depicts the addict as master of the universe. Aided by alcohol or other drugs, addicts maintain an image of being in control, needing no one, being all-powerful and unconstrained by limitation. In its publication *Twelve Steps and Twelve Traditions* (1952) Alcoholics Anonymous describes this spiritual state as "self-will run riot." In this position, alcoholics are in the complementary, or one-up, position to others. They insist on "power over." This is very similar to the dominant discourse on power in the larger society.

Alcoholics cannot maintain this state, because they are not perfectible and are never really beyond needing others. They need a drug to bolster their illusions. The drug, which they use to maintain the illusion of remaining in control, then paradoxically renders them powerless and out of control. They topple from Olympus. At the bottom, they experience themselves as shame bound, as nothing, as inadequate. Here they have "hit bottom, surrendered" (Alcoholics Anonymous, p. 19). Now they are teachable; they acknowledge their powerlessness, the unmanageability of their life. They accept help from others.

Paradoxically, once they admit powerlessness, addicts receive the power

FIGURE I-I   THE PRIDE CYCLE

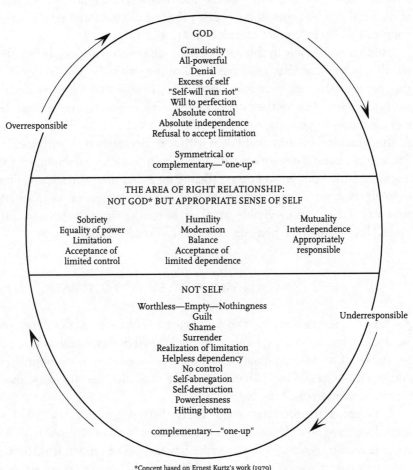

GOD

Grandiosity
All-powerful
Denial
Excess of self
"Self-will run riot"
Will to perfection
Absolute control
Absolute independence
Refusal to accept limitation

Symmetrical or
complementary—"one-up"

Overresponsible

THE AREA OF RIGHT RELATIONSHIP:
NOT GOD* BUT APPROPRIATE SENSE OF SELF

Sobriety	Humility	Mutuality
Equality of power	Moderation	Interdependence
Limitation	Balance	Appropriately
Acceptance of	Acceptance of	responsible
limited control	limited dependence	

NOT SELF

Worthless—Empty—Nothingness
Guilt
Shame
Surrender
Realization of limitation
Helpless dependency
No control
Self-abnegation
Self-destruction
Powerlessness
Hitting bottom

Underresponsible

complementary—"one-up"

*Concept based on Ernest Kurtz's work (1979)

to rebuild their life. Berenson (1991) says, "Optimally powerlessness is a way-station between control and empowerment" (p. 75). The addict is now in what Figure 1-1 depicts as the middle zone of right relationship. Addicts at this point have an appropriate appreciation for their interconnectedness and interdependency with others. They accept limited control ("I cannot take the first drink"). They accept limited dependence on a community that acknowledges interconnectedness. The zone of right relationship is the zone of limitation, humility, moderation, balance, and mutuality. In terms of race and gender issues, it is a zone of sharing of power and psychological androgyny. This is "correct complementarity."

Addicts do not stay in this zone of right relationship for long before they tell themselves that they got sober because they were the chosen one, that they got sober because they were smart. They believe that they survived the earthquake not because they were lucky but because they were special. Before long, they begin to inch up to the top of the cycle again. They might not do this with alcohol, they might do it with sex, they might do it with cocaine. They might substitute working an eighty-hour week or gambling, or they might substitute power over others. Before long they are vulnerable again to toppling. If at the top they suffer from "self-will run riot," an excess of self, destruction of the self is inevitable and they are back down at the bottom of the cycle. Hubris calls forth nemesis. Grandiosity breeds self-destruction.

THE POWERLESSNESS OVER ADDICTION

CLEARLY, POWER AND POWERLESSNESS are key ideas in the dominant paradigm for addiction treatment in the United States, which is based on the model of treatment promoted by AA. This organization maintains general service offices in more than forty-three countries, and there are meetings in more than one hundred.

Let's look at the first steps in the Twelve Step program of AA: "[We] admitted we were powerless over alcohol and that because of it our lives had become unmanageable." Whatever the language of surrender, it is through accepting powerlessness over addiction that the addict is empowered to resume a sober life. A context for recovery from addiction provides a space where the addict can replace false pride in "power over" with healthy pride in "power to." Such a context promotes interconnectedness and community, a recognition of one's interdependence with others. It is a corrective context, correcting for the false beliefs in absolute power and autonomy. This context need not be the twelve-step programs and their derivatives. However, the *principles* of the twelve-step programs—primarily, accepting that one is not God and accepting "limited control" and "limited dependence" (Kurtz, 1982)—are, I believe, fundamental to recovery from addiction.

The principles of a twelve-step program are actually more syntonic with the values of origin of marginalized groups than they are with the values of the culture's dominant group. Living in the zone of right relationship is fundamentally more in concert with the values of those whose values have traditionally fallen outside the dominant discourse of "power over." It is precisely the "power over" of the dominant discourse that requires the in-depth ego deflation of hitting bottom. Native Americans, African Americans, Latinos, and Asian Americans—all prescribe the humility, balance, moderation, mutuality and acceptance of limitation that characterize the zone of right relationship, which is inherent in the recovery process.

THE DOMINANT DISCOURSE ON DIFFERENCE

DESPITE A GROWING ethnic diversity in the U.S. population, it is still White male Euro-American ideas about power that prevail. Those ideas are refuted by a program of recovery that values "power to" and avoids "power over." Sixty-five years from now the White Euro-American majority will be in the minority in the United States. The continuing ethnic shift in our population will present rich and exciting opportunities for learning and experiencing different cultures. It will also necessitate a shift in the power structure at every level of society. When the present majority becomes the minority, White Euro-Americans will have to integrate a new reality about their power position: their dominance in the United States is eroding.

ASKING THE CULTURALLY POWERLESS TO ACCEPT POWERLESSNESS IN RECOVERY

THE DOMINANT DISCOURSE tells us that everyone can attain "power to," but this is a falsehood in a society that still oppresses and marginalizes so many groups: women, people of color, the poor, the differently abled, and so on. Addiction helps those without power feel temporarily powerful. Although it can frequently substitute an illusory, distorted feeling of power for real empowerment, ultimately it robs the powerless of any chance to have "power to."

It is difficult to ask a person who is part of a powerless group to accept powerlessness. We need, then, to separate powerlessness due to oppression from powerlessness due to the addiction, which may have arisen to ease the pain of the original powerlessness. Only then can we ask members of already disempowered groups to accept powerlessness over their addiction. We cannot ask disempowered peoples to fight the "disease" of alcoholism without also locating this "disease" within a larger social system whose diseases include racism, sexism, classism, and oppression of all kinds.

Powerlessness, as Alcoholics Anonymous uses it, means relinquishing power over the addiction or relinquishing illusory power over one's self and others in exchange for the power to be in community and the power to direct one's own life. Such acceptance of powerlessness over the chemical (as opposed to "power over") is itself an empowering act.

White Bison, a Native American Indian consulting group, teaches a road to sobriety that integrates the medicine wheel with the twelve-step teachings of AA to adapt substance abuse recovery to Native American culture. In an ongoing dialogue with Richard Simonelli, a staff member of White Bison, I exchanged views on the pride cycle and its application to American Indian groups. In personal correspondence with me in 1997, Simonelli wrote the following:

> What hit me immediately is that the band running through the middle of the pride cycle (the zone of right relationship) might be called the Red Road in the current Indian sobriety movement. The Red Road is free of harmful extremes and cultivates human decency. What also struck me is that the top of the pride cycle really characterizes most of our culture. The dominant culture plays God while those who are different are forced to the bottom of the pride cycle. Is it any wonder that there is so much addiction and hurt?
>
> My other reflection is about powerlessness and surrender. Since the White male system is about dominance and power, it is natural that an alcoholic would finally feel humbled when he hits bottom. He finally meets something that is more powerful than he—alcohol, which is cunning, baffling, powerful. Since he's on a power trip, he calls it "powerlessness" when he finally meets something bigger than he is. He surrenders to something that has bested him. It's the language of dominance and challenge, win and lose. An Indian person who still lives in his or her culture might not use the same language. Power is not the issue. Rather, it's simple healing from misuse/abuse of a substance. . . . A traditional Indian lives in harmony with the forces of life. You might say he or she lives in surrender. But there is a language gap there. Surrender is harmony, but a person can have "power with" rather than "power over" while living in harmony. I think Indians see these distinctions intuitively.

This passage illustrates beautifully how even our language of recovery uses the language of the dominant discourse to explain what it is we are recovering from. Addicts in AA say, "[We] admitted we were powerless over alcohol and that because of it our lives had become unmanageable." In the dominant discourse, pride is in having power and in managing one's life. Addicts have to admit that addiction robs them of power and of the ability to manage. Other treatment groups may use language that is more meaningful to them. Many of these groups start by rewording the Twelve Steps. One Native American first step reads as follows: "We admit that because of our abuse of alcohol and other drugs, we have been unable to care for ourselves." In this example, one's recovery is from the inability to take responsibility for caring for oneself.

In *Many Roads, One Journey*, Charlotte Kasl offers sixteen steps for "discovery and empowerment." The first step reads as follows:

"We admit we were out of control with/powerless over——, but have the power to take charge of our lives and stop being dependent on substances or other people for our self-esteem and security."

The universality is striking. Each version of the first step in an addiction treatment program requires that the addict realize that he or she is not the Higher Power. Each version of the program stresses balance, interconnectedness, "power to," and "power with." These are precisely those values that the dominant discourse has minimized. I am not implying that all addicts need to get clean and sober through a twelve-step program of recovery. I am suggesting that addicts recover in a context that stresses community, interconnectedness, deflation of false pride or ego, and acknowledgment and subsequent healing of shame. I am further suggesting that this context approximates the values of origin of many groups that are not White and Eurocentric.

THE SHAME OF DIFFERENCE AND EMPOWERMENT THROUGH COMMUNITY

I HAVE DISCUSSED HERE the vicious cycle of power and powerlessness, how power needs constant reinforcement to maintain itself and how any hint of powerlessness may give rise to attempts at "power over." Power and powerlessness are reciprocally related. They may be external or internal. Both may provoke shame.

There is a human hunger to belong. Our initial feelings of powerlessness and shame are often inseparable from experiences of difference. Difference, like power, is relational, interactional. It is a feeling that is experienced only in particular contexts. My ecology—that is, my race, gender ethnicity, religion, class, or sexual orientation—may make me feel a difference that is profoundly alienating, in either the context of my traditional culture of origin or in the context of the culture I am acculturating to. A Latina adolescent who wants the freedom to go out with her girlfriends and faces her mother's restrictions and anxieties about the threat to her virginity if she is given freedom may feel ashamed of being different (Garcia-Preto, 1998). A college-educated Anglo woman who has been sexually molested (as have many female addicts) may feel a shame she attributes to being different. An African American male who is lighter skinned than his siblings may be tormented for looking different. Shame frequently arises from feeling different whether or not that difference is discriminated against by society in a particular instance, and whether the shame is created by external or internal circumstances.

Finally, the shame that attends addiction can be a shame that robs the addict of all dignity, all hope. Since shame does not heal in isolation, some sort of healing group context is optimal for healing shame. As Kurtz (1982) points out, "The typical meeting of Alcoholics Anonymous is a model of the living out of the shared honesty of mutual vulnerability openly acknowledged that the historical narrative has pointed out to be the essential dynamic of AA therapy" (p. 75).

Lili

Lili, a recovering alcoholic and heroin addict is Chicano and Navaho. Lili learned at a tender age the price that is too frequently paid for being different:

"In public school all of us who spoke any language other than English were severely punished . . . my brother was three years older and I was six . . . I noticed that if any of us spoke our native language the White teachers, because that's all there was, would either smack us on the hand or hit us on the head. I was so tiny . . . would just observe, I remember once that my oldest sister disappeared from the classroom . . . they had locked her up in the cellar because she wouldn't speak English that day . . . and my brother had already been to the cellar; he had been whipped with paddles, and he had been whipped with horse harness straps, and his hands had bruises from rulers, his head had bumps . . . and he was a lot slower at learning . . . they threatened to take him to the outhouses and hang him upside down inside the toilet . . . he was bigger and stronger . . . he was bigger and they couldn't hit him so easily any more . . . he would take the paddles away . . . they dragged him out of the room . . ."

Through a blend of Alcoholics Anonymous and return to her cultural traditions, Lili experienced the liberation that comes from locating powerlessness in the addiction experience and then claiming the power of community.

MIKE

Throughout this chapter I have inveighed against the White heterosexual male Euro-American dominant discourse. However, the White heterosexual male Euro-American often experiences himself as different and feels inadequate to embody dominant values.

Mike was the youngest child of seven and the only boy in an Irish Catholic family. His sisters dressed him in doll's clothes. His mother insisted that he quit the football squad after a high school injury. His father, however, shamed him for any indication that he was less than a 100 percent man. Mike enlisted in the Marines and saw action in Vietnam, where he was severely wounded and saw several of his buddies die. He came into therapy to explore his fears of weakness, fears that had made him increasingly vulnerable to drinking and using drugs. His greatest shame was that he remembered longing for his mother when he was wounded. He wondered whether that made him homosexual.

LARRY

Larry, a recovering addict, tells the following story:

"In the spring of 1946 I was born an outcast on the Ki-on-twog-ky (Cornplatter) reservation in the state of Pennsylvania, the ancestral land of the Seneca Indian. Today it is the Kinzua Valley, now covered by water. Being born neither White nor *o(h)n-weh-o(h)n-weh* (of the real people), I wondered which race would claim me. To which culture did I belong? I soon lost any identity I may have had, resenting the Senecas, hating White society, and angry at both. I would get even! I would show them! Prejudice, racial slurs, hatred, and indifference were my life. I did not fit in the workplace, the social circle, even religion. So alcohol became my master and I turned my back on everything. My spirit was dead. My life of self-destruction had begun. For the next three decades I saw the edge of the world through the bottom of a whiskey, wine, or beer bottle." (*Grapevine*, October 1997, p. 34).

Marta and Rachel

I led a small group in an exploration of difference, using some questions about ethnicity from Pinderhughes' 1989 work, *Understanding Race, Ethnicity, and Power*. A woman in the group named Marta told us the following about herself: "I am Mexican American; I grew up on the border, on the southernmost tip of New Mexico, five miles from the Mexican border, but I am sixth generation here in the United States. My family does not remember when we came over . . . but to look at me people don't think that."

Marta's family had been in New Mexico for many generations before the United States, in the war with Mexico, annexed the lands in 1848. *Respeto* formed the basis of her interpersonal relationships with the Mexican American community, and she experienced little or no prejudice until she went to college and interacted with the dominant Anglo culture. Then her story changed. She experienced discrimination based on her skin color and she also experienced loneliness in her family of origin: "I am the first woman who is educated, and like many of you I feel different and not fully accepted . . . I mean my family is very proud of me but I am isolated." Marta experienced herself as different not only from her culture of origin, but also from the dominant culture. She experienced difference based on ethnicity, education, gender roles, and acculturation.

Of course, one need not turn to alcohol or drugs in an effort to cope with feelings of being different. One might, for example, seek empowerment through education. Education moves one to a less vulnerable place on the external hierarchy of oppression. However, the internal pain of shame may still be there. Rachel, another woman in the group who had not become addicted spoke: "I find this very difficult. My ethnic background is mixed. My father is Jewish and my mother is German. There was conflict in my family whenever the news came on television. At one point I thought I could have created a group around being Jewish, but I could not swallow the traditional Jewish upbringing because of my feminism. I did not know which of my identities to choose—Germany or Palestine." This woman's shame lay in having no reference group.

Neither Rachel nor Marta were addicts. Although they had to struggle with the pain of difference, they did not have the additional struggle of addiction. Lili, Mike, and Larry, on the other hand, felt the initial powerlessness over the shame of difference, but they had the secondary shame of the addiction, as well.

I remember hearing a television star talk at an AA meeting about the five words that changed his life, words that were spoken to him by his sponsor: "I know how you feel."

RONALD

The red sandstone cliffs of Canyon de Chelly rise two thousand feet from the valley floor. Ronald, my tour guide, and I stand before the petroglyphs, next to the dry wash and under the golding cottonwoods. We have just shared our personal histories of addiction and our roads to recovery. We are in awe at our commonality.

Ronald is Navaho. He had four brothers once. A drunk driver killed one, cirrhosis claimed another, a third hanged himself, and a fourth died in a bar fight. Now there is only Ronald. He hasn't had a drink in eight years. He is fifty-three now. When he was nine, he was sent off the reservation to boarding school. He can neither read nor write in his own language.

Ronald's Nation has the power to keep us Anglos from Canyon de Chelly unless we let them guide us. Ronald doesn't think about his power that way, however. He thinks in terms of protecting the land. I have the power of money to hire Ronald to give me a private tour. I have not always had power. I am a woman, never married, only child of a first-generation Bohemian father and a second-generation Irish English mother. Because of my white skin, I don't have trouble hailing a taxi in New York City. I was, however, paid less than a man for similar work for most of my career.

Ronald and I have each known the powerlessness of addiction, which nearly destroyed us. Now we share the power of the past in this sacred place, the power of the ancient ones who came before, the power of community, and the power of a belief system that transcends our differences of gender and class and ethnicity and our ideas of "race." We share the power of having embraced the powerlessness over addiction, thereby finding the liberating empowerment of connectedness and community. This kind of power and powerlessness each of us knows, despite our differences. This kind of power and powerlessness is in a language each of us speaks, a voice each of us owns.

To create a recovery context for others, we must understand the nature of power and powerlessness in different cultures. We must relanguage powerlessness to refer to the addiction and create other kinds of empowerment that do not include "power over" but liberate us to find "power to." We must understand the particulars of another's shame story. We must be able to say to one another, "I know how you feel."

References

Alcoholics Anonymous World Services, Inc. (1952). *Twelve Steps and Twelve Traditions.* New York: Author.

Alcoholics Anonymous World Services, Inc. (1976). *Alcoholics Anonymous* (3rd. ed.) New York: Author.

Alcoholics Anonymous World Services, Inc. (1997, October). *Grapevine,* p. 34.

Almeida, R. (1994). Expansions of Feminist Family Theory Through Diversity. In M. McGoldrick (Ed.), *Re-Visioning Family Therapy: Race, Culture, and Gender in Clinical Practice.* New York: Guilford Press.

Bacigalupe, G. *El Latino: Transgressing the Macho.* In press.

Baker-Miller, J. (1976). *Toward a New Psychology of Women.* Boston: Beacon Press.

Bateson, G. (1972). *Steps to an Ecology of Mind.* New York: Chandler.

Beattie, M. (1987). *CoDependent No More.* New York: Harper/Hazelden.

Bennett, L. A., & Ames, G. M. (Eds.). (1985). *The American Experience with Alcohol: Contrasting Cultural Perspectives.* New York: Plenum Press.

Bepko, C., & Krestan, J. A. (1985). *The Responsibility Trap: A Blueprint for Treating the Alcoholic Family.* New York: Free Press.

Berenson, D. (1991). Powerlessness—Liberating or Enslaving? Responding to the Feminist Critique of the Twelve Steps. In C. Bepko (Ed.), *Feminism and Addiction* (pp. 67–81). New York: Haworth Press.

Boublil, A., Maltby, R., Jr., and Schönberg, C.-M. (1990). *Miss Saigon: A Musical;* adapted from the original French lyrics by A. Boublil; additional material by R. Maltby, Jr. [printed music]. Milwaukee: Hal Leonard.

Boyd-Franklin, N. (1989). *Black Families in Therapy: A Multisystems Approach.* New York: Guilford Press.

Caetano, R. (1989). Concept of Alcoholism Among Whites, Blacks, and Hispanics in the United States. *Journal of Studies on Alcohol, 50*(6), 580–582.

Cahalan, D., Cisisn, I. H., & Crossley, H. M. (1969). American Drinking Practices: A National Study of Drinking Behavior and Attitudes. New Brunswick, NJ: Rutgers Center of Alcohol Studies; New Haven, CT: College & University Press.

Crowfoot, J. & Chesler, M. (1996). White Men's Roles in Multicultural Coalitions. In B. Bowser & R. Hunt (Eds.), *Impacts of Racism on White Americans.* (pp. 202–229). Thousand Oaks, CA: Sage.

Douglas, M. (Ed.). (1987). *Constructive Drinking: Perspectives on Drink from Anthropology.* New York: Cambridge University Press.

Ebb, F., McNally, T., & Kander, J. (1992). *Kiss of the Spiderwoman* (A Musical).

Espiritu, Y. L. (1997). *Asian American Women and Men.* Thousand Oaks, CA: Sage.

Falicov, C. J. (1995). Training to Think Culturally: A Multidimensional Comparative Framework. *Family Process, 34*(4), 373–388.

Falicov, C. J. (1998). *Latino Families in Therapy*. New York: Guilford Press.

Fine, M., Weis, L., Powell, J., & Wong, L. (Eds.). (1997). *Off White: Readings on Race, Power and Society*. New York: Routledge.

Fleming, C., & Manson, S. (1990). Native American Women. In R. Engs (Ed.), *Women: Alcohol and Other Drugs* (pp. 143–148). Dubuque, IA: Kendall/Hunt.

Foulks, E. F., Wintrob, R. M., Westermeyer, J., & Favazza, A. R. (Eds.). (1977). *Current Perspectives in Cultural Psychiatry*. New York: Spectrum.

Garcia-Preto, N. (1998). Latinas in the United States. In M. McGoldrick, (Ed.), *Re-Visioning Family Therapy* (pp. 330–346). New York: Guilford Press.

Gates, H. L., & West, C. (1996). *The Future of the Race*. New York: Knopf.

Goodrich, T. J. (1991a). Women, Power and Family Therapy: What's Wrong with This Picture. In T. J. Goodrich, (Ed.), *Women and Power* (pp. 3–35). New York: Norton.

Goodrich, T. J. (1991b). *Women and Power*. New York: Norton.

Hare-Mustin, R. T. (1994). Discourse in the Mirrored Room: A Postmodern Analysis of Therapy, *Family Process, 33*(1) (March): 19–35.

Hayton, R. (1994). European American Perspective: Some Considerations. In J.U. Gordon (Ed.), *Managing Multiculturalism in Substance Abuse Services* (pp. 99–116). Thousand Oaks, CA: Sage.

Helzer, J. E., & Canino, G. J. (Eds.). (1992). *Alcoholism in North America, Europe, and Asia*. New York: Oxford University Press.

Ho, M. K. (1987). *Family Therapy with Ethnic Minorities*. Newbury Park, CA: Sage.

Horney, K. (1937). *The Neurotic Personality of Our Time*. New York: Norton.

Kasl, C. D. (1992). *Many Roads One Journey: Moving Beyond the Twelve Steps*. San Francisco: Harper Perennial Library.

Kliman, J. (1998). Social Class as a Relationship: Implications for Family Therapy. In M. McGoldrick (Ed.), *Revisioning Family Therapy: Race, Culture and Gender in Clinical Practice* (pp. 50–61). New York: Guilford Press.

Krestan, J. (1989). Alcoholism, Family Therapy and Pride. In K. Tilley (Ed.), *Building Bridges, Creating Balance* (a monograph of AAMFT San Francisco Annual Conference Plenary Presentations). Washington, DC: American Association of Marital and Family Therapy.

Krestan, J. (1991). The Baby and the Bathwater. In T. Goodrich, (Ed.), *Women and Power* (pp. 229–233). New York: Norton.

Krestan, J., & Bepko, C. (1990). Codependency: The Social Reconstruction of Female Experience. *Smith College Studies in Social Work, 60*(3), pp. 216–232.

Kurtz, E. (1982). Why AA Works: The Intellectual Significance of Alcoholics Anonymous. *Journal of Studies on Alcohol 41*(1), 38–80.

LA Times, Nov. 9 1994, p. D5.

Malcolm, E. (1986). *Ireland Sober, Ireland Free: Drink and Temperance in Nineteenth-Century Ireland*. Syracuse, NY: Syracuse University Press.

Maney, K. (1998 March 4). Gates Takes on Senate: Microsoft Chief Plays Role No Business Giant Ever Has. *USA Today*, pp. 1–2.

Martindale, D., & Martindale, E. (1971). *The Social Dimensions of Mental Illness, Alcoholism, and Drug Dependence*. Westport, CT: Greenwood Press.

McClelland, D. C., Davis, W. N., Kalin, R., & Wanner, E. (1972). *The Drinking Man*. New York: Free Press.

McGoldrick, M., & Giordano, J. (1996). Overview: Ethnicity and Family Therapy. In M. McGoldrick, J. Giordano and J. K. Pearce (Eds.), *Ethnicity and Family Therapy* (2nd ed., pp. 1–27). New York: Guilford Press.

McGoldrick, M., Giordano, J., & Pearce, J. K. (1996). *Ethnicity and Family Therapy* (2nd ed.). New York: Guilford Press.

McIntosh, P. (1998). White Privilege: Unpacking the Invisible Knapsack. In M. McGoldrick (Ed.), *Revisioning Family Therapy: Race, Culture and Gender in Clinical Practice* (pp. 147–152) New York: Guilford Press.

Mezzich, J. E., & Berganza, C. E., (Eds.). (1984). *Culture and Psychopathology.* New York: Columbia University Press.

Morrison, T. (1998) Home. In W. Lubiano (Ed.), *The House that Race Built.* New York: Vintage Books.

Pinderhughes, E. (1989). *Understanding Race, Ethnicity, & Power.* New York: Free Press.

Pittman, D. J., and Snyder, C. R. (Eds.).(1962). *Society, Culture and Drinking Patterns.* New York: John Wiley.

Sebastian, L. (1992). *The Chaco Anasazi.* New York: Cambridge University Press.

Simonelli, R. (1998). Personal correspondence with J. A. Krestan.

Singer, M., Valentin, F., Baer, H. and Jia, Z. (1992). Why Does Juan Garcia Have a Drinking Problem? The Perspective of Critical Medical Anthropology. *Medical Anthropology, 14,* 77–108.

Tiebout, H. (1954). The Ego Factors in Surrender in Alcoholism. *Quarterly Journal of Studies on Alcohol, 15,* 610–621.

United Nations (1944). The United Nations Development Report. New York: United Nations Development Programme.

USA Today (March 4, 1998), p. 1.

Zack, N. (1995). Introduction. In N. Zack (Ed.), *American Mixed Race: The Culture of Microdiversity* (pp. xv–xxv). Lanham, MD: Rowman and Littlefield.

Chapter Two

Kaleidoscopes and Epic Tales: Diverse Narratives of Adult Children of Alcoholics

Laura Chakrin Cable

The singular action of moving out of denial about alcohol's effect on my family opened many doors to healing. Behind one door was grieving the many losses due to alcohol and learning to rebuild a healthy self in the process. Another door had the beautiful surprise of learning about and celebrating resiliency—my own, my family's and my tribe's.
ANNA LATIMER

Our lives are in our own hands. We intend collectively to reverse
the negatives and to make a more positive future first of all
for ourselves, as well as for our children, for others we love,
and for those who love us.
FRANCES BRISBANE

To tell a story about your life turns it into a history, one that can
be left behind, and makes it easier for you to create
a future of your own design.
DAVID EPSTON

HISTORICAL CONTEXT: THE ACOA MOVEMENT

ONCE UPON A TIME North American children learned to read with Dick and Jane. The White, Christian, blond-haired children lived with their mother, father, cat, and dog in a clean house on a tree-lined street. They epitomized normality, inhabiting a landscape with the Beavers, Ozzie and Harriet, and families like the one in *Father Knows Best*. These families captured the attention of the baby boomers of the 1950s and early 1960s.

In the 1970s and 1980s, as boomers grew old enough to tell their own truths, therapists and writers documented the stories of adults who had been raised with one or more chemically dependent parents. Popular authors (Black, 1981/1987; Wegscheider-Cruse, 1983; Woititz, 1983/1990) articulated experiences that many had secretly and shamefully endured. The national media reflected the power of this story, and the Adult Children of Alcoholics (ACOA) movement was born (Middelton-Moz, 1990; Sher, 1991).

Public stories described the trauma of being raised in a family impaired by substance abuse. Other adults related to the ACOA experience, and the national conversation expanded to one about adult children raised in "dysfunctional families" (Sher, 1991; Wolin, 1991). Many adults found comfort in the proliferating books and self-help groups and were validated in their experience of having been parented in what they considered an inconsistent, neglectful, or abusive manner.

The widespread identification with the ACOA movement triggered another debate, one reflected in humor and cultural essays. The famous cartoon of the large auditorium with a solitary person sitting beneath the banner ANNUAL CONVENTION OF ADULT CHILDREN OF NORMAL FAMILIES expressed awareness of how profoundly Americans resonated with the ACOA movement. Critics voiced concern that true abuse was being trivialized by mixing it with relatively minor family problems and that we were becoming a nation of victims (Kaminer, 1992; Wolin, 1991). Some therapists argued that the ACOA movement was an example of how pathology-based the mental health field had become:

> Recovery got out of control, and spread across our country like wildfire, turning us into a nation of emotional cripples. . . . For the survivors of troubled families, the fad is lethal, as the very strengths that enable children of hardship to prevail are being twisted around, labeled as illnesses, and identified as the cause of lifelong pathology. (Wolin, 1991, p. 3)

Since then, various schools of therapy have embraced a more strengths-oriented, solution-focused and resiliency-based approach (e.g. Miller, 1992; O'Hanlon, 1994; Walsh, 1996, 1998; White, 1995; White and Epston, 1990; Wolin & Wolin, 1993).

The dominant discourse about ACOA issues was also limited by its one-size-fits-all flavor. With notable exceptions (Ackerman, 1986; Brisbane & Stuart, 1985; Middelton-Moz, 1989), the popular and clinical literature omitted discussion of racism, gender, class, sexual orientation, or issues of migration and cross-cultural dynamics. On the basis of a rigorous critique of the literature, Sher (1991) concluded, "Despite the multiracial and multicultural nature of our society, most of the published research fails to address the effects of parental alcoholism on individuals of different racial and ethnic backgrounds" (p. 173). Claudia Black's important later work, *Double Duty* (1990), recognized this gap and acknowledged how other issues, including race and ethnicity, interact with parental alcoholism.

The concepts that underlie narrative therapy provide a framework with which to incorporate an awareness of the influences of culture, class, and racism as well as a recognition of strengths and resilience. The purpose of this chapter is to offer ideas for understanding and working with clients of diverse backgrounds whose lives have been affected by parental substance abuse. These ideas draw from a narrative approach (White and Epston, 1990), a multidimensional cultural comparative framework (Falicov, 1995), and a resiliency-based perspective (Palmer, 1997; Walsh, 1996, 1998; Wolin, 1991; Wolin and Wolin, 1993).

The reader may hold two images in mind through this chapter: the kaleidoscope and the epic tale. The kaleidoscope, with its numerous fragments of multicolored glass, presents endless variety when shifted even slightly. When held to the light, its designs appear different than when turned to shadow. The relationship of its contents and its relationship to the holder and the setting all impact its particular loveliness.

The epic tale records acts of courage and power. Heroes and heroines triumph over unthinkable tests to their endurance and resilience. Tragedies are often suffered, one journeys to new destinations, and individual fates intersect with broader forces of history.

While many sources have been consulted in the writing of this chapter, my orientation is that of a therapist who sits in a room and talks with individuals and families who arrive at the door with pain and hope. My task is to help them turn the kaleidoscope, to see the fragments of their lives in a fresher and clearer way, one that may allow something different to happen. As people tell their stories of what has happened so far and what they want to happen in the future, it is often the case that those who have endured the most adversity see only their inadequacies. When we talk together, they begin to recognize the courage and stamina already apparent in their past, traits that can help guide them toward a future more worth living.

Working Definitions and Assumptions

For the purposes of this chapter, the terms ACOA and *adult child of a substance abuser* will be used interchangeably; that is, they may refer to the adult child of an alcoholic or of an abuser of any other drug. Culture is defined as "a broad multidimensional concept that includes but is not limited to ethnicity, gender, social class, and so forth" (Hardy and Laszloffy, 1995, p. 228). Ethnicity "refers to the group(s) from which an individual has descended and derives the essence of her/his sense of 'peoplehood'" (Hardy and Laszloffy, 1995, p. 229). Individuals cannot be understood out of their cultural context, and yet context does not cause behavior. Here, as in so many areas, a dialectic allows one to see aspects of reality that are made invisible if one uses too narrow a lens.

Dialectical thinking is "any systematic reasoning, exposition, or argument that juxtaposes opposed or contradictory ideas and usually seeks to resolve their conflict" (*Merriam-Webster's Collegiate Dictionary*, 9th ed., s.v. "dialectic"). It is a "both-and" perspective rather than an "either-or" viewpoint. As clinicians we can be more useful to our clients if we can incorporate multiple, sometimes contradictory, frameworks with which to understand our clients' situations than if we try to fit our clients into reductionist frameworks.

The Increasing Need to Develop Cultural Competence

The prevalence of adult children of substance abusers is difficult to ascertain for various methodological reasons (Windle, 1997). However, Windle reports a recent estimate of twenty-two million children of alcoholics (not other drug abusers) over age eighteen. Research indicates that an increase in substance abuse problems is frequently correlated with immigration and acculturation (Gordon, 1981; Heath, 1987, p. 34; Hoffman, 1994). In the United States, the number of non-European immigrants continues to rise; the Census Bureau predicts that the percentage of non-Hispanic Whites will decrease from 72.3 percent in 1998 to 52.8 percent in 2050 (U. S. Bureau of the Census, 1996, 1998). Therefore we can predict an increase in the number of ACOAs from diverse cultural backgrounds.

Researchers have documented an underutilization of treatment resources and Al-Anon by minority groups (Finn, 1994; Wolf/Altschul/Callahan, 1996). At least among family therapists, an overwhelming percentage of clinicians are White (Green, 1998, p. 94). Given the increasing number of immigrants, the underutilization of services by non-Whites, and the fact that children of addicts are at high risk of developing their own chemical dependency problems (Sher, 1997), there is a compelling need to increase our effectiveness with children of substance abusers of all cultural and racial backgrounds. A better understanding of the cultural issues of minorities will help us develop even clearer and more effective therapy for members of White populations (Green, 1998).

LITERATURE REVIEW: ADULT CHILDREN OF ALCOHOLICS FROM DIVERSE CULTURAL BACKGROUNDS

THERE IS A PAUCITY of research about children of substance abusers from a cross-cultural perspective (Sher, 1991). Research for this chapter included exploration of the literature in the fields of substance abuse prevention and treatment, mental health, and family therapy. Given the limitations of the professional literature, both fiction and other nonfiction sources were also consulted. In addition, representatives of Al-Anon's Public Information Service and various agencies and organizations were interviewed.

Ten interrelated themes emerged from this exploration concerning ACOAs from diverse cultural backgrounds. These themes are discussed in the following pages.

CULTURE AND SUBSTANCE ABUSE

Jellinek (1962) recognized that there were different meanings and forms to alcoholism, depending upon one's cultural group. For example, problems with alcohol in Finland often took the form of weekend binge drinking with violent outbursts, while in France there was little drunkenness but significant medical problems caused by daily drinking and high tolerance. In recent decades, anthropologists and alcoholism researchers have conducted considerable research and analysis concerning substance use, misuse, and treatment in various cultures (e.g., Douglas, 1987; Heath, Waddell, and Topper, 1981; Klingemann, Takala, and Hunt, 1992). This depth of research has not yet been conducted with children of alcoholics as the focus.

The Eurocentric Perspective

Most popular and clinical ACOA literature is embedded in the dominant discourse of the patriarchal, White European-American culture. Assumptions are made about normality without acknowledging how much of what is considered normal is related to one's culture. Most empirical research has been conducted on White populations (Rodney, 1996; Sher, 1991) and includes little or no reference to how race, racism, or cultural factors affect ACOA issues.

The absence of recognition of cultural issues is hardly unique to the ACOA literature; similar concerns have been raised about social science (Walsh, 1993, p. 21), family therapy (McGoldrick, 1998) and other aspects of clinical practice: "Much of our theory has shared this bias, which universalizes the experience and social context of the White middle class" (Akamatsu, 1998, p. 129). The pervasiveness of the White perspective reflects the fact that members of a dominant culture are not aware of their own status of privilege: "I have come to see white privilege as an invisible package of unearned assets which I can count on cashing in each day, but about which I was 'meant' to remain oblivious" (McIntosh, 1998, p. 148). Howard (1991) noted that even anthropology reflected this Eurocentric bias: "Cultures organized around the wisdom of a set of stories that are quite different from our (i.e., Western) dominant cultural tales were labeled as backward or primitive cultures" (p. 191).

Clinicians must be aware of their own assumptions about what is normal and "move beyond the myth that one type of family is the paragon of virtue to be emulated by all families and that all others are inherently deficient" (Walsh, 1993, p. 19). If we are not aware of our assumptions about what is normal, we run the risk of imposing our own values upon people who live in different contexts and who might prefer different norms.

Risk and Resilience: Multiple Factors

Two fairly distinct bodies of literature about ACOAs have developed. Sher (1997) reviewed both the clinical and research literature about ACOAs and concluded that "perhaps the most significant revelation about COAs that the research community has established is how difficult it is to make valid generalizations" (p. 248). The only significant exception involves the increased risk of alcoholism among offspring of alcoholics: "In fact, there is probably no more robust finding in the area of alcohol research than the finding that COAs are somewhere between 2 and 10 times more likely to develop alcoholism than non-COAs" (Sher, 1997, p. 249).

The general consensus among researchers is that multiple variables affect the risk and resilience for children of alcoholics. These include length and severity of parent's substance abuse; the child's age and gender; the presence of other supports, traumas, and psychosocial problems; ethnicity and race; economic issues; and treatment involvement (Windle, 1997, p. 189). Tweed and Ryff (1991) articulated the need to identify factors that lead to more positive outcomes; Werner (1986) concluded that resilience can be increased by "constitutional characteristics of the child, and by qualities of the early caregiving environment" (p. 39). The preservation of family rituals appears to reduce intergenerational transmission of alcoholism (Wolin, Bennett, Noonan, and Teitelbaum, 1980). In addition, certain psychological stances have been associated with increased resilience (Wolin and Wolin, 1993).

Some research indicates that pessimistic expectations held by clinicians can in turn lead to exaggerating the pathology of children of alcoholics (Burk and Sher, 1990). Sher (1997) concluded that "many of the popular portrayals of COAs are clearly overgeneralizations and have the potential to be harmful" (p. 253). Rodney (1996) argued for recognition of the failure of research to confirm the ACOA traits repeatedly cited in the popular literature.

"NORMALITY" AND ACOAS

Woititz (1983/1990) stated: "Adult Children of Alcoholics guess at what normal is. The significance of this statement cannot be overestimated, as it is their most profound characteristic. Adult children of alcoholics simply have no experience with what is normal" (p. 22).

The Children of Alcoholics Foundation (COAF) developed a parenting program called Discovering Normal (Bush and Lang 1992), which illustrates both the significance of the concept of "normality" and the potentially harmful effects of confusing "normal" with "healthy" or "culturally dominant." The program's purpose is to help parents who had grown up in alcoholic homes improve their parenting skills, with hopes of breaking the cycle of familial alcoholism. The title of the program reflects the concern expressed by many ACOAs that their lack of knowledge of what is normal impairs their parenting. One of the goals of the program is to help participants recognize that there is a wide range of normal parenting behaviors and that there are also ways of parenting that are less healthy than others. The program offers in-depth and extremely valuable psychoeducation about parenting. However, it does not address cultural issues that impact what is perceived as normal family functioning in such areas as the boundaries between parent and child, the standard for expression of emotion, and expectations about autonomy and interdependence. Undoubtedly, a second edition of this extremely useful resource would reflect the development of the field and would attend more to cultural issues. In fact, the foundation's more recent training program, for college counseling centers, does have a key unit about cultural issues that must be understood in working with students who are children of alcoholics (Children of Alcoholics Foundation, 1997).

UNDERUTILIZATION OF TREATMENT RESOURCES BY CULTURAL MINORITIES

Language presents the most obvious barrier for immigrants and some Native American minorities. However, even when language is not the salient issue, significant research indicates underutilization of treatment resources by minorities. Finn (1994) reported that members of cultural minorities initiate and complete substance abuse treatment at a lower rate than those of cultural majority groups. They are also "less likely to reduce or eliminate substance abuse during or after treatment" (Finn, 1994, p. 325). Bell (1990) reported that African Americans initiate teatment at a later stage of substance abuse than Whites, which decreases the efficacy of treatment (pp. 16–17).

Kuramoto (1997) noted that various factors may lead to problems with Asian American and Pacific Islanders accessing and utilizing treatment (p. 96). Twelve-step groups involve face-to-face contact and catharsis, which is often experienced as unfamiliar and uncomfortable for Asian Americans (F. Kuramoto, personal communication, August 12, 1998). For example, among Southeast Asians, attendance at AA and NA (Narcotics Anonymous) is usually court-ordered and is perceived as extremely shameful, though it can be useful (H. Phengsomphone, personal communication, August 13, 1998). Concerning Hispanics, Delgado (1997) has argued that "failure to provide culture-specific services throughout the entire continuum [of substance abuse treatment] will in all likelihood result in poor use of services" (p. 41).

Surveys conducted by Al-Anon indicate that 93 percent of its members within the United States identify as White, 3 percent as Hispanic, 1 percent as Black, 1 percent as Asian, and 1 percent as "other." Interestingly, Whites are a much smaller percentage of Alateens: 80 percent White, 11 percent

Hispanic, 3 percent Native American, 3 percent Black, 1 percent Asian, and 3 percent "other" (Wolf/Altschul/Callahan, Inc., 1996). In both parts of Al-Anon, however, the membership does not reflect the demographics of the United States. The organization is aware of this problem and is concerned about finding ways for Al-Anon to become more accessible to diverse people (C. Ricewasser, personal communication, August 1998). Al-Anon publishes material in Spanish and has hundreds of groups throughout the world, including many in Central and South America. There are at least six Hispanic Central Service offices throughout the United States.

"THE MAP IS NOT THE TERRITORY": A CAUTION ABOUT CULTURAL CATEGORIES

Cultural competence involves both awareness and sensitivity. Awareness requires "exposure to content highlighting the unique aspects of various cultural groups," while sensitivity is "primarily an affective function; an individual responds emotionally to stimuli with delicacy and respectfulness" (Hardy and Laszloffy, 1995, p. 227). In discussing ACOAs and culture, one is faced with a dilemma: How do you increase your awareness of any generalizations that can be made about groups while remaining sensitive to individual differences? For example, perhaps this chapter should be divided into sections about Native Americans, African-Americans, Hispanics, Asian Americans, and Jews. Why not?

The first problem with categorizing people into ethnic and racial categories is that the major ethnic or racial categories contain numerous subgroups with very different characteristics. For example, in 1993 there were 341 different Native American tribes recognized by the federal government and 111 entities seeking federal recognition (Moran and May, 1997, p. 3). The socially constructed term *Latino/Hispanic* (Delgado, 1997, p. 36) includes numerous and quite diverse subgroups from the Caribbean and from North, Central, and South America. Gray (1997) has argued that most research has not addressed the heterogeneity among Black Americans, who include African Americans, African Caribbeans, Africans from Central and South America, and recent immigrants from Africa. African Americans have diverse religious affiliations and worldviews. *Asian/Pacific Islander* refers to more than sixty different ethnic/racial groups and subgroups (National Clearinghouse for Alcohol and Drug Information, 1998). Differences among Jewish Americans include nation of origin or of ancestors' origin, stage of acculturation, and degree of religious observance.

A second problem with categorizing people is the increasing number of those of mixed heritage, for whom ethnic and racial identification is not a fixed state but rather a part of a changing and constructed identity. "America is becoming a mestizo nation" (Martinez, 1998, p. 262). Julia Alvarez wrote, "I discovered that there were others out there like me, hybrids who came in a variety of colors and whose ethnicity and race were an evolving process, not a rigid paradigm or a list of boxes, one of which you checked off" (1998, pp. 146–147). Another biracial writer stated, "In the 1990s, I'm still an aberration, but in another ten, twenty, thirty years, Americans will look at each other and—just like they do with me now—really not know who someone is by their face" (See, 1998, p. 137).

A third problem with categorization is the bias embedded in the language of the categories. In some cases, words used to categorize one's ethnicity can contain the oppression one is seeking to resist. For example, as Castillo (1994/1997) has noted: "'Hispanic,' the ethnic label for all people who reside in the United States with some distant connection with the culture brought by the Spaniards during the conquest of the Americas, is a gross misnomer. The word promotes an official negation of people called 'Hispanic' by implying that their ethnicity or race is exclusively European rather than partly Native American (as are most Chicanos/as) or African American (as are those descendants of the African slave trade along the Caribbean coasts)" (pp. 266–267).

A fourth problem is that the process of categorizing easily slides into perceiving people as objects, an outcome that can be disempowering. The most powerful healing relationships are those in which the therapist believes in the client's ability to become an active agent in his or her own life, an author of his or her own life story. The greater the client's trauma and oppression, the more necessary is the therapist's faith in resilience and possibility. Indeed, one of the Twelve-Steps slogans is "Expect a miracle." Buber (1957/1996) articulated the power of the I–Thou relationship: "The language of objects catches only one corner of actual life. The It is the chrysalis, the You is the butterfly" (p. 69). If a therapist perceives a client as a "Thou," or a subject, rather than an "It," or an object, there is more possibility to imagine and result in change.

SUBSTANCE ABUSE AND OPPRESSION

Alcoholism has devastated the indigenous people of our continent. Middelton-Moz (1986, 1989, 1990; also with Dwinell, 1986) has written extensively about the trauma of parental alcoholism, racism, and oppression among Native Americans. She emphasized the critical issue of enormous unresolved grief at the loss of culture, connection, kinship, and self-esteem. For those who had been taken away from their families and sent to boarding schools, there was the loss of family and parenting. Native Americans often completed treatment for alcoholism without any attention being paid to their cultural stories, values, or beliefs.

The literature about substance abuse treatment of African Americans recognizes the importance of addressing racial oppression: "Attempts to understand individual and group behavior in general and AOD [alcohol and other drug]-related behavior in particular must acknowledge the role that racism plays" (Gray, 1997, p. 66). Bell (1990) asserted, "For historic reasons of racism and oppression, [B]lack people have developed a strong racial identity that most [W]hite people don't have" (p. 46). Anderson (1986) addressed the importance of incorporating racial identity and other aspects of the African American experience into treatment: "This Experience involves history, society's view of [B]lacks, [B]lack self-concept, racial identity, the civil rights movement, socioeconomic factors, and racism" (p. 209). She argued that "one cannot assume that [B]lack adult children of alcoholics will relate to what we already know about ACOAs and co-dependency. Many have commented 'That is not me!' when presented with the information" (p. 216).

Brisbane and Stuart (1985) found minimal involvement of Black women in Al-Anon or COA groups. They identified a taboo among Blacks against saying anything about one's mother that might be perceived as disrespectful, even if she was an alcoholic. "Projection of a good home front is protection against what is seen as negative intervention by schools, police, and other social agencies. But what works in response to negative external forces often works against finding solutions to internal problems" (p. 211). The author bell hooks (1995) articulated the impact of racism on the field of mental health:

> Within institutions shaped by [W]hite supremacist capitalist patriarchal biases, there is little hope that individuals who are interested in developing psychological theories and practices that address the dilemmas facing African Americans will find support. When this reality is linked to a culture of shame within diverse [B]lack communities that silences attempts by [B]lack folks to name our woundedness, a climate of repression prevails. (P. 138)

Migration and Acculturation

Migration can lead to dynamics similar to those caused by parental alcoholism. Oliver-Diaz and Fiqueroa (1986) identified some common themes of children of alcoholics and children of immigrants. For example, there is often a role reversal with parents; for immigrants, it is because children often have better language skills and knowledge about how to negotiate American systems. There is commonly in the children of immigrants embarrassment about the parents' behaviors and guilt about this embarrassment, which parallels the embarrassment experienced by children of substance abusers. "The feelings of mistrust, guilt, confusion, isolation, and fear are as true for children of acculturation as for children of alcoholics" (Oliver-Diaz and Fiqueroa, 1986, p. 55). Clearly, the implication is that in treating children the clinician must address acculturation issues as well as alcoholism issues.

Spirituality

Al-Anon grew out of Judeo-Christian roots, but a large number of Asian Americans practice Buddhism, Confucianism, and animism (Kuramoto, personal communication, August 12, 1998). There are also a growing number of Muslims in the United States. The whole area of spiritual issues in therapy offers rich possibilities for exploration.

Oliver-Diaz and Fiqueroa (1986) recognized the importance of addressing spiritual beliefs among Hispanic children of alcoholics who have been impacted by the

> fundamentalist Christian belief that equates alcoholism with sin. . . . Understanding the disease concept gave them real relief. Once they understood that their parents had a disease and were not at fault, they were able to let go of their belief that their parents were doomed 'sinners' and to grasp the possibility that a loving God would not eternally damn the victim of an illness that preys upon the body, mind, and soul. (P. 56)

Spiritual issues are important for Jewish ACOAs to deal with if they are to utilize the Twelve Steps approach of Al-Anon. Many Jews wrestle with conflicts and discomfort about attending meetings that are often in church basements and frequently involve reciting the Lord's Prayer. A group called

Jewish Alcoholics, Chemically Dependent Persons and Significant Others (JACS) is a volunteer, non-profit self-help organization developed to support Jews coping with substance abuse. JACS disseminates literature through its newsletter and Web site, which examines connections between the Twelve Steps and helps reconcile Jewishness with twelve-step programs (e.g., Almoni, 1987; Roberts, 1997; Twerski, 1985).

Cultural Sources of Resilience

A prominent theme in the literature is that adult children of alcoholics find sources of strength and resilience in the nurturant parts of their cultural community and heritage. This dynamic has been identified by writers of all cultural groups.

Middelton-Moz (1986) emphasized the healing potential of opening up communication about issues of loss between members of a family or tribe. "Most often, when communication in families is reestablished and the family shares its grief together, there is a new sense of power in the family. A reconnection with the greater community develops, as well as a sense of responsibility to the kinship network" (p. 64). Pride develops, which counters the shame and disempowerment of addiction and oppression.

Moran and May (1997) report that lower rates of substance abuse have been noted among Native American youths with "strong attachments to families in which culture and school are valued" (p. 8). They also indicate that recent research has found "higher self-esteem and more internal locus of control, and fewer problem behaviors among American Indian adolescents who identified strongly with both their American Indian culture and Western culture versus those who identified with only one or with neither" (p. 11).

The National Association of Native American Children of Alcoholics (NANACOA) grew out of the COA movement. In 1988 a group of Native Americans attended a conference of the National Association of Adult Children of Alcoholics. According to Anna Latimer (personal communication, May 15, 1998), then executive director of NANACOA, the conference was quite informative, and yet there was a sense of something missing. The group retreated for its own meeting to address this; they formed a talking circle and asked people to pray. The participants identified a need to incorporate spirituality and humor and, especially, a focus on the group as opposed to the individual.

This emphasis on "we-ness" is integral to traditional Native American culture and has been reclaimed by NANACOA. "The welfare of the people was what was important. In ceremonies held early in their lives, children were taught to think of what was best for the tribe as a whole. Being selfish or thinking only of oneself was unheard of" (National Association of Native American Children of Alcoholics, 1996, p. 9).

The purpose of NANACOA is to promote healing in indigenous people from the effects of alcoholism, historical trauma, and racism. Healing occurs on an individual level and in the context of the family and tribe, through spirituality, ritual and ceremony, and cultural values that emphasize connectedness. Part of the mission is to recognize and build on the survival against centuries of oppression. As Latimer puts it, "When obstacles are put in your way it forces you to dig deeper."

The expression "getting on that red road" refers to the process of healing; the "recovery process is the recovery of human beingness." Part of the process is removing the effects of alcohol so that "what's already there can blossom." What is already there includes traditional wisdom, which has been passed along not necessarily through book knowledge but primarily through "the way one lives, the way one is taught to behave." The young are encouraged to seek out elders who can share their knowledge.

In 1995, NANACOA and three other national Native American organizations developed the Healing Journey Accord, a ten-year plan whose goal is stated as follows: "We envision that by the year 2005, we will have strong, healthy communities which can nurture and support the spiritual, cultural and economic growth of individuals and families" (National Association of Native American Children of Alcoholics, 1996, p. 5). This accord specifies strategies for each of the participating organizations. Individual recovery is linked with communal well-being.

Recent writing and research has explored the value of incorporating an Afrocentric orientation into substance abuse prevention and treatment (hooks 1993). Gray (1997) reported that a fundamental component of an Afrocentric model is to "build self-esteem by developing an identity that begins with African origins rather than slave origins" (p. 73). Madhubuti (1997) described how he overcame the legacy of poverty, racial oppression, and his mother's substance abuse and early death: "My own transformation came about as a direct result of being introduced to African (Black) ideas that did not insult my own personhood, but guided me, invigorated me, and lifted me beyond the white supremacist theories that confined me and my people to the toilets of other people's promises and progress" (p. 449).

Delgado (1997) emphasized the need for substance abuse treatment to understand and collaborate with "natural support systems" in the Hispanic/Latino community. JACS sponsors regular retreats for "recovering alcoholics, chemically dependent persons, significant others, and family members to explore values and spiritual resources within Judaism that may support and strengthen their recovery" (Jewish Alcoholics, Chemically Dependent Persons and Significant Others, 1998).

POSTMODERNISM, SOCIAL CONSTRUCTIONISM, AND OTHER BIG IDEAS: WHAT DO THEY HAVE TO DO WITH ACOAs?!

MODERNIST THOUGHT HOLDS that there is an external truth. The implication for this issue is that there is a category "Adult Children of Alcoholics" and that members of this category share many common traits and would benefit from a particular mode of therapy. If particular members do not believe they suffer from those traits, they could be seen as being "in denial." Postmodern thought, on the other hand, offers new and extremely useful ideas for increasing resilience among ACOAs and for integrating issues of diversity into the discussion.

Postmodern thought views reality through multiple lenses and recognizes that there are multiple realities, each with its own internal validity. Social constructionism postulates that the particular version of reality held by an individual is shaped by the person's social context and is particularly influenced by the way that language shapes his or her perception of reality.

Narrative therapy, as articulated by White and Epston (1990), is based on the notion that "we live by the stories that we have about our lives, that these stories actually shape our lives, constitute our lives, and that they 'embrace' our lives" (p. 14). A fundamental concept is that "people are not problems, problems are problems." People may suffer from "problem-saturated" descriptions of themselves that constrain their behavior and imprison them in self-defeating patterns. Narrative therapy is an approach that can incorporate "local" and scientific knowledge to help people develop stories about their life that allow growth and empowerment.

LOCAL KNOWLEDGE

Local knowledge is the experience people have of their own life. An individual may contact a therapist for an initial session using popular expressions to describe various problems; for example: "I grew up in a dysfunctional family, and I can't cope with intimate relationships." Or a colleague may refer a person for therapy by saying, "She is really codependent." However, "except in very general terms, it is not possible to predict the effects of the problem in advance of meeting with the persons concerned" (White and Epston, 1990, p. 49). Local knowledge is defined as that experience of individuals that arises from their own personal life. It is "experience-near" rather than scientifically based.

Foucault (1980) asserted that local knowledges have been "subjugated" in modern society, that is, "disqualified as inadequate to their task or insufficiently elaborated: naïve knowledges, located low down on the hierarchy, beneath the required level of cognition or scientificity" (p. 82). As mental health professionals, we may be so imbued with our expert knowledge that we do not listen carefully and truly empathically to the people sitting in front of us.

An important aspect of respecting local knowledge is to understand problems in the context of an individual's life. We maximize the options for clients to change their relationship to their problems by eliciting their own local knowledge, which is, by definition, more complete and nuanced than any description that could be provided by an unknown scientist who does not know all the myriad variables of a person's situation.

SCIENTIFIC KNOWLEDGE

Scientific knowledge is based on empirical research. There are pieces of this knowledge base that can provide clarity and useful information to adult children of alcoholics when presented in a psychoeducational format. The most important information to communicate is the well-researched risk factors for offspring of alcoholics to develop alcoholism themselves. It is as important for ACOAs to know about this as it is important for anyone else with a family history of a particular disorder to know about transmitted risk factors; given such knowledge, those at risk can make informed choices about how they will monitor their own health and choose to respond to any early warning signs of the disorder.

The following are other examples of information about alcoholism that can be useful for clients in making sense of their own stories: the common stages of alcoholism, what happens during a blackout, the fact that alcohol affects women differently at various points in their menstrual cycle and that the process of alcoholism is often "telescoped" for women in the sense that the stages seem to occur in a more rapid progression. For example, one client found that her anger toward her mother became more manageable when she recognized that her mother's failure to acknowledge incidents while drinking could be indicative of blackouts rather than of malicious ly-ing. As she more clearly understood the biological impact of alcohol, she was able to achieve a level of understanding of her mother that allowed her to recognize her mother's strengths while she continued to set limits on her mother's behavior.

THE USEFULNESS OF A NARRATIVE APPROACH

NARRATIVE PERSPECTIVE INVOLVES helping clients tell their own story, their own preferred story. "Once we recognize that there are many sto-ries that may fit any individual's life, we are freed from having to discover the ultimate truth about a client's life. . . . Our job is only to help them find the creativity and wisdom they need to find their own truths and heal their own lives" (Penn, 1991, p. 45).

Narrative ideas lead to a basic dissonance with the whole concept of ACOAs, because the latter concept conflicts with the belief that people are not problems, problems are problems. Where, then, can one place the pop-ular and clinical literature about effects of parental alcoholism? This litera-ture is most useful as examples of local knowledge. The popular classic books can be introduced as versions of reality, as lenses through which it might be useful to view one's own story. In addition, we can offer stories of individuals who come from diverse cultural backgrounds and who have traveled various pathways to successfully battle the effects of alcoholism and addiction.

THE INTERACTION OF CULTURE AND ACOA ISSUES

HOW DOES CULTURE interact with ACOA issues? First and most obvi-ously, each person affected by parental substance abuse is a member of various overlapping cultures and subcultures, as defined by such variables as ethnicity, geography, class, religion, and sexual orientation. These factors interact to form "ecological niches" (Falicov, 1995) and "multiplexities" (Cornel West, quoted in Akamatsu, 1998; see also Kliman, 1994). For ex-ample, Debra is a fifty-five-year-old African American accountant living in Connecticut who attends Baptist services and has family in Georgia, with other relatives originally from the Cape Verde Islands. Nicole is a twenty-five-year-old nurse's aide living in a tenement in Providence, Rhode Island, who escaped Liberia during the recent civil war and has no religious affiliation. Both are dark-skinned, and both report parental substance abuse. Yet there are fundamental differences between these women; they occupy different ecological niches. To be most useful, therapy must acknowledge their specific realities in addition to the more traditionally defined ACOA issues.

Second, cultures set norms for what is acceptable and shameful, valued and discouraged, publicly celebrated and privately endured. Loud debates and intense emotional displays are considered signs of comfort and love in one family, while another household perceives the same behavior as rude and disrespectful. Norms exist not only for general behavior but also for substance-related practices. In some cultures it would be considered rude to host a wedding with no alcohol, while in others it would cause dismay to have an open bar. In one community it is assumed that New Year's Eve is a time for getting drunk whereas in another a toast of champagne is expected and in yet another only nonalcoholic beverages are regularly set out. In one neighborhood a man is not considered to be a man unless he occasionally gets drunk with his buddies; in another a dinner drink is suspect (and one may end up discreetly shooting heroin). A Puerto Rican volunteer with Al-Anon (Carmen N., personal communication, August 1998) noted that some members of her community have a deeply held belief that it is a man's right to become intoxicated and verbally abusive and that it is the woman's duty to accept this treatment. Indeed, women who attend Al-Anon or ACOA often face censure from their families. She noted how difficult it is to break the cycle of "adult children of adult children of adult children."

Addiction affects particular families differently in part because various subcultures have different norms for family and social behaviors. Some cultures favor high degrees of autonomy and separation by the young adult; other groups encourage highly interdependent patterns and very close relationships between generations. The ACOA movement evolved into the movement against "codependency" and promoted "taking care of oneself." Feminist critics have discussed the movement's inherent devaluing and pathologizing of traditionally female characteristics of caretaking (Krestan and Bepko, 1990). The codependency movement comes out of a European-American middle-class tradition, does not fit everyone's realities (Inclan and Hernandez, 1992), and "might err by unwittingly defining recovery and normality as the client's and family's ability to incorporate values, beliefs, and behavior that are more congruent with the ways of the Anglo culture than with their own" (p. 247). The impact of "normality" is discussed later in further depth.

Third, children of alcoholics suffer from erosion in the addict's connection with his or her community and traditions (Favazza, 1981; Westermeyer, 1981). The concept of "suspended ethnicity" (Westermeyer, 1981, p. 48) is implied in the words of a Mexican American (quoted in Favazzo, 1981, p. 88): "I am a heroin addict first and a Chicano second. Maybe one day when I kick the habit, I'll become a Chicano again." There is evidence that disrupted family rituals contribute to increased rates of transmission of alcoholism (Wolin, Bennett, Noonan, and Teitelbaum, 1980). While this research was conducted on White middle- and upper-class families, one could hypothesize that it can be generalized to other racial and socioeconomic groups and that the preservation of rituals and connections increases the likelihood of more positive outcomes for adult children of alcoholics.

Fourth, some aspects of American culture are oppressive for people of color and ethnic minorities, as well as for other less privileged groups, such as poor people, gay men, lesbian women, and the physically disabled. "Racism and discrimination can tip the scales of risk and resiliency for these children, placing them in uniquely vulnerable positions, especially those who have been cut off from their histories and discouraged from identifying positively with their culture of origin" (Vasquez, quoted in Brooks and Rice, 1997, p. 191).

Fifth, the trauma of racism—and the denial of racism—is woven into the fabric of American culture. It is distressing for most therapists to confront the extent to which racism and oppression affect our everyday life of and that of our clients. "We have found that because many individuals are unaware of the existence and effects of a pro-racist ideology, the process of effectively challenging it is extremely difficult, both in and out of therapy. After all, one cannot actively resist a phenomenon to which one is oblivious" (Hardy and Laszloffy, 1998, p. 124).

Traumatic realities are difficult to confront. There is such dissonance between the way we want to see ourselves and the flawed reality of our society. Of the phenomenon of cultural denial of trauma, Herman (1992) wrote:

> The knowledge of horrible events periodically intrudes into public awareness but is rarely retained for long. Denial, repression, and dissociation operate on a social as well as an individual level. The study of psychological trauma has an 'underground' history. Like traumatized people, we have been cut off from the knowledge of our past. Like traumatized people, we need to understand the past in order to reclaim the present and the future. Therefore, an understanding of psychological trauma begins with rediscovering history. (P. 2)

Finally, the process of recovery can be understood as a cultural transformation: some people who confront parental addiction break intergenerational patterns of behavior. "Individuals involved in self-help and 12-step recovery programs acquire a new language of recovery that structures behavioral change and the uncovering of deep beliefs and feelings. A language of recovery provides a sense of order and a vocabulary to describe and validate what was previously denied" (Brown, p. 228).

Black (1990) expanded her original model of ACOAs to include those who identified an additional factor—such as race, history of sexual abuse, or presence of an eating disorder—alongside the presence of a parent with alcoholism. This was an attempt to acknowledge how crucial are other realities in addition to parental substance abuse. A limitation of the "double duty" model is the number of people with multiple issues: the African American divorced daughter of an alcoholic, who is in recovery for her own drinking and who has a history of physical abuse; the Korean-born young man adopted by a White Jewish couple who later divorced after the father's alcoholism progressed; the Italian American woman who had multiple abusive and substance-abusing male figures in and out of her house during her childhood and who now simultaneously struggles with her own gambling, her Puerto Rican husband's episodic cocaine abuse, and her children's school problems.

"Don't Talk, Don't Trust, Don't Feel": Parallels Between the Family, Community, and Society

"Don't talk, Don't trust, Don't feel" (Black, 1981/1987). These rules resonate powerfully with so many adult children of substance abusers and other trauma. They are embedded in the broader culture in a way that maintains oppression. The subjugation of the child in an alcoholic family parallels other forms of oppression such as those based on color, culture, gender, and sexual orientation.

"Don't Talk." Pinderhughes (1998) described the "vulnerability to responding to the pain of oppression by sealing off the pain, not talking about it, not asking, not trying to understand" (p. 197). The author bell hooks wrote, "Only as African Americans break with the culture of shame that has demanded that we be silent about our pain will we be able to engage wholistic strategies for healing that will break this cycle" (1995, p. 144).

"Don't Trust." Distrust of the oppressor is a survival skill used by subju-

gated people everywhere. Perpetrators of abuse are notoriously devious in their methods. Herman (1992) detailed the ways that abusers try to use subtle forms of coercion to gain control. Subjugated people learn to be streetwise, to be hypervigilant, to observe the oppressor with exquisite sensitivity, just as a young child learns to open the door slowly, on coming home from school, to gauge her parent's level of sobriety.

Bell (1990) argues that African Americans' distrust of the dominant culture reduces the use of treatment: "When an individual is concerned about the alcohol or other drug use of a family member, there is frequently little trust in outside resources available to the family. The family often views treatment as culturally insensitive and, more important, as being generally ineffective." (p. 13).

"Don't Feel." Numbing and restricted range of emotions are classic symptoms of posttraumatic stress disorder (Herman, 1992). Educators and therapists often encounter students "whose poor school performance and learning problems are linked to their efforts to keep hidden emotionally laden, overwhelming events of loss and abuse" (Pinderhughes, 1998, p. 197).

IMPLICATIONS FOR THERAPY

THEORETICAL IMPLICATIONS FOR THERAPY

THE ACOA STORY as described in the self-help literature has merit, as does the emerging story of the "resilient self" and other tales. As therapists we should invite our clients to tell rich stories of themselves, because opportunities for healing can be mined from the infinite complexity of an individual's story. "All of our story threads—the ones we favor and the ones we do not—make up the ever-undulating tapestry of who we are, the culture of the self" (Pare, 1996, p. 34).

Each therapy is a novel situation. As therapists we must view each client as representing a unique culture. There is not a regular therapy for "mainstream" people and separate ethnic therapies. Understanding someone's cultural issues is a part of empathy (Di Nicola, 1997).

"The therapist is a master conversationalist artist, an architect of dialogue" (Anderson and Goolishian, 1988, p. 384). In particular, White and Epston have developed the idea of the "externalized conversation," an approach in which the therapist helps the client examine how "the Problem" has affected him or her and how it has, all too frequently, "recruited the person into assisting the problem (White, 1995). The art and craft of therapy involves striking various balances, for example, developing sufficient rapport and empathy so that clients experience enough safety, respect, and acceptance to communicate the problem or pain that is bringing them to therapy while also conveying to them one's belief that they are capable of making changes to find a solution. There is, ideally, a balance between offering useful new information and possible narratives while also eliciting the client's own resources and narratives.

Therapists must assume responsibility for raising the topic of culture and racism. This requires the development of skill and sensitivity, just as therapists have over time developed skill in addressing the previously taboo issues of death and sexual abuse. "Because of the toll that a pro-racist ideology takes upon relationships of all types, it represents a serious impediment to the treatment process—one that therapists must assume an active role in confronting and resisting" (Hardy and Laszloffy, 1998, p. 124).

The tyranny of "normality" should be confronted. The issue of normality is frequently raised by many ACOA and non-ACOAs in therapy. For example, Mary, a forty-five-year-old office worker, was raised by a physically abusive mother and an alcoholic father. She described how often she finds herself staring at the NORMAL setting of her washing machine and wondering, What is normal?; Mary wishes she could simply push a switch to put her life on a normal setting. Ralph, a thirty-five-year-old speech therapist, struggles every time he wants to ask his partner to make a change. "How do I know if what I feel and what I want is normal or if I am just being a selfish child? After all, I grew up in a dysfunctional family."

There are difficulties with the impact of the concept of normality on therapy. First, it can be related to the use of therapy as a form of social control—to help a person adjust to a "normal" social order that may be dominant and destructive. The most obvious example of this is the widespread use of Valium by unhappy housewives in the 1950s.

Second, individuals may believe that if they could only figure out how to act normal, their emotional pain will cease. In fact, behaving in a conventional and socially acceptable way may be a skill they choose to utilize in certain situations, but they may decide that to oppose what is conventional is the most productive route to being in the world.

Third, what is normal is culture bound. The distress a person experiences may be related to the inherent conflict of living in a multicultural situation where several norms are mutually contradictory. What is normal for a particular ethnic or racial subgroup may be unhealthy for a particular individual, yet it may be harder for the person to resist the pressure to conform because of the larger context of racism or the stress of migration. In addition, the cultural norm may be overly constraining for the person. Weingarten (1995) asserts that "we must be able to identify cultural premises that constrain us and others" (p. 2) and must engage in conversations that allow the client to challenge these cultural beliefs.

Finally, the concept of normality can be used as ammunition between family members. For example, partners can argue about whose perspective is more normal, meaning correct. Or a family member accuses another family member of being abnormal, which might mean wrong or inadequate or simply different.

The whole notion of normality may need to be deconstructed (White, 1995, p. 24) in the therapist's mind and, when appropriate, in the clinical encounter. What does a client mean by "normal"? How, in his opinion, would things be different if he were more "normal"? Does she want to fit into the stereotypical nuclear family with a dominant husband to whom she graciously submits? Does she feel like a failure because after divorcing her abusive husband she believes she is raising her children in a broken family? Does the client, wishing to overcome the profound shame that has shadowed him since childhood, envision fitting in as the necessary route to avoid humiliation? Does she want to know some useful strategies for managing a toddler, which she did not learn in her family of origin?

Finally, we must examine the implications of the term *dysfunctional family*. The notion of dysfunctionality must be disentangled from ideas of diversity and difficulty or suffering. The belief that one's problems stem from being raised in a dysfunctional family can be liberating, because it allows one to feel less shame about one's perceived inadequacies. However, this belief can also belittle one's parents in a way that can sever ties to roots of meaning and resilience. For example, what is the difference between (1) perceiving that your African American parents struggled to cope with alcoholism, in a society that judged it as a moral failure, while they battled racial oppression and (2) labeling them as dysfunctional parents?

GUIDELINES

1. *Know what you know.* Own your clinical experience and empirical knowledge. Even if each family is approached as unique, previous knowledge is useful. As in anthropology, "although one starts any effort at thick description, beyond the obvious and superficial, from a state of general bewilderment as to what the devil is going on—trying to find one's feet—one does not start (or ought not) intellectually empty-handed" (Geertz, 1973, p. 27).

2. *Know what you don't know.* Assume a stance of curiosity and naïveté

(Dyche and Zayas, 1995). Recognize that each person who steps into your office is a unique and mysterious individual who lives within multiple contexts. However, know where to go for more information about a particular ethnic group (e.g., McGoldrick, Giordano, and Pearce, 1996); seek out that information and be aware of it, yet do not assume that the generalization actually applies to this new person. Be a "highly informed 'not-knower'" (Laird, 1998, p. 30). "Conducting therapy, learning a language, entering another culture are activities that require childlike qualities—the ability to see things freshly, to suspend one's disbelief" (Di Nicola, 1997, p. 313).

3. *Work with the client to discover what he or she knows.* Clients come to us aware of their woundedness; we can help acquaint them with their competence and resilience. "How did you manage to go on despite the repeated sexual abuse?" "How were you able to concentrate on school with so many fights at home?" "Was there a relative who also coped with so much adversity, who helped you to learn how to do that?" Exploring unique outcomes in depth roots the alternative skills and story.

4. *Support connections with others who can share useful knowledge.* Refer clients to appropriate readings, local cultural organizations, and Web sites (encourage those without computers to explore the public library). Present twelve-step groups as sources of information, support, and alternative ways of looking at the world, as offered meaning, as possible stories to draw from. As Davis and Jansen (1988) have written about Alcoholics Anonymous, "in the narrative framework, people joining AA are not help seekers in search of treatment, but story tellers who through telling and listening transform their lives" (p. 173). When appropriate, inform people that organizations like Al-Anon/ACOA are great resources for some people, that you would encourage them to try it, that Al-Anon flourishes in many foreign countries and is beginning to examine ways of being more accessible to people of all cultures and races. Some ACOA groups are not affiliated with Al-Anon. In the author's experience, those that *are* affiliated are preferable because they adhere to Al-Anon standards. Express curiosity about their experience, opinions, and ideas about how any weaknesses in these organizations could be ameliovated. Establish contact with local Al-Anon/ACOA folks. Particular AA meetings have evolved and have been successfully adapted to various cultural groups (Amodeo, Robb, Peou, and Tran, 1996; Gordon, 1981; Hoffman, 1994). Writers have explored the connections between the Twelve Steps of Alcoholics Anonymous and particular spiritual traditions to facilitate connections for such groups as Jews and Native Americans (Blackfeet Chemical Dependency Program, 1996; Olitzky and Copans, 1991).

PRACTICAL IMPLICATIONS FOR THERAPY

1. Therapy is guided by the client's presenting problem. The presenting problem should not be seen as symptomatic of underlying "unresolved ACOA issues." If the therapist believes that parental substance abuse has affected the presenting problem, this idea can be raised in a transparent way as an offered, not imposed, meaning.

2. Develop a cultural genogram. The genogram is a wonderful tool for contextualizing a particular situation (McGoldrick and Gerson, 1985). The creation of a genogram should routinely include questions about substance abuse, ethnicity, resilience. Melina (1989) described ways of incorporating adoption stories into the genogram. In the process of constructing a genogram, the therapist and client access local knowledge, particular language (Anderson and Goolishian, 1988), family themes (Papp and Imber-Black, 1996), "cultural stories" (McGill, 1992), and images of resilience (Walsh, 1996), all of which can later be built upon.

3. Present "expert knowledge" *as offered meaning or information* (White, 1995, p. 30). For example, information about addiction and common dilemmas faced by other families can be offered, with humility, as being of some possible use to a client, rather than presented with the arrogant certainty that the therapist "knows best."

CASE STUDY: JENNIFER'S STORY

Jennifer was referred for therapy by her supervisor, who was concerned that her angry outbursts at work were interfering with her job performance. The employee assistance counselor who made the referral noted the presence of ACOA issues. Jennifer worked in middle management in an insurance company. She had significant technical skills but had a reputation for being very critical of her coworkers. Jennifer was single, though she lived with her boyfriend of ten years; neither had any children.

Jennifer had been in individual and group therapy since age eleven, when her mother insisted that she see a psychiatrist. She had been shuttled between her parents' houses after they divorced, when she was three years old. Her father, who was Puerto Rican, gradually became disengaged and lost contact with her. Her mother, who was Jewish, drank heavily, which contributed to her involvement with a series of three boyfriends, each of whom moved in and brought with him various substances that he was involved with. Jennifer, an only child, had focused all of her energies on succeeding at school; she was devastated when her mother sent her to live with maternal grandmother at age fifteen, because she could no longer "handle" her. At that time Jennifer was sent to a new school, which had none of the advanced courses she had been preparing herself for. Her grandmother was deeply shamed by her daughter's alcoholism, lifestyle, and biracial child and periodically erupted in anger at Jennifer, cursing and belittling her.

Jennifer smoked marijuana heavily in college. After several leaves of absence she graduated, found work, and was promoted in her company. She visited her grandmother and mother regularly, although each visit was unsettling. In fact, she visited on Saturdays in order to have Sunday to recuperate before returning to work.

Jennifer was referred to Al-Anon/ACOA as part of her therapy. However, the two local groups were both in churches, and she felt extremely uncomfortable attending the meetings. She also complained that she felt worse after attending each of the meetings and simply did not return. She identified with what she read in Janet Woititz' *Adult Children of Alcoholics* and believed she had a big need to control things at work.

Jennifer was seen weekly for twelve weeks, biweekly for several months, and then monthly. Initially the focus was on helping her to be more appropriately assertive at work and to vent her anger in therapy. Early on, we identified her status as an adult child of an alcoholic. We focused on how she had managed to become so successful at school and in her career despite the incredible disruptions throughout her childhood. How had she concentrated on learning what she needed to learn in order to graduate and pass her exams? What resources had she called into play in order to find her own apartment and become financially independent and professionally competent? How had she learned to overcome the racism and anti-Semitism from within her family and in the community? What skills allowed her to navigate through the seductions of addiction?

During the course of her therapy, Jennifer began to own her strengths as well as her vulnerabilities. She recognized that she was energetic and goal oriented, and she reached out to teachers and supervisors who could teach her needed skills. She began to trust her own perceptions, emotions, and opinions. She gradually learned to transfer her assertiveness at work to her personal life. Changes in Jennifer led to confrontations with her grandmother, mother, and eventually her boyfriend. She set limits in her relationships with them. Jennifer developed a sense of pride in her success in overcoming so much adversity.

CONCLUSION

THE CONCEPT OF Adult Children of Alcoholics has allowed many people to understand the way substance abuse intruded on their development. Increasing demographic and cultural complexity in North American society requires recognition of clients' ecological niches, including the interactive effects of multiple variables including race, ethnicity, and class. A narrative framework lends itself well to incorporating these multiple factors and perspectives into understanding people who come to us with problems and asking for help.

Earlier, the reader was asked to hold the images of the kaleidoscope and the epic tale while reading this chapter. How do these metaphors relate to therapy with children of substance abusers?

The image seen in a kaleidoscope is composed of many elements. The more diverse the elements, the more potentially different images can be formed. In addition, the appearance of the composition is affected by the degree of light and the perspective and position of the beholder. Our clients' lives are composed of infinite numbers of variables. As therapists, we have more ability to instill hope and possible motivation for change if we encounter our clients with an awareness of their richness and complexity, than if we reduce them to generalizations and objects. The ability to see someone's life from multiple perspectives, incorporating multiple elements, allows for greater opportunities to visualize pathways to change.

One of the pitfalls of the ACOA movement was the temptation to see oneself as a victim. Holding the concept of the epic tale, the therapist can hear an individual's story with an attention to ways the client demonstrated active coping. Such instances can be witnessed, recognized and amplified in the therapeutic relationship so that the client develops increasing awareness and ownership of the capacity to write his or her own future to the extent that is possible. Larger social forces of class, racism, and migration can be validated. The wishes expressed in the Serenity Prayer, so important to the Twelve Step program, can thereby be addressed: to have the serenity to accept those things that cannot be changed, to have the courage to change those things which can be changed, and to have the wisdom to know the difference.

References

Ackerman, R. J. (Ed.). (1986). *Growing in the Shadow: Children of Alcoholics.* Pompano Beach, FL: Health Communications.

Akamatsu, N. N. (1998). The Talking Oppression Blues: Including the Experience of Power/Powerlessness in the Teaching of 'Cultural sensitivity.' In M. McGoldrick (Ed.), *Re-Visioning Family Therapy: Race, Culture, and Gender in Clinical Practice* (pp. 129–143). New York: Guilford Press.

Almoni, P. (1987). Lord's Prayer at AA Meetings. Retrieved October 11, 1998, from World Wide Web: http://www.jacsweb.org/jacspack/articles/peloni.html.

Alvarez, J. (1998). A White Woman of Color. In C. C. O'Hearn (Ed.), *Half and Half: Writers on Growing Up Biracial and Bicultural* (pp. 139–149). New York: Pantheon Books.

Amodeo, M., Robb, N., Peou, S., & Tran, H. (1996). Adapting Mainstream Substance-Abuse Interventions for Southeast Asian Clients. *Families in Society, 77,* 403–412.

Anderson, H., & Goolishian, H. A. (1988). Human Systems as Linguistic Systems: Preliminary and Evolving Ideas About the Implications for Clinical Theory. *Family Process, 27,* 371–393.

Anderson, S. E. (1986). Working with Black Adult Children of Alcoholics. In R. J. Ackerman (Ed.), *Growing in the Shadow: Children of Alcoholics.* Pompano Beach, FL: Health Communications.

Bell, P. (1990). *Chemical Dependency and the African-American: Counseling Strategies and Community Issues.* Center City, MN: Hazelden.

Black, C. (1987). *"It will never happen to me!"* New York: Ballantine Books. (Originally printed 1981, Denver: M.A.C.)

Black, C. (1990). *Double Duty: Dual Dynamics Within the Chemically Dependent Home.* New York: Ballantine Books.

Blackfeet Chemical Dependency Program. (1996). *Recovery Journal.* Browning, MT: Author.

Brisbane, F. L., & Stuart, B. L. (1985). A Self-Help Model for Working with Black Women of Alcoholic Parents. *Alcoholism Treatment Quarterly, 2*(3/4), 199–129.

Brooks, C. S., & Rice, K. F. (1997). *Families in Recovery: Coming Full Circle.* Baltimore: Paul H. Brookes.

Brown, S. (1992). *Safe Passage: Recovery for Adult Children of Alcoholics.* New York: Wiley.

Buber, M. (1996). *I and Thou* (W. Kaufman, Trans.). New York: Touchstone Edition. (Original translation published 1957)

Burk, J. P., & Sher, K. J. (1990). Labeling the Child of an Alcoholic: Negative Stereotyping by Mental Health Professionals and Peers. *Journal of Studies on Alcohol, 51*(2), 156–163.

Bush, I. R., & Lang, M. E. (1992). *Discovering Normal: A Parenting Program for Adult Children of Alcoholics and Their Partners.* New York: Children of Alcoholics Foundation.

Castillo, A. (1997). A Countryless Woman: The Early Feminista. In I. Reed (Ed.), *Multi-America: Essays on Cultural War and Cultural Peace* (pp. 261–279). New York: Penguin Books. (Reprinted from *Massacre of the Dreamers: Essays on Xicanisma* by A. Castillo, 1994, Plume)

Caution, G. L. (1986). Alcoholism and the Black Family. In R. J. Ackerman (Ed.), *Growing in the Shadow: Children of Alcoholics.* Pompano Beach, FL: Health Communications.

Children of Alcoholics Foundation. (1997). Workshop 5: Understanding Cultural Differences. In *The Options Program: Mastering the Challenges of College Life* (pp. 91–117). New York: Author.

Davis, D. R. & Jansen, G. G. (1998). Making Meaning of Alcoholics Anonymous for Social Workers: Myths, Metaphors, and Realities. *Social Work, 43*(2), 169–182.

Delgado, M. (1997). Hispanics/Latinos. In J. Philleo & F. L. Brisbane (Eds.), *Cultural Competence in Substance Abuse Prevention* (pp. 33–54). Washington, DC: National Association of Social Workers Press.

Di Nicola, V. (1997). *A Stranger in the Family: Culture, Families, and Therapy.* New York: Norton.

Douglas, M. (1987). *Constructive Drinking: Perspectives on Drink from Anthropology.* New York: Cambridge University Press.

Dyche, L., & Zayas, L. H. (1995). The Value of Curiosity and Naivete for the Cross-Cultural Therapist. *Family Process, 34,* 389–399.

Falicov, C. J. (1995). Training to Think Culturally: A Multidimensional Comparative Framework. *Family Process, 34,* 373–388.

Favazza, A. (1981). Alcohol and Special Populations. *Journal of Studies on Alcohol,* Suppl. 9, 87–98.

Finn, P. (1994). Addressing the Needs of Cultural Minorities in Drug Treatment. *Journal of Substance Abuse Treatment, 11*(4), 325–337.

Foucault, M. (1980). *Power/Knowledge: Selected Interviews and Other Writings, 1972–1977* (C. Gordon, L. Marshall, J. Mepham, K. Soper, Trans.; C. Gordon, Ed.). New York: Pantheon Books.

Geertz, C. (1973). *The Interpretation of Cultures.* New York: Basic Books.

Gordon, A. J. (1981). The Cultural Context of Drinking and Indigenous Therapy for Alcohol Problems in Three Migrant Hispanic Cultures: An Ethnographic Report. *Journal of Studies on Alcohol,* Suppl. 9, 217–240.

Gray, M. (1997). African Americans. In J. Philleo & F. L. Brisbane (Eds.), *Cultural Competence in Substance Abuse Prevention* (pp. 55–81). Washington, DC: National Association of Social Workers Press.

Green, R.-J. (1998). Race and the Field of Family Therapy. In M. McGoldrick (Ed.), *Re-Visioning Family Therapy: Race, Culture, and Gender in Clinical Practice* (pp. 93–110). New York: Guilford Press.

Hardy, K. V., & Laszloffy, T. A. (1995). The Cultural Genogram: Key to Training Culturally Competent Family Therapists. *Journal of Marital and Family Therapy, 21,* 227–237.

Hardy, K. V., & Laszloffy, T. A. (1998). The Dynamics of a Pro-Racist Ideology: Implications for Family Therapists. In M. McGoldrick (Ed.), *Re-Visioning Family Therapy: Race, Culture, and Gender in Clinical Practice* (pp. 118–128). New York: Guilford Press.

Heath, D. B. (1987). A Decade of Development in the Anthropological Study of Alcohol Use: 1970–1980. In M. Douglas (Ed.), *Constructive Drinking: Perspectives on Drink from Anthropology,* (pp. 16–69). New York: Cambridge University Press.

Heath, D. B., Waddell, J. O., & Topper, M. D. (Eds.). (1981). Cultural Factors in Alcohol Research and Treatment of Drinking Problems. *Journal of Studies on Alcohol,* Suppl. 9.

Herman, J. L. (1992). *Trauma and Recovery.* New York: Basic Books.

Hoffman, F. (1994). Cultural Adaptations of Alcoholics Anonymous to Serve Hispanic Populations. *International Journal of the Addictions, 29,* 445–460.

hooks, b. (1993). *Sisters of the Yam: Black Women and Self-Recovery.* Boston: South End Press.

hooks, b. (1995). *Killing Rage; Ending Racism.* New York: Henry Holt.

Howard, G. S. (1991). Cultural Tales: A Narrative Approach to Thinking, Cross-Cultural Psychology, and Psychotherapy. *American Psychologist, 46*(3), 187–197.

Inclan, J., & Hernandez, M. (1992). Cross-Cultural Perspectives and Codependence: The Case of Poor Hispanics. *American Journal of Orthopsychiatry, 62*(2), 245–255.

Jellinek, E. M. (1962). Cultural Differences in the Meaning of Alcoholism. In D. J. Pittman & C. R. Snyder (Eds.), *Society, Culture, and Drinking Patterns* (pp. 382–389). New York: Wiley.

Jewish Alcoholics, Chemically Dependent Persons and Significant Others (JACS). (1998). *Announcement of 40th Spiritual and Communal Gathering.* New York: Author.

Kaminer, W. (1992). *I'm Dysfunctional, You're Dysfunctional.* New York: Addison-Wesley.

Kliman, J. (1994). The Interweaving of Gender, Class, and Race in Family Therapy. In M. P. Mirkin (Ed.), *Women in Context: Toward a Feminist Reconstruction of Psychotherapy* (pp. 25–47). New York: Guilford Press.

Klingemann, H., Takala, J.-P., & Hunt, G. (Eds.). (1992). *Cure, Care, or Control: Alcoholism Treatment in Sixteen Countries.* Albany, NY: State University of New York Press.

Krestan, J., & Bepko, C. (1990). Codependency: The social reconstruction of female experience. pp. 216–232. In J. Laird (Ed.), *Smith College Studies in Social Works*, 60(3). Northampton. MA: Smith College School of Social Work.

Kuramoto, F. H. (1997). In J. Philleo & F. L. Brisbane (Eds.), *Cultural Competence in Substance Abuse Prevention* (pp. 83–125). Washington, DC: National Association of Social Workers Press.

Laird, J. (1998). Theorizing Culture: Narrative Ideas and Practice Principles. In M. McGoldrick (Ed.), *Re-Visioning Family Therapy: Race, Culture, and Gender in Clinical Practice* (pp. 20–36). New York: Guilford Press.

Latimer, A. M. (1997). Welcome to NANACOA's Web Site. Retrieved July 18, 1998, from World Wide Web: http://www.nanacoa.org/welcome.cfm.

Madhubuti, H. R. (1997). Cultural Work: Planting New Trees with New Seeds. In I. Reed (Ed.), *MultiAmerica: Essays on Cultural War and Cultural Peace* (pp. 443–450). New York: Penguin Books. (Reprinted from *Claiming Earth: Blacks Seeking a Culture of Enlightened Empowerment*, by R. H. Madhubuti, Third World Press)

Martinez, R. (1998). Technicolor. In C. C. O'Hearn (Ed.), *Half and Half: Writers on Growing Up Biracial and Bicultural* (pp. 245–264). New York: Pantheon Books.

McGill, D. W. (1992). The Cultural Story in Multicultural Family Therapy. *Families in Society*, 339–349.

McGoldrick, M. (Ed.). (1998). *Re-Visioning Family Therapy: Race, Culture, and Gender in Clinical Practice.* New York: Guilford Press.

McGoldrick, M., & Gerson, R. (1985). *Genograms in Family Assessment.* New York: Norton.

McGoldrick, M., Giordano, J., & Pearce, J. K. (Eds.). (1996). *Ethnicity and Family Therapy* (2nd ed.). New York: Guilford Press.

McIntosh, P. (1998). White Privilege: Unpacking the Invisible Knapsack. In M. McGoldrick (Ed.), *Re-Visioning Family Therapy: Race, Culture, and Gender in Clinical Practice* (pp. 147–152). New York: Guilford Press.

Melina, L. R. (1989). *Making Sense of Adoption: A Parent's Guide.* New York: HarperCollins.

Middelton-Moz, J. (1986). The Wisdom of the Elders: Working with Native American and Native Alaskan Families. In R. J. Ackerman (Ed.), *Growing in the Shadow: Children of Alcoholics*, pp. 57–70. Pompano Beach, FL: Health Communications.

Middelton-Moz, J. (1989). *Children of Trauma: Rediscovering Your Discarded Self.* Deerfield Beach, FL: Health Communications.

Middelton-Moz, J. (1990). *From Nightmare to Vision: A Training Manual for Native American Children of Alcoholics.* Seattle, WA: National Association for Native American Children of Alcoholics.

Middelton-Moz, J., & Dwinell, L. (1986). After the Tears: Working Through Grief, Loss, and Depression with Adult Children of Alcoholics. In R. J. Ackerman (Ed.), *Growing in the Shadow: Children of Alcoholics*. (pp. 225–234). Pompano Beach, FL: Health Communications.

Miller, S. D. (1992). The Symptoms of Solution. *Journal of Strategic and Systemic Therapies*, *11*(1), 1–11.

Moran, J. R., & May, P. A. (1997). American Indians. In J. Philleo & F. L. Brisbane (Eds.), *Cultural Competence in Substance Abuse Prevention* (pp. 1–31). Washington, DC: National Association of Social Workers Press.

National Association of Native American Children of Alcoholics (NANACOA). (1996, September). *Healing Our Hearts: The Newsletter for NANACOA*. Seattle, WA: Author.

National Clearinghouse for Alcohol and Drug Information. (1998). Asian/Pacific Islander Americans. Retrieved August 4, 1998, from World Wide Web: http://www.health.org/pubs/primer/api.htm.

O'Hanlon, B. (1994, Nov./Dec.). The Third Wave. *Family Therapy Networker*, 19–29.

Olitzky, K. M., & Copans, S. A. (1991). *Twelve Steps to Jewish Recovery: A Personal Guide to Turning from Alcoholism and Other Addictions*. Woodstock, VT: Jewish Lights.

Oliver-Diaz, P., & Fiqueroa, R. (1986). Hispanics and Alcoholism: A Treatment Perspective. In R. J. Ackerman (Ed.), *Growing in the Shadow: Children of alcoholics* (pp. 45–56). Pompano Beach, FL: Health Communications.

Palmer, N. (1997). Resilience in Adult Children of Alcoholics: A Non-Pathological Approach to Social Work Practice. *Health and Social Work, 22* (3), 201–209.

Papp, P., & Imber-Black, E. (1996). Family Themes: Transmission and Transformation. *Family Process, 35*, 5–20.

Pare, D. A. (1996). Culture and Meaning: Expanding the Metaphorical Repertoire of Family Therapy. *Family Process, 35*, 21–42.

Penn, P. (1991). Letters to Ourselves. *Family Therapy Networker, 15*(5), 43–45.

Pinderhughes, E. (1998). Black Genealogy Revisited: Restorying an African American Family. In M. McGoldrick (Ed.), *Re-Visioning Family Therapy: Race, Culture, and Gender in Clinical Practice* (pp. 179–199). New York: Guilford Press.

Roberts, S. (1997). Lord's Prayer in Twelve Step Meetings: A Thesis Introduction. Retrieved October 11, 1998, from World Wide Web: http://www.jacsweb.org/bookshelf/articles/stephan.html.

Rodney, H. E. (1996, July). Inconsistencies in the Literature on Collegiate Adult Children of Alcoholics: Factors to Consider for African Americans. *Journal of American College Health, 45*, 19–25.

See, L. (1998). The Funeral Banquet. In C. C. O'Hearn (Ed.), *Half and Half: Writers on Growing Up Biracial and Bicultural* (pp. 125–138). New York: Pantheon Books.

Sher, K. J. (1991). *Children of Alcoholics: A Critical Appraisal of Theory and Research*. Chicago: University of Chicago Press.

Sher, K. J. (1997). Psychological Characteristics of Children of Alcoholics. *Alcohol Health and Research World, 21*, 247–254.

Sher, K. J. (with P. Mothersead). (1991). The Clinical Literature. In K. J. Sher (Ed.), *Children of Alcoholics: A Critical Appraisal of Theory and Research* (pp. 148–170). Chicago: University of Chicago Press.

Tweed, S. H., & Ryff, C. D. (1991). Adult Children of Alcoholics: Profiles of Wellness Amidst Distress. *Journal of Studies on Alcohol, 52*(2), 133–141.

Twerski, A. J. (1985). Spirituality, Prayer, the Twelve Steps and Judaism. Retrieved October 11, 1998, from World Wide Web: http://www.jacsweb.org/jacspack/articles/twerski1.html.

U.S. Bureau of the Census. (1996). Resident Population of the United States: Middle Series Projections, 2035–2050, by Sex, Race, and Hispanic Origin, with Median Age. Retrieved October 25, 1998, from World Wide Web: http://www.census.gov/population/projections/nation/nsrh/nprh3550.txt

U.S. Bureau of the Census. (1998). Resident Population of the United States: Estimates by Sex, Race, and Hispanic Origin, with Median Age. Retrieved October 2, 1998, from World Wide Web: http://www.census.gov/population/estimates/nation/intfile3-1.txt

Walsh, F. (Ed) (1993). *Normal Family Processes* (2nd ed.). New York: Guilford Press.

Walsh, F. (1996). The Concept of Family Resilience: Crisis and Challenge. *Family Process, 35*, 261–281.

Walsh, F. (1998). Beliefs, Spirituality, and Transcendence: Key to Family Resilience. In M. McGoldrick (Ed.), *Re-Visioning Family Therapy: Race, Culture, and Gender in Clinical Practice* (pp. 62–77). New York: Guilford Press.

Wegscheider-Cruse, S. (1983). *The Family Trap: No One Escapes from a Chemically Dependent Family* (3rd ed.). Rapid City, SD: Nurturing Networks.

Weingarten, K. (Ed.). (1995). *Cultural Resistance: Challenging Beliefs About Men, Women, and Therapy.* New York: Haworth Press.

Werner, E. E. (1986). Resilient Offspring of Alcoholics: A Longitudinal Study from Birth to Age 18. *Journal of Studies on Alcohol, 47*(1), 34–40.

Westermeyer, J. (1981). Research on Treatment of Drinking Problems: Importance of Cultural Factors. *Journal of Studies on Alcohol,* Suppl. 9, 44–59.

White, M. (1995). *Re-Authoring Lives: Interviews and Essays.* Adelaide, S. Australia: Dulwich Centre Publications.

White, M., & Epston, D. (1990). *Narrative Means to Therapeutic Ends.* New York: Norton.

Windle, M. (1997). Concepts and Issues in COA Research. *Alcohol Health and Research World, 21*, 185–191.

Woititz, J. G. (1990). *Adult Children of Alcoholics* (rev. ed.). Deerfield Beach, FL: (Originally published 1983) Health Communications

Wolf/Altschul/Callahan, Inc. (1996). *Al-Anon/Alateen Membership Survey.* New York: Author.

Wolin, S. (1991, November). Discovering Resiliency: Children at Risk. *The Addiction Letter,* Special Suppl, 1–4.

Wolin, S. J., Bennett, L. A., Noonan, D. L., & Teitelbaum, M. A. (1980). Disrupted Family Rituals: A Factor in the Intergenerational Transmission of Alcoholism. *Journal of Studies on Alcohol, 41*(3), 199–214.

Wolin, S. J., & Wolin, S. (1993). *The Resilient Self: How Survivors of Troubled Families Rise Above Adversity.* New York: Villard Books.

CHAPTER THREE

CULTURALLY SPECIFIC ADDICTION RECOVERY FOR NATIVE AMERICANS

Don Coyhis

INTRODUCTION

Richard Simonelli

W E ARE LIVING in a time of great renewal for the Indigenous people and communities of North America. For the first time since European contact with the Western Hemisphere in 1492, Native American culture is finally beginning to receive the legal, religious, and ethical rights that the dominant society has enjoyed. In concert with women and cultures of color, American Indians have struggled greatly since the 1950s and 1960s for inclusion into the White Male System and acceptance of their own ways. Now that Indians have won some of the first battles for equal rights, a period of healing emotional and social wounds has taken hold in Indian Country, even as the struggle for more visible rights continues.

The 1990 Census reports a total Native American population of approximately 1.9 million people. States with the largest populations are Oklahoma, California, and Arizona in that order, but Indians can be found anywhere in North America. A therapist or addictions counselor in any geographic region might find his or her next new client to be an Indian person. The term "Indian Country" is often taken to mean all of North America because Indians are at last able to take advantage of educational, residential, and employment opportunities throughout the land.

There are at least four distinct eras which have affected Indian cultures in the United States. From 1492 to approximately 1890 Native people experienced the long four hundred years of Euro-American contact and conquest in which American Indian culture and the traditional ways of life were lost or threatened. This period of military and physical subjugation ended abruptly with the massacre of some three hundred Lakota people at Wounded Knee, South Dakota, on December 29, 1890, considered to be the last "battle" of the Indian Wars. The period of contact and conquest is different for different regions of North America, but by 1890 the pattern of military subjection begun with Columbus was complete.

The period from about 1880 to approximately 1950 witnessed a federal policy of assimilation toward Native Americans. The United States Government sought to assimilate Indian tribes into the dominant culture of the land. Indian boarding schools were one of the primary weapons used to break down Indian identity during this period by forbidding Native language and culture at every turn. Another was the breakup of reservations by allotting the land to individuals rather than the tribal entity.

The termination era was a period from about 1945 until the late 1960s when federal Indian policy sought to divest itself of its historic trust and treaty responsibilities to Indian tribes. Its primary weapon was the 1953 House Concurrent Resolution 108, which sought to terminate the tribal status of tribes over which federal responsibility was thought unnecessary. Before this era ended, approximately one hundred Indian tribes, bands, and *rancherías* had lost their status as Indian entities, thus becoming subject to state laws and losing all semblance of the sovereignty which history and treaty had accorded the Native peoples of North America.

The self-determination era began with the civil rights fervor of the Lyndon B. Johnson presidency and passage of the Indian Civil Rights act of 1968; it continues today. Landmarks of the beginning of self-determination at the grassroots include publication of Vine Deloria Jr.'s book, *Custer Died for Your Sins* (1969); the occupation of Wounded Knee, South Dakota, in 1973 by The American Indian Movement (AIM); the occupation of the Bureau of Indian Affairs (BIA) offices in Washington, D.C.; and the occupation of the former Alcatraz prison in California by newly energized Native Americans. But as the 1980s wore on, it became very clear that there could be no lasting gains for Native Americans, no sovereignty for reservation lands, no success in education, no access to jobs and no rebuilding of the culture without widespread sobriety and recovery from alcohol.

The sobriety movement began to gather force in Indian Country in the mid to late 1980s. It is growing stronger and becoming more effective, but the urgent need for large-scale sobriety among Indian people calls for a more culturally specific recovery model. The Indian sobriety movement uses various approaches to sobriety. One of the common threads is pride: pride in tradition, pride in culture, pride in being Indian. Using one's culture as an adjunct to recovery provides an ally which unlocks emotional energy in the service of sobriety.

In 1988 an Indian man of the Mohican Nation named Don Coyhis had a vision. In that vision he saw a white buffalo (bison) come out of a mist and turn its head to look directly at him. In keeping with his own Native tradition, he later visited an Elder in order to ascertain the meaning of his vision. The Elder told him the vision concerned his role in healing the People. White Bison, Inc., an American Indian nonprofit corporation, was founded by Coyhis in 1989 with the goal of contributing to the Indian sobriety movement. White Bison's first mission was the dream of achieving 95 percent sobriety among Indian youth by the year 2000. White Bison's teaching programs throughout the '90s have all been directed towards its primary mission.

American Indian teachings are traditionally presented within the oral tradition by talks, discussions, and sharing within a talking circle. The teachings which follow are presented in Don Coyhis' story voice with facts and ideas carefully woven into the narrative. This chapter of White Bison's approach to the sobriety movement is much as it would be presented orally to a gathering of family therapists and addictions counselors.

SUBSTANCE ABUSE AND CULTURAL ISSUES IN INDIAN COUNTRY

From Talks by Don Coyhis

WHAT ARE SOME of the main recovery and sobriety issues in Indian Country? This section provides an overview of issues and culture for helping professionals who may see Native American clients.

We would like to share some knowledge about Native American culture with helping professionals who might see our Indian people as clients. We would also like to share both facts about life in Indian Country as well as some of the Medicine Wheel teachings which have been given to us by our Elders. As you know, there is a great deal of alcohol and substance abuse in Indian communities. There is also a lot of unhappiness because so many families are dysfunctional. What are some of the issues in our Indian communities that contribute to this?

First of all, I think you have to break away from what you might have learned about Indian people from television or old media stereotypes. The many social and environmental issues of Indian country are often distorted when presented to the general public. There are 547 federally recognized tribes in the United States, and the tribes have different cultures from one another. It is important to remember that each nation is traditionally like a separate country as far as their culture is concerned. When treating a Native person be aware that there is great diversity among Indian cultures (May and Moran, 1995).

The American Indian population in the United States is a little over two million people. Of that two million, maybe two-thirds live in urban settings such as major cities, and the other third will be on reservations. Of that two-thirds in urban centers, about 50 percent of those will go from reservation to city, moving back and forth on a regular basis. There is a lot of movement in our population. It is also important to realize that there is a large population of Indian people who don't know about their Indian culture. In the 1950s, '60s, and '70s Indians were regularly adopted out of Native families, so even though they look Indian, I think you have to be careful making any assumptions about how much they are connected to their culture. And related to that, some people who have lost much of their culture are turning back to the culture for recovery (Trimble, Fleming, Beauvais, and Jumper-Thurman, 1996).

It is also good to realize that many Indian people are from two or more tribes. They may be enrolled in their mother's tribe, or they might be enrolled in their father's tribe. So I think the first question to ask is, What tribe is this person from? Then find out if he or she was raised on the reservation. I think the next thing one needs to ask is whether they were raised in a traditional way. "A traditional way" means that they probably had grandparents, parents, or a family which has been steeped in the traditional knowledge of their culture. Next, it is very important to know if they speak their language. These questions are important because if your client is a traditional person steeped in their culture, then it is very appropriate treatment to have knowledge of that culture, or the spirituality of that person, and to work with them on the basis of their spirituality and culture. It is also important to know if a person is of mixed blood—Indian and non-Indian. Many of our people are mixed-bloods or "breeds," and may experience racism from more than one culture (Trimble, 1995).

Another important body of information is about family history. Learning about Indian family history is similar to standard mental health procedure but with the understanding that the extended family is very important in Indian culture. Were they raised by their grandparents? It's not uncommon in Indian country, especially in traditional systems, to be raised by other than just your parents. Sometimes the extended family is very involved in the child rearing (May and Moran, 1995).

The next thing I think which is very important to understand in working with someone who has come to seek help, is that many Indian people struggle with Alcoholics Anonymous, and traditional people struggle with Alcoholics Anonymous the most. This is because, and I say this respectfully, that AA was created and initially designed by two white middle-class males. Many AA concepts come out of white male thinking. If an Indian person enters a recovery process using a Euro-American style of thought, they usually have a very difficult time associating with or assimilating into that kind of program (Simonelli and Ferrigno, 1993).

As a therapist or addictions counselor takes a drug- or alcohol-use inventory for an Indian person, it should also be kept in mind that use of solvents, glue, or other kinds of inhalants is more common in native communities than in non-Indian culture at this time. It is quite rampant, actually, and is at crisis levels in some communities (May and Moran, 1995).

Fetal alcohol syndrome/fetal alcohol effect (FAS/FAE) is another result of alcohol use in Indian country which is much higher than in the wider society. Native Americans suffer from FAS at a rate 33 times as great as Caucasians, almost 5 times as great as African Americans, 37 times more than Hispanics and almost 100 times that of Asians. Fully a quarter of the Indian community is affected either by FAS or FAE. As a result of FAS there are Attention Deficit Disorder (ADD) children in Indian communities in higher percentages than in the surrounding society. Individuals suffering from ADD will exhibit behavior problems that include anger or disruptiveness. It is important to have knowledge about FAS or ADD in Indian Country because some therapeutic solutions, such as counseling or working the Twelve Steps, can be undermined by individuals with untreated FAS or ADD (Hornby, 1994; Wescott, 1990; see also Kifaru in the list of resources at the end of this chapter).

The Indian boarding school is another area a therapist or counselor needs to know something about if he or she sees Native American clients. Indian people were sent to boarding schools in large numbers beginning in the last quarter of the nineteenth century. This continued all the way into the 1970s. One of the earliest boarding schools was the Carlisle School in Pennsylvania, founded by General William Pratt in 1879. Pratt's motto was "Kill the Indian and save the man," so that tells you why Indian boarding schools have hurt Indian people and communities to such an extent. BIA boarding schools also carried the slogan "Tradition is the enemy of progress."

Many children, their parents, and grandparents attended boarding school. The behavior of current generations will be characterized by a certain type of boarding school behavior. This includes very low self-esteem, negativity towards their own Indian culture, loss of language and learned helplessness. Indians were taught in the boarding schools to hate their Indianness. They were shamed for being Native Americans. Their mouths were washed out with soap for "speaking Indian." Even though this has stopped in recent years, such dislike of one's own culture is often carried inside a person, which is called "internalized oppression" (Rose, 1995). It is appropriate to approach problems related to the Indian boarding schools as a post-traumatic stress disorder (Kifaru).

Many Indian people today are turning back to the values of their culture in drug and alcohol recovery. The cultural self-hatred learned at the boarding schools can interfere with a person's recovery based on culture. It is important to ask a client whether their parents or grandparents attended boarding school. A person coming in for treatment can have boarding school behavior even though they didn't attend boarding school. It's intergenerational stuff that has created inherited family dysfunction unique to Indian Country.

Boarding schools are just one example of the many incidents of historical trauma and cultural oppression which Indian cultures have experienced. Loss of lands and language, cultural shame, racism, poor educational and economic opportunities, and high rates of alcoholism have led to high Indian suicide rates. The suicide rate in Indian communities in the age group of 15 to 25 years of age is three times what it is in non-Indian communities. Most Indian people know someone who has committed suicide or has attempted to. It is very likely that someone seeking help in drug or alcohol recovery is carrying suicide issues from his or her community (May, 1994).

Another thing to be aware of is whether an Indian client—man or woman—is a veteran. The Elders have told us that Indian communities won't heal from drug or alcohol problems until the veterans have been properly welcomed home in cleansing and healing ceremonies. At some point in treatment a client might want to participate in ceremonies appropriate to their own tradition. This is different from the needs of the wider society in recovery. It is also necessary to be aware that Indian men generally don't have satisfactory roles in their communities. Even though they may have served their country in military service, they find themselves cut off from jobs and community life for diverse reasons (Trimble, 1995).

Sexual abuse among Indian people is also much higher than in the general society. If a person were raised on a reservation I would estimate somewhere between 75 to 85 percent of the women probably experienced some form of sexual abuse. Do not be surprised if over 50 percent of the men in our Indian communities have also experienced sexual abuse.

On reservations where you have high alcoholism you will also have a high incidence of violent behavior. By the time many Indian people end up in treatment, or by the time they seek help, a high percentage have experienced severe verbal abuse and physical violence, resulting in low self-esteem. It's important not to confuse low self-esteem in Indian people with lack of eye contact. It is culturally appropriate not to look people in the eye in many Indian cultures. When you see a person acting like that, it doesn't mean that there's something wrong with them. Actually it means there's something right with them. It's often a mark of respect to avoid eye contact. I believe real lack of self-esteem originates with the community. It's something you grow up in.

Suppose we describe the Indian community as a forest with many different kinds of trees. Each one of the trees represents an individual in the community and perhaps a social issue. Some of the trees are alcoholic trees. Then there are trees which are married to alcoholic trees. There might be codependency trees, ACOA (adult children of alcoholic) trees, sexually abused trees, and some trees which are doing the sexual abuse.

There are a lot destructive emotions in this forest; that's the environment most of our kids grow up in. If you look at the roots of the trees symbolizing the culture, and if you were to go down through layers of earth surrounding the roots, first you'd find a layer of anger. Deeper than that you'll find a layer of guilt, and deeper than that you'll have a layer of shame. At the greatest depth you would encounter a base of fear. Anger, guilt, shame, and fear [are] expressed at the community level because the dysfunctional cultural roots determine the behavior of individual trees. When these adult trees get married and they have children, the little trees grow up in a soil of anger, guilt, shame, and fear. That's how it is in our Indian communities.

When you look at what it means to be an Indian some will say, "I'm traditional." A traditional is someone who's grown up with some knowledge of the old culture. Then you have the urban Indian, a person who could be a full blood, could be three-quarters, or half, or a fourth, but they will be Indians who have grown up in the cities. They might look Indian but they probably don't have knowledge of the culture. You can't make the assumption just because a person will say "I'm a full blood" that they are living in a cultural way. Some may never have been to a reservation, or have only visited.

Another bit of information that's useful to know when seeing Native clients is whether they are part of a clan or society. Some tribes still have clan systems that people belong to, so you hear words like "clans," and you'll hear words like "society." Those identities refer to sub-cultures inside of tribes. If you can find out what clans or tribal societies an individual is in, then you will know something about how they were raised. You can ask them about this or you can read something about it.

Returning to the analogy of an Indian community as a forest, some of those trees are called "breeds." These are people who are combinations of cultures or ethnicities. They could be a combination of two or three tribes, or be Indian and white, Indian and black, or Indian and Asian; but they're called breeds. Breeds are often looked down upon, especially by traditional people. So you have traditional trees, you have urban trees, you have the breed trees, and then you have the Res (reservation) Indian trees. Many Indian people who live on reservations don't practice the culture, or they've lost a lot of that culture, especially on reservations that are located near big cities. Many Indians living on reservations have been assimilated into the wider culture. Nevertheless, whether those Indian communities are urban or reservation based, what you are dealing with at the community level is community anger, guilt, shame, and fear. So Indian individuals are the product of an environment that is very, very dysfunctional.

The Healing Forest model was developed to deal with the fact that Indian communities as a whole exhibit dysfunctional behavior. Let's say you have a hundred-acre forest which is diseased. Then suppose you take one tree out and bring it to a nursery. You nuture it, give it vitamins, make it well and make it mentally healthy. When the tree is healthy you bring it back home to the community, to the culture, to the original sick forest. It will always take on the nature of what it returns to. It is very difficult for a well tree to join a diseased forest and not get the disease. The Healing Forest model says that a community-wide change program is needed to augment any individual drug and alcohol recovery in Indian country or individuals will have a difficult time maintaining sobriety. A Native American in treatment for drug or alcohol problems may travel back and forth to his or her community, creating a condition for relapse (May and Moran, 1995; Simonelli, 1993a).

One thing which is very significant to know when you work with Indian people, probably more so than most races or cultures, is that they differentiate between spirituality and religion. Christian missionaries have been working in Indian communities for a long time. There are strong Baptist, Catholic, Episcopal, Jehovah's Witnesses, Mormon, and the presence of many other Christian sects in Indian communities. So there is a lot of religion in Indian Country. But in addition to that, many Indian people have a strong sense of spirituality separate from religion. It's important to be clear about how they perceive "religion," on the one hand, and how they perceive the experience of "spiritual," on the other hand. I think Native people differentiate religion and spirituality more than most people do. They probably don't mean that they are a Catholic or a Lutheran, and so on when they say "spiritual." It is possible for them to have two paths. For example, Pueblo people in the Southwest have been successfully mixing Catholicism and their traditional spirituality for almost four hundred years. This ability allows Native people to utilize both their culture and their Christian religion in their drug or alcohol recovery process. It is important for a therapist or counselor to find out very early if their Indian client is walking two roads.

A spiritual approach to recovery is very important for Indians. No matter what you say about Indian spirituality, it is always tied to the earth or to nature. For Indian people, nature of the earth is a source of spirituality. So to say "spiritual" means that you are a student of the earth teachings. Religion is a term different than spirituality. Spirituality refers to an unseen world that the senses cannot detect and see. It is different than Indian culture. Culture is an expression of spirituality. In the Mohican language we say, "Quina-mon-tha Te she la ma qua," which means, "How are you with the Creator?" or "How are you standing spiritually?" Your own client will probably have a greeting in his or her own language which will carry a similar meaning.

Focusing on meaning to life will contribute greatly to an Indian person's recovery. Questions like, Why are you here? What is your life's purpose? and What is your greater good? make sense to an Indian. The greatest teacher for finding meaning to life is to go out in nature. We have vision quests in our traditions to find this meaning to life. In the Indian way you always look at the big picture first. Then you come back down and work the small. Foundation building doesn't work with Native people. If a therapist or counselor can get an Indian client to talk about their life's meaning, they will come alive. In our work in Indian country we understand addictions to be by-products of spiritual dis-ease. It is probably true in the wider society too. Addictions express a general crisis in spirituality and loss of true purpose.

Next, considering education, it is important to know that the high school dropout rate is very high among some of the tribes. You can't make an assumption that a person knows how to read really well; he may be able to read, but not to understand, because over the years reading hasn't been encouraged in Indian communities. So don't assume that if you give a Native client a book they will get as much out of it as you might think. If a therapist or counselor determines in the normal intake process that a client can't read well, then you'll want to use audiotapes or video resources (see the list of resources at the end of this chapter).

I think it is also important during the original assessment process with an Indian client to find out if they have any elders that they go to or use. It could be a grandpa, an uncle, a relative or it could just be somebody in their community that they talk to. It may be possible to get these elders or mentors to support them in the recovery process. But in any case, I think you'll have a tendency to see Native people become pretty quiet, especially when they come into recovery. They have a hard time expressing themselves, and I believe that has a lot to do with the trust level, based on experiences in the past. You won't find them to be really talkative.

There are a number of trust issues an Indian person may be holding, especially if they come from a reservation setting. Most Indian people have experienced racism. In an Indian's experience, negative comments or body language from other people about being Indian are commonplace. It happens to Indians just by being around the community. People are treated poorly, so there is a tendency to shut down, a tendency to stuff things. I believe it is an issue of trust instead of physical caution or survival that is involved. So, in other words, I think it's really important to gain that person's trust (Rose, 1995).

Trust issues are not in the physical or the "seen" world. Trust is about understanding spirit and intent. Spirit and intent [are] about the interconnectedness of human beings. Indian people can especially sense interconnectedness. In an interconnected system people can detect your true thoughts. If my words and my thoughts and feelings are congruent, then my spirit and intent is in alignment and you can tell. This is where trust comes from. If I say words and don't mean them, then I am out of spirit and intent and that creates mistrust. It has nothing to do whether you are Indian or non-Indian. The human being picks up on spirit and intent. If you are working with an Indian person and you want to gain their trust, just speak the truth. It's not so much how you get an Indian to trust you, but rather, how do you get this *human being* to trust you? Indians are spirits walking around in an earth suit just like everyone else. Look beyond the earth suit and go heart to heart. If you are sincere and talk to people in what Indians call a "good way," you'll get trust right away. But it is also important for a therapist or counselor to be cautious with a client because Indian people might bullshit you; for example, about race. I think the issue is not to focus on race, because sometimes you'll get drawn into a race discussion. A client might use that as an excuse. The issue really is alcohol abuse. Always bring the conversation back to alcohol, not to race, or issues of racism.

Sometimes there is conversation about whether Indian people are more physically susceptible to alcohol than others. I think that taking a family history we only know that if there is alcohol with the mom or dad or with the grandparents, there's a high chance, probably higher than other cultures, that once it runs in the family it will be rare if a person is not affected by it. Sooner or later all family members are affected by it, but I'm not sure that we understand why that is; we just know that it is. I don't think there is any final understanding about this. There are studies that indicate it is a community issue, some are saying it's an environmental issue, some say there is nothing else to do but drink in Indian communities, so people just end up drinking. In our healing work we treat it like a myth and tell Indian people they are *not* more physically susceptible to alcohol than non-Indians. We tell them that no physiologic predisposition to alcohol has been documented in scientific studies to date (May, 1994).

Indian communities, especially reservations, are economically depressed. There are many reasons for this, but on reservations the work ethic plays some role. In a reservation setting, due to high rates of welfare or nepotism, I don't think you see a strong built-in work ethic as you do in white cultures. There are certain things which are more significant than work. Church ceremonies, certain culture events, times when the salmon are running, or hunting, are often a high priority. That sometimes gets Indian people in trouble because they will go to sundances or things like that instead of working. These are value differences which have hit Indian communities very hard (May and Moran, 1995).

We have talked about some of the issues surrounding drug and alcohol abuse among Indian people which a helping professional might find useful to be aware of. The heart of the sobriety movement in Indian country revolves around a return to cultural values and ways, at the same time that an individual is participating in the wider society. Just as they say a picture is worth a thousand words, we feel it is important for sobriety and recovery counselors to hear Indian people talk about the problems and solutions in their own voices. We recommend the video *The Red Road to Sobriety—Video Talking Circle* very highly. In it you will see and hear Native Americans speak of their recovery journeys and you will learn of other sobriety-related issues in Indian Country (Kifaru).

Teachings of the Medicine Wheel

From Talks by Don Coyhis

THE PHILOSOPHY BEHIND the Medicine Wheel teachings will probably be familiar to Native Americans no matter what their individual tribal backgrounds. When recovery therapy is aware of or even utilizes the world-view of the Medicine Wheel, a step towards culture-specific counseling for American Indians has been taken.

In July of 1991 we had the opportunity to bring together a group of Native American Elders from many of the different tribes. They gathered from the Oneida Nation, the Hopi Nation, the Navajo or Diné, the Nez Perce, the Blood Reserve in Canada, the Dakota Nation, and from many others. The Elders have a great contribution to make to us, to our tribes, to our organizations, and to individuals. We asked the Elders at this conference, "What is it that you would like to tell the world about what is going on with the mother earth and her inhabitants? What is it that you could tell us about building families? What is it you could tell us about communities? What is it you could tell us about relationships?"

They told us that as a result of the many changes taking place at this time the Great Spirit was going to cause a distribution of new types of gifts, new healing gifts that would be given to many, many people. They said all of the people would begin to come together from all of the directions—from the red direction, from the yellow direction, from the black direction, and from the white direction. They called this new period we were entering a coming-together time. We also know it as a time of multiculturalism greater than the world has ever seen.

As we discussed these things with the Elders at that gathering, we asked them about a particular community we were working in. This community was a Native American community, and in this community the average life span was 37.6 years. This particular community had just one high school graduate. It had about 85 percent alcoholism among people over the age of twelve, and less than 8 percent of their people lived to be over 43.

In a sense we were asking the Elders, "Is it too late?" Is it possible to take a community and turn it around? They told us that contrary to how things look in society and in the world—we might see a lot of confusion, a lot of abuse, a lot of dysfunction, a lot of broken families—if you have a community that is in a downward spiral, it can be brought back. That community can be brought back to what the Elders call the Red Road or the right road—the right way of thinking. They said we would be able to do that if we were to follow certain natural principles and laws. When the Elders say "Walk the Red Road," they mean the big system that the Great Spirit put into place.

They used an element called the Medicine Wheel to help us see in this new way and to walk the Red Road. The Medicine Wheel is a very ancient Native way of teaching. Not all tribes have a Medicine Wheel. Of the tribes that do, many of them are different from one another. A good way to look at it is that each tribe, each nation, is like a separate country; it's a sovereign nation. Because our Native people did not have a way to write languages, the Elders of each tribe used to teach us by symbols and by pictures. So the Medicine Wheel is the teaching that the Elders taught us.

The Medicine Wheel is basically a circle teaching. It is a way of teaching, and a way of sharing knowledge, information, or concepts that align with the system that the Great Spirit put into place a long time ago. The Medicine Wheel teachings explain that anything growing always grows as a system of circles and cycles, not as a linear system in a strictly linear way. Whether it's animals, plants, or organizations, anything that's growing, anything that has life, always grows following circular or cyclic principles. One of these principles is that of the four directions: east, south, west and north. Each of these directions has qualities and powers associated with it. The Medicine Wheel teaches about a cycle of life. In the east you have the direction of the baby or infanthood; in the south lies the direction of the youth; in the west would be the direction of the adult; and the north is the direction of the elder. So, the cycle of life is baby, youth, adult, and elder. There is also a cycle of seasons: spring, summer, fall, and winter, associated with the four directions. There are four directions of human growth—the emotional, the mental, the physical, and the spiritual, also linked to the four compass directions. Different colors are often associated with the Medicine Wheel. For example, the Lakota Nation of the Northern Plains utilizes red for the east, yellow for the south, black for the west and white for the north. The color scheme will vary with the particular tribal culture.

We were also told that the system the Creator put into place is a balanced system. Whether we are talking about the system at the level of an atom, or about life, there always seem to be two roads. It's a balanced system with two polarities. For example, there is plus-minus, man-woman, here-there, up-down, boy-girl, east-west, north-south and good-bad, just to name a few possibilities. We live in a system of opposites and Medicine Wheel teaches about bringing that system to balance.

They also told us that in the system the Creator put into place there are two worlds that exist—there is a seen world and there's also an unseen world. The seen world we might call the physical world, and the unseen world today we might call the spiritual world. If we, as human beings—in building our families, or running our organizations—live our lives and direct our thinking to be in harmony with the principles, laws, and values of both the physical and spiritual worlds, we will see certain positive results in our lives and in our organizations. They also said we have the option of living out of harmony. Then we will see different results in our lives; we'll see a lot of confusion, a lot of chaos, a lot of fighting, a lot of injustice, a lot of fault-finding, a lot of conflict, a lot of attack between one another—which we do see today.

As the Native American Elders spoke to us during the summer of 1991 they kept returning to one basic idea. [What] they told us is that the system which is going to make everything work, to bring back harmony, to help us find a peaceful time, is a system of circles and cycles. We need to know that things go in seasons. There is a repetitiveness to all that happens. It is a balanced system. It is also a polarity-based system. And within this balanced, harmonious system, there is a system of justice. Justice, by the way, should not be confused with what we say is "fair." Fair, in a sense, is an ego word. "Fair" says if you do it my way it's fair, if you don't do it my way, that's unfair. The system of justice that the Elders have told us about is something that the human being cannot touch. It's bigger than the human being, sort of like the law of gravity. But it is still there, it is actively working.

Another thing they told us about the system that the Creator put into place, is that it is an interconnected system. All too often we are taught about separation. We make decisions based on what our eyes can see, we make decisions based on what our ears can hear, we make decisions based on what we can smell or what we can measure. But if we just give that a little thought—especially with the help of modern technology—we are able to come to terms with the fact that there is a world beyond our sight, there is a world beyond our senses. We have developed certain types of electronic equipment, such as electronic microscopes or telescopes and other instruments that you see in the medical field which allow us to see into the unseen world. They told us is that the system that we live in is interconnected, interdependent, and all things are in relationship with one another.

In many of the Native ceremonies you will hear people say "We are related to one another." The Lakota people say, "Mitakuye Oyasin," which means "for all my relations." The Elders have shared with us the Native understanding that all things are related and connected. There is a level in the unseen world where we are all connected to one another. When we look at our families, and when we look at our organizations, we need to understand and look at things as being integrated, interconnected, and coupled. For example, one of the teachings of the Medicine Wheel says that The Honor of One is the Honor of All. And if that is true, then The Pain of One is the Pain of All. In an interconnected system, because everything is connected, if there is pain somewhere, then that pain is everyone's pain. If something happens in one side of the system, whatever happens there is always felt through the entire family or organization.

Another thing that the Elders have taught us about this interconnected system is that it is an evolving system. "Evolving" means it is designed with a mechanism that is constantly changing. The teachings of the Medicine Wheel say this: that which is built is constantly being destroyed; that which is loose is being used to build new things. For example, if you were to take and build, say, a log cabin out in the woods, and you do nothing to maintain that log cabin, it would be just a matter of time, without anyone doing anything, that it would start to crumble. It would start to return to the mother earth. And then it would just finally be absorbed and you wouldn't even know it was there. So they told us that all these things which are built are constantly being changed, and in a sense they're being destroyed. That means if you have an organization that's running really fine, it won't stay that way forever because the system that the Creator put into place is constantly changing.

One consequence of a constantly changing, polarity-based system is the reality of conflict and struggle. Everything in the universe grows and changes through a process of struggle and conflict, leading to clarity and understanding, then back to conflict, struggle and change again. The Elders told us that is a natural part of growth and a natural part of an interconnected system. We usually hate it when conflict begins. But the teaching says, "When the struggle starts, get happy." It means a change is starting to occur. If there's no struggle, the odds aren't too good that anything of significance is going to occur. They taught us that conflict is a friend, not an enemy. Struggling is part of growing. If we find ourselves out of harmony, we often need to struggle to get back to it. Conflict is a guidance system, it's a friend. Did you ever notice how good you feel when you get clarity after a conflict?

The Elders also told us that if we want to see what is going on in a system, we need to look inside of ourselves, we have to look into the unseen world. If we want to participate in and feel this interconnectedness of the system, then we ourselves must live in a harmonious, balanced way. There are four directions of inner growth needed for us to find the principles, laws, and values of interconnected systems. Those directions are the emotional, the mental, the physical, and the spiritual. If we want to get to our place of power, if we want to find our place of harmony, then it is by working with ourselves in those four directions that such growth will be achieved. Balance in those four directions is what allows us to see in the unseen world.

The unseen world isn't just empty space. The unseen world is a living web which is active, has depth, dimension, power, principle, and intelligence. Love already exists in the unseen world. The seen world is very spacious because objects are separated by space. But there is no space in the unseen world. It is full of life and energy even though to the eye it looks like there is nothing there. There is really more activity in the unseen world than in the seen world. The unseen world is also where principles, laws, values, beliefs, and thinking originate. Elements and situations taking place in the seen world at one time originated in the unseen world. If there is physical sickness, such as a drug and alcohol problem, then you have to go do the work in the unseen world in order for healing to take place.

The teachings on the alignment of spirit and intent were one of the greatest gifts we received during the Elders' Gathering. If my thinking, feelings and decisions are in harmony with the principles, laws, and values of the Medicine Wheel—if my thoughts are aligned with that spirit and intent— you can tell because you and I are connected. Because we're connected, you can also tell if I function out of harmony with spirit and intent. In other words, if I lie or use manipulative words, or if I function outside of truth, you can tell because we're connected in the unseen world of spirit. The Medicine Wheel teachings express a worldview which will be recognized by Tribal people the world over. They are akin to the emerging ideas in systems theory which are just becoming popular in today's culture.

When our thoughts are in harmony with spirit and intent, others can usually sense our true meaning, or the spirit behind the words that we say, because we're connected in the unseen world. It's not the words that make it so. It's the meaning in the spirit and the power of that intent behind the words that make it so. Organizations and families, also, have spirit and intent. Teams have spirit and intent. Cities have spirit and intent. Everyone can tell about spirit and intent.

The Medicine Wheel teachings are recognized by all Indigenous peoples because in their own cultures they are taught that the universe operates on circular or cyclical principles. Perhaps 80 percent of all tribes have some form of a Medicine Wheel. One hundred percent of tribes practice circle teachings, one way or another. There might be different symbols or colors, depending on what the tribe values. They learned about circle or cycle systems by observing nature. For example, they watched the fish come into their streams, and they watched the fish go away. Then, when a certain berry appeared on a plant they noticed the fish came back. They began to see the pattern of repetitive relationship. So as we teach in that way to diverse tribes they never say what they are hearing is wrong. They will say, "Our understanding is just like that, only we substitute something else for some particular thing you have said." Also, since one of the most important Indian values is respect, they show respect for truthful ideas rather than saying they are wrong because they differ from their own ways, as the dominant society tends to do.

All life occurs within the circle of nature and all things are connected and dependent upon one another. Discord in any area of life can affect other areas and create imbalance, even if the connections aren't obvious. Severe imbalance causes substance abuse and addiction. The Elders have told us that we must start to think circles, think balance, think polarity, think connectedness, and to realize that there is a seen world and an unseen world. It is only when we make our choices and decisions from both of those worlds— both from the unseen and the seen world—that we can start to make better choices and decisions. Too often today we are just making decisions from the seen world. As we traveled around the country to various communities, we started to sense that our families, our organizations, and our tribes have lost the spiritual way. We have forgotten to make spiritual laws a part of our daily decisions, for individuals, organizations, and communities alike. The Medicine Wheel teachings are a way to get back to the harmony which the Great Spirit placed in life.

NATIVE AMERICAN VALUES AND BEHAVIORS

From a Talk by Don Coyhis

INDIAN VALUES have been passed through families and reservation communities over many generations. They are often diametrically opposed to some of the values of Western society. Here is a reflection on Native values and behaviors, and an intimate insight into ceremony.

Certain values place us in harmony with the principles, laws and values of the unseen world, but there are other values which take us out of harmony. What we call the Traditional Indian Values come from tribes, communities, or cultures which traditionally valued harmony and lived in ways to promote harmony. Today, Indian people live in a world having a value system that seems to work for the contemporary world, but which is not necessarily in harmony with the Ways of Indian cultures. We would like to present a list contrasting what we call Traditional Indian Values with Euro-American Contemporary Values. You'll notice that the topics in the list are actually a mixture of values, behaviors, attitudes, and orientations to living. We would also like to speak about twelve out of this list of thirty topics so that helping professionals might better understand their Native American clients. We always have to keep in mind the fact that any individual Indian person will lie somewhere on a spectrum between "very traditional" and "very acculturated." The individual might be moving either towards or away from Native culture in a search for a healthy bicultural identity. Any individual client will exhibit a mixture of both columns of values or behaviors from this list. We would first like to speak about cooperation (May and Moran, 1995, and Trimble, Fleming, Beauvais and Jumper-Thurman, 1996).

TABLE 3-1

TRADITIONAL INDIAN VALUES	CONTEMPORARY EURO-AMERICAN VALUES
Cooperation	Competition
Group Emphasis	Individual Emphasis
Modesty, Humility	Self-Importance
Individual Autonomy	Interference / Involvement
Passivity / Calmness	Activity / Restlessness
Generosity	Saving
Patience	Impatience
Nonmaterialism	Materialism
Work to Meet Need	Puritan Work Ethic
Time—Always With Us	Time—Use Every Minute
Orientation to the Present	Orientation to the Future
Pragmatic, Practical	Theoretical
Respect for Age	Respect for Youth
Right-Brain Orientation	Left-Brain Orientation
Cooperate with Nature	Control over Nature
Religion—Way of Life	Religion—Segment of Life
Spiritual-Mystical	Skeptical
Personal Caution	Personal Openness
Listening—Observation Skills	Verbal Skills
Indirect Criticism	Direct Criticism
Extended Family	Nuclear Family

Cultural Pluralist	Assimilationist
No Eye-to-Eye Contact	Eye-to-Eye Contact Important
Self-Exploratory Child Rearing	Strict Discipline
Restitution	Punishment
Character=Source of Status	Degree=Source of Status
Bilingualism	Monolingualism
Illness=Imbalance(s)	Illness=Physical Issue
Belief in the Unseen	Belief in the Seen / Proven
Respect for Tradition	Progress-Oriented

THIS CONFLICT IN VALUES CREATES STRESS, ANXIETY AND FRUSTRATION

Prepared by Joann Sebastian Morris (Chippewa / Oneida)

COOPERATION

One of the traditional values is cooperation. By contrast, in the non-Indian community you'll see that competition is valued. In organizations which are designed to compete, everyone is ranked and people are taught to struggle or strive against others. A competitive system has a strong tendency to put an emphasis on your *doing*. But cooperative values place a strong emphasis on your *being*. There is a difference between the two. Competitive systems focus on the physical or seen world while cooperative systems first honor the unseen world of the spirit. Cooperative systems have more potential to accomplish things in the physical world without falling out of harmony with the principles, laws, and values which maintain health and happiness, [and are] discussed in the Medicine Wheel teachings. The social systems currently in place too often look at us as our *doing*, and they say *do* differently in order to change. But the Indian way says we're not human doings, we're human beings. If we want to change the *doing* in a healthy way, we have to examine our need for competition. We can do this by changing our being. And the way to change our being is to change our intent. Our intentions or thinking processes lie in the unseen world and the twelve-step process is one way to examine and change our intent.

GROUP EMPHASIS

Traditional Indian values have a group emphasis, in contrast to the individual emphasis which you find in the non-Indian community. When you are working with Indian people, to isolate them individually, or to make them better or worse than the group, will create a tendency for a person to withdraw. Traditionally, the first decision is always for the good of the tribe; then the clan and the group are considered. You are not supposed to put yourself first. But in the non-Indian community there is emphasis on "I," "Me," "My," "I did it," or "I'm better than . . ." That kind of emphasis will embarrass an Indian person. We're taught not to think that way. We are taught to think that we are just a small part of something big; we are not the center of the universe.

PATIENCE

Another strong value in any Indian community is patience. This is in contrast to impatience, or always looking on to the next thing. Impatience is actually a form of anger. When you are working with an Indian person in recovery you have to be patient. For example, in the white world you might say, "What do you think?" and it is conventional for a person to come right back and tell you what they think. In the Indian community when you say, "What do you think?" a person will usually stop and think about it. Time will go by and then he or she will tell you what they think. Sometimes it will appear that a person is nonresponsive or is not a fast or quick thinker. An Indian person first listens before responding; listening is patience. You will notice a timing phenomenon in conversations or in counseling sessions involving an Indian client. You've got to be patient. Don't come back and ask another question if there isn't an immediate answer forthcoming.

NONMATERIALISM

Indian people are brought up with a strong emphasis on nonmaterialism. In the white culture the emphasis is materialistic, or directed more towards the seen world. So, if you are trying to motivate a client to find purpose by talking about getting a house or a car it won't have much impact. In our cultures we have Give-Away ceremonies or Potlatches where you give away what is valuable to you. This emphasizes the nonmaterial side of things. The recovery or counseling strategy for an Indian person has to first work with change in the nonmaterial or unseen world inside a person. Then more tangible physical changes will occur.

WORK TO MEET NEED

The work ethic between Indian and non-Indian cultures is also different. In the Indian way we work to meet needs, but in the white culture you'll see a "Go! Go! Go!" kind of pressure in most activity. It's more accelerated, aggressive, and productivity-oriented. Sometimes you'll see an Indian person quit and go home after they have worked and have enough. This leads to the stereotype that the Indian person is a bad worker. This especially happens if there are ceremonies to attend or if hunting or fishing season is on. When they have enough they are content; there may not be the drive to be successful at work. By contrast, the Puritan work ethic is restless and never content. It leads to accumulating surplus wealth, or as an Indian might say, hoarding. These aren't moral judgments as much as they are value differences.

RIGHT-BRAIN ORIENTATION

Native people also have a high inclination to be right-brained. In Euro-American cultures there is more of a tendency to be left-brained. To be left-brained means to value and utilize the line, list, sequence, logic, order, fact, outlines, and taking things apart. But Indian culture is more right-brained, valuing and using rhythm, music, song, dance, creativity, picture, vision, story and imagery. So, suppose you have a left-brained person trying to counsel a right-brained person. They might say, "There are four steps in order to do this," or "Here's the formula to do that." This creates a conflict of innate capability. When working with Indian people it is often better to talk in story language, or ask them to tell you, as the counselor, what something might mean in terms of their own culture. When working with an Indian person, think "story" rather than facts or information. The facts will come out of the story in their own time and way.

COOPERATE WITH NATURE

It is the Indian point of view to cooperate with nature. In the white point of view you control it. People who control become takers, characterized by being self-centered, territorial, and possessive. When you value control over nature, then you are always striving to place your mark on the world. It shows itself in every area, from how the house and yard are kept, to the workplace and on into relationships. You always have to be in control, to dominate and to conquer. But Indians look at it differently. You work with nature or the situation you are in. You understand that everything is interconnected. One of our values is to "share the deer." It's the opposite of control; it's about sharing, it's about flow, it's about balance and it's about rhythm. Our ceremonies guide us in how to live those values. So for example, if the counselor says, "Take control of yourself," or "You've got control of your life," as part of the counseling process, an Indian person would instinctively interpret that as untrue. A Native person was probably raised to believe the Creator runs everything. When we work in counseling with one another as Indian and non-Indian, you'll see a different "thought" or philosophy operating. A therapist can "cooperate with nature" by recognizing those differences and using them, rather than discounting them.

RELIGION—WAY OF LIFE

In the traditional Indian way I think you'll also see that religion is a way of life rather than a part of life. This relates to spirituality being different than religion for Indian people. Religion isn't something you participate in just one day of the week. So for example, in the Indian way you never separate church and state. Being spiritual, or religious, is a way of life. When this is so, discussions about leadership or running a community are not separate from the spiritual well-being of the people who make up the community. Important meetings in Indian communities are almost always begun with prayer and ceremony. Of the many different tribal nations that make up Turtle Island or North America, there are many different Indian religions, or as we call them, "Ways." "Ways" refers to different religions or cultures. As we teach in Indian communities around North America, we present a spirituality that most Indians recognize. But we never try to impose a particular set of Ways on the people we are visiting. They have their own religion and culture. They recognize a way of life in the Medicine Wheel teachings, for example, but these don't replace their own specific Indian religions.

LISTENING/OBSERVATION SKILLS

Another Indian value is expressed by the fact that Indian people have very good listening skills. They listen more than they talk. This might be interpreted as being shy, not interested, passive or inactive. In the white way, people like to talk a lot. They are more verbal. Indians listen a lot more than they talk, but that doesn't mean there is something wrong. If as a counselor you ask a question and want an answer, you'll see a difference in the conversation dynamics with an Indian client. Dialog is not valued in the same way as it is in the non-Indian or Western system. Native people also value observation skills. Indigenous traditional knowledge systems placed a very high value on observing the world, and those skills have been preserved in the culture. A therapist might think that they are observing the behavior of an Indian client, but they need to realize that they also are being observed. Perhaps not with clinical skills, but your client is watching your body language, tone of voice, and whether you are being true. The counselor is being observed, not as a non-Indian person (which might be a political or racial stance) but for the feeling of his or her spirit. If they detect that your spirit is not right, then they will shut down. The therapist might conclude that the client is not responding to treatment, but maybe it is the outcome of a different cultural value or emphasis that is being experienced.

NO EYE-TO-EYE CONTACT

In some of our Native cultures you will see different habits or behaviors around eye contact. I estimate that about 50 percent of the tribal cultures don't maintain eye contact. I think many of these tribes are in the West. Indian cultures function as an interconnected system. The first level of connectedness is when the gaze of two people's eyes physically meets. A second later there is a feeling which goes across that connectedness. When the feeling goes across, that's when you acknowledge. It is a second level of connectedness. In the Indian way, you don't just look at a person and nod. You look at someone, that feeling connects, and then you nod. Indian culture values respect; we are taught to show respect. The object of respect could be an Elder, or it could be a boss or a counselor.

So, suppose an Indian person wants to talk to someone whom he or she respects. First they will look into each other's eyes and let the connectedness feeling happen. Then the Native person would look down out of respect. Lowering the head or eyes means that respect is being shown for the other person. It doesn't mean the client is not listening. But some cultures say you are not listening unless your eyes meet. Yet, you can have two people whose eyes meet but who are not listening to each other because they are not honoring the second-level connectedness. In my Mohican culture the second level of eye-connectedness is called Na-tash-nay-ya, which means "touch-love" in English. It is a touch of love and it is a feeling. This connectedness is maintained by talking to the person. Then, when they speak, in order to keep that connectedness you have to listen. If an Indian person is talking and you are thinking about what you are going to say to them next, you break the connection. If your thoughts drift off and you are having a conversation with yourself you lose the connection. If you lose the connection you lose the Indian.

CHARACTER—SOURCE OF STATUS

In Indian Country, status is related to a person's character. In white culture the more degrees you have or your level of education often determines your status. So, an associate degree is the beginning, a bachelor's is next, a master's means you are almost there, and a doctorate means you are god. And nobody questions a god. But a person with a doctor's degree could be very dysfunctional and sick. In Indian culture a person is always working towards being an Elder. There are Elders and then there are old people. Being old does not automatically make you an Elder. An Elder is someone who has developed themselves in a balanced way; that [is what] gives [an Elder] status. It is important when counseling people from an Indian culture to see if they have an Elder who will help them. Just as some people will go to a minister and some people will go to a counselor, an Indian person will often seek an Elder's guidance. We value our Elders. Status in Indian country means that you have worked on yourself.

RESPECT FOR TRADITION

Another value which I think is very important is respect for tradition. The white way, by contrast, is very progress-oriented. Contemporary culture is always progressing and progressing. It is never satisfied and it is never content. It's really never happy. If an Indian person is trying to figure out a life problem he or she might say to themselves, "What would grandpa or grandma say about this?" Then they might reflect on where grandpa or grandma got their understanding. They would see they got it from *their* grandpa or grandma. And their reflection would take them backward in time. At some point there had to have been original teachings given which started to get passed down. That's why we have such a strong emphasis on tradition. It's not about living in the old way, like in tipis or hunting and gathering, but respect for tradition says you have a respect for the old way of thinking. You bring the old way of thinking to today's problems.

BELIEF IN THE UNSEEN

In Indian culture the strongest belief is belief in the unseen world or the spirit world. In white culture the strongest belief is in the seen world. Seen world people say, "Where are the numbers? Where is the data? Where is the graph? Where are the statistics?" They say, "Build a model. Where is the proof? If you can't see it, it's not true." By contrast, a person from an Indian culture believes in the unseen world, which manifests in visions, dreams, prayers, inspiration, urges, hunches, vision quests, ceremony, sweat lodges, or the power of the Channupa (Sacred Pipe, in the Lakota language). That is where the real power lies. You go into the sweat lodge to access the unseen world. In fact, you can't even see in the sweat lodge. What does that mean in terms of recovery? As a counselor you can say, "If you don't get God in your life, you're not going to get sober. If you don't get your creator in your life, you're not going to make it. If you don't pray and ask for help and guidance, then you're not going to get there." Some treatment programs are publicly funded, which means you have to separate church and state. This forces treatment into the seen world. You can't talk about religion, you can't talk about God, and often you can't start the session with Indian-style prayer.

Belief in the unseen world is so strong for an Indian person that if you can convince a Native person in recovery to get up in the morning and pray with the eagle feather, and smudge with sage or cedar in a shell, then positive changes will happen. It is appropriate for a non-Indian therapist to make this kind of suggestion if he or she is sincere and has understood about these Ways. It is also appropriate, if the counselor has knowledge of what the eagle feather means—how to hold it, how to treat it, and how to smudge with sage or cedar—for a non-Indian helping professional to participate in such a ceremony.

The best way to incorporate the eagle feather and a smudging ceremony into a counseling session is to invite the client to share his or her own feather and sage or cedar if it seems appropriate. It must be remembered that federal law does not permit non-Indians to own eagle feathers or wings, but Indian people can share these elements with others. We would like to speak a little about the significance of the eagle feather and the smudging ceremony.

Non-Native culture might think that an eagle feather is just the feather of a large bird. If you look at the eagle feather in the spiritual world, it is alive. It's not a dead feather, it actually has life in it. Everything in the world is designed with a purpose. All entities of nature have a reason for being here; they are all what we call "medicine." Some animals are eaten, some carry pollen, some keep other populations from growing too large. God has given a unique blessing to every animal. The eagle feather has many teachings in it. In the old days it was always believed that the eagle carried prayers off to the Creator, or God, or whatever, because it flew so high in the sky. That's the basis of importance for an eagle feather and that's why they are so highly respected. So, can you imagine the power of holding the eagle feather and praying with it? It is not like any other feather. That feather is alive. When you hold it, the eagle feather is connected to the spirit world. When you are finished praying it is customary to wrap it in a red cloth for protection and to keep it really safe. When an Indian person gets an eagle feather it changes his or her life. It makes them feel like they are home. Praying with an eagle feather accelerates a person's shift in awareness; changes will start to happen.

To make a smudge, you take sage or cedar leaves, or whatever plant is appropriate in your region, and burn them in a shell or other non-metallic container. Next, you pass the feather through the smoke, west to east and north to south. When the smoke touches the feather it makes the feather alert. When you pray, the meaning behind your words goes into the smoke. What's important is the meaning behind the words, not necessarily the words themselves. For example, if you pray, "God, help me to get sober," and you really want to get sober, it doesn't matter how you start, what your words are, or if you can't put the words together properly. The sage or cedar smoke takes the meaning behind your words and carries it to the creator. If the Medicine Wheel teachings or other contact with Native culture has triggered sincere curiosity in these ways, it would be appropriate to incorporate them in a session with an Indian person. You'll have to feel out and evaluate it on a case-by-case basis.

AN OVERVIEW OF THE TWELVE STEPS

From Talks by Don Coyhis

THE TWELVE STEPS of Alcoholics Anonymous become more useful to Native Americans when the whole Twelve-Step process is placed into a culturally specific context. This section describes one way of accomplishing this and mentions the Talking Circles and Healing Circles which have helped so many people to recover.

We want to look at the Twelve Steps of Alcoholics Anonymous as a process which an Indian person can use to place their lives back into harmony with the principles, laws, and values of Native culture. Some Indian people have trouble with the Twelve Steps because the Twelve Steps were originated by two white males in the 1930s and the AA program still carries that cultural direction. But many Indian people have also found sobriety by working the Twelve Steps. Our Elders say that if you understand the Twelve Steps in an Indian way, you'll find that they are in alignment with traditional Indian values. We want to talk about using the Twelve Steps in a way that is culturally specific to Indian people by bringing the Steps into alignment with our circle thinking and the Medicine Wheel (Simonelli and Ferrigno, 1993).

The Medicine Wheel teaches about the four directions of life—east, south, west and north—and the principles and gifts associated with each direction. The Elders tell us that there are powers, spirits, or helpers connected with each direction; if you face a particular direction when you are seeking to accomplish something, those helpers will come. If you face that direction something will happen, like the magic inside where an idea comes from, for example.

When we pray to the east in the morning when the sun first comes up, you'll notice everything is waking up. The flowers are waking up, the insect nation is starting to crawl around, the birds start their singing, the animals begin to appear; but none of that happens until something happens in the east. So they say that when we pray, if we face east, then something happens to us. Now if you don't believe this is so, sometime when you're out praying, face the other way. Put your back to the east and look to the west; do the same thing and see if it will be any different. If you face the west you will have a hard time.

Many Native people have found sobriety by working the Twelve Steps just as they are presented in the Big Book of Alcoholics Anonymous. But others might want to change the wording so they will sound closer to an Indian way of thinking or feeling. No matter how they are worded, each of the Steps carries a principle or spiritual gift which a person must connect with on the road to recovery.

TABLE 3-2

Twelve Steps and Twelve Principles

An Alternate Wording of the Twelve Steps

STEP 1   **HONESTY**
We admitted we were powerless over alcohol—that we had lost control of our lives.

STEP 2   **HOPE**
We came to believe that a power greater than ourselves could help us regain control.

STEP 3   FAITH
We made a decision to ask for help from a Higher Power and others who un-derstand.

STEP 4   COURAGE
We stopped and thought about our strengths and our weaknesses and thought about ourselves.

STEP 5   INTEGRITY
We admitted to the Great Spirit, to ourselves, and to another person the things we thought were wrong about ourselves.

STEP 6   WILLINGNESS
We are ready, with the help of the Great Spirit, to change.

STEP 7   HUMILITY
We humbly ask a Higher Power and our friends to help us to change.

STEP 8   FORGIVENESS
We made a list of people who were hurt by our drinking and want to make up for these hurts.

STEP 9   JUSTICE
We are making up to those people whenever we can, except when to do so would hurt them more.

STEP 10   PERSEVERANCE
We continue to think about our strengths and weaknesses and when we are wrong we say so.

STEP 11   SPIRITUAL AWARENESS
We pray and think about ourselves, praying only for the strength to do what is right.

STEP 12   SERVICE
We try to help other alcoholics and to practice these principles in everything we do.

To work the Twelve Steps in an Indian way they are placed in a circle, not in a line or a list. Steps 1, 2 and 3 are placed in the east, which is the direction of the infant and of springtime. Those working the first three steps actually face east and call in those powers while sitting at a table or on the ground. Facing east and working Steps 1, 2, 3, the intent is to find a relationship with the Creator, God, or the Great Spirit. It is necessary to first make a relationship with the Creator before the other steps will reveal their gifts.

Once we get through Steps 1, 2, and 3, the work will switch and we face the south for Steps 4, 5, and 6. The south calls in the gifts of the youth and the summer season. These are the inventory step, the step that reveals the defects of character, and the step expressing the willingness to change. We begin to make an authentic relationship with ourselves for the first time while working Steps 4, 5, and 6. Facing south we begin to get answers to the questions, "Why am I? Who am I? and Where am I going?"

Next we go to the west in order to work Steps 7, 8, and 9. The west is the direction of the adult and the autumn or harvest season. These are the steps about making amends. If I hurt someone, then I have to go set it right. Whatever I have done, I have to correct it as part of facing the western direction. This is the direction to find a relationship with others.

Once we have worked the steps of the western direction, then we go to the north to work Steps 10, 11, and 12. The north is the elder direction and the season of winter. They are maintenance steps which allow us to remain in harmony with the large system of the whole world. This Twelve-Step journey is one that we take in a circle. Working the Twelve Steps in a Native way, we go through a new set of steps every year.

The Medicine Wheels of different Native traditions often have animals associated with each direction. In one tradition the east is the direction of the eagle, the south is the direction of the mouse, the west is the direction of the bear, and the north is the direction of the buffalo. In many of our cultures, animals will come help us for certain things because they're our relatives. When you face west, working Steps 7, 8, and 9, for example, bear medicine might start to come into your life. All of a sudden you'll start to see signs pertaining to the bear; you'll see things that catch your eye to help (Four Worlds Development Project, 1984, 1985, 1989).

Let's take a journey through these Twelve Steps now—not to talk about how to work them, but just to see the big picture. The Medicine Wheel teaches about the eagle and the mouse. The eagle flies overhead and sees the big picture while the mouse is down on the ground taking care of details. The eagle might see forests and meadows while his brother the mouse is concerned with tufts of grass and little seed cones. Both play a role in the balance of the Medicine Wheel. So let's take an eagle's view of the Twelve Steps.

One of the things about the steps is that they are built on human junk. If you are resentful, hateful, angry, self-pitying, or judgmental, that's what the steps are designed to handle. If you're an angel you will have a hard time with this because this is based on junk. These steps are not designed for perfect people, they are designed for people who are way off track from the Creator's system. They are designed to help you get back on track. That's why I like them, because they're not for perfect people, they're for imperfect people.

The AA wording for Step 1 is *We admitted we were powerless over alcohol, that our lives had become unmanageable.* Some Indian groups have reworded the Twelve Steps to be in better alignment with Native thinking. The Umatilla tribe of Oregon, through The Umatilla Tribal Alcohol Program, has created an Indian version of the Steps that is used in the "Medicine Wheel and the Twelve Steps" recovery program. We use their wording in this writing. Their version says, *We admitted we were powerless over alcohol—that we had lost control of our lives.* In both cases, the principle of the step is honesty. We have to admit that our lives are broken (White Bison: Video Set and Workbook).

Step 1 has two parts to it. The first part of Step 1 has to do with me admitting I'm powerless over alcohol, drugs or whatever. I need to admit it to myself, my innermost self. It's not something glib like "Oh yeah, I got a problem." You have to admit it to yourself inside. Then the second part of the step is to look at unmanageability in my life. Unmanageability means "[In] what areas of my life am I functioning way out of alignment with the Great Spirit system?" To work the second part of Step 1 there are nine areas of life that are evaluated. These are: personal relationships, emotional nature, misery, depression, making a living, uselessness, fear, unhappiness, and help to others. These can be evaluated by making mind maps and discussing them with a sponsor, sobriety elder, or other brothers and sisters.

We would like to say a little bit more about wording of the Twelve Steps at this point. Minorities and women often have difficulty with the idea of admitting powerlessness in the traditional AA wording of Step 1. Minorities and women have been disempowered from the White Male System for a long time. Theirs is a journey of empowerment, so it may not seem right to take the first Step using the word "powerless." Another version of Step 1, used by the Indian Brotherhood, says, *We admit that because of our abuse of alcohol and other drugs, we have been unable to care for ourselves.* There are also versions of the Twelve Steps which say it in a way that is nonoffensive to women. The main thing is not to let the wording of the Steps get in the way of the life-saving benefits of the program. Each special group can word it so that they can work it (Simonelli and Ferrigno, 1993; Wilson Schaef, 1981).

Step 2 says, *Came to believe that a power greater than ourselves could restore us to sanity.* An Indian wording for Step 2 is *We came to believe that a power greater than ourselves could help us regain control.* The Principle for Step 2 is hope. You catch sight of the possibility that your life can be put back on track.

When we go to Step 2, we take the nine areas that you have from Step 1 and describe what it would be like for each of these nine areas if our lives were run by the Creator—in other words, if our lives were working. The concept in Step 2 is that we always move towards and become like that which we think about. In fact, we move towards and become like that which we think about whether it's good for us or not. We look at those areas where our lives are unmanageable and ask ourselves what our lives would like in these nine areas if our lives were under control. Thinking always drives behavior, so we set a target or a vision for each of the nine areas to guide us as we work the remainder of the steps.

Once we create the vision in Step 2, we go on to the third step, *Made a decision to turn our will and our lives over to the care of God as we understood him*. In the Indian way we might say, *We made a decision to ask for help from a Higher Power and others who understand*. The principle of the third step is faith.

I don't need to clean up my act in order to turn over my life and will to the care of a Great Spirit. He'll take it as it is. He takes the whole package because that's his deal. He says, "I'll take your good, I'll take your bad. I'll take your strengths, I'll take your weaknesses. I'll take the shit, I'll take everything you've got going right now. If you will turn all that over to me, then I will work on you some." The third step is about a decision to get the Creator involved. It takes a step of faith.

Once we've completed Step 3, we face south and start on Step 4. The AA way says, *Made a searching and fearless moral inventory of ourselves*. An Indian wording of Step 4 goes like this: *We stopped and thought about our strengths and weaknesses, and thought about ourselves*. The principle behind this step is courage.

Inventory is where I first look inside of myself. The first three steps in the east were about finding God; but now I've got to work on me. Now you've got to make a relationship with yourself. You do this in three ways. The first inventory is on resentments. In other words, there are people that I can't stand; I hate them. So here are my resentments. The second part of the inventory is to work on fears, and the third part of the inventory is to work on sex. There is a process to do this. For the resentment inventory, you take a sheet of paper and create five columns on it. For the fear inventory you make a list of information that's four columns wide. The sex inventory has seven columns.

As you work through Step 4, the fourth column of the resentments inventory is information that you will use in Step 6 and in Step 7. We're building a structure which will become the individual's sobriety. The fifth column in the resentment inventory and the seventh column in the sex inventory is information you will need in Step 8 and Step 9. That's why you can't just jump up and say, "Well, I like Step Nine the best, I think I'll do that first." No, it's got to go in order because you find things in the process to be used later on.

Once the Step 4 inventory is complete, it is necessary to read it over and to admit that this is it—this is what I did, this is how I feel, and this is how I see it. But you've got to admit it to yourself, to another person, and to the Great Spirit that this is how that is. This is Step 5. The standard wording for Step 5 is *Admitted to God, to ourselves, and to another human being the exact nature of our wrongs.* An Indian wording is *We admitted to the Great Spirit, to ourselves, and to another person the things we thought were wrong about ourselves.* You've got to find a trusted friend to do that. The fifth step can also be done in the sweat lodge holding an eagle feather. If one of the trusted friends is a pipe carrier, the two can smoke the Channupa together as they work the step. Step 4 and Step 5 reveal my character defects to me. Selfishness, self-centeredness, anger, envy, jealousy, dishonesty, and other disharmonies will become clear. Working Step 5 awakens the principle of integrity in us.

An Indian view of the Twelve Steps continues in this way, awakening the principles of willingness, humility, forgiveness, justice, perseverance, spiritual awareness, and service as we continue with Steps 6 through 12.

An Indian person works the Twelve Steps from a spiritual perspective. What is a spiritual person, anyway? Well, the process is a little like an airplane and a guided missile. Let's say an airplane is being followed by a guided missile—a heat-seeking missile. The guided missile will follow an airplane's exhaust. So as the missile follows the airplane and the airplane moves to evade it, then the missile will detect less heat as it advances. It says to itself, "Whoops, I'm off track from the target." Then it sends a feedback signal to an engine to get it back on track. Then suppose the missile sinks below the exhaust. It goes, "Whoops, too low." Then it adjusts and gets back on track. The airplane keeps moving and pretty soon the missile is off track again. "Whoops, too high; too far left; too far to the right . . ." And that's what it does in order to follow the airplane. It's constantly hunting around: off track, back on track. Off Track, back on track. Over and over.

The vision that we create in Step 2, in our minds and written down, is the vision of where we're headed. As we clear up the wreckage of our past, we become better and better at chasing the vision. Suppose part of my vision is to create myself an image of a spiritual warrior, a positive warrior. When I act in a nonspiritual way, I get off the track. When I get off track, I feel tension in my system; that's the feedback. Every human being's feedback is some type of anxiety, stress, or tension. The meaning of that anxiety, stress or tension is that you're off track. Whoops! Correct for the mistake and get back on track.

A spiritual person is somebody who goes through the day and gets on and off track maybe thirty to fifty times. A spiritual person is a person who screws up thirty to fifty times a day and keeps coming back. That's a spiritual person. A spiritual person is not someone who's perfect—a spiritual person is always getting off track, on track, off track and on track, all day long. But getting on track to a vision is working Steps 3 to 12 so the vision of Step 2 can be realized.

Step 12 says, *Having had a spiritual awakening as a result of these steps, we tried to carry this message to alcoholics, and to practice these principles in all our affairs.* The Indian version says, *We try to help other alcoholics and to practice these principles in everything we do.* Step 12 is about serving our brothers and sisters. The principle is service.

"Having had a spiritual awakening . . ." It doesn't say maybe. It's quite clear. Having had a spiritual awakening as a result of these steps, that's the message we carry to our brothers and sisters who aren't there yet. What is this spiritual awakening? It's the vision that you set in Step 2. And that's all you get for that particular journey around the Twelve Steps. That's why we go through them again on a yearly basis, to redo the vision so that we continually grow, going on to do the next thing.

The Twelve Steps carry the principles which I need to live my life in a good way. I get certain results in my life if I am honest, I get certain results in my life if I have faith, I get certain results in my life if I have forgiveness, and so on through all twelve principles. We have the ability to be peaceful warriors, even, just to have peace of mind. It's a menu of things that we can choose. So it doesn't matter how far off track we got, working steps is about allowing us to come back and find the Red Road or the decent, spiritual way, no matter where we are, what we've done, what's going on, or what voice from our past told us that we're not going to make it. Working steps is a way for us to come back and get on track.

It makes more sense to me when I look at the Steps in the Indian way. At an Indian Twelve-Step group which I attend we meet in a circle. We take turns reading from the Big Book in one hand, holding an eagle feather in the other. We fold up the tables and sit in a circle of chairs. As soon as we started doing that, more Indians began showing up. We smudge with sage or cedar or sweetgrass to start the meeting. When we do it that way, our Medicine is good. These cultural ways help us to be clear and to walk in balance.

Perhaps the most important thing for anyone helping another person is to be aware that if you haven't healed yourself you are not going to be able to heal others. You have to be walking the Red Road or the good road yourself. It doesn't matter how much head knowledge you have. So, for example, you have to become a patient person or you have to become a good listener. You have to change yourself. If an Indian client asks you, "What do you think?" you will find yourself pausing before answering them. Gandhi said, "We must be the change we wish to see in the world." As a counselor or therapist you must be the change you wish to see in the client.

If the Medicine Wheel teachings have triggered curiosity about Native culture in non-Indian counselors, we encourage them to seek opportunities for further learning. If the opportunity presents itself, go into the sweat lodge and see what happens there. In most Indian cultures there are no expectations of an outsider. Ask your own client about their culture of origin. If you or your healing center will have regular contact with Native Americans, it is appropriate to seek out an advisory board of Indian Elders to support you in your work. A Native advisory board can provide cultural connections for the client at timely junctures of treatment (Wilson Schaef, 1995).

We also encourage helping professionals to understand and use the power of the Talking Circle. In a Talking Circle, people speak one at a time and listen to one another. Indians will talk in circles more than they will talk at tables or respond to lectures. A circle fits with their culture. Talking Circles allow each person to be heard, giving them a stake in the outcome of the proceedings. The outcome might be their own sobriety (Wisdom Circles; Simonelli, 1999).

The Healing Circle is another group-process methodology which supports the sobriety journey for both Native and non-Native people. The Healing Circle can be a very powerful and intense emotional experience for participants. Specific emotional wounds are brought up, shared within the ceremony of the Healing Circle, and let go under the direction of a person who knows how to conduct a Healing Circle. Use of both the Talking Circle and the Healing Circle can cause a shift in an individual which may greatly speed up addictions recovery (Simonelli, 1999).

We are honored to have shared this cultural information with the readers of this book. Our vision is that all four nations, directions and ethnicities—the red, the yellow, the black, and the white—will find wellness with each other during the coming together time which has been spoken of in our prophecies.

CASE STUDY

EDDY

Eddy is a Cherokee mixed blood ("breed") in his thirties who is presently incarcerated. He remembers drinking by the age of five, smoking marijuana at seven or eight, and injecting drugs by the time he was twelve. Driving under the influence (DUI) and violence were constant companions throughout his teens and early twenties. Eddy has an eighth-grade education and was arrested fifty-six times by the time he was finally incarcerated for armed robbery and assault. From his vantage in prison he looks back on ruined marriages and four children. In his own words, "I had drunk everything from rubbing alcohol to moonshine. I had done every drug I can think of, from sniffing paint thinner to taking LSD. I had absolutely nothing to show for my life but a twenty-two-year prison sentence."

As he began serving his sentence, Eddy vowed never to use alcohol and drugs again. His mind began to clear only because substances weren't easily available in prison. Early in his sentence he stayed sober by weight lifting, playing basketball and handball, and by force of will. He did not connect with counseling or a specific program at this point, and even though he was not "using," as he puts it, "I was still an emotional and psychological wreck, still acting out my inner life with violence."

Like many urban Indians who grew up in the '50s, '60s, and '70s, Eddy's Cherokee roots did not run deep. His Indian heritage consisted of some vaguely remembered songs from childhood and some contact with the reservation culture which he was near until the age of four. But then something happened to change his life. One day in the early part of his sentence an old Indian inmate came up to him and invited him to the sweat lodge, which Indian prisoners were allowed by virtue of the Native American Religious Freedom Act. That experience changed him and he grew to love traditional drumming and singing. He was at peace as long as he was participating in those activities, but he had not truly entered recovery yet.

At approximately this time Don Coyhis came to Eddy's prison and through a very far-sighted institutional attitude to offender-rehabilitation programs, was able to introduce the "Medicine Wheel and the Twelve Steps" program to the Indian inmates. Eddy was finally able to connect with recovery concepts because he heard them taught in a culturally appropriate manner. During the next year Eddy and fellow inmates circled up to watch the videos which were left by Coyhis. Those Indian inmate circles amounted to an extended family which further kindled his desire for sobriety. Eddy was on the verge of entering recovery, but there was still something missing. He needed a true AA sponsor in order to actually work the Steps. It turned out that the head of offender programs for the state prison system was himself an avid Twelve-Step person and was able to sponsor Eddy in actually working his recovery program.

Using his own cultural tools and the teachings of the Medicine Wheel provided the key to open the lock which gave Eddy an ability to work the Twelve Steps and to enter recovery. Eddy uses the sweat lodge as an integral part of his Twelve-Step process. His experience working the First Step is an example of the role culture and spiritual fellowship can play in causing positive change. He says, "When I went to the sweat lodge to make this commitment I explained to the brothers what I was about to do. It was suggested that I go in only with the Creator while they circled the lodge. As I went in, and the flap was closed, I received an overwhelming vision of my First Step. I felt totally powerless, like I was at the mercy of the Creator. Someone reached in and threw a big handful of cedar on the twelve stones that seemed to be dancing at the center of the lodge. And with all the humility of remembering that my kids were calling someone else 'daddy,' I asked the Creator for help and made the commitment.

"Things seemed to be working in slow motion as my past history rolled across the stone people (sweat lodge stones) and my vision overrode those memories. The blood of the Creator ran down my face for what seemed like all day. And then someone opened the door. I cannot describe the washing feeling that came over me as I crawled on my hands and knees out of the lodge. The Great Spirit had made a deal with me and I knew instinctively that my sponsor would know what to do. I was ready to face the South in recovery."

For Indian people the correlation between incarceration and drug and alcohol abuse is almost 100 percent. Eddy is now eligible for parole and his own fledgling sobriety is acting as a model and a resource for others in prison, both of Native and non-Native backgrounds. He reports that other ethnic groups are working the Twelve Steps in prison, using the Medicine Wheel principles to assist in their own sobriety.

REFERENCES

Deloria, V., Jr. (1988). *Custer Died for Your Sins: An American Indian Manifesto;* with new preface. Norman: University of Oklahoma Press.

Four Worlds Development Project (1984 1985, 1989). *The Sacred Tree: Reflections on Native American Spirituality.* Lotus Light, PO Box 2, Wilmot, WI 53192; phone: (800) 826-4810; ISBN: 0941524-58-2.

Hornby, R. (1994). *Alcohol and Native Americans.* Mission, SD: Sinte Gleska University Press.

Lobo, S. and Talbot, S. (1998). *Native American Voices: A Reader.* New York: Addison Wesley Longman Educational Publishers.

May, P. A. (1994). The Epidemiology of Alcohol Abuse Among American Indians: The Mythical and Real Properties. *American Indian Culture and Research Journal, 18*(2), 121–143.

May, P. A. & Moran, J. R. (1995). Prevention of Alcohol Abuse: A Review of Health Promotion Efforts Among American Indians. *Journal of American Health Promotion, 9*(4), 288–299.

Rose, L. R. (1995, Spring). Healing from Racism. *Winds of Change, 10*(2), 14–17.

Simonelli, R. (1993a, Spring). The Healing Forest. *Winds of Change, 8*(2), 18–22.

Simonelli, R. (1993b, Winter). Seeds of Diversity: A Training Program Based on Native American Principles and Values. *Winds of Change, 8*(1), 28–36.

Simonelli, R., & Ferrigno, B. (1993). Alcoholic Recovery and the 12 Steps. *Winds of Change, 8*(3), 41–47.

Simonelli, R. (1995, Summer). The Healing Wind, *Winds of Change. 10*(3), 16–20.

Simonelli, R. (1999, Spring). A Native American Approach to Diversity. *Winds of Change, 14*(2), 16–21.

Trimble, J. E. (1995). Toward an Understanding of Ethnicity and Ethnic Identity, and Their Relationship with Drug Use Research. In G. J. Botvin, S. Schinke, & M. A. Orlandi (Eds.), *Drug Abuse Prevention with Multiethnic Youth* (pp. 3–27). Thousand Oaks, CA: Sage.

Trimble, J., Fleming, C., Beauvais, F., & Jumper-Thurman, P. (1996). Essential Cultural and Social Strategies for Counseling Native American Indians. In P. Pedersen, J. Draguns, W. Lonner, and J. Trimble (Eds.), *Counseling Across Cultures* (4th ed., chapter 8). Thousand Oaks, CA: Sage.

Utter, J. (1993) *American Indians—Answers to Today's Questions.* Lake Ann, MI: National Woodlands.

Wescott, S. M. (1990). Time to Address a Preventable Tragedy. *Winds of Change, 5,* 30–34.

Wilson Schaef, A. (1981, 1992). *Women's Reality.* San Francisco: HarperCollins.

Wilson Schaef, A. (1995). *Native Wisdom for White Minds.* New York: Ballantine Books.

RESOURCES

Wisdom Circles (an organization dedicated to the Talking Circle Process). 3756 Grand Ave., Suite 405, Oakland, CA 94610; phone: (510) 272-9540.

For a comprehensive print and video catalogue, "American Indian Books," contact AISES (American Indian Science and Engineering Society), 5661 Airport Blvd., Boulder, CO 80301; phone: (303) 939-0023.

For the video *The Red Road to Sobriety: Video Talking Circle,* contact Kifaru Production, 1550 California St. 4275, San Francisco, CA 94109; phone: (800) 400-VIDEO.

The following materials are available from White Bison, Inc., 6145 Lehman Drive, Suite 200, Colorado Springs, CO 80918-3440; phone: (719) 548-1000; Web site: *www. whitebison.org.*

"Message to the Younger Brother." A prison prevention video for Native Americans.

"Message to the Younger Sister." A prison prevention video for Native Americans.

"The Medicine Wheel and the 12 Steps for Men." A video set and workbook.

"The Medicine Wheel and the 12 Steps for Women." A video set and workbook.

CHAPTER FOUR

ADDICTION TREATMENT FOR JEWISH AMERICANS AND THEIR FAMILIES

Jeffrey Ellias-Frankel, Alan Oberman, and Kelly Ward

INTRODUCTION

THE USE OF an ecological approach to study Jewish addiction belongs to the social science tradition of Gregory Bateson. His discussions about the importance of context in understanding behavior underlie our view, that understanding and treating addiction requires information about its context.

This chapter develops the viewpoint that forms of Jewish addiction, and the most likely routes and barriers to recovery, may be conditioned by the Jewish experience in history. We postulate a dialogical process by which individual consciousness may be affected by historical group experience. Profound historical events may leave their mark in the form of themes that subsequent generations must address. How particular Jewish family members engage these Jewish themes impacts their functioning and dysfunctioning—including their addictions. We theorize that a family's response to an ethnic theme affects the pride and shame structure of its members. We examine several ethnic themes and relate them to idealized Jewish male and female self-images. Shame that cannot be regulated is seen as a significant risk factor for addiction. We present a variation on a family treatment model that considers issues that recovering Jews must confront.

CAUTIONS IN APPLYING THE ECO-ETHNIC APPROACH

THE ECOLOGICAL APPROACH usefully focuses our attention on a complex array of population and environment interactions that are likely to be valuable for developing population-level interventions. However, clinicians are advised to be cautious when applying such observations directly to a particular addict and his or her family. For example, the fact that abuse of prescription medication is one of the more common drug routes for Jewish addicts suggests a range of potential population-level prevention programs and should direct the clinician to inquire about a family's use of doctors and medication. However, we have encountered a number of Jewish alcoholics who would never consider pharmaceutical abuse. We believe that although psychotherapy addiction treatment, practiced within an ethnically sensitive framework, must use generalized observation as the basis for specific inquiries about the addict and his or her family, clinicians must not trust their prior "knowledge" more than the data they generate through proper questioning. For example, the widely held but erroneous belief that alcoholism is not a problem among Jews has led many therapists away from a thorough assessment.

Knowledge of the cultural values of Jews as a group is a useful place to begin to learn how to learn from the particular family. For example, in formulating initial therapeutic actions with the family it is helpful to know that although women are most often the gatekeepers of the Jewish family, a Jewish husband's pride is likely to be wounded unless his role is acknowledged. Clearly, looking at the ethnic level of an ecological perspective can be both valuable and hazardous, since it sometimes illuminates important patterns and sometimes obscures them. In this case, "the wisdom to know the difference" depends upon clinicians' ability to perceive data that doesn't fit their expectations.

WHAT IS A JEW?

AN OLD JOKE says, "Two Jews meet and there are three opinions." The debate over the definition of Jewishness, and who has the power to define who is a Jew, has always been intense—and continues to be so even today. Perhaps because Judaism began as an idea (a difference or distinction from the dominant culture) and Jews continued as a minority for most of their history, they have been very sensitive to group membership issues. Of course, too frequently the definition of a Jew was of great concern to anti-Semites, with lethal consequences for the Jews. However, the current debate is between those who officially (and sometimes unofficially) represent the various groups of Orthodox and non-Orthodox Jews, and the social and political consequences are difficult to foresee. The defining criteria used in this chapter ignore the questions of that debate. In this chapter we are concerned with behavioral patterns; therefore, our focus is on people whose family history or present choices subject them to common forces and to some degree a shared destiny. We as clinical professionals recognize that it is not necessary for clients to consciously identify with their Jewish heritage for their behavior and their family's behavioral patterns to be connected to certain Jewish themes.

It is important to note that substantial social and behavioral differences among subpopulations of Jewish communities exist; these must be considered when designing group-level or individual and family-level interventions. For example, differences exist between Sephardic Jews (descendants of Spanish Jews) and the more numerous Ashkenazi Jews (descendants of Western European Jews) on matters as diverse as food preferences and gender relationships. An intermarriage between these two groups sometimes meets with a great deal of family disapproval.

JEWISH THEMES

THE CONCEPTS OF national and ethnic character have been used to explain psychological and behavioral differences between groups. We reject this way of capturing distinctions among people. The notion of an ethnic character is trait based, implying a static or fixed identity. We subscribe to a dynamic or relational concept whereby the dialectic between people and social context continues over time, mutually shaping both the people and their context. There is a need for a construct that enables us to capture meaningful patterns for Jews as a group and for individual differences among Jews and that is also sensitive to change over time. The concept of an ethnic theme appears to be a viable approach.

An ethnic theme is operationally defined as the dialogue that ensues when constellations of issues or events confront a people and either latently or manifestly invite a set of responses. The ethnic theme does not determine a particular response but rather poses an overt or covert question to which members of the group may have dissimilar responses. For example, the event and issue of persecution invites a response from Jews that takes diverse forms. A fear of publicly displaying imperfection and an obsessive need for financial security may both be responses to the cultural legacy of persecution and exclusion. The meaningfulness of a given theme for an individual may vary in relation to time, place, and personal variables.

We believe that knowing about the ethnicity of one's client enables one to begin with a set of probable themes and inquire about how they may relate to a particular family's functional and dysfunctional patterns. Sensitivity to these themes is essential not only for establishing rapport but also for crafting interventions that are culturally compatible. Incompatible interventions are not likely to be sustained. For example, one naive clinician recommended that a Sephardic woman consider a weekend trip with some friends she met in school; she in her way and her husband in his let the therapist know that the clinician really didn't understand the "community."

In the following sections we relate the concept of ethnic themes to the effect of shame and the dynamics of addiction. These themes have been selected because at this historical moment they appear relevant both to Jews as a people and to family processes involved in the dynamics of addiction.

SECURITY

"Az der soineeh falt, tor men zich nit fraien, ober men haibt im nit oif [when your enemy falls, don't rejoice, but don't pick him up either]."

Personal and group security is a salient theme for Jewish people. Events in both the ancient and modern worlds have left generations with the question of how to maintain individual and collective survival. The world, particularly the non-Jewish world, is perceived as a potentially dangerous place. The destruction of the ancient Temples (A.D. 70), the Inquisition (1500s), Russian pogroms (1860s), and the Holocaust (1940s), have left a residue of a unique but profound insecurity. Despite considerable access to wealth and power, many Jews experience collective and individual vulnerability. Tobin (1988), writing about American anti-Semitism, notes that despite a decrease in the frequency of anti-Semitic events many Jews report a kind of background wariness in which they attempt to determine if a particular anti-Semitic comment or incident is an isolated event or part of some trend signaling the beginning of more dangerous times. Jews must confront the reality that a number of times in the past what they gained was lost, what they built was destroyed. The repetitive cycling from safe to unsafe, powerful to powerless, has made the theme of security a dominant one. From this perspective, the establishment of the state of Israel, the respect for education, and the individual quest for money and symbols of status may be viewed as responses to the always present question "How can we survive in a potentially hostile world?"

While the theme of security is important for most Jews, gender role prescriptions interact with it and lead to different sets of issues and conflicts for men and women. In the past, life within the walls of the family home was the province of Jewish women. They were responsible for preparing the next generation, that is, for socializing their children into appropriate roles, and in this sense they were responding to the security needs of the family and the people. Men were responsible for earning sufficient money to provide for the material and status needs of the family. Historically, they were also the ones who studied the Torah and contributed to the religious continuity of the community. We discuss in later sections of this chapter how gender and Jewish theme issues interact to form particular pride dynamics that manifest in addiction-related behaviors.

IDENTITY

"Az ich vel zein vi yener, ver vet zein vi ich [if I would be like someone else, who would be like me]?"

The question "Who is a Jew?" is relevant on an individual level to the question "Who am I?" While the latter question has universal significance, the Jews' place in history makes it a particularly salient one for the individual Jew. Sartre (1948), writing about anti-Semitism and Jewish identity, stated "The inauthentic Jew flees Jewish reality and the anti-Semite makes him a Jew in spite of himself. However, the authentic Jew makes himself a Jew, in the face of all and against all" (p. 137). While one can argue whether authenticity requires that one claim one's Jewishness in any particular form, we believe that authenticity demands a response to the question "Who are you in relation to your Jewishness?"

The Diaspora meant that Jews would spend generation after generation in countries beyond Palestine as sometimes welcome and sometimes unwelcome guests. Without a sense of place in which to root their identity, they were defined and defined themselves both as outsiders and as members of the "Jewish community." The Enlightenment, with its universalist beliefs, led to a loosening of the boundaries between the Jews and their surrounding culture. This eventuated in a diminished sense of community but not in permanent acceptance by the non-Jewish majority. The definition of oneself and the degree of one's identification as a Jew began to emerge for consideration by the Jewish individual. Even the possibility of "passing" began to grow, as greater mobility meant the opportunity to reinvent oneself. Immigration to the United States in the nineteenth and twentieth centuries left Jews with multiple identity components to integrate: many immigrants, who had to learn English to function in their new country, arrived speaking both Yiddish and the language of their former homeland. The influences of universalism and rationality were dominant in America, and the myth of the melting pot was appealing to many Jews. For some, the decision to anglicize one's name embodied a hope for a new future and a severing of an identity connected to the past; this was simultaneously a strategic decision designed by the immigrant to change others' perceptions of him and an important step in re-defining himself. As overt anti-Semitism in this country began to wane after the Holocaust, the pressure to include Jewishness in the definition of self further diminished.

As external threats to survival became less apparent to the Jew, the need to feel one's group identity diminished—perhaps to the point of creating an internal threat. Moreover, the question "Who am I?" is not solely a question about individual identity. The identity of Jewish families is also a concern— not only to parents, who often transmit confusing messages to their children, but also to those who worry about the survival of the Jews as a people. The 1990 National Jewish Population Survey indicates that the structure of Jewish families is changing. Since 1985, twice as many mixed marriages have been created as marriages where both spouses are Jewish. Less than 30 percent of children born to mixed marriages are being raised Jewish. Jewish parents who perhaps took their Judaism for granted are often dismayed at their children's lack of Jewish identity. Synagogues attempt to respond to the perceived problem by reaching out to young families. Perhaps because of a concern for continuity, establishment Judaism supports a traditional definition of the Jewish family. Childless couples and gay and lesbian couples, who also search to define an identity that includes their Judaism, are still not likely to feel validated within mainstream Judaism.

SUFFERING

"Az men ken nit iberhalten dos shlechteh, ken men dos guteh nit derleben [if you can't endure the bad, you'll not live to witness the good]."

Suffering is closely related to the themes previously discussed. Herz and Rosen (1982) note the centrality of suffering for the Jewish family and link it to the Jewish experience of external persecution. They contrast this with the Irish perspective on suffering, which is linked to punishment for sin. Jews often take pride in their ability to persevere despite pain. This may be connected to two historical aspects of the Jewish experience: (1) An intermittently harsh external reality requires the ability to come to terms with suffering, so that the hope required for survival can be maintained. The belief that life can go on despite suffering is related to the coping one does through anticipatory grieving; the capacity to be aware of and even take pride in one's pain means that one will be more likely to be prepared. (2) The need to maintain a collective identity among a people geographically dispersed and united by various degrees of adherence to a set of religious teachings can be met through sharing the visceral common bond of suffering.

The relationship between pride and suffering is an important one. Rosen and Weltman (1996) note that the burden of being a Jew is often worn with pride. We might conjecture that pride in suffering the pain that results from one's Jewishness is in part a defensive response to the shame felt as a result of anti-Semitic judgment. Recently, a colleague shared her response to a conversation with a Jew who converted to Christianity: when describing a religious service for Jews who have come to believe that Christ was the messiah, the converted Jew used the term *completed Jews*. While many feelings were evoked and some shared, our colleague recognized her need to defend against the judgment of incompleteness. Sharing such stories of "feeling wronged" with those who identify with them may serve to help Jews repair the momentary wounds. On a far more profound level, the Holocaust memorials and the undiminished interest of many Jews in matters relating to the Holocaust underscore the centrality of suffering in Jewish lives (Rosen and Weltman, 1996). We think the public nature of participation in Holocaust memorial services and even attending Holocaust museums is in part healing, because the public sharing of such suffering validates, reassures, and undoes the shame associated with victimhood.

The Jewish relationship to suffering is not limited to suffering directly because of one's Jewishness. Rosen and Weltman (1996) and Zborowski's (1969) study *People in Pain* assert that Jews complain about their symptoms in a way that communicates that they "hardly expect better treatment from life" (Rosen and Weltman, 1996, p. 616). Paradoxically, although Jews may expect to suffer, they are often heavy consumers of medical and mental health services aimed at alleviating their pain.

While both Jewish men and women address the theme of suffering in their lives, culturally defined gender differences exist. Traditionally viewed as innately more expressive, Jewish women are likely to be more direct in articulating their suffering. Jewish men, on the other hand, often take pride in their ability to suffer in (almost) silence.

ADDICTION IN THE JEWISH COMMUNITY

THE MYTH OF THE SOBER JEW

The most important fact to grasp about Jewish addiction is that it exists and is significantly underdiagnosed and undertreated. Given a tradition of overutilization of medical services, this lack at first appears paradoxical. The reasons lie both within and beyond the community. "Shikker Iz a Goy [The Drunk Is a Gentile]" is the title, both descriptive and proscriptive, of a Yiddish folk song that linked Jewish identity with sobriety. Snyder (1958) posited that the explanation for Jewish sobriety could be found in their internalization of a historical view that drinking to excess is a gentile (in contrast to Jewish) trait, and in the belief that a Jew who drinks reflects negatively upon Jews as a group. The literature on Jewish alcoholism has argued that this group pride may have served as a protective mechanism. However, the group pride issues may, in part, also account for why the myth of the sober Jew has been so persistent. Despite the fact that for more than twenty-five years there has been a literature that challenges the myth (see Keller, 1970; Schmidt and Popham, 1976; Wislicki, 1967), Jewish alcohol and substance abuse addiction remains little discussed outside of a small but growing circle.

The apparent sobriety of Jews has been of interest for many years. Immanuel Kant, writing in the 1700s, observed, "Jews do not get drunk because they are exposed through their eccentricities and alleged closeness to the attention and criticism of the community, and thus, cannot relax in their self control, for intoxication, which deprives one of their cautiousness, would be a scandal for them" (Jellinek, 1941, pp. 777–778). The internalized need for cautiousness perhaps served as an additional protective mechanism for many years. Guests cannot afford to make too big a mess, and Jews have almost perpetually been in a host–guest relationship. A number of studies from the early 1900s through the 1980s reported that Jews generally were moderate in their consumption of alcohol (Cahalan and Cisin, 1968; Nusbaumer, 1981; Riley and Marden, 1947; Snyder, 1958). However, this older epidemiological research concerning Jewish substance use has been criticized as seriously flawed (Adlaf, Smart, and Tan, 1989; Heath, 1991). Researchers have difficulty defining whom to count as a Jew and disentangling this variable from other socioeconomic ones. Also, self-report about behavior that is culturally unacceptable is likely to be significantly distorted. There is little hard data to support either historical or current prevalence or incidence rates. Twerski and Twerski (1994), experts in the field of Jewish addiction, note with some irony, "With all the theory and research in print, there is no reputable source of empirical data indicating the incidence of alcohol or drug addiction in the Jewish population . . . Those in the treatment field note that for the affected individual and family, the incidence is 100%" (p. 4). Levin (1992) writes, "When one attempts to examine the facts behind the folklore, one finds few recent studies comparing substance abuse rates by religious affiliation" (p. 3). Nevertheless, the myth of sobriety has had serious negative unintended consequences.

The origins of the myth may have once been rooted in reality. Keller (1970) argued that prior to the establishment of the second Temple (approximately 500 B.C.), drunkenness was common among Jews but that after the banishment of pagan worship and the integration of drinking into religious ceremonies, drunkenness was negatively viewed by the community. Perhaps the religious value of moderation, the pride of not being *shikker* like the gentiles, and the fear of calling attention to oneself and one's community served for generations as protective mechanisms.

JEWISH DENIAL

"A Yid a Shikker, zoll Geharget veren [a Jew who is a drunk may he get killed]."

At present, the myth of Jewish sobriety serves to support individual, family, community, and treatment provider denial and thus threatens Jewish lives. Twerski and Twerski (1994) note that denial concerning Jewish addicts is particularly severe: "The scope of who manifests the denial is vast, which results in multiple levels of resistance"(p. 6). To an increasing number of addicts, their family members, their clergy, and those in their recovery system, it is painfully apparent that Jews abuse alcohol, hallucinogens, opiates, prescription drugs, gambling, sex, and food. Levin (1992), using a Delphi technique to survey a national panel of experts in the area of Jewish addiction, concludes, "The panel saw the addictive behavior of Jews as highly similar to that of gentiles." However, she notes, "An important exception to the panel's minimization of the uniqueness of the Jewish population was that Jews were seen as having significant attitudinal and emotional blocks to seeking treatment, particularly within the Jewish community, due to denial of the problem and judgmental treatment by other Jews."

This distinguishing feature of Jewish addiction has relevance for assessment, prevention and treatment. The Jewish (and non-Jewish) denial of

Jewish addiction is perpetuated by the ways that Jews perceive and respond to problems. Zborowski (1969) noted that Jews, compared to other ethnic groups, seemed to be less stoic and to even enjoy their "patienthood." Jewish common wisdom notes the Jewish affinity with medicine in the following joke: "If you can't become a doctor, the next best thing is to consult one." Thus, Jewish denial of addiction is reinforced by a reliance on physicians for vague physical or even behavioral problems. The desire and means to find the best possible professional often results in Jewish clients consulting specialists who know little about addiction. Addiction training among medical doctors has been late in coming. Psychologists and social workers, too, generally receive little training. It is sometimes a "hard sell" to get a Jewish family with an addicted member to see that the best helping professional for their situation is an addiction counselor who may not have a PhD and who may not even be Jewish.

Denial is also strengthened by what may be a common Jewish pathway to addiction: rather than a progression from recreational use and abuse, a more common Jewish route may begin from the desire to relieve suffering. Spiegal (1986), reviewing case studies of Jewish alcoholics, concludes, "They drank primarily to relieve stress and psychic discomfort; social drinking was minimal" (p. 1). Levin (1992) reports that her panel of experts believed that sedatives and tranquilizers represented the greatest problem to the Jewish community (p. 86). These substances, prescribed to reduce discomfort, are culturally compatible with the theme of suffering discussed earlier in this chapter. The language of suffering is familiar to Jews. Therefore, action to reduce suffering is comprehensible. Taking a drink or a pill to ease suffering is acceptable; using substances just because they are fun is not. Since suffering justifies the drink or drug and since suffering continues because of the drink or drug, continued use is justifiable. In contrast to those whose addiction begins with recreational use, "suffering pathway" addicts and their families don't have to confront the reality that what once began as fun is no longer fun.

There are several other factors that are particularly salient within Jewish families that support denial. Herz and Rosen (1982) note the centrality of the family in Jewish life. Religious teachings and the previously discussed theme of security may account for a view of the family as sacred. The consequent emphasis on emotional closeness makes the stakes of confronting a family member's apparent addiction feel that much higher. This, coupled with the intense shame that the addict and the entire family are likely to experience if the news gets out, provides strong motivation for denial. The particularly intense motivation to deny is often combined with a verbal and cognitive style that facilitates obfuscation. The Jewish tradition of "learning" the Torah involves the vigorous examination of multiple interpretations; indeed, verbal skills are highly valued even in more secular families. A people who can reframe persecution in terms of being "chosen" can reframe compulsive behaviors in a number of interesting but potentially destructive (if not fatal) ways.

ADDICTIONS OF CHOICE

Unfortunately, the extent and pattern of addiction within the Jewish community is unknown. However, there are some soft indices. Levin's (1992) panel estimated that 8.6 percent of Jews had an alcohol problem and 10.5 percent had a drug problem in 1991. Our own clinical experience varies. However, our Jewish clients demonstrate that food, drugs, and gambling, followed by alcohol, are the addictions of choice. Levin's (1992) expert panel did not include food addiction among those they considered. Although tests for statistical differences among the panel's ranking of abused substances were not reported, the category of "Sedative/Tranquilizer" received a mean severity score of 2.08 (where 1 = Severe and 5 = No problem); painkillers received a score of 2.25; gambling, 2.42; cannabis and cocaine, 2.67; and alcohol, a 2.83. Other observational data reported by Arnie Wexler, an international consultant in gambling treatment, suggests that approximately 40 percent of the membership of Gamblers Anonymous in American metropolitan areas are Jewish. Concern about Jewish cocaine use is reflected in the fact that in the mid-eighties a national cocaine hotline reported that almost 20 percent of its calls were from Jewish people. Benzion Twerski (1987), a noted specialist in addiction among Jews, believes that dual addiction in Jews may be higher than for the general public.

The consensus among Jewish addiction specialists is that while all forms of addiction occur in the Jewish community, alcoholism among Jews is increasing. In addition, drug addiction, gambling, and food addiction may be overrepresented in the Jewish population. It is likely that some of the cultural patterns previously discussed have influenced these choices. One hypothesis is that the increase in alcoholism is a result of acculturation, with Jewish identity being of decreasing importance to Jews (Snyder, 1958; Zimberg, 1986). The relatively high frequency of prescriptive drug abuse is likely connected to its availability and to the community's sanction of the use of drugs to deal with "pain and suffering."

Linn (1986), writing about gambling in the Jewish community, notes that some combination of religious beliefs and the Jews' precarious place in

history creates a setting favorable to recreational gambling. His work connects an interest in gambling to the theme of Jewish security by postulating
the survival value of a "capacity to eroticize anxiety" (Linn, 1986, p. 342).
The ability to transform the unpleasant possibility of loss to the pleasurable
excitement of a game of chance serves a valuable cultural function for a
people with a history of repetitive losses. Additionally, since in ancient Jewish writings the decisions apparently made by chance often reflect the will
of God, some pathological gamblers may be soliciting some external manifestation that they are loved by God.

The Jewish relationship with food has been material for endless jokes
and family stories. Recently, one of us heard our eighty-seven-year-old
mother-in-law reminisce about how as she was leaving the house fifty years
ago to give birth to one of her children her own mother-in-law tried to get
her to take food for the car ride to the hospital (when she refused, claiming
nausea, her mother-in-law insisted that she needed food for strength). With
a nod to her own overattachment to food as a source of pleasure, she added,
"You know, if she had offered me those spinach knishes she used to make, I
would have taken them." The Jewish mother, traditionally the emotional
center of family life, often found/finds herself depleted as she nurtures children, husband, and parents. The comfort of food is always at hand without
imposing on anyone. Filling your own emptiness in a way that may lead to
continued isolation and emptiness is unfortunately not a big step from
preparing food for those you love.

DYNAMICS OF JEWISH ADDICTION

NEITHER DATA NOR theories exist to suggest that the processes of addiction are different for Jews than for non-Jews. However, the most common pathways to addiction may be different, as may the addictions of
preference, the problem of denial, and the shame and pride profiles. Nevertheless, we make the assumption (as others have about the general population) that addiction among Jews is a systemic process in which the addictive
behavior "affects and is affected by change and adaptation at many different
systemic levels including the genetic, physiological, psychological, interpersonal and spiritual" (Bepko and Krestan, 1985, p. 5). This section of our
chapter integrates the model of addiction presented in *The Responsibility
Trap* (Bepko and Krestan, 1985) and in Donald Nathanson's 1992 work on
pride and shame with some of the dynamics and themes that Jewish men
and women confront.

The Krestan–Bepko model of addiction offers a powerful and complex analysis of the dynamics of alcohol addiction, which we believe is applicable to many other forms of addiction. Their systemic perspective unites the addictive behavior with family dynamics and gender roles. Their framework permits the view of addiction as a cyclical process in which the addictive behaviors are seen in part as a consequence of a distorted relationship between self and other. The lack of appropriate complementarity in the self–other relationship (extreme power imbalances) is itself seen as a consequence of a gap between the idealized self and the experienced self. This gap often leads to an extreme and rigid pride system in which the "unacceptable aspect of the self" is denied by the self and by the other. Addiction-related experiences of the self are often the only opportunities to express the "disowned" aspects of the self (e.g., the "fiercely independent man" who becomes dependent or the "other-oriented mother" who loses focus on the needs of others only when she is gambling). While a detailed exposition of this model is beyond the scope of this chapter, the model's utility for bringing an ethnic perspective to understanding addiction is noteworthy. Bepko and Krestan (1985) cogently argue that the culture has prescribed male and female roles in ways that often makes the gap between idealized and experienced self so large that the discrepancy, in combination with other factors, makes addiction more likely. Their work focused on the gender aspect of the developing self and examined its relationship to addiction. We believe that by augmenting this model through the inclusion of additional dimensions of the self, we can arrive at a theoretically interesting and clinically useful formulation for working with Jewish (and non-Jewish) addicted families.

Nathanson looks at the dynamics of shame from a developmental perspective and includes the gender/sexuality dimension as only one of a number of developmental issues. He argues that pride is attached to the successful acquisition of each step of the individual's growth and development and that shame is attached to each failure. Which aspects of growth and development are viewed as important is, we believe, a matter of the value complex in which the individual lives. Feminists have justly critiqued developmental theorists for their claim of universality and have suggested that more appropriate female developmental milestones be used when thinking about females (McGoldrick, 1989). However, from a clinical perspective, we believe that it is most important to understand how the individual, as well as his or her family and reference group, views various developmental tasks. Nathanson's generalized schema suggests that there are opportunities to develop pride (and shame) at a number of different developmental points. These include the development of size and strength, dexterity and physical skill, independence, cognitive ability, communication and interpersonal skills, and sense of self, gender identity, and sexuality. It is our position that this schema, like all developmental models, must be viewed in light of the particular culture in which the individual lives. Understanding the ways an ethnic group values developmental tasks for the two sexes will bring us closer to understanding the shame dynamics within that group. Furthermore, by integrating this understanding with the Bepko and Krestan (1985) model of addiction, we can better comprehend the role culture plays in addiction formation and treatment.

The gap between the idealized and experienced self that forms the well of shame can best be viewed as multidetermined and multidimensional. The dominant culture, one's ethnic subculture, and one's class subculture all potentially contribute to the individual's internalization of the ideal. Clinicians must assess how a particular individual constructs this ideal. Additionally, we understand that an individual's view of self is conditioned by the successes achieved and the failures sustained at multiple developmental points. Therefore, a complete "shame history" must follow a developmental review that is sensitive to ethnic differences.

PRIDE, SHAME, AND ETHNIC THEMES

NATHANSON (1992) QUOTES a humorous exchange that illustrates the dilemma of competing cultural standards in matters of shame and pride. He writes that Sylvia Fine, a screen and song writer, was challenged by a rival who saw her after a recent nose job. "Sylvia, darling, I see you have cut off your nose to spite your race." "Yes," came the swift answer. "Now I am a thing of beauty and a goy forever" (p. 449). Significant deviation in size or shape of the body or a body part is one of the earliest sources of shame for the developing child. Culture communicates to children which of the developmental dimensions are essential to the developing self and which are more peripheral. Plastic surgeons and eating disorder clinics address some of the needs of those for whom the pride and shame issues of size and shape have become central.

It is our thesis that the ethnic themes of a culture play a significant role in determining which pride and shame matters are viewed as especially significant, as well as what the ideal of any given attribute should be. For example, it is our experience that height and strength are generally not particularly core attributes about which American Jewish men or women feel pride or shame. A history that teaches that survival goes to the clever, not the tall and strong, seems a likely explanation. But it is a particular family's response to an ethnic theme that will most heavily determine the nature of the individual's own idealized standard. For example, many Jewish families respond to the theme of security in a way that intensifies pride in cognitive ability and intensifies shame in failure to achieve in this domain. Without sufficient healthy mechanisms for dealing with the painful shame associated with this kind of failure in such a family, the individual is at greater risk to engage in potentially addictive affect-modifying behaviors. However, a minority of Jewish families may respond to the security theme in a way that intensifies pride in dexterity and physical skill. In these families a small, weak boy is more likely to experience intense shame. Should he fail to develop sufficient mechanisms for coping with this shame, he too would be at increased risk for addiction. Therefore, one cannot assume which are the pride and shame issues for a particular addicted Jewish family. Knowledge of salient ethnic themes enables the clinician to explore with a particular family how those themes were interpreted and, in the post-sobriety phase of treatment, to address the intra- and interpersonal shame dynamics. It should be noted that while we view ethnic themes as important determinants of pride and shame intensifiers, we recognize the contribution of other significant factors, including family history, social network, biology, and social class. A thorough assessment must address these and consider them in light of the client's culture.

If we employ an ecological framework and look beyond the general culture's contribution to "generic" individuals' (male and female) idealized and experienced selves, we can see how these selves are influenced by ethnic status. That is, we might assume that Jews are each subject to varying degrees of both the general culture's and the Jewish culture's contribution toward their idealized and experienced selves. Moreover, it is also reasonable to assume that the cultural message from the general or dominant culture regarding appropriate role behavior will vary in accordance with one's ethnic status. Although it has not been empirically tested, it seems plausible that the dominant non-Jewish culture has ideas about the expected and acceptable behavior for Jewish men and women that may be different from its view of other ethnic groups and different from the Jewish culture's view. Tobin (1988) reports poll results from 1940, 1964, and 1981 that indicate an increase in the belief that Jews have too much power in the business world. We can only wonder whether we are more likely to see a female or a Jewish president of the United States first. The notion of a Jewish female president seems like the beginning of an ethnic or sexist joke. The internalization of both dominant and ethnic role prescriptions have clear implications for the parts of ourselves that we are most likely to take pride in or feel shame about and disown. It is our belief that the gap between the experienced and the idealized self, which is seen as playing a pivotal role in addiction, can be best appreciated when one understands more about the specific ecology of the self.

ECOLOGY OF THE JEWISH SELF

MALES

"Di libeh iz zis, mit broit iz zi besser [love is sweet, but with bread it's better]."

Herz and Rosen (1982) note that historically "men and boys were expected to be free from worldly tasks so they could 'learn' (study the Torah)." In this patriarchal culture those (males) gifted enough would pray, analyze, and debate all day with other males. Perhaps as a derivative of this pattern, and of the historical need to use one's wits as opposed to brawn to survive, intellect was and is one of a Jewish male's prime attributes. Intellectually unsuccessful Jewish males suffer from their own self-judgments as well as from the judgments of peers and family. The humorous response to the stereotype of the Jewish parent *kvelling* about (taking pride in) "my son the doctor" belies the shame, for child and parent, associated with "my son who has to work with his back because he can't work with his head." While the ideal Jewish man responds to the security theme by being smart, that is clearly not enough. It appears that as Jewish men have become more secular, they have not migrated back to their homes but rather to their offices. In large measure, women continue to have the responsibility for and the power in the home. "Success outside the family was achieved at the cost of relative devaluation of the husband/father in ongoing family life" (Herz and Rosen, 1982, p. 375). This success does not subtract from the shame associated with the Jewish male's failure to enter the role of husband/father. In most families, and perhaps linked to the security theme, marrying successfully and having children is a source of pride if accomplished and a source of shame if not. From our clinical experience, it appears that shame associated with Jewish divorce seems to be magnified by the failure it represents to the extended family and the community.

As in many cultures, secular Jewish men were traditionally viewed as being responsible for providing well for their family. How well Jewish men provided was often not just a matter of comfort but survival. However, the inability to know how much is enough has perhaps led to a legacy in which it is difficult for Jewish men to feel good about themselves unless they work unreasonable hours or produce increasingly large sums of money. Jewish men still take pride in providing enough so that their wives don't have to work. Couples will often protect this pride and disavow the necessity of the wife's income even in the face of obvious need. Closely akin to pride and shame associated with being a provider is the issue of pride and shame at being able to accept dependency needs. Jewish men, like most men in this culture, are likely to have experienced shame when they were accused of not acting like a "big boy." Being called a *mensch* is one of the highest accolades one can be accorded. Translation of this term is difficult, but it means being a good human being, that is, someone who has a clear sense of his identity and is competent, responsible, and generous. Few would associate being dependent with being a *mensch*.

Emotional expressiveness and responsiveness are increasingly desirable traits for Jewish men—but not necessarily at the cost of their ability to provide. These characteristics are not always central to the Jewish male's ideal self and therefore often do not create important pride or shame issues. However, there clearly is a limit to acceptable expressiveness. The Jewish theme of suffering often manifests in the female *and* male pastime of *kvetching* (ritualized complaining). Complaining about one's suffering in some part of one's life—physical aches and pains, one's job, aggravation from family members, is permissible among friends and colleagues up to a threshold, beyond which one becomes known as a *kvetch*. This is a shaming appellation. Jewish men often take pride in suffering in near silence and look disdainfully at those who inordinately *kvetch*. While expressiveness, including anger and tenderness, is not outside the range of acceptable Jewish male repertoires, acknowledgments of financial and intellectual "underfunctioning" and emotional dependency needs often are.

The themes of security, suffering, and identity energize particular shame and pride issues for Jewish men. The shame and pride matrix is different for Jewish women, but the themes can still be seen as motivating certain skills, behaviors, and attributes.

FEMALES

"Der man iz der balebos—az di veib zaine lozt [the husband is the boss—if his wife allows]."

Jewish women must integrate paradoxical messages about themselves. While Orthodox men offered prayers of gratitude that they were not born female, women exercised control over major aspects of family life. For generations, Jewish women have also worked outside the home, providing financial support while their husband studied the Torah, or more recently medicine, law or business.

The role conflict between being a homemaker and pursuing a career and the sometimes conflicting aspects of self that these roles demand often leave Jewish women particularly pained. As opportunities for achievement for women have expanded, so have the opportunities for shame. The family has always been at the secular and religious center of Jewish life. In the nomadic existence of the Jewish people, the family was the nexus of survival and identity. Women have been viewed as the heart of the Jewish family, and those aspects of women (nurturer, organizer, communicator, regulator of interpersonal relationships) that contribute to the maintenance of the family are culturally prized. A Jewish woman gets the message that these dimensions should be core components of her self and that she should feel pride at her accomplishments in these dimensions and shame at her failures. However, increasingly, achievement in the academic, professional, or business world is also valued for Jewish females—this despite the fact that the personal characteristics that often correlate with achievement, namely, ambition, assertiveness, and viewing work as a priority, are still often viewed with ambivalence. Therefore, as we look at the gap between the idealized and the experienced self for Jewish females, we encounter several potential problems. Women who have received cultural support for both traditional homemaking and outside-the-home work may feel "wrong" even when seeming to perform culturally sanctioned roles. There are significant challenges for women who have received not only family support for multiple role performances (homemaker and professional) but also validation for the variety of necessary personal characteristics (e.g., nurturer and ambitious). While the culture may "permit" certain behaviors and experiences within a particular gender, it also "requires" some others. Increasingly, Jewish women are "permitted" to be personally ambitious but are still often "required" to be emotional caretakers.

As acculturation continues, the Jewish theme of identity is increasingly echoed not just in terms of who you are in relationship to your Judaism but in terms of who you are. Having a well-developed sense of self is now valued relative to an older standard in which being helpmate and supporter were sufficient. While there are many reasons to believe this form of valuing one-self is an important advance, clinicians need to know the potential for and to be on alert to identify increasing amounts of shame in women for not knowing who they are or what they want. Opportunities that become requirements always carry the risk of shame. Similar to the sense-of-self issue is the issue of dependence versus independence. Historically, the theme of security found a response in Jewish families that nurtured female dependence. However, this appears to be less and less true. Jewish women are still more immune than men to "shame attacks" for being dependent, but this is changing as well.

Jewish women have been in the forefront of modern feminism. However, integrating a feminist identity with a Jewish identity still remains a daunting task fraught with possibilities for shame. The paternalistic legacy of five thousand years is echoed in traditional religious life as well as in traditional family life. There are some important exceptions, and the number of female non-Orthodox religious leaders is growing. But often the issue of integrating these two aspects of female Jewish identity is addressed either by creating alternative cultural communities or by splitting one's identity. Years ago one of us knew an orthodox Jewish feminist who confided that the alternative religious services, with their equal emphasis on the male and female images of God, just didn't feel true. Today it is getting easier to find rabbis, texts, and rituals that acknowledge and celebrate the feminine aspects of God and that reflect back to women an image that allows them to perceive the divine within.

SUBPOPULATION VARIATIONS

When considering the cultural influences on the development of the idealized image of the Jewish male self and the Jewish female self, one must be aware of the significant differences among Jewish subpopulations. Generalizations that fail to take this into account are likely to lead to false conclusions and faulty clinical interventions. For example, subpopulations within the Jewish world differ significantly in the width of their role prescriptions. Orthodox Ashkenazi observers of the religious tradition maintain sharper divisions between the sexes with regard to sex roles; in fact, men and women literally sit apart in synagogues. Generally, a larger family and strong traditions of the mother as the organizing force of the home leave less room for an Orthodox woman to consider commitment to a career outside the home. Compared to women of other Jewish subpopuluations, she is more likely to experience deep shame for neglecting her domestic responsibilities if she pursues a career and she is less likely to experience shame for not achieving outside of the family. In contrast, Reform and Conservative Ashkenazi Jews permit men and women to worship together and are more likely to view aspects of their lives from nonreligious as well as religious perspectives. These secular perspectives account for the greater role conflict. If these Jewish men and women choose to have fewer children and to experience a broader range of role choices, they are more likely to experience both internal and marital conflicts.

Like the more Orthodox Ashkenazi, the subpopulation of Sephardic Jews (Jews whose ancestors passed through Spain, Greece, and a number of Middle Eastern countries) have, generally speaking, a narrower band of sex role choices available. These frequently insular communities do not offer many models that support a wide range of diverse social behavior. More often than in other Jewish subpopulations, there is a clear standard of what it means to be a good Jewish man and a good Jewish woman. These roles are distinct, and the shame for failure is greater. The much larger group of Ashkenazi is far more diverse, and role expectations are less rigid.

There are other differences among the various Jewish subpopulations that include, but are not limited to, average socioeconomic status, average educational level, average age of marriage, and even susceptibility to certain inheritable diseases. Since it is the subpopulation that may form the reference group for clients, clinicians are advised to become acquainted with the ecology of the various Jewish populations with which they are likely to work.

THE RELEVANCE OF THE JEWISH ADDICT'S JEWISHNESS

WHILE IMPORTANT DISTINCTIONS must be made between the subpopulations of Jews, it is also important for those treating the Jewish addict to recognize that the apparent relevance of the addict's Jewishness will vary significantly among cases. While it is likely that family dynamics around the addiction and internalized self-images will to some degree reveal echoes of long-forgotten Jewish roots, treatment strategies must give priority to immediately relevant variables. For some clients, these variables will include aspects relating to their ethnicity; for others, ethnicity may emerge indirectly or perhaps not at all as a significant factor in their treatment.

Assessment is an ongoing part of our treatment. It always begins with consideration of the presenting problem and includes the development of a three-generation genogram. The basic structure of the family; a chronology of major changes, including entrances and exits from the family; the addiction status of family members; the general patterns of closeness, conflict, and cutoffs—are all indicated on the genogram. The ethnic origins of each side of the family are noted. Intermarriage is rarely a neutral event for Jewish families. When there are ethnic differences between spouses, we inquire at an appropriate time about the impact of those differences and attempt to determine how the problem is perceived, how the couple generally relates to each other, and how the extended families reacted to the marriage. In constructing the genogram, we have observed that when addiction is not the presenting problem, as is most often the case with Jewish families, specific inquiry about immediate and extended family involvement with gambling, drinking, and prescription and illegal drug use sometimes precipitates the first recognition of a family pattern. In contrast, it is our experience that members of interethnic marriages are more often cognizant of at least some of these addictive patterns.

Augmenting the genogram with the social atom, a sociometric tool developed by Moreno (1985), offers a valuable perspective on the external and internal life of our clients. In our variation on Moreno's technique, clients are given unlined paper and instructions about how to represent their social worlds. They are instructed to represent people, things, and activities in a size and proximity to the self that represents their importance and relevance. This nonverbal technique is particularly difficult and valuable for Jewish clients, who often use verbal defenses to mask unacceptable realities. Use of the social atom technique and the ensuing conversations about it indicate a good deal about not only clients' relationships with their addictions and with their Jewishness but also their perception of the relationship between the two. Since the social atom tells us something about perceived reference groups, it is often a valuable introduction to the pride and shame issues that will emerge in treatment. It also communicates potential conflicts before clients may be ready to verbalize them. A social atom of a man in early recovery who positions AA between himself and the drink and positions his wife, children, parents, and "the community" on the other side of himself may be in danger of a slip. As treatment continues, changes in the client's social atom productions can serve to document to therapist and client the development of a more balanced and integrated social world. Initial social atoms that omit any reference to Jewish people or Jewish things may indicate a cutoff; however, it is usual for Reform Jews to omit direct reference to their Jewishness.

The activities, people, and things that clients represent on their social atom can be examined for clues about how immediately relevant their Jewishness is. It is important to note that this is likely to change over time. For example, many Jewish clients report greater sensitivity to their Jewishness as they first begin to attend AA meetings, which are often held in churches. When some aspect of their ethnicity is specifically referenced in the social atom—or, for that matter, in conversation—it is likely to be an important factor to consider in constructing interventions.

In the sections that follow we examine treatment issues for Jewish families from the perspective of the three-stage treatment model developed by Bepko and Krestan (1985). At the end of the discussion of each stage, we present a case illustration of the issues and interventions.

Pre- and Post-Sobriety Treatment Issues for the Jewish Family

Pre-Sobriety

Following Krestan and Bepko's model for treating alcoholic families, we conceptualize three phases of treatment: pre-sobriety, adjustment to sobriety, and maintenance of sobriety. Our experience, and that of others who write about Jewish addictions (Levin, 1992), is that the fundamental processes of addiction and treatment are similar for Jews and non-Jews. A major distinguishing feature for Jewish alcoholics concerns the issue of denial. Fully understanding the degree of shame underlying Jewish denial is important. According to Bepko and Krestan (1985), "Treatment in pre-sobriety is the treatment of denial" (p. 970). In addition to all the other sources of shame that all addicts experience and attempt to disavow, Jewish addicts often feel their addiction is a betrayal of their Jewish community, if not their identity.

Bepko and Krestan's descriptions of direct and strategic approaches to dealing with denial are applicable to many Jewish clients as long as the therapist keeps in mind the concept of systemic levels of denial. Twerski and Twerski (1994) and others have articulated the phenomenon of the extension of denial beyond the bounds of the individual and family to include the community as well. In light of the pervasiveness of the denial, therapists are ill-advised to take a direct approach in labeling a drinking, drug, or gambling problem without first assessing a motivated family member's ability to connect with community resources that support Jewish sobriety. These may include knowledgeable clergy, members of Jewish Alanon (or some other twelve-step program), or recovery treatment groups with other Jewish members. In the absence of this connection, the motivated and receptive family member is likely to be placed in an extremely difficult position if he or she joins the therapist in asserting the existence of an addiction problem. Clearly, the more important the client's identity as a Jew, the more difficult the position. One solution to this dilemma is to enlarge the treatment unit and include appropriate extended family or, as Abraham Twerski (1994) has suggested, to employ a network therapy approach in which family and social support are included in the office-based therapy.

Once there is sufficient support to see, speak, and live the truth, Jewish pre-sobriety treatment proceeds just about the same as non-Jewish treatment. However, involving the addict and co-addict in a twelve-step program may be more difficult for Jewish clients. There is literature available from JACS (Jewish Alcoholics, Chemically Dependent Persons and Significant Others) that relates the twelve steps to Judaism (*Rabbi Steinman JACS Journal*, 1984; *Rabbi Twerski JACS Journal*, 1986). However, often Jews believe such a program is not for them. Meetings are frequently held in churches, and often the customs of a particular meeting (e.g., reciting the Lord's Prayer and praying on bended knees) are distinctly non-Jewish. The therapist is advised to anticipate this resistance and openly discuss the issue with clients and to suggest attendance at meetings where there is likely to be at least one other Jewish person or provide background material that helps Jewish clients see the compatibility between Judaism and twelve-step programs. One of us has successfully responded to clients who balked about twelve-step meetings being too gentile by asking "What religion was your dealer [or bartender or bookie]?" or "If you were strung out, would you buy drugs from a gentile or wait to find a Jewish dealer?"

Finally, we recognize that there may be a limited number of circumstances where attendance at twelve-step meetings is so culturally dystonic for a client that it may distract from recovery at a given point in time. It is sometimes difficult to distinguish between resistance to recovery and genuine cultural concerns. In such instances, consultation by client and therapist with a religious leader trained in addiction treatment is warranted, even if such consultation can only be obtained by telephone. When detoxification and inpatient rehabilitation is necessary, it is important to consider whether the treating facility has experience dealing with the religious and dietary requirements of observant Jews. Even for nonreligious Jews, an environment that contains other recovering Jews will more likely enable clients to deal with the intense isolation and shame that they may carry. Referral to such facilities and programs can often be made by the closest Jewish Family Service Agency with an addiction counselor on staff.

Case Study

Family A came to therapy seeking help for an adolescent son acting out in school. Development of the genogram indicated that the parents were both second-generation Eastern European Reform Jews. The parents denied concern about their child's use of drugs and initially denied any family history of addiction. Structural family assessment indicated a perverse triangle with the mother in the distant and subordinate position and the father and son in covert alliance. It took several sessions of careful questioning with various combinations of family members (including the adolescent's older sister) to discover that the father was an early-stage functional alcoholic and the mother had a serious spending addiction problem. Over the course of several months, the parents were given behavioral management strategies designed to realign the family hierarchy. As the clinician's initial success deepened his rapport with the family, he was able to more directly challenge the addictive patterns. Simultaneously providing literature on alcohol and drug abuse and on spending addiction was particularly useful in enabling the family to look at the addictions without disturbing the parents' balance of pride. The father ultimately agreed to a ninety-day abstinence contract and attendance at AA meetings conditional upon his wife's abstinence from credit card use and attendance at Debtors Anonymous meetings.

Adjustment to Sobriety

Bepko and Krestan (1985) write that the goal of the adjustment-to-sobriety phase of treatment is to "help the family deal with the after shocks of sobriety" in ways that prevent both relapse and symptom shifting (p. 127). The fundamental clinical issue of the co-addict's need to construct a redefinition of self that is not based on emotional or physical overfunctioning is particularly charged for Jewish men and women. The centrality of the family in Jewish life and the previously discussed Jewish themes of identity and security come together at this juncture of treatment. If a Jewish husband's hunger for identity has made him overfunction in the role of protector and provider and if he has taken great pride in that role, he will have a difficult time as his wife's recovery leaves her better able to protect, and perhaps even provide for, herself. He will need a good deal of support from peers to forge a new basis for self-esteem. As she recovers, she will need a good deal of support to deal with a variation of the deep shame that many recovering women feel. The shame is for not fulfilling her own, her spouse's, her children's, her parents', and her community's image of her role as ultimate caretaker of others. There are many humorous, as well as disparaging, jokes about Jewish mothers, and they almost all involve her overconcern for others, especially her children. Additionally, there are few precedents in her community for the necessary frequent absences to attend twelve-step or therapy meetings. When we meet resistance to this, we ask the family to regard the addiction as a cancer and the AA meetings as an equivalent to radiation therapy. Medical metaphors are often quite helpful.

Many Jewish women may have a somewhat easier time dealing with the role of recovering co-addict than their non-Jewish counterparts. Since the Jewish culture has been generally more liberal in supporting the role of women professionals (while not abandoning its sanctioning of the caretaker role), support from the therapist to relinquish her overfunctioning role can often be experienced by the wife with a sense of relief. Following her spouse's sobriety, the co-addict's pride system is often assaulted by the loss of the overfunctioning caretaker role. However, for many Jewish women this can be attenuated by the knowledge that there are other culturally valued things that she does or could do.

The Jewish male addict's challenge is to deal with the shame that he has let everyone down. Since he may view his addiction as failing not only his nuclear family and family of origin but also the Jewish people, he needs a context to heal this shame. For many, connecting or reconnecting with a spiritual framework is an important component at this phase. Additionally, many states have organized weekend retreats for Jews in recovery. These retreats offer Jewish men and women in recovery an opportunity to deal specifically with the issues of shame, isolation, and denial. Moreover, since there is such a tremendous degree of diversity among recovering Jews in the way they manifest their spirituality, these retreats are often opportunities for Jews who have moved away from traditional means of observance to find fellow seekers. The spiritual part of recovery poses problems for the Orthodox Jew, who may believe that he is unacceptable to God. A Jewish recovery experience provides a safe context for exploring these issues.

CASE STUDY

Family B presented for marital therapy, upon referral from Mrs. B's psychiatrist. She had been treating her for several years for her anxiety symptoms. The husband's complaints about Mrs. B's absences from the home during times when she was responsible for the children, as well as careful tracking of presumably social drinking, led the therapist and the husband to conclude that Mrs. B was abusing both prescription drugs and alcohol. Mrs. B ultimately agreed to enter rehab after Mr. B, with the support of his good friends and the family's enlightened rabbi, took a stand and threatened a separation. Care was taken to find a rehab facility that had Jewish females in recovery. Although the B family was not very religiously observant, they were uncomfortable attending AA and Al-Anon meetings in a church. The therapist introduced the couple to another recovering Jewish couple, and this buddy system seemed to put them more at ease. It is noteworthy that the initial referring psychiatrist has since entered a recovery program herself.

MAINTAINING SOBRIETY

In the maintaining-sobriety phase, dysfunctional family relationships that would threaten sobriety if left untreated are addressed. Aspects of family relationships that limit family members from fully experiencing and expressing themselves while sober are challenged. Specifically, we work with the intra- and interpersonal pride/shame systems of family members. Within the more insulated Jewish communities, this is often a difficult phase to successfully resolve. Role prescriptions are not only narrowly defined but feedback for norm violation is often swift and to the point.

Shaming interactions are common. One man in recovery was given a seemingly simple task of making the next set of social plans for the couple. Both he and his wife reported that his efforts to break out of his customary role in the family led to humor-disguised criticism by both her friends and his. The couple tried to resolve the conflict between their community's rigid role prescriptions and their own felt need for more role flexibility by deciding to act as if they were following the community-prescribed roles when they were in public while they were privately working at establishing more flexible and balanced role relationships at home. Ultimately, they decided that they could not rewrite the rules of their relationship and continue to live in the community.

With members of the more mainstream Reform and Conservative communities, clinicians can worry less about community censure but must address the individual pride systems of husband and wife. Bepko and Krestan (1985) write about the rigid posture of self-justification and the need to be right that often characterize alcoholic family systems. The historical need for Jews to live by their wits, coupled with a tradition of learning through argumentation, may have left a particularly potent legacy for many Jews of the need and ability to prove that they are right. Escalating pride wars are the result. Working in individual, group, and conjoint sessions, the therapist must help family members examine their shame-avoiding strategies and come to a deep level of acceptance of their own imperfection.

Another Jewish variant on pride issues that must be addressed in this phase of treatment concerns the Jewish theme of suffering. Since many Jewish men take pride in their ability to suffer in near silence whereas Jewish women may feel pride in their ability and willingness to visibly sacrifice and suffer "for the sake of the family," couples may have a pride struggle over who suffers the most. Occasionally, humor helps both spouses gain perspective about the irony of competing for this prize. Working to help individuals make explicitly clear what they need and what they are capable of and finding ways for them to deeply experience their own and their partner's right to a meaningful and joyful life is the essence of this end phase of treatment.

CASE STUDY

Family C came to treatment following referral from a fellow Gam-Anon member. Mr. C had been in GA (Gamblers Anonymous) for several years. Mrs. C had been attending Gam-Anon meetings for two and a half years. They came for treatment to specifically address the issue of a lack of a real relationship with each other. Mr. C complained bitterly that Mrs. C was never happy and complained often. After he left his stockbroker job and went into business with his brother she complained about his long hours and meager pay. Mrs. C reported that while she was grateful that her husband's gambling had stopped, she was jealous of the relationship some of her friends seemed to have with their husbands. The therapist took a good deal of time developing a genogram and had the couple create their representations of their social atoms. The genogram indicated a history of estrangements that occurred when some family member's pride was mortally wounded. Using this as an entry to explore the pride systems of the couple, the therapist was slowly able to help each of them come to terms with a good deal of the unresolved shame of their lives. Mrs. C's exploration of her feelings about her inability to have children and Mr. C's exploration of his inability to meet his father's expectations led to painful moments that the couple could share in an empathic connection. The oscillations between attacking the other and attacking the self diminished greatly as the couple's relationship became more of a context for healing old pride injuries.

CONCLUSION

W E HAVE TRIED to demonstrate that the processes for treating addicted Jewish families are no different from those used for treating other families. The content of the treatment may vary, since pride patterns may differ. Cultural resources and obstacles may require clinical flexibility to assist clients in following though on twelve-step and other programs. We think that many kinds of therapies, when presented by a culturally competent therapist, can be effective in treating Jewish families.

Lynch and Hanson (1992) define cultural competence as a way of thinking and behaving that enables a member of one culture, ethnic, or linguistic group to work effectively with members of another. We believe that the unit of cultural competence ought to include the client, the therapist, and the supervisor or co-therapist. There is reason to believe that the most therapeutic means of providing addiction treatment for Jewish addicts involves a culturally diverse team. With such team, whether as co-therapists or as supervisor and supervisee, we believe that a kind of binocular vision is made available to the client; that is, assessments that include the challenging perspectives of both a friendly "foreigner" and a fellow traveler reduce each clinician's blind spots and increase therapeutic creativity. While the financial constraints of managed care have reduced our ability to provide co-therapy for individual families, we are about to develop marital group therapy with a culturally diverse therapy team.

REFERENCES

Adlaf, E. M., Smart, R. G., & Tan, S. H. (1989). Ethnicity and Drug Use: A Critical Look. *The International Journal of the Addictions, 24*(1), 1–18.

Bepko, C., & Krestan, J. A. (1985). *The Responsibility Trap.* New York: Free Press.

Cahalan, D., & Cisisn, I. H. (1968). American Drinking Practices: Summary of Findings from a National Probability Sample. *Quarterly Journal of Studies on Alcohol, 29,* 130–151.

Council of Jewish Federations. (1991). *Highlights of the CJF 1990 National Jewish Population Survey.* New York: Author.

Heath, D. B. (1991). Uses and Misuses of the Concept of Ethnicity in Alcohol Studies: An Essay in Deconstruction. *The International Journal of the Addictions, 25*(5A & 6A), 607–628.

Herz, F. M., & Rosen, E. J. (1982). Jewish Families. In M. McGoldrick, J. K. Pearce, & J. Giordano, (Eds.), *Ethnicity and Family Therapy* (pp. 364–392). New York: Guilford Press.

Inkeles, A. (1997). *National Character.* New Brunswick: Transaction Publishers.

Jellinek, E. M. (1941). Immanuel Kant: On Drinking. *Quarterly Journal of Studies on Alcohol,* 1(4), 777–778.

Jellinek, E. M. (1960). *The Disease Concept of Alcoholism.* New Haven, CT: Hillhouse Press.

Keller, M. (1970). The Great Jewish Drink Mystery. *British Journal of the Addictions, 64,* 287–296.

Levin, K. B. (1992). *Addictive Behaviors in the Jewish Community: A Delphi Investigation.* Unpublished doctoral dissertation, Rutgers, The State University of New Jersey.

Linn, L. (1986). Jews and Pathological Gambling. In S. J. Levy, & S. B. Blume, (Eds.), *Addictions in the Jewish Community.* (pp. 337–358) New York: Commission of Synagogue Relations.

Lynch, E., & Hanson, M. (1992). *Developing Cross-Cultural Competence.* Baltimore: Paul H. Brookes.

McGoldrick, M. (1989). Women Through the Life Cycle. In M. McGoldrick, C. Anderson, & F. Walsh (Eds.), *Women in Families.* New York: Norton.

McGoldrick, M., & Gerson, R. (1985). *Genograms in Family Assessment.* New York: Norton.

McGoldrick, M., Pearce, J. K., & Giordano, J. (Eds.). (1982). *Ethnicity and Family Therapy.* New York: Guilford Press.

Moreno, J. L. (1985). *Psychodrama.* Ambler, PA: Beacon House.

Nathanson, D. (1992). *Shame and Pride: Affect, Sex, and the Birth of the Self.* New York: Norton.

Nusbaumer, M. R. (1981). Religious Affiliation and Abstinence: A Fifteen Year Change. *Journal of Studies on Alcohol,* 42(1), 127–131.

Riley, J. W., Jr., & Marden, C. F. (1947). The Social Pattern of Alcoholic Drinking. *Quarterly Journal of Studies on Alcohol,* 8(2), 265–273.

Rosen, E., & Weltman, S. (1996). Jewish Families: An Overview. In M. McGoldrick, J. Giordano, & J. K. Pearce, (Eds.), *Ethnicity and Family Therapy* (2nd ed.; pp. 611–637). New York: Guilford Press.

Sartre, J. P. (1948). *Anti-Semite and Jew.* New York: Schocken Books.

Schmemann, S. (1998 January 27). "'Who's a Jew' Puzzle Gets More Tangled. *New York Times,* p. A7.

Schmidt, W., & Popham, R. E. (1976). Impressions of Jewish Alcoholics. *Journal of Studies on Alcohol,* 37(3), 931–939.

Snyder, C. R. (1958). *Alcohol and the Jews.* Carbondale, IL: Southern Illinois University Press.

Spiegal, M. (1986). Profile of the Alcoholic Jew. *British Journal of Alcohol and Alcoholism,* 16(3), 141–149.

Tobin, G. A.(1988). *Jewish Perceptions of Anti-Semitism.* New York: Plenum Press.

Twerski, B. (1987, May). *Alcoholism in Jews: Shattering the Myth of Sobriety.* Paper presented at American Psychological Association Annual Meeting, New York.

Twerski, B., & Twerski, A. (1994, May). *Treating Jewish Substance Abusers.* Paper presented at American Psychological Association Annual Meeting, Philadelphia.

Wislicki, L. (1967) Alcoholism and Drug Addiction in Israel, *British Journal & Addictions,* 62, 367–373.

Zborowski, M. (1969). *People in Pain.* San Francisco: Jossey-Bass.

Zimberg, S. (1986). Alcoholism Among Jews. In S. J. Levy, & S. B. Blume, (Eds.), *Addictions in the Jewish Community.* New York: Commission of Synagogue Relations.

RESOURCES

Jewish Family Service Agency (local chapters)

Jewish Alcoholics, Chemically Dependent Persons and Significant Others (JACS) phone: (212)397-4197; Web site: http://www.jacsweb.org.

Exodus Hospital Drug/Alcohol Rehabilitation Program, Miami, FL; phone: 1-800-443-DRUG.

New Direction Project, The Rabbinical College of America, Morristown, NJ; phone: (783) 267-1443.

CHAPTER FIVE

ADDICTION, AFRICAN AMERICANS, AND A CHRISTIAN RECOVERY JOURNEY

Deniece J. Reid

> The major Black cultural response to the temptation of despair
> has been the Black Christian tradition—a tradition dominated
> by music in song, prayer, and sermon.
> CORNEL WEST (1996, P. 101)

> One cannot stagger into freedom.
> REV. JESSE JACKSON

THERE IS AN Ethiopian proverb that states, "A disease which is concealed cannot be cured." This African wisdom accurately reflects the experience of addiction in the lives of African Americans and their families. The disease of addiction in its various stages and styles has brought about much disease, disorganization, discomfort, and disruption in African American families and communities.

Denial, enabling, and lack of understanding of addiction are primary contributing factors in the continuous contagious spread of addiction, with its illness of body, mind, and spirit. A "cure," meaning a sense of recovering wholeness, can only be experienced when an African American can courageously say, "I'm sick and I want to be sane and sober. I'm drowning and I need a recovery lifeline. I'm a dead man [woman or child], barely walking and I need some solid sober ground to stand on."

This chapter discusses some of the cultural contexts, realities, healing, and hope of the addiction experience of African American families.

> Some estimates suggest that 16% of African Americans are alcoholics, and 32% have used illicit drugs. Figures vary, but it is clear that crack cocaine and heroin have reached epidemic problems, along with associated problems like AIDS (Gordon, 1994).

"Some indicators of community well being suggest that rural Black communities may be as vulnerable [to AOD, i.e., alcohol and other drugs of abuse] as their urban counterparts." (Dawkins and Williams, 1997, p. 484).

Drug and alcohol-using African Americans have higher rates of AOD-related health problems than do users from other ethnic groups (Herd, 1995).

African American families are known to be spiritual, strong, supportive, and resilient. The different historical, cultural, and socialization experiences of African American families have contributed to some often distinct experiences of and responses to addictions in African American family systems. It is important to recognize some of these distinctions in order to understand some of the emotional and familial dynamics of African American families when faced with the addiction of a loved one.

Historically, survival of the extended family has been one of the most important values in African American tradition. This commitment to family evolved from the longstanding African allegiance to the tribe. Nancy Boyd-Franklin (1989), an African American family therapist, comments, "The emphasis in African culture was the survival of the tribe rather than the individual, the nuclear family, or even the extended family" (p. 8). A traditional African philosophy expressing the tribe or family versus the individual is "I am because we are, and because we are, therefore, I am" (Mbiti, 1969, p. 108). These traditions are contrary to Western European familial values, which focus on individuation, differentiation, and boundaries. For instance, in the chemically dependent African American family, so-called enabling may be the family's attempt to ensure "tribal survival."

The historical context in which tribal/familial survival became so critical was the slavery period. The impact of slavery was one of the cruelest attempts to destroy the African family, traditions, and values. Family members were separated and lost during slave trade. Traditional food, language, and spiritual rituals were often forbidden. African slaves struggled to maintain these family values and traditions by practicing African marriage rituals, informally adopting slave children when their parents were sold or killed, and singing "Negro" spirituals with hidden messages of escape, liberation, and/or rebellion (Giddings, 1984). This struggle has continued into contemporary times. Hines and Boyd (1982) state, "It is from this heritage of shared loyalty and strong kinship bonds that African Americans descend. Reliance on a kinship network, not necessarily drawn along blood lines, remains a major model for coping with the pressures of an oppressive society" (p. 87). These historical struggles of African families have contributed to the contemporary strengths of African American families as we face various oppressive, destructive experiences today, including addictions.

African American sociologist Dr. Robert Hill (1972), responding to the Moynihan report and other deficit models of Black family life, identified the following five prevalent strengths of the African American family. Although Pinderhughes and others also recognize that strengths may start as a response to victimization, nonetheless the strengths Hill identified in 1972 are still relevant. Hill outlined the major strengths as:

1. Strong kinship bonds
2. Adaptability of family roles
3. Strong work orientation
4. High achievement orientation
5. Strong religious orientation.

These five strengths are functional, familial foundations.

Most clinicians are aware of the importance of the extended family network in African American families: the informal adoption system; the presence of "secondary family members" (mostly children), and augmented families where children who live in the household are not blood-related to anyone (Boyd-Franklin, 1989). Deficit models of African American family structure have perpetuated a myth that the African American family has always been matriarchal or matri-focal. In 1960 only 22 percent of Black families were female headed. Now, reality has seemingly caught up with perception. Recent changes in African American family organization have sent the escalation of female-headed single-parent families up to 57 percent (Billingsley, 1992).

Kinship bonds, whatever the family forms, have historically been a foundation of strength in African American families. The crushing effects of addictions have chipped away at these bonds. When addictions reside in African American families and communities, strong kinship bonds become loose destructive relationships. African American families, friends, and community relationships that were built on trust begin to break down because of the addict's lying and stealing. Communication breaks down and tension builds up. Family members and elders in the community are not respected, and they are fearful of the addict. For the African American addict, instead of the strong kinship bonds being a source of strength, they become a resource for acquisition of drugs and alcohol. Kin become prey.

> Blacks have a proportionally higher than average incidence of heart disease and stroke, homicide and accidents, cancer, infant mortality, cirrhosis, and diabetes (Gordon, 1994).

When addiction enters the home, the adaptability of family roles may quickly deteriorate into an absence of clear boundaries and unhealthy roles. As Boyd-Franklin (1989) points out, role flexibility can easily become boundary confusion. African American family members become stuck in certain survival roles, in order to maintain equilibrium and a sense of stability in the family and community. The pressure of these roles also contributes to many physical illnesses of family members because of the stress of the secrecy and shame of the addiction. Many children have an early entry into parental roles, such as care of younger children due to parents' illnesses or their preoccupation with the addict. The children also are exposed to the legal system from witnessing violence and arrests, and they frequently accompany adults on prison visits. The family members are "forced" into roles, resulting in the loss of flexibility and freedom.

> It has been estimated that illegal drugs constitute an economic incentive to see drugs consumed in the community. According to a 1986 National Institute on Drug Abuse study of drug-related deaths in 27 metropolitan areas across the country, Blacks accounted for 25% of the victims (Gordon, 1994, p. 65). "Combating the drug problem is complicated because drugs are big business in America."

When addiction is the employer, the strong work orientation in African American families turns into entrepreneurial zeal in pursuing illegal opportunities for monetary gain. Selling drugs becomes an avenue for a continued supply, immediate gratification, and easy provision of material items. Dealers of drugs (not users) have a detrimental impact on the African American strong work ethic, because they become negative role models in the African American community. They become addicted to a lifestyle of immediate gratification/gain and poisonous power. The relationship of drugs to crime in Black communities cannot be overestimated.

When addiction becomes head of the household, the high achievement orientation in African American families becomes exclusively "addiction" focused. The greatest achievement for the addict becomes acquiring the drug or the high. The addict's pride is built around his or her manipulation skills. The addict exists with a "distorted" sense of power and control of his or her dependency. The African American family's sense of achievement is established by their ability to control the addiction. Also, the family hero has to work very hard to keep the family feeling good about themselves and to compensate for the family's high level of shame. A systemic cycle starts as the family's attempts at control and the addict's attempt at control become a mutually escalating symmetrical battle.

> The economic impact of crime, disease, disability, drug abuse, and related problems like AIDS compounds the already polarized economic structures of Black communities. Glick (1997) states that, "The poverty rate has continued to be about two or three times as high for Black families as for all families" (p. 134).

When addiction becomes a family member's "God," the strong religious orientation in African American families becomes spiritually and morally diluted. The addiction is worshipped at the addict's altar of false hope, peace, and strength. Spiritual commitments are often manipulated and shortlived if the addict is not sincere about recovery. Often African American family members may get angry with God if their loved one continues in his or her addiction. However, this anger or disappointment is usually temporary because God continues to be the family's only hope for recovery, and for the addict's return to the cultural and spiritual family strengths, values, and beliefs.

CULTURAL/SOCIO-ECONOMIC FACTORS OF AFRICAN AMERICAN USE/DEPENDENCY AND ADDICTIONS

FOR AFRICAN AMERICANS, various usage, dependencies, and addictions have often times been a method of coping with the painful familial/societal experiences of oppression, racism, poverty, and loss. Some lines from the poem, "The Meanings of Alcohol to Black America" (Harper, 1976) still ring true today; and various other addictions can be added to explain the "coping," compensating usage of chemicals among African Americans.

ALCOHOL . . . that joy juice which serves a quasi suicidal means of
tuning out painful realities, . . .
ALCOHOL to the Black community is that omnipresent catalyst that
frees anxiety, jealousy and anger; that causes one to avenge the self from
the lowest depth of insult in the only way he or she knows—by assaulting,
by fighting, by destroying.
ALCOHOL keeps the Black man from going crazy in a castrating and
racist world . . . so necessary to pump life into a body and community of
hopelessness and despair; so necessary for social intercourse, relaxation,
partying and psychological survival; so "good" but yet so "bad". (Pp.
33–34)

Some related responses of African American addicts, when asked about
their usage and addictions and painful emotional life experiences, include:"I
just got so frustrated when I couldn't get a job"; "I feel like somebody when
I'm in a relationship no matter how unhealthy"; "It just wasn't getting any
better"; "I couldn't see the light at the end of the tunnel, just the tunnel"; "I
got tired of waiting and doing the right thing." These responses become ra-
tionalizations: ". . . So I started using . . . picked up again . . . started gambling . . . bought some sex . . . got on the pipe . . ."

Peter Bell (1990) considers addiction the by-product of racism, poverty,
and lack of opportunity. These factors are also associated with other types of
chemical use. However, Bell (1984) also states that racism and oppression
must not be permitted to excuse or enable AOD abuse.

> In a study of drug-related deaths in 27 urban areas, Blacks repre-
> sented 25% of the victims . . . this was reported by a 1986 National In-
> stitute on Drug Abuse . . . survey (Gordon, 1994, p. 65) among African
> Americans from differing socioeconomic statuses.

HOMELESS ABUSERS

The African American skid-row or homeless chemical abusers usually work
on a day-to-day basis if they work at all, getting spot jobs as a dishwasher,
or at a car wash. They live to get the next bottle or fix, whether indulging
alone or in groups. The poverty-stricken African American chemical
abusers in both urban and rural communities use chemicals to ease the per-

sonal/economic tensions of an "oppressive" life experience (unemployment, crime, racism).

> Blacks are more apt than Whites to be a victim of violent crimes, including rape, assault, robbery, and homicide. "The typical American has a 1-133 chance of being murdered. However, for Black males the chances are 1-in -21" (Gordon, p. 64).

The chemical becomes a short-term ego-booster. The less stable, low-income African American chemical abusers with unstable employment are often seen drinking and using on the street corners, steps, and alleys. They are members of visible bottle gangs or known street users.

OTHER ABUSERS

The more stable low-income African American chemical abusers do most of their using in their own homes or the homes of friends; they are seldom members of bottle gangs or public/street users. Middle-class African American chemical abusers often have many of the same types of usage patterns as their White counterparts. The majority of their usage occurs at house parties, conventions, vacations, neighborhood cocktail lounges, and lodges. They are often loyal lodge and church members. The same patterns of usage in White and Black communities are seen with other addictive behaviors such as gambling, relationships, etc.

The addict's ultimate goal is to experience power and control, because one's world and life circumstances seem so out of control. Ironically, power is never truly experienced and control is always out of reach when a drink, a line of a chemical, a roll of the dice, or an unhealthy relationship are the only means of achieving the goal. When the addict realizes that using doesn't work to meet insatiable needs and unattainable goals, he or she stands confronted by addictive ditches, detours, and crossroads. Here, at the turning point, opportunities to share the realities about addictions and the hope for recovery can meet each other.

One method of "hope-filled" treatment for African Americans was developed by Peter Bell, an African American addictions consultant. Bell (1990) emphasizes the importance of an "Environmental-Secondary theory" that is responsive to cultural issues and relates to underlying causes of addictions such as crime, unemployment and family instability. His methods have received great support among African Americans. His theory explores the "whys" of addictions as well as the "how" to recover. For African Americans, many life experiences with the dominant society are "heartfelt" and often "heart-broken." Treatment that deals with "heart matters" is treatment that will effectively make a difference in the life of a recovering African American.

HEART MATTERS: THE EMOTIONAL SYSTEM

FOUR PREVALENT EMOTIONS experienced in the lives of African Americans that are associated with the "whys" of addictions are: guilt, shame, anger, and grief. Toxic guilt and shame, unresolved grief, and repressed anger are commonly underlying root causes/experiences that African Americans share as they tell their addiction story.

GUILT AND SHAME

Chemical addiction is often an action taken to relieve the pain of toxic shame and guilt, and to have a sense of well-being. However, the pain returns when the effects of the chemical are gone. More chemicals are taken, and the cycle begins again. Ramsey (1988) comments that "a basic description of chemically dependent people is that they are guilt-ridden people" (p. 88). Chemical addiction can result in dysfunctional behavior which results in the addict feeling guilty, and this guilt gets transferred into shame. The addict tries to change or control the addictive behavior when she or he feels the internalized message change from "what I did was bad" to "what I did was wrong, and I must be a bad and weak person for doing it." This final attitude illustrates the bridge from guilt to shame in addiction. Guilt and shame are necessary emotions/issues to address in treatment with African Americans. In my counseling experience, addicts frequently struggle with shame and guilt issues surrounding their addiction and addictive behavior (stealing, prostitution, or incarceration may result in hitting bottom). Addiction-related experiences such as dealing, arrests, drug busts, family arguments, violence, unemployment, financial difficulties, and health problems are usually highly emotional and highly publicized in some African American neighborhoods via media or police interventions. It seems that everyone in the neighborhood and eventually the town knows about "the incident" by eyewitness or word of mouth. The addict and family become headlines for "neighborhood shaming news." These experiences may be coupled with other verbal or nonverbal cultural/societal/familial toxic guilt and shame based messages of inadequacy and incompetence. The addict and family may feel non-redemptive, ostracized, and stigmatized. These internalized messages, stigmas and experiences need healing recovery.

> Prison surveys in 1984 showed that 40% of all prison inmates in the country were Black. For youths, this number jumped to 61% (Gordon, 1994, p. 62).

GRIEF

African Americans experience loss at various levels. Physically, it may be loss of human life; concretely, loss of housing; emotionally, loss of personal peace; societally, loss of opportunity. Addicts additionally experience loss of spirituality. Losses are a common occurrence in the daily lives of many African Americans that range from the legacy of the slave experience, to crime in the streets, to drug overdoses. African Americans suffer loss due to their high health risks and mortality rates. Losses outside the nuclear family may be as important as a nuclear family loss, due to the strong kinship network among African Americans (Hines, 1991). There is often little or no time to emotionally prepare for and/or grieve one loss before the next loss occurs.

> There is a difference of better than five years in the relative life expectancies for Blacks and Whites; Black infant mortality continues to be twice the rate of Whites (Gordon, 1994).

Given these realities, the grief journey for African Americans is often confusing, complex and uncharted. Frequent cultural messages such as "be strong," "you are the man of the house now," "you promise me to take care of——" have suppressed, repressed and expressed grief in unhealthy and addictive ways.

Complicated and unresolved grief can be an underlying cause of addictions. Addicts commonly experience difficulty handling intense emotional feelings, and the addictions often relieve the intensity. Effective grief work involves an ego structure that will allow oneself to feel the pain of loss and to experience the intensity of feelings that arise throughout the process. Without this ability, pathological reaction to unresolved grief develops (Goldberg, 1985). Chemical addiction has been a pathological reaction to grief experiences. Grief is a reaction to the loss of a person or thing to which one has become attached. It can be very painful and frightening and therefore it is often avoided and/or repressed. It is important for a person to accept the "need" to grieve. The result of appropriate grieving is making the loss real inside of self that has been an established reality outside of self. For African Americans, addictions give a false sense of "moving on" when one's grief/healing journey never started. In my clinical experiences with African Americans, I have found that often their addictions started when they experienced the death of a family member/friend, a job termination, an eviction, a chronic illness, or other losses. During these losses, emotional conflicts can occur because family secrets and unresolved relationship issues often surface. The survivors are left with painful baggage to carry and/or unexpected responsibilities; and addictions and silence are chosen to help carry and lighten the load of a painful loss/grief experience. However, I have discovered that educating African American addicts about the dynamics of grief and processing the true pain of the losses has greatly assisted in lightening the load and making the grief journey a real healthy step toward recovery and wholeness.

ANGER

A fourth prominent emotional issue often associated with addictions for African Americans is anger. Anger is a normal human emotion. Yet, it is one of the most difficult emotions to understand and/or manage. For addicts, anger is often expressed in extreme and/or inappropriate manners such as verbal or emotional abuse, violence, silence and isolation. It is often accompanied by fear and guilt. It is a difficult emotion to define, yet the common thread that is often experienced by many includes feelings of being unappreciated, belittled, taken for granted, helpless, or insignificant (Carter 1983).

Homicide rates and suicide rates are connected with rage. These feelings are indeed a part of the cultural/societal threading of life stories that have angered many African Americans. Also, environmental struggles (territorial gangs) and a sense of vulnerability and powerlessness due to racism and oppression (Boyd-Franklin, 1989) are other contributing factors of African Americans' anger experiences. Once again, these feelings and factors have been shared by many African American addicts who chose addiction as a means of expression, ventilation and compensation. Consequently, African

American addicts have experienced serious consequences surrounding expression of anger such as violence, arrests, and loss of family. Providing opportunities for the healthy expression of anger, educating about anger dynamics (personal/societal) and anger management and assessing the type of anger an addict experiences are effective treatment techniques to utilize with African American addicts to decrease consequences and increase understanding and control of anger. Release from the bondage of anger can enable African American addicts to focus and to be free to recover.

Ultimately, when an "understanding and working" light is shed on these four core emotional issues, African American addicts and their families begin to experience hopeful turning points in recovery. These turning points have been witnessed in personal and family lives when addiction ceases, denial is broken, trust is built, connection with God is renewed, and commitment to the recovery process increases.

GENDER FACTORS OF AFRICAN AMERICAN ADDICTIONS

GENDER ISSUES IN FAMILY TREATMENT

In recovery treatment with family members, it is important to be sensitive to cultural, emotional, and relational gender issues. These issues are often demonstrated among family members by overprotective behavior, withholding information, and testing the treatment person's cultural sensitivity and genuine respect for family's feelings and pain. For example, an African American mother will often protect her son from judicial consequences (jail) by minimizing addiction behavior, because she fears for her son's physical and emotional treatment in correctional facilities. Also, I have found that it is helpful for the treatment person to share the disease concept of addictions with African American family members. African Americans are often unfamiliar with this concept and it helps to shift the blame/shame/guilt thinking of the addict and family members. Education about the addiction process and dynamics, cultural and spiritual sensitivity, and respect for the family's desire and courage to learn and recover are important foundations for effective family treatment.

Given the high incidence of AIDS, violence and violent deaths, and the disruption of family life that is addiction-related, I have witnessed a growing "weariness" of behavior that "robs one of life" among African American men, women, and adolescents. We are seeking preventive, proactive treatment programs and services that are "life-giving" culturally, emotionally, and spiritually. Doctors Daryl Rowe and Cheryl Grills (1993) support this realization in their article, "African Centered Drug Treatment," as they share their insights:

> . . . effective drug abuse treatment and recovery must emphasize the acquisition of power (spiritual, personal, familial, communal, institutional and cultural . . .). . . . Empowering African Americans facilitates their ability to define, decide and determine the direction and course of [their] individuated and collective lives. Thus, intervention systems that require African Americans to further relinquish power (personally, spiritually, culturally) are psychologically damaging. . . . Effective drug abuse treatment and recovery must emphasize the positive potential of human behavior based on a value system and sense of order committed to the greater good of humankind. Treatment strategies that simply emphasize the cessation of addictive behaviors without refocusing individuals toward the production of the life sustaining activities are insufficient. . . . For African Americans, it is more appropriate to consider that any individual's drug abuse treatment and recovery . . . is actually a healing of the African American community . . . [This African centered transformative healing of addictions consists of]: . . . seven fundamental constructs which are consciousness, character, conduct, collectiveness, competence, caring and creed. . . . These characteristics provide an [outline] for defining positive culturally congruent behavior for African American relationships with self, family, community, and the world at large. (Pp. 26–27)

THE AFRICAN AMERICAN MALE

An African American male addict often feels that he has little or no control of his life and destiny. Therefore, addictions can provide a means of control and/or coping. Ironically, the use of addictive substances creates the opposite of their intended purposes, resulting in increasingly less control/coping, and often a disastrous destiny.

Particular abuse has been associated with various social and legal difficulties of African American males. Some empirical studies suggest a relationship between chemical use and illegal activities. Many reported incarcerations are the result of drug-related crimes or legal offenses committed by African American males while under the influence of a chemical substance. Researcher Myers (1989) reports, "Blacks were 25% more likely than Whites to be incarcerated for drug offenses, especially for Black drug traffickers, and especially during the most intense years of legislation (1980–1982)" (pp. 298–299). Too often, the chemical abuse issue is not part of the rehabilitation process.

> Barry McCaffrey, Director of the Office of National Drug Control Policy in Washington, D.C., has stated that "the current federal sentencing policy has produced disproportionally severe punishment for African Americans. According to the most recent figures, African Americans constitute 15 percent of cocaine users. However, 38 percent of those charged with powder cocaine violations, and 88 percent of those convicted of crack cocaine charges, are Black. For crimes involving 50 to 150 grams of cocaine, crack defendants received median sentences of 120 months in prison compared to 18 months for powder. Since nearly all cocaine is smuggled into our country and transported over state lines in powdered form (one gram of powder cocaine converts into .89 grams of crack), the federal sentencing disparity has produced long incarceration for low-level crack dealers rather than for international, interstate, and wholesale traffickers." (McCaffrey, 1997)

The socioeconomic status of many inner city African American males, with accompanying unemployment and pressure from loan sharks, frequently leads to excessive "escape" chemical use. Another study (Fagan, 1994) reports, "the expansion of the drug economy in the 1980s created opportunities for income and drug use that have been well exploited by inner-city residents. Participants in drug use and selling were people who were not well matched to the rapidly changing formal labor market . . . and they were very well matched to the labor market for drug distribution" (pp. 193).

The African American male tends to also experience more chronic physical illnesses and health problems than the general adult population. Cirrhosis rates and AIDS-related deaths are high among African American male alcoholics and intravenous drug users. Health problems associated with chemical abuse are seldom identified as a primary concern among some African American males. They seem to disregard excessive chemical use as a problem requiring medical attention. Unfortunately, when medical treatment is pursued by African American males, their illnesses are frequently at terminal stages and early deaths occur. Paradoxically, many African American males have been culturally and socially taught messages such as, "control your hurts and pain" and do not show "weaknesses" (Boyd-Franklin,

1989). These messages of survival have caused many African American males to barely survive because they have had to deny their emotional struggles and numb their pain with chemical poisons and other addictions.

Given these cultural, societal, and emotional realities for African American males, I have found that recovery treatment needs to encompass a holistic approach. Medical needs, societal oppression, emotional struggles (especially anger, shame, guilt, and grief) and life skills (communication, conflict resolution, vocational training) should be addressed in treatment.

THE AFRICAN AMERICAN FEMALE

Historically, the African American female's identity has been viewed by her and those close to her in the descending order of mother, wife, grandmother, sister, aunt, and person. Her status/identity may fluctuate between these different roles; however, most often she operates in the role of person last and least.

Family therapists Hines and Boyd-Franklin (1982) describe African American females as: "often more actively religious than their males. They tend to be regarded as 'all sacrificing' and the 'strength of the family'" (p. 89). Their identity is most likely tied to their role as mothers (1982). This role/status can be very stressful, confusing, and ultimately destructive to the African American female addict because it keeps her in a responsibility/loyalty bind with her family, and in a high state of denial of her addiction. In many instances, the African American family will exhibit two extremes of reaction (persecution and protection) toward their female chemical abuser family member. She will be persecuted for being an alcoholic/addict because of an old gender/cultural belief and message that "the hand that rocks the cradle shouldn't be shaky." The family will usually protect the female chemical abuser's "maternal image" by keeping her addiction a family secret and becoming her "treatment" providers (i.e., taking care of children, promoting geographical cures by sending her to relatives in the South, etc.). Ultimately, enabling the African American female chemical abuser and her denial becomes so strong that she considers outside treatment a violation of her respect/obligation to her family and self. This loyalty backfires when the continuous pressure of putting up a sober front in the presence of family and/or community increases the anger and blame toward family along with the addictive cycle. Often this results in crisis (i.e., leaving home, child abuse, or public intoxication).

It is imperative to understand this cultural gender issue of the African American female's relationship to the "mother figure/role" regarding addiction factors. McGee and Johnson (1985) emphasize this importance in their description of this dynamic: ". . . there is a common myth of the Black superwoman. This myth holds that Black women can withstand any amount of pain and keep on working, especially in order to support our families. This myth has kept many of us from taking care of ourselves very well because we feel we must take care of everyone else first . . . often we will not reach out for help. . . ." (p. 7).

Given these cultural, emotional and spiritual realities for African American females, I have found that recovery treatment needs to assist the addict in working through these "assigned" roles and expectations. Addressing issues of shame, grief, guilt and anger, and giving permission to acknowledge her "own" personal and emotional needs are key "breakthrough" recovery factors for the African American female.

AFRICAN AMERICAN ADOLESCENTS

Adolescence is a time of confusion, change and conflict. This time of growth may be characterized by trial and error, ups and downs, ambivalence and a great deal of experimentation. A youth who is poorly prepared to enter adolescence will use and/or abuse chemical substances in order to cope with changes, conflicts, problems, low self-esteem, uncomfortable situations and everyday stresses.

For the African American adolescent, this stage in the life cycle is compounded by various cultural, socioeconomic, and environmental factors which make the pulls toward chemical abuse a tremendous struggle. Many urban African American youths have been unsuccessful with this struggle, and there is monumental concern about the devastating effects of chemical abuse/addiction in their lives.

Environmentally, the urban African American adolescent is heavily exposed to chemical use, abuse and addictive behavior on the streets. These adolescents are physically surrounded in their communities by numerous liquor stores, bars, billboards, and crack houses, which are often located next to their homes, churches, and schools (Harper, 1976). Alcoholic beverages are "packaged" under very innocent and inviting labels, bottles, colors, tastes, and prices. For example, the inexpensive, sweet taste of a wine cooler called "Breezer" is accepted as a way for an African American adolescent to "chill" (to relax or hang out while partying). This exposure and accessibility to chemicals and addictive activities heightens the African American urban adolescents' acceptance and likelihood of using and abusing alcohol and other drugs, as well as participating in other addictive activities.

One of the most prevalent and poisonous lures among urban African American youth today is involvement with the drug industry. In some cases, "entry-level" positions for teenage drug pushers pay thousands of dollars a week. Some teenagers who sell "crack" own luxury autos, much gold jewelry and designer clothes. Since the unemployment rate among African American teenagers is 37 percent, it is not surprising that drug dealers exploit this recyclable labor force (*Ebony*, August 1989). The use and sale of chemicals among African American adolescents exists in suburban and rural communities as well.

Paradoxically, the losses of many young lives, futures, and self-respect have far outweighed any monetary or material gains that African American youths have obtained as participants in the drug industry. Bell (1990) says, "Black on Black murder is the leading cause of death in Black males from 15 to 44 years of age and the leading cause of death in Black females from 15 to 34 years of age" (p. 19). Stevenson (1997), reviewing the research, claims that "exposure to violence in any form, or the perception that one is in danger, tends to influence the youth's development of anger management and violence expression behaviors" (pp. 39–40). Stevenson (1997) also says, "The image of the African American male youth as aggressive, criminal and dangerous influences how these young men develop gender identities. These images are both rebelled against and appropriated for the purpose of demonstrating power within a powerless context" (p. 40).

CHEMICAL ABUSE PREVENTION AND TREATMENT STRATEGIES FOR AFRICAN AMERICAN YOUTHS

A panel of African American experts in the alcohol field asked hundreds of African American individuals in three communities this question: "What motivates African American youth to drink?" Their conclusions were:

1. Their value system
2. The influence of role models
3. The influence of the media
4. Other factors, such as unemployment and easy access to liquor.

Prevention and treatment measures should focus on these areas (National Institute of Alcoholism and Alcohol Abuse). These prevention and treatment strategies must also target other chemical substances such as crack, cocaine, heroin, and marijuana.

1. Specific: Alcohol/chemical substance education in the schools, peer alcohol/chemical substance educator programs, encouragement of responsible role modeling, support of zoning restrictions to remove bars and taverns from close proximity of schools and churches, etc.

2. Nonspecific: Values clarification and related activities to improve decision-making skills, projects aimed at developing coping skills, projects that teach alternative methods of relaxing (i.e., sports, recreation, etc.). Also, alternative educational and employment training programs are needed for African American youths because patterns of heavy alcohol/chemical abuse may occur during high school dropout and unemployment experiences (ages 17 to 22 years).

Contemporary programs and services that include cultural history education and cultural enhancement have also been effective prevention and treatment strategies with African American adolescents. Cultural connections are important for African American adolescents to experience in order to begin to stand on a solid, rich, strong historical foundation when current ground and life experiences are shaky, shifty, and unstable.

Rites-of-passage programs have been used in many churches, community centers, and social service programs. A center for substance abuse programs in Ohio called "The Comprehensive African American Services Project" included a rites-of-passage protocol that addressed gender relationships, race relations, self-discipline, community service, entrepreneurship, and Council of Elders for youth ages 13 to 22. This program has been effective in reducing high-risk community based factors (Signs of Effectiveness, CSAP, 1987).

This type of program also counteracts the destructive rites of passage that are part of the drug culture for African American adolescents, such as participation in crime, and teenage sex and pregnancy. Criminal activity, and "doing time" without becoming an informant, often increase status in peer groups. Adolescent relationships and pregnancies are also ways to prove adulthood and to gain status, attention, and "hopeful" commitment from another person (Bell, 1990).

SPIRITUAL FORMATION OF THE AFRICAN AMERICAN CHRISTIAN

LET US TAKE a closer look at the spiritual formation and belief system of African Americans. Traditionally, spirituality and religion have been a very central and unified portion of the life of Africans and African Americans. Wade Nobles (1980), an African American psychologist, discusses this strong foundation of spirituality and religion, by noting that "many African languages did not have a word for religion as such. Religion was such an integral part of man's [human] existence that it and he [the human being] were inseparable. Religion accompanied the individual from conception to long after . . . physical death" (p. 25).

> The 1997 Yearbook of American and Canadian Churces lists U.S. religious bodies with more than 60,000 members. There are more than 76 denominations or religions listed. The overwhelming majority of African Americans are Christians, usually part of a Protestant tradition.

Specifically, African American Christian theology has two foundational connections. The African-Hebraic tradition encompasses the total life: spiritual, social, and economic. The slave experience connects African Americans to the Exodus event and the Christ event. Reverend Cecil Cones (1976) describes African American Christian theology and these connections: ". . . because of their African understanding of life, African American people opened themselves up to a reality that was beyond rationality . . . therefore able to get an insight into a divine reality . . . embracing God and giving their total lives to God, they became free . . . they began to create a new kind of religious experience and way of life made possible both by their world view and their encounter with Almighty Sovereign God in the midst of slavery" (p. 45).

African American spiritual formation can also be understood by recognizing the importance of the concept of "core beliefs." Theologians Mitchell and Lenter (Wimberly, 1991) define core beliefs as "deep metaphors or images that point to the plot or directions of life; they undergird the behaviors of people . . . for African American Christians, deep metaphors are related to the life, death, and resurrection of Jesus Christ, who liberates the oppressed and cares for the down trodden . . . is informed by the Exodus story and God's involvement with God's people" (p. 12).

HISTORICAL ROLES OF THE AFRICAN AMERICAN CHURCH

Historically, the African American church played a major role in conveying strength, hope and a message of escape from the hardships and heartaches of slavery. The African American church assisted in keeping slavery in perspective; slaves knew that this horrible experience was not a permanent condition. The African American church gave them a "trouble don't last always" state of mind. African American slaves found spiritual comfort and opportunity for social expression in the church. It was the only institution that African Americans could call their own. It belonged exclusively to African Americans and their community. At this time, the African American church functioned in many roles. It was a center for religious devotion and ceremony, a school, a political meeting hall, a community recreation and social center, and a haven for fugitive slaves.

Slavery was a very lonely, isolated, alienated living experience. It was a violation of being, an abandonment. Therefore, spiritual fellowship and human contact were very important and much appreciated by African American slaves. It was spiritually, emotionally, and physically inspiring to gather together with hearts in accord to edify, strengthen, encourage, and love one another. Wallace Smith (1985) describes the African American church as "a place of relationship. The church is family. Slave owners did everything humanly possible to destroy the African American family. The church kept the concepts of family alive. God was the parent, and those who gathered came together as a few of God's 'helpless children'" (pp. 17–18). Through a relationship with God, the African American slaves, in their state of powerlessness, believed there would be a time when they would be empowered. The slaves realized that their ability to endure the hardships of slavery could only be possible if the Godcoming was already in their hearts. Often, at a spiritual gathering, an experience of freedom occurred when a slave felt a "touch" from the Holy Spirit. The slave would respond with dancing, crying, jumping, and shouting, because briefly he or she felt released from oppression. Dr. Joseph Durham (1972) describes the birth of the African American church: "The African American church was born out of protest. It was the African American slave's instrument to protest against the White man's [society's] definition of the African American . . . as a piece of property; and to refuse the view that God ordained African American people to be slaves."

E. Franklin Frazier (1974), an African American who devoted his academic study to the subjects of the African American family and church, summarizes the tremendous impact of these historical roles on the lives of African Americans with the following statement: "For the slaves who worked and suffered in an alien world, religion offered a means of catharsis for their pent up emotions and frustration . . . the Negro could give expression of his/her deepest feelings and at the same time achieve status and a meaningful existence, the Negro church provided a refuge in a hostile White world . . . They retained their faith in God and found a refuge in their churches" (p. 44).

THE FUNCTION OF THE AFRICAN AMERICAN CHURCH IN THE SPIRITUAL IDENTITY FORMATION OF AFRICAN AMERICANS

In addition to the historical roles of the African American church, there are three primary functions that have chronologically contributed to the spiritual identity formation of the African American.

In his book, *The Church in the Life of the Black Family*, Wallace Smith (1985) describes these three functions of the African American Church as three shared realities of the African American family/church. These are the realities of suffering, inclusiveness, and hopefulness. His idea of community is not simply used to describe a particular geographical location residence of African Americans. It is describing a group of people with common historic, social, cultural, and spiritual experiences.

The first shared experience of the African American Church and family that Smith refers to is the reality of a suffering community. Suffering has been a foundational and consistent experience for most African Americans, the joining factor of African American families and churches. Smith shares that the African American Church became a "source of nurturance and socialization" and that the African American extended family provided a model of social welfare and concern for the church (Smith, 1989). The African Americans shared material supplies (food clothing, shelter) and addressed educational and political injustices. Suffering was shared, thereby decreasing its impact on individual, familial, and systemic levels among African Americans.

The second shared experience of the African American Church and family that Smith refers to is the belief in an inclusive/adoptive community. In the religious and family structure of the West African Ashanti tribe (many African Americans are descendants of this tribe) the elders are honored, the women are highly respected, and the children closely protected. Culturally, the male was responsible for the primary leadership of the family and the female was responsible for the socialization of the family. The male was the head and the female was the heart of the tribe.

Historically, the inclusive/adoptive community experience in the African American church family was not always a family in which one's membership was based on human blood kinship. Spiritually this kinship and community were established through shared belief in salvation based on the redeeming blood of Jesus Christ and shared membership in the church. Smith explains this spiritual kinship dynamic: "Black family as an inclusive community was also an adoptionist community. The inclusion into membership was the saving of a sinner and also the grafting into the entire reality of that church a new family member, who, in turn became a full participant in the life and customs of that church. It is here that the black church as extended family obtains much of its identity. For black people a family member is not one who necessarily shares same blood kinship. He or she is one who has come to share one's loves, pains, and struggles mutually" (pp. 26–27).

Presently, this inclusive community experience in many African American churches/families provides a sense of worth when African Americans experience worthlessness in society.

The third experience of the African American Church and family that Smith refers to is the shared attitude of a hopeful community. In spite of the most inhumane, oppressive situations and experiences of slavery, and in spite of the present-day experiences of discrimination and racism, African Americans have demonstrated the ability to hold on to continue to hope for something better. This attitude of hope is reflected in the sermons and spiritual songs of African American Christians. James Evans (1992), an African American theologian, comments on this consistent, hopeful theology of African Americans. He shares that African American religion/theology is a story expressed and experienced in three stations of time: past, present, and future. The past provides a firm foundation of historical hope through God's acts of deliverance and the African Americans' acts of determination. The present provides an experience of a believing community of African Americans that continue to keep hope alive and keep liberation a practicing reality. The future provides room for African Americans to extend our faith, trust, and hope in God, who remains faithful throughout all stations of time to attain complete justice for the oppressed (Evans, 1992). Hope in God has been one of the spiritual handles that African Americans have learned to grip tightly to endure the storms of life.

A comprehensive description of these shared experiences and the functions of the African American Church is expressed by James Joseph (Raboteau, 1978): "The African American church has always been a special kind of community. It has always been the one place where the local doctor and the local chicken thief might share a pew. It can embrace wide social differences because it is a community with a shared sense of history. As a human community, its concern is . . . to make human life more humane. As a spiritual community it embraces both the living and the living dead . . . not only to proclaim a message but to accomplish a mission" (p. 40).

The church also functions currently as a base from which to launch effective prevention programs for AOD abuse. In a recent CSAP study, Johnson et al. conclude: "This study strongly suggests that prevention of alcohol and other drug use among young adolescents can be achieved by implementing a church community-based program targeting family resilience" (p. 306).

The African American church does not function perfectly. However, it is one of the constant institutions and available experiences for African Americans. A strong ecological perspective in the cultural lives of African Americans has a genuine spiritual connection to our addictions and recovery experiences.

SPIRITUALLY EFFECTIVE AND INEFFECTIVE RECOVERY MODELS FOR CHRISTIAN AFRICAN AMERICANS

In my experience as a pastoral counselor, I have found that spiritually overt, biblically related recovery treatment has been extremely effective for African Americans who are recovering Christians. Historically, the Bible has made sense out of life for African Americans and has been a source and resource that has sustaining truth and trust for African Americans.

One effective, healing use of scriptures in recovery counseling is a technique that facilitates growth and yet is simultaneously authoritative. African American pastoral counselor Edward Wimberly (1994) describes this counseling technique and compares it with a "nongrowth-authoritarian" counseling technique. He says that author*itarian* uses of scripture seek to make children of the counselees and frustrate the growth of persons toward their full possibilities as human beings. He says that author*itative* uses of scripture aim to appropriate those dimensions of scripture that support the empowering of humans to become full and responsible participants in life (Wimberly, 1994).

I have conducted individual and group counseling sessions utilizing this technique with biblical characters and experiences in addressing emotional/recovery issues of surrender, trust, guilt and shame, loss, forgiveness, personal responsibility, and love. These counseling experiences have enabled recovering addicts to integrate and internalize God's strength, grace, and love, as they faced painful, embarrassing realities about their addiction.

A spiritual conflict with the twelve-step programs for African American Christians is the vagueness of the identity of God as discussed in AA. The term often used in twelve-step circles is "God as we understand him." AA groups tend to discourage specific religious discussion and encourage a more generic spirituality. Christian recovery counselors (Hemfelt, Minirth, Fowler, Meier, 1991) express this conflict: "We've found that our patients have had difficulty walking through the twelve-step process in full recovery without the involvement of this God of the Old and New Testaments."

Earlier discussion about the spiritual formation of African Americans emphasized our spiritual identity and relationship with the personal Judeo-Christian God of the Bible. Numerous African American recovering addicts have expressed their frustration at not being allowed to identify and express their feelings about their gratitude, strength, and personal relationship with Jesus Christ. Subsequently, many twelve-step Christian groups have started in African American churches where African American recovering addicts are at liberty to identify their Judeo-Christian God and discuss racial issues. These addicts have reported a more spiritually relevant recovery experience. The twelve-step groups with a biblical perspective and use of scriptures have been widely welcomed by African American recovering Christian addicts. These groups foster an experience of unconditional acceptance, personal responsibility, discipleship, and spiritual growth.

The Twelve Steps seen from a biblical perspective can be likened to a journey/process of addiction/recovery. Steps 1, 2, and 3 are Surrender steps, Steps 4 and 5 Spiritual and Moral Inventory steps, Steps 6 and 7 Miracle Transformation steps, Steps 8 & 9 Restitution steps, Steps 10 and 11 Daily Maintenance steps, and Step 12 a Transcendence and Evangelism step.

It is also important that the recovering Christian addict connect with a local church for additional discipline and spiritual growth. Pastoral counseling or professional counseling should be available for other personal and family issues.

SPIRITUALLY WORKING THE TWELVE STEPS

I have found that a spiritually responsive presentation of the twelve steps, from a spiritual perspective, for African American Christians in recovery is the concept of a spiritual journey with the following associations and goals (Recovery Publications, 1988, p. xii).

Peace	Step One	is about recognizing our brokenness.
with	Step Two	is about the birth of faith in us.
God	Step Three	involves a decision to let God be in charge of our lives.

Peace with Ourselves	Step Four	involves self-examination.
	Step Five	is the discipline of confession.
	Step Six	is an inner transformation sometimes called re-pentance.
	Step Seven	involves the transformation or purification of our character.
Peace with Others	Step Eight	involves examining our relationships and prepar-ing ourselves to make amends.
	Step Nine	is the discipline of making amends.
	Step Ten	is about maintaining progress in recovery.
Keeping the Peace	Step Eleven	involves the spiritual disciplines of prayer and me-ditation.
	Step Twelve	is about ministry to others.

The utilization of this format makes a connection between twelve-step program principles and African Americans' spiritual/biblical principles, convictions, and goals. It has been applicable for recovery from all types of addictive behaviors and relationships. On this journey of recovery, the African American travels along the road of spiritual surrender and growth, personal responsibility, and relational health, healing, and wholeness.

CONCLUSION

As we come to the end of this chapter and recovery journey, I leave you with one of my most personal, effective, and rewarding clinical/spiritual treatment interventions that I share with African-American recovering addicts and their family members. This treatment technique is inclusive of all that has been discussed in this chapter. It includes cultural, spiritual, biblical, emotional, communal, and familial factors and recovery needs of African American families. It is in building what I call a Spiritual Recovery Support System.

1. I share the roles and functions of five types of supportive people (originated by MacDonald, 1986).

2. I also identify these five people as equivalent to related biblical characters (utilizing the growth-facilitative, authoritative use of scripture).

3. I apply these five supportive roles to recovery needs.

4. I ask the counselee to identify and secure five people in their lives who can be members of their personal "Spiritual Recovery Support Group."

The Spiritual Recovery Support System is clinically/biblically presented as follows:

BIBLICAL EXAMPLES

ROLE	REFERENCE	FUNCTION
1. A Sponsor or Mentor	Mary and Elizabeth St. Luke, Ch. 1	A person who can disciple the recovering person/family member offering "strength, experience, hope" and resources.
2. An Affirmer	Paul and Timothy 2 Timothy, Ch. 1	A person who can encourage the recovering person/family member offering praise and value to recovery efforts and accomplishments. A personal cheerleader.
3. A Corrector	Nathan and David 2 Samuel, Ch. 12	A person who can confront the recovering person/family member offering corrective truth in love when the recovery journey gets inconsistent or dishonest.
4. An Intercessor	Jesus and struggling believers St. Luke, Ch. 22	A person who can pray for or with the recovering person/family member offering conscious, constant contact with God for recovery needs and help as a prayer partner.
5. A Partner	Elijah and Elisha 2 Kings, Ch. 2	A person who can "lighten the load" for the recovering person/family member offering concrete, practical assistance (child care, transportation) to ensure recovery work/commitments.

Many individuals and families have found that implementing this "Spiritual Support System" has decreased personal isolation, negative stigmatism, and sense of hopelessness and has increased cultural/communal kinship bonds and spiritual connections on the recovery journey.

I have joyfully shared the building of this "Spiritual Recovery Support System" in my Sunday Worship Sermons, individual/family counseling sessions and cultural seminars. It works! I believe that no African American (or anyone) should take the recovery journey alone.

As an African American clinician and clergy person, I believe that providing cultural/spiritually sensitive counseling with:

A listening ear
A caring heart
An encouraging word
A praying spirit

and together journeying with an African American addict/family to:

Communicate with one another
Listen to one another
Reason with one another
Learn from one another
Work with one another

the treatment/recovery experience for the African American can be filled with the blessings of:

Healed and healthy relationship
Renewed mind and hope
Wise choices and direction
Changed heart and personal responsibility
Liberated spirit and redemptive love of God.

REFERENCES

Barnes, C. (1989). *Treatment of the Chemically Dependent Black Female: A Cultural Perspective*. New Orleans: Southern University Substance Abuse Department.

Bell, P. (1984, Fall). Cultural Aspects of Chemical Abuse in the Black Community. *DAC Bulletin*, 1–2.

Bell, P. (1990). *Chemical Dependency in the African American*. Center City, MN: Hazelden Foundation.

Billingsley, A. (1992). *Climbing Jacob's Ladder*. New York: Simon and Schuster.

Boyd-Franklin, N. (1989). *Black Families in Therapy: A Multi-Systems Approach*. New York: Guilford Press.

Brisbane, F. (1988 August/September). Black Children of Alcoholic Parents: Why They Resist Treatment and How to Get Them Involved. *Minority Issues: Adolescent Counselor*.

Brisbane, F., & Wombe, M. (1985). *Treatment of Black Alcoholics*. New York: Haworth Press.

Carter, L. (1983). *Good 'N' Angry*. Grand Rapids: Baker Book House Co.

Center of Substance Abuse Prevention. (1993). *Signs of Effectiveness in Preventing Alcohol and Other Drug Problems*. (DHHS Publication No. SAM 93–2001).

Collier, A. (1989, August). To Deal and Die in L.A. *Ebony*, p. 108.

Cones, C. (1976). Mind, Body, and Soul. In *Southern Exposure: On Jordan's Stormy Banks*. Institute for Southern Studies vol. *IV*(3) pp. 44–53.

Davis, F. T. (1973). *Alcoholism Among American Blacks*. New York: National Council on Alcoholism.

Dawkins, M. & Williams, M. (1997). *Substance Abuse in Rural African American Populations*. In E. B. Robertson, Z. Sloboda, G. M. Boyd, L. Beatty, & N. Kozel (Eds.), *Rural Substance Abuse: State of Knowledge and Issues*. (Research monograph No. 168). Rockville, MD: National Institute on Drug Abuse.

Dewart, T. (1988) *The State of Black America*. New York: National Urban League.

Durham, J. (1972). *Civil Rights*. Elgin, IL: David Cook.

Durham, J. & Coleman, C. D. (1972). *The Story of Civil Rights as Seen by the Black Church in America*. Elgin, IL: David C. Cook.

Evans, J. H. (1992). *We Have Been Believers: An African-American Systematic Theology*. Fortress Press. 1992.

Frazier, E. F. (1989). *The Negro Church in America*. (Originally published 1964.) Published with C. E. Lincoln, *The Black Church Since Frazier*. New York: Schocken Books. (Originally published 1974.)

Gates, H. L., Jr., & West, C. (1996). *The Future of the Race*. New York: Knopf.

Glick, P. (1997). Demographic Pictures of African American Families. In H. P. McAdoo (Ed.), *Black Families*. Thousand Oaks, CA: Sage.

Goldberg, M. (1985). *Loss and Grief: Major Dynamics in the Treatment of Alcoholism*. Hawthorne, NJ: Hawthorne Press.

Gordon, J. (1994). African American Perspective. In J.Gordon (Ed.), *Managing Multiculturalism in Substance Abuse Services*. Thousand Oaks, CA: Sage.

Harper, F. D. (1976). *Alcoholism Treatment and Black Americans*. Rockville, MD: National Institute on Alcohol Abuse and Alcoholism.

Hemfelt, R., Minirth, F., Fowler, R., & Meier, P. (1991). *The Path to Serenity*. Nashville, TN: Thomas Nelson Books.

Herd, D. (1985). A Review of Drinking Patterns and Alcohol Problems Among U.S. Blacks. In U.S. Dept. of Health and Human Services, Secretary's Task Force on Black and Minority Health (Eds.), *Chemical Dependency and Diabetes* (Vol. VII, pp. 75–140). Washington, DC: U.S. Government Printing Office.

Hill, Robert (1972). *The Strengths of Black Families*. New York: Emerson Hall.

Hines, P. (1991) Death and the African-American Culture. In F. Walsh and M. Mc-Goldrick (Eds.), *Living Beyond Loss* (pp. 183–194). New York: Norton.

Hines, P. & Boyd-Franklin, N. (1982). Black Families. In M. McGoldrick J. Pearce & J. Giordano, (Eds.), *Ethnicity and Family Therapy* (pp. 84–107). New York: Guilford Press.

Holinger, P. C., Offer, D., Barter, J. T. & Bell, C. C. (1994). *Suicide and Homicide Among Adolescents*. New York: Guilford Press.

Jackson, J. (1990). Suicide Trends of Blacks and Whites by Sex and Age. In D. Ruiz (Ed.), *Handbook of Mental Health and Mental Disorder Among Black Americans*. Westport, CT: Greenwood Press.

Johnson, K., Bryant, D., Collins, D., Noe, T., Strader, T. & Berbaum, M. (1998, July). Preventing and Reducing Alcohol and Other Drug Use Among High-Risk Youths by Increasing Family Resilience. *Social Work, 43*(4), 297–308.

MacDonald, G. (1986). *Renewing Your Spiritual Passion*. Nashville, TN: Thomas Nelson.

McCaffrey, B. R. (1997, Oct. 5). Race and Drugs: Perception and Reality: New Rules for Crack Versus Powder Cocaine. *Washington Times*.

McGee, G. & Johnson, L. (1985). *Black, Beautiful and Recovering*. Center City, MN: Hazelden Foundation.

Myers, M. A. (1989). Symbolic Policy and the Sentencing of Drug Offenders. *Law and Society Review, 23*(2), 295–315.

Nobles, W. (1989) *Expert Advisory Roundtable on African American Issues*. GA: Office of Substance Abuse Prevention.

Pinderhughes, E. (1982). Afro-American Families and the Victim System. In M. McGoldrick, J. Pearce, & J. Giordano (Eds.), *Ethnicity and Family Therapy* (pp. 108–122). New York: Guilford Press.

Poussaint, A. F. (1990). The Mental Health Status of Black American, 1983. In D. S. Ruiz & J. P. Comer (Eds.), *Handbook of Mental Health and Mental Disorder Among Black Americans*. New York: Greenwood Press (reprinted from Dewart, T. [1989]. *The State of Black America*. New York: National Urban League).

Prugh, T. (1986/1987). The Black Church: A Foundation for Recovery. *Alcohol Health and Research World, 11*(2) 52–54. Rockville, MD: U.S. Dept. of Health, Education, and Welfare.

Raboteau A. (1979). Slave Religion: The "Invisible Institution." In J. W. Blassingame, *The Slave Community: Plantation Life in the Antebellum South*. New York: Oxford University Press.

Ramsey, E. (1988). From Guilt Through Shame to AA: A Self-Reconciliation Process. In P. Potter-Efron (Ed.), *The Treatment of Shame and Guilt in Alcoholism Counseling* (pp. 87–107). New York: Haworth Press.

Recovery Publications. (1988). *The Twelve Steps: A Spiritual Journey*. San Diego: RPI Publishing.

Rowe, D., & Grills, C. (1993). African Centered Drug Treatment: An Alternative Conceptual Paradigm for Drug Counseling with African American Clients. *Journal of Psychoactive Drugs, 25*(1) 21–33.

Smith, W. (1985). *The Church in the Life of the Black Family*. Valley Forge, PA: Judson Press.

Stevenson, H. C., Jr. (1997). Missed, Dissed, and Pissed: Making Meaning of Neighborhood Risk, Fear and Anger Management in Urban Black Youth. In L. Comas-Diaz (Ed.), *Cultural Diversity and Mental Health* (Vol 3, no. 1, pp. 36–52). New York: Wiley.

Washington, J. (1964). *Black Religion*. Boston: Beacon Press.

Washington, J. (1978). *Black Religion and Public Policy*. Philadelphia: University of Pennsylvania Press.

Williams, B., Richardson, T., & Watson D. (1991) *Recovery for the African American Family*. Center City, MN: Hazelden Foundation.

Wimberly, E. (1991). *African American Pastoral Care*. Nashville, TN: Abingdon Press.

Wimberly, E. (1994). *Using Scripture in Pastoral Counseling*. Nashville, TN: Abingdon Press.

CHAPTER SIX

ADDICTION RECOVERY AMONG WEST INDIANS

Amy Bibb and Georges J. Casimir

U NDERSTANDING AND WORKING with addictions among West Indians is an enigmatic process. Addressing the social and psychological scope of addictions entails many paradoxes and contradictions. Holding individuals personally accountable must be balanced with knowledge of the powerful social, geographic, and economic forces that created and now maintain the flow of alcohol and drugs abroad and in North America. It is important to attend not only to the psychological and clinical dilemmas that substance abusers face but also to their social and community context. Addiction is extremely personal and yet extremely global.

SCOPE AND LIMITATIONS OF TREATMENT AND RESEARCH

T HE CLINICIAN/RESEARCHER working in addictions among West Indians in the United States faces a number of obstacles. There is a paucity of current and historical data and literature on West Indian substance abuse in the United States. This reflects the broader limitations of the addictions field; that is, current addictions treatment and research on people of African ancestry in general is limited. Use and abuse of substances prior to enslavement and colonization is even less understood. This has significant implications for West Indians, since many, although not all, are of African ancestry.

Another obstacle to treatment and research on West Indian substance abuse in the United States is the comparatively small, yet quite diverse, population; West Indians are descended from people from many different countries. Attending to West Indian phenomena, whether general or specific, is not a priority in the addictions field. Moreover, when specific findings are documented, they may reflect global trends that do not describe

173

experiences of the largest West Indian populations in the United States. The 1980s transshipment of cocaine from the Bahamas to the United States resulted, among many things, in the publication of one of the most comprehensive reports on addictions in the West Indies (Allen 1987a, b, c). That report provides vital information on clinical, research, and policy initiatives pertaining to Bahamians residing in the Bahamas. Ironically, the experiences of Jamaicans, Haitians, and Trinidadians, who constitute the largest number of West Indians in the United States, remain underdescribed in the addictions literature; that is, reports on the West Indian experience often lack specificity and statistical data. In the United States, West Indians may be categorized as "other," along with many other people of color who are not African American.

Finally, cultural beliefs about taboo matters like substance abuse are often shrouded in secrecy. West Indian preference for privacy and even secrecy may contrast with the relative openness of many Americans and the recent "outing" of taboo subjects in North America. Under these circumstances, the paucity of treatment approaches, data, and published reports on West Indian addiction in the United States is not surprising.

In this chapter we use existing publications and data to explain the etiology of substance abuse in West Indian populations living in the United States. Relevant substance abuse patterns in the West Indies are described. First we present a historical background, including trends, the social context, and the impact of the drug trade in the West Indies. The remainder of this chapter addresses addictions in the social context of West Indians living in the United States. We conclude with an outline of gaps in the current literature as well as recommendations for future interventions and research. The relationship between the globalization of substance trading, use and abuse, and past and current cultural beliefs and practices will be the primary focus of this chapter.

Overview

ADDRESSING PRIDE AND shame issues is an integral part of treating any addict, no matter the cultural background. Pride and shame have particular significance for West Indians, whose history is fraught with paradox. The dialectic between expectations of personal responsibility and cognizance of external forces beyond individual control is a recurring theme in their lives. Routine assumptions about personal responsibility, self-determination, and external locus of control parallel the range of beliefs and explanations about addictions. The conservative end of this continuum frames addiction as indicative of loose or relaxed moral values. Addiction in this context is viewed as a phenomenon that can be willed away. Proponents of this view may be less likely to accept the disease model, believing that a "just say no" philosophy is the antidote to this problem. External determinants such as physiological, genetic, and environmental risk factors are likely to be discarded or minimized.

Some West Indians take pride in a relatively conservative, rigid worldview. Many believe in pulling themselves up by their bootstraps, a process that may require a high level of compliance and endurance of daily emotional assaults. However, challenge, rebellion, and revolution are also aspects of their history. They have fought and survived under colonialism, despite many past (and more recent) defeats. Pride about their heritage is intermingled with shame about their oppression and second-class status under the yoke of racism, classism, sexism, and national chauvinism. Some experience ambivalent allegiance to their African heritage as well as to the European powers who colonized them.

West Indians who emigrate to the United States add another layer of complexity to their experience. It is here where their past experiences are compared and contrasted with North American life. In this context, differing belief systems and values may either clash, intermingle, or be integrated in a cohesive manner. These social phenomena do not necessarily correlate with a propensity toward addiction, yet understanding the broader social context allows clinicians, practitioners, and policymakers to design appropriate, realistic interventions.

West Indian migration to the United States began in the early nineteenth century (Brice-Baker, 1996). By the end of the century, migration was nominal; it is estimated that the number had risen to only one thousand per year (Ueda, 1980, as quoted in Brice-Baker, 1996). Significant increases in migration have occurred in recent decades; some studies indicate that in the years 1981–1991 approximately one million Caribbean immigrants lived in the United States (Brice-Baker, 1996, p. 86). The 1990 United States Census tallied West Indians residing in the United States as follows: 159,167 West Indians; 435,024 Jamaicans; 289,521 Haitians; 76,270 Trinidadians and Tobagoans; 61,530 from the Dutch West Indies; 37,819 from the British West Indies; 35,455 Baijians (Barbadians); 22,922 from Belize; 21,081 Bahamians; 7,621 from the U.S. Virgin Islands; 4,941 Bermudians; and 4,139 other West Indians.

It is unlikely that any formalized census will accurately depict the ethnic diversity or numerical makeup of any cultural group. Undocumented immigrants and refugees are not reflected in these numbers, and therefore one can only approximate the size of the various West Indian populations in this country. In addition, recent immigration laws have affected the transmigrating patterns of these immigrants. Obtaining a green card or residency, under certain circumstances, does not guarantee continued occupancy in the United States. West Indians who lack U.S. citizenship risk expulsion and repatriation if they are charged with a minor criminal offense (e.g., jumping a subway turnstile). Repatriation is possible despite years of residency in the United States, and whether or not West Indians have any family in their homeland.

The terms *West Indian* and *Caribbean* are often used interchangeably to describe geographical location as well as ethnic/cultural heritage. The Caribbean is composed of twenty-seven island and mainland territories and is associated with various linguistic groups and a mélange of races, cultures, ethnicities, and classes (Sunshine, 1994, preface). The West Indies are part of the Caribbean and are divided into the Greater Antilles, the Lesser Antilles, and the Bahamas (Brice-Baker, 1994, as quoted in Augeli, 1973). West Indians of African ancestry who were colonized by the British (i.e., Jamaicans, Trinidadians, Bahamians) as well as Haitians (who were colonized by the French) will be the focus of this chapter.

HISTORY

CHRISTOPHER COLUMBUS' EXPLOITS in the West Indies in the late 1400s marked the beginning of colonization for the region. During this period the indigenous population, consisting of Arawak Indians in the Bahamas and Greater Antilles and Caribe Indians in the Lesser Antilles, resisted yet ultimately succumbed to the Spaniards. The Spaniards' armor-covered horses and superior weaponry defeated the Arawaks; forced labor completed their destruction. Many died from smallpox, starvation, and abuse. Following the unsuccessful enslavement of Amerindians, Spain turned to African slaves supplied to them by Portuguese traders (Sunshine, 1994, p. 10).

The French, Dutch, and British subsequently followed Spain in their quest for land, power, and slave labor. In the Lesser Antilles, the Caribes put up a prolonged resistance against the French and British invaders in the early seventeenth century. By the mid-seventeenth century, the Europeans had forced the Caribes into the mountainous regions of Dominica and Saint Vincent; these environs were natural fortresses that enabled the Caribes to further resist the Europeans. Europeans eventually recognized these regions as under Caribe control by signing a treaty in 1660. The Caribes continued to raid European settlements from this region for the remainder of the century (Sunshine, 1994, p. 11).

During the sixteenth and seventeenth centuries, colonists utilized slave labor to make their fortunes in the production of tobacco and sugar. By the late 1700s, the soil was depleted and the slave population enraged. The advent of the Industrial Revolution and sugar's declining economic value culminated in a period of economic and social crisis for the colonies. Violent slave revolts occurred throughout the West Indies. The Haitian Revolution in 1804 resulted in establishing Haiti as the first independent Black republic in the Western hemisphere. Similar revolts occurred throughout the West Indies, yet none resulted in independence. Contrary to popular myth about moral imperatives, the emancipation of slaves in the French and British colonies occurred only when slavery became unprofitable. Declining profits and rising violence culminated in slaves in British colonies being freed on August 1, 1834, and in emancipation of the French islands in 1848. Indentured servants from India, Asia, and Europe were subsequently brought into the West Indies in order to avoid a "free" labor market (Sunshine, 1994, p. 15). Animosity between indentured servants and freed slaves was inevitable as they competed for subsequent paid labor; racial tensions between these groups were rooted in the colonizers' deliberate attempts to exploit and divide them.

West Indian independence in the truest sense did not occur upon the emancipation of slaves. Planters immediately made ex-slaves "apprentices," obligating them to perform forty and a half hours of weekly unpaid labor in an attempt to tie them to plantations. Ensuing riots forced planters to abandon "apprenticeship" four years later (Sunshine, 1994, p. 15). Neocolonization quickly replaced colonization, with the United States joining European powers in maintaining economic, militaristic, and political power over West Indians. West Indian economic isolation forced many countries to rely on North American markets to survive. Concurrently, the United States' evolving capitalism was producing more goods than domestic markets could absorb. The consequent economic depression in the 1880s caused business interests to seek and acquire new markets and areas for investment abroad. At the time, the United States coveted Caribbean trade and seized this opportunity to fulfill its expansionist dream. Commercial and maritime rights to the West Indies were granted to the United States during this period (Sunshine, 1994, p. 29). Thus, the road was paved for United States' intervention in the region.

Impact of Foreign Intervention

CORRELATIONS BETWEEN West Indian colonization, foreign intervention, and the evolution of substance abuse have not been widely studied or documented, but evidence points to a relationship in neighboring regions. The Spaniards learned of the Incan practice of chewing coca leaves in the 1500s. Subsequent explorers reported that chewing of the leaf increased the Indians' endurance, enabling them to work harder and eat less food at higher altitudes. By 1569 Spaniards capitalized on this practice in their attempts to recruit Indian workers for intensive labor (Allen, 1987a, pp. 7–8). It would be important to determine whether similar foreign manipulation of substance use occurred in the West Indies. Foreign intervention, particularly U.S. intervention, is currently proliferating in the West Indies. While foreign countries have reduced the amount of goods they import from the West Indies, goods are imported into the region at high cost. Moreover, financial assistance that would allow countries to resume production of their own goods is meager. At present, many countries rely on tourism and a service economy to survive. Political unrest, unemployment, and emigration have increased. These are some of the factors that have contributed to the proliferating transhipment trade and the resulting increase in abuse of illicit substances in the region.

Many foreign tourists associate sun, fun, and relaxation with a Caribbean vacation. The use and abuse of alcohol and illicit drugs are noticeably absent from enticing commercials and print ads, yet they are covertly linked with the marketing of a "party time" atmosphere of these vacations. Tourists may presume that *ganja* and a Jamaican holiday are synonymous or that unlimited access to cocaine and alcohol can be obtained in any West Indian island or country.

The past and current crack cocaine abuse, both in the West Indies and in North America, is less publicized. Neither popular culture nor the advertising industry has chronicled the ensuing impoverishment of social communities in the West Indies and the deterioration of the social fabric of life in North America. This deterioration occurred in the 1980s in Trinidad and Tobago (Beaubrun, 1987, p. 168) and in the Bahamas (Humblestone and Allen, 1987, p. 121) and in the 1990s in Haiti (Haiti Parolysis, 1998). Both Trinidad and the Bahamas share an ideal location among trafficking routes from South America (e.g., Peru, Bolivia, Colombia) to North America and Europe. The Bahamas, an archipelago of seven hundred islands and cays (the majority of which are uninhabited), offers numerous areas for easy transfer (Allen, 1987a, p. 11; Jekel, 1987, p. 108).

PATTERNS OF DRUG TRANSSHIPMENT AND ABUSE

A VARIETY OF FACTORS precipitated the proliferation of freebase cocaine. During the 1980s, producers and traffickers discovered that cocaine was more profitable and safer to produce and ship than marijuana. It commanded a higher price per ounce and was easier to dispose of if enforcement authorities were approaching. The increase in production and shipment of cocaine correlated with a sharp increase in supply and a consequent drop in prices in the Bahamas in 1982 and 1983 (Jekel, 1987, p. 108).

The drop in prices of street cocaine posed problems for drug pushers, since there was no corresponding increase in demand for cocaine powder. Pushers were aware that freebase cocaine was far more addictive than the powder form and that a sales increase would result if users switched to freebase. Pushers began producing their own "rocks" of freebase cocaine and limiting the sale of cocaine to this form. Other shrewd marketing schemes were devised. For example, these rocks of freebase cocaine were sold in small plastic vials that were easily returnable for cash; as customers reappeared for a cash refund, they returned to the pusher who in turn sold them more drugs (Jekel, 1987, p. 108).

What followed was a surge in hospitalizations due to an increase in acute intoxications, bizarre and violent behavior, and drug-related psychoses. Further, freebase addicts were funneled into the criminal justice system, as they frequently resorted to violent crime to support their habit. McCartney and Neville (1987, p. 163) noted the higher ratio of inmates with drug problems as compared to patients hospitalized for the same reasons. They hypothesized that the inability to treat addiction and obtain funding for larger hospital units would result in addicts' incarceration rather than treatment.

Despite cocaine's destructive nature, societal perception of it has fluctuated over time. It was initially perceived as curative at best or (at least in powder form) as a comparatively benign drug. It was frequently used as an anesthetic. In the United States it was used as an ingredient in patent medicines, tonics, and soft drinks during the late nineteenth and early twentieth century (Johnson, 1987, p. 33). Is cocaine addictive? If so, how is this measured? Differing criteria are used to ascertain addiction and, hence, to fuel the debate. Traditional ideas about addiction presumed the presence of physical dependence based on tolerance and withdrawal symptoms (Beaubrun, 1987, p. 169). Some maintain that cocaine is both physically (physiologically) as well as psychologically addictive (Allen, 1987c, pp. 19, 208). Opponents counter by comparing the sequelae of cocaine use with those associated with other substances. They assert that abuse of cocaine, unlike that of alcohol and opiates, can be stopped abruptly without medical risk and without requiring subsequent drugs to wean the user. Inadequate distinction over cocaine's various forms may further fuel the debate; that is, many may concur that cocaine in powder form is not physiologically addictive but that freebase is.

What actually happens when someone smokes "rock" cocaine? In the Bahamas many smoke the rock in a homemade pipe called a *camoke*. Foil paper is stretched over a glass to create various holes, enabling the user to inhale (waft) the crack when it is ignited by cigarette ash. It is estimated that 80 percent pure cocaine vapor reaches the brain in eight seconds, causing intense euphoria. This rush, sometimes referred to as "Christmas" or "joy," lasts about two minutes and is followed by a glow that continues for another ten to twenty minutes; it is marked by a sense of supreme confidence, well-being, and drive (Allen 1987a, p. 17).

Succeeding highs are less intense and of shorter duration and are associated with increasing dysphoria and anhedonia upon crash. The dopamine stored in the pleasure centers of the brain are depleted, and the pleasure threshold associated with simple daily acts is raised. Dopamine depletion results in a supersensitivity of the receptors on nerve cells, creating a biologically based craving for cocaine that is similar to hunger and thirst (Washton, 1987, p. 46). Upon frequent cocaine use, this dysphoria leaves the user unsatisfied, unhappy, and with terrible mood swings. Many users report abusing other substances to alleviate the unpleasant aftereffects; increased use and abuse of alcohol and marijuana are common (Allen, 1987, p. 211; Washton, 1987, p. 55).

WOMEN AND ADDICTION

CHANGING TRENDS IN West Indian women's use and abuse of substances merit examination. These changes have been carefully documented in the Bahamas. A shift occurred in Bahamian women's hospitalization patterns for substance-related admissions during the 1980s. For women, the cocaine epidemic peaked in 1984, when nearly as many female drug abusers were hospitalized as were female alcohol abusers. Prior to 1984 a steady but small number of drug-related first or repeat admissions transpired (Dean-Patterson, 1987, p. 149).

Rigid gender role expectations can exacerbate the shame women addicts experience and can therefore maintain their chemical dependence (Bepko and Krestan, 1985). Like nonaddicted women, they may not fulfill unrealistic caretaking functions that are embedded in stereotyped, patriarchal assumptions; however, they may also fail to perform minimal, routine tasks that are not based on sexist assumptions. Many risk being reported to authorities for neglectful or abusive treatment of their children; often this culminates in the children's removal from the mother's custody (Wallace, 1992, p. 316, 1995, p. 475; Dean-Patterson, 1987, p. 153). This is especially true for women of color in general and for African American and West Indian women in particular. Gender role expectations clearly affect male–female relationships. Male partners can become abusive when they believe their mate is not fulfilling the prescribed standards for a girlfriend, wife, or mother.

Various authors have described the vicissitudes African American women face when they are addicted (Richie, 1996; Wallace, 1995). They delineate how multiple oppressions (racism, sexism, and classism) interlock and maintain their subjugation. These phenomena apply to the West Indian woman as well. Addictions fuel this vicious cycle. Many women are introduced to illicit drugs by men, including friends, boyfriends, spouses, pimps, and drug dealers. Their addiction often forces them to formally or informally prostitute themselves in order to maintain their habit. The reverse is also true: many prostitutes are introduced to drugs by pimps in an attempt to increase their dependence upon them. They may be forced to perform a wide range of sexually degrading acts in order to obtain more cocaine. Inevitably, many of these women engage in criminal activities other than prostitution. In New York City, the number of African American women charged with felonies has raised the rate of incarceration to record levels (Richie, 1996).

Author Beth Richie's (1996) research illustrates the range of attitudes African American women have about battering and addiction. The majority of women who were battered cited the battering as preceding the addiction. For them drug use was a way to create emotional intimacy and establish a deeper connection with partners (pp. 123–124). A minority of battered women attributed the onset of drug abuse more directly to being physically battered. Nonbattered women tended to describe their initiation to drug use as voluntary rather than coerced. This group was more likely to become involved in selling drugs for their own profit and used drugs as a public and social, rather than private, activity (p. 125). Richie notes, "Contrary to the findings from the African American non-battered women who associated drug use with an increase of violence in their lives, the African American battered women tended to believe that using drugs enhanced their safety. For many it was a way to create a sense of intimacy with their violent partners or to avoid a violent episode" (p. 150).

These distinctions provide a more complex picture of battering and addiction. It is important to understand that women's addiction can occur in conjunction with, or apart from, domestic violence and that addiction may precede or follow domestic violence and other social risk factors. While causality is paramount, the mere linkage between the two social ills should not be minimized; these associations expand the context and our understanding of addictions. Further research might reveal whether or not the aforementioned risks are manifest in West Indian women in the West Indies as well as in North America.

The numerous assaults on self-esteem that addicted women experience perpetuate vicious cycles. Drug use reinforces a negative self-image, rendering the attainment of both realistic and unrealistic expectations even more remote. If the cycle of blame and self-hate continues, women lose perspective on strengths and qualities that would facilitate positive change. Self-medication through continued abuse of drugs only provides temporary relief. "Gender entrapment" (Richie, 1996) is an apt descriptor of a cycle in which many women get caught. Gender oppression contributes to their participation in illegal drug activity, which in turn hastens the physical and emotional injuries they sustain. Clinical interventions must account for the idiosyncratic needs of women in an environment that is often racist, sexist, and classist. These interventions will have limited utility if they are not accompanied by attempts at changing dominant social, psychological, and legal assumptions and practices within the wider culture.

GAYS AND LESBIANS AND ADDICTION

RIGID GENDER ROLES inhibit and stereotype the lives of gays and lesbians as well as straight men and women (Green, 1994, 1996). Unlike the latter, gays and lesbians are not afforded the freedom to express their sexual choices or orientation. This has particular relevance for gay and lesbian addicts. Causal inferences between addiction and sexual orientation cannot be made. What is clear is that some gays and lesbians are addicts and that dilemmas posed by heterosexism, among other factors, can be associated with their addiction. In past decades, many gays and lesbians lacked social settings where they could interact without threat or ostracism: Outside of their homes, bars were one of the few settings where they could socialize. Unfortunately, it was and is a breeding ground for alcohol and drug abuse. Gays and lesbians who struggle over whether, when, and how to come out may find a temporary, albeit dangerous, refuge in the use of substances. The closeted existence that some are forced or choose to take can further mask the addiction they contend with. Isolation due to closeted sexual identity may exacerbate secrecy around their addiction.

One can hypothesize that being gay, addicted, and West Indian entails being in constant jeopardy. Heterosexism and homophobia are prominent in many cultural/ethnic groups; West Indian culture is not immune to this tendency. Already stigmatized in the wider culture owing to their racial/ethnic origins and to their substance dependency, West Indian lesbians and gays may not wish to make their sexual orientation known. Some West Indian lesbians have emigrated from their homeland believing that coming out in the United States will be relatively easier; many conclude that anonymity is greater in the heterogeneous United States than in the smaller interconnected communities in the West Indies (Greene, 1994). The closeting of sexual orientation, abroad and in the United States, prevents West Indian gays and lesbians from seeking services that would cater to their specialized needs. It would be interesting to discover whether or not gay/lesbian West Indian substance abusers also share the belief that anonymity is greater in the United States, and whether or not their addiction affects decisions regarding migration.

BELIEFS, MISCONCEPTIONS, AND HELP-SEEKING BEHAVIOR

ACKNOWLEDGING THE NEED for help is a core clinical issue for any substance abuser. It is widely recognized as a preliminary yet crucial start and is incorporated in the initial steps of self-help groups like Alcoholics Anonymous (AA) and Narcotics Anonymous (NA). Recovering substance abusers, their family members, and addiction professionals understand the addict's avoidance of help owing to matters of false pride and shame and therefore never minimize the importance of these factors.

The meaning of pride and shame differs in West Indian and mainstream American culture, and this difference will, consequently, influence West Indians' help-seeking patterns in this country. The AA/NA concept of false pride (i.e., pride that is self-defeating rather than self-enhancing) may be foreign and even unfathomable to them, as pride is frequently seen as a positive, motivating force. Similarly, shame does not have the derogatory, limiting connotation for West Indians that it may have in the twelve-step culture. Many in the step programs view addicts as particularly vulnerable to shame. They may be seen as predisposed to it for characterological rea-

sons or because of guilt over their addiction. Either of these causal explanations is viewed as exacerbating an addict's tendency to continue abusing
and perpetuating a vicious cycle (i.e., "character defects" or shame or guilt
leads to abuse, which leads to continuing character defects or shame or guilt
and more abuse). Although never pleasant, being shamed or ashamed (like
the cultivation of pride) can be viewed by West Indians as valuable and
necessary in order to move on and up in life. Generally, pragmatic approaches to problems and vulnerabilities are valued; protracted processes
that might enhance insight may be viewed by West Indians as indulgent
and unnecessarily time-consuming.

Clinicians must view the pragmatic viewpoint of West Indians dialectically, particularly when it pertains to addictions: pragmatism can function
as an invaluable coping skill yet also as a mechanism for denial and minimization of problems. The term *alcoholic* or *substance abuser* may not be part
of the West Indian lexicon. Alcoholics are frequently viewed as people who
like to drink, and drug abuse may only be recognized when it is exhibited in
its most blatant form. These addictions are acknowledged with greater ease
when they present with other medical or psychiatric symptoms. Alcoholism, for example, may be noted when a West Indian patient has been
hospitalized for medical reasons (Ketty Rey, personal communication, September 1998). When circumstances other than addiction challenge the fa-
cade of wellness and strength, subsequent acknowledgment of addiction
may be easier to tolerate.

Clinicians should look for obvious and obtuse modes of drug and alcohol
use among West Indians. Like members of other cultures, West Indians will
ingest alcohol and drugs both in social settings (e.g., bars, parties, formalized
celebrations) and via street life. Overt and covert religious and spiritualistic
practices may provide a social context where alcohol in particular is ingested and potentially abused. Various authors have described the role of
European-based religions (e.g., Catholicism, Protestantism) in combination
with, or syncretized with, African-based religions and spiritualistic practices
(*vodun, obeah, Santeria*) in the West Indies (Bibb and Casimir, 1996; Brice-
Baker, 1994, 1996; and Gopaul-McNicol, 1993). Alcohol is integrated into
many of the rituals associated with these forms of observance.

Although religious and spiritualistic beliefs and practices do not necessarily condone and promote the abuse of alcohol, alcohol abusers may drink
excessively during religious rituals in an attempt to mask their addiction. In
this context, the sequelae of drinking can easily be attributed to "bad spirits" rather than to alcoholism. The use of roots and herbs can be traced back
to African-based religious practices and is especially valued among less as-

similated West Indians. The roots and herbs can be ingested in many ways, including being mixed with high levels of alcohol. Ingestion of these drinks can be frequent and habit forming. This drinking pattern is not limited to use in the West Indies; it is found in the United States as well (Franz Jerome, personal communication, September 1998). The assistance of West Indian spiritual leaders, including pastors, ministers, and priests, as well as non-Western healers like spiritists, priestess's *mambos*, and *houngans*, can be helpful in addressing addictions. Outsiders attempting to cultivate relationships with them should be respectful and not hasten the process. Often such relationships evolve only when outsiders prove their commitment and interest to the community over time.

The health and social problems related to addiction differ among and within West Indian countries. Efforts to simply import prevention programs or mass media slogans (e.g., "just say no") in the United States as well as in the West Indies are likely to fail. Characteristics and dimensions of substance abuse differ between immigrants from upper-class metropolitan areas and those living in rural settings. Technological advances have not successfully addressed the strengths and limitations of indigenous belief systems of health, healing, and illness. West Indians of different class and educational levels require different specific prevention strategies. Modern communication technologies are most effective with upper-class education sectors whereas direct interpersonal approaches are needed with poor rural populations.

One can hypothesize that substance abuse is especially closeted in the West Indian community. Many West Indians advise themselves against "airing dirty laundry" in public. Secrecy and protection of privacy are time-honored practices (Bibb and Casimir, 1996). They pride themselves on their accomplishments despite great odds and may not wish to tarnish their image. People who are victims of racism may be reluctant to publicly acknowledge universal vulnerabilities such as substance abuse as well as vulnerabilities created and maintained by a racist context. Brice-Baker (1994, 1996) has noted the differing assumptions between West Indians and African Americans regarding racism in the United States. Both populations may share ambivalent feelings about the Unites States; however, West Indians may be more optimistic about their ability to advance despite racism. Consequently, some West Indians may be less strident in articulating racism than some African Americans. In addition, West Indians might believe that acknowledging substance abuse might refute a self-determining, self-reliant philosophy.

Compared to African Americans (who have legal U.S. citizenship and are comparatively assimilated into North American culture), West Indians experience racial vulnerability, shame, and the consequences of exposure differently. Again, this may affect the extent to which they reveal substance abuse—or whether they acknowledge it at all. Lacking citizenship can be construed as a source of shame for some. West Indians may internalize xenophobic beliefs that imply that they are not "legitimate" or "good enough" by U.S. standards. Shame and vulnerabilities over lack of citizenship may exacerbate the tendency to hide other problems, such as substance abuse; West Indians who believe that "foreigners" are not welcome under ideal circumstances may well believe that they will be viewed even less favorably if they acknowledge an addiction.

Fear of legal repercussion will impact West Indians' willingness to expose themselves. Recent émigrés may be cautious about revealing their addiction, fearing criminal charges and possible expulsion and repatriation. Cautiousness occurs even in the absence of criminal charges. Examples can be cited from within the Haitian community. During the 1980s faulty assumptions resulted in the classification of Haitians as a risk group for AIDS, a classification that barred many from gaining entrance or a continued stay in the United States (Bibb and Casimir, 1996). As a result, many non-Haitians viewed Haitians as deviants and undesirables; the leap or linkage to criminal behavior was easy for some to make in this uninformed context. Some Haitians became self-deprecating despite the fact that no evidence existed of criminal activity. Indeed, methods used in detaining HIV-infected Haitian refugees at Guantanamo Naval Base parallel those used in the detainment of criminals. Currently, Haitians may guard against substance exposure, fearing it will provide yet another phenomenon to marginalize them. While erroneous linkages to AIDS were made because of Haitians' ethnic origin rather than drug abuse per se, they may refrain from discussing any taboo subjects, fearing increased stigmatization.

TREATMENT MODELS

TRADITIONAL ADDICTION TREATMENT models rarely address the particular needs of people of color, women, lesbians, or gays. The field must begin to redress this limitation yet must incorporate models proven successful within dominant cultures when appropriate. A multimodal approach is frequently the treatment of choice for substance abuse in general and for cocaine (especially freebase) abuse in particular. Group therapy, twelve-step programs, and frequent urine testing are cited as particularly effective

(Washton, 1987, p. 58). Clinicians disagree about the efficacy of inpatient versus outpatient treatment for cocaine addicts (Allen, 1987c, p. 209; Carroll, Keller, Fenton, and Gawin, 1987, p. 76). Those who assert that cocaine is physically addictive advocate hospitalization whereas opponents maintain that outpatient treatment is sufficient. Generalized utilization of cognitive behavioral techniques, as well as their applied use in relapse prevention, is indicated. Individual treatment as well as multifamily group therapy are also recommended (Carroll et al., 1987, p. 98).

Systemic approaches to addiction include treatment with alcoholics and their family members as described by Bepko and Krestan (1985). Models of treatment for drug addicts and family members have been described by Stanton, Todd and associates (1982). Systemic models frequently attend to the multiple contexts in which problems are embedded. A strong argument can be made for an integrative treatment approach (i.e., combining group, individual, systemic, and community interventions). The range of content areas, treatment interventions, and research data make a definitive systematic evaluation and treatment plan within the addictions field almost implausible. Many advocate a disciplined yet eclectic approach that can be tailored to the myriad stages of addiction relapse and recovery (Carroll et al., 1987, p. 100).

Religiosity is an important predictor of abstinence and recovery from substance abuse. Internalized religious faith often provides meaning for life and appears to be associated with reduction in substance abuse. It is likely that the increased sense of community experienced within a religious group militates against substance abuse. Many persons in "recovery" drift toward some kind of religious community (Allen, 1987, p. 23). Religious and spiritual beliefs are a cornerstone of twelve-step programs such as AA and NA. The spiritual, religious orientation of twelve-step programs will probably appeal to many West Indians. However, the group participation that is also an integral part of AA and NA is likely to be a deterrent; self-disclosure in groups may be viewed as an inappropriate expression of private business. West Indians may likely believe that being in a room with others, even if one does not speak, does not provide enough anonymity. They may avoid group psychotherapy for similar reasons (Ketty Rey, personal communication, September 1998).

Working with West Indian substance abusers requires that the therapist understand and respect their cultural worldview and practices as well as address and even challenge beliefs when they maintain addictive behaviors. Utilizing a cultural framework that is both separate from and integrated with traditional Western approaches is appropriate when working with immigrants residing in the United States. Westernized approaches are more likely to occur when outside agents and institutions require intervention (e.g., hospitalization, or protective services) since many West Indians tend to solve problems on their own or seek intracommunity resources to assist them.

Need for Research and Treatment Agenda

Various treatment modalities and techniques for addicted persons have been described in the literature; however, the experience of West Indian addicts in the United States has been underdescribed. Numerous questions abound. What is the explanation for this gap in services, research, and policy? It is implausible to assert that substance-abusing West Indians do not exist in the United States.

Inadequate documentation by drug treatment centers may partially explain the paucity of information concerning West Indian addicts. Hospitals, clinics, and rehabilitation centers in New York City, for example, frequently categorize patients according to race; it is unclear whether they also classify for ethnicity. Many addicts may be identified as Black yet not necessarily as Jamaican, Haitian, Bahamian, and so on. I conducted an informal survey of agencies servicing West Indians. Numerous cross-searches between West Indians and substance abuse were conducted, but no agencies in the New York City area were cited. Although agencies may be servicing this population, they do not appear to be advertising or documenting this trend. Recent inquiries revealed that no twelve-step programs were conducted in Haitian *Kreyol* (Creole) in Brooklyn. This is a significant finding, as the majority of Haitians in New York City reside in this borough. Interestingly, twelve-step meetings in other languages exist, including Polish, Russian, and Spanish (the latter are newly established groups). Twelve-step meetings have been held in certain West Indian countries. Participation appears particularly high in the Bahamas (McCartney and Neville, 1987, p. 163). Whether Bahamian participation is transferred upon migration to the United States is unknown.

Numerous research questions can be posed concerning the West Indians' relationship to substance abuse. Do major cities with significant West Indian populations other than New York City classify data differently? It would be interesting to note whether Miami, Florida, which has a sizable West Indian population classifies by race and ethnicity. Other questions should be explored: Do West Indians with longer residency in the United

States differ from recent West Indian émigrés? That is, do second- or even third-generation West Indian Americans adopt differing values over time? Do they assimilate? If so, are these patterns of assimilation similar or dissimilar to the way African Americans have assimilated to North American culture? What impact, if any, do these differences and/or similarities have on substance abuse? What are the particular needs of addicted, battered West Indian women? Addicted gay and lesbian West Indians?

The transshipment of cocaine from the West Indies to the United States has been described. The indirect transmission of substance abuse practices from the United States to the West Indies is existent yet not widely documented. West Indians repatriated from the United States back to the Caribbean because of criminal charges may be engaging in illegal drug activity in their homeland. It appears that the practices they were exposed to or engaged in in the United States has increased the level of drug activity in their native countries (Franz Jerome, personal communication, September 1998). What is the extent of travel for drug traffickers, pushers, and addicts in these two regions? If substantiated, how might this travel impact global and market forces as well as the individual and community response to addiction? One might hypothesize that within the West Indian community, addicts, particularly those who are in crisis, are less likely to emigrate to the United States. Obtaining another "high" might take priority over immigration.

SUMMARY

BIASES EMBEDDED IN ethnic/racial, gender, class, and sexual orientation inequities severely limit minority access to addiction treatment services. Comprehensive services for the relatively privileged private sector increase while they simultaneously decrease in the public sector (Wallace, 1992). Global trends (i.e., transshipment of illicit substances despite government interdiction) further complicate an already complex social phenomena. Archibald stresses that success will be isolated and temporary without coordination: "Drug traffickers are multinational corporations with highly developed systems including marketing specialists, promotion specialists, training for couriers. They have it in their power to change the political map of the world. In contrast, the addictions field is rife with territorialism and mutual disdain, specialty for specialty, group for group" (Archibald, 1986, as quoted in Allen, 1987, p. 215).

Multidisciplinary interventions, provided by various professionals who treat drug addiction, are particularly indicated in an era of massive international, national, state, and municipal funding cuts. If inroads are to be made in the war on drugs and alcohol, addiction, health, and mental health professionals, as well as researchers and policymakers, will have to attend to the needs of third-world people in particular. Dominant classes have historically disenfranchised them and then ignored their ensuing social and psychological problems. Paradoxically, racism may cause people of color to exacerbate this phenomenon: fear of inequitable repercussions (i.e., incarceration, expulsion, repatriation), as well as a desire to avoid further stigmatization, cause them to hide such universal vulnerabilities as drug and alcohol addiction. Innovative research and clinical and social services must be developed for and by West Indians, who are frequently viewed as the minority within minority populations in the United States.

The authors wish to thank Franz Jerome, Dorie Clay, and Ketty Rey for their helpful comments on an earlier version of this chapter.

REFERENCES

Allen, D. (1987a). History of Cocaine. In D. Allen (Ed.), *The Cocaine Crisis* (pp. 7–13). New York: Plenum Press.

Allen, D. (1987b). Modes of Use, Precursors, and Indicators of Cocaine Abuse. In D. Allen (Ed.), *The Cocaine Crisis* (pp. 15–26). New York: Plenum Press.

Allen, D. (1987c). Cocaine Addiction: A Socio-Ethical Perspective. In D. Allen (Ed.), *The Cocaine Crisis* (pp. 207–219). New York: Plenum Press.

Archibald, D. (1986). Coordinated Anti-Drug Action Is Imperative. *The Journal, 15*(2), 1, as quoted in Allen, 1987c.

Augeli, J. P. (Ed.). (1973). *Caribbean Islands*. Grand Rapids, MI: Fidler, as quoted in Brice-Baker, 1994.

Beaubrun, M. (1987). Cocaine Update. In D. Allen (Ed.), *The Cocaine Crisis* (pp. 167–173). New York: Plenum Press.

Bepko, C., & Krestan, J. (1985). *The Responsibility Trap: A Blueprint for Treating the Alcoholic Family*. New York: Free Press.

Bibb, A., & Casimir, G. J. (1996). Haitian Families. In M. McGoldrick, J. Giordano, & J. K. Pearce (Eds.), *Ethnicity and Family Therapy* (2nd ed.). New York: Guilford Press, pp. 97–111.

Brice-Baker, J. (1994). West Indian Women of Color: The Jamaican Woman. In L. Comas-Diaz & B. Greene (Eds.), *Women of Color: Integrating Ethnic and Gender Identities in Psychotherapy*. New York: Guilford Press.

Brice-Baker, J. (1996). Jamaican Families. In M. McGoldrick, J. Giordano, & J. K. Pearce (Eds.), *Ethnicity and Family Therapy* (2nd ed.). New York: Guilford Press.

Carroll, K., Keller, D., Fenton, L., & Gawin, F. (1987). Psychotherapy for Cocaine Abusers. In D. Allen (Ed), *The Cocaine Crisis* (pp. 75–105). New York: Plenum Press.

Dean-Patterson, P. (1987). Cocaine and the Bahamian Woman: Treatment Issues. In D. Allen (Ed.), *The Cocaine Crisis* (pp. 145–159). New York: Plenum Press.

Gopaul-McNicol, S. (1993). *Working with West Indian Families*. New York: Guilford Press.

Green, R., Bettinger, M., & Zacks, E. (1996). Are Lesbian Couples Fused and Gay Male Couples Disengaged? Questioning Gender Straightjackets. In J. Laird & R. Green (Eds.), *Lesbians and Gays in Couples and Families* (pp. 185–230). San Francisco: Jossey-Bass.

Greene, B. (1994). Lesbian Women of Color: Triple Jeopardy. In L. Comas-Diaz & B. Greene (Eds.), *Women of Color: Integrating Ethnic and Gender Identities in Psychotherapy*. New York: Guilford Press.

Haiti Paralysis Brings a Boom in Drug Trade. (October 27, 1998). *New York Times*, p. A1.

Humblestone, B., & Allen, D. (1987). The Bahamas and Drug Abuse. In D. Allen (Ed.), *The Cocaine Crisis* (pp. 119–123). New York: Plenum Press.

Jekel, J. (1987). Public Health Approaches to the Cocaine Problem: Lessons from the Bahamas. In D. Allen (Ed.), *The Cocaine Crisis* (pp. 107–116). New York: Plenum Press.

Jekel, J., Allen, D., Podlewski, N. C., Patterson, S. D., & Cartwright, P. (1987). Epidemic Freebase Cocaine Abuse: A Case Study from the Bahamas. In D. Allen (Ed.), *The Cocaine Crisis* (pp. 125–138). New York: Plenum Press.

Johnson, E. (1987). Cocaine: The American Experience. In D. Allen (Ed.), *The Cocaine Crisis* (pp. 33–44). New York: Plenum Press.

Krestan, J., & Bepko, C. (1993). On Lies, Secrets, and Silence: The Multiple Levels of Denial in Addictive Families. In E. Imber-Black (Ed.), *Secrets in Families and Family Therapy* (pp.141–159). New York: Norton.

McCartney, T., & Neville, M. (1987). Treatment Approaches to Cocaine Abuse and Dependency in the Bahamas. In D. Allen (Ed.), *The Cocaine Crisis* (pp. 161–165). New York: Plenum Press.

Richie, B. (1996). *Compelled to Crime: the Gender Entrapment of Battered Black Women*. New York: Routledge.

Stanton, M. D.; Todd, T. C., & Associates (1982). *The Family Therapy of Drug Abuse and Addiction*. New York: Guilford Press.

Sunshine, C. (1994). *The Caribbean Survival, Struggle and Sovereignty: Ecumenical Program on Central America and the Caribbean* (EPICA publication, 3rd printing). Washington, DC.

Ueda, R. (1980). West Indians. In S. Thernstrom, A. Orlov, & O. Handlin (Eds.), *Harvard Encyclopedia of American Ethnic Groups*. Cambridge, MA: Harvard University Press.

Wallace, B. (1992). Toward Effective Treatment Models for Special Populations: Criminal, Pregnant, Adolescent, Uninsured, HIV-Positive, Methadone-Maintained, and Homeless Populations. In B. Wallace (Ed.), *The Chemically Dependent Phases of Treatment and Recovery*. New York: Brunner/Mazel.

Wallace, B. (1995). Women and Minorities in Treatment. In A. Washton (Ed.), *Psychotherapy and Substance Abuse: A Practitioner's Handbook*. New York: Guilford Press.

Washton, A. (1987). Cocaine: Drug Epidemic of the '80's. In D. Allen (Ed.), *The Cocaine Crisis* (pp. 45–63). New York: Plenum Press.

CHAPTER SEVEN

TREATING ASIAN/PACIFIC AMERICAN ADDICTS AND THEIR FAMILIES

Peter Chang

VIGNETTE 1

QLB, a forty-three-year-old Cambodian acupuncturist, was referred for treatment following charges that he had committed insurance fraud with the state. He was extremely distraught over the charges, insisting he was innocent of any misconduct, and sought help in resolving the matter, claiming that he had "difficulty thinking clearly." Careful inquiry soon revealed an individual who experienced severe insomnia, nightmares, and agitation for much of the seven years since his arrival to the United States. He was rarely able to sleep more than two or three hours at a time and often had terrifying dreams that would awaken him. He lived alone, near his office, and was able to tolerate such a regimen with the aid of frequent naps and, over the past year and a half, the increasing use of alcohol and a variety of narcotic agents and barbiturates, which he was able to "borrow" from a pharmacist friend.

VIGNETTE 2

FS was a thirty-seven-year-old divorced Japanese American who had lost her job after a random test revealed drugs in her urine. She had been employed for twelve years as a bus driver in a safety-sensitive position and had been a stellar employee up to the time of her termination. FS denied any history of drug abuse and attributed her positive test response to some amphetamines her brother had "slipped" into her coffee one morning. She was emotionally and financially drained from trying to contest her dismissal and regain her job, as well as from raising two children alone with no spousal or familial support. She had few friends or family contact and spent most of her time at home "watching TV." Her presentation was one of great sadness, and she would cry softly as she described how she had always tried to "do the right thing," and how desperately quiet and lonely her personal life was.

VIGNETTE 3

CYW was incarcerated on charges of being an accomplice to murder. He was an ethnic Chinese who had been in this country almost ten years, and was married with two children and employed full time prior to his arrest. CYW readily admitted that it was his gun that was used in the murder, although he was not present when the shooting occurred. Evaluation revealed a complex set of circumstances, including evidence that his wife was a heavy gambler who owed a considerable sum of money. CYW also reported experiencing a fuguelike state for several days prior to the shooting during which he was unable to sleep, felt dissociated, and experienced a constant rush of thoughts and ideations. He never spoke to anyone in his family during this time and, other than chance encounters with a few acquaintances, kept entirely to himself.

VIGNETTE 4

AA is a thirty-three-year-old married Filipina who sought consultation after her husband discovered that she had accumulated an enormous debt over several years' time, necessitating the couple's filing for bankruptcy. Repeated attempts at persuading the husband to participate in treatment failed, and it was decided that AA would come on her own, despite my pessimism about treatment outcome. AA had some understanding of her husband's fury at her for what she had done, yet she continued her own outbursts of anger at him in response to the slightest provocation. History taking revealed that AA was an only child—unusual for her culture—and that her excessive spending habits preceded her marriage. She and her mother even had their own code words to signal whenever AA needed more money to pay off new debts and prevent her husband's ire.

INTRODUCTION

As THESE VIGNETTES SHOW, Asians and Asian Americans engage in a variety of addictive behaviors. While epidemiologic data indicates lower rates of prevalence as compared with other ethnic populations (see Zane and Sasao, 1992, for an excellent review and critique of this research), anecdotal evidence suggests that these figures are rising and may not fully reflect the unique patterns and characteristics of addiction among Asian and Pacific Islander groups. Rates of alcoholism and general substance abuse, for example, are low relative to other ethnic populations (Akutsu, Sue, Zane, and Nakamura, 1989; Varma and Siris, 1996) but gambling and nicotine addiction appear to be disproportionally high in comparison (World Health Organization, 1997). In addition, newer forms of addictive behaviors, such as compulsive shopping and addiction to the Internet (Young, 1998), appear to be increasing. This chapter reviews specific background and etiologic factors important to the understanding and treatment of addiction among Asian and Pacific Islander groups and outlines suggestions for a more culturally syntonic therapy protocol.

ASSESSMENT

EFFECTIVE TREATMENT MUST, of course, begin with an accurate assessment of the individual, his or her relevant background, precipitating circumstances, and significant aspects of psychological functioning. Most experts agree that addictions are multidetermined (Margolis and Zweben, 1998; Schuckit, 1995), and for persons of Asian ancestry it is essential to understand their unique cultural backgrounds and level of acculturation if proper treatment is to occur. Important regional, national, and ethnic distinctions exist among Asians and Pacific Islanders, and these are compounded by significant differences in migration patterns and subsequent experiences in the United States (Takaki, 1989). While this chapter cannot begin to thoroughly cover the unique characteristics and customs of each specific group, several broad topics can be addressed. These include family structure and process, cultural values, gender roles, and styles of communication within traditional Asian cultures. In addition to understanding these broad topics, the therapist must assess the addict's and family's level of traditionalism and acculturation to American values. How long a person has been in the United States, whether the native dialect or English is spoken at home, and which family members still live in the homeland are crucial determinants of the person's sense of self and worldview.

To begin, it is important to recognize how addicts identify themselves. Most foreign-born individuals refer to themselves by their nationality of origin and prefer to be recognized as such. Whether they are from one of the Asian continental cultures or a Pacific island one, the issue of national origin must be addressed clearly and accurately in order to not offend potential clients. The possibilities, of course, are numerous and include cultures as diverse as those of Bangladesh, Burma, Cambodia, China, India, Japan, Korea, Laos, Nepal, Pakistan, Thailand, Tibet, and Vietnam, to name only a few. For Pacific Islanders the distinctions are no less important and include an even greater array of cultures, such as those from Borneo, Guam, Indonesia, Malaysia, Micronesia, the Philippines, Samoa, Singapore, Sri Lanka, and Tonga, among others.

What people call themselves is, of course, as much a political statement as a designation of identity (Shankar, 1998). While the majority of new or recent immigrants refer to themselves by their nationality of origin, younger as well as American-born individuals of Asian or Pacific Islander descent increasingly prefer to append the term *American*. As a group, Asian Pacific Americans are important to distinguish from their foreign-born counterparts, whose values and practices are often much different from theirs. In addition, there are growing numbers of mixed-race individuals of Asian or Pacific Islander descent, especially from countries with historical involvement with the U.S. military, such as Japan, Korea, the Philippines, and Vietnam (Kim, 1981). These distinctions may be subtle, but they are important clues to factors that can be further assessed by the therapist and amplified as time permits.

The contrasts among the various nationalities, however, are enormous. Asians and Pacific Islanders share no common ancestry, language, or religion. While similarities may appear to an outsider, most Asians recognize significant differences between themselves, especially with respect to neighboring countries. For example, a H'mong from the mountains of Laos will likely be Buddhist in her beliefs and can speak, but likely not write, her native language (Moore, Keopraseuth, Leung, and Chao, 1997), while an ethnic Chinese from neighboring Vietnam may be more Confucian and/or Catholic and may speak and write French as well as Chinese and Vietnamese, reflecting that country's long history of colonization (Leung and Boehnlein, 1996).

Compounding these religious and linguistic distinctions are vastly different political and cultural histories. Many Chinese, for example, who lived through the Cultural Revolution under Mao Tse-tung experienced severe deprivation and starvation along with physical and psychological traumas that are incomprehensible to those born later. Most Koreans to this day have missing family members whom they have not seen in the decades since the separation of their country into North and South. More familiar, perhaps, in the American consciousness, as a result of the Vietnam War, are Southeast Asians, but the specific experiences of the Cambodians, H'mong, Laotians, Mien, Thai, and Vietnamese are still relatively obscured (Kamm, 1998). Furthermore, as in many parts of the world, there are often historically deep and intense animosities between neighboring countries, and these differences do not easily disappear as their citizens arrive in the United States. A common mistake by therapists unfamiliar with such histories is to combine all Asian clients into one treatment group, thus neglecting the sometimes profound differences that may still exist.

In addition to their unique history and circumstances prior to arrival in the United States, each Asian group has its own pattern of migration to this country as well as its own subsequent experiences here (Takaki, 1989). While some (mostly the Chinese, Filipinos, and Japanese) came to the United States as early as the 1800s and played important roles in the developing history of this country, others are relatively new (e.g., the H'mongs, Moluccans, and Tamals) and are just beginning to be recognizable groups of their own. Many of the early immigrants were poor, single males while a large number in recent years, especially those from India and Korea, are highly educated and come with a family. Lastly, Asians migrate under such vastly different conditions that even within one family there may be members who arrived years apart as well as others still left behind. In addition, their experiences subsequent to arrival in the U.S. are often quite different. While most have encountered racial discrimination and prejudice in the U.S., none have endured the degree of indignation, humiliation, and maltreatment associated with the forced incarceration of Japanese Americans in internment camps during World War II (Nagata, 1990, 1991; Takaki, 1989).

Such distinctions serve to remind us of the complexities inherent in assessing and treating Asian Pacific American and Pacific Islander addicts. Clearly, the differences between the various groups are more than semantic distinctions. Although the terms *Asian*, *Asian American*, and *Pacific Islander* are necessarily aggregative, they connote significant aspects of the individual's phenomenal world and important differences in customs, values, and beliefs. They also alert clinicians to the essential task of ascertaining their clients' background through observation and through questions such as the following: How do clients and their family appear in mannerism and dress?

Where were they born? How old were they before leaving their homeland? Who was the primary caretaker in their childhood? How did they come to this country? How long have they been here? Do they speak their native language at home? What is their degree of immersion in their traditional culture versus adaptation to more Western customs and beliefs? Careful assessment reveals important details about an individual's ethnicity, religious beliefs, class, and socioeconomic background.

Beyond their semantic significance, the terms (Asians and Asian Americans or Pacific Islanders versus Pacific Americans) also suggest a continuum of psychological adjustment spanning both a traditional heritage and a more Western, or Americanized, context. Simply put, all Asian Pacific Americans come from families that were at one time Asian or Pacific Islander. At the same time, all Asians and Pacific Islanders who are now here in the U.S. are in the process of becoming Americans. While risking reliance on stereotypes, these initial aggregates of nationality and generation level also highlight important contrasts in attitudes, behaviors, and customs, contrasts that serve as an essential basis for accurate assessment and treatment of an individual's addiction. Because this chapter focuses on the family ecology of the addicts, the term *Asian* will be used as a general reference for all those who share Asian or Pacific Islander ancestry, including both those who are foreign born as well as those born in this country.

To illustrate briefly, two groups of Asians have become increasingly recognizable in the United States over the past two decades—the Koreans and the H'mongs. While the Koreans are largely educated professionals from a highly stylized culture with thousands of years of history (Kim, 1997), the H'mongs (together with the Miens) are a nomadic people from an agrarian culture with mainly oral traditions and little in the way of cultural artifacts (Moore et al., 1997). Subsequent to their arrival in this country, the former have occupied a largely middle-class stratum with very different rates of addiction and psychiatric problems than the latter, who, along with Cambodians, manifest extremely high rates of psychiatric symptomatology (Kinzie et al., 1990; Westermeyer, 1988).

For most Asians, it is essential to know the individual's life experiences prior to coming to the United States, as these serve as the larger context for subsequent addictive behaviors. Some people come with previous histories of addiction, most often to alcohol and opium (Lee, 1992; Westermeyer, 1971). When the city of San Francisco, for example, opened its first methadone clinic over twenty years ago, the largest ethnic population represented among its clientele were Chinese "gentlemen" opium addicts (Tavano, 1998). It is not uncommon for many older foreign-born individuals to have still unresolved significant physical and psychological trauma when they arrive here in this country (Kinzie et al., 1990). Most Asian cultures have experienced profound turmoil—war, famine, and other political and natural disasters—throughout their history and into this century. When the stress of living through such turmoil is compounded by the additional stresses and hardship of the migration process itself (Chang, 1995; Sluzki, 1979), the consequence is often an emotionally fragile and psychologically weakened individual who is especially vulnerable to the availability of drugs in this country. For example, just knowing the nationality and age of QLB, the client described in Vignette 1, immediately signaled in me an important working hypothesis: he was involved in the horrible genocide during his country's political struggle with the Pol Pot regime, and his nightmares are the psychological sequelae from that experience. Similarly, AA's nationality and status suggested significant experiences related to being an only child in a Catholic family that valued multiple offspring.

Cultural Context

Given the political and cultural histories of countries throughout Asia, it is clear that Asians do not represent any one monolithic group so much as an exceedingly diverse aggregate of customs, languages, affinities, and systems of beliefs (Lee, 1997; Nakamura, 1964; Takaki, 1989). These countries and nationalities can be vastly different from one another—in size, religious orientation, linguistic base, economic and political history, and social orientation. Over 40 ethnic and nationalistic groups exist, representing over 30 distinct primary languages and a greater mix of religious beliefs than in any other part of the world. While the dominant religions are Buddhism, Christianity, Hinduism, and Islam, numerous lesser religions exist, including Judaism, Taoism, and various animistic systems, such as Shintoism and *khwaan*, a belief in soul spirits (Phillips, 1965). Even within a single country, significant differences can exist, especially if it is a geographically vast one such as India or the People's Republic of China.

Families Within the rich diversity of customs, values, and beliefs, certain salient commonalities do appear across many Asian cultures. First and foremost is the importance of the family and an adherence to social hierarchy (Hsu, 1970; Shon and Ja, 1982). Western conceptions of individuality and the many related notions of self, autonomy, choice, and privacy are rarely condoned. Instead, it is the family, not the individual, that is the primary social unit (Markus and Kitayama, 1991). One subtle but common indication of this is the fact that in many parts of Asia it is the family name that is introduced first, before the given name of the individual, during social in-teractions. The family is also defined more broadly than is customary here in the United States. It includes not only the immediate nuclear unit but also the many extended relationships. Many Asians, for example, consider their grandparents and aunts and uncles, especially paternal ones, as integral members of their family. Traditionally, families are patrilocal, with multiple generations living together or in close physical and emotional proximity. They also operate according to strict hierarchical rules. Elders and parents are accorded the most respect and influence, while younger family members are expected to be deferential and obedient and, above all else, to put the elders' wishes and well-being before their own.

Given this centrality of the family in most Asian cultures, it is essential to assess the role of the family when working with any Asian addict. The presence and influence of the family, especially the elders, cannot be under-estimated. Even when significant members are absent, for example, through nonmigration, loss, or emotional estrangement, their psychological influ-ence is often still profound. Moreover, because of the patterns of migration among many Asian groups, it is more the norm for an Asian family to in-clude individuals with significantly different levels of acculturation (or, conversely, different degrees of attachment to their traditional customs and values). The assessment of an Asian addict, then, must include that of his or her most important emotional and psychological unit before treatment can properly occur.

Relationships Because Asian cultures are so family centered and socially contextualized, maintaining family obligations and the accompanying re-sponsibilities of filial piety that surround each individual is perhaps the dominant concern in the life of most Asians. This responsibility typically falls most heavily on the oldest child, especially if it is a son. One's sense of self and social status is reflected largely in how well one upholds his or her family obligations, especially through bringing honor to the family. The concept of "face" embodies such values, and one strives always to acquire or maintain face (*yao lien* in Chinese) rather than to lose it (*diu lien*). Having face is to feel honorable, virtuous, and respectable, while losing face brings profound shame and dishonor to the individual as well as to the family. Self-esteem is inextricably tied to the reflected esteem from others (Norbeck and DeVos, 1972), and how one feels about one's self is intimately tied to one's fulfillment of family obligations (Roland, 1988). This identity between per-sonal experience and social appraisal as embedded within relationships is also similar to the concepts of *amae* and *omoiyari* among the Japanese (Doi, 1962; Lebra, 1984). And there is no better way to maintain face than to show respect and bring honor to one's family and ancestors. Conversely, violating or not upholding familial and social standards brings tremendous shame and a profound loss of face to the individual in most Asian cultures.

Another derivative of these values is that of shaming as a form of social, especially parental, discipline and motivation. Children are typically disciplined through two methods: physical punishment and emotional shaming (Tseng, McDermott, Ogino, and Ebata, 1982). Parents will publicly and explicitly reprimand a child who they feel has brought embarrassment and dishonor to the family through some transgression. The child not only is admonished for the misdeed but is especially reprimanded for causing shame to the family through his or her lack of forethought and judgment (Tang, 1992). Children learn early on the many and subtle ways in which they can avoid such negative reinforcement, and the lessons thus instilled during childhood serve as the basis for powerful mechanisms of social control among adults. One learns to anticipate the reactions of others carefully, as well as to manage their likely judgment of one's actions. Families are also accustomed to anticipating such judgment from their surroundings and are ever vigilant about whether their members may be transgressing.

A common consequence of such customs is the tendency for families who encounter situations or behaviors they find nonconforming or unacceptable to minimize, deny, reject, or ostracize the culpable individual. Families either pretend that there is no problem or admonish and severely criticize the offending individual. They ultimately seek to either reject the person or hide the problem from public view. For the addict, of course, this furthers the sense of profound emotional isolation that has often already preceded the addiction process and adds to its negative spiral. Whether the family's response is intended as punishment or is simply a manifestation of severe cultural strictures against reflected shame, the effect is inevitably negative for everyone within the system.

Socially stigmatized behaviors, such as mental illness and drug abuse, are treated especially harshly. This is reflected in the late entry to and low utilization rates of mental health services that are often reported for Asian communities (Leong, 1986; Snowden and Cheung, 1990; Sue, Fujino, Hu, Takeuchi, and Zane, 1991). It is also reflected in the following anecdote: An alcoholic client recalled being locked in the family basement for over a year of his childhood because he was too hyperactive at school. Amazingly, his two siblings expressed surprise at this recollection, as they had no memory of their brother's absence during that entire time. Everyone agreed, however, that this confinement was entirely consistent with their parents' values and behaviors, and the client's siblings had no doubt that it did occur.

One ramification of the importance of familial and social relationships is the complexity of managing the multiple familial and social relations and obligations (e.g., *giri* in Japanese). It is, therefore, entirely pragmatic how Confucian values have come to dominate so much of Asia (Cleary, 1992; Nakamura, 1964). Confucianism is not so much a religion as it is a social contract. It offers, in its elaborate prescriptions for social conduct, a convenient protocol for what would otherwise be even more exceedingly complex interactions. Each individual has his or her place in society, as determined by age, gender, and family status. In turn, each person must revere "heaven, earth, the emperor, parents, and one's teachers, in that order" (Leung and Boehnlein, 1996, p. 296). This sense of hierarchy is even reflected in the language. In Chinese, for example, a constellation of terms exists just to identify and connote family relationships (Hsu, 1970). Each term signifies the rank of a family member, by both age and gender, in relationship to the speaker and must be strictly adhered to in all formal interactions. In addition, a distinction is drawn between those on the father's side of the family and those on the mother's so that each individual's exact role and position within the larger family is specified (Hsu, 1970). A familiarity with the native language, then, allows an exact understanding of the structural and, more importantly, possible emotional relationship between each family member and the reference person.

Gender Roles Another common characteristic is gender bias and the imposition of strict gender roles both within and outside the home. Other than some Pacific Islander groups and in isolated parts of the continent, (Mead & Metraux, 1970), most Asian cultures are historically patrilineal and patrilocal and favor male offspring over female. Consequently, women often grow up feeling devalued and suffer emotional and psychological consequences from these sexist customs throughout their lives (Mah, 1998). For example, a Japanese father may address the son at any time, whereas the mother only speaks to the daughter if both parents are present (Tseng et al., 1982). As has been true historically for many other cultures worldwide, it is the male's responsibility to manage all the "outside" affairs and provide financial support for the family (Chang, 1996); women, on the other hand, are responsible for "inside," or family, matters, especially those involving the children. An ironic extension of this custom is that while sons are often accorded more privileges than their sisters, it is often the mother of the sons who has the most power and influence within the family as they become older (Shon and Ja, 1982).

Constricted gender roles are often compounded by the custom of arranged, or exchange, marriages within many Asian cultures. Historically in Asia and parts of the Pacific, couples marry not so much for romantic love as to maintain family status and obligations or for economic reasons, such as in the case of the many "picture brides" who came to the United States earlier this century (Takaki, 1989). Even in contemporary times, it would be a mistake to assume that an Asian couple "chose" to marry each other or that the foundation of any marriage is a shared romantic affinity between the spouses. Instead, it is the families that arrange the marriage, and the prospective bride and groom sometimes do not even see each other, much less know one another, until shortly before the wedding. One client, married for twenty-five years, met her husband for the very first time on the tarmac of a U.S. airport after leaving Korea just hours earlier. Violating such customs can sometimes have drastic, even deadly, repercussions (Bearak, 1998; Hoge, 1997).

This practice has obvious implications for subsequent marital interaction and family functioning. A marriage that is rooted in fulfilling a family obligation or social arrangement operates very differently from one based on strong romantic feelings of love or on an affinity between the partners. Under the former circumstances, a husband's marital infidelity is not uncommon whereas dominance and control over the family, especially the children (and particularly the sons), are the contrasting uxorial manifestations. The irony is that such marriages are often quite enduring, although not necessarily tranquil or harmonious (again because of the social obligation inherent in the union). Domestic violence and spousal abuse are also unfortunate consequences of such arranged marriages in many Asian communities (Masaki and Wong, 1997).

Another custom that was common until recently is that of multiple marriages on the part of the male. Historically, as a reflection of class differences as well as ethnic ones, men have been permitted to have more than one wife, either openly or secretly. For some Asian families that have migrated to the United States, the "secret" wives and children left behind become the source of great animosity and bitterness, especially if they surface years later to the surprise of those here in this country.

Communication Another dominant characteristic of Asian culture is the hierarchy within a family and in the broader society between older and younger members. Age, longevity, wisdom, and life experiences are highly valued in traditional Asian cultures, and significant rules of conduct exist to operationalize these values. Elders and those of a higher social status are to be respected, and one way to show respect is to honor their wishes and opinions. This precludes openly disagreeing with them or, at times, even voicing one's personal opinion for fear that doing so may precipitate conflict, displeasure, or disappointment. Children learn to carefully differentiate between what is acceptable or safe to express and what is not. The unspoken rule is this: when in doubt, remain silent. Similarly, children are taught not to ask too many risky questions, especially provocative ones that may make an elder uncomfortable or feel put on the spot. Instead, it is more important to remain quiet in order to avoid the possibility of conflict. These habits and behaviors have obvious parallels to observations of alcoholic families in the United States (Black and Bucky, 1986; Wegscheider, 1981), but they seem paradoxical in cultures that are so prescriptive in terms of social structure and interpersonal relationships.

The learned silence and concern about propriety undoubtedly serve as the basis for another common characteristic among many traditional Asians: indirect communication. Given the strictures against offending an elder or person of higher social status yet the human need to voice one's own thoughts and needs, many traditionally raised Asians have learned subtle and indirect ways to express themselves. Especially when a restrictive environment is compounded by a political climate that is severely oppressive—as is true even today in such communist or dictatorial countries as North Korea, Burma/Myanmar, and the People's Republic of China—the ability to communicate in veiled or indirect ways becomes an important pragmatic and survival skill. This approach is then generalized to any new situation where the circumstances or outcomes are uncertain, such as when one emigrates and finds oneself in a strange, new environment.

Relative to Americans, who place a high value on directness and being assertive, most traditional Asians hold the exact opposite belief about communication. For them, to be boastful is to be shameful, and to bring attention to oneself is to be boastful. And to be direct is to risk being confrontational. Confrontation is considered to be socially rude, as it ignores one's obligation to maintain face in relationship to others. Conversely, to be discreet, modest, indirect, and circumspect is highly valued, as it allows one to convey one's thoughts without challenging or, worse yet, possibly insulting the other person. The ability, then, to maintain these social graces is seen as the highest form of social skill and is an integral aspect of either face-keeping or face-saving. Similarly, the experiencing of strong emotion is also to be avoided, as is the expression of strong, intense feelings and affect, especially interpersonally or in public. To express such feelings risks causing discomfort or embarrassment to others, thus bringing shame to oneself.

It is no accident, then, that Asian languages tend to be more metaphoric and analogic in contrast to English. Where words have unique definitions and specific meanings in English, the opposite is often true in Chinese,

Hindi, Japanese, and Korean, where meanings may change with the twist of a sound or a shift in tonal inflection, a reflection of these cultures' emphasis on nonconfrontation and public deference between individuals. An exaggeration of this involves beliefs and superstitions held by some, especially members of the older generation. For example, many buildings in Hong Kong and southern China (and here in the United States, for that matter, where there are high concentrations of Chinese, as in the Chinatowns of San Francisco, New York, and Boston) do not have a fourth floor, since the word in the Cantonese dialect for four sounds too much like the word for death. Taken out of context, this appears to be a primitive superstitious belief, but it is perhaps a culture's way of protecting its members from casual confrontation with certain harsh and unpleasant realities (Schweder 1991).

Harmony Great value is placed on the experience of stillness and inner peace in many traditional Asian cultures, especially those with a strong Buddhist or Taoist heritage. Perhaps because of the dominance of the traditional family structure described above and a need by individuals to counterbalance its emotional density, many Asian cultures have spiritual teachings that emphasize the need for inner harmony, as well as harmony with the natural order. The classic Taoist text, for example, begins with these words:

> *The Tao that can be told is not the eternal Tao.*
> *The name that can be named is not the eternal name.*
> *The nameless is the beginning of heaven and earth.*
> *The named is the mother of ten thousand things.*

And further: "Empty yourself of everything. Let the mind rest at peace" (Feng and English, 1972).

This sense of harmony is also reflected in classical Chinese paintings, in which a common theme is a solitary scholar or hermit in a mountain setting. Similarly, the idealized Zen rock garden, or *sekitei* in Japan, is prized for its evocation of serenity and calmness in the participant viewer. Other customs and practices that also reflect such an emphasis include the many forms of meditation and certain martial arts, such as *aikido, chi gong, tai chi,* and classical *kung fu*. All rest upon a common suspicion of worldly chaos and turmoil and offer instead a trust in inner tranquility or harmony. The seeking of inner resolution and harmony with nature through solitude and meditation is no doubt best understood within its specific cultural contexts, but notions as diverse as nirvana in Buddhism and "no mind" in Soto Zen (Suzuki, 1956) share this underlying commonality (Smith, 1986). The paradox, of course, is that such beliefs and practices should come from those very tradition-bound cultures that are so characterized by social conformity and population density.

Migration and Loss. Out of context, the customs and values described thus far not only lose their meaning but seem dysfunctional in their distortion. This is inevitably the case as a result of migration. Like many immigrants who have historically relocated under conditions of duress, most Asians have come to the United States because of economic or social hardship (Takaki, 1989). Migration is the one common experience of all Asian and Pacific Islander groups in this country. For example, the largest subgroup in the United States has until recently been the Cantonese from southern China. Their migration was due in large part to the historical ravages by the Yangtze River of south and central China. Local peasants call this body of water "China's Sorrow" in reference to the frequent floods and devastation it has caused, including the deaths of countless hundreds of thousands over the centuries. This struggle continues today, as the Yangtze is at the center of one of the great ecological controversies of our time. The People's Republic of China has begun construction of a huge dam to block the river's flow, a dam that will also inundate thousands of archaeological treasures. Still, a year as recent as 1998 brought yet another reminder of the ravages of flooding; thousands of lives were lost and hundreds of thousands displaced in the Yangtze Valley alone (Poole, 1998).

Along with the move from one country to another, there is always loss. Rarely does the entire family move, especially as family is defined in Asian cultures. Indeed, the majority of first-generation Asians experience their families as incomplete (Chang, 1995). And in cultures that are constructed around the family as the core social and emotional unit, family members who do not move, migrate, or relocate constitute significant losses in the lives of those who do. Sometimes a child or young adult is sent by the family as an emissary of sorts, with others following over time. Or a parent will migrate and then send for one or more of the others. It is not uncommon for families to spend years apart before members are able to rejoin one another. During the interim, some members die, others are born, and the family changes in significant ways—sometimes without an individual's knowledge. As these and other losses become too overwhelming, the ability to adequately mourn is also compromised. As in many cultures worldwide, mourning in Asian cultures is a familial and community experience (Bateson, 1994), and when it is the family or community itself that is to be mourned, another form of silence often sets in, the silence of solitary grief and mourning (Chang, 1995; Jordan, Kraus, and Ware, 1993).

It is again paradoxical that the communication within many immigrant Asian families in the United States, who come from cultures so often seen as highly family based, can be severely constrained and problematic. This is sometimes attributed to the generation gap or to intergenerational conflict, which is typically understood to be between those who are foreign born ("first generation") and those who are American born ("second generation"). Conflict may also exist between family members of markedly different levels of comfort and acculturation with American norms versus traditional Asian ones. There are, of course, many reasons for this. Traditional gender roles are one obstacle, especially between husbands and wives. And if the marriage is an arranged one without the base of affection between the spouses, the likelihood of effective communication, as between two respectful partners, can be compromised or reduced. The customs and norms that worked for family members in their homeland, when the family was surrounded by a supportive larger social ecology, no longer do so here. The father's distance from the family, which was once culturally syntonic, becomes an added liability to the family system here in the United States, where the entire structure and process of the family is different. Now women are accorded more equal status, children no longer show the customary deference to their elders, the aged lose their significance as the keepers of social and familial tradition, and society as a whole espouses different virtues and aspirations than before.

A second common experience for most Asians in coming to the United States is that of discrimination and racial prejudice. When compounded by the further confusion and trauma of American racial bias and discrimination, many Asian families begin a downward spiral fueled by overwhelming stressors and unfamiliar social landmarks. This is evident not only for many recently immigrated families but even for those who have been here for decades and generations. FS, the subject of Vignette 2 in the beginning of this chapter, was a *Sansei*, a third-generation Japanese American whose parents were interned in one of the many camps set up by the U.S. government during World War II for American citizens of Japanese descent. Like many of her background (Nagata, 1990, 1991), she grew up in a household dominated by silence, as her parents, especially her father, were too stunned and shamed by their experience to be able to express themselves. They sealed off their pain behind a wall of total avoidance and silence regarding their lives during the war years to such an extent that their children grew up in an emotional vacuum. It is almost axiomatic in clinical practice that one will find that the families of many Asian clients, especially the more traumatized or those with serious disturbances, share this characteristic. The deprivation and isolation these individuals experienced in their families of origin serve as potent precursors to a variety of psychological ills, addiction being one of the increasingly common ones, as we are now witnessing.

One end result of this process is increased isolation and loss of social support, coupled with a sense of estrangement from the dominant culture. Despite the outside perception of Asians as a model minority—hardworking, industrious, and family oriented—emotional estrangement and isolation are more often the "inside" experience for many Asian immigrants. This is due to two common factors: First, the loss of family as it is defined in most Asian cultures leads to a loss of self, identity, and belonging. Second, many feel cut off from the dominant society in this country through the cumulative experiences of discrimination, marginalization, and racism (Takaki, 1989). Until recently, for example, no positive Asian American role models were presented by the mass media or were featured in the field of sports or in popular entertainment (Mok, 1998).

Addiction. Finally, it is important to understand the history, role, and conceptions of addictive agents and addictions prevalent in Asian cultures. Historically, the most common forms of addiction for Asians have been to gambling, nicotine, alcohol, and opium, because of the widespread acceptance of their usage. Alcohol and opium, for example, have long been valued for their social and medicinal properties (Booth, 1998; Vallee, 1998; Westermeyer, 1991) while betting and gambling, along with cigarette smoking, occupy significant social functions, especially among males.

Alcohol is commonly ingested during important social rituals such as celebrations and funerals, and sometimes great quantities are consumed, particularly by the men (Wang et al., 1992). This practice is most common in modern urban Japan and Korea (Chung, 1992), where public intoxication is viewed without stigma and is easily accepted as normal social group behavior. Solitary drinking, however, is rarely condoned, and solitary intoxication is viewed with great suspicion and disdain. Similarly, the use of opium is either accepted or stigmatized, depending on its social context. In addition, some Asian cultures view opium use as a privilege of the aged, to ease their physical distress as well as to prepare them for transition to an afterlife (Booth, 1998).

Betting and gambling pervade many contemporary Asian cultures and are popular pastimes that take multiple forms, for example, horse racing, the card game *pai gow*, cockfights, gaming, and *mah-jongg*. Practically anything with an element of chance and competition can become the basis for betting and gambling, which are practiced with fervor by both men and women. There are open stalls on Tokyo streets where passersby can place bets, and it has been said that the national sport of the Philippines is betting and gambling (Fernandez, personal communication, August 8, 1998), a status no less likely in many other parts of Asia.

Equally prevalent in many Asian countries is cigarette smoking. Since there has been easy acceptance of such behaviors for much of this century, cigarette smoking, along with nicotine addiction, has reached epidemic proportions in recent years and is now the leading health risk among Asian males overseas (World Health Organization, 1997).

These practices of betting, gambling, and smoking, along with the importance of maintaining face within Asian cultures and a general lack of understanding about the addictive process, often result in a tremendous tolerance within Asian families for an addict's behavior. Whatever the explanation, many addicts are able to continue their addictive habits, without sanction by the family, while everyone colludes to hide the problem from outside attention. One client dropped out of college because he had gambled all of his tuition money away and could not tell his family. Another declared bankruptcy after she lost all the proceeds from her family business at the card table. Yet another underwent five detox programs within two years through the creative use of "business trips" in order to not alarm his spouse. Addicts are reluctant to acknowledge their problems, much less ask for help, feeling that to do so would be to impose on others or risk bringing shame to the family. At the same time, others are reluctant to confront the addict, because to do so violates the dominant social concern regarding face. Inevitably, the result is an enabling cycle that perpetuates the addictive process and leads the problem to a much later stage before it comes to any outside attention. This is, unfortunately, where many courses of treatment must begin.

TREATMENT

TREATMENT OF ASIAN, Asian American, and Pacific Islander addicts must be based on a thorough assessment and understanding of pertinent data. Given the customs described above, it is essential to begin with both a standard diagnostic workup of the type and severity of the addiction (Schuckit, 1995) as well as an assessment of the individual's degree of acculturation. (A common source of conflict in many Asian families is the variation in times of arrival in the United States by various family members along with different developmental stages upon arrival, thus leading to asynchronous rates of adjustment to this culture.) In addition, for those more traditional in their beliefs and upbringing, ethnic background and national identity must also be accurately identified. These preliminary clues provide early guidance for how to best proceed clinically with one's client. Even preliminary and basic identifying information, such as name, age, and other demographic data, begins to inform the treatment approach. For example, QLB's name and age suggested that he was someone who was likely affected by the mass genocide that occurred in Cambodia during the early 1970s and provided a working hypothesis about his symptoms (Kinzie et al., 1990). Noting FS's ancestry, age, and English fluency suggested that she was likely Japanese American with a family history involving the internment camps (Nagata, 1990, 1991). Both CYW's and AA's names identified their ethnicity and nationality, and their respective vignettes provided specific clues about unique family histories, migration experiences, and likely premorbid patterns.

Clinically, the overriding task is to address the multiple issues that involve the family of the addicted individual within the context in which treatment is to occur. A few unique treatment programs now exist in the United States that are specifically designed for Asian and Pacific Islander addicts (e.g., Asian American Recovery Services in San Francisco, the Asian American Drug Abuse Program in Los Angeles, and the National Asian/Pacific American Families Against Substance Abuse). They provide more comprehensive service than programs designed for the general public as well as specific treatment components addressing the various issues described above. An ideal program would include native language services for the many different ethnic groups, separate treatment groups for each gender, a spectrum of therapy modalities for the addict and his or her family, and psychoeducational components addressing the appropriate level of familiarity with Western as well as traditional concepts of disease and treatment.

Most treatment of Asian clients, however, probably still occurs within the general outpatient mental health system of this country, whether private or public. The challenges to a clinician in such circumstances can be particularly daunting. Sue's (1977) findings of two decades ago still hold in many circumstances: most Asian, Asian American, and Pacific Islander clients in a public mental health setting will likely not return for more than a handful of treatment sessions, if at all.

Focusing just on the addicted individual is rarely successful. Whether the family is to be actively included or not, it remains a central issue in the addict's overall treatment (Inaba, Cohen, and Holstein, 1997; Margolis and Zweben, 1998). This is particularly true for Asian addicts, but owing to the various factors outlined above, engaging their families often presents special dilemmas and challenges. Given what has been said about the importance of the family for persons of Asian and Pacific Islander descent, it is not surprising that in every one of the vignettes presented at the beginning of this chapter the family was a dominant etiologic factor. Thus, every effort should be made to engage the family of the Asian addict as part of ongoing treatment (Margolis and Zweben, 1998; Stanton and Todd, 1981). While the family's involvement may present additional complexities for the clinician, the necessity cannot be overstated; moreover, Asian families can be especially compliant with treatment, given their cultural values regarding authority and conformity. It is also important to look past the family's "cultural mask" (Montalvo and Gutierrez, 1983) in order to better understand the hidden issues unique to each addict that are crucial for effective intervention. The decision, however, about whether the addict is to be seen with the family or separately should be based on clinical exigencies.

Because of the centrality of the family for most Asian addicts (Lee, 1997; Shon and Ja, 1982), it is imperative that treatment planning begin as early as possible with active consideration of the family's role in the person's addiction as well as treatment and recovery. The intense psychological relationship that characterizes many Asian individuals and their family is the *sine qua non* of systemic family theory. This intensity does not mean, of course, that there is necessarily affection or even a positive relationship with the family but simply that the family occupies perhaps the dominant role in the life of most Asians. It is, therefore, essential to assess the individual's addiction process with respect to the family's level of functioning. All the classic constructs upon which the field of family therapy is based—scapegoating, fusion, emotional cutoffs, triangulation, and so forth (Nichols and Schwartz, 1995)—pertain.

Mindful of Asian cultural characteristics, as described earlier in this chapter, I routinely ask clients to identify all those whom they grew up with and I then compare those named with family members who actually live here. Especially for those foreign born, this inquiry may be simply "Before you came to this country, who all were part of your family?" followed by "And who do you live with here now?" This simple exercise often reveals large voids in the family composition and possibly in the client's phenomenal world. Asian clients often experience great difficulty attempting to speak with their family, particularly the parents or elders, about a personal matter. It is as difficult for addicts to verbalize their feelings and concerns as it is for their family members to listen and hear what is meant and said. This becomes a recursive pattern of repeated rebuffs and nonspecific answers that often ends in frustration and feelings of futility. The therapist must establish clear and direct ways to address hidden apprehensions if overall treatment is to be successful.

Care must also be exercised that the therapy not violate gender roles or cross-generational boundaries in communication. AA's husband, for example, eventually did participate in treatment but only after careful focus and coaching on how she might approach him with her concerns. An offer was also extended by the therapist that he could come and "just listen," if he wished, and he was assured that if he wished to speak (and most likely complain about her), she would not argue back and would make every effort to listen to his complaints. These are, of course, simple convening strategies (Stanton and Todd, 1981; Tiesman, 1980) that the therapist must be prepared to flexibly adopt in order to involve the critical family component of a client's life. Other strategies include attempts to engage the family by requesting their help with one's therapeutic role. Fathers are sometimes particularly reluctant to participate, and it may be necessary to find exceptional ways to reach out to them, such as by visiting the home initially (Shon and Ja, 1982). A straightforward problem-solving approach is often most effective. It is the therapist's privilege as a "doctor" to ask careful questions, as long as they are pertinent to the client's care. As Sue and Zane (1987) have suggested, Asian clients respond best to therapists who are expert and credible and can offer concrete suggestions or advice about their distress.

At the same time, there is always a fine (and often fragile) line between soliciting a family's help and the possibility of arousing their discomfort. For Asians, disclosing about one's self, especially one's private emotions or feelings, is often neither a familiar nor an acceptable practice. The tendency to engage in indirect communication is typically operative, as is a prohibition regarding the expression of personal needs, problems, and concerns. Being directive in treatment, therefore, is not *ipso facto* therapeutic. The use of models of intervention emphasizing confrontation or direct, explicit verbal exchange between clients (as in certain types of group approaches), between family members (especially cross-generational), or between client and therapist is likely to be not only ineffective but, worse yet, detrimental.

Assuming that outpatient therapy can proceed on a regularly scheduled weekly basis is often erroneous, and a choice needs to be made between maximizing impact and ease of regularity. Some Asian clients are unfamiliar with Western models of treatment and, instead, follow a more "drop jin" or crisis orientation (Chien and Yamamoto, 1982). They may feel devalued or rejected when a therapist only spends fifty minutes with them unless a thorough explanation is given about the therapist's plan of approach. One strategy is to schedule ample time beyond the standard therapy hour for one's first meeting with the entire family—on the assumption that it may be the last. The extra time allows enough critical history and information to be acquired and affords an opportunity to create enough psychological impact so that even if the family does not return, sufficient change has occurred to begin a process of perturbation (Hoffman, 1981; Maturana, 1974). Whatever discomfort may occur during this critical first meeting can be worked through if the therapist is skilled enough to "hold" the anxiety (Winnicott, Shepherd, and Davis, 1989) of family members so that they can learn to survive their apprehension and recognize that there can be sufficient gain to warrant their return to the therapist's office. It is also effective sometimes to strike while the iron is hot and meet with the family for a second session sooner than the standard one-week follow-up schedule in order to solidify the developing therapeutic relationship with everyone.

When successful, of course, simply engaging the family in the addict's ongoing treatment is an important step in countering the enormous sense of shame and isolation that the addict typically experiences. It is a clear measure of the skill of the therapist to successfully engage family members and facilitate their involvement in the addict's recovery process while at the same time challenging them to learn new, more functional ways of relating to one another.

Working carefully with the elders in the system is of paramount importance. They are often the most traditional in their values and orientation and the least accustomed to Western views and models of treatment and psychotherapy. At the same time, they are likely the "carriers" of unresolved loss, previous trauma, and other pathologies (Kao and Lam, 1997). When unresolved issues and trauma are identified at an earlier generational level, it is all the more crucial to address these issues without causing the family to experience its elders as being embarrassed or threatened. Great respect must be shown to these family members, along with a genuine indication that the therapist "knows" and understands their pain and suffering. The tendency of family members, sometimes especially the addict, is to protect the parents or elders from any sense of discomfort or shame, and it is essential for the clinician to be ever mindful not to rush in too quickly to areas of vulnerability. One technique is to initially join with the family at the broad experiential level—sharing their pain, grief, or any other aspect of salient traumatic experience—without pushing for details that may be embarrassing or threatening to the family.

At the same time, it is important to be as concrete and specific as possible in proceeding with the process of treatment. Instead of talking about subjective feelings, as may be the custom for many Western clients (and therapists), it is important to focus on more tangible and behavioral matters. Identify triggers for the addictive cycle, track the cycle components for the client and the family, discuss how progress will be noted and documented, and establish, at least implicitly, a contract (including homework, if appropriate) so that the family is clear about what they may expect from the therapist as well as from the therapeutic process.

Given the common orientation among Asians to somatic experiences rather than emotional ones (Kleinman and Good, 1985; Tung, 1991), an important first step for many clients is to learn about their inner subjective world and understand that they have personal feelings, emotions, needs, and desires. Tools and techniques involving creative or expressive arts may be especially useful in this regard. Clients will also likely need the therapist's help in experiencing new behaviors within the therapy session. Role-playing a difficult or vulnerable situation is often helpful in order to provide a tangible experience of this sort. Similarly, helping the addict to predict the inevitable relapses can be particularly effective, as is identifying more soothing but nontoxic alternatives to the addict's substance of choice. These interventions help enhance the therapist's expertise and credibility and serve as a "gift" to the client (Sue and Zane, 1987).

Other psychoeducational approaches include offering handouts in the native language, addressing the importance of dietary changes, suggesting remedies (such as melatonin) for common sleep disturbances, and teaching pain management techniques and relaxation exercises. Calling a physician whom the therapist can work with during the session is another way to emphasize the importance of taking treatment seriously. One can then discuss the appropriateness of adjunctive therapies—such as acupuncture and innovative pharmacologic agents such as acamprosate, bupropion, naltrexone, and nicotine gum—directly in front of the client and the family. While somewhat controversial (Morrow, 1998; Noble, 1999), these pharmacologic agents are likely to be more culturally syntonic for many Asian clients than talk therapy alone and deserve greater consideration by the health care and treatment communities.

When family issues are clearly identified that pertain to one individual's addiction, such as a parent's unresolved trauma or loss, these attendant issues must then be incorporated into the treatment plan, along with a further assessment of family members' accessibility for continued exploration of such issues. For example, when AA reported that she was an only child and had come to the United States by herself, careful inquiry revealed a sense of shame and guilt for leaving her family that served as a hidden source of stress from the very beginning of her marriage. Excessive shopping became both a way to fill the void and isolation in her life and a familiar means to remain attached to her mother. Similarly, QLB's losses were exactly at the core of his trauma. He was, to his knowledge, the only member of his family still alive. Much of his dream content was related to his having been forced to witness his wife and children being shot after she was caught stealing some rice to feed them. His life was spared because of his medical skills and because his captors wanted to make an example of him in their terrorist campaign.

Loss in FS's case was less obvious. Her parents were alive but not so emotionally present for her for much of her life. Her brother, with whom she had been very close during childhood, had become severely drug addicted as an adolescent. Emotionally impoverished as an adult, FS remained isolated from her family, yet she was devoted to her parents and bound by their sense of shame about her brother's problems. Outwardly she was a model employee, but inwardly FS became more and more depressed and desperate in her private search for meaning and emotional affection. A recently soured relationship finally left her vulnerable to her brother's "solution"—getting high as an alternative to her inner pain.

For CYW, loss was in the form of leaving his grandmother behind when he came to the United States. She had been his caretaker and he was very attached to her, more so than to his mother, who had left him behind as an infant to flee China. When CYW was finally able to join his mother, first in Hong Kong and later in the United States, his grandmother decided that she was too old and frail to leave her home, thus forcing him to make an extremely difficult choice. He felt torn between staying with his grandmother to care for her and coming to the United States, the land of opportunity, to start a new life with his mother and sister. He chose the later but was consumed with guilt, longing, and concern for his elderly grandmother until she died, two years after he left. He married his wife that same year and was alarmed when he learned, shortly afterward, of her gambling habit. He and his wife lived with his mother, who disliked his wife. CYW felt increasingly estranged from both women, yet he felt obligated to maintain his responsibilities as a son and husband.

In examining these vignettes more closely, another theme that emerges, beyond that of loss, is the emotional isolation and impoverishment in these clients' lives, especially within the family. Asian addicts commonly report that their family is the last place where they can confide, yet it is the primary source of their frustrations and the major object of their concerns.

Whether these concerns are about the well-being of their parents or about their own experience of being overwhelmed by the family's problems and needs, the cultural norms regarding hierarchy and obligation often result in Asian addicts' inability to affect their concerns. The implicit cultural expectation is typically for the addict to put the family's needs and well-being before his or her own. At the same time, cultural norms also prohibit the expression of disagreement with elders or even the raising of any concern that may cause discomfort and embarrassment. The experience of futility and psychological numbness that ensues is often accompanied by a deep sense of anger and bitterness that further amplifies the emotional separation and isolation of the addict within the family. This may explain why the drug of choice in Asian American communities is the sedative (Inaba et al., 1997, p. 410), which allows addicts to further numb their feelings without risking the eruption of unacceptable behaviors that violate cultural standards. Because the family occupies such a dominant role in the life of most Asians and because it is highly likely that salient but vastly different generational values will exist within the family, the treatment of Asian, Asian American, and Pacific Islander addicts is necessarily a complex and challenging process.

REFERENCES

Akutsu, P. D., Sue, S., Zane, N. W. S., & Nakamura, C. Y. (1989). Ethnic Differences in Alcohol Consumption Among Asians and Caucasians in the United States: An Investigation of Cultural and Physiological Factors. *Journal of Studies on Alcohol, 50*(3), 261–267.

Bateson, M. C. (1994). *Peripheral Visions: Learning Along the Way.* New York: HarperCollins.

Bearak, B. (1998, September 19). Caste Hate, and Murder, Outlast Indian reforms. *New York Times,* p. A3.

Black, C., & Bucky, S. F. (1986). Interpersonal and Emotional Consequences of Being an Adult Child of an Alcoholic. *International Journal of the Addictions, 21*, 213–231.

Booth, M. (1998). *Opium: A History.* New York: St. Martin's Press.

Chang, P. (1995). *Migration and Family Process.* Invited address, American Family Therapy Academy Conference, Cambridge, MA.

Chang, P. (1996). *The Role of Fathers in Chinese Families.* Paper presented at the American Family Therapy Academy Conference, Sante Fe, NM.

Chien, C. P., & Yamamoto, J. (1982). Asian-American and Pacific Islander Patients. In F. X. Acosta, J. Yamamoto, & L. A. Evans (Eds.), *Effective Psychotherapy for Low-Income and Minority Patients* (pp. 117–145). New York: Plenum Press.

Chung, K. L. (1992). Alcoholism in Korea. In J. Helzer & G. Canino (Eds.), *Alcoholism in North America, Europe and Asia* (pp. 247–286). New York: Oxford Press.

Cleary, T. (1992). *The Essential Confucius.* San Francisco: HarperCollins.

Doi, T. (1962). Amae: A Key Concept for Understanding Japanese Personality Structure. In R. J. Smith & R. K. Beardsley (Eds.), *Japanese Culture: Its Development and Characteristics.* Wenner-Gren Foundation for Anthropological Research.

Doi, T. (1969). Japanese Psychology, Dependency Need and Mental Health. In W. Caudill & T. Lin (Eds.), *Mental Health Research in Asia and the Pacific.* Honolulu: East-West Center.

Feng, G.-F. & English, J. *Lao Tsu: Tao Te Ching.* A new translation by Gia-Fu Feng and Jane English (1972). New York: Random House.

Helzer, J. E., & Canino, G. J. (1992). *Alcoholism in North America, Europe and Asia.* New York: Oxford University Press.

Hoffman, L. (1981). *Foundations of Family Therapy.* New York: Basic Books.

Hoge, W. (1997, October 18). Marked for Death, by Their Families. *The New York Times,* p. A4.

Hsu, F. L. K. (1970). *Americans and Chinese.* Garden City, NY: Doubleday.

Huang, P. P.-F., Chang, R. I. F., Chao, H. H., Hsia, L., & Wang, Y. C. (1967). *20 Lectures on Chinese Culture.* New Haven, CT: Yale University Press.

Inaba, D. S., Cohen, W. E., & Holstein, M. E. (1997). *Uppers, Downers and All-Arounders: Physical and Mental Effects of Psychoactive Drugs.* Ashland, OR: CNS Publications.

Jordan, J. R., Kraus, D. R., & Ware, E. S. (1993). Observation of Loss and Family Development. *Family Process, 32,* 425–440.

Kamm, H. (1998). *Cambodia: Report from a Stricken Land.* New York: Arcade.

Kao, R. S.-K., & Lam, M. L. (1997). Asian American Elderly. In E. Lee (Ed.), *Working with Asian Americans* (pp. 208–223). New York: Guilford Press.

Kim, B.-L. C. (1981). *Women in Shadows: A Handbook for Service Providers Working with Asian Wives of U.S. Military Personnel.* La Jolla, CA: National Committee Concerned with Asian Wives of U.S. Servicemen.

Kim, B.-L. C. (1996). Korean Families. In M. McGoldrick, J. Giordano, & J. K. Pearce (Eds.), *Ethnicity and Family Therapy,* (2nd ed., pp. 281–294). New York: Guilford Press.

Kinzie, J. D., Boehnlein, J. K., Leung, P. K., Moore, L. J., Riley, C., & Smith, D. (1990). The High Prevalence Rate of PTSD and Its Clinical Relevance Among Southeast Asian Refugees. *American Journal of Psychiatry, 147,* 813–917.

Kleinman, A. M., & Good, B. (1985). *Culture and Depression.* Berkeley, CA: University of California Press.

Lebra, T. S. (1984). *Japanese Patterns of Behavior.* Honolulu, HI: University of Hawaii Press.

Lee, C. K. (1992). Alcoholism in Korea. In J. E. Helzer & G. J. Canino (Eds.), *Alcoholism in North America, Europe and Asia* (pp. 247–286). New York: Oxford University Press.

Lee, E. (Ed.). (1997). *Working with Asian Americans.* New York: Guilford Press.

Leong, F. T. L. (1986). Counseling and Psychotherapy with Asian-Americans: Review of the Literature. *Journal of Counseling Psychology, 33,* 196–206.

Leung, P. K., & Boehnlein, J. (1996). Vietnamese Families. In M. McGoldrick, J. Giordano, & J. K. Pearce (Eds.), *Ethnicity and Family Therapy* (2nd ed., pp. 295–306). New York: Guilford Press.

Mah, A. Y. (1998). *Falling Leaves: The True Story of an Unwanted Chinese Daughter.* New York: Wiley.

Margolis, R. D., & Zweben, J. E. (1998). *Treating Patients with Alcohol and Other Drug Problems: An Integrated Approach.* Washington, DC: American Psychological Association.

Markus, H. R., & Kitayama, S. (1991). Culture and the Self: Implications for Cognition, Emotion, and Motivation. *Psychological Review, 98,* 224–253.

Masaki, B., & Wong, L. (1997). Domestic Violence in the Asian Community. In E. Lee (Ed.), *Working with Asian Americans*. New York: Guilford Press.

Maturana, H. (1974). Cognitive Strategies. In H. Von Forester (Ed.), *Cybernetics of Cybernetics* (pp. 457–469). Urbana, II: University of Illinois.

Mead, M., & Metraux, R. (1970). *A Way of Seeing*. New York: Morrow.

Mok, T. A. (1998). Getting the Message: Media Images and Stereotypes and Their Effects on Asian Americans. *Cultural Diversity and Mental Health, 4*, 185–202.

Montalvo, B., & Gutierrez, M. (1983). A Perspective for the Use of the Cultural Dimension in Family Therapy. *Family Therapy Collections, 6*, 15–32.

Moore, L. J., Keopraseuth, K.-O., Leung, P. K., & Chao, L. H. (1997). Laotian American Families. In E. Lee (Ed.), *Working with Asian Americans*. New York: Guilford Press.

Morrow, D. J. (1998, July 31). Curbing the Urge to Drink: Drug to Treat Alcoholism Sets Off Controversy in U.S. *The New York Times*, pp. B1, 4.

Nagata, D. (1990). The Japanese American Internment: Exploring the Transgenerational Consequences of Traumatic Stress. *Journal of Traumatic Stress, 3*, 47–69.

Nagata, D. (1991). Transgenerational Impact of the Japanese American Internment: Clinical Issues in Working with Children of Former Internees. *Psychotherapy, 28*, 121–128.

Nakamura, H. (1964). *Ways of Thinking of Eastern Peoples: India-China-Tibet-Japan*. Honolulu, HI: University Press of Hawaii.

Nichols, M. P., & Schwartz, R. C. (1995). *Family Therapy: Concepts and Methods* (3rd ed.). New York: Allyn and Bacon.

Norbeck, E., & DeVos, G. (1972). Culture and Personality. In F. Hsu (Ed.), *Psychological Anthropology in the Behavioral Sciences*. Cambridge, MA: Schenkman.

Noble, H. B. (1999, March 2). New from the Smoking Wars: Success. *The New York Times*, pp. D1–2.

Phillips, H. P. (1965). *Thai Peasant Personality*. Berkeley: University of California Press.

Poole, T. (1998, August 9). Fast Rising, Deadly Yangtze Floods Worst in Decades. *San Francisco Chronicle*, p. A 20.

Roland, A. (1988). *In Search of Self in India and Japan: Toward a Cross-Cultural Psychology*. Princeton: Princeton University Press.

Schuckit, M. A. (1995). *Drug and Alcohol Abuse: A Clinical Guide to Diagnosis and Treatment* (4th ed.). New York: Plenum Press.

Shankar, L. D. (1998). The Limits of (South Asian) Names and Labels. In L. D. Shankar & R. Srikanth (Eds.), *A Part, Yet Apart* (pp. 49–66). Philadelphia: Temple University Press.

Shon, S. P., & Ja, D. Y. (1982). Asian Families. In M. McGoldrick, J. K. Pearce, & J. Giordano (Eds.), *Ethnicity and Family Therapy* (1st ed., pp. 208–228). New York: Guilford Press.

Shweder, R. A. (1991). *Thinking Through Cultures: Expeditions in Cultural Psychology*. Cambridge, MA: Harvard University Press.

Sluzki, C. (1979). Migration and Family Conflict. *Family Process, 18*, 379–390.

Smith, H. (1986). *The Religions of Man*. New York: Harper & Row.

Snowden, L. R., & Cheung, F. K. (1990). Use of Inpatient Mental Health Services by Members of Ethnic Minority Groups. *American Psychologist, 45*, 347–355.

Stanton, M. D., & Todd, T. C. (1981). Engaging "Resistant" Families in Treatment: Principles and Techniques in Recruitment. *Family Process, 20*, 261–293.

Sue, S. (1977). Community Mental Health Services to Minority Groups. *American Psychologist, 32*, 616–624.

Sue, S., Fujino, D. C., Hu, L. T., Takeuchi, D., & Zane, N. (1991). Community Mental

Health Services for Ethnic Minority Groups: A Test of the Cultural Responsiveness Hypothesis. *Journal of Consulting and Clinical Psychology, 59,* 533–540.

Sue, S., & Zane, N. (1987). The Role of Culture and Cultural Techniques in Psychotherapy. *American Psychologist, 42,* 37–45.

Suzuki, D. T. (1956). *Zen Buddhism: Selected Writings* (W. Barrett, Ed.). Garden City, N Y: Doubleday.

Takaki, R. (1989). *Strangers from a Different Shore: A History of Asian Americans.* New York: Penguin Books.

Tang, N. M. (1992). Some Psychoanalytic Implications of Chinese Philosophy and Child-Rearing Practices. *The Psychoanalytic Study of the Child, 47,* 371–389.

Teisman, M. W. (1980). Convening Strategies in Family Therapy. *Family Process, 19,* 393–400.

Tseng, W. S., McDermott, J. F., Ogino, K., & Ebata, K. (1982). Cross-Cultural Differences in Parent–Child Assessment: USA and Japan. *International Journal of Social Psychiatry, 28,* 305–317.

Tung, M. P. M. (1991). Symbolic Meanings of the Body in Chinese Culture and "Somatization." *Culture, Medicine and Psychiatry, 18,* 483–492.

Vallee, B. L. (1998, June). Alcohol in the Western World. *Scientific American,* pp. 80–85.

Varma, S. C., & Siris, S. G. (1996). Alcohol Abuse in Asian Americans. *The American Journal on Addictions, 5,* 136–143.

Wang, C.-H., Liu, W. T., Zhang, M.-Y., Yu, E. S. H., Xia, Z.-Y., Fernandez, M., Lung, C.-T., Xu, C.-L., & Qu, G.-Y. (1992). Alcohol Use, Abuse, and Dependency in Shanghai. In J. E. Helzer & G. J. Canino (Eds.), *Alcoholism in North America, Europe and Asia* (pp. 264–286). New York: Oxford University Press.

Wegscheider, S. (1981). *Another Chance: Hope and Health for the Alcoholic Family.* Palo Alto, CA: Science and Behavior Books.

Westermeyer, J. (1971). Use of Alcohol and Opium by the Meos of Laos. *American Journal of Psychiatry, 127,* 1019–1023.

Westermeyer, J. (1988). DSM-III Psychiatric Disorders Among Hmong Refugees in the United States: A Point Prevalence Study. *American Journal of Psychiatry, 145,* 197–202.

Westermeyer, J. (1991). Historical and Social Context of Psychoactive Substance Disorders. In R. J. Frances & S. E. Miller (Eds.), *Clinical Textbook of Addictive Disorders* (pp. 23–40). New York: Guilford Press.

Winchester, S. (1996). *The River at the Center of the World.* New York: Henry Holt.

Winnicott, C., Shepard, R., & Davis M., (Eds.), (1989). *D. W. Winnicott: Psycho-Analytic Explorations.* Cambridge, MA: Harvard University Press.

World Health Organization. (1997). *Tobacco Epidemic in the Western Pacific* (N175, Fact Sheet). Geneva, Switzerland: Author. (Retrieved from http://www.who.ch/).

Young, K. S. (1998). *Caught in the Net: How to Recognize the Signs of Internet Addiction.* New York: Wiley.

Zane, N. W., & Sasao, T. (1992). Research on Drug Abuse Among Asian Pacific Americans. *Drugs and Society, 6* (3–4), 181–209.

CHAPTER EIGHT

ADDICTION TREATMENT FOR MEXICAN AMERICAN FAMILIES

Moises Barón

INTRODUCTION

THE 1990 U.S. population statistics reveal that there are about 21.4 million Hispanics residing in this country, out of a total United States population of approximately 246 million. This number does not reflect undocumented Hispanics who may be in this country illegally. The majority of Hispanics residing in the United States are people of Mexican origin (63 percent), who reside primarily in the Southwest; mainland Puerto Ricans (12 percent), who live principally in the Northeast; and Cubans (5 percent), who live primarily in the Southeast (Padilla and Salgado de Snyder, 1995; Ruiz and Langrod, 1992, 1997). Demographic projections indicate that Hispanics will become the largest minority group in the United States between the years 2000 and 2010. It is estimated that by the year 2020 there will be approximately 54.3 million Hispanics residing in this country (Aponte and Crouch, 1995; Holmes, 1998). The growth in the Mexican American population has been fueled by higher than average birthrates and by an ongoing process of legal and illegal immigration.

Mexican Americans trace their origins as a group in this country to 1848, when Mexico surrendered its northern territory. The current pattern of legal and illegal immigration began during World War II. At that time the United States was short of labor and entered into an agreement with Mexico to obtain a steady supply of cheap labor. After the war this arrangement continued and developed into the well-known Bracero Program (Padilla and Salgado de Snyder, 1995). Although this program ended in the late sixties, Mexicans continued to cross the border in an effort to find employment and better financial and social opportunities. Currently, a significant proportion of the Mexican American population is composed of immigrants and the children of immigrants born in this country. The majority of Mexican American families currently residing in the United States are undergoing a cultural transition and are also facing the many stressors and challenges associated with trying to learn a new language and integrate into a new society and way of life. Some consequences of this process can be discerned by examining current demographic data. Hispanics as a group are overrepresented among the poor and the unemployed and often live in substandard housing (Sue and Sue, 1990). Ninety percent of Hispanics live in large urban centers, and the majority have semi-skilled occupations. Compared to the non-Hispanic White population, Mexican Americans are younger (median age, 23 versus 33 years), earn less (median family income, $21,000 versus $33,000); are undereducated (years of education completed for individuals aged 25 and older, 10.8 versus 12.7), and have higher high school dropout rates (8.5 percent versus 5.2 percent) (Padilla and Salgado de Snyder, 1995).

From their analysis of the data, Padilla and Salgado de Snyder (1995) conclude, "All social indexes point to the fact that Hispanics, especially youths, constitute a population that is at high risk for experiencing a greater incidence of physical and psychological problems." (p. 121).

PATTERNS OF ALCOHOL AND DRUG USE AMONG MEXICAN AMERICANS

The review of demographic data suggests that Mexican Americans confront major socioeconomic challenges in their quest for educational, career, and economic advancement. Moreover, these economic challenges may translate into stresses that can lead directly or indirectly to the use of drugs or alcohol. We know that the abuse of alcohol, with the behavioral and physical problems that ensue, is becoming a major health issue for certain segments of the Mexican American population (Gilbert and Cervantes, 1986b; Ruiz and Langrod 1992, 1997).

A comprehensive review of the literature by Gilbert and Cervantes, in 1986, revealed that Hispanic ethnicity is a significant predictor, together with age and gender, in defining patterns of alcohol use and incidence of alcohol-related problems. A second major finding by these researchers was that the characteristic drinking patterns of ethnic groups in the United States strongly resemble the patterns of consumption in their countries of origin (Gilbert and Cervantes, 1986b).

Results of the 1993 National Survey on Drug Abuse indicate that Hispanics have a lower rate of illicit drug use when compared to the general population. There is a slightly higher rate of crack and heroin use. The information available suggests that the incidence and prevalence of alcohol use by Mexican Americans vary by region or state.

Mexican American and Anglo men appear to have similar patterns of alcohol use (Gilbert and Cervantes, 1986b). Although the percentage of males who drink is similar for the Mexican American and Anglo groups, Mexican Americans tend to drink more frequently to the point of intoxication. In addition, Mexican American males seem to experience more alcohol-related problems and show a greater incidence and chronicity of heavy drinking into middle age in contrast to the general population, where the incidence of heavy drinking decreases with age. Another significant finding is that when subjective measures are utilized, Mexican American males tend to perceive themselves less frequently as excessive drinkers than do non-Hispanic White males. It appears that Mexican culture imposes few limits on drinking behavior in men, so that even drinking behavior that is considered problematic in U.S. culture may be normative in Mexican culture (Gilbert and Cervantes 1986a). Both in Mexico and in the United States, the heaviest drinking appears to occur among middle-aged men.

Studies conducted in Texas and California suggest that Mexican Americans show a greater tendency to drink outside the home, such as in dance clubs and bars, than do members of the general population. This pattern may be partially due to the significant oversupply of alcohol outlets in urban areas with a high Mexican American concentration (Gilbert and Cervantes, 1986b). These results suggest that drinking is a social activity for Mexican American males, who may not drink at home in front of other relatives as frequently as do other individuals in the general population. This pattern of drinking may partially explain the greater incidence in Mexican American males, compared to the general population, of such alcohol-related problems as car accidents and driving while intoxicated (Gilbert and Cervantes, 1986a).

The available information indicates that Mexican American women drink significantly less than men. Interestingly, Mexican women appear to have lower rates of alcohol consumption and higher rates of abstention than Mexican American and non-Hispanic American women (Gilbert and Cervantes, 1986a). This finding suggests that Mexican cultural norms regulating drinking center around *who* may drink rather than *how* one should drink. Most ethnic groups regulate how one should drink. Basically, in Mexican culture, women and children are greatly restricted from drinking. In contrast, men are allowed to drink with little prescription made as to when, where, and how much (Gilbert and Cervantes, 1986b; Padilla and Salgado de Snyder, 1995; Smith-Peterson, 1983).

Research on Hispanics' use of illicit drugs also indicates that there are certain important cultural correlates. It appears that the finding of an apparently lower rate of use of most illicit drugs by Hispanics may be mediated by level of acculturation. In a review of the literature, Ruiz and Langrod (1992, 1997) report that the stronger the ties of Hispanics to Hispanic culture, the less likely the use of drugs. Conversely, the stronger the ties to American culture, the more likely the drug use. The issue of acculturation and its implications for treatment of Mexican Americans will be discussed later in this chapter.

SUBSTANCE ABUSE TREATMENT SERVICES FOR MEXICAN AMERICANS

A PERSON'S ETHNICITY and culture partially determines the context in which substance abuse takes place, the meaning given to it, the degree of tolerance and acceptability and the kinds of expectations encountered. Failures to acknowledge cultural variables in substance abuse problems have perpetuated stereotypes, lack of understanding, and treatment ineffectiveness (Smith-Peterson 1983). In contrast to their lower than average use of other health- and mental-health-related services, Mexican Americans do not underutilize alcohol treatment services (Gilbert and Cervantes, 1986a).

A substantially higher percentage of Mexican Americans are in alcohol treatment involuntarily than is the case for the rest of the population in treatment. Mexican Americans seeking alcohol rehabilitation services tend to primarily utilize outpatient settings and tend to underutilize detoxification interventions and residential programs. Mexican American males account for a significantly higher percentage of treatment utilizers in comparison with the larger population, where the ratio of male and female clients is not as skewed as in the Mexican American group. Finally, Mexican American clients who do utilize alcohol rehabilitation services tend to come from more stable family environments than do clients from other ethnic groups (Gilbert and Cervantes, 1986a).

The research and literature reviewed clearly indicate that alcohol and substance abuse are significant problems for Mexican Americans. However, there appears to be little systematic information about the usefulness of different approaches in treating addiction for the Mexican American population (Gilbert and Cervantes, 1986a; Gloria and Peregoy, 1995; Ruiz and Langrod, 1997; Smith-Peterson, 1983). For example, despite the call for culturally congruent and appropriate therapeutic interventions, more than half of Hispanics who utilize mental health services terminate therapy after only one session (Cheung, 1991; Sue and Sue, 1990; Sue and Zane, 1987). Difficulties regarding the best way to incorporate ethnicity and culturally related variables in the treatment of ethnic minority individuals can also be found in the family therapy literature.

Falicov (1995) summarizes the efforts of family therapists to find a way to incorporate culture and ethnicity into their conceptual frameworks and treatment by describing four positions. These positions are also helpful in examining the different treatment interventions that have been developed to treat alcohol- and drug-abusing Mexican Americans and other ethnic minority groups.

UNIVERSALIST POSITION

The universalist position holds that families are more alike than different and that the relevance of culturally related variables is minimal. Advocates of this approach assume that there is uniformity among families and their experience of the family life cycle (Falicov, 1995). Treatment proceeds from a view of drug and alcohol abuse as universal problems. Those who hold this position believe there is no need to develop treatments specifically for different ethnic groups or to use transcultural adaptations of the Alcoholics Anonymous doctrine and programs. Denial, enabling and codependency are seen as dynamics present in all family systems where alcohol or drugs are a central organizing principle. Cultural expertise is viewed as helpful but not central to treatment. Universalists believe that interventions and methodologies can be developed without much consideration of the cultural beliefs, attitudes, and characteristics of individual clients.

Universalist assumptions may incline the therapist to pathologize culturally congruent behavior that deviates from established mainstream norms. A review of the substance abuse treatment literature indicates that some minority individuals and families are not helped by universal interventions that disregard their cultural context.

PARTICULARIST POSITION

The particularist position is the opposite of the universalist in that it presupposes that every family is unique. This position requires the therapist to be respectfully curious when engaging the family in conversations related to family structure, customs, and beliefs in order to learn their uniqueness (Falicov, 1995).

A particularist therapist would not translate research findings into clinical hypotheses. That is, although research suggests that Mexican American males tend to drink more heavily when they do drink, a particularist would not ask, "Is this the case with this particular client I am working with?" Nor would a particularist ask, "What are the implications of such finding for developing an appropriate treatment plan?" Although this position, unlike the universalist one, stresses the need for the therapist to focus on individual differences and idiosyncrasies, it fails to consider the potential impact of broader social and ecosystemic issues such as acculturation, migration, minority status, and the influence of society as a whole.

ETHNIC FOCUS POSITION

The ethnic focus position posits that the differences between culturally diverse families are primarily because they have different ethnicities. This position urges the therapist to have a sociological understanding of the traits, beliefs, and customs of the different ethnic groups represented in his practice. The therapist then views the clients from an ethnically aware position (Falicov, 1995). The ethnic focus position has been popularized by McGoldrick, Pearce, and Giordano (1982, 1996). While McGoldrick and Giordano (1996) have emphasized that ethnicity is a key variable for assessment and intervention and should always be included in a clinical assessment, they have emphasized that it is not the only factor and that therapists are not cultural anthropologists and cannot possibly understand more than a few groups in any depth. Nevertheless, they believe that therapists should develop an appreciation for cultural patterns based on ethnicity, beginning with their own, and attend to potential cultural differences in their understanding of problems and their solutions as they work with clients in therapy. Indeed, their preference is to teach clinicians awareness of ethnic differences through focusing on specific differences in patterns of expression of pain, attitudes toward health care professionals, and the differential meaning of the notion of "family" to different groups.

Although McGoldrick and Giordano (1996) acknowledge that it is important for therapists to learn how to think culturally, and acknowledge the intersections of race, class, and gender with ethnicity, the prescription appears to be to learn and become aware of the characteristic values, ideas, behaviors, and norms of the specific ethnic groups with which one may come into professional contact. Following an ethnic focus perspective can be useful in that content information about a specific ethnic group can be utilized to generate hypotheses.

However, although an ethnic focus position emphasizes awareness of cultural issues in a person's and family's functioning, it does not provide a conceptual model to help determine how a person's expression and experience of ethnicity can be influenced by a variety of factors, including socioeconomic status, degree of acculturation, religion, and other contextual variables. In addition, an ethnic focus perspective does not provide a conceptual framework to help determine to what extent a person's behavior is a manifestation of pathology, a cultural norm, or a combination of both. Hence, the approach is vulnerable to clinical applications that may minimize these other variables and/or possibilities. An ethnic-focused drug and alcohol therapist might place much emphasis on ethnic-based research findings or writings and would search for culturally congruent and ethnic-specific interventions.

An example of such an approach in the treatment of Hispanic substance abuse clients is outlined by Gloria and Peregoy (1995). These authors describe a model for treatment that stresses the importance of family therapy, gender roles, and a number of variables that are defined as being central to Hispanic cultures (e.g., congeniality, personalism, familism, and spiritualism). Gloria and Peregoy indicate that these factors need to be incorporated into an assessment in order to gain cultural understanding of the sustaining factors in and the attributed meaning of substance use or abuse. The implication of such an approach is that a therapist must incorporate the prescribed approaches and identified variables whenever working with Hispanic clients. Yet an ethnic focus runs the risk of stereotyping and overgeneralizing. This approach does not allow at times for an individualized assessment and intervention; rather, it runs the risk of categorizing the client and his or her problems with prescriptive methodologies. Another potential limitation of such an approach is the belief that therapists who do not have knowledge of the culture or ethnicity of their clients may not be able to effectively work with clients or their families. This limitation is similar to the erroneous belief that an ethnic minority client will always benefit from working with a therapist from the same minority group (Sue, 1988).

Multidimensional Position

Several authors have attempted in the recent past to develop more inclusive and comprehensive models to help mental health providers learn how to think culturally and how to incorporate into their clinical work culturally related constructs in an effective and meaningful manner (Boyd-Franklin, 1989; Falicov, 1988, 1995; Jones, 1985; Sue and Zane, 1987). "A multidimensional position seeks to address the complexities not covered by the previous three positions" (Falicov, 1995, p. 375).

Culture involves differences in worldviews, beliefs, and behaviors that result from the amalgam of contexts and variables that shape each individual's uniqueness from and similarity to others. These variables involve, among others, the person's ethnicity, gender, sexual orientation, education, socioeconomic status, personal experiences, religion, minority status, abilities, and disabilities. The significance of these variables in defining a person's culture can vary depending on the context.

On the basis of this definition of culture it is possible to identify different "cultural groups" in a more varied and fluid manner than by using only an ethnic-focused approach (e.g., first-generation Mexican American males as opposed to just Mexican American). This definition and framework function to define culture in a way that is similar to a camera. If one is interested in taking a picture of a landscape, one can use a wide-angle lens and capture in one frame most of the area in question. But such an approach loses detail. In contrast, if one is interested in taking a picture of a particular part of the landscape, one could use a telephoto lens and capture in the picture the desired area but with the loss of its context.

Defining few parameters of inclusion (e.g., ethnicity) allows generalizations about a specific group, but this approach may lack reliability and validity. On the other hand, if one defines a group's culture utilizing more parameters of inclusion (e.g., ethnicity, nationality, gender, and religion), it becomes more difficult to make generalizations but one's method gains in reliability and accuracy. It is important that the therapist have the ability to approach a client's or family's assessment in a fluid manner.

Sometimes it is helpful to start the assessment process with a wide-angle lens in order to get a global understanding of the potential issues and variables one may need to incorporate in such an assessment (i.e., knowledge of universal information related to the presenting problem and the client's ethnicity). This process, though, needs to be completed by a thorough assessment of individual issues and differences (i.e., particularist focus) utilizing a "telephoto" approach.

Falicov's (1995) "multidimensional comparative framework" is based on the notion that by identifying a family's combination of multiple contexts and partial cultural locations, one can identify or define such a family's ecological niche. The identification of such an ecological niche allows the therapist to identify the family's position relative to dominant cultural values. Falicov (1995) suggests that such analysis be conducted along four key comparative parameters: ecological context (i.e., where and how the family lives), migration and acculturation, family organization (i.e., structure, including composition of the dominant dyad), and family life cycle (i.e., how developmental stages and transitions in the family life cycle are culturally patterned). Falicov's model is extremely useful in that it allows a therapist to understand the complexity of the interplay of different contextual variables in understanding the influence of culture and culturally related variables.

Although this model allows for cross-cultural comparison along the four key parameters, it does not address the importance of also identifying the relative significance of a particular context or parameter in shaping and defining the cognitive and behavioral manifestations of a person's or family's culture.

THE INTEGRATIVE CROSS-CULTURAL MODEL (ICM)

BUILDING ON THE multidimensional perspectives of several authors (Falicov, 1988, 1995; Jones, 1985; Sue, 1988; Zane, 1987), I developed a metamodel that incorporates their strengths, as Falicov recommends (1995), into a "meta position relative to current prevailing theories and techniques" (p. 386). The metamodel is intended to help the therapist integrate the complex individual, family, and culturally related variables that underlie and color the beliefs, cognitions, and behaviors—both adaptive and maladaptive—presented by individuals and families in clinical situations.

The Integrative Cross-Cultural Model (Figure 8–1) is based in part on Jones' model (1985), which was developed with Black American clients. Jones identifies four sets of interactive factors to be considered when working with minority clients: (1) Personal Experiences and Endowments, (2) Influence of Native Culture, (3) Reactions to Racial Oppression, and (4) Influence of the Majority Culture (Jones, 1985).

The relative contributions of each set must be considered in order to understand a client's presenting problem. The ICM expands this approach by defining similar "domains of inquiry," which constitutes a more comprehensive assessment of external and internal influences and organizes them into four main areas: (1) Individual/Systemic Variables and Dynamics, (2) Culturally/Ethnically Related Variables, (3) Dominant Group Influences, and (4) Minority Group Experiences

Individual/Systemic Variables and Dynamics are the factors most clini-

FIGURE 8–1

INTEGRATIVE CROSS-CULTURAL MODEL (ICM)

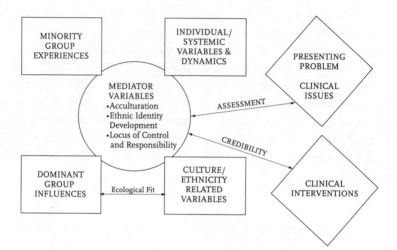

cians incorporate into an assessment: neurobiological conditions, developmental issues, family-of-origin dynamics, childhood experiences, education, and so on. In assessing a drug and alcohol problem, one would question the client about substance use, frequency, presence of tolerance or withdrawal symptoms, alcoholic family dynamics, centrality of alcohol in his or her life, and so on.

Culturally/Ethnically Related Variables comprise the set of beliefs, values, cognitions, and patterns of behavior that are related to or shaped by the client's native culture or ethnic group. In the assessment of substance abuse, variables to consider would include culturally based beliefs about drinking and sobriety, differences in help-seeking behavior, family organization, family life cycle, hierarchies, gender roles, parenting, and so forth.

Dominant Group Influences identify the extent to which the individual or family incorporates beliefs, values, attitudes, and patterns of behavior characteristic of the dominant culture. In the area of substance abuse, we would examine the extent to which the individual's or family's beliefs about alcohol and drug use, misuse, abuse, and dependence are congruent with the dominant society's norms. In addition, we would need to explore the client's family dynamics; his or her beliefs about the subjects of abstinence, sobriety, help-seeking behavior, and the use of twelve-step programs; and the extent to which these are consistent with the dominant group's norms.

Minority Group Experiences refers to the impact of a minority person's or family's exposure to differential treatment by members of the society's dominant group and other minority groups, especially in terms of such variables as personality development, beliefs, attitudes, and the origin and maintenance of the presenting problem. Mexican Americans, like other minority groups, are exposed to discrimination, prejudice, and/or oppression. Whether such incidents are acute and blatant or subtle and pervasive, they can have significant impact on personality development and can sometimes shape a minority individual's sense of self, experience of the environment, and future interactions with members of the dominant group. Because these experiences can have different effects on individuals owing to the many situational, environmental, and personal variables involved, it is important to assess their prevalence and impact on a case-by-case basis. For some individuals and families, exposure to prejudice and discrimination can contribute to the development and maintenance of a substance abuse problem.

While these four lines of inquiry allow the therapist to structure an assessment that discerns the relative impact of many variables on the development and maintenance of the problem, they do not account for the relative contributions of factors grouped within each domain. This limitation is inherent in many culturally comparative models. For example, there may be two Mexican American families with drug- or alcohol-related problems that present similar dynamics and socioeconomic and demographic variables, but the significance or contribution of the culturally related variables may differ between them. Rather than assume that both families need to be treated in a similar manner, we might first determine the relevance of each domain of inquiry so as to individualize the assessment and interventions and avoid generalizing or stereotyping. In this connection we suggest an examination of three important processes as mediator variables.

MEDIATOR VARIABLES

The significance of level of acculturation, ethnic identity development, and worldviews in the assessment and treatment of minority individuals and families has been extensively documented in the literature (Caetano and Mora, 1988; Falicov, 1988, 1995; Marin and Posner, 1995; Neff and Hoppe, 1992; Neff, Hoppe, and Perea, 1987; Sue and Sue, 1990). In the ICM model, these variables are employed as mediators, because they provide a context in which to understand the extent to which a person's subjective experience of self and the environment is shaped by the four domains of inquiry. Individual or family profiles based on the mediator variables can determine the extent to which each of the domains impacts, shapes, or contributes to the maintenance and development of the problem. Such profiles can help the clinician to conceptualize the presenting problem and generate a working hypothesis about how much emphasis to place on each area of inquiry.

ACCULTURATION

A frequently cited definition of acculturation, provided by Redfield, Linton, and Herskovitz (1936), holds that it occurs when members of different cultures come into continuous contact, which results in changes to the original culture pattern of one or both groups. Acculturation is seen as a dynamic, bidirectional sociocultural interaction whereby a person adopts, or fails to adopt, the customs, beliefs, and norms of an alternate culture while retaining, or failing to retain, norms of his or her native culture. The degree of incorporation of the dominant group's norms and values together with the degree of retention of the norms and values of the original culture determines the level or extent of acculturation: traditional, bicultural, or acculturated (Berry, 1980; in Arevalo, 1987; Padilla, 1980). Individuals or families at a traditional level of acculturation preserve the majority of their native customs and values and have not incorporated many of the dominant culture's schemas because of discrimination, inability to learn the language, segregation, or lack of opportunities (Baron and Heras, 1991). The bicultural individual has integrated some of the customs and values of the new culture and retains some of his or her original culture. The success of the blend is determined by the compatibility of the traditional and dominant cultural norms and the amount of effort required to make the change. Acculturated individuals appear to prefer the customs and values of the dominant culture and are often unfamiliar with the customs of their family's native culture.

An individual's level of acculturation has a significant impact on the assessment of the family and its members and, consequently, on the development of an effective intervention plan. Use of acculturation as a mediator variable leads to the hypothesis that when families or individuals are traditional, it will be important for the clinician to examine the culturally or ethnically related variables in order to understand the presenting problem. In such cases, a culturally congruent approach based on knowledge of the client's culture and use of the ethnic focus position may be most appropriate; conversely, if the client appears to be more acculturated, an ethnic focus approach may lead to erroneous generalizations. For more acculturated individuals, variables related to the domain of Dominant Culture Influences may be more useful in conducting an assessment and developing an effective intervention. For Mexican American clients presenting with substance abuse problems, it is imperative to determine the level of acculturation at the outset. If the client exhibits traditional characteristics, it is necessary to evaluate the influence of acculturative stress, marginalization, alienation, lack of opportunity, and social barriers. In addition, the presenting problem should be examined from a cultural perspective that incorporates an understanding of the norms, values, beliefs, and expectations of Mexican American culture. A similar approach, however, would not be successful with an acculturated individual who has a similar substance abuse problem. With such an individual, the values, norms, beliefs, and expectations of the dominant culture may be experienced as more congruent than those ascribed to Mexican American culture.

The assessment of level of acculturation as an initial step is not meant to provide the clinician with a definitive answer about the relevance of the different domains to the presenting problem. Rather, the advantage of conducting the assessment in this manner is that one can develop hypotheses to guide the assessment process while minimizing the possibility of stereotyping. In addition, the assessment of a client's level of acculturation supports an appraisal of the degree of ecological fit between the individual, his or her family, and the dominant group (Falicov, 1988). The greater the dissonance between the family's values, beliefs, and expectations and the dominant group's norms, the more likely the family is to experience conflict and acculturative stress. This stress and lack of fit may, in turn, influence the development or maintenance of substance abuse problems.

Several authors (Ramirez, 1977; Rueschenberg and Buriel, 1995) have suggested that the process of acculturation of Mexican Americans is different from that of other immigrant groups in the United States. Previous assimilationist models of acculturation were based on the experience of European immigrant families at the turn of the century (Rueschenberg and Buriel, 1995). For families of Mexican descent, however, acculturation to U.S. society may be better explained by a bicultural model. As a result of many sociocultural and ethnohistorical variables, Mexican immigrants and their families often exhibit biculturalism, with family life in the home reflecting a more traditional or Mexican orientation and activities in the community reflecting a more dominant group orientation (Rueschenberg and Buriel, 1995).

This alternating biculturalism has important clinical implications.

When assessing the members of a family, it is important to understand that they may exhibit outward characteristics and behaviors of acculturation while their behavior and beliefs within the family are likely to be more traditional. A Mexican American client's beliefs about use, misuse, abuse, and dependence on alcohol and drugs may vary according to his or her degree of acculturation. Even though it may appear that the client holds the dominant group's beliefs about substance abuse because he or she appears to be acculturated—as indicated, for instance, by fluent English—it is possible that the client's beliefs may actually be more consistent with a traditional stance. Members of a family will acculturate at different rates, thereby exacerbating tensions between parents and children, between spouses, and between siblings. Intrafamilial dissonance is not uncommon in first and second-generation immigrant families, because one generation, as a result of their socialization with the dominant culture, may exhibit behavior that is not syntonic with the family's culture of origin. This point of cleavage or lack of fit between the values and beliefs of the dominant culture and those of the culture of origin can result in significant intergenerational conflicts that surface as a variety of seemingly unrelated problems. When assessing a first- or second-generation Mexican American family, it is also important to consider the factors that led to and affected their immigration to this country, as these can also have far-reaching implications (Falicov, 1996).

Ethnic Identity Development

Ethnic identity development is a concept adopted from earlier models that recognize that minority individuals may undergo a developmental process as they attempt to understand their experience as a member of a minority group (Oler, 1989; Sue & Sue, 1990). These models give the clinician a conceptual framework from which to gain an understanding of a minority individual's level of cultural or ethnic identity development and, consequently, a means of better understanding their subjective experience of themselves and the world around them.

The racial/cultural identity development (R/CID) model (Sue and Sue, 1990) provides the clinician with a means of determining clients' perspective on their ethnic identity. The R/CID model comprises five stages, each with four corresponding beliefs and attitudes. "These attitudes/beliefs are an integral part of the minority person's identity and are manifest in how he/she views (a) the self, (b) others of the same minority, (c) others of another minority, and (d) majority individuals" (Sue and Sue, 1990, p. 96).

The five stages are as follows: conformity, dissonance, resistance/immersion, introspection, and integrative awareness (Sue and Sue, 1990 p. 97).

A person's stage of ethnic identity is relevant to treatment. For example, Mexican Americans who are conforming to the dominant culture may actively try to distance themselves from their culture of origin and may try to incorporate the values, expectations, and beliefs of the dominant culture as they understand them. Such individuals may seek out a clinician from the dominant group owing to their belief in the superiority of the dominant group. For clients manifesting conformity-stage characteristics, the Culture/Ethnic Related Variables domain may be less helpful to the clinician in developing a comprehensive conceptual understanding of the presenting problem. Also, clients may attempt to minimize the variables related to the fourth domain, Minority Group Experiences, because of their need to downgrade that which makes them different from the dominant group. In contrast, clients manifesting characteristics congruent with the resistance/immersion stage of ethnic identity development (R/CID) may exhibit a clear preference for working with a minority therapist. Such clients' substance abuse problems may also be related to tensions and conflicts associated with their experiences of mistrust and tension with dominant group individuals or institutions. For such individuals, the second and fourth domains acquire more significance in the clinician's attempts to understand the presenting problem and its context; the third domain, Dominant Group Influences, in turn, may not be as useful, other than to identify beliefs and expectations that the person may reject or actively resist. When working with an individual in the resistance/immersion stage, it becomes imperative to address these issues as part of the assessment process in order to determine the need to develop therapeutic interventions that will be received as useful rather than actively resisted because they represent the views of "them" rather than "us." As clinicians assess their clients' level of R/CID they should bear in mind that an individual may not progress through each of the R/CID stages in order and that one stage is not necessarily more desirable than another. Actually, R/CID can frequently be thought of more usefully as a contextual set of responses than as a developmental process. Therefore, it is recommended that R/CID be appraised as part of a comprehensive assessment process not only to determine the impact that the individual's experiences as a minority group member may have had in the development of the problem but also to help develop hypotheses about the relative impact that the variables related to each one of the four domains may have had in the development and maintenance of such a problem.

TABLE 8–1

RACIAL/CULTURAL IDENTITY DEVELOPMENT MODEL

Stage One: Conformity
1. Preference for dominant culture values
2. Lacks awareness of an ethnic perspective
3. May exhibit negative attitudes toward self and others who are members of an ethnic minority group
4. May accept and believe stereotypes prevalent in society about self and group
5. Naïveté with regard to issues of integration, prejudice, and differential treatment

Stage Two: Dissonance
1. Experiences confusion and conflict about values and beliefs developed in Stage One, a process that may be gradual or precipitated by external events
2. Actively questions dominant culture values
3. Becomes aware of issues involving racism, sexism, and oppression
4. Identifies with the history of own culture group
5. Has feelings of anger and loss
6. Seeks sense of belonging

Stage Three: Resistance/Immersion
1. Actively and forcefully rejects and distrusts the dominant culture
2. Demonstrates greater identification with own culture group
3. Immerses in own group's ethnic history, traditions, foods, language, etc.
4. Begins to exhibit activist behavior with motivation toward combating oppression, racism, and sexism
5. Might separate from the dominant culture
6. May develop prejudices toward majority group

Stage Four: Introspection
1. Questions rigid rejection of dominant culture values
2. Experiences conflict and confusion regarding loyalty to one's own cultural group and personal autonomy
3. Struggles for self-awareness continuously

Stage Five: Integrative Awareness

1. Resolves many of the conflicts of Stage Four
2. Has a sense of fulfillment regarding personal cultural identity
3. Increased appreciation for other cultural groups, as well as for dominant cultural values
4. Selectively accepts or rejects dominant culture values based upon prior experience
5. Is motivated to eliminate all forms of oppression

Adapted with permission from *Counseling the Culturally Different* (2nd ed.) by D. W. Sue and D. Sue. New York: Wiley, 1990.

WORLDVIEW: LOCUS OF CONTROL AND RESPONSIBILITY

Sue and Sue (1990) point out that "it has become increasingly clear that many minority persons hold views different from members of the dominant culture" (p. 137). Furthermore, how people perceive their relationship to the world and their environment appears to be correlated with their cultural upbringing and life experiences. Several models and frameworks have been advanced for understanding differences among individuals and groups with regard to worldviews (Ibrahim, 1985; Kluckhohn and Strodtbeck, 1961). One such model attempts to integrate the way in which ethnicity and culture-specific factors may interact to produce differences in worldview among peoples from diverse backgrounds (Sue and Sue, 1990). This model identifies two factors that are important in understanding people with different psychological orientations.

Locus of Control. This dimension is based on the idea that people adopt one of two perspectives pertaining to their belief about their ability to control themselves and the world around them. For example, individuals with an internal locus of control believe that they can shape their own fate whereas those with an external locus of control believe that the future is determined by forces beyond their control, such as luck or chance. Individuals with an internal locus of control present traits and characteristics that are highly valued in U.S. society, such as such as being strongly motivated to succeed and being deeply involved in social activities (Sue and Sue, 1990).

Locus of Responsibility. This dimension, based on attributional theory, measures the degree of responsibility or blame placed on the individual or the system. Individuals with an internal locus of responsibility believe that their successes or failures are due to their own efforts or shortcomings whereas individuals with an external locus of responsibility believe that regardless of what they do, their successes or failures are determined by social, cultural, or environmental forces (Sue and Sue, 1990). Gaining an understanding of a client's psychological orientation pertaining to these two dimensions of worldview can help the clinician understand how the client experiences the presenting problem and its possible solutions. For instance, if a woman with a substance abuse problem has an external locus of control and responsibility, she may feel impotent to change her condition owing to the indomitable forces she feels she is facing. She may blame her drinking on the fact that she is a minority individual who constantly experiences prejudice and discrimination. Taken to an extreme, such an individual may not only learn that she is helpless in the face of perceived negative societal forces but she may come to expect such helplessness and may in effect give up trying to control situations that may in fact be controllable. For such an individual, drinking may also become a means of escaping some of the difficulties associated with this problem.

In addition to aiding in the conceptualization of the problem, an assessment of the client's worldview may help the clinician identify potential problems he or she may encounter with treatment. For example, minority individuals with external loci of control and responsibility may see their relationship with a dominant-group clinician as representative of the relationship between the dominant and minority groups and may not take seriously the clinician's efforts to instill in them a sense of control over the course of their lives (Sue and Sue, 1990). In addition, such individuals may interpret their substance abuse problems as being externally motivated (i.e., fate, bad luck), which in turn may lead them to feel that there is no point in seeking help. Sue and Sue further point out that racism and oppression are important contributors to a minority person's worldview.

MEXICAN AMERICAN FAMILIES

ATTEMPTS TO INCORPORATE knowledge of Hispanic culture and research on Mexican Americans into clinical work can lead to stereotyping and overgeneralization. However, this knowledge can be valuable if it is utilized within a multidimensional perspective to better understand the behaviors, beliefs, patterns of interactions, responses, and emotions of the individuals we are treating. Some of the elements of a multidimensional perspective are described in terms of how they may impact the development, maintenance, and treatment of substance abuse problems in Mexican American families.

Although Mexican Americans have been the subject of inquiry for several decades, the existing literature does not yield a clear picture of this group's characteristics and patterns of functioning (Rueschenberg and Buriel, 1995). Empirical studies have revealed that there is a great degree of within-group variability, which is due in part to differences in level of acculturation, education, and ethnic identity development.

Two important internal aspects of functioning differentiate Mexican American families from the prototypic American nuclear family. First, Mexican American families are typically embedded in an extended family network (Falicov and Karrer, 1980). Strong ties with siblings and extended family members are stressed and valued throughout life. Family members are expected to share in the family's functioning, adaptation, survival, and responsibilities. Affiliation and the incorporation of these values are supported by clear hierarchies. Mexican American men and women, as well as children, try to achieve smooth, pleasant relationships that avoid conflict. These relationships in turn are based on *respeto*, a Spanish term that means more than "respect." It denotes elements of emotional dependence and dutifulness that are not as clearly conveyed by the English word. Indirect, implicit, or covert communication is consonant with Mexicans' emphasis on family harmony, on getting along and not making others uncomfortable; assertiveness, openly expressing differences of opinion, and demanding clarification are seen as rude or insensitive to others' feelings.

The second internal aspect of functioning that characterizes Mexican families is the importance of the mother–child relationship as the central family dyad (Falicov, 1988). The centrality of the mother–child dyad appears to be rooted in Mexican history. Ninety percent of modern Mexico's population is *mestizo* (mixed Indian and Spaniard heritage). Alan Riding (1986), in his book *Distant Neighbors*, wrote, "On August 13, 1521, heroically defended by Cuauhtemoc, Tlatelolco fell into the hands of Hernan Cortes. It was neither a triumph or a defeat: it was the painful birth of the mestizo nation that is Mexico today" (p. 3). Mexico's *mestizaje* began with the mating of Spanish men and Indian women. These relationships were not based on a need for procreation (many of the Spaniards already had families back in Spain) but rather on a need to gratify sexual desires. The children born from these relationships grew up in a family environment in which the father was rejecting and distant. In contrast, the mother was perceived as nurturing, mistreated, dominated, and abnegated. Since she could not expect to have the father figure satisfy her needs for companionship, partnership, and support, she concentrated all of her caring, nurturing, and affectional needs on her children, especially male children, who in a way filled the void created by the absent male figure. *Mestizo* children experienced much conflict and confusion in this environment, as well as difficulties with identification. They re-created in their own families what was observed at home and perpetuated the dynamic (Ramirez, 1977; Riding, 1984).

From a family systems perspective, this history suggests a possible origin for the centrality of the mother–child dyad in Mexican families, as well as for other dynamics, such as *machismo*. This internal aspect is important to understand, because many principles of family organization (i.e., rules, roles, expectations, and types of family subsystems) vary depending on the dominant dyad (Falicov, 1988). It is not uncommon to find that a Mexican American's expectations are different from those that characterize American culture. These differences in turn color and shape the way a family may experience and respond to a family member's substance abuse problems.

An external aspect of functioning that is central to understanding Mexican American families is religion. Roman Catholicism provides continuity for more than 90 percent of Mexican Americans (Falicov, 1996.) Catholic beliefs reinforce the ethnohistorically based expectations for the roles played by men and women in relationships and within the family. Folk medicine and indigenous spirituality may coexist with mainstream religion and medical practice. For example, *curanderos* (folk healers) are consulted for many maladies and are often trusted for sicknesses with psychological components. The coexistence of Catholicism and folk practices also has its roots in ethnohistory. After the conquest, the Spaniards initiated the task of converting the native population. The result of this process can be observed in current Mexican religious practices, which reflect the influence both of the Spaniards' Catholicism and of the native population beliefs. The Virgin of Guadalupe, Mexico's most important religious figure, exemplifies the ideal characteristics of every Mexican's mother (i.e., devoted to her children, saintly, abnegated, nurturing) (Ramirez, 1977; Riding, 1984). One can still see traces of the native population's beliefs in folk healing practices and the idolization of saints. Understanding the Mexican and Mexican American religious and spiritual belief system can be of great significance in the assessment and intervention of substance abuse problems.

TREATMENT CONSIDERATIONS

When a Mexican American family seeks services for substance abuse problems, it is necessary for the clinician to first assess level of acculturation, ethnic identity development, and worldview. This assessment allows the clinician to construct a profile that in turn will help guide the evaluation process and the development of a culturally congruent treatment plan.

ACCULTURATION

Although Mexican Americans may exhibit a more acculturated set of behaviors in their interactions with the dominant group, it is possible that at home they may manifest behaviors and beliefs that are more traditional and congruent with Hispanic culture (Rueschenberg and Buriel, 1995). The more traditional their values, the more important it is to consider ethnic and cultural variables in the development and maintenance of the problem behavior. In addition, the process of acculturation itself and the potential differences in degree of acculturation among family members become sources of conflict often contributing to substance abuse problems (Arevalo, 1987; Falicov, 1988; Ruiz and Langrod, 1997).

Mexican Americans with a more traditional degree of acculturation may ascribe little credibility to the therapeutic process, because in Mexican culture mental health services have not achieved the level of acceptance that is more characteristic of the dominant culture. For a Mexican American, the need to seek help for a substance abuse problem may feel incongruent and undesirable. There is a Mexican saying that *la ropa sucia se lava en casa* (dirty clothes should be washed at home). Moreover, one often finds among Mexican Americans an attitude of permissiveness that encourages the use of alcohol among men and discourages them from seeking help for alcohol addiction from outsiders (Smith-Peterson 1983; Riding, 1984; Ruiz and Langrod, 1997). Drinking tends to be associated with socializing and celebrating, and it also allows for the expression of otherwise unacceptable emotions (i.e., pain, sadness, weakness). "Although being drunk, high, or inebriated is not glorified, the macho attitude does suggest that a man should be able to drink and hold his liquor. The more he can do this, the more of a man he is . . . if a man admits that he cannot handle his liquor, that he has a drinking problem, he is then also admitting that he doesn't have control. This may be experienced as an admission of weakness" (Smith-Peterson, 1983, p. 375).

As part of the initial assessment, then, the therapist identifies the extent to which the client and family subscribe to traditional Mexican beliefs about alcohol and drinking. Such beliefs may color the client's ascription of credibility to a therapist who questions alcohol consumption. In working with Mexican American males, it is important to remember that apparent resistance to treatment may be rooted in an unwillingness to admit a lack of control or weakness and that it may be necessary to reframe the problem as an issue that feels more credible to the client.

The process of "motivational interviewing," with its emphasis on a directive, client-centered style, has proven effective for helping clients explore and resolve ambivalence about changing their substance abuse patterns (Rollnick and Morgan, 1995). An important component of motivational interviewing is the process of exposing a discrepancy, for example, between future goals and current behavior (Rollnick and Morgan, 1995). Although *machismo*-related attitudes and beliefs may make it difficult for some Mexican American males to acknowledge the need for change, *machismo* also involves a "father's dedication to his children and his responsibility for the family's well being" (Falicov, 1996, p. 176). Thus, the desirable meanings of *machismo* can be utilized to help a client question the discrepancy between these positive role expectations and the negative impact that his drinking has on the fulfillment of his responsibilities. From this perspective, *machismo* may become a bridge, rather than an obstacle, to developing readiness for change.

Mexican American women too may find it difficult to seek help with a substance abuse problem. Although men's drinking may be socially sanctioned, women are restricted from drinking (Gilbert and Cervantes, 1986a; Padilla and Salgado de Snyder, 1995). It is not uncommon to observe family members sanctioning a father's or son's drinking and harshly castigating a mother's or daughter's drinking. In fact, a traditionally acculturated Mexican American woman will expect to be subjected to a double standard and to be judged more harshly than males.

Ethnic Identity Development

The integrative cross-cultural model (ICM) stresses the need to evaluate the client's ethnic identity development (EID). Many Mexican Americans experience episodes of prejudice, discrimination, or differential treatment. These experiences echo the discrimination that is also prevalent in Mexico, where people can be treated differently based on the color of their skin or their ancestry. Exposure to differential treatment can affect one's sense of ethnic identity and one's vulnerability to psychosocial problems. As Falicov (1996), quoting Padilla, writes, "Many social ills that affect minorities who have been discriminated against, such as drugs, alcohol, teen pregnancy, domestic violence, gangs and AIDS, are visited upon Mexican Americans; they appear even more frequently in the second and third generations than in the first" (Padilla, 1995, p. 173).

When clients present with beliefs regarding their ethnic identity and the dominant group that are consistent with either the dissonance or the resistant/immersion stages of EID, it is important to consider the contribution Minority Group Experiences may have in the development and maintenance of the problem behavior. Individuals in the dissonance and resistance/immersion stages of EID are characterized by questioning, confusion, possible mistrust of the dominant group, a need to identify with their own group or culture, and at times an "us versus them" attitude or feeling. When such individuals are exposed to these experiences, they may at times utilize alcohol or drugs to numb themselves, that is, to find refuge or relief from what may be experienced as a hostile, unwelcoming, or discriminating environment. Feelings of resistance and dissonant expectations may influence clients' perceptions of the clinician's credibility, especially if the clinician is perceived or experienced as a representative of the dominant group. Under these conditions, the process of establishing a trusting therapeutic relationship may be difficult to achieve unless these issues and their current manifestations are openly addressed with the client.

Mexican American clients with substance abuse problems who manifest behaviors consistent with the conformity stage of EID will most likely exhibit a different set of behaviors and expectations than those just described. Such individuals may have come to accept the stereotypes prevalent in society about themselves and their group, may display a naïveté regarding issues of integration and differential treatment, may exhibit a preference for dominant cultural values, and may lack an ethnic/cultural perspective. They may end up developing difficulties with self-esteem. If a substance abuse problem is present, it is probably related to self-deprecating beliefs and feelings. For such individuals, the therapist's ethnicity may not be as significant a factor. In fact, they may actually prefer to work with a member of the dominant group.

Clients who exhibit attitudes consistent with Stages 4 (introspection) and 5 (integrative awareness) of EID have come to be more selective in their beliefs. Their attitudes regarding self, their own group, and the dominant group are most likely contextual and more fluid than the attitudes of those in earlier stages of EID and depend on ecological, experiential, and personal factors.

WORLDVIEW: LOCUS OF CONTROL AND RESPONSIBILITY

The ICM proposes worldview as the third mediator variable for the clinician to consider in the assessment process. An examination of clients' locus of control and locus of responsibility indicates a systemic relationship between (1) the way in which they may conceptualize their substance abuse problem, (2) their help-seeking behavior, and (3) their worldview (which in turn can be influenced by the person's difficulties with substance abuse). For example, Mexican American clients with an external locus of control and an internal locus of responsibility are most likely going to manifest dynamics and characteristics consistent with the EID conformity stage (Sue and Sue, 1990). It may be helpful for such individuals to identify the extent to which their efforts to acculturate and their confusion with regard to their own culture may be contributing to their substance abuse problem. Mexican American individuals who believe in external control and external responsibility may feel a sense of helplessness or hopelessness about the difficulties and stressors they are experiencing with regard to their minority status and may respond by giving up. Drinking or using drugs is, of course, but one way in which people may end up coping with these feelings in an effort to seek relief. For such individuals, the consequences of drinking may come to reinforce their feelings of helplessness and worthlessness, which in turn may further exacerbate their drinking problem. In an effort to help these clients effectively address their drinking problem, it may be necessary to acknowledge their experience as a member of a minority group and to help identify ways of coping in a more adaptive manner.

THE IMPORTANCE OF FAMILY AND FAMILY THERAPY

Over the last sixty years, family models that address substance abuse have evolved into complex and comprehensive paradigms that emphasize the multiple determinants of substance use disorders, the multiple factors that maintain these disorders, and the complex interrelationships between the substance user and the family (McCrady and Epstein, 1996). Chemical dependency is currently conceptualized by some authors as a "biopsychosocial disorder whose occurrence, longevity, severity, and response to treatment are largely influenced by familial and social factors" (Stellato-Kabat, Stellato-Kabat, and Garrett, 1995, p. 314). In the absence of awareness of disease or when social or cultural norms condone or permit the abuse of a substance, families display a tendency to adapt to the resulting dysfunction by integrating the sickness into everyday life. Stellato-Kabat, Stellato-Kabat, and Garrett (1995) state:

> In the case of chemical dependency, this adaptation is reflected in the integration into family life of routine abusive drinking and drugging

and the family's accompanying patterns of denial, minimization, and rationalization. The popular term codependency reflects the family's adaptive strategy for maintaining family functioning. (P. 315)

The family and its interactions are the basis of Mexican culture (Falicov, 1996; Rueschenberg and Buriel, 1995). Affiliation and cooperation are stressed, and these values are in turn supported by clear hierarchies in which men are usually the undisputed figures of authority. It is also expected that family members will try to achieve smooth and pleasant relationships that avoid confrontation and conflict. The use of indirect, implicit, or covert communication is consonant with Mexican American families' emphasis on harmony (Falicov, 1996; Sue and Sue, 1990). It is not uncommon, then, that when a Mexican American develops a substance abuse or dependence problem, the family's "culturally congruent" behaviors and responses may come to exacerbate the problem and contribute to the development of what Steinglass, Bennet, Reiss, and Wolin (1987) describe as the "alcoholic family." In other words, the behavior of the chemically dependent person shapes the compensatory and defensive behaviors and patterns of interaction of the rest of the family. Since, as previously stated, Mexican American males are more likely to exhibit problems with alcohol abuse and dependence than are Mexican American women (Gilbert and Cervantes, 1986b) and since in Mexican American families it is not unusual to observe a hierarchy based on gender that is rooted in ethnohistorical factors, it is to be expected that family members may not be able to address openly or confront the substance abuse problem.

FIGURE 8-2

	MARITAL DYAD	INTERGENERATIONAL DYAD (Traditional Mexican American Family)
Principles of Organization		
(Nuclear Family)	Marital Bond Discontinuity	Intergenerational bond Continuity
(Extended Family)	Exclusiveness Symmetry	Inclusiveness of others Complementarity
Marital Relationship is characterized by:		
Boundaries	Clear and firm Equal proximity to children	Clear but permeable Unequal proximity to children

FIGURE 8–2 *(continued)*

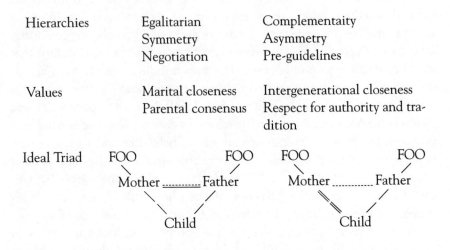

	MARITAL DYAD	INTERGENERATIONAL DYAD (Traditional Mexican American Family)
Hierarchies	Egalitarian Symmetry Negotiation	Complementaity Asymmetry Pre-guidelines
Values	Marital closeness Parental consensus	Intergenerational closeness Respect for authority and tra- dition

Adapted with permission from "Learning to Think Culturally in Family Therapy Training" by C. J. Falicov. In H. Liddle, D. Breunlin, and D. Schwartz (Eds.), *Handbook of Family Therapy Training and Supervision.* New York: Guilford Press, 1988.

Actually, it would be culturally congruent for family members to attempt to placate the alcoholic and adjust to the behavior if it is exhibited by the head of the household, who is perceived as the undisputed authority figure. These dynamics in family members could in turn be labeled by a clinician as codependency and enabling. Although descriptively it is possible that this may be an accurate statement, subjectively it may be incongruent for some Mexican American women to hear that their culturally rooted responses are pathological or inappropriate. Likewise, culturally based beliefs may make it difficult for the Mexican American man to recognize the dysfunctional aspects of his drinking behavior if, in his mind, he is fulfilling his role as provider. Previously outlined research findings (Gilbert and Cervantes, 1986a, 1986b; Ruiz and Langrod, 1997; Smith-Peterson, 1983) indicate that Mexican American males may perceive their drinking as being socially sanctioned and expected, may manifest a greater incidence of intoxication episodes, and may tend to minimize the significance of their drinking behavior even when it becomes problematic. A man may feel a sense of entitlement to do as he sees fit, as long as he fulfills his obligations as head of the household. In my clinical practice, I have consulted on many occasions with Mexican American women who approach extended family members for advice in an effort to seek support from them because of their husband's alcoholism. It is not uncommon for them to hear this response: "As long as you have a home, a husband that returns to you, and food on the table, what are you complaining about?" Such dynamics may create a reality for the family where the pain, confusion, and despair associated with the drinking behavior is not openly discussed (sometimes not even acknowledged) or is minimized. In addition, they may lead to the development in family members of compensatory behaviors and roles (e.g., overfunctioning) that are, at the same time, culturally congruent but dysfunctional, in that they further exacerbate and perpetuate the problem behaviors.

Considering the above-mentioned dynamics and the fact that research findings suggest that Mexican Americans who exhibit alcohol or substance abuse problems have more stable family environments than addicts from other ethnic groups (Gilbert and Cervantes, 1986b), the significance of family therapy as a desirable unit of treatment is clear. Family therapy is congruent with the value system of the Mexican American culture. Several authors (Steinglass et al., 1988; Stellato-Kabat et al., 1995) have proposed treatment models to use in work with families afflicted by substance abuse. The principles outlined in those models could be very effective with Mexican American families. However, one should also focus on the role mediator variables may have in the development and maintenance of the problem, on the ascribed and achieved credibility of the therapeutic interventions, and on the difficulties that the individual and family may have in acknowledging the need for help. As previously stated, motivational interviewing techniques may be of great help in increasing the individuals and family's readiness for change. In addition, knowledge of culturally based values may help the clinician reframe obstacles into opportunities. For example, the value placed by Mexican Americans on family loyalty and interdependence—which, as we have seen, could on the one hand lead to the development of enabling behavior—could be used to recruit family members to help in the addicted member's recovery, that is, they can be encouraged to see that this is a preferable way of being loyal and fulfilling one's role within the family. In addition, it may be helpful to remember that for many Mexican American families the intergenerational dyad is the primary principle of organization. An understanding of the dynamics that characterize such family structure (see Figure 8–2) may guide the clinician to intervene in a culturally congruent manner. For example, it may be frequently useful to consider the incorporation of extended family members in family treatment when such intervention may be useful and appropriate.

Once an individual and his or her family acknowledge the need for help, twelve-step groups may be suggested as a congruent intervention. Catholicism has significantly influenced the development of Mexican culture. Many Mexican Americans may find twelve-step groups congruent with their religious beliefs and their spiritual convictions. Utilizing the mediator variable profile (see Figure 8–1) will help clients identify the group they may experience as being most beneficial. For some, this will be a Spanish-speaking group; others may prefer to attend a group with people from the dominant culture.

Mediator variables can be utilized by the clinician to customize such interventions, to make appropriate use of cultural knowledge, and to utilize in a culturally congruent manner the information that has been generated by research and other clinicians' experiences.

CASE STUDY

The following case example illustrates the use of the ICM model in the assessment and treatment of a Mexican American family:

Mr. and Mrs. Deleon, a first-generation Mexican American couple, called to make an appointment with me at the insistence of their seven-year-old son's teacher. Mr. Deleon was born and raised in a small town in the state of Jalisco. He worked in construction and had a tenth-grade education. He was fluent in English but preferred to communicate in Spanish with his wife and family. Mrs. Deleon was born and raised in the border town of Tijuana. She was the youngest of eight siblings and worked half-time as a housekeeper. During the initial interview, Mr. and Mrs. Deleon stated that their son, Raul, had been experiencing some behavioral problems at school. Although he was doing well academically, his behaviors had become very disruptive in the classroom during the last year. Mr. and Mrs. Deleon indicated that they had also observed some of those disruptive behaviors at home. They were concerned that Raul was now hitting his younger sister and was constantly fighting with his older brother. In describing the problem, Mr. Deleon expressed frustration and concern over the fact that his son was being so disrespectful. The parents reported that in addition to their three children, Mrs. Deleon's mother also lived with them. She had moved in after her husband died and helped Mrs. Deleon by caring for the children and doing the housework while Mrs. Deleon was at work.

After the initial appointment, Mrs. Deleon called to confirm the time for a follow-up session. During the phone conversation, she disclosed her concerns about her husband's excessive drinking. She also stated that she believed this was part of the reason why her son was acting out. She explained that lately Mr. Deleon had been spending more and more time drinking during weekends and was failing to fulfill his promises to take the children on outings. In addition, the children had witnessed them arguing on several occasions. Mrs. Deleon denied any incidents of abuse or domestic violence and stated that she was not afraid of her husband. When questioned, she explained that she did not bring this information up during the intake interview because she did not know how to address it. Mrs. Deleon agreed to discuss her concerns with her husband during the following appointment.

In the course of the second appointment, Mrs. Deleon was able to tell her husband that she had called me to express her concerns about his drinking. He became annoyed but expressed a willingness to address the issue—to prove that he did not have a drinking problem. Mr. Deleon continually stated during this interview that none of his behaviors interfered with his responsibilities and obligations to his family. With pride he indicated that he worked hard to provide his family with a good life. He explained that he liked to go out and drink with his coworkers three or four afternoons a week and that during weekends he relaxed by drinking beer. He indicated that he worked hard and did not see a problem with the idea of having some time to unwind with his friends before coming home. He also explained that work was stressful and demanding. While talking about his job, he explained that he had a good relationship with his coworkers, most of whom were also Mexican American. However, he reported some problems and tension with his supervisor and the owner of the company. He stated, "You know how it is here in America: we do the hard work but the gringos make the big money."

Assessment Using the ICM

As previously stated, the ICM (see Figure 8–1) directs the clinician first to construct a profile utilizing the three mediator variables. This profile in turn allows the clinician to hypothesize about the possible contribution of each one of the four domains of inquiry (Individual/Systemic variables, Cultural/Ethnic variables, Dominant Group Influences, and Minority Group Experiences) to the development and maintenance of the client's presenting problem.

The information collected during the intake interview indicated that Mr. and Mrs. Deleon were first-generation Mexican American immigrants who, like many other immigrants, were exhibiting a bicultural and alternating degree of acculturation. The family structure, the couple's preference to speak Spanish with each other, and their description of the problem further suggested that they probably exhibited behaviors at home and harbored expectations that were consistent with a more traditional level of acculturation. In addition, it was also clear that family members were exhibiting different degrees of acculturation. Mrs. Deleon's mother spoke only Spanish and was most likely at a traditional stage. On the other hand, the children, although also bicultural, were most likely more acculturated than their parents. Mr. Deleon's statements about the majority group and his feelings about work pointed to the possibility that he harbored feelings and beliefs consistent with the dissonance or resistance/immersion stage of EID. His statements during the initial assessment also pointed to an external locus sense of control and an external locus of responsibility. This worldview orientation suggested that he perceived the difficulties and conditions in his environment as inevitable and placed responsibility on the system or on external factors.

Mr. Deleon's profile led to the development of a number of hypotheses that in turn helped guide the assessment and treatment plan. A thorough exploration of the variables related to the first domain, Individual/Systemic variables, revealed that Mr. Deleon's drinking pattern was consistent with a DSM-IV diagnosis for Alcohol Dependence (American Psychiatric Association, 1994). In addition, it was learned that Mr. Deleon had been exposed to alcoholism in his family of origin. His family background and the fact that he grew up in a culture that was more tolerant of his excessive drinking were factors that contributed to his minimization of the problem. Mr. Deleon's worldview was also consistent with his drinking and suggested that this behavior served, at least in part, the function of helping him cope with an environment that he perceived as stressful, nonsupportive, and discriminatory, an environment over which he felt he had little or no control. The assessment of the family's acculturation indicated that variables related to the second domain, Cultural/Ethnic variables, were of great significance in understanding the presenting problem. From this perspective, Mrs. Deleon's behavior and her effort to share her concerns about her husband's drinking were assessed as being culturally congruent, suggesting that the family's expectations and beliefs with regard to Mr. Deleon's drinking needed to be thoroughly assessed (i.e., What role did Mrs. Deleon play at home? Did she experience a need or pressure not to confront her husband? Did she perceive her husband's behavior as congruent with her beliefs and socialization? Was her way of responding to her husband's problem leading her to enable his drinking?). In addition, it was determined that Mr. Deleon's minimization of his drinking problem needed to be understood in the context of Mexican culture's more lenient beliefs and attitudes toward male alcohol drinking patterns. The role played by extended family members was also hypothesized as an important area of assessment. Of great concern was the family's potential to respond to the problem through culturally congruent behaviors that were likely to perpetuate the dysfunction by creating an enabling environment. Despite the fact that the family was working with a bilingual Hispanic therapist, the level of ascribed credibility was hypothesized as being low. This hypothesis stemmed from the assessment of Mr. and Mrs. Deleon's degree of acculturation, from the fact that the family did not self-refer, and from the fact that the family identified Raul as the patient. In addition, it was hypothesized, given the couple's level of acculturation, that seeking help from a professional to address such private matters as Mr. Deleon's drinking would probably not feel congruent with their accustomed ways of managing problems. The information generated by the assessment of Mr. Deleon's level of EID suggested that variables related to the third domain of the ICM, Minority Group Experiences, needed to be thoroughly explored and considered in the formulation of the problem. It was clear that Mr. Deleon was harboring some feelings of resentment, which probably were contributing to his drinking. His problems with adaptation to a new culture and environment were also hypothesized as an area in need of intervention. In addition, his perceptions with regard to issues related to recovery, abstinence, rehabilitation services, treatment and so on needed to be identified to ensure that the proposed interventions were not experienced as incongruent, thus further lowering the clinician's level of credibility for this client.

Many of the above-mentioned hypotheses were confirmed in the context of the treatment. The initial emphasis was placed on building credibility. Motivational interviewing techniques were utilized to help build discrepancy, that is, to help Mr. Deleon see the contrast between his perception of what his role as a father and provider needed to be and the negative impact that his drinking was having on his family, especially his son. In addition, Mr. Deleon and his wife received psychoeducation and a "professional's confirmation" that his drinking was indeed a serious problem. From this perspective, Raul's behavior was reframed as an attempt on his part to communicate to his father the distress and concern he was experiencing, rather than as evidence of a lack of respect. Mrs. Deleon's behavior (i.e., talking with me privately about her husband's drinking) was reframed as a manifestation of the conflict she was experiencing between the respect she had for her husband and the concern she had for his well-being. In an effort to join with Mr. Deleon, I initially placed emphasis on acknowledging the great deal of pressure he was experiencing. With help he was able to realize that his work environment was recreating for him some of the dynamics he had experienced growing up in an alcoholic family with an unresponsive and at times abusive father. Once greater credibility was established, Mr. Deleon agreed to a trial of abstinence. He was sure he would be able to control his drinking for three weeks. His inability to do so helped me emphasize the fact that he had a problem that required help. He agreed to attend AA meetings, and the family continued participating in family sessions. Needless to say, Raul's problems disappeared shortly thereafter.

This case illustrates the fact that the ICM can be useful at the initial phase of treatment, when the clinician is conducting an assessment, building a therapeutic alliance, and developing a treatment plan with an ethnically or culturally diverse client or family. It is during this initial stage of treatment that knowing "how to think culturally" (Falicov, 1988) is of great significance. Knowledge of culture can only be effective if clinicians have a conceptual framework that allows them to utilize such information in an effective and individualized manner.

REFERENCES

American Psychiatric Association. (1994). *Diagnostic and Statistical Manual of Mental Disorders* (4th ed.). Washington, DC: American Psychiatric Association.

Aponte, J. F., Crouch, R. T. (1995). The Changing Ethnic People of the United States. In J. F. Aponte, R. Y. Rivers, & J. Wohl (Eds.), *Psychological Intervention and Cultural Diversity*. Boston: Allyn and Bacon.

Arevalo, L. E. (1987). Distress and Its Relationship to Acculturation Among Mexican Americans. Doctoral dissertation, California School of Professional Psychology, San Diego.

Barón, M., & Heras, P. (1991, November 1–8). *Acculturation*. Academy of San Diego Psychologists Newsletter.

Boyd-Franklin, N. (1989). *Black Families in Therapy*. New York: Guilford Press.

Caetano, R., & Mora, M. (1988). Acculturation and Drinking Among People of Mexican Descent in Mexico and the United States. *Journal of Studies on Alcohol, 49*(5), 462–471.

Cheung, F. K. (1991). The Use of Mental Health Services by Ethnic Minorities. In H. F. Myers, P. Wohlford, & L. P. Echeoredia (Eds.), *Ethnic Minority Perspectives on Clinical Training and Services in Psychology*. Washington, DC: American Psychological Association.

Falicov, C. J. (1988). Learning to Think Culturally in Family Therapy Training. In H. Liddle, D. Breunlin, & D. Schwartz (Eds.), *Handbook of Family Therapy Training and Supervision*. New York: Guilford Press.

Falicov, C. J. (1995). Training to Think Culturally: A Multidimensional Comparative Framework. *Family Process, 34*, 323–388.

Falicov, C. J. (1996). Mexican Families. In M. McGoldrick, J. Giordano, & J. Pearce (Eds.), *Ethnicity and Family Therapy* (pp. 169–182) (2nd ed.). New York: Guilford Press.

Falicov, C. J., & Karrer, B. (1980). Cultural Variations in the Family Life Cycle: The Mexican-American Family. In E. Carter & M. McGoldrick (Eds.), *The Family Life Cycle: A Framework for Family Therapy*. New York: Gardner Press.

Gilbert, M. J., & Cervantes, R. C. (1986a). Alcohol Services for Mexican Americans: A Review of Utilization Patterns, Treatment Considerations and Prevention Activities. *Hispanic Journal of Behavioral Sciences, 8*, 191–223.

Gilbert, M. J., & Cervantes, R. C. (1986b). Patterns and Practices of Alcohol Use Among Mexican-Americans: A Comprehensive Review. *Hispanic Journal of Behavioral Sciences, 8*, 1–60.

Gloria, A. M., & Peregoy, J. J. (1995). Counseling Latino Alcohol and Other Substance Users/Abusers. *Journal of Substance Abuse Treatment, 13*, 119–126.

Holmes, S. A. (1998, August 16). Figuring Out Hispanic Influence. *The New York Times*.

Ibrahim, F. A. (1985). Effective Cross-Cultural Counseling and Psychotherapy: A Framework. *The Counseling Psychologist, 13*, 625–638.

Jones, A. C. (1985). Psychological Functioning in Black Americans: A Conceptual Guide for Use in Psychotherapy. *Psychotherapy, 22*, 363–369.

Kluckhohn, F. R., & Strodtbeck, F. L. (1961). *Variations in Value Orientations*. Evanston, Il: Row, Patterson.

Marin, G., & Posner, S. F. (1995). Role of Gender and Acculturation on Determining the Consumption of Alcoholic Beverages Among Mexican Americans and Central Americans in the United States. *International Journal of Addictions, 30*(7), 779–794.

McCrady, B. S., & Epstein, E. E. (1996). Theoretical Bases of Family Approaches to Substance Abuse Treatment. In F. Rotgers, D. S. Keller, & J. Morgenstern (Eds.), *Treating Substance Abuse* (pp. 117–142). New York: Guilford Press.

McGoldrick, M., Pearce, J. K., & Giordano, J. (Eds.). (1982). *Ethnicity and Family Therapy*. New York: Guilford Press.

McGoldrick, M., Giordano, J., & Pearce, J. K. (Eds.). (1996). *Ethnicity and Family Therapy* (2nd ed.). New York: Guilford Press.

Neff, J. A. (1986). Alcohol Consumption and Psychological Distress Among U.S. Anglos, Hispanics and Blacks. *Alcohol and Alcoholism, 21*(1), 111–119.

Neff, J. A., & Hoppe, S. K. (1992). Acculturation and Drinking Patterns Among U.S. Anglos, Blacks, and Mexican Americans. *Alcohol and Alcoholism, 27*(3), 293–308.

Neff, J. A., Hoppe, S. K., & Perea, P. (1987). Acculturation and Alcohol Use: Drinking Patterns and Problems Among Anglo and Mexican American Male Drinkers. *Hispanic Journal of Behavioral Sciences, 9*(2), 151–181.

Oler, C. H. (1989). Psychotherapy with Black Clients' Racial Identity and Locus of Control. *Psychotherapy, 26*(2), 233–241.

Padilla, A. M., & Salgado de Snyder, V. N. (1995). Hispanics: What the Culturally Informed Evaluator Needs to Know. In A. Padilla (Ed.), *Hispanic Psychology*. Thousand Oaks, CA: Sage.

Ramirez, S. (1977). *El Mexicano: Psicologia de Sus Motivaciones*. Mexico City: Editorial Grijalbo, S.A.

Redfield, R., Linton, R., & Herskovitz, M. J. (1936). Memorandum for the Study of Acculturation. *American Anthropologist, 38*, 149–152.

Riding, A. (1984). *Distant Neighbors: A Portrait of the Mexicans*. New York: Vintage Books.

Rogler, L., Cortes, D., & Malgady, R. (1991). Acculturation and Mental Health Status Among Hispanics: Convergence and New Directions for Research. *American Psychologist, 46*(6), 585–597.

Rollnick, S., & Morgan, M. (1995). Motivational Interviewing: Increasing Readiness for Change. In A. M. Washton (Ed.), *Psychotherapy and Substance Abuse: A Practitioners Handbook*. New York: Guilford Press. (pp. 179–191).

Rueschenberg, E. J., & Buriel, R. (1995). Mexican American Family Functioning and Acculturation. In A. Padilla (Ed.), *Hispanic Psychology. Critical Issues in Theory and Research*. Thousand Oaks, CA: Sage.

Ruiz, P., & Langrod, J. G. (1992). Substance Abuse among Hispanic-Americans: Current Issues Future Perspectives. In J. Lowinson, P. Ruiz, R. Millman, & J. Langrod (Eds.), *Substance Abuse: A Comprehensive Textbook* (2nd ed.) (pp. 868–874). Baltimore: Williams & Wilkins.

Ruiz, P., & Langrod, J. G. (1997). Substance Abuse among Hispanic-Americans: Current Issues Future Perspectives. In J. Lowinson, P. Ruiz, R. Millman, & J. Langrod (Eds.), *Substance Abuse: A Comprehensive Textbook* (3rd ed., pp. 705–711). Baltimore: Williams & Wilkins.

Smith-Peterson, C. (1983). Substance Abuse Treatment and Cultural Diversity. In G. Bennett, C. Vouvkis, & D. Woolf (Eds.), *Substance Abuse: Pharmacologic, Developmental and Clinical Perspectives*. New York: Wiley.

Steinglass, P., Bennet, L. A., Wolin, S., & Reiss, D. (1987). *The Alcoholic Family*. New York: Basic Books.

Stellato-Kabat, D., Stellato-Kabat, J., & Garrett, J. (1995). Treating Chemical-Dependent Couples and Families. In A. M. Washton (Ed.), *Psychotherapy and Substance Abuse: A Practitioner's Handbook* (pp. 314–330). New York: Guilford Press.

Substance Abuse and Mental Health Services Administration. (1994). *National Household Survey on Drug Abuse: Populations Estimates 1993* (DHHS Publication No. (SMA)94-3017).

Sue, D. W., Sue, D. (1990). *Counseling the Culturally Different* (2nd ed.). New York: Wiley.

Sue, S. (1988). Psychotherapeutic Services for Ethnic Minorities: Two Decades of Research Findings. *American Psychologist, 43*(4), 301–308.

Sue, S., & Zane, N. (1987). The Role of Culture and Cultural Techniques in Psychotherapy: A Critique and Reformulation. *American Psychologist, 42*(1), 37–45.

Treadway, D. (1989). *Before It's Too Late: Working with Substance Abuse in the Family*. New York: Norton.

U.S. Bureau of the Census. (1991). *Current Populations Report* (Series P-20, No. 449).

Wallace, C. B. (1995). Women and Minorities in Treatment. In A. M. Washton, (Ed.), *Psychotherapy and Substance Abuse: A Practitioner's Handbook* (pp. 470–492). New York: Guilford Press.

CHAPTER NINE

PUERTO RICAN FAMILIES AND SUBSTANCE ABUSE

Miguel Hernandez

SOLUTIONS TO ALCOHOL and other drug (AOD) abuse problems must include an understanding of the direct impact that multiple ecological contexts have on the family's life. Exploring these contexts will help us decide which parameters most demand our attention as we work with addictive families. By multiple ecological contexts I am not referring only to the role that sociopolitical and socioeconomic forces have in shaping the family's life. I am also interested in exploring how culture, ethnicity, race, social class, religious background, and the history of a particular ethnic minority group interact with addiction problems.

In this chapter I propose that by exploring the impact that these contexts have on the life of Puerto Rican immigrant families living in the United States, a clinician will be better able to identify and interpret the text of the family's narrative. This text includes the family's experiences with colonialism, immigration, acculturation, social marginality, racism, and political oppression, as well as its members' own personal and familial stories. The emotional reactions and the cognitive meanings attributed to these experiences can promote feelings of inadequacy, anger, confusion, low self-esteem, isolation, and a pervasive sense of shame and powerlessness. These meanings and feelings, similar to those associated with addiction, most be explored within the family's experience as an ethnic minority. Only then can one appreciate the complexities of ethnic minority addictive families and their struggles in trying to overcome such problems.

This chapter was written to provide a critical review of important concepts to be considered when working with Puerto Rican immigrant families living in the United States. The ideas presented may not necessarily apply when working with families living in Puerto Rico itself. In addition, it should be noted that these ideas have grown out of eight years of clinical work with poor first-, second-, and third-generation immigrant Puerto Rican families living in New York City. They are the result of clinical observations rather than scientific research. Furthermore, these ideas are not meant to represent a theory of addiction in Puerto Rican families. The constructs that I present here have been useful to me in organizing my thinking and informing my actions when doing clinical work with addictive immigrant families. Finally, I wish to inform the reader that my thinking is influenced by my own subjective experience as a family therapist, as a man, and as a recent immigrant from Puerto Rico living in New York City.

PUERTO RICO: THE HISTORICAL CONTEXT

PUERTO RICO WAS colonized by Spain in the sixteenth century. At the time, the island was inhabited by Taino Indians. It is believed that most of the Taino died of hunger, overwork, or suicide, if they were not killed by the Spaniards shortly after the invasion. The Spaniards forced the surviving men to work for them under exploitative conditions. They raped and otherwise sexually exploited the surviving women, forcing them to become their consorts. Even though the Taino's way of life was destroyed shortly after the invasion, their strong legacy persists in our language, physical attributes, and culture (Garcia-Preto, 1996). The Taino influence is less visible, however, than the Spanish influence in our culture.

During the first colonial period in Puerto Rico, Spaniards imposed on the Taino their language, culture, and religion, as well as their political and economic ideology. Specific elements of the Spanish legacy include the family's patriarchal structure, the double standard for men and women regarding sexual behavior, and values such as familism, personalism, machismo, and marianismo. The Spanish also left a worship of Catholic values and a value structure that prizes class and prestige based on family heritage and economic power (Garcia-Preto, 1996; Ramos-McKay, Comas-Diaz, and Rivera, 1988).*

During the 16th century, Spaniards brought African slaves to the island to work in the production of sugar cane. Although these slaves were not

---

*The concept of familism stresses family loyalty and interdependence among its members by reinforcing cooperation over competition. Personalism is a cultural concept that emphasizes the personal quality of any interaction. Machismo is a value dictating that the male is considered superior to the female based solely on his gender. In the counterpart of the latter, marianismo (a value based on the cult of the Virgin Mary), women are considered spiritually superior to men and, therefore, capable of enduring all suffering inflicted by men.

segregated by the Spaniards to the extent that slaves were by the British in other colonies in America (Skidmore and Smith, 1995), they nonetheless suffered the same horrors as slaves in the United States and elsewhere. African slaves brought to our culture their language, food, religion, values, and traditions, as well as the fatalism of an enslaved race. This fatalism is still present in the rich cultural mix of the island (Garcia-Preto, 1996).

In 1898 the United States colonized Puerto Rico after taking the island as war booty in the Spanish-American War. For a time the island was assigned an ambiguous status that did not allow statehood, because its citizens were considered "racially inferior" (Skidmore and Smith, 1992). With the Jones Act of 1917, Puerto Ricans were granted U.S. citizenship, and since then the fused relationship between Puerto Rico and the United States has been filled with contradictions and dependency.

Under U.S. dominance there was less economic and political autonomy than Puerto Rico had enjoyed under the Autonomous Charter, which Spain had granted in 1897. Although that charter had been opposed by some Puerto Ricans who felt it did not go far enough, it did give Puerto Ricans the right to full representation in the Spanish Congress (i.e., Puerto Ricans could elect a voting representative to the Spanish Congress), the right to participate in negotiations between Spain and other countries in matters affecting the commerce of the island, the right to ratify or reject commercial treaties affecting Puerto Rico, and the right to frame tariffs and fix customs on imports and exports (Rodriguez, 1991; Skidmore and Smith, 1995). These rights were not retained under U.S. possession. At the present time, Puerto Rico is still represented in the U.S. Congress by a resident commissioner who cannot vote. Although Puerto Ricans living on the island may be party members and may participate in the primaries, they cannot vote for president, nor can they send representatives to the Senate or the House of Representatives (Garcia-Preto, 1996). However, the president and Congress can (and do) send Puerto Rican males to fight in U.S. wars. In addition, Puerto Rico today does not have much control over its commerce, has no local control over customs, does not receive federal assistance programs such as Supplemental Security Income (SSI), and is economically dependent on the United States.

The changes experienced by the Puerto Rican economy after the U.S invasion were dramatic. The economy went from a diversified subsistence economy producing four basic crops for export (tobacco, cattle, coffee, and sugar) around the turn of the century to a sugar-crop economy, with 60 percent of the sugar industry controlled by U.S. absentee owners. The decline of the cane-based industry (combined with no reinvestment) and continued population growth in the 1920s resulted in high unemployment, poverty, and desperate conditions in Puerto Rico. These factors propelled the first waves of Puerto Rican migrants to search for a better life. The 1930s saw more migration, as workers sought to deal with the stagnant economy on the island (Rodriguez, 1991).

In the 1940s, World War II boosted the flagging economy somewhat. The Puerto Rican government initiated a series of reforms and entered into what has been variously called its "state capitalist development phase" and its "socialist" venture. A series of government-owned enterprises were established and run by the Puerto Rican Development Corporation. Influenced by the New Deal philosophy, this program stressed goals of "social justice and economic growth." Had this program succeeded, Puerto Rico would have achieved greater economic independence. However, these efforts were frustrated by a combination of technical problems and ideological opposition from the U.S. Congress.

In 1948 Puerto Rico elected its first governor, and in 1952 it became a commonwealth. With this later change, Spanish was reinstituted as the language of instruction in public schools, and English became the second language. This was an important period in Puerto Rican history. Between 1947 and 1951 the Puerto Rican government, in conjunction with the U.S. government, developed a strategy designed to attract U.S. industrial capital to develop the island's economy. Long-term tax exemptions and cheap labor were among the incentives offered to U.S. industrialists in a strategy called Operation Bootstrap (Skidmore and Smith, 1992). U.S. industrialists, wanting to deal with what was regarded as an excessive population that would hinder economic growth, used Operation Bootstrap as an escape valve by promoting massive emigration of Puerto Ricans to the U.S. as well as the sterilization of low-income women, sometimes without prior consent, through a so-called family planning program (Facundo, 1991).

Although much in Puerto Rico improved during this period, including education, housing, electrification, and the quality of drinking water, sewage systems, roads, and transportation facilities, Operation Bootstrap did not work as planned (Facundo, 1991). The industries, which were highly mechanized, did not absorb the expected number of people into the workforce, particularly during the phase characterized by the establishment of huge petrochemical and pharmaceutical plants on the island. Thus, the escape valve for emigration was left open. Emigration from Puerto Rico to the United States became the only choice for those who lost their jobs and were looking for a better life. Emigration, however, was a survival strategy that did not work for all of those who left our country (Facundo, 1991).

The majority of Puerto Ricans who migrated had to deal with racism and discrimination not only because they were considered foreigners (even though legally they were—and are—U.S. citizens) but also because they were poor. During the earlier migration years, Puerto Rican immigrants were ready to assume the jobs that nobody else wanted and the salaries that others could not afford to live with (Facundo, 1991). The immigrants were ready to pay this economic price to pursue the concept of subjective happiness found through the achievement of the American dream of economic success. However, the effects of migration, the consequent changes in socioeconomic status, the process of cultural transition, and the disruption of social support networks due to the experience of relocation had a dramatic impact on family structure and normal developmental process.

It is important to note that Puerto Rican family life had already experienced great disruption owing to the imposition of a developing industrial capitalist state that had challenged the way the family had previously been organized when the island had an agrarian economy and a coexisting agrarian–capitalist socioeconomic order. In our preindustrial capitalist society, agricultural work that was centered in the family or the village was the predominant and necessary condition for the maintenance of life. The family was the organizational unit for the natural processes of life, such as eating, sleeping, sexuality, sickness, education, and productive labor. Cooperation between adults and the division of labor along sex lines were practices that also resulted in increased interdependence. Since the family's maintenance was based on the subsistence agriculture derived from the family's labor on their property, there existed only minor divisions between family life and productive work. Because benefits were derived from ownership of private property and the efforts of everyone, the responsibilities and status of all family members remained fairly uniform (Inclan, 1980). During this preindustrial period, self-esteem and prestige were a product of wisdom and knowledge, which could be attributed to life experience and old age, and the family's search for well-being (physical and emotional) was based on its ability to produce its own goods and satisfy its own needs. The material need for interdependence that existed during this period had among its sociological manifestations the development of large and extended families and the encouragement of family clans based on geographical proximity. Family cohesion and collaboration were the psychological expressions of a strong value system (Inclan, 1980).

With the development of industrialism, however, there was such a separation created between family work and wage work that the economic functions of the family became obscured. The work that was completely removed from the family or village and centralized in the large industrial work centers was done by men, and the work done in the house was relegated to women. Children were removed from the duties of "family labor" and their time was organized around education and other activities peripheral to the family's life. A family's prestige and self-esteem became functions of its members' participation in wage labor and their acquisition of material goods from earned money that was not derived from the family's enterprise. During this period, *machismo* began to be institutionalized. Productive work was considered a male responsibility. Men who once measured their success by being a good "family man" (by spending time with family members, and providing for them) no longer found family-centered activities so rewarding. Home became not a place of joy but only a refuge from low wages, labor abuse, and a sense of powerlessness in the new socioeconomic order (Inclan, 1980). Work began to be understood as necessarily and intrinsically undesirable and unrewarding. Because of the low wages they earned, the work abuse they tolerated, and their need to maintain a home that they were not supposed to allow the problems of the work place to infiltrate, men found it difficult to carry all the responsibilities for the family's economic survival. Women were supposed to derive their satisfaction from supporting their husband, taking care of the home, being in charge of the child rearing, and providing whatever they could to promote the family's emotional happiness so that their husband would experience home as a refuge. The search for happiness and for the family's identity began to be perceived as a separate and subjective realm outside of the productive work process (Inclan, 1980).

Further family disruption at the microsystemic level was experienced when women were incorporated into the productive work process. By the 1940s there were larger numbers of women operatives (rural or urban) than men. The same held true for professionals, although this may be partially explained by the large percentage of women teachers in the labor force. Teaching became a central area of development under the new economic order in as much as the government attempted to make education a priority in achieving the new status of a commonwealth (Skidmore and Smith, 1992).

The incorporation of women into the labor force occurred when men were displaced from their jobs. This economic fact provided the conditions for further disruption of family life and for a redefinition of roles and hierarchical structure. In joining the labor force, women, faced the dilemma of going against a foreign concept of family life and facing its consequences, which generated questions like these: Am I a bad mother? Is my husband a poor husband for not providing for us? Can I feel good about working? Do I have to do wage work and also housework? Men faced similar questions: Am

I useless as a father, husband, man? Is my wife going to become independent of me and leave me? Is my role to do housework? These personal concerns were complicated by changes in parental child rearing functions, the socializing role of schools, community life involvement, the amount and function of leisure time, the nature of mother–child and father–child relationships, the relationship with extended family, and the meaning and duration of marriage. Indeed, overall structural changes in a new social and economic order resulted from the overall cultural and political changes associated with a fast Americanization of the country and from the new economic patterns ushered in by industrial capitalism (Inclan, 1980).

Within this context of change and subjective struggle for adaptation, Puerto Rican families began to migrate to the United States. Those who made it were forced to deal with a new socioeconomic and cultural system that directly affected family life.

History for both groups—migrants and those left on the island—does not end with the 1940s. For both groups, changes in family life have been directly affected by the socioeconomic reality of the United States, by our reality as a colony, and by worldwide changes that have occurred since then. Puerto Ricans living on the mainland have been witness to the subtle infiltration of the colonialism that shaped our national character and what it means to be Puerto Rican. For instance, the fifties brought to Puerto Rico the all-American notion of the perfect world, including the concept of the nuclear family, a male-dominant social structure, the perfect economic working middle-class dream, as well as the rush for new technology and a social hierarchy defined by what you do instead of who you are. The sixties brought the sexual revolution, the drug subculture, the women's liberation movement, racial and ethnic pride, political awareness about the impact of war and the need for world peace, and political paranoia about communism. The seventies were the years of confusion. A new social order was established, and contradictory cultural messages (i.e., a worldview supporting the value of being socially and politically committed versus a fatalistic worldview leading to a blasé attitude toward life) affected our sociocultural system in the same ways that they affected the American culture.

While political awareness facilitated the growth of independence movements in Puerto Rico, the economic recession experienced in the United States affected the national economy, forcing a second mass migration to the States. During this decade, circular migration patterns became very popular among Puerto Ricans. The mainland culture began to be exposed to the New York Puerto Rican culture with the first massive re-migration of New York Puerto Rican migrants who returned to the island. The eighties brought the Generation X phenomena, Reagan's politics, the fears of nuclear war, further infatuation with technology, the ideology of rescuing the world from socialist and communist dictators who threatened freedom, and interest in economic world power. Present times are about the struggles of postmodern ideas and their impact on political, social, and cultural values. Puerto Ricans living on the island are reflecting on the impact of the one hundredth anniversary of U.S. colonization. Technology and globalization are eliciting important philosophical reflections among intellectuals and creating confusion among the general population. Racism, feminism, the male movement, and the gay and lesbian struggles have become core causes in the new sociopolitical order. New immigrants and the growing influx of newcomers are impacting the Puerto Rican culture as well as the island's economy. Conservatism among those in power in Puerto Rico is in constant struggle with a country that is trying to redefine the new Puerto Rican reality. Violence and an underground drug subculture threaten personal and national security. A growing economic recession caused by the conservative political leadership in Puerto Rico is directly influencing the personal, familial, community, social, and political experience of Puerto Ricans living on the island today.

The story for those who migrated to the States evolved within the complex sociocultural, socioeconomic, and political contexts of life in the United States. The migration of Puerto Ricans after the U.S. takeover has been classified into three major periods.

The Pioneers

During the first period of Puerto Rican migration, 1900–1945, the pioneers arrived. The majority of these pioneers settled in New York City. At the beginning of the twentieth century, the Puerto Rican community was generally made up of well-to-do merchants, political activists closely allied with the Cuban revolutionary movement, and skilled workers, many of whom were skilled tobacco workers. By the first quarter of the twentieth century, the Puerto Rican community was described as consisting of people who were employed in predominantly working-class occupations (Skidmore and Smith, 1992).

The Great Migration

The second phase of Puerto Rican migration, 1946–1964, is known as the great migration because this is when the largest numbers of Puerto Ricans arrived in the United States. During this period, settlement in new areas of New York, and in New Jersey, Connecticut, Chicago, and other areas of the country took place, but the bulk of the Puerto Rican population continued to reside in New York City. The composition of the migrant population continued to be diverse, but there was a strong working-class base. In the 1940s the migrant population was urban, skilled, and predominantly female. In the 1950s the migrant population was described as predominantly male, unskilled, and rural. By the early 1960s the followers were younger in age, of diverse class origin, and largely from a rural background.

THE REVOLVING DOOR MIGRATION

The last period of Puerto Rican migration, 1965 to the present, is termed the "revolving door migration, or circular migration." It involves a fluctuating pattern of net migration as well as greater dispersion to other parts of the United States. Those in this migration group include graduate students, scholars, young professionals, and the working poor. During the last ten years the migrant population has included highly skilled professionals who worked for American companies in Puerto Rico before those companies closed operations on the island and relocated in the States.

The Puerto Rican presence in the United States has presented an enigma to the host country. As a racially diverse group, Puerto Ricans have challenged the racial order based on the White–Black dichotomy. Puerto Ricans constitute an ethnic group but more than one racial group. From the U.S. perspective there are both White and Black Puerto Ricans. However, ethnically Puerto Ricans belong to a single group. Thus, Puerto Ricans find themselves caught between two polarities and at a distance from both groups. Puerto Ricans define themselves in terms of ethnicity more than in terms of skin color. The U.S. imposition of race over ethnocultural identity has created severe strains on Puerto Ricans living in the States. Whereas the perception of Puerto Ricans by North Americans is based on race, the subjective experience of Puerto Ricans is based on ethnocultural factors. Thus, there is an experience of constant dissonance between the way they are perceived and the way they perceive themselves. This experience on one hand, has perpetuated the sense of isolation and marginalization experienced by Puerto Ricans in the United States, but on the other hand, has encouraged the strong cultural affirmation existing in their communities.

This, however, is not to be confused with the fact that there is racism among Puerto Ricans themselves. Like other Caribbean islands, Puerto Rico has a wide range of racial denominations. For example, dark-skinned

Puerto Ricans are *morenos* or *prietos* (Blacks); less dark are *trigueños* (olive-skinned, dark-complexioned); lighter Puerto Ricans are considered *grifos* or *jabaos* (light skin with kinky hair); *indio* (bearing Indian characteristics) or *blanquitos* (white skin with Caucasian features). The color classification has implications for what is considered attractive (the whiter the person, the more attractive) (Ramos-McKay, Comas-Diaz, and Rivera, 1991), intelligent (Blacks are considered genetically inferior), and socially superior (Whites have more social power than Blacks). When dark-skinned Puerto Ricans who are not considered Black on the island (*trigueños, jabaos,* or *indios*) migrate to the United States, where they are considered Black, a major crisis in identity develops. A more complex and painful experience is when within the same family some members are considered Black and others not. Usually, this creates unspoken family tension.

A strong ethnic identification among Puerto Ricans living in the States has been evident since the migration during the 1940s. Puerto Rican immigrants transplanted their culture and language to their *barrios* and, in comparison with other ethnic immigrant groups, have resisted assimilation even during periods of intense repression. The prevalence of Spanish–English bilingualism among Puerto Ricans in New York City suggests a broad allegiance to maintaining Spanish as a marker of cultural, social, and political identity. The 1990 census data also indicate that a very high percentage of Puerto Ricans in New York City speak Spanish at home. Moreover, there is continuing evidence that both first and second generations identify themselves as Puerto Ricans, use Spanish at home, and view Puerto Rican culture as a positive influence. From my clinical experience it is evident that young Puerto Ricans are retaining their Puerto Rican heritage as a symbol of their identity even when they were not born in Puerto Rico and have little direct connection with the island. This phenomenon can be better understood if one explores the cultural legacy that Puerto Ricans have given to urban culture in the United States.

The Puerto Rican community in New York, almost from the moment of its inception, has developed its own rich traditions in literature, music, visual arts, sports, and the street hip-hop culture. As early as 1928, Puerto Ricans living in New York created a musical tradition of lyrics that narrated our history, the struggles of migration, the realities of our communities, and our various idiosyncrasies as a community in transition. The evolution of Latin jazz, salsa, hip-hop, and Latin rap has kept the Puerto Rican culture alive within the community. Another example of our devotion to our culture is El Museo Del Barrio (the Community's Museum), on Fifth Avenue's "museum row," a museum that represents the community that gave birth to it. Along with the Bronx Museum of Arts, El Museo Del Barrio has become a leader and an important outlet for the exhibition of Puerto Rican and other Latino art. Satellite galleries have accompanied both museums, so that art has become more accessible to all community residents.

Puerto Ricans living in the States have also made role models out of Puerto Rican heroes such as baseball player Roberto Clemente. In the political arena, recent years have seen Puerto Rican members of Congress, whose success is a source of pride for the community. In addition a strong movement among poets, writers, actors, and arts promoters has created a Puerto Rican presence in New York City culture that is echoed throughout the nation, as Puerto Ricans have re-created communities in other cities. In sum, by taking their culture to the streets, resisting assimilation, and keeping Spanish alive, Puerto Ricans have made New York a bilingual city in the same way that Cubans made Miami a bilingual city.

However, the reluctance to leave behind one's cultural roots cannot be seen purely as the result of internalized pride and cultural affirmation. The long-lasting quality of Puerto Rican identity is also related to the disadvantaged position of the group as a whole and to the continual revitalization of ethnic symbols through the process of circular migration. It has been argued that bilingualism and biculturalism are necessities for Puerto Ricans who are involved in the constant back-and-forth migration to and from the island. Even for those who are not involved in this circular migration pattern, it is important to be both bilingual and bicultural in order to function in the Puerto Rican community, familial networks, and the host community.

Residential segregation or concentration has also had an impact on the ethnic identification of Puerto Ricans. Having migrated from a segregated colony, many Puerto Ricans find themselves once again segregated. They tend to work in similar job sectors, and many live in ethnically homogeneous areas. Thus they are marginalized, just as they were while living on the island. It is important to understand how this segregation occurs and is maintained: Residential segregation determines educational options, particularly in the early grades. Subsequent educational attainment determines labor market power (i.e., technical or professional skills), which in turn determines income. Income, in large part, determines housing options. Segregation is further reinforced by racism and ethnic prejudice and by political strategies that limit the resources available to homogeneous ethnic communities.

The living conditions for many Puerto Ricans are below the poverty level. As a group, Puerto Ricans are not prospering as other migrant groups are. Social problems such as teen pregnancy, school truancy, substance abuse, gang violence, and unemployment are present concerns in our communities. Invisibility, racism, and prejudice are strong forces in maintaining the Puerto Rican community's marginalization from the dominant culture. Finally, the legacies of a complex colonial history, an unusual migratory pattern, and the reaction of the receiving society to a different and complex immigrant group have created a unique context that must be explored and considered when addressing the psychosocial problems that attack the Puerto Rican community.

The Sociocultural Context of Alcohol Use in Puerto Rico

In Puerto Rico one of the biggest industries is the production and sale of rum. The sale of beer and other alcoholic beverages is common almost everywhere. While beer is considered a light alcoholic drink, and rum mildly alcoholic, drinking whiskey, scotch, or any other alcoholic beverage that is drunk straight is considered to be strong and serious drinking. Regardless of the alcoholic beverage of choice, drinking is common in Puerto Rico, and different kinds of alcoholic beverages are consumed on almost every occasion. In fact, drinking alcohol is an essential part of socializing with friends, closing business deals, participating in family celebrations, and relaxing. Drinking is used to help tolerate the heat, to release tension, to calm sorrows, to celebrate. Alcohol is consumed alone or with company, at home or in bars or restaurants, at the beach or in parks; indeed, it is consumed almost everywhere.

Puerto Rican women are much less likely to be drinkers than Puerto Rican men, but they do drink more than women of other ethnic groups. They usually drink quietly and always within the context of a social activity, that is, with company. A woman who drinks alone or in the company of a group of men or as frequently as men do is considered either a drunk or sexually promiscuous (or even a lesbian). Heavy drinking in women is also considered low-class, regardless of social status. If a woman's drinking gets out of hand, it is extremely embarrassing for the family, since women are supposed to keep their place and behave as respectable ladies. Alcoholism in a woman is likely to cause the breakup of her marriage, the loss of parental rights after a divorce, termination of employment, and a cutoff from the woman's family of origin. An alcoholic woman is considered to be unfit to be a mother, a wife, and a respectable community member. Even after rehabilitation, women are more likely than men to be labeled as an alcoholic.

The story for men is quite different. Heavy drinking among men is tolerated by Puerto Rican society. Indeed, social support is provided for excessive drinking. For example, problem drinkers are sheltered by friends and even relatives in order to escape public recognition and censure. Additionally, heavy drinking is associated with being macho, and it is supported by the *machismo* ideology. According to Abad and Suarez (1974), Puerto Rican men are subjected to intense degrees of stress throughout their lives in their attempts to achieve an ideal macho self-image. Meeting the standards of what defines a man as macho becomes an organizing force in the development of their self-esteem and self-image and determines social approval of their role as a man. Abad and Suarez posit that Puerto Rican males may turn to alcohol as a source of dependency gratification, as a release of anxiety and tension, or as a means of fantasizing *machismo* characteristics in themselves.

In Puerto Rico, men have rituals that celebrate drinking and manhood. For instance, on Fridays after work men usually gather in bars, parks, and even in the streets to celebrate the end of the week. These "social Fridays," as they are called, are about meeting friends to drink, to talk about "men's stuff," to release the tensions of work, to vent the frustrations of family life, and, more importantly, to escape from wives, children, and responsibilities. While a man is out drinking with friends, it is not uncommon for his wife or even mother to be at home preparing a special meal (usually a thick soup) to feed him to help cure the next day's hangover. Moderate drinking at home is tolerated even when it becomes a daily activity. While drinking within what is defined as a social event (i.e., drinking with company), regardless of the amount and frequency, is tolerated, drinking alone is considered a problem. Alcoholism among men is usually seen as a weakness of the soul and will. Puerto Rican women tend to tolerate their husband's alcoholism more than do women of other ethnic groups. Caring for a husband while he is drunk, making excuses for his social dysfunction, tolerating his violence, and other forms of codependency are reinforced by cultural and social values such as *marianismo* and familism, which encourage sacrifice, abnegation, loyalty toward men, keeping the family together, and supporting family members in trouble at all cost. In fact, the wife of an alcoholic is more likely to seek support to endure her suffering than to seek change in her role or situation, since the latter may demand a transgression of her expected role as a woman (Inclan and Hernandez, 1992). Thus, the family will probably not seek help for an alcohol-related problem until it has become so serious that someone outside the family—a friend, the family doctor, a spiritual leader, a school authority, or, in many cases, the police—intervenes. Social censure and shame usually have a positive impact during the course of treatment, with feelings of guilt and repentance usually being the beginning steps toward recovery. Bolstered by education and AA supportive services, spiritual guidance, and extended family and community support, an alcoholic can achieve healing and sobriety (B. Velez-Purcell, personal communication, 1998).

The reader is reminded that while these patterns are relevant to traditional Puerto Ricans living on the island, there are significant variations within the population, owing to class, education, socioeconomic status, and generation. For instance, many Puerto Rican feminist women do not respond to the rigid role expectations described above. Likewise, some feminist men will at least struggle with the rigid expectations of the *machismo* ideology. Education, social class, and exposure to Americanization are mediating factors in some of the behaviors and responses described above. Additionally, urban reality is completely different from rural reality. For instance, urban adolescents begin drinking at an early age and drinking is considered by those in their immediate environment to be a normal developmental milestone. In the countryside, drinking at an early age is punished by the community and considered to be social deviance. Social status also affects the response toward heavy drinking. A professional woman who meets her colleagues for a couple of martinis after work is considered glamorous and assertive. A poor woman who has a couple of beers at the local *bodega* is seen at best as a *borracha* (drunk) and as worst as a *mala mujer* (bad woman). Likewise, a group of professional men meeting for an extended lunch to close a deal while sipping expensive wine are considered to be working whereas a group of construction workers drinking beer with their lunch under the shade of a tree to escape from the heat of the noonday sun are considered lazy bums who are stealing money from their employer. When a drunk heterosexual man becomes loud and expressive (establishing physical contact) with his friends, he is considered manly, but a gay man will be accused of making sexual advances to his friends and any physical contact with another man will be seen as misconduct. Finally, drinking is socially accepted among the young crowd but punished and ridiculed among the elderly (B. Velez-Purcell, personal communication, 1998).

The Sociocultural Context of Alcohol Use Among Puerto Ricans Living in the United States

Alcohol consumption among Puerto Ricans has a different meaning in the United States. Within this new cultural context, Puerto Rican attitudes toward alcohol consumption are considered socially and culturally deviant. For instance, the amount of alcohol intake that is tolerated in Puerto Rico is considered evidence of alcoholism in the United States. To the American culture, drinking in the streets while playing dominoes is considered low-class, if not barbaric. In New York City, local businesses have closed their stores during Puerto Rican Pride Day, fearing that participants will get drunk and cause a riot (although this has never happened in the history of this celebration). Social drinking among Puerto Ricans has been associated with crime and violence, and police tend to be less tolerant of public drinking by Puerto Ricans than by members of any other ethnic group (De La Rosa, 1991). Puerto Rican men have been stereotyped as drunks, and alcohol consumption has been defined as one of the causes for their social marginality. Therefore, Puerto Ricans, after migration, have come to view cultural patterns of alcohol consumption as shameful activities, since they are socially condemned by the dominant culture. The consequences of these cultural changes are numerous.

For instance, because women tend to acculturate faster than men, Puerto Rican women in the United States tend to be less tolerant of their husband's drinking habits, even when the amount of alcohol he consumes is the same as before migration. Children also become less tolerant of their parents' drinking habits, which usually become a source of shame to them as evidence that their parents are not behaving like mainstream Americans (Inclan and Hernandez, 1992). The reality for women in the United States is not so different from that in Puerto Rico. In the new context, heavy alcohol consumption is socially punished and public social drinking is a source of shame for their husbands and families (Inclan and Hernandez, 1992).

When drinking becomes a problem, acculturation will impact the response of Puerto Rican immigrant families to the problem. Puerto Rican immigrant women tend to seek outside help for their husbands more often than do women living on the island. School personnel, church leaders, and community workers (social workers, psychologists, and substance abuse counselors) support women seeking help without blaming them for breaking family loyalties. Divorce and separations due to alcohol abuse are more common among Puerto Ricans living in the States than among those on the island. Alcohol-related violence and alcohol abuse are less tolerated among highly acculturated Puerto Rican immigrants.

These new attitudes, however, do not mean that there is less alcohol abuse among Puerto Rican immigrants in the States. Actually, alcohol abuse is very common among immigrants, since they frequently use alcohol as a tranquilizer in order to numb the pain associated with their new minority status. Migration-induced changes, such as acculturation, change in social status, rupture of social supportive networks, and unresolved mourning issues associated with the uprooting experience, are severe strains in the immigrant's life (Hernandez and McGoldrick, 1998).

When Puerto Ricans migrate to the States, they are immersed in a different cultural context, a different socioeconomic hierarchy, and a hostile environment full of racism and ethnic prejudice. Coping and adapting to their new environment, as well as dealing with new and unexpected migration-induced challenges, creates a unique psychosocial reality with potential detrimental consequences. Erosion of self-esteem, loss of self-confidence and a sense of mastery, internalized shame and anger, and a sense of confusion are some of the emotional issues experienced by immigrants as they try to cope with their new environment. These issues are usually related to the experiences of poverty, unemployment, social isolation, discrimination, lack of resources, sociopolitical marginality, and cultural shock (Hernandez and McGoldrick, 1998). Therefore, when exploring the cultural context of alcohol consumption among Puerto Ricans living in the States, clinicians must explore the complex web of emotional and psychosocial experiences induced by migration, cultural transition, and ethnic minority status.

For instance, one of the most difficult experiences Puerto Ricans face by migrating is that of being uprooted. This involves breaking previous strong ties and alliances with relatives and friends and leaving behind what is known and familiar. Multiple losses evoke a complex mourning experience (Hernandez and McGoldrick, 1998). It is important to understand that while the grief of the bereaved can often be traced to the nature of the relationship with the deceased, the immigrant's experience of loss is vague and pervasive. Immigrants mourn not only the loss of relationships but also the loss of what is familiar and known, the loss of what Tichio (1971) refers to as the "average expectable environment." The inability to trace the sense of loss to a tangible object makes the mourning experience difficult, and feelings of confusion and profound sadness are common. In the Puerto Rican experience, women tend to process these emotions more easily, as they are provided with social and cultural permission to be emotional and to openly express their suffering. Men, however, must be strong and endure pain in order to be considered a man. Drinking then becomes an outlet for expressing their emotions. Crying and other manifestations of pain that are expressed when a Puerto Rican man is drunk are tolerated by his internalized *machista* ideology (Hernandez, 1996). Consequently, alcohol intake usually increases shortly after migration, and it is not uncommon for Puerto Rican men to gather to drink and talk about their feelings about the uprooting experience.

Acculturation to U.S. society challenges traditional Puerto Rican gender roles. Women are often first to obtain jobs, because they are more open to performing menial tasks or because the available jobs are seen as more appropriate for females. Through their work, women usually develop an outside network that exposes them more rapidly to the new culture. Even when they are not part of the workforce, women develop social relationships more quickly than men, since they meet others in the course of carrying out traditional duties such as shopping and caring for children. This exposure provides new strategies to negotiate their traditional gender roles, and the impact of new gender behaviors is felt in the family when women begin to demand more participation in home care from children and husbands. New behaviors unbalance the family's structure, particularly the marital dyad's traditional power structure. For example, a traditional husband, who is used to being the main provider and protector of his family, will resent the changes and will challenge the newly acquired independence of his wife by reclaiming old role patterns. Women are often accused of abandoning their culture and family, but in my experience many women try to reassume old roles out of guilt and confusion; they isolate themselves from friends and work extra hard to please their husband. Their resulting discontent usually is manifested in somatization, depressive symptoms, or relational conflicts. Drinking and addiction to prescribed drugs often seem to them to be the only way to deal with their problems (Hernandez, 1996; Hernandez and McGoldrick, 1998).

Traditional Puerto Rican masculine gender roles are also challenged by the new cultural environment. Without the public recognition given by the cultural notion of *machismo* and without the strong patriarchal ideology to which they are accustomed, many Puerto Rican men feel they have lost their power. Their new ethnic minority status and social invisibility invalidate them in their traditional domain, the public sphere. Losing power in the public sphere owing to racism, ethnic prejudice, and (paradoxically) societal change toward gender equality has a direct impact on a man's family life. Alcohol abuse and alcohol-related violence, anxiety, and depression are common manifestations of its effects (Hernandez, 1996).

Finally, poverty, segregation, unemployment, lack of supportive resources, racism, and prejudice all contribute to increasing alcohol use among Puerto Rican immigrants as a way to escape their difficult psychosocial reality.

THE SOCIOCULTURAL CONTEXT OF SUBSTANCE ABUSE IN PUERTO RICO

WHILE ALCOHOL IS tolerated in the Puerto Rican culture, abuse of other substances is socially punished and considered deviant behavior. The use of marijuana, cocaine, crack, and other chemical substances is associated with crime and violence; even when it is employed recreationally, drug use is considered abuse (De La Rosa, 1991). A substance abuser is considered a weak soul, a person without morals or will power. In Puerto Rico, drug addiction is considered such a significant social transgression that social shame becomes a powerful component of drug treatment.

Studies about substance abuse in Puerto Rico have tended to focus on the poor. Until very recently it was viewed as a common problem among young, poor men who did not work and who had chosen the easy way in life. The problem was seen as confined to facilities known as *caseríos* (low-income public housing projects), where drug-related crimes were common problems (and usually ignored by the authorities). In contrast, nowadays the subculture associated with illegal drugs has affected most of Puerto Rican society with violent crimes such as kidnapping, car hijacking, robbery, and murder. The problem affects all social classes, and the acknowledged victims include the poor as well as the rich. Likewise, the common user is no longer seen only as the young, poor man living at the projects; currently, substance abuse is identified with all social classes and backgrounds. In other words, the traditional stereotyped image of the substance abuser has shifted, as the drug culture has become more visible and menacing to all social spheres, including the powerful social class. In these days your next-door neighbor, a middle-class kid living in the suburbs, and the prestigious lawyer from a private corporate law firm are all seen as potential drug abusers. In fact, drug use is so spread out among the social classes that *puntos* (drug-infested areas where illegal substances are sold) are no longer located only at the *caseríos* and drugs can be bought almost anywhere. Dealers and pushers can be singled out in public places that are usually frequented only by upper- and middle-class Puerto Ricans. They are usually recognized by their stereotypical "new rich" image: they carry expensive cellular phones and beepers, wear expensive jewelry and designer clothes, drive expensive cars, and show off their economic opulence by carrying a lot of cash. In fact, there are rumors that houses in the new expensive suburbs can only be bought by drug dealers, since they are the ones on the island who have the economic means to afford these mansions (B. Velez-Purcell, personal communication, 1998).

While there has been a changing trend across social classes, drug abuse in Puerto Rico continues to be more common among teenagers and young adults. The statistics show that the rates are higher for men than for women. Social punishment of addicted women appears to be a factor in this phenomenon. Alcoholism and addiction are considered the worst character traits a Puerto Rican woman can have. There is a social stereotype that addicted women are promiscuous, that they are unable to fulfill the roles of spouse and mother. Such transgressions of *marianista* values are socially punished by the withholding of any respect, empathy, or compassion for women who are substance abusers. Young addicted women are usually cut off from their family of origin. Married women are abandoned by their husband, and mothers lose custody of their children owing to court decisions that reflect society's bias against female addicts. Communities tend to alienate addicted women to the extent of denying them any support even for recovery. In fact, it was not until very recently that the Puerto Rican Social Service Department addressed the need for specialized treatment centers for addicted women. The proposed approach would include issues pertaining specifically to the female addicted population. For example, addicted women are more at risk of being physically and sexually abused than men. They become silent victims and up to now have received little help from authorities even if the abuse is reported.

In contrast to women, men who are drug abusers receive less severe treatment from their family and community. Usually supported by his mother, the young male addict is most likely to stay home, where denial, tolerance, and forgiveness tend to perpetuate the problem. The cultural belief that mothers need to endure suffering and show self-abnegation for the sake of their family reinforces these codependent behaviors. Not doing so tends to be considered a transgression of a woman's role and responsibility. Addiction among Puerto Rican men is also excused by society as the result of external pressures such as lack of work or peer pressure and as a rite of passage for becoming a man. Society sees the addicted man as a weak, confused individual who needs spiritual counseling in order to gain a sense of morality and responsibility. This belief is so ingrained that the most successful treatment approach in Puerto Rico uses social punishment and spiritual guidance as the main forms of intervention. Confrontative therapies are also used in order to generate social and moral shame as the first steps toward recovery.

At the sociopolitical level, the drastic increase in the drug epidemic in

Puerto Rico has forced authorities to administer severe punishment for drug-related crimes and even to use the Civil Guard and other military forces to control drug activities in the *caseríos*. A discussion of the reasons for Puerto Rico's drug epidemic is beyond the scope of this chapter. However, an understanding of the drastic increase of substance abuse in Puerto Rico should include an analysis of the political and economic situation of the island, its present relationship with the United States, and the impact of a hundred years of colonization and oppression by the American government.

As a closing remark about substance abuse in Puerto Rico, I would like to report that I could not find anything in the literature about drugs among the gay and lesbian community on the island. From personal conversations with gay activists on the island, I have gathered information that describes patterns of drug abuse among the Puerto Rican gay and lesbian community that are similar to those noted in the States. Among gay men, recreational drugs are considered an essential part of the social life of clubs and bars. Stimulants are often used to endure the long hours of partying. Abuse is often associated with self-medication for the unbearable feelings resulting from the experience of oppression in the Puerto Rican homophobic culture, from the pressure of maintaining a "closeted" life and social isolation, and from being cut off from family and community. The problem tends not to be openly discussed owing to the weak political power of the gay community in Puerto Rico. However, in recent years gays have become more open and politically involved.

While substance abuse is a concern among gay men on the island, lesbian activists do not consider it a problem among their community (personal communication). Age appears to be an important factor, and abuse is most common among young adults and teenagers. Alcohol tends to be more common for the middle-aged and is equally consumed by gay and lesbian Puerto Ricans on the Island.

THE SOCIOCULTURAL CONTEXT OF SUBSTANCE ABUSE AMONG PUERTO RICANS LIVING IN THE UNITED STATES

SUBSTANCE ABUSE IS a real threat to the Puerto Rican communities in the United States. Studies have shown that Puerto Ricans living on the mainland are twice as likely to have used illegal drugs when compared to Mexican Americans and Cubans. Further, it has been reported that single Puerto Rican males between the ages of eighteen and twenty-four have the highest prevalence of illegal drug use among Hispanics living in the United States. Compared to females, Puerto Rican males have a higher incidence of drug abuse, which has been correlated with their higher incidence of death in cities such as New York (De La Rosa, 1991). Compared to other males, many poor, urban Puerto Rican males, who become victims of violent crime, murder, overdose, or AIDS, are dying at a drastic, high rate. In the best cases, they end up being incarcerated, homeless, or addicted to methadone. These tragic endings are usually the culmination of experiences such as social, economic, and political deprivation; lack of family and community support; racism and ethnic prejudice; and internalized oppression.

Substance abuse has been so normalized in the development of Puerto Rican men that many have viewed experimenting with drugs as a normal milestone in the process of becoming a man. Exposed to the drug subculture when they are very young, many Puerto Rican men living in urban U.S. cities begin using illegal substances between ages thirteen and fifteen. Recreational use becomes a problem once it is learned that it is better to feel numb than to face the pain experienced by oppression and racism. Peer pressure to use drugs is usually supported by the social pressure of fitting into the stereotyped role that society defines for them. That is, young Puerto Ricans internalize the messages they hear from the dominant group, such as the following, which a fifteen-year-old patient reported hearing from a schoolteacher: "Spiks are lazy, stupid, and the best thing they do is getting girls pregnant. . . . They don't do nothing but get high and become graduated bums." In many cases, these stereotyped views of who we are become a self-fulfilling prophecy owing to a socially supported sense of not having a future, choices, or control over whether we can become part of society's dominant group. Therefore, racism, ethnic prejudice, and oppression are important variables to explore in understanding this psychosocial phenomenon in a Puerto Rican client. These experiences also need to be contextualized within the Puerto Rican client's migration history and process of cultural transition.

Migration is a multigenerational experience through which a family loses social status, self-esteem, and mastery while coping with contradictory values and belief system conflicts associated with the acculturation process. Adaptation to the new environment demands that immigrants deal with changes while processing the massive losses due to the uprooting experience. In addition, they have to cope with the unexpected experience of ethnic prejudice, racism, and social marginality associated with their immigrant status. Rather than achieving the American dream and being part of mainstream America, immigrants are always at the periphery of mainstream society, experiencing a marginal and oppressed psychosocial reality that has a serious impact on their emotional, cognitive, behavioral, and ecological life. Without community support, immigrant families are left alone, having only each other to depend on for surviving the unknown and unexpected experiences of immigration. For the sake of the family, and consistent with the values of familism, family members tend to suppress their own emotional needs in order to preserve family functioning and to protect the family from the complex outside forces that threaten the system. This strategy usually results in family members isolating themselves from each other; they keep secret their discontent with their new reality and attempt to diminish the impact on themselves of the forces of prejudice, racism, and oppression in their life (Hernandez and McGoldrick, 1998). Husbands and wives do not share with each other their experiences at work, at the market, with the school authorities, with the neighbors, and so on. Children do not share their experiences with parents, peers, teachers, or authority figures. In order to concentrate and survive the stress associated with being an immigrant, many family members (especially men) try to keep their concerns from the family.

In my experience, the high prevalence of substance abuse among Puerto Rican immigrants is correlated with their individual unresolved mourning issues, acculturation conflicts, internalized oppression, and sense of personal failure in achieving the American dream. The dynamics related to migration-induced stress are similar for cases of substance abuse and cases of alcohol abuse. A difference, however, rests on how the use of illegal substances becomes more ecologically suitable for poor urban immigrants. In many ways the drug subculture is experienced by drug users as a private community, a refuge from the oppressive forces that affect their lives. Many young Puerto Rican men have told me that the rituals associated with buying, selling, and using drugs make them feel important and powerful. Within the underground social order they have an important status over White kids who "don't know enough about the street" in order to understand the business. In fact, drug activity became the central organizing force in the development of gangs in New York City. Substance abuse has also become a requirement in order to be considered a "good homeboy." It is experienced as something American and different from drinking. It is even perceived among the youngsters as something glamorous and cool. Again, I am convinced that it is related to the internalization of the stereotyped roles (and oppression) that are given to Puerto Rican males by the dominant group.

Family responses to substance abuse among Puerto Ricans living in the United States are no different from the responses of families living on the island. However, because of migration-induced stresses it is important to use a sociopolitical lens in order to understand the role that racism, ethnic prejudice, and oppression have in the development and manifestation of substance abuse.

CLINICAL ISSUES

Substance abuse among Puerto Rican immigrants should always be contextualized within their migration experience and their oppressed reality as an ethnic minority group. Rather than as an illness, I prefer to conceptualize it as a symptom of the complex urban psychosocial reality experienced by oppressed groups. In applying this approach, the biological and psychological dynamics of addiction should not be ignored. I do, in fact, tend to use an "illness model of practice," but the concept is expanded to include the toxicity of our social environment and the recognition of the dramatic impact that the hidden forces of oppression have on our lives. The goal of this approach is to connect the political context with the client's personal experience. To this end, the work is centered on deconstructing the idea of addiction as a private, problem and on understanding and treating it as a social and community problem.

ACCEPTING THE PROBLEM

In my experience many clients begin treatment once the substance abuse problem has been recognized—either by the addict or a family member or by someone out side the family, such as a counselor or teacher. Recognizing the problem does not necessarily means taking responsibility for its origin and treatment. I strongly believe that alcohol or drug abusers have to be held accountable for their behaviors. Because of this, my first clinical move is always to track the underfunctioning behaviors and to explore how the family has responded to them. The central behavior I look for is control, or the lack of it, as it relates to substance abuse. I have found it useful to define addiction as the result of not having control over one's life. This metaphor allows me to position myself as a therapist who seeks to help the family and client explore the multiple causes for the development of such a condition. I explain my belief that this condition is the result of internal and external experiences that we are not always aware of. Among those external experiences that have an enormous impact on our internal world is the ethnic minority experience. It affects how we feel, think, and behave. In addition, the metaphor of not having control captures the reality of oppressed individuals, and my clients become very curious about exploring issues of oppression in therapy. I believe that by using political language early on I am setting the tone of the treatment and validating the need to have conversations about issues that are usually not discussed.

In setting up the case, I use a lot of self-help jargon, which I find relevant to the dominant belief that abusers are weak souls. The spiritual tone and nonblaming aspect of this jargon allow me to talk about the process of addiction in a language that is familiar to clients; the self-help movement's emphasis on spirituality and its public recognition of the spiritual realm are important features for Puerto Rican clients. For families that practice *espiritismo* or Santeria, the central principle of exploring the forces that are causing the addiction becomes very useful and culturally syntonic with the belief that one's life is affected by unknown spiritual forces.

During the assessment phase I also look for the family's strengths in the areas of coping with their ethnic minority reality. This validates their efforts to defend their culture and preserve the language and encourages their sense of pride in preserving their ethnic cuisine and other traditions. I plead with family members to remember the value of familism and ask them to be supportive and empathic with the abuser; I encourage abusers to recognize that they need their family to keep them on the road to recovery. In talking about familism, I always try to normalize and contextualize overfunctioning patterns as signs of love and of family loyalty. The family, however, is also invited to reflect on whether or not these patterns have perpetuated the abuser's underfunctioning. I talk a lot about how love can hurt and about the predicaments that result from some of our cultural norms. Again, my goal is to validate, support, and at the same time challenge some of our beliefs by introducing and reflecting on evidence that rigid practices can cause problems.

I must alert the reader to the fact that my own Puerto Rican heritage allows me to use language and my knowledge of ethnohistory and cultural details to connect with the family faster than would otherwise be possible. I also believe that my strong directive approach and my technique of letting the family know that I have skills to help them provides a sense of relief for my clients. Seeking mental health services (or any other kind of outside intervention for the family) is not a common practice for many Puerto Rican families. When they do seek help, I feel that it is better for the clinician to be directive and to have a concrete plan of action; this usually provides for clients a sense that change can be generated.

In helping family members to accept the problem of substance abuse, my intentions are to join and engage them by using cultural metaphors and validating ethnic realities; this furthers recognition of the role that oppression has on our lives, signifies acceptance of spiritual values, and makes possible educational work on addiction and its relation to not having control.

SETTING UP EXTERNAL SUPPORTS

Establishing a commitment to abstinence is the result of a process. I never expect a client to become abstinent before starting treatment. Allowing abusers to understand that they do not have control over the substance includes accepting relapses. Before suggesting self-help referral, I prefer to talk with abusers about their tales of losing control over their use of a substance. I emphasize tracking the sequences of behaviors and try to elicit the feelings they experienced and the thoughts they had about themselves when they saw once again that they were unable to control themselves. On many occasions, I have these conversations with the family in the room; I do so if I feel that family members can have compassion for the client and can therefore be supportive and accept the fears, pains, and anger the client feels for being a failure. I try to weave into the conversation the similarities between these experiences in failing to control substance use and experiences in failing to control racism and prejudice. I also share the similarities between feeling the shame of substance abuse and feeling ashamed about being an ethnic minority. Clients are usually confused by my permissiveness, which works very well with the normal oppositional attitudes of adolescents and young adults. They also react with confusion to my decision to emphasize issues of race and oppression while discussing their failure at self-control. Pushing the issue helps me to make my point, which is that every time one loses control, one is falling into the trap of reacting and not reflecting, that is, one is giving in to an impulse that perpetuates oppression.

During this work I like to include a psychoeducational piece with family members that emphasizes the stresses that young adults experience in being an ethnic minority at school, in the neighborhood, and in the context of the larger culture. Issues around peer pressure and internalized oppression are also presented. Again, being directive and laying out the facts while always showing support and social empathy facilitates the process.

Having initiated these conversations, I like to invite abusers and their families to visit a self-help group. I only use groups that are all-Latino—and, if possible, Puerto Rican—and that address issues of culture and other matters of concern to their communities. In New York City, there are groups that foster support with a strong political twist; these groups are very successful with young adults and adolescents. If Latino groups are not available, I recommend groups that are racially and ethnically diverse, and I encourage my clients to bring into the discussions in these groups the ideas that we explored in their treatment sessions. I also invite my clients' sponsors to our sessions, where I expose them to my thinking and explain to them my philosophy of treatment.

Other support groups include church, prayer, or Bible study groups, empowerment groups, immigrant support groups, and groups that works with political and social issues. I tell my clients that being politically and socially involved is the best antidote for feeling that you do not have control.

TALKING ABOUT THE ISSUES

The question of when and how a therapist should bring issues of race and oppression into the treatment is always an issue. As a Puerto Rican man with a strong Spanish accent, I have no choice but to address it from the very beginning. I always begin my sessions by introducing myself to my clients and offering information about my immigrant status, my class background, my race, my sexual orientation, and my experiences with cultural transition and by sharing my beliefs about how larger contexts affect our lives. Being transparent about myself with my clients is not a clinical strategy but more a manifestation of how I work. Usually, such honesty sets the tone of how I am going to work and address the issues that bring us together.

Explaining my theory and way of working also helps clients not to feel awkward in talking about these difficult issues in such an open manner. When working with substance abusers, I also lay out my beliefs about addiction, its causes, etiology, and manifestations and do so from a sociopolitical and biopsychosocial perspective.

In addressing the themes of oppression, I use many of my personal experiences and bring into the room the voices of other clients and thus the benefit of their experiences, insights, and reflections about issues of oppression, racism, ethnic prejudice, internalized homophobia, and migration-induced realities. The central theme I try to discuss is how by losing control and becoming addicted the client has fallen into the trap of acting out the stereotyped view that the dominant group has about Puerto Ricans. I tell my clients that every time they lose control, they become another number in the statistics that prove to "them" that Puerto Ricans are "spiks who don't do nothing but get high." Talking about the impact that poverty, migration, and ethnic minority reality have on our lives is done to contextualize addiction within a sociopolitical context. Throughout this process encouraging polarization between "us" and "them" is the beginning of the conversation. Identifying "them" and "us" is the first step in recognizing our marginal, or oppressed, position as well as in identifying who is the oppressor. Dissecting the differences between "us" and "them" become an exploration of our stereotyped views of the oppressor and of other ethnic groups, encourages discussion of our views of our own group, and enables clients to confront their internalized oppression. We then confront our ethnic shame and identify how we perpetuate the stereotypes by conforming to the roles assigned to us by the dominant culture. In order to facilitate the discussion, it is important for me to introduce topics such as poverty, teen pregnancy, the high number of school dropouts and incarcerated men, and the high rates of unemployment. I am always impressed by the reactions I get when I share the census statistics on issues such as poverty and unemployment. Seeing the numbers and reading reports on the alarming reality of the Puerto Rican community help clients to connect the personal with the political.

PRIDE VERSUS SHAME

Oppression does not occur without a context. For Puerto Ricans, as for any other ethnic minority group living in the United States, community and personal problems should always be contextualized within the group's migration history. Expanding the perspective in order to explore the multigenerational impact of migration helps to normalize and validate the experiences of oppression from a psychohistorical perspective. Using this "culture and migration dialogue" approach, I lead the clients into an open discussion about their migration history. This exploration includes their reasons for migration and the history of their adaptation, as well as a detailed tracking of the three migration-induced transitions: acculturation, loss of social status, and loss of support networks. Dissecting the stories about these processes brings up issues that directly relate to the addictions. For instance, exploring how clients reconcile their culture of origin with the host culture has given me the opportunity to address the generational conflicts that often exist between parents and children owing to differing degrees of acculturation. Using a simple scale of 1 to 10, I ask parents and their children to rate how Puerto Rican they feel. Very often the discrepancies that exist between the members of a family—children will usually rate themselves as more Americanized—provide an open forum to address the conflicts about values and belief systems that result from acculturation. Having children share with their parents the things they are learning from the new culture and asking parents to share the values that orient their decisions on discipline helps both parents and children to contextualize their actions and normalize the distance between then; such discussions also help to decrease parental fears of losing their children to the new culture. Within this framework, I am able to help children to talk with their parents about the peer pressure they experience in school and about how the use of drugs or alcohol may be seen as a way to fit into the new environment. Talking about acculturation stresses also helps to contextualize the overfunctioning patterns of familism and *marianismo*. From this perspective, I can discuss with clients how our values orient our choices of coping with problems such as addiction, and I can suggest the need to find ways of caring for our family members without supporting the underfunctioning patterns related to addiction. Uncovering the stresses due to acculturation is also very helpful in discussing the shame that family members experience if they have an alcoholic father. Having family members talk to each other about their fears of being perceived as different from those in the new environment and about their wish to "fit in" helps to contextualize family members' anger and distancing from the addicted member.

Discussing the emotional impact of losing social status owing to migration has helped many of my male clients to contextualize their addiction as a self-medicating strategy for coping with the pains of racism and prejudice. Helping families to understand the stresses of not having a support network validates their sense of isolation and explains how very often the family feels they have limited resources to address crises. Becoming aware of the impact that migration and acculturation processes have on our lives is a liberating experience that helps migrant families to understand their very complex psychosocial reality. I strongly believe that in order to have a future clients need to understand their present within the context of their past history. To do this, it is important to have a sense not only of one's personal history but also of the history of one's ethnic group and one's country of origin. Eliciting pride by helping migrant families to recognize their survival skills and their skills for adaptation helps to reinforce positive self-esteem and a sense of mastery.

Pride is also an important concept to reflect on with addicts. Helping these clients to reconnect with cultural values like self-respect helps to reframe recovery as a process of getting control over the addiction and learning how to respect themselves so that others can respect them and accept them as members of a family and a community.

SPIRITUALITY

As previously mentioned, the Puerto Rican culture places a strong value on spirituality. Our culture is rich in rituals and is heavily influenced by

Catholicism. We believe in the power of God, Jesus Christ, the Virgin Mary, and other saints. Even when a family does not actively observe religious practice, religious values influence the way family members each experience their life. Regardless of their religious practices, Puerto Rican families believe in God or in the existence of a greater power. Enduring suffering, practicing forgiveness, and repentance are values that we can access when working with addiction. Because of its compatibility with these values, the philosophy of self-help groups is very useful in treating addiction among Puerto Ricans. In fact, many successful treatment programs on the island are based on religious conversion as the main intervention in recovery. The desire to turn their life around and live a Christian life and the support of a religious community have been known to work in helping addicts to get control over their addiction and maintain abstinence.

I like to use spirituality as a resource in different ways. For example, I use religious institutions as a concrete resource by inviting a religious figure, such as a priest or a pastor, to participate in therapy sessions and by encouraging my clients to attend a religious service. In my experience, this works very well with parents and sometimes with the siblings of the addicted member. Adolescents, however, do not necessarily engage well with religious activities. In those cases, I like to expand the definition of religion by talking about spirituality. Focusing on ideas about what is good and what is bad, morality, the power of the unknown, and the meaning of believing in a greater power affords me a forum in which I can elicit conversations about the meaning of life. I encourage praying and other rituals for the addicted family member as a way of eliciting hope for recovery. I reinforce connection with a church as a way of breaking the family's isolation and promoting the development of connections with the community.

I draw upon basic beliefs—that God is in charge, that he will never turn his back on you, and that he works in mysterious ways—to elicit hope and patience in working toward recovery. The idea that healing the soul is part of the treatment is, in my way of working, an important belief. By bringing spirituality into the room and making it part of my language, I am in many cases also helping the family to embrace once again values that were abandoned because they were defined as old-fashioned and dystonic with the new environment.

Spirituality also allows me to address how oppression has affected a client's soul by destroying self-esteem, self-respect, self-dignity, and a sense of self-worth. Again, drawing upon the cultural values of self-respect, honor, and dignity, I have the opportunity to talk about how we feel when we lose those values and how we can work to gain them back.

CLOSING REMARKS

THROUGHOUT THIS CHAPTER I have discussed some ideas to be considered when working with Puerto Rican families who are victims of addiction. The central organizing principle of these ideas is the belief that larger ecological forces have a direct impact on families and on individual lives. In the case of poor Puerto Rican families living in the United States, migration issues, sociopolitical oppression, and ethnic marginality have created a unique psychosocial reality that affects family members' level of functioning and adaptation to the host environment. Leaving these issues out of treatment will be detrimental for clients. I believe that therapy is a liberating experience in which we can transform our lives by learning how to reflect on the issues that affect us, thus expanding the views that we have about our lives and making concrete changes that leave us feeling that we have inner and outside resources to overcome adversity. Learning how to expand the lens that we use to explore our predicaments and knowing how to contextualize our lives within the larger context is an empowering experience. In working with addiction, I have learned from my clients the value of having conversations about these issues and have seen its positive impact on recovery. For many of my clients recognizing and validating their experience of oppression has changed their lives in deep and meaningful ways.

I must alert the reader that contextualizing is never about justifying choices or toxic behaviors. The goal of such a rich process is learning to connect the personal with the political and doing so with an understanding that problems are the result of complex processes. Learning how to reflect on the impact of social, political, and psychosocial forces decreases the potential for reacting impulsively and maximizes the chance to better control the future. I believe that addiction among ethnic minority clients is a self-destructive and reactive behavior embedded in oppression. Recovery will only be achieved by becoming aware of its impact and by understanding its effects on our lives.

REFERENCES

Abad, V., & Suarez, J. (1974). Crosscultural Aspects of Alcoholism Among Puerto Ricans. In *The Proceedings of the Fourth Annual Alcoholism Conference* (pp. 282-294). Washington, DC: National Institute of Alcohol Abuse and Alcoholism.

De La Rosa, M. (1991). Patterns and Consequences of Illegal Drug Use Among Hispanics. In M. Sotomayor (Ed.), *Empowering Hispanic Families: A Critical Issue for the '90s* (pp. 39–58). Milwaukee, WI: Family Service America.

Facundo, A. (1991). Sensitive Mental Health Services for Low-Income Puerto Rican Families. In M. Sotomayor (Ed.), *Empowering Hispanic Families: A Critical Issue for the '90s*. (pp. 121–140). Milwaukee, WI: Family Service America.

Garcia-Preto, N. (1996). Puerto Rican Families. In M. McGoldrick, J. Giordano, & J. K. Pearce (Eds.), *Ethnicity and Family Therapy* (2nd ed., pp. 183–199). New York: Guilford Press.

Hernandez, M. (1996). Central American Families. In M. McGoldrick, J. Giordano, & J. K. Pierce (Eds.), *Ethnicity and Family Therapy* (2nd ed., pp. 214–224). New York: Guilford Press.

Hernandez, M., & McGoldrick, M. (1998). Migration and the Family Life Cycle. In B. Carter & M. McGoldrick (Eds.), *The Expanded Family Life Cycle: Individual, Family, and Social Perspectives* (3rd ed., pp. 169–173). Boston: Allyn and Bacon.

Inclan, J. (1980, April 10). The Economic History of Puerto Rico: A History of the Family. Paper presented at the 57th Annual Meeting of the American Orthopsychiatric Association, Toronto (pp. 1–24).

Inclan, J., & Hernandez, M. (1992). Crosscultural Perspectives and Codependence: The Case of Poor Hispanics. *American Journal of Orthopsychiatry, 62*(2), 245–255.

Ramos-McKay, J., Comas-Diaz, L., & Rivera, L. (1988). Puerto Ricans. In L. Comas-Diaz & E. E. H. Griffith (Eds.), *Clinical Guidlines in Crosscultural Mental Health* (pp. 204–232). New York: Wiley-Interscience.

Rodriguez, C. E. (1991). *Puerto Ricans Born in the U.S.A.* Boulder, CO: Westview Press.

Skidmore, T. & Smith, P. (1992). *Modern Latin America*. London: Oxford University Press.

Tichio, G. (1971). Cultural Aspects of Transference and Counter-Transference. *Bulletin of the Menninger Clinic, 35*, 313-334.

CHAPTER TEN

ADDICTION AND GROUPS OF EUROPEAN ORIGIN

Jacqueline Hudak

THIS CHAPTER EXPLORES the connection between a family's ethnic background and its relationship to addiction. While no one factor has been found to cause the disease of addiction, research has revealed that attitudes toward drinking and socially sanctioned drinking practices are important considerations in the development of the disease (Vaillant, 1995). Field studies have found that demographic categories play an important role in alcoholism. Cahalan and Room (1974) identified youth, lower socioeconomic status, minority status (Black or Hispanic), and other conventional ethnic categories (Irish vs. Jewish or Italian) as predictors of drinking problems. Greeley and McCready (1980) identified "ethnic drinking subcultures" and found that they have withstood the otherwise apparent assimilation into mainstream American culture.

Cultural differences are critical factors in the recognition by family, friends, and coworkers that one's drinking has reached problematic proportions. "Tremendous variability persists—even in the wave of widespread publicity regarding the nature of alcoholism as a "disease"—in people's inclination to deny, ignore, adjust to, or confront the drinking patterns of those around them" (Bennett and Ames, 1985, p. 4b).

There are fifty-three categories differentiating families of European ethnicity in the United States. The largest groups are German, English, and Irish. Most of these families have been here for three generations or more and consider themselves American. Their struggles against discrimination have largely faded. A large percentage marry outside their ethnic background. These groups of European origin were some of the first immigrants to this country. Even when clinicians treat second- or third-generation family members, who consider themselves American, they can often detect the nuances and intricacies of European family life that link to a client's ethnic heritage. For example, issues about emotional closeness and distance or about group affiliation versus individual freedom are connected to ethnic background. This is particularly interesting to think about in the context of addiction. Issues about pride and shame are integral to understanding the addictive process. These issues are present for members of each ethnic group, whose own drama about immigration and acculturation affects their sense of ethnic pride. Although research and models for treatment are largely based on the population of European ethnicity, the impact of ethnicity on the addictive process for clients and their family is rarely addressed.

This chapter addresses the clinical needs of American families whose ancestors were of European origin. It provides the clinician with new questions to ask when thinking about addiction in these groups. Case studies are provided to help translate this thinking into action in the therapy room. My goal is to create a context for this discussion that is inclusive of the above-mentioned issues and to then move to more central issues about gender, power, and privilege, issues that have for so long been obscured in our conversations, thinking, and research on addiction. Genetic factors, as well as the cultural context in which the disease develops, are also central to this discussion. Since Alcoholics Anonymous (AA) is the dominant model of treatment for addiction, AA as a social construct will be examined in light of its fit with particular cultures.

Some of the questions about the impact of culture on addiction are not easily answered. For example, because European groups have largely assimilated and presently seek to identify themselves as American, it is difficult to tease out the differences in sociopolitical power between each group. In general terms, we know, for example, that the Irish, German, and Anglo populations have become more assimilated and subsequently have had more privilege than the descendants of Italian or Polish immigrants. At different points in U.S. history it has been more dangerous for some group—at some points Irish, at other times German, Polish, or Italian—to claim their heritage. This means that at such times members of that group had difficulty getting a job or were discriminated against in some other way. Yet they always had the option of disguising or relinquishing their ethnic background in ways that were and are not available to African American or other immigrants of color. The fact that these groups were White afforded them advantages not available to people of color.

Although the immigration experience did eventually translate to privilege for members of these European groups, they encountered discrimination at first in a variety of ways. An interesting theme that emerges in writings about these groups is the importance of stoicism in their lives. The ability to feel pain and not let it show was a survival tool for many immigrant groups. It was communicated in hushed tones in the early, crowded settlements, stops on the way to fulfillment of the American dream: "Don't let it show." "Don't show your weakness." No doubt this survival tool had a strong connection with the immigrants' relationship to alcohol, which could function either to inhibit or permit the expression of those painful feelings (Bepko and Krestan, 1985). This is most evident when the variable of gender is taken into account: a woman, not socialized to show anger, could do so under the influence of alcohol; likewise, a man, not socialized to be emotionally vulnerable, could do so after a few beers.

IRISH FAMILIES

"The drunkard was treated with care and affection, with a special connotation of sympathy, love, and pity. He was sometimes envied by the sober" (Bales, 1962, p. 170).

W E BEGIN WITH the Irish. Much has been written about their propensity for hard drinking and their tolerance for excessive drunkenness. Whiskey, or aqua vitae, was first used in Ireland only as a medicine. The Irish historian Moorewood (1824) states it "was considered a panacea for all disorders, and the physicians recommended it to patients indiscriminately for preserving health, dissipating humors, strengthening the heart, curing colic, dropsy, palsy, quarantine fever, stone, and even prolonging existence itself beyond the common limits".

Bales (1946) suggests that the prevalence of this utilitarian attitude toward drinking partly explains the historically high rate of alcoholism among the Irish. The prevailing attitudes in a culture toward the use of intoxicants is important in assessing its members' to alcoholism. For the Irish, alcohol had a functional value. It served a purpose and filled a need and thus could be viewed as a necessity in life.

Between 1840 and 1860, more than a million Irish peasants immigrated to the United States. No other country has given up a greater proportion of its population to the United States (McGoldrick, Giordano, and Pearce, 1996). The majority of these immigrants left to escape British oppression. They frequently settled in large urban areas such as New York, Chicago, Boston, and Philadelphia. At one time the Irish were among the ethnic groups most discriminated against in America. They were thought to be dirty, lazy, rowdy, and, above all, drunkards (Clark, 1973; Curtis, 1971). Irish immigrants started out on the side of the oppressed, but they soon learned of their ability to define themselves as members of the dominant (White) group (Ignatiev, 1995). They moved quickly toward this redefinition of themselves by giving up previously held alliances with groups such as the antislavery movement. By the second generation, the Irish thought of themselves primarily as American.

Some scholars believe that the nine-hundred-year history of oppression by the English has a strong connection to the propensity toward heavy drinking on the part of Irish men. O'Connor (1996), who views alcoholism as a "major public health problem among Irish Catholics," suggests that Irish drinking patterns were shaped by a sense of cultural inferiority resulting from the oppression experienced by the Irish on both sides of the Atlantic. Alcohol was perceived as the balm to soothe the pain of powerlessness. Indeed, the victimization of Irish men is evident in most theories regarding Irish culture, and fosters the sentiment that they should be treated specially. Denied their right to inherit from their fathers, Irish families were often tied to paying very high rents. This, combined with the horror of extreme poverty and famine, leads O'Connor (1996) to suggest genocide. "Even if genocide was not consciously intended, the forced migration after the famine of two million Irish Catholics to North America and elsewhere in the world jeopardized the nation's future by destabilizing the intellectual, cultural, and political life of the country" (p. 128).

Eventually the Irish did, for the most part, flourish in the United States. Therefore, it may be difficult to view them as a group that at one time was rendered nearly extinct. O'Connor proposes that alcohol mediated their internal conflict between self-destruction and self-preservation. This feeling of cultural inferiority may still exist, despite the present-day trappings of success and power for Irish American families.

The political and social history of Ireland as a colonized nation also impacts the ways in which women function in Irish families. Catholicism in Ireland created a paradoxical quality to the Irish woman's role: she was expected to be strong and subservient at the same time. Mothers were expected to rule the family with an iron hand but remain subservient to the teachings and traditions of the Catholic religion. Irish women have little expectation of or interest in being taken care of by a man (McGoldrick et al. 1996). An Irish wife is likely to try to do everything by herself, and asks for little help.

The Irish are the only European group in which the emigration of women to the United States far surpassed that of men (McGoldrick, 1996, p. 557). In this country, as in their homeland, Irish women continued to be reluctant about marrying and enjoyed a range of options regarding careers in teaching, nursing, or the convent.

In general, the Irish adapted well and eventually flourished. Saloons and the church were the focal points of their community. Their values permitted them to accommodate to U.S. society without giving up their deeply rooted culture. Catholic schools transmitted Irish cultural values to generations of Irish American children. Alcohol was integrated into virtually all aspects of Irish life. Stivers (1976) suggests that drinking was important among Irish immigrants as a "national identifying trait": "In Ireland, drink was largely a sign of male identity; in America it was a symbol of Irish identity" (p. 129). Thus, hard drinking made one "more Irish." The stereotype of the Irish American as a drunkard intensified and became institutionalized in a number of ways. These included employment practices (men were sometimes partially paid in whiskey), job and police discrimination, and treatment in the popular culture (Stivers, 1976). An example of the latter is the caricature of the Irishman in theatrical productions, in which the Irish character was always seen carrying and drinking from a bottle of whiskey.

The clinician who treats an Irish family should be aware that loyalty to each other, privacy, and suffering will dominate the family's process. Although the Irish demand total loyalty from family members, this demand, along with many other feelings, is unexpressed. A bond of protective privacy will block discussion, no matter how blatant or obvious the problem or feeling. The Irish think of problems as a private matter between themselves and God. They do not discuss problematic issues outside the family, often choosing instead to turn to spiritual practices. The lighting of candles, saying novenas or the Rosary, and daily attendance at Mass are common ways for both men and women to handle problems. Congruent with the teachings of Catholicism, the concept of suffering, or the notion that everyone has a cross to bear, is central to the thinking of Irish families. This concept of suffering is further reinforced by the spiritual belief that it is only in the afterlife that one will be freed of the pains and burdens of being on earth. A high tolerance for emotional pain is inevitably the result of such a belief system, which places the notion of suffering at the core of the way things are "supposed to be." Catholic teachings are replete with stories about martyrs who suffered in the name of God. Thus, suffering and emotional pain are normalized in Irish families. It is probable, then, that individual family members who are drinking heavily may not notice that anything is wrong.

Let us consider how the values and family structure intrinsic to Irish culture relate to the treatment of addiction in Irish families. What are children taught about alcohol use in their families? Recalling the utilitarian approach to alcohol use that is embedded in the culture of the Irish, the clinician must assess to what extent this posture toward alcohol as a necessary part of everyday life continues to exist. Many clients do tell stories about the medicinal use of alcohol in their family: a shot of whiskey might be expected to cure menstrual cramps, a headache, or the common cold. Further, Vaillant (1995) describes the use of alcohol in Irish families, as compared to those from Mediterranean cultures, and hypothesizes that this to some extent also accounts for the higher rates of addiction. Although food dulls the effect of alcohol, the Irish tend to drink high-proof liquor without food. They also tend to drink outside the home, away from the family, such as at local pubs. There is a high tolerance in the Irish for both drinking and drunkenness, and the alcoholic is seen as an object of pity or amusement rather than criticism (Walsh 1987).

In Irish culture, women's alcohol use and addiction often become obscured in a discussion that has for so long focused on the male alcoholic. We know that women tend to use alcohol in isolation and continue to function, often in ways that men do not. Irish women, although not as heavy drinkers as Irish men, do drink more than women from other ethnic groups (Johnson, 1991). Disinhibition or loss of control in any form in Irish women, who tend to drink at home and alone, is considered extremely embarrassing for the family.

The family clinician needs to pay particular attention to the patterns of women's drinking in Irish families, as it may often go unnoticed or remain secret owing to this embarrassment. Questions should be formulated in the context of care and concern about the woman's health, and the clinician should assume a nonblaming stance. The family may need to be educated about alcoholism in general and the particular health consequences for women. Typical barriers to treatment for women include lack of alternative means of child care and intense shame. The clinician should be aware of and strategize to accommodate both of these concerns.

The clinicians need to be aware that they are treating families who view a tremendous amount of drinking as normal. Indeed, they may present with other problems, such as marital discord, affairs, young children with school problems, or acting-out adolescents. Since the family may not view drinking as the problem despite the family history, the onus of responsibility is on the clinician to explore this issue. A thorough assessment of drinking behavior across generations should be done despite this potential protestation of the client: "This has nothing to do with what's happening today!" In fact, Bepko and Krestan (1985) always assess the existence of alcoholism, assuming that it exists "unless proven otherwise."

Clinicians must be aware of their own family issues with addiction. Denial about one's own issues makes it difficult to recognize and treat others.

This awareness is tantamount to good addiction treatment. Denial in clients is a prevailing symptom of the disease; it is present in varying degrees, depending upon the family's presentation for treatment.

The value of loyalty to one's family, combined with the acceptance of suffering and the notion of drinking as normal, can create a formidable climate within which the clinician must begin to address addiction in an Irish family. Although deeply concerned or angered by a loved one's drinking, an Irish person may perceive confrontation over the drinking as a act. The family clinician must reframe this confrontation as an act of love and concern on behalf of someone who needs help. But compassion needs to exist together with accountability; the clinician must challenge the family's acceptance of alcoholism, particularly in men, as normal or inevitable. Since the family process is systemic, in a heterosexual relationship a woman should be coached to become aware of the ways in which she has overfunctioned for her husband. This overfunctioning behavior should not be framed as an illness, which is common in the language of Al-Anon, but rather as a protective response to a family crisis that is no longer helpful.

The lack of expression of feeling in an Irish family can also be a complication. The clinician must guide the family with clear interventions, such as "Tell your father how his drinking has impacted you." The deep sense of personal responsibility among the Irish can foster movement toward recovery. Also, their spiritual connection is consistent with the tenets of AA. For centuries the Irish have turned to God for help. They should be encouraged to attend AA and Al-Anon early in treatment.

CASE STUDY

Patty and Ed entered treatment for marital counseling after twenty-six years of marriage. They had three grown children: two sons and a daughter. Ed, a second-generation Irishman, was a self-employed carpenter who worked sporadically and brought in income inconsistently. Some years earlier Ed had lost his seat on the New York Stock Exchange, owing to drinking and embezzlement. He had at least five citations for drunk driving and had lost his license. Patty, who was also second-generation Irish, was the supervisor of nursing for a large hospital.

The presenting problem was Patty's concern for Ed's health. He was a diabetic, and refused to follow treatment for it or see a doctor for other medical concerns. When asked to elaborate further, Patty said that Ed had been impotent for some time.

Patty and Ed had disparate views of their history together. Despite his numerous citations for drunk driving and employment history, Ed denied he was an alcoholic. He continued to drink, sometimes falling asleep at the dinner table. The couple fought bitterly about this in sessions and appeared quite embarrassed by their very different views of their history together.

The children were brought into a session and were quite reticent to talk about their father's alcoholism. Although they could agree that sometimes he got "carried away" (a familiar refrain), their assessment of his behavior never went beyond that and they did not see his drinking as a problem.

Ed's drinking needed to be reframed as alcoholism for the couple and family; both were encouraged to attend twelve-step meetings, and Patty complied. She began to view the primary health problem as alcoholism. Ed continued to attend therapy—and to drink.

The couple soon reported that the sessions had become too emotionally painful. They were unused to such frank discussion about their problems and remained completely polarized about their views on Ed's drinking. Eventually Ed made the decision to stop drinking as the only way to "shut Patty up." He was able to remain without liquor for some time. Patty continued in Al-Anon and decided to remain in the marriage. She stated that she was quite satisfied that Ed had stopped drinking and really did not expect the marriage to improve beyond that. Patty, as is common for Irish women, was used to her very high level of functioning, and she did not look to Ed for emotional support and comfort.

This case is a good illustration of the impact of ethnicity on the development and maintenance of addiction in Irish families. The norm of suffering and an almost unquestioning acceptance of negative events and consequences serve to sustain the heavy drinking. The description of Patty—as an extremely competent woman with very little need or expectation of emotional support from her husband or children—is so very consistent with Irish women. These gender roles persist to an alarming degree in present-day Irish American families.

Even though Ed did stop drinking, this was framed only "as a way to shut Patty up." Although this was our desired outcome, his reasoning completely dismisses Patty's valid concerns and obscures the history relevant to his abuse of alcohol. It was the family's, in particular Patty's, acceptance of this outcome that prohibited the clinician from pressing for sobriety in AA, which would have fostered further behavioral changes.

GERMAN FAMILIES

THE IMAGE OF the German *fräulein* in a traditional costume with a trayful of beer steins is familiar to many. German beer gardens and the annual Oktoberfest are synonymous with this culture. Although known for its beer production and consumption, Germany also produces wine, in the Rhine Valley region of the country. Compared to associations to the image of the suffering Irish "drunkard," associations with German drinking are more about fun, sport, outdoor activities, and a national holiday. In German culture, there is a strong emphasis on outdoor physical activity, such as hiking, skiing, or skating, and such activity often involves the whole family (Vogt, 1995). Men in Germany do drink large quantities of alcohol. Beginning in their teenage years, they are encouraged to drink with their peer group and in the company of other men. Women drink only moderately: drunkenness in women is considered inappropriate (Vogt, 1995).

Germans are the largest and oldest immigrated group in the United States. The 1990 census counted fifty-eight million Americans of German heritage. The official beginning of German immigration was marked by the arrival of the *Concord* in 1683, although there were German settlers in Jamestown as early as 1607 (Furer, 1973). Pennsylvania leads as a home for Germans, followed later by Cincinnati and other large cities of the Midwest, particularly in Wisconsin (Winawer and Wetzel, 1996). Immigration declined in the twentieth century, with New York leading as home to German Americans until 1970. German Americans made significant contributions to new methods of agricultural production and were noted for their technical abilities in the fields of engineering and science (Billigmeier, 1974).

Since German Americans have become so well assimilated into the dominant culture, we can hypothesize that their levels of alcohol use are consistent with those in the general (White) population. That is, men would generally consume more than women, with the highest consumption rates being for those aged eighteen to twenty-nine (Hudak, Krestan, and Bepko, 1999).

Despite their numbers, German Americans are often less visible than other groups. This is due to physical characteristics, intermarriage and assimilation, and the two wars of the twentieth century. The wars had tremendous impact on a person's propensity to identify as German and resulted in a great loss of ethnic identity and pride. Xenophobia was intense during World War I, and suppression of German language and culture was pervasive. World War II left German Americans few positive cultural ties with which they could identify. Thus, one's German roots were toned down and expressed carefully or secretly (Winawer and Wetzel, 1996).

The cultural identity of families that immigrated to the United States was determined by the region from which they emigrated and also by their religion. Cultural unity was limited. For example, Catholic Germans were likely more traditional and subject to the authority of the church whereas Protestants placed a higher value on the role of individual responsibility (Winawer and Wetzel, 1996). Gender roles were rigid, with the women assigned to "children, kitchen and church" (Winawer and Wetzel, 1996, p. 505).

German society is highly structured, with clear boundaries both in and outside the home. There is a more subtle style of communication in the German family, than in, for example, the more verbal Italian family. German Americans come to treatment when they feel they have no alternative. Privacy is highly valued, and conflicts that are experienced as embarrassing are to be contained within the family. Germans are known to employ emotional restraint: they rarely show emotion openly or in public. The clinician may find that they talk about intensely painful issues with little or no affect. This lack of display should not be confused with a lack of feeling, however; Germans are sentimental and loyal.

German American fathers are known for being rather stern and strict, and family history may reveal corporal punishment used as discipline. Fathers may also be emotionally distant. They have a strong work ethic and are quite successful in their careers.

Highly assimilated Germans and those who have intermarried may have to be guided by the clinician to explore their ethnic background. They may be reluctant, especially if there is any shame about being German. Family history, particularly if members had any involvement with war crimes, may contain deeply buried family secrets (Winawer and Wetzel, 1996). One can easily see the kind of trepidation clients deal with in telling their story.

In addition to shame about ethnic issues, it is also important to consider clients' shame regarding their inability to stop using an addictive substance. Negative feelings about one's ethnicity and the need to keep them secret are an important part of the context within which the addiction develops. The clinician must carefully tend to these layers of shame. Clients' ingestion of the addictive substance, alcohol or otherwise, is meant to change their experience of themselves.

It is often difficult to admit addiction when one is a member of a group with such privilege and has had "everything, that is, secure home, stable financial picture, a good education—in short, access to everything American. Indeed, German American parents of an addicted child may feel this strongly.

The restrained emotional climate in a German American family can serve to inhibit the addictive process. Drunkenness that results in emotional upheaval is not tolerated, particularly if it is public and brings embarrassment to the family. However, alcohol can also serve to ameliorate this emotional constraint, permitting outbursts in the privacy of the home.

Family life is highly valued in German American families. Aunts, uncles, cousins, and so on are usually part of a well-organized family structure that has regular contact or a strong emotional connection to the family being treated. Clinicians should use the extended family to carefully track the presence of others in the family who are in recovery and could be a resource to the client or family. The family clinician should fully explore issues of addiction and recovery in the extended family as well and whenever possible include family members in treatment.

Work and education are highly valued by German Americans. Families may have motivation to change if the addiction has decreased functioning in either area. Families may tolerate drinking by their college-age children, but they become gravely concerned if it impacts on their grades. Expectations are generally high for the children of this group, as well as for the parents themselves.

German Americans generally respond well to authority, so the clinician can be straightforward and confront the alcoholism. Gender roles in these families tend to be traditional and somewhat rigid. Alcohol use should be tracked carefully in couples presenting for marital treatment with this ethnic background, since alcohol can be a regulator for issues such as emotional closeness and distance and acting in or out of one's gender role (Bepko and Krestan, 1985).

It is likely that the adolescent phase of the life cycle will be most impacted by addiction in German American families. The fact that German Americans rarely talk openly about struggle creates particular difficulty for them during their teenage years, when the developmental task is to struggle about everything. The authoritarian posture assumed by fathers in these families contributes to the inhibition of this process of challenge and yearning to be on one's own.

Case Study

The S family called for consultation about their seventeen-year-old son, Alex. Recently, his grades had been dropping, and he seemed depressed and isolated. He was a junior in high school, so the parents were quite anxious about how this would affect his college admissions process. Alex was the oldest of three children and had two younger sisters, ages fourteen and ten. The girls were doing well academically and excelled in sports.

Mr. S had a PhD in engineering and did quite well with a local firm. Mrs. S had a bachelor's degree from an Ivy League school and worked outside the home prior to the birth of her children. She was active in community organizations and was on the board of education for her children's school district.

During the first interview, the family related their concerns about Alex's sullen behavior. Mrs. S revealed that there was an incident about six months prior when they returned home late one evening to find Alex "passed out" on the couch, smelling of alcohol. Alex denied that he had been drinking. The family had little conversation about this incident afterward.

Family history revealed that Mr. S had "some German" in his background, among other ethnicities. When asked to elaborate further, Mr. S talked about his paternal grandfather's immigration to this country: "I don't know what he did, and I don't want to know." He was also unclear about family members on his maternal side.

Mrs. S was a fourth-generation descendant of English–German heritage. She knew that her ancestors had come over in the 1700s but knew little about the family story other than the fact that they were successful farmers who owned a good deal of land.

The family presented as congenial and polite; the parents seemed confused by Alex's lack of interest in moving forward with his life. It was clear that they cared deeply about one another, but this was not expressed with words. Each parent presented as trying to do a good job for the sake of helping their children get ahead in life.

During an individual interview, Alex reported drinking both alone and with a few peers several times a week. He related feeling very distant from his father in particular. Alex eventually contracted with the clinician to attempt to stop drinking and to inform his parents about his consumption. Alex's parents were shocked to learn of the extent of his drinking. Mr. S was obviously furious. Still, few words were exchanged.

Several months later the family called in crisis to report that Alex was again caught drinking. The parents began to explore inpatient hospitalization for Alex, who agreed to go. Mr. S was quite intolerant regarding his son's need for hospitalization. He could not understand Alex's inability to stop on his own, as promised, and he stated that he was "humiliated" by the thought of the community finding out. His focus was very future oriented. He displayed little patience with the process of taking a family history. In fact, he was visibly distressed when the clinician asked about his own family background.

Mrs. S was desperate to get help for her son, at any cost. She began to challenge Mr. S's posture about his family background, and marital struggles began to surface. Mrs. S pleaded with her husband to talk about his family, particularly the paternal side. With much reluctance he began to share the story of his father's involvement with the war as a member of the German army. This was a fact he had wanted to keep hidden. It soon became clear that the intense pressure felt by Alex to succeed, to "do right" and bring honor to the family name, was connected to the secret about his grandfather. Mr. S's shame and inability to express his grief were palpable; he was horrified by his father's deeds but loved him still. This energy was put into his relationship with Alex, as if to counter the loss from the previous generation.

The process of simultaneously working on the addiction and the ethnic shame issues worked well for Alex. His relationship with alcohol had provided the desired emotional distance from his demanding father. Now, without the alcohol, he needed to manage his relationship with his father in a new and better way. His parents' ability to explore their past took the constant focus off Alex and his future achievements.

Alex returned to his community and attended AA meetings, where he met peers who were also learning not to use drugs or alcohol. The family continued in therapy to define more clearly how to manage the life cycle issues associated with adolescence.

ANGLO AMERICANS

"An Anglo American may drink a great deal without noticing that it is a problem. Cocktails before dinner, wine with dinner, and an after dinner aperitif may be regarded as gracious living, a matter of pride, not embarrassment" (McGill and Pearce, 1996, p. 458).

THE UNITED KINGDOM consists of England, Wales, Scotland, and Northern Ireland. The UK may be grouped with Protestant cultures that have considerable ambivalence about alcohol, even though there is widespread use and a general acceptance of it. In the UK, alcohol consumption is not especially high, but alcohol misuse has long been regarded as a major national problem (Plant, 1995).

Approximately seventy million Americans (one quarter of the population) have ancestors who descended from the English colonists counted in the first United States census of 1790. These early colonists came in search of religious freedoms; they were not victims of famine or extreme poverty. They came with the notion that America was the land of opportunity, a land where individuals could achieve untold fortune if only they were willing to work hard. This theme prevails today in Anglo American families. They have been calling themselves American for a long time: "They fought the English 200 years ago to be American, not English" (McGill and Pearce, 1996, p. 460). They came to this country early, and became part of the dominant culture. Their wealth and privilege are highly visible in our culture, despite the norm in many families to not talk about such issues.

Individual freedom and psychological individualism are the values that most distinguish Anglo American families from other American families. The clinician sitting with an Anglo American family will note that family members are expected to be strong and independent and to "make it alone." Self-control is highly valued in these families, with little tolerance for public displays of emotion or conflict. Normal drinking may involve consumption of large amounts of alcohol by a member of the family, but there is no tolerance for drunkenness. Indeed, drunkenness is viewed by Anglo Americans as a shameful loss of self-control that must be stopped or hidden. Starting treatment can be difficult and embarrassing for these families, since alcoholism is often viewed as a personal failure or shortcoming.

Once treatment begins, an Anglo American family will want to clearly define the problem and then work hard toward the resolution. However, while family members may readily perceive the problem as alcoholism, they are often quite unrealistic about the process leading toward sobriety. They may desire a quick "fix" and have a difficult time understanding the alcoholic's struggle to stay sober. The family may continue to doubt the disease concept of alcoholism, which runs counter to their belief that "you can achieve anything." Since their orientation about self-control is so strong, they may insist upon viewing the problem as a personal shortcoming.

The values of strength of will and self-control make it especially difficult for Anglo American clients to surrender to the fact that they are out of control of their drinking. They may make many fruitless attempts to control their drinking on their own, which adds to their sense of inadequacy and shame. Even in sobriety, they may view themselves, or be viewed by others close to them, as weak. Their financial resources can often access good treatment facilities or keep hidden the problem drinking for many years.

Functioning at a high level is a central value in these families. It seems that as long as a man continues to function in his job, it is difficult to confront him about his drinking. Particularly if the job is high paying and prestigious, the family is apt to maintain the notion that so long as his work is not interfered with, he is fine. If the drinking of such an individual does interfere with his employ, he, as a valued, high-level executive, would no doubt be encouraged to attend an inpatient recovery program, which would be paid for by the company, with his job waiting for him upon his discharge.

The clinical picture for a woman in such families is somewhat different, and more frightening. We know that women tend to drink in isolation (Bepko and Krestan, 1985) and that their addictions can remain hidden for years. We know too that they can easily become cross-addicted. Data indicates that their addictions are often misdiagnosed. They are at risk for overdose from a combination of alcohol and prescription drugs. Like men, women are expected to work hard and to be successful. While the arena of success for men is the more public work sphere, for women it is generally the home and children, along with perhaps various charity activities. Even though an Anglo American woman may have attended one of the best colleges and may even have worked successfully for some years, the birth of children necessitates negotiation of who will be responsible for their care on a daily basis. Often it is the woman who will give up her job, even if the couple is fortunate enough to have live-in child care.

The stress of giving up one's job to be at home, along with the isolation, can be difficult. Often the husband is working long hours. The norm in Anglo American families of strength of will and independence does not promote the open discussion of emotional issues such as loneliness or feeling about dependency. A woman in such a situation might seek solace by consulting a doctor, who may prescribe antidepressants. This need for help may be viewed by those in her family as a crutch that can isolate and depress her further. The use of alcohol on a regular basis as part of gracious living further complicates this picture, since it can serve to restrain or promote the expression of feelings. It is easy, then, to see how the process of addiction can be superimposed on this picture. Further, it is important to note the special circumstances for women: drunken, out-of-control behavior is not tolerated in them and, unlike men, they have no (corporate) support system to help move them discreetly into recovery.

Children in Anglo American families are raised to be responsible and self-contained. Parents will frequently pay for treatment for them but remain reluctant to become too involved. A parent might remain in denial for a long time about a child's problem, so long as the child continues to play sports or make good grades in a prestigious school. A family may experience the addiction of a member with a deep sense of embarrassment and as a personal shortcoming on the part of the alcoholic.

The first step of the AA's Twelve Steps program—surrendering that one is powerless over one's drinking—is the very antithesis of Anglo American individualist thinking. Thus, the clinician should have many conversations with the client about this particular aspect of treatment and recovery.

CASE STUDY

Fran was a thirty-four-year-old married woman with an eighteen-month-old son. Her husband was a partner in a prestigious law firm begun by his grandfather. Fran's complaint was her husband's drinking. She had been concerned about it for quite some time: even prior to the marriage she had discussed it with her husband and the cleric during their prenuptial counseling.

Fran was the youngest of three daughters. Her mother was a successful educator, her father a real-estate professional. Fran enjoyed the privileges of a private education and membership in private country clubs. She had a master's degree in education and had spent years teaching at an elite preschool. She left this job, which she loved, when the family moved to the suburbs, and she then devoted her time to raising her child and decorating their large home.

Rob, her husband, grew up in New England and had a similar background. He was the oldest child of three and the only son. His parents were both physicians. He too enjoyed a private education. Indeed, it was as if he were groomed from early life for his present position.

Rob did not view his drinking as a problem; in fact, he felt quite entitled to enjoy an expensive bottle of wine. He saw the presenting problem as his wife's lack of adjustment to suburbia and felt the solution was for her to become involved in charities and sports. He refused to entertain the notion of either stopping or decreasing his alcohol intake.

Fran entered a woman's group whose members were struggling

with issues of addiction in their families. She resisted the recommendation to attend Al-Anon, because of her concern about the alcoholism in her family becoming known in the community. She began to explore the use of alcohol in her family of origin and to question the level of use by both of her parents, concluding, "I now realize the level of tension and anxiety that exists before my father has his first martini." Like so many in Anglo families, Fran simply never paid attention to the often large quantity consumed as a daily ritual of the cocktail hour.

Fran's parents and sisters came into treatment with her. They immediately sought to know what the problem was and how to fix it. They had a difficult time dwelling on any emotions, particularly Fran's grief and pain about her dissolving marriage.

Rob eventually responded by filing for divorce from Fran. It was as if he viewed the marriage relationship as a contract between the two, a contract that Fran broke.

SCOTS AND SCOTCH-IRISH

Section Contributed by Jo-Ann Krestan

Today, more than ten million United States citizens claim Scottish or Scotch-Irish ancestry. Products of the Scottish Reformation, both the Scots and the Scotch-Irish are primarily of Presbyterian heritage, having rejected the Anglican and Roman Catholic Churches to embrace a Calvinist tradition. Hess (1995) says, "The issue of descent is somewhat confused, as not all historians and social scientists count Scotch-Irish as a culturally distinct group" (p. 200). The discussion here is primarily of the Scotch-Irish, except where specifically noted.

In the 1600s the British had lured Scottish subjects to Ireland in an effort to control that "savage, uncivilized" population. But the Scots, who already felt inferior to the British were, naturally, deeply resented by the Irish whom they were sent to control. They, in turn, looked down on the Irish and kept their distance from them. When the opportunity came to emigrate to the United States, the Scots seized it eagerly.

Between 1680 and 1840, over seven hundred thousand Scots and Scotch-Irish emigrated to the United States. The Scots emigrated primarily in clans, while the Scotch-Irish came largely as individuals or as families. The effects of two mass migrations—the first from Scotland to Ulster in the early 1600s amid poverty and political provocation and the second from Ulster (as well as directly from Scotland) to the United States in search of religious freedom—made for a people who were "practiced in abandoning their past" (Blethen and Wood, 1997, p. 2). They survived by borrowing useful cultural elements from others. Once in this country, the Scotch-Irish had the least likelihood of all ethnic groups to identify ethnically and the greatest tendency to marry out.

Upon entering first the colonies and then the United States, Scotch-Irish artisans and laborers sought life in cities like Philadelphia. The farmers moved inland, creating settlements from Georgia to Nova Scotia. They claimed the hillier, less hospitable land not yet settled by the Germans and the English who had preceded them. Eventually, the Scotch-Irish claimed the entire backcountry of the Appalachian Mountain range. Scots and Scotch-Irish claimed Nova Scotia (New Scotland) and much of the down east coast of Maine. There, settling land grants heavily promoted in Scotland by the grantors, they worked in the fisheries and also in the fur and lumber industries. Farming was harder, but they introduced the potato plant; today, Aroostook "the County" Maine is known for potato production on a large scale.

New England was less hospitable to Presbyterianism than the Mid-Atlantic states were. Willis (1859) claimed that New England was the "peculiar land of Congregationalism or Independency" (p. 24). Actually, the belief systems of the two denominations were very similar, but governmental structures within them differed.

Despite their skill at adopting other people's ways, the Scotch-Irish also developed an extremely strong culture of their own. Gradually the Appalachian region became almost synonymous with the Scotch-Irish culture, which tended to absorb the cultures of the earlier English and Germans. The coast of northern New England is heavily Scotch-Irish. Nashville, Tennessee and Branson, Missouri, in the Ozarks, persist as the homes of bluegrass. One can still hear Gaelic spoken and see the "clog" danced.

Mountain Moonshine

Wake up wake up darlin' Corey
What makes you sleep so sound?
The revenue officer is comin'
Gonna tear your still house down . . .

This folk ballad conjures up the stereotype of the mountaineer moonshiner. According to Alan Lomax (1947), it is based on a Kentucky "moonshinin' gal," who represented a frontier type well known in the hill country. The stereotype also still persists of uneducated, inbred "hillbillies" with names like Lil' Abner from places with names like Dogpatch. A *New York Times* article on August 1, 1998, discusses the persistence of these stereotypes in a discussion of the media coverage of the Clinton affair.

Scotch whisky is still considered the national drink of Scotland (1994). The Scots, who migrated first to northern Ireland and then to the colonies, came with a taste for whiskey and a skill at distilling and exporting spirits. In the United States they converted corn to liquor, which was easier to transport out of the mountains than corn—and more profitable. They created a lucrative industry in the Appalachian backcountry, which provided moonshine that was primarily created for export but was also put to some personal use (alcohol was used for sore throats and poultices). In the late 1700s the United States government tried to regulate this industry. The Scotch-Irish, fierce believers in individual rights and well accustomed to fighting oppressive governments, were outraged. They became proficient at evading the revenuer as their production and consumption of moonshine went underground. Having honed their fighting skills in the border wars between England and Scotland, and later against the Irish, the Scotch-Irish brought here an appetite for combat and adventure that served them well against the government. Violence was not uncommon in their fight to preserve their survival economy and protect their individual rights.

The Scotch-Irish also brought a fierce insistence on religious freedom. They were heavily persecuted in Ulster by the English, who would not permit marriages in the Presbyterian church, labeling them unions of "fornication." The Scotch-Irish fiercely defended their faith. These Presbyterians, and later Baptists, Methodists, and other conservative Protestants, were characterized by a very extreme theology. The rigidity of Calvinist control, with its stringent prescriptions for behavior yet egalitarian governing structure, can be symbolized by the stereotypes of the dour Scot and the determined moonshiner who would bow to no authority to pay taxes. Good or evil, Black or White, kin or enemy, extreme breeds extreme.

Not surprisingly, the Scotch-Irish have a profound ambivalence toward alcohol that many researchers (Ames, 1985; Cahalan et al., 1969; Heath, 1995) claim typifies a peculiarly Protestant belief system. Edwards (1985) points out that the same preacher might accept a jug of whiskey for payment and then condemn drinkers to hell from the pulpit. Calvinist theology doesn't exactly encourage dancing in the streets. Work is all-important, and carousing and partying take place only when the work is done. Behavior that becomes out of control owing to liquor produces terrible guilt. The cycles of sin and redemption find expression in a high prevalence of both binge drinking and abstinence, in the use of alcohol as a home remedy for virtually every ill, and in the temperance movements spawned by Protestantism. These seemingly contradictory values of origin are expressed in the saying "Praise God and pass the ammunition."

The Scotch-Irish emphasis on individual rights heavily influenced the politics of the United States. The election of Andrew Jackson made American politics a populist democracy. Like the English and the Germans before them, the Scots and the Scotch-Irish were among the earliest colonists. Together they created the dominant White Anglo Saxon Protestant culture.

CLASS, CLAN, AND GENDER

The Scotch-Irish are extremely sensitive to class issues. My Scotch-Irish friend Hattie's first inquiry about people I want to introduce her to is whether they look down on other people. She is a typical Down-Easter, that is, fiercely self-reliant, proud to a fault, and with a profound disdain for those who think they are better than other people. Her family's farm sustained four generations: they spun their own wool, stored clams dug in summer in cornmeal in the barn so they could have chowder all winter, cut their own ice from the mill pond.

Many of the wealthiest people in New England, stalwarts now of the large, white Congregational churches that grace the little towns of Maine, New Hampshire, Vermont, and Massachusetts, are also of Scots or Scotch-Irish ancestry. Their reputation for being thrifty is synonymous with what we think of as a Yankee virtue. Pretentiousness is eschewed.

Then there is Appalachia and an entire culture of the rural, particularly the Southern rural, poor. The Scotch-Irish of Appalachia are characterized by a high incidence of domestic violence, chronic malnutrition, and high infant mortality (Hess, 1995).

The extreme isolation of rural settlements, particularly in the Appalachians, Nova Scotia, and the Ozarks, intensified in the Scotch-Irish a natural reliance on family. "The family, then, becomes a clan with intense loyalty toward one another. Even when family members do not like each other very much, they are tradition bound to defend and protect their own from outsiders and alien institutions, such as schools, government offices, and social and health care agencies" (Edwards, 1985, p. 141). A man from the Ozarks put it to the author succinctly by saying, "We'uns don't like outsiders."

Edwards (1985) points out that the educated mountaineer often lives within two cultures: the mainstream culture, as typified by the schools and other institutions in the community, and his own subculture, with its extremely rigid set of rules. Individuals who leave home and seek their education and fortune elsewhere may be suspect for disloyalty, particularly if they do not travel back to attend the ubiquitous family reunions, birthday celebrations, and other festive occasions. Family members may feel that such individuals think they are "beyond them."

It is disloyal in Scotch-Irish families to call a loved one an alcoholic, and it would be an act of desperation to seek help from outsiders. The concept of "enabling" in traditional alcoholism treatment would characterize most families that have drinkers. The family protects its own even at its own expense. Addicts themselves also will have trouble seeking outside help, because of strong family loyalties. This is true across classes.

This overprotectiveness in Appalachia is also tied to highly conservative and traditional gender roles. Although some women drink (women had an active role in the underground economy of whiskey production), their drinking is strongly proscribed. Edwards (1985) claims that they are quite literally "closet drinkers" (p. 136). The more typical job for a woman is to protect her man and his soul. He is expected to drink; she is expected to provide sanctuary for him, forgive him, overfunction for him. Men are the head of the household, and the rigidity of traditional gender role definition is reinforced by the fundamentalist religions.

PLACE

Another folk ballad captures the rural Scotch-Irish love of place: *Oh Shenandoah, I long to see you . . . way, hey, you rolling river.*

Few Scotch-Irish leave home, and when they do they long to return. This homesickness complicates their going for alcoholism rehabilitation to urban centers. Their values of origin include a fierce attachment to kinfolk or clan, stubbornness, and a mistrust of outsiders. They also value autonomy in a context of Calvinist fatalism.

FAMILY THERAPY AND ADDICTION

The Scotch-Irish, with their history of self-reliance, are not likely to seek psychological help, but if they do, the clinician must bear in mind that a personal relationship must be established with the family to gain the beginnings of trust. The Scotch-Irish family has all the properties of a closed system. Clinicians need to understand the importance of religion and family to these people, their fierce love of place, and their sensitivity regarding class.

Drinking is very ingrained in Appalachian culture. It is also ingrained in those on the New England coast. We tend to think of alcoholism when we think of Appalachia; however, Maine has its share. Alcoholism is as characteristic of the well-to-do of Scotch-Irish ancestry as of the poor.

An outsider should use caution before applying labels like "addiction" or being confrontational with family members. Challenging traditional gender roles will likely produce tremendous resistance. Alcoholics themselves are more likely to talk with their pastor than to seek therapy, and abusive drinking, although often considered a sin, may be tolerated with a sense of resignation (Ames, 1985). Addiction and its behavioral consequences are not seen as out of the ordinary. There is, arguably, more tolerance for addiction in Appalachia and the Ozarks than in New England or the Mid-Atlantic, where the Scotch-Irish are not the predominant group.

I (J. K.) consulted at a mental health center in the Appalachians at the juncture of North Carolina, Virginia, and Tennessee. (In doing family-of-origin work with the clinicians themselves, all of them from the region, I found that virtually all the clinicians on the staff had a history of alcohol abuse or domestic violence in their own family of origin.)

In one case, when I met my client's Scotch-Irish family of origin for the first time, I greeted them first in the driveway. They had arrived in a camper. I spent fifteen minutes or so with the family discussing the merits of various campers (i.e., vans, truck campers, Class C versus Class A rigs, and tag-alongs). I told the clients that I was in the market for a camper and solicited their advice. I would have been highly reluctant to initiate such a boundary crossing with a family of a different ethnicity but felt, in this case, that the context demanded it.

When I first moved to Maine from a location fifty miles from Manhattan, I consulted with a series of Scotch-Irish families. Unaccustomed to the degree to which these families were closed systems, I frequently moved too quickly to confront the family secrets. As a consequence, families did not return for a second or third session.

Whether the family clinician is working with a middle-class, suburban WASP family or a poor, rural WASP family, if their ancestry is Scotch or Scotch-Irish, certain characteristics will often surface. The clinician will be struck by their clannishness, stubbornness, and frequently taciturn manner. As Hess (1995) notes, "Scots are relatively unscathed by any ethnic stereotyping; however, the phrase, 'cold as Presbyterian charity' reflects the long-standing belief that Scots are dour and stingy" (p. 1201). The hard work and thrift that were so valued in the building of this country are traits that those of Scotch and Scotch-Irish ancestry are still proud of. But it is the fierce pride in the rights of individuals to think what they please and to be independent that will be most troublesome for the clinician working with an addictive family. If, however, the clinician manages to successfully refer the family to a twelve-step program, the spiritual and somewhat puritanical framework of AA is ideally suited for Scotch and Scotch-Irish Americans. The clinician might well stress the anonymity of the program (to respect the closed nature of the family system) and appeal to the family's strong work ethic by talking about the "working" of the steps. Finally, a sensitivity to the family's reluctance to seek outside help, coupled with an emphasis on the spiritual nature of the AA program, will be helpful.

ITALIAN FAMILIES

"May God protect me from those who don't drink."

IN ITALY, there is hardly any type of human activity that does not relate to wine consumption. Drinking wine is very much a part of this culture; it imparts graciousness, relaxation, celebration, and health.

Research has indicated that Mediterranean cultures typically have low rates of alcoholism. In Italy, this is despite the fact that alcohol production is a major industry (where vineyards cover 10 percent of the country's surface) and 10 percent of the country's gross national product involves the making of wine. Wine is seen as nourishment. An association between wine and blood is learned early and is emphasized in the Catholic teachings. During the celebration of Mass, wine is turned into blood, symbolizing the blood of Christ, which is received in the sacrament of Communion. Italians speak about wine promoting "good blood," among its many other health benefits. Indeed, this belief is reinforced by the fact that the water in very highly populated areas of southern Italy is unsafe owing to high mineral and bacteria content (Pisani, 1991).

In Italy there tends to be "regulated abuse," that is, ritual occasions where people are expected or encouraged to get drunk, as in certain rites of passage, such as joining the draft or marrying. However, there is much emphasis placed on the negative effects that heavy drinking can have on work and sociability. Although there exists no moral stigma on heavy drinking as such, the culture does tend to blame people who have no control, since such behavior threatens the values of sociability. A man unable to master his drinking is not a "real" man (Cottino, 1995).

Researchers have noted that sobriety is more commonplace in Italy than drunkenness, even in light of the large amount of wine being consumed (Moss and Cappannari, 1960). However, the Italian cirrhosis rate is one of the highest in Europe (Whitehead and Harvey, 1974). Thus, the incidence of drunkenness in a society is not a sufficient indicator of that culture's relationship to alcohol.

Between 1900 and 1910, two million Italians, mostly peasants from southern Italy, immigrated to this country (Giordano and McGoldrick, 1996). These immigrants tended to be poor and less educated than others in Italy. They came to escape poverty, and the United States represented opportunities for both education and work. They tended to settle in "little Italies" in the Mid-Atlantic states and New England (Johnson, 1991).

Italian culture was not consistent with the American values of independence and personal freedom. Family affiliation was paramount for these early immigrants. Their values included adaptability and stoicism, and they took pride in their resilience and ability to cope. "To counter the harshness and fatalism in their daily lives, Italians mastered the ability to fully savor the present, particularly with family gatherings and community festivals" (Giordano and McGoldrick, 1996, p. 568).

As more and more Italian immigrants came to this country, prejudice against them grew. This may have had to do with their darker skin color, their emphasis on family loyalty and affiliation, or social class. Nonetheless, they were considered dangerous and criminal (we are all familiar with the popular image of the Mafia, a violent group of men who engaged in illegal operations). Gambino (1974) suggests that the southern Italian social structure was firmly transplanted in the United States. This structure involved social controls that dealt swiftly and firmly with any family member that displayed any behavior that would bring shame upon the family.

The family continues to provide a strong sense of security and identity for many second- and third-generation Italian Americans. They turn first to the family for help in solving problems and hold the strong belief that the family should intervene in matters of emotion or the heart. Thus, we often find that families of Italian heritage will wait a long time before entering therapy. When they do, they often feel that their love should have been able to resolve the problem for their family member. This has tremendous implications for the treatment of the Italian American family struggling with addiction. To fathers, the need for treatment implies that they are not capable of remaining in control of their families. Mothers blame themselves for not being able to fix the problem.

In an attempt to explain the lower rates of alcoholism in members of Mediterranean cultures, Vaillant (1995) cites their tendency to consume low-proof alcohol (wine) with food and in the presence of the family. There is a low tolerance for those who cannot handle their liquor or who shame the family by their behavior.

Simboli (1985) tested the hypothesis that Italian American drinking behavior is directly related to generational membership, a correlation mainly mediated by the process of acculturation. He found that alcohol consumption went from moderate drinking among first-generation Italians to heavy drinking among those of the second and third generation, with wine being the primary choice for the first generation and beer and hard liquor being preferred by the second and third. He concluded that his study supported his hypothesis and that acculturation into American society produces an increase in problem drinking.

This change in drinking practices from one Italian American generation to the next illustrates how acculturation produces tension in families as children grow up and begin to conform to the culture's dominant values (in this case, about the use of alcohol). Tension between generations exists over other values as well, as even today Italian Americans are ambivalent about moving up the socioeconomic ladder. Despite their rise to the middle class and the professions, Italian Americans often verbalize a sense of inferiority and a lack of acceptance of their own success (Giordano, 1994). This conflict often fosters shame and identity confusion. In this context, it is not surprising that an increase in problem drinking is seen in second- and third-generation Italian Americans; issues about shame set the stage for addictive behavior and are a large part of the context in which it occurs.

The family clinician working with an Italian American family should carefully track the use of substances by all members across generations, since Italian Americans often do not recognize when drinking has become problematic. This is because alcohol, particularly wine consumption, has been so much a part of daily life and because rates of alcoholism have been historically low.

Many therapists have also noted the propensity toward gambling on the part of Italian American men. This can take many forms, such as "going to the track" or placing bets by "calling the bookie." Although this behavior is certainly not limited to Italian American families, it is worth noting and deserves some research on its own. The clinician should track the gambling tendencies in the family: Who goes to the track? How has this impacted the family's ability to manage financially? Is the family under financial pressure or in debt because of this behavior?

The need to go outside the family for help can be particularly disturbing for Italian American parents. They may be at a loss to understand the need for a loved one to attend AA or GA—even once the problem has been defined. Their thinking is, "Why can't the family just provide this help? We'll do it; we'll take care of it now that we know what the problem is." Italian Americans have difficulty with the concept—so prevalent in Al-Anon and so necessary to recovery—of "detachment" from the addict. That emotional process is the antithesis of Italian American family values.

The clinician may need to also carefully assess the family's understanding of the problem. Italian Americans, particularly older ones, can be superstitious about why illness or tragedy befalls them. Education about addiction is important to counter some of the fears that may accompany these beliefs.

Affiliation with the Catholic Church continues to be strong for Italian Americans. Unlike the Irish, who experience the authority of the church, Italians tend to perceive God as a "benign friend" and are drawn to the church for the pageantry, family celebration, and ritual (Giordano and Mc-Goldrick, 1996). Thus, if the family can accept the need to attend AA, the spiritual component of the program and the connection to God make this treatment approach a good fit for this group.

Since Italians believe so strongly about not bringing shame upon the family, it is important in therapy to have discussions about how the addiction has affected family members. Although they tend to be expressive in therapy, Italians often do not talk about some of the more painful issues, instead tending to "dance around" them (Giordano and McGoldrick, 1996). The clinician should be aware that family members could be quite angry at the alcoholic for bringing the family to the attention of "outsiders" and for not being able to control his or her use of alcohol or drugs. Further, the Italian American values of coping with difficulty on one's own, resilience, and stoicism run counter to some of the behaviors promoted in AA, such as talking to a sponsor, asking for help, and "sharing" one's experience.

Unlike the Irish, German, and Anglo groups, Italians have struggled with the integration of dominant American values in their family lives. The notion of individual achievement versus group affiliation is a present-day struggle for many third-generation Italian Americans. Alcohol again can function to mediate this conflict, either allowing the individual to go a distance from the family or to stay close.

CASE STUDY

Mary V, a fifty-year-old second-generation Italian American, entered treatment for depression. She had been married for twenty-three years to a man of Anglo origin and was the mother of a son, Tony, who was twenty-two, and a daughter, Carmie, who was fifteen. Tony was cut off from the family and living on his own. This was extremely painful to Mary, who felt she was not fulfilling her role as a mother to this young man. Mary described much conflict around this role, as she discussed the differences between her maternal behaviors and those of her mother.

Soon after Mary entered treatment, it became clear that Tony had a drinking problem ("He went away to college and drank for seventy days straight"). His parents had "rescued" him from several situations with the police. Eventually, he was brought up on charges of stealing computers from the college and embezzling from a bank.

Mr. and Mrs. V had sought therapy at times in the past, and Tony had been given several diagnoses, including conduct disorder and personality disorder as well as alcoholism.

The clinician suggested to Mr. & Mrs. V that if Tony was indeed an alcoholic, pointing out that he sounded like one, his alcoholism was the primary problem to work on. The parents were encouraged to attend Al-Anon and become further educated about the nature of addiction. This enabled them to depersonalize the issues at hand and helped them view Tony's behavior as a part of his disease and less as a personal affront to them.

Tony remained very connected to his family emotionally, particularly to his mother, and willingly attended family sessions. Because conflict could become so intense between Tony and his mother, the clinician encouraged Mr. V to come forward and take more responsibility for his son. The parents explored the option of hospitalization for Tony, and after yet another crisis Mr. V pleaded with his son to enter inpatient treatment. Tony did so, allowing his parents for the the first time in more than a year to feel that he was safe.

After several weeks in the hospital Tony began to disclose that although he understood that alcohol was a problem and that he needed to get sober, his main addiction was gambling. He described a long history of varied and extensive gambling activities.

POLISH FAMILIES

THE STORY OF alcohol consumption in Poland is closely tied to its political history. For centuries, alcohol production and consumption were controlled by its rulers. As recently as 1980, "the political regime was blamed for pushing alcohol in order to manipulate a 'drunken society' more easily, and to maximize their revenues" (Moskalewicz, 1985). Poles readily admit that heavy drinking has always been a part of their culture and that "vodka is even more deeply enshrined in the Polish tradition than it is in the Russian" (Folwarski and Marganoff, 1996, p. 663).

Between 1870 and 1914, over three million illiterate Polish peasants immigrated to the United States. They settled in the large industrial cities of the Northeast and Midwest, in neighborhoods organized around the Catholic church (Freund, 1985). Being Polish was synonymous with being Catholic. Polish beliefs are not unlike those of the Irish, with suffering and martyrdom at the core of their ideology about life. The attitude toward alcohol that they brought with them was that it was a necessary part of socializing and a symbol of hospitality; it was used for sealing contracts as well as marking life events (Freund, 1985). The local ethnic saloon played a dominant role in the lives of those immigrants, as it was reminiscent of the neighborhood tavern in Poland. Some authors have noted the sheer number of these saloons in Polish American communities: there were usually two or three at every street intersection (Zand, 1961). There was great tolerance for heavy drinking, but limits on drinking were recognized. Drinking was frowned upon if it caused one to neglect family or church responsibilities (Freund, 1985).

The involvement with ethnic saloons was predominately male. "Standing rounds" and frequent drinking of toasts were common rituals. Men could appear successful by buying the standing rounds, which included a shot and a beer for each patron (Freund, 1985). This kind of drinking was strictly a male activity, associated with strength and manhood. Although women were allowed to drink, their drinking was usually part of some ritual, as in a toast. They were never to drink in the company of men. "A woman was expected to show deference by turning her head when she accepted a drink from a man" (Freund, 1985, p. 88). There was tremendous stigma attached to any woman who drank to excess.

Polish immigrants were among the most disadvantaged in that they experienced extreme discrimination and bigotry. Perhaps owing to their level of illiteracy on their arrival in this country, they were generally thought of as "moronic" (Folwarski and Marganoff, 1996). This in turn fostered a deep sense of shame; Polish Americans change their names more than any other ethnic group (Folwarski and Marganoff, 1996). It also fostered an extreme sense of nationalism, and their opposition to authority became a main tool of survival. Children in Polish American families were expected to be obedient, to contribute to the family, and to take care of their parents. Stoicism was highly valued, and any feelings and expressions of need for emotional connectedness were strongly prohibited. Feelings of emotional need were not considered normal and were often associated with feelings of shame (Folwarski and Marganoff, 1996). Children grew up with alcohol used as a regular part of religious, ethnic, and family celebrations and were accustomed to the high degree of tolerance for drunkenness on the part of men.

Freund (1985) conducted a study of Polish American drinking practices in the social clubs of Rhode Island. He found considerable persistence in attitudes and behaviors in the Polish American community over time. He did find that younger generations have different drinking practices and have not joined the social clubs so prevalent for first- and second-generation Polish Americans. Further, he found a generational shift in attitudes toward drinking: specifically, younger generations perceive drinking in less positive terms than do previous generations and are more open to seeking help, especially from AA, for drinking problems.

Folwarski and Marganoff (1996) discuss the alcoholism problem in their writing about Polish American families: "Resistance to acknowledging or recognizing alcohol as directly related to family problems is stronger in Polish families than in many other ethnic groups" (p. 663). Although this resistance may be difficult to measure, the clinician working with a Polish American family must keep in mind the history of alcohol in this culture, specifically, the fact that it may function to ameliorate the shame associated with being Polish. For example, since alcohol was a way for a man to build status by providing "standing rounds" in the local saloon, it became associated with economic success. Further, since stoicism in this group was necessary in the face of such intense bigotry and since it functions to inhibit the expression of feelings, particularly the need for emotional contact, alcohol became the vehicle that allowed expression of feelings associated with being vulnerable or needy.

The inability to negotiate conflict is also a common theme for Polish families. It is not uncommon when taking a family history to notice patterns of cutoff between family members that last many years. This can be particularly threatening in a subculture that experiences such hostility from the dominant group; since members of the subculture tend to be more dependent on each other, the emotional impact of a cutoff becomes amplified. Here too alcohol can have different effects, sometimes inhibiting further expression of loss around important relationships and sometimes promoting it.

In an ethnic group that so values stoicism and minimizes the need for emotional expression and connectedness, it is indeed difficult for a family to acknowledge that a member's drinking is resulting in behaviors that are hurtful or troublesome. The clinician must frame inquiries about the behaviors in terms of having "concern" about the family member rather than ask the family to directly list their hurts or grievances. The family will feel more comfortable talking about facts and specific instances of the behaviors and staying away from the emotional context. The clinician should spend time getting to know family members before making any quick moves to ask them to consider alcohol, however obvious, as the problem.

Generational membership is also an important consideration in treating Polish American families for addiction. Since there is data that indicates a shift in thinking about the effects of alcohol, it is wise to invite children and grandchildren to therapy sessions when working with adults in their fifties and beyond. The behavior of adolescent clients may well express the conflict inherent in members of a group that demands obedience to parents as well as opposition to authority.

CASE STUDY

Zach was a twenty-six-year-old man referred to an outpatient clinic after inpatient hospitalization following a serious suicide attempt. He had overdosed on a variety of prescription medications and alcohol.

Zach, who lived alone in a large city, had a history of seeing psychiatrists for depression and anxiety. He was an only child, and his parents lived a considerable distance away. It was evident from family history that Zach's father was an untreated alcoholic, and that there was alcoholism on both sides of his family. Zach described his ethnic background as "some Polish, I think."

Zach was a gay man who was not out to his parents or to anyone at work, where he was employed as an assistant chef. His community gathered in the local gay bars, which he frequented, although he reported that he tried "not to drink too much anymore."

The clinician began to discuss with Zach his drinking history, as well as his father's. Zach described many of the drunken scenes he had witnessed while growing up, but he had never spoken directly to either of his parents about his father's drinking. He complained of a distant relationship with them, although it was clear that he cared a great deal for them. They had visited him in the hospital, seemed genuinely confused by his suicide attempt, and did not know how to help their son.

The clinician suggested that Zach attempt to not drink. This posed a problem for Zach, since he would then be almost completely isolated socially. The clinician then suggested gay AA and Al-Anon meetings, to which Zach reluctantly agreed. Zach was also coached to have conversations with both of his parents about family history. He learned that his paternal grandfather had immigrated to this country as a young man and had changed his named to an abbreviated version (which the family still used) shortly thereafter to hide the fact that he was Polish.

It was clear that Zach had much to sort out regarding the shame attached to his addiction. The history of the bigotry encountered by earlier generations of his family, current heterosexism, and his own internalized homophobia created a context that was critical to an assessment of how alcohol functioned for him. Zach finally succeeded with his "no drink" contract, but he was able to do so only after making connections with sober men. It was in the gay recovery community that he began to explore the many complex layers of addiction and their connection to being gay in a homophobic culture. It was only after Zach had established sobriety and a sense of community that his family-of-origin work could begin.

References

Applebome, Peter. (1998, August 16). It's Not Called Arkansas for Nothing. *The New York Times*, Week in Review, p. 3.

Ames, G. M. (1985). Middle Class Protestants: Alcohol and the Family. In L. A. Bennett and G. M. Ames (Eds.), *The American Experience with Alcohol: Contrasting Cultural Perspectives* (pp. 435-438). New York: Plenum Press.

Bales, R. F. (1946). Cultural Differences in Rates of Alcoholism. Quarter Four of *Studies on Alcoholism*, 6, 480-499.

Bales, R. F. (1962). Attitudes Toward Drinking in the Irish Culture. In D. J. Pittman & C. R. Snyder (Eds), *Society, Culture and Drinking Patterns*. New York: Wiley.

Barlow, J. (n.d.). Tulip: The Five Points of Calvinism. Web site: www.users.globalnet. co.uk/~gospel/tulip.htm. Retrieved July 1998.

Bennett, L. A., & Ames, G. M. (1985). Alcohol Belief Systems in a Pluralistic Society. In L. A. Bennett, & G. M. Ames, (Eds.) *The American Experience with Alcohol: Contrasting Cultural Perspectives*. New York: Plenum Press.

Bepko, C., & Krestan, J. (1985). *The Responsibility Trap: A Blueprint for Treating the Alcoholic Family*. New York: Free Press.

Billigmeier, R. H. (1974). *Americans from Germany: A Study in Cultural Diversity*. Belmont, CA: Wadsworth.

Blethen, T., & Wood, C. (1997). *Ulster and North America: Transatlantic Perspectives on the Scotch-Irish*. Tuscaloosa, AL: University of Alabama Press.

Cahalan, D., Cisisn, I. H., & Crossley, H. M. (1969). *American Drinking Practices: A National Study of Drinking Behavior and Attitudes*. New Brunswick. NJ: Rutgers Center of Alcohol Studies; New Haven, CT: College & University Press.

Cahalan, D., & Room, R. (1974). *Problem Drinkers Among American Men*. New Brunswick, NJ: Rutgers Center for Alcohol Studies.

Clark, D. (1973). *The Irish in Philadelphia*. Philadelphia: Temple University Press.

Cottino, A. (1995). Italy. In D. B. Heath (Ed.), *International Handbook on Alcohol and Culture*. Westport, CT: Greenwood Press.

Curtis, L. P. (1971). *Apes and Angels*. Washington, DC: Smithsonian Institution Press.

Davies, N. (1992). *Heart of Europe: A Short History of Poland* (rev. ed.). New York: Oxford University Press.

Donaldson, G. (1980). Scots. In S. Thernstorm, A. Orlov, & O. Handlin (Eds.), *Harvard Encyclopedia of American Ethnic Groups*. Cambridge, MA: Harvard University Press.

Edwards, G. T. (1985). Appalachia: The Effects of Cultural Values on the Production and Consumption of Alcohol. In L. A. Bennett & G. M. Ames (Eds.), *The American Experience with Alcohol: Contrasting Cultural Perspectives* (pp. 131–146). New York: Plenum Press.

Folwarski, J., & Marganoff, P. (1996). Polish Families in Ethnicity and Family Therapy. In M. McGoldrick, J. Giordano, and J. Pearce (Eds.), *Ethnicity and Family Therapy* (2nd ed., pp. 658–687). New York: Guilford Press.

Freund, P. J. (1985). Polish American Drinking: Continuity and Change. In L. A. Bennett and G. N. Ames (Eds.), *The American Experience with Alcohol: Contrasting Cultural Perspectives (pp. 77–92)*. New York: Plenum Press.

Furer, H. B. (Ed.). (1973). *The Germans in America 1607–1970*. Dobbs Ferry, NY: Ocean.

Gambino, R. (1974). *Blood of My Blood: The Dilemma of Italian Americans*. New York: Doubleday.

Giordano, J. (1994, June 13). The Shame We Share in Secret. *Newsday*, p. 25.

Giordano, J., & McGoldrick, M. (1996). Italian Families. In M. McGoldrick, J. Giordano, & J. Pearce (Eds.), *Ethnicity and Family Therapy* (2nd ed., pp. 567–582.). New York: Guilford Press.

Greeley, A., & McCready, W. C. (1980). *Ethnic Drinking Subcultures*. New York: Praeger.

Heath, D. B. (1995). *International Handbook on Alcohol and Culture*. Westport, CT: Greenwood Press.

Hess, M. (1995). Scottish and Scotch-Irish Americans. In J. Galens, S. Malinowski, R. J. Vecoli, N. Schlager, R. V. Young, and A. Sheets (Eds.), *Gale Encyclopedia of Multicultural America* (1995). (Vol. 2, pp. 1198–1209). Detroit: Gale Research.

Hudak, J., Krestan, J., & Bepko, C. (1999). Alcohol Problems and the Family Life Cycle. In B. Carter and M. McGoldrick (Eds.), *The Expanded Family Life Cycle* (3rd ed.). Needham Heights, MA: Allyn and Bacon.

Ingnatiev, N. (1995). *How the Irish Became White*. New York: Routledge.

Johnson, P. B. (1991). Reaction Expectancies of Ethnic Drinking Differences. *Psychology of Addictive Behaviors*, 5(1), 36–40.

Jones, M. (1980). The Scotch-Irish. In S. Thernstorm, A. Orlov, & O. Handlin (Eds.), *Harvard Encyclopedia of American Ethnic Groups*. Cambridge, MA: Harvard University Press.

Lomax, A. (1947). *Folk Song U.S.A.* New York: Duell, Sloan, & Pearce.

McGill, D., & Pearce, J. (1996). "American Families with English Ancestors from the Colonial Era: Anglo Americans in Ethnicity and Family Therapy." In M. McGoldrick, J. Giordano, & J. Pearce (Eds.), *Ethnicity and Family Therapy* (2nd ed., pp. 431–466). New York: Guilford Press.

McGoldrick, M. (1996). Irish Families. In M. McGoldrick, J. Giordano, and J. Pearce (Eds.), *Ethnicity and Family Therapy* (2nd ed., pp. 544–566). New York: Guilford Press.

McGoldrick, M., Giordano, J., & Pearce, J. (Eds.). (1996). *Ethnicity and Family Therapy* (2nd ed.). New York: Guilford Press.

Moorewood, S. (1824). An Essay on the Inventions and Customs of Both Ancients and Moderns in the Use of Inebriating Liquors. London: Longmans, Hurst, Rees, Orme, Brown and Green.

Moskalewicz, J. (1985). Monopolization of the Alcohol Arena by the State. *Contemporary Drug Problems*, 18(3): 407–416.

Moss, L. W., & Cappannari, S. C. (1960). Folklore and Medicinals in the Italian Village. *Journal of American Folklore*, 73, 95–102.

O'Connor, G. (1996). Alcoholism in Irish American Catholics: Cultural Stereotypes versus Clinical Reality. The *American Journal on Addictions*, 5(2), pp. 124–135

Peele, S. (1984). The Cultural Context of Psychological Approaches to Alcoholism: Can We Control the Effects of Alcohol? *American Psychologist*, 39, 1337–1351.

Pisani, P. T. (1991). Historical Aspects of the Vine and Wine in Italy *Alcologen*, 3, 21–29.

Simboli, B. (1985). Acculturated Italian-American Drinking Behavior. In L. Bennett & G. Ames (Eds.), *The American Experience with Alcohol* (pp. 61–76). New York: Plenum Press.

Spidell, D. (1998). The Scots/Irish Immigration of the 1700s. Retrieved July 30, 1998, from World Wide Web: http://www.zekes.com/~dspidell/ulster.htm.

Stivers, R. (1976). The Hair of the Dog: Irish Drinking and American Stereotypes. University Park: Pennsylvania State University Press.

Vaillant, G. E. (1995). *The Natural History of Alcoholism Revisited*. Cambridge, MA: Harvard University Press.

Vogt, I. (1995). Germany. In D. B. Heath (Ed.), *International Handbook on Alcohol and Culture* (pp. 88–97). Westport, CT: Greenwood Press.

Walsh, D. (1987). Alcohol and Ireland. *British Journal of Addiction*, 82, 118–120.

Whitehead, P. C., & Harvey, C. (1974). Exploring Alcoholism: An Empirical Test and Reformation. *Journal of Health and Social Behavior*, 15, 57–65.

Willis, W. (1859). Scotch-Irish Immigrations to Maine and a Summary History of Presbyterianism: An Address Before the Society, Jan. 27, 1858. In *Collections of the Maine Historical Society* (Vol. 6). Portland, ME: Brown Thurton.

Winawer, H., & Wetzel, N. (1996). German Families. In M. McGoldrick, J. Giordano, & J. Pearce (Eds.), Ethnicity and Family Therapy (2nd ed.). New York: Guilford Press.

Zand, H. S. (1961). Polish-American Leisureways. *Polish American Studies*, 18, 34–36.

INDEX

Abad, D., 265
acculturation, 56, 230–32; of Hispanics, 222; of Italians, 308; of Jews, 132–33; of Mexican Americans, 239–40; of Puerto Ricans, 267, 269; of West Indians, 189, adolescents, 10; African American, 159–61; Jewish, 138; Native American, 57; Polish American, 313
Adult Children of Alcoholics (ACOA), 6, 45–71; case vignette of, 69–71; cultural issues of, 48–59; historical context of, 45–47; implications for therapy for, 65–71; interaction of culture and issues of, 61–64; narrative approach to, 61; Native American, 83; "normality" and, 51–52; oppression and, 54–55; parallels between family, community, and society for, 64–65; postmodernist and social constructionist views on, 59–61; risk and resilience of, 50–51; underutilization of treatment resources by, 52–53; working definition of, 48
African Americans, 1, 4, 7, 28, 35, 38, 185–86, 189, 284; adolescent, 159–61; adult children of alcoholics, 61, 67; categorization of, 53, 54; cultural/socioeconomic factors of addiction in, 149–52; distrust of dominant culture by, 64–65; emotional issues of, 152–55; gender issues for, 27, 155–59, 181; and Integrative Cross-Cultural Model, 227; oppression of, 22, 24, 55, 150; spirituality of, 26, 161–68; underutilization of treatment resources by, 52
AIDS, 145, 155, 157, 240, 273; classification of Haitians as risk group for, 186
Al-Anon, 49, 55, 62, 68, 70, 135, 290, 291, 300, 310, 314; "detachment" from addict in, 309; Judeo-Christian roots of, 56; Public Information Service, 49; underutilization by minorities of, 52–53

Alateens, 51
Alcoholics Anonymous (AA), 28, 32, 34, 36–39, 41, 68, 81, 285; African Americans in, 166–68; Anglo Americans in, 299; Irish Americans in, 290, 291; Italian Americans in, 309; Jews in, 135, 136, 140; Mexican Americans in, 250; Native Americans in, 102–10; Polish Americans in, 312, 314; power issues and, 15, 17, 18; Scots and Scotch-Irish in, 306; underutilization by minorities of, 52; West Indians in, 183, 187
alcoholism, 38, 39, 41, 284; among African Americans, 145–46, 159, 160; among Anglo Americans, 296–300; among Asian/Pacific Americans, 194, 197, 200, 207; cross-cultural literature on, 5; among German Americans, 292, 294–96; among Irish Americans, 286–91; among Italian Americans, 306–10; among Jews, 116, 122–25, 127; among Mexican Americans, 220–23, 232, 242, 245–50; among Native Americans, 54–55, 81–83, 87, 111; parental, see Adult Children of Alcoholics; among Polish Americans, 310–14; powerlessness and, 28, 31, 36; pride cycle and, 32; among Puerto Ricans, 264–69; among Scotch-Irish, 302–6; values of origin and, 26; among West Indians, 180, 184–85, 187
Almeida, R., 7, 24, 28, 31
Alvarez, Julia, 54
American Family Therapy Academy, 2
American Indian Movement (AIM), 78
anger, African American feelings of, 154–55
Anglo Americans, 221, 284, 285, 296–300, 309; case vignette of, 299–300
animism, 56, 198
anti-Semitism, 118, 119, 121

317

DATE DUE

New Trails

Twenty-three
Original Stories
of the West
from Western Writers
of America

New Trails

Edited by John Jakes
and Martin H. Greenberg

INTRODUCTION BY JOHN JAKES

DOUBLEDAY

New York London Toronto Sydney Auckland

PUBLISHED BY DOUBLEDAY
a division of Bantam Doubleday Dell Publishing Group, Inc.
1540 Broadway, New York, New York 10036

DOUBLEDAY and the portrayal of an anchor with a dolphin
are trademarks of Doubleday, a division of
Bantam Doubleday Dell Publishing Group, Inc.

Page 307 constitutes an extension of this copyright page.

Library of Congress Cataloging-in-Publication Data

New trails: twenty-three original stories of the West / edited by Martin H. Greenberg
   and John Jakes; introduction by John Jakes.—1st ed.
      p.   cm.
      1. Short stories, American—West (U.S.)   2. American fiction—
   20th century.   3. West (U.S.)—Fiction.   4. Western stories.
   I. Jakes, John, 1932–   . II. Greenberg, Martin Harry.
   PS561.N47   1994
   813′.01083278—dc20   94-9525
   CIP

ISBN 0-385-46990-X
Copyright © 1994 by John Jakes and Martin H. Greenberg
All Rights Reserved
Printed in the United States of America
November 1994
First Edition

10   9   8   7   6   5   4   3   2   1

Contents

Introduction

YOU ARE ABOUT to set out on a journey into virgin territory. This is a collection of new, never-before-published short stories by members of Western Writers of America. Each story comes from a certified professional, because only pros are eligible to join the national organization. There hasn't been an anthology like this one in twenty or thirty years (that I know about, anyway).

But there's something even more exciting. This book not only presents writers whose successful careers span several decades—Elmore Leonard and Elmer Kelton are notable examples—but also presents stories from a new generation of writers taking the western in new directions.

The work of these strong, fresh voices frankly came as something of a revelation to me, and to my co-editor and friend, Dr. Martin H. Greenberg, after we issued a call for material over a year ago.

Yes, we received, and chose, any number of traditional westerns —stories that descend directly from masters such as Zane Grey and Louis L'Amour. But there were fewer of this kind than we expected, and fewer utilizing the historic West, though these are represented. Among the history-based submissions, several involved Custer and events central or peripheral to the Little Big Horn massacre—an interesting comment on what still fascinates writers.

Along with traditional stories—the kind Marty and I have enjoyed for years—a great many came in that made us blink. Strong and interesting trends became apparent.

First, more women are writing westerns—and writing them from a woman's perspective. No more hiding behind initials, as Dorothy Johnson did when she was "D. M. Johnson." Understandably, this was her defense against a backlash of male chauvinism from readers and editors. To this new wave of feminine subjects and perceptions in the western, we say hurrah.

Next, more stories are being written about Native American characters. No longer are Indians the stereotypical bad guys. Another turn for the better.

Finally, we received a large number of stories set in the contemporary West. This kind of tale has already whipped up a tempest within WWA; some members insist that "real" western stories can only be set in the years from 1865 to about 1900. Marty and I have a more inclusive view; we have included several contemporary pieces.

But why this kind of collection at all?

For some years, the West as a subject for short stories, novels, feature films, TV movies-of-the-week, drifted into a sort of limbo. In Hollywood, where the western was once a staple, it was all at once taboo; killed off, some say, by the special effects and razzle-dazzle novelty of films such as *Star Wars*.

The perception that westerns were passé was suddenly challenged by the extraordinary ratings of the *Lonesome Dove* miniseries. To this was added a huge box office and crossover audience (people from many age groups) for *Dances with Wolves*.

Then came the watershed summer of 1992: Michael Mann's spellbinding visualization of *The Last of the Mohicans*, plus Clint Eastwood's *Unforgiven*, immediately labeled a classic. Both pictures were hits. As a result, there are presently twenty-five or thirty theater and TV westerns ready for air, in production, or in development.

Which only proves what a lot of us knew all along: on the page or the screen, the western never really lost its appeal. Some people just thought it did.

Dale Walker, current president of WWA, put it this way in a column in the *Rocky Mountain News:*

> The West is *not* dead, my friends—though there seems to be a small cottage industry, centered mostly among academic critics of American literature, dedicated to pronouncing, with a suspicious level of glee, the death of the western. These premature burial notices, cropping up with regularity in books, popular magazines and scholarly journals, are written by western history reconstructionists, political correctness drones and certain other

scholar-morticians who seek to embalm western fiction without first checking its pulse.

Dale wrote that in the fateful summer of '92.

Through the lean times, a few publishers such as Doubleday and Bantam Books continued to believe there was an audience for the well-done western novel. Bantam author Louis L'Amour demonstrated it resoundingly during the later years of his long career.

Because I'd like to see the western short story make a comeback too, I proposed doing this book. Markets for shorts are almost nonexistent today, save for the new *Louis L'Amour Western Magazine*.

Doubleday and Bantam backed the idea; Marty Greenberg, who has edited something over five hundred anthologies as of this date, enthusiastically signed on as co-editor; and we issued our invitation to members of WWA to send us their best.

You're holding the result. It mixes traditional stories by old hands with westerns by newer authors who have responded to a changing world with changing creative approaches.

So if you've been hankering for some western tales in shorter lengths, you've come to the right book.

Read on!

—JOHN JAKES
October 1993

New Trails

"Hurrah for Capt. Early"

Elmore Leonard

THE SECOND BANNER said "HERO OF SAN JUAN HILL." Both were tied to the upstairs balcony of the Congress Hotel and looked down on La Salle Street in Sweetmary, a town named for a copper mine. The banners read across the building as a single statement. This day that Captain Early was expected home from the war in Cuba, over now these two months, was October 10, 1898.

The manager of the hotel and one of his desk clerks were the first to observe the colored man who entered the lobby and dropped his bedroll on the red velvet settee where it seemed he was about to sit down. Bold as brass. A tall, well-built colored man wearing a suit of clothes that looked new and appeared to fit him as though it might possibly be his own and not one handed down to him. He wore the suit, a stiff collar and a necktie. With the manager nearby but not yet aware of the intruder, the young desk clerk spoke up, raised his voice to tell the person, "You can't sit down there."

The colored man turned his attention to the desk, taking a moment before he said, "Why is that?"

His quiet tone caused the desk clerk to hesitate and look over at the manager, who stood holding the day's mail, letters that had arrived on the El Paso & Southwestern morning run along with several guests now registered at the hotel and, apparently, this colored person. It was hard to tell his age, other than to say he was no longer a young man. He did seem clean and his bedroll was done up in bleached canvas.

"A hotel lobby," the desk clerk said, "is not a public place anyone can make theirself at home in. What is it you want here?"

At least he was uncovered, standing there now hat in hand. But then he said, "I'm waiting on Bren Early."

"*Bren* is it," the desk clerk said. "Captain Early's an acquaintance of yours?"

"We go way back a ways."

"You worked for him?"

"Some."

At this point the manager said, "We're all waiting for Captain Early. Why don't you go out front and watch for him?" Ending the conversation.

The desk clerk—his name was Monty—followed the colored man to the front entrance and stepped out on the porch to watch him, bedroll over his shoulder, walking south on La Salle the two short blocks to Fourth Street. Monty returned to the desk, where he said to the manager, "He walked right in the Gold Dollar."

The manager didn't look up from his mail.

Two riders from the Circle-Eye, a spread on the San Pedro that delivered beef to the mine company, were at a table with their glasses of beer: a rider named Macon and a rider named Wayman, young men who wore sweat-stained hats down on their eyes as they stared at the Negro. Right there, the bartender speaking to him as he poured a whiskey, still speaking as the colored man drank it and the bartender poured him another one. Macon asked Wayman if he had ever seen a nigger wearing a suit of clothes and a necktie. Wayman said he couldn't recall. When they finished drinking their beer and walked up to the bar, the colored man gone now, Macon asked the bartender who in the hell that smoke thought he was coming in here. "You would think," Macon said, "he'd go to one of the places where the miners drink."

The bartender appeared to smile, for some reason finding humor in Macon's remark. He said, "Boys, that was Bo Catlett. I imagine Bo drinks just about wherever he feels like drinking."

"Why?" Macon asked it, surprised. "He suppose to be somebody?"

"Bo lives up at White Tanks," the bartender told him, "at the Indin agency. Went to war and now he's home."

Macon squinted beneath the hat brim funneled low on his eyes.

He said, "Nobody told me they was niggers in the war." Sounding as though it was the bartender's fault he hadn't been informed. When the bartender didn't add anything to help him out, Macon said, "Wayman's brother Wyatt was in the war, with Teddy Roosevelt's Rough Riders. Only Wyatt didn't come home like the nigger."

Wayman, about eighteen years old, was nodding his head now.

Because nothing about this made sense to Macon, it was becoming an irritation. Again he said to Wayman, "You ever see a smoke wearing a suit of clothes like that?" He said, "Je-sus Christ."

Bo Catlett walked up La Salle Street favoring his left leg some, though the limp, caused by a Mauser bullet or by the regimental surgeon who cut it out of his hip, was barely noticeable. He stared at the sight of the mine works against the sky, ugly, but something monumental about it: straight ahead up the grade, the main shaft scaffolding and company buildings, the crushing mill lower down, ore tailings that humped this way in ridges on down the slope to run out at the edge of town. A sorry place, dark and forlorn; men walked up the grade from boardinghouses on Mill Street to spend half their life underneath the ground, buried before they were dead. Three whiskeys in him, Catlett returned to the hotel on the corner of Second Street, looked up at the sign that said "HURRAH FOR CAPT. EARLY" and had to grin. "THE HERO OF SAN JUAN HILL" my ass.

Catlett mounted the steps to the porch, where he dropped his bedroll and took one of the rocking chairs all in a row, the porch empty, close on noon but nobody sitting out here, no drummers calling on La Salle Mining of New Jersey, the company still digging and scraping but running low on payload copper, operating only the day shift now. The rocking chairs, all dark green, needed painting. Man, but made of cane and comfortable with that nice squeak back and forth, back and forth . . . Bo Catlett watched two riders coming this way up the street, couple of cowboys . . . Catlett wondering how many times he had sat down in a real chair since April twenty-fifth when war was declared and he left Arizona to go looking for his old regiment, trailed them to Fort Assinniboine in the Department of the Dakotas, then clear across the country to Camp Chicamauga in Georgia and on down to Tampa where he caught up with them and Lt. John Pershing looked at his twenty-

four years of service and put him up for squadron sergeant major.
It didn't seem like any twenty-four years . . .

Going back to when he joined the First Kansas Colored Volunteers in '63, age fifteen. Wounded at Honey Springs the same year.
Guarded Rebel prisoners at Rock Island, took part in the occupation of Galveston. Then after the war got sent out here to join the
all-Negro 10th Cavalry on frontier station, Arizona Territory, and
deal with hostile Apaches. In '87 went to Mexico with Lt. Brendan
Early out of Fort Huachuca—Bren and a contract guide named
Dana Moon, now the agent at the White Tanks reservation—
brought back a one-eyed Mimbreño named Loco, brought back a
white woman the renegade Apache had run off with—and Dana
Moon later married—and they all got their pictures in some newspapers. Mustered out that same year, '87 . . . Drove a wagon for
Capt. Early Hunting Expeditions Incorporated before going to
work for Dana at White Tanks. He'd be sitting on Dana's porch
this evening with a glass of mescal and Dana would say, "Well,
now you've seen the elephant I don't imagine you'll want to stay
around here." He'd tell Dana he saw the elephant a long time ago
and wasn't too impressed. Just then another voice, not Dana's, said
out loud to him:

"So you was in the war, huh?"

It was one of the cowboys. He sat his mount, a little claybank
quarter horse, close to the porch rail, sat leaning on the pommel to
show he was at ease, his hat low on his eyes staring directly at
Catlett in his rocking chair. The other one sat his mount, a bay,
more out in the street, maybe holding back. This boy was not at
ease but fidgety. Catlett remembered them in the Gold Dollar.

Now the one close said, "What was it you did over there in
Cuba?"

Meaning a colored man. What did a colored man do. Like most
people the boy not knowing anything about Negro soldiers in the
war. This one squinting at him had size and maybe got his way
enough he believed he could say whatever he pleased, or use a tone
of voice that would irritate the person addressed. As he did just
now.

"What did I do over there?" Catlett said. "What everybody did,
I was in the war."

"You wrangle stock for the Rough Riders?"

"Where'd you get that idea?"

"I asked you a question. Is that what you did, tend their stock?"

Once Catlett decided to remain civil and maybe this boy would go away, he said, "There wasn't no stock. The Rough Riders, *even* the Rough Riders, were afoot. The only people had horses were artillery, pulling caissons with their Hotchkiss guns and the coffee grinders, what they called the Gatling guns. Lemme see," Catlett said, "they had some mules, too, but I didn't tend anybody's stock."

"His brother was a Rough Rider," Macon said, raising one hand to hook his thumb at Wayman. "Served with Colonel Teddy Roosevelt and got killed in an ambush—the only way greasers know how to fight. I like to hear what you people were doing while his brother Wyatt was getting killed."

You people. Look at him trying to start a fight.

"You believe it was my fault he got killed?"

"I asked you what you were doing."

It wasn't even this kid's business. Catlett thinking, Well, see if you can educate him, and said, "Las Guásimas. You ever hear of it?"

The kid stared with his eyes half shut. Suspicious, or letting you know he's serious, Catlett thought. Keen-eyed and mean; you're not gonna put anything past him.

"What's it, a place over there?"

"That's right, Las Guásimas, the place where it happened. On the way to Santiago de Coo-ba. Sixteen men killed that day, mostly by rifle fire, and something like fifty wounded. Except it wasn't what you said, the dons pulling an ambush. It was more the Rough Riders walking along not looking where they was going."

The cowboy, Macon, said, "Je-sus Christ, you saying the Rough Riders didn't know what they were *doing*?" Like this was something impossible to believe.

"They mighta had an idea *what* they was doing," Catlett said, "only thing it wasn't what they *shoulda* been doing." He said, "You understand the difference?" And thought, What're you explaining it to him for? The boy giving him that mean look again, ready to defend the Rough Riders. All right, he was so proud of Teddy's people, why hadn't he been over there with them?

"Look," Catlett said, using a quiet tone now, "the way it was, the dons had sharpshooters in these trees, a thicket of mangoes and palm trees growing wild you couldn't see into. You understand? Had men hidden in there were expert with the rifle, these Mausers they used with smokeless powder. Teddy's people come along a ridge was all covered with these trees and run into the dons, see, the dons letting some of the Rough Riders pass and then closing in on 'em. So, yeah, it was an ambush in a way." Catlett paused. "We was down on the road, once we caught up, moving in the same direction." He paused again, remembering something the cowboy said that bothered him. "There's nothing wrong with an ambush—like say you think it ain't *fair?* If you can set it up and keep your people behind cover, do it. There was a captain with the Rough Riders said he believed an officer should never take cover, should stand out there and be an example to his men. The captain said, 'There ain't a Spanish bullet made that can kill me.' Stepped out in the open and got shot in the head."

A couple of cowboys looking like the two who were mounted had come out of the Chinaman's picking their teeth and now stood by to see what was going on. Some people who had come out of the hotel were standing along the steps.

Catlett took all this in as he paused again, getting the words straight in his mind to tell how they left the road, some companies of the Tenth and the First, all regular Army, went up the slope laying down fire and run off the dons before the Rough Riders got cut to pieces, the Rough Riders volunteers and not experienced in all kind of situations—the reason they didn't know shit about advancing through hostile country or, get right down to it, what they were doing in Cuba, these people that come looking for glory and got served sharpshooters with Mausers and mosquitos carrying yellow fever. Tell these cowboys the true story. General Wheeler, "Fightin' Joe" from the Confederate side in the Civil War now thirty-three years later an old man with a white beard; sees the Spanish pulling back at Las Guásimas and says, "Boys, we got the Yankees on the run." Man like that directing a battle . . .

Tell the *whole* story if you gonna tell it, go back to sitting in the hold of the ship in Port Tampa a month, not allowed to go ashore for fear of causing incidents with white people who didn't want the men of the Tenth coming in their stores and cafés, running off their customers. Tell them—so we land in Cuba at a place called Daiquiri . . . saying in his mind then, Listen to me now. Was the Tenth at Daiquiri, the Ninth at Siboney. Experienced cavalry regiments that come off frontier station after thirty years dealing with hostile renegades, cutthroat horse thieves, reservation jumpers, land in Cuba and they put us to work unloading the ships while Teddy's people march off to meet the enemy and win some medals, yeah, and would've been wiped out at El Caney and on San Juan Hill if the colored boys hadn't come along and saved Colonel Teddy's ass and all his Rough Rider asses, showed them how to go up a hill and take a blockhouse. Saved them so the Rough Riders could become America's heroes.

All this in Bo Catlett's head and the banners welcoming Capt. Early hanging over him.

One of the cowboys from the Chinaman's must've asked what was going on, because now the smart aleck one brought his clay-bank around and began talking to them, glancing back at the porch now and again with his mean look. The two from the Chinaman's stood with their thumbs in their belts, while the mounted cowboy had his hooked around his suspenders now. None of them wore a gunbelt or appeared to be armed. Now the two riders stepped down from their mounts and followed the other two along the street to a place called the Belle Alliance, a miners' saloon, and went inside.

Bo Catlett was used to mean dirty looks and looks of indifference, a man staring at him as though he wasn't even there. Now the thing with white people, they had a hard time believing colored men fought in the war. You never saw a colored man on a U.S. Army recruiting poster or a picture of colored soldiers in newspapers. White people believed colored people could not be relied on in war. But why? There were some colored people that went out and killed wild animals, even lions, with a spear. No gun, a spear. And made hats out of the manes. See a colored man standing there in front of a lion coming at him fast as a train running down grade, stands there with his spear, doesn't move, and they say colored men can't be relied on?

There was a story in newspapers how when Teddy Roosevelt was at the Hill, strutting around in the open, he saw colored troopers going back to the rear and he drew his revolver and threatened to shoot them—till he found out they were going after ammunition. His own Rough Riders were pinned down in the guinea grass, the Spanish sharpshooters picking at them from up in the blockhouses. So the Tenth showed the white boys how to go up the hill angry, firing and yelling, making noise, set on driving the garlics clean from the hill . . .

Found Bren Early and his company lying in the weeds, the scrub —that's all it was up that hill, scrub and sand, hard to get a footing in places; nobody ran all the way up, it was get-up a ways and stop to fire, covering each other. Found Bren Early with a whistle in his mouth. He got up and started blowing it and waving his sword— come on, boys, to glory—and a Mauser bullet smacked him in the butt, on account of the way he was turned to his people, and Bren Early grunted, dropped his sword and went down in the scrub to lay there cursing his luck, no doubt mortified to look like he got shot going the wrong way. Bo Catlett didn't believe Bren saw him pick up the sword. Picked it up, waved it at the Rough Riders and his Tenth Cav troopers, and they all went up that hill together, his troopers yelling, some of them singing, actually singing "They'll Be a Hot Time in the Old Town Tonight." Singing and shooting, honest to God, scaring the dons right out of their blockhouse. It was up on the crest Catlett got shot in his right hip and was taken to the Third Cav dressing station. It was set up on the Aguadores River at a place called "bloody ford" being it was under fire till the Hill was captured. Catlett remembered holding on to the sword, tight, while the regimental surgeon dug the bullet out of him and he tried hard not to scream, biting his mouth till it bled. After, he was sent home and spent a month at Camp Wikoff, near Montauk out on Long Island, with a touch of yellow fever. Saw President McKinley when he came by September third and made a speech, the President saying what they did over there in Cuba "commanded the unstinted praise of all your countrymen." Till he walked away from Montauk and came back into the world Sgt. Major Catlett actually did believe he and the other members of the Tenth would be recognized as war heroes.

He wished Bren would hurry up and get here. He'd ask the hero of San Juan Hill how his heinie was and if he was getting much unstinted praise. If Bren didn't come pretty soon, Catlett decided he'd see him another time. Get a horse out of the livery and ride it up to White Tanks.

The four Circle-Eye riders sat at a front table in the Belle Alliance with a bottle of Green River whiskey, Macon staring out the window. The hotel was across the street and up the block a ways, but Macon could see it, the colored man in the suit of clothes still sitting on the porch, if he tilted his chair back and held on to the window sill. He said, "No sir, nobody told me they was niggers in the war."

Wayman said to the other two Circle-Eye riders, "Macon can't get over it."

Macon's gaze came away from the window. "It was *your* brother got killed."

Wayman said, "I know he did."

Macon said, "You don't care?"

The Circle-Eye riders watched him let his chair come down to hit the floor hard. They watched him get up without another word and walk out.

"I never thought much of coloreds," one of the Circle-Eye riders said, "but you never hear me take on about 'em like Macon. What's his trouble?"

"I guess he wants to shoot somebody," Wayman said. "The time he shot that chilipicker in Nogales? Macon worked hisself up to it the same way."

Catlett watched the one that was looking for a fight come out through the doors and go to the claybank, the reins looped once around the tie rail. He didn't touch the reins though. What he did was reach into a saddle bag and bring out what Catlett judged to be a Colt .44 pistol. Right then he heard:

"Only guests of the hotel are allowed to sit out here."

Catlett watched the cowboy checking his loads now, turning the cylinder of his six-shooter, the metal catching a glint of light from the sun, though the look of the pistol was dull and appeared to be an old model.

Monty the desk clerk, standing there looking at Catlett without getting too close, said, "You'll have to leave . . . Right now."

The cowboy was looking this way.

Making up his mind, Catlett believed. All right, now, yeah, he's made it up.

"Did you hear what I said?"

Catlett took time to look at Monty and then pointed off down the street. He said, "You see that young fella coming this way with the pistol? He think he like to shoot me. Say you don't allow people to sit here aren't staying at the ho-tel. How about, you allow them to get shot if they not a guest?"

He watched the desk clerk, who didn't seem to know whether to shit or go blind, eyes wide open, turn and run back in the lobby.

The cowboy, Macon, stood in the middle of the street now holding the six-shooter against his leg.

Catlett, still seated in the rocker, said, "You a mean rascal, ain't you? Don't take no sass, huh?"

The cowboy said something agreeing that Catlett didn't catch, the cowboy looking over to see his friends coming up the street now from the barroom. When he looked at the hotel porch again, Catlett was standing at the railing, his bedroll upright next to him leaning against it.

"I can be a mean rascal too," Catlett said, unbuttoning his suitcoat. "I want you to know that before you take this too far. You understand?"

"You insulted Colonel Roosevelt and his Rough Riders," the cowboy said, "and you insulted Wayman's brother, killed in action over there in Cuba."

"How come," Catlett said, "you weren't there?"

"I was ready, don't worry, when the war ended. But we're talking about *you*. I say you're a dirty lying nigger and have no respect for people better'n you are. I want you to apologize to the Colonel and his men and to Wayman's dead brother . . ."

"Or what?" Catlett said.

"Answer to me," the cowboy said. "Are you armed? You aren't, you better get yourself a pistol."

"You want to shoot me," Catlett said, " 'cause I went to Cuba and you didn't."

The cowboy was shaking his head. " 'Cause you lied. Have you got a pistol or not?"

Catlett said, "You calling me out, huh? You want us to fight a duel?"

"Less you apologize. Else get a pistol."

"But if I'm the one being called out, I have my choice of weapons, don't I? That's how I seen it work, twenty-four years in the U.S. Army in two wars. You hear what I'm saying?"

The cowboy was frowning now beneath his hat brim, squinting up at Bo Catlett. He said, "Pistols, it's what you use."

Catlett nodded. "If I say so."

"Well, what else is there?"

Confused and getting a mean look.

Catlett slipped his hand into the upright end of his bedroll and began to tug at something inside—the cowboy watching, the Circle-Eye riders in the street watching, the desk clerk and manager in the doorway and several hotel guests near them who had come out to the porch, all watching as Catlett drew a sword from the bedroll, a cavalry saber, the curved blade flashing as it caught the sunlight. He came past the people watching and down off the porch toward the cowboy in his hat and boots fixed with spurs that chinged as he turned to face Catlett, shorter than Catlett, appearing confused again holding the six-shooter at his side.

"If I choose to use sabers," Catlett said, "is that agreeable with you?"

"I don't have no *saber*."

Meanness showing now in his eyes.

"Well, you best get one."

"I never even had a sword in my hand."

Irritated. Drunk, too, his eyes not focusing as they should. Now he was looking over his shoulder at the Circle-Eye riders, maybe wanting them to tell him what to do.

One of them, not Wayman but one of the others, called out, "You got your .44 in your hand, ain't you? What're you waiting on?"

Catlett raised the saber to lay the tip against Macon's breastbone, saying to him, "You use your pistol and I use steel? All right, if that's how you want it. See if you can shoot me 'fore this blade is sticking out your back. You game? . . . Speak up, boy."

In the hotel dining room having a cup of coffee, Catlett heard the noise outside, the cheering that meant Capt. Early had arrived. Catlett waited. He wished one of the waitresses would refill his cup, but they weren't around now, nobody was. A half hour passed before Capt. Early entered the dining room and came over to the table, leaving the people he was with. Catlett rose and they embraced, the hotel people and guests watching. It was while they stood this way that Bren saw, over Catlett's shoulder, the saber lying on the table, the curved steel on white linen. Catlett sat down. Bren looked closely at the saber's hilt. He picked it up and there was applause from the people watching. The captain bowed to them and sat down with the sergeant major.

"You went up the hill with this?"

"Somebody had to."

"I'm being recommended for a medal. 'For courage and pluck in continuing to advance under fire on the Spanish fortified position at the battle of Las Guásimas, Cuba, June 24, 1898.' "

Catlett nodded. After a moment he said, "Will you tell me something? What was that war about?"

"You mean why'd we fight the dons?"

"Yeah, tell me."

"To free the oppressed Cuban people. Relieve them of Spanish domination."

"That's what I thought."

"You didn't know why you went to war?"

"I guess I knew," Catlett said. "I just wasn't sure."

To Challenge a Legend

Albert Butler

THE NOSE OF THE BULLET had flattened against the bone. I took it from the shelf, holding the misshapen .45 slug in the palm of my hand, thinking of the pain it had caused all these years. And I had been the cause of it.

Tears came to my eyes even now as my thoughts went back to that time, waiting with my mother on the depot platform, for the 12:15 train . . .

Whoooo . . . oooo came the distant sound. Soon the engine burst into view, around the curve by the river, smoke puffing from its stack, streaming back over the mail and baggage and passenger cars. With a flare of steam, the whistle pounded my ears and the platform vibrated, and when the last note faded, I could hear the rhythmic clanging of the engine's bell, the screeching of brakes.

I felt a hand on my shoulder and I looked up and my father was standing beside me looking so handsome in his station agent uniform. He smiled at me and I thought for sure I'd be a railroad man when I grew up. But the train had stopped and two women got off the first passenger car and then I saw Grandpa Hawke and I knew I wanted to be just like him.

Someone shouted something from a car two or three back and my grandfather stopped and looked that way. I couldn't see who it was because of the baggage cart on the platform and then Grandpa saw us and waved and hurried toward us.

I remember he hugged my mother and kissed her on the cheek

and said, "You're beautiful as ever, Prissy Powell." He tousled my hair. "How are you, Billy?" He shook hands with my father and I swelled with pride when he turned back to me and said, "My— you're getting to be a big young man."

Since we lived only three blocks away, we walked home. Grandfather carried his heavy carpetbag; he let me carry a small but quite heavy leather bag. Father said he'd bring a large package wrapped in heavy brown paper when he came home.

I had seen my grandfather only once before and I didn't remember him very well. He and Mother talked a long time to "catch up" as she called it. My grandmother Hawke had died when Mother was born, so she grew up living with the Fields, her grandparents.

"Well, young man, we need to get acquainted," Grandfather said at last. "Come on up while I unpack."

"Yes, sir," I said. "I'll be right there."

I ran to my room and got *the* book. I stopped a moment at the top of the stairs to catch my breath. Grandfather heard me and called, "Come on in, Billy."

He'd put his derby hat on the bureau along with his tie. "Making myself comfortable," he said, taking off his coat and vest. "Can you reach high enough to hang these up?"

"Yes, sir."

The room only got used when someone came to stay and I looked around for a place to put *the* book. A big old trunk sat in one corner so I laid the book there.

After we got his clothes put away, he sat in a chair next to the bed and patted the cover. "Come sit here and tell me about school —about yourself."

"Yes, sir."

I couldn't wait any longer. I didn't want to talk about me. I got *the* book from the trunk and came and sat down on the bed. "Grandpa—I've read these stories so many times I know them almost word-for-word."

The wrinkled cover showed a drawing of my grandfather with a gun in each hand belching flames. It didn't look much like him because in the drawing his mustache was bigger and he wore a big broad-brimmed hat and a vest with a star pinned on it. The title said *The Exploits of Ross Hawke: Frontier Marshal* by Ned Buntline.

He took the book from me and held it at arm's length and said, "I didn't think any of these were still around."

"Yes, sir. I got it last year when we lived in Omaha. A kid in my school had it and he didn't believe it was about my grandfather. I traded him a mouth organ for it."

Grandpa Hawke reached for a pair of glasses on the bureau and put them on. He looked at the book's cover, thumbed through a few pages before giving it back to me. "Billy—these are mostly just stories. Made-up stories."

I remember that I felt shocked when he said that. "But you— you were a marshal like it says."

Grandpa nodded. "I only met Ned Buntline once. Talked maybe an hour. Not even his real name. Judson. Something like that."

"He says you were a marshal in Ellsworth and Abilene and Wichita. And a U.S. deputy marshal for Judge Parker."

Grandpa took his glasses off. "Buntline was right about that. Now all those things he said I did—well, they're pretty farfetched. I guess folks get some pleasure from reading them."

Grandpa put his glasses back on the bureau. "You take Bill Cody —he's quite a man, but Ned Buntline's stories made him into a myth. Now I'm just *me*. Walking the streets, waiting around to head off trouble before it starts; riding long miles through the Nations isn't very exciting, Billy. If someone wrote about those things, no one would read it."

"What about that time in Abilene? When you faced those seven Texas men all alone?" I found the chapter headed OUTDRAWS SEVEN DESPERADOES. "It says Marshal Hawke drew both guns before any of those 'seven murderous desperadoes' hands touched the butts of their weapons.' "

"First, Billy, there were five men, not seven. Second, I never carried two guns. Third, those men were trail hands. One, Adam Schmitz, owned the herd they'd driven up from Texas. The City Council passed an ordinance making it illegal to carry a gun in town and they didn't like it. The year before, the men had pretty much had their way, hurrahing the town—riding up and down the streets firing their guns. I told them we wanted them to have a good time, but they'd have to check their guns in the marshal's office until they were ready to leave for their camp outside of town, or home.

"Well, one of the hands said, 'Marshal, you care to count, you see five of us and one of you, so what's it going to be?' I simply told him whatever happened I figured I could get off one shot and they'd have to bury their boss, Adam Schmitz, or pack his body all the way back to Texas. So Schmitz said to his men he thought it best they comply and they all went in the office and left their guns and we didn't have any trouble."

I remember sitting there on the bed, wide-eyed, and I said, "Weren't you scared, Grandpa?"

"You bet. I don't think those men were feeling all that good right at the moment either. They were hard-working ranch hands, not desperadoes, and they knew I meant what I said."

"What about that time in the Indian Nations when you rode into that camp where there were a dozen outlaws and you told them they were under arrest and they pulled their guns and you shot four of them and the rest surrendered?"

Grandpa didn't say anything for a moment. "A dozen?" He glanced at the Ned Buntline book on the bed beside me. "I never did read all of that nonsense. A dozen men? Well, Billy, to show you how smart I was, I didn't even see that camp. In fact, I would have ridden on past if those men hadn't taken a shot at me. I didn't have any place to hide and I turned my horse and rode in and they were shooting and I shot back." He shook his head. "A *dozen* men! Two. There were two, Billy. One was only seventeen. I always felt bad about that."

I hopped off the bed. "Grandpa! I'll be right back."

I ran downstairs to my room and reached under the pillow for the wooden revolver my father had made for me. Now as I remember it was only a flat piece of wood cut with a grip and a hole for the trigger guard, the barrel partly rounded. Proudly, I ran back upstairs and handed it to Grandpa Hawke. "Well, Billy," he said, "this is a good-looking revolver. A Colt?"

"Yes, sir. Just like yours."

When he gave it back, I said, "Grandpa, can I see your revolver?"

"Mine? Where would it be?"

I pointed to the leather bag I'd carried from the train depot.

Grandpa Hawke just looked at me without saying anything. Finally he got up and unstrapped the bag that he'd left on top of the bureau. He held up his razor and a box of cigars. "Looks like that's about all that's in here, Billy."

"Please, Grandpa."

Grandpa Hawke carefully lifted his revolver out of the bag, the barrel resting against the palm of his left hand. It was a Colt single-action army model.

"Can I hold it, Grandpa?"

"No, Billy. It's loaded. Five cartridges. You always leave the chamber under the hammer empty to avoid accidents. You already knew that, didn't you?"

"Yes, sir . . . Can I see the notches?"

"Notches?" He shook his head. Gripping the barrel tightly with his left hand, he let me see the smooth walnut grip. "It makes a good story, I guess. I never knew anyone who did it."

"Wes Croy does. He has three of 'em."

"This Croy—you know him?"

"Talked to him once. He doesn't really live here, but he comes here some and he's my friend Jay Mason's cousin."

Grandpa Hawke put his revolver away and said, "Billy, your mother says your teacher tells her you are the best pupil she has."

I remember that I sort of shrugged.

"So what would you like to be when you grow up?"

"A marshal just like you."

"Well, I'm not a marshal anymore, Billy. That was quite a few years back."

"I could still be one—like you, Grandpa." I pointed my wooden revolver at the window and said, "Bang! Bang! Got 'em both."

I remember Grandpa Hawke looked at me and sat down. "A man has to fit his time, and change when times change. The country is growing up, just like you, Billy. We'll always need lawmen, but mostly we're going to need people who can think and learn to do new things. Why, last week I read in a Kansas City newspaper about this inventor, Edison. He's built some kind of machine that makes pictures that move. Besides, you can never be like someone else. You have to be *you;* do the things your mind and hands let you do best."

That night after supper, Grandpa Hawke asked me to open the paper-wrapped package my father had carried home. When I started untying the string and the paper loosened, I could smell leather. Inside was a beautiful handbag for Mother, a belt and gloves for my father, and a short deerskin coat for me with fringes and some silver decorations. I went and hugged Grandpa, then I put the coat on and it was a bit too big. Grandpa laughed and said, "Had to guess some at your size, Billy. You wait—come winter, you'll be filling it out and another year or two you won't be able to get it on."

All of the gifts were made by Grandpa Hawke in his Kansas City leather works and I knew I'd keep my coat even when I could no longer wear it.

If ever there was a time in your life you'd like to take back, the next few days would haunt me for years. Often I'd wake up with a start and see every detail and feel the hurt.

Grandpa Hawke had walked downtown to talk to Asa Gordon at the tannery about some leather he wanted to buy. It was almost summer and I went barefooted, the dirt soft and warm, over to Jay Mason's place, my wooden revolver tucked in the waistband of my trousers. Jay was sitting on the porch and I sat down beside him and told him how my Grandpa Hawke had come to visit and how he'd shown me his Colt revolver. Jay had heard me talk about him a million times and borrowed my Ned Buntline book and read all the stories about Grandpa.

I remember the screen door opening behind us but I didn't look around because I thought it was Jay's mother or his sister, Nan. "Boy," someone said, "you tell that old windbag granpa of yours I'm lookin' for him, and when I find him . . ."

I looked over my shoulder and Jay's cousin Wes Croy was standing there. Quick as a wink his hand flashed to the revolver at his hip and whipped it out of the holster and the hammer clicked back and the barrel was pointed right at me.

"Wes! Don't you be scaring that boy!" Jay's mother called.

He grinned and tilted the barrel up and let the hammer down and holstered his revolver. "Come on, Hank. My whistle is gettin' dry."

Wes Croy stepped down off the porch followed by Hank Dixon and Hank stumbled like he'd already been drinking too much. He used to help out some at the depot until my father said he let him go because he caught him going through some passengers' bags. Hank had a revolver, too, but there were a lot of ranches in the area and most of the hands wore guns and carried rifles in saddle boots when they came to town.

Everything had happened so fast the fear didn't catch up with me for a minute. Then I started to shake and I said something to Jay about having to get home.

I remember I hardly ate any dinner and I could hardly look at

Grandpa Hawke. I wanted to tell him about Wes Croy and I didn't know quite how.

"Billy," my mother said, "you don't look like you feel very good. Why don't you go take a nap? Your grandfather and I haven't had a chance to really talk since he got here."

"You get to feeling better," Grandpa said. "I'll take all of you to the Palace Theater tonight."

I went to my room and I knew I couldn't sleep. I fluffed up my pillow and sat on my bed and thumbed through the Ned Buntline book, looking at the illustrations. I wanted to keep believing every word despite what my Grandpa Hawke said. I finally closed my eyes and I could see my grandpa out in the middle of the street, walking toward Wes Croy and Hank Dixon, and both of them reaching for their guns and Grandpa's Colt revolver appearing like magic, bucking, smoking, and Wes and Hank lying in the dirt . . .

I didn't know how long Grandpa planned to stay, but at supper he said he was going to leave the next day on the twelve-fifteen train.

I had to put on shoes and wear my Sunday clothes, and we walked to the Palace Theater. There were a lot of people and it got hot inside and I sat next to Grandpa Hawke and felt very proud. A traveling troupe put on a play and there was a lot of shouting, the women in the play crying; finally a man shot the one making the women cry and when the gun went off Grandpa's arm bumped me.

When we started outside, Grandpa held on to my hand. People were crowded around in front of the theater and I saw Wes Croy and Hank Dixon, and Wes yelled something at Grandpa Hawke.

"This way," I heard my father say. Grandpa's hand gripped mine tightly as we squeezed past people, out of the light, and down a narrow alley between the theater and Brock's Mercantile.

My father and mother were ahead of us, and when we reached the end of the alley, they hurried along the back of Brock's and no one said anything until we were on the street that led to our house.

With a sigh, Father said, "I feel better now."

"Is he still angry with you?" my mother asked.

"I don't think so. He isn't very bright," and I knew he was referring to Hank Dixon. "That Croy—he's the bad one."

Grandpa said, "Sorry to cause so much trouble."

Nothing more was really said when we reached home and I was sent off to bed soon after. I could hear them talking in the parlor for a long time before I went to sleep.

I suppose the muffled voices woke me. Father had always got up early; he had to be at the station when the 6:10 morning train came through, but I seldom ever heard him. He'd fix some coffee and let Mother sleep, then come home for his breakfast at eight.

I got out of bed and crept to the door and listened and I could hear Mother, Father, and Grandpa Hawke talking in the kitchen. Then I heard the front door open and close. Pretty soon the crack of light under the door went out. The soft steps I knew were those of my mother going back to bed. Why didn't I hear Grandpa Hawke go back upstairs? No matter how quiet you tried to be, the stairsteps always creaked.

Dawn light spilled around the edges of my bedroom window shade as I pulled on my shirt and trousers. Quietly, I slipped out of my room, tiptoed across the cold linoleum kitchen floor, past the warm cookstove, to the front door. We never locked the door and in a minute I was outside.

The town was still asleep; a rooster crowed, the only sound until I neared the depot. One of the men pulled a cart loaded with mail sacks and boxes across the platform. Then I saw Grandpa Hawke standing at the end of the platform smoking a cigar. "Grandpa!" I called, running through the cindery dirt, up the slope to the level of the platform.

"Billy! What are you doing here?"

"Are you leaving, Grandpa? You didn't say good-by."

I stood looking up at him and he didn't say anything for a moment. Then he touched a hand to my shoulder, pulled me close, and I could feel the revolver under his coat.

"You said you were going home on the twelve-fifteen."

"Sorry, Billy. I decided to leave earlier—after you were in bed."

"Why?"

"Well—there are some things I'd forgotten about I have to do." His hand tightened on my shoulder. "Billy—you better run on home."

Grandpa had glanced over his shoulder, and when I looked, I saw two men coming along the dusty street to the depot. The sun wasn't quite up but I could see it was Wes Croy and Hank Dixon.

"Billy!"

Grandpa Hawke sounded gruff and he gave me a little push and I knew there was going to be some kind of trouble. Instead of going home I ran along the tracks to the water tank about a hundred feet from the station and ducked behind one of the big wooden tower legs.

"Hawke!" Wes Croy called, when he and Hank stopped walking. "You tryin' to run away?"

I remember when he said that I suddenly felt sick. Was my grandpa scared? Was that why he hadn't said good-by to me last night—why he'd decided to take the morning train? Then I saw his cigar go sailing and he slowly lowered his arm to his side. "I don't want any trouble with you."

"Old man—I do believe you're a coward! I see that grandson of yours hidin' under the water tank over there. He thinks you are some kind of hero and now he's gonna be disappointed, you tryin' to sneak outta town."

"There's no need for you to do this, Croy. So you are good with a gun. I accept that. You don't have to prove it to anyone."

"I do for a fact. I beat a man like Ross Hawke with all the stories they tell like in that book Billy Boy's so proud, ever'body'll know I'm the best."

Grandpa Hawke said, "I'm not going to fight you," and turned his back. In a second or two splinters flew from the platform by Grandpa's feet, the boom of Wes Croy's gun reverberating across town. Grandpa Hawke slowly turned and the sun, now peeking over the horizon, outlined him against the sky. This time I saw flames shoot from Wes Croy's revolver and Grandpa staggered and two shots sounded almost simultaneously and Wes—facing slightly uphill—seemed to stand on his toes then go over backward like he'd been hit with a sledgehammer.

By the time I saw Grandpa Hawke's Colt, it was pointed at Hank Dixon. Hank whirled around, stumbled to one knee, got up and ran as fast as he could go back down the street.

"Grandpa!" I ran to him. When I reached him, his revolver was poked behind the waistband of his suit and he was getting his coat off.

My father and the baggagemen were there in another minute. My father took one look, said, "Billy—go get Doc Waters!"

The rest remains somewhat a blur. Grandpa Hawke had been hit in the left shoulder and Doc Waters put on a big bandage to stop the blood. "You'll have to come down to my office," Doc said. "All right," Grandpa told him.

By that time Marshal Turner and one of his deputies were there. Grandpa Hawke said, "I didn't intend to kill him. My eyes aren't what they used to be."

Grandpa Hawke had to stay over two days for an inquest. No one could find Hank Dixon, but several people testified that Wes Croy had been talking about killing Grandpa Hawke and the coroner's jury brought in a verdict of justified self-defense.

I could hardly look at my Grandpa those two days without feeling that none of it would have happened except for me. I hid the Ned Buntline book away. And the day Grandpa Hawke went home, I burned my wooden revolver in the kitchen cookstove . . .

Memories. They came flooding back. Grandpa Hawke buttoned his shirt collar, put his coat on, and reached for his cane. "I don't need to come back?"

"No. Everything looks fine." I held out the .45 slug. "Do you want it?"

He shook his head.

I dropped the old slug in a waste container, walked to the door, held it open, then followed Grandpa Hawke out on the covered entrance. The sun was shining. A beautiful day. He turned and ran his fingers over the raised lettering of the nameplate beside the door: W. ROSS POWELL M.D.

"Grandfather . . ." I began. For the first time in all the years I brought myself to tell him about that day at Jay Mason's house. "You see, it would never have happened if I hadn't been bragging and Wes Croy learned that you were at our place."

"No, no. He was on the train I came on. Someone pointed me out and he challenged me. He'd been drinking and I thought at first he'd forget about it when the liquor quit talking."

Another piece of memory fell in place. That day at the depot— someone had called to Grandpa Hawke when he got off the train.

He took his glasses from his coat and put them on. Once more he ran his fingers over the nameplate. "I'm glad that boy, Billy, decided to be himself. After all these years it's a great relief to be rid of the pain."

"Yes," I said. "It certainly is."

Wildfire

Marianne Willman

"LOOKING MIGHTY PURTY today, Miss Parmenter."

Annie looked up from her baking chores. Seth Begley stood just inside the lean-to that was her summer kitchen, idly chewing on the butt of his cigar. Annie read derision in his voice. She had no illusions as to her beauty. She was homely and she'd known it all her twenty-four years. Thread-thin and freckled as a wild bird's egg. Mama had told her that often enough.

She fixed Seth with a wide blue stare. "I am not going to sell you my land, Mr. Begley. No matter how many hollow compliments you may pay me. And I'll thank you not to come sneaking around my place again."

"Wasn't sneaking . . . Ma'am. My horse is down at the creek. Thought it'd be a nice morning for a little walk. And some neighborly talk." His thin face hardened. "I like to do business in a right friendly fashion. When folks'll let me."

Annie didn't challenge the implied threat but she didn't intend to sell her land to him or anyone. The land was all she had left, the only thing that was really hers. She punched the heavy dough down with her knuckles, pretending it was Seth Begley's face. Childish, she knew, but immensely satisfying.

"Ain't you gonna offer me anything to drink? Cold buttermilk or hot coffee, either one'll do. I'm not hard to please."

She slapped the floured dough into a mound and punched it down so hard she lost a hairpin and a wisp of hair tumbled loose at her nape. Begley noticed the color then, red-gold and fine as floss. It was the only pretty thing about her. He came a little closer.

"Is it true what they say about redheads? Being fiery and passionate and all?"

She was too mortified and angry to answer his impertinence in the way that he deserved. Face flaming, she buried her floury hands in the bread dough when she really wanted to box his ears soundly. It wouldn't do to antagonize him right now while they were still negotiating for her rights to the creek. Pounding and punching the dough instead of Seth Begley, she struggled with her temper. It was her greatest flaw and Ma had warned her time after time to mend her hotheaded ways.

Seth watched her with growing interest. With the high color in her face and her hair coming loose in wisps, Miz Annabel Parmenter was looking better and better. There might be other ways to bring her round his thumb than his original plan. He reached out and fingered one of her curls. Annie jerked away with an angry exclamation but Seth grinned more widely.

"Right pretty hair. Bright as a new penny and a might softer. Better watch out, Miz Parmenter, or one of them Comanche braves'll have your scalp dangling from his belt." He lit the cigar and puffed a cloud in her direction. "They're raiding again hereabouts. Winged one yestidy. Damn savage tried to steal my horse."

Annie had never liked Seth Begley, but she'd never been afraid of him, either. Something had changed. Her skin crawled. Not knowing the best way to react, she did what she'd done in the past when he'd pestered her: She ignored him so thoroughly he grew tired of needling her.

He blew out a blue cloud of cigar smoke. "Play your little games, Miz Parmenter. You're gonna have to talk to me sooner or later. You can't keep a spread going alone, even with them two Whistler boys helping out when they can." He shambled into a patch of strong morning sun. "I'll be back. You can count on it."

There was no response except for the angry flush staining Annie's face and throat. Begley frowned in aggravation. Compliments and intimidation hadn't worked. So far. But he'd be back. He certainly would.

Leaning past Annie, he dumped the long gray ash of his cigar over the tops of two loaves of dough already rising on her worktable. Annie's arm swung round to slap him. Seth caught her wrist and their eyes locked. "Let go of me, at once!" She'd meant her voice to sound strong and steady. It came out in a hoarse squawk. Seth laughed, held her arms long enough that the fear showed in her eyes, then shoved her against the table and sauntered out.

A woman alone had to be careful whom she antagonized, but Annie was suddenly terrified beyond caution. She grabbed her always-loaded rifle and racked the shell into the chamber as she followed him to the door. He didn't see her raise the rifle to her shoulder and aim, but the whine and zing that followed got his immediate attention. Whirling around he saw her aiming again. The explosion of dirt and gravel was too close to his heels for comfort.

Annie faced him coolly. "The next one will be a lot closer, Mr. Begley. I'd advise you to get on your horse and *git!*"

He got. But as he wheeled his sorrel, he called back to her. "And I'd advise you to light out of here within the week, Miz Parmenter. 'Cause your creek is gonna be drier than dirt—and if any of your cattle stray onto my propity, they's gonna die of lead poisoning."

"Vulture! Jackal!" she called out to his retreating form, and dashed a sting of angry tears from her eyes. Mama would have been upset to know that Annie had threatened a man with a rifle—but a lady could only hold so much in. She would never give up this land her parents had fought and died for. Not for a dozen Seth Begleys.

She had regained her equilibrium by afternoon when the new bread was baked and the little house was filled with its warm, yeasty flavor. Annie enjoyed baking. There was something rewarding about seeing quick results from her labor. Less frustrating than wresting crops from the Texas soil.

Her Pa had worked hard to plant and harvest their land and she'd worked right along beside him. Mama had always been too delicate. As her hopes of a fine estate and an elegant, eligible daughter had faded beneath the harsh sun, so had she.

After Mama's death everything had begun to fall apart, beginning with Pa. "I never should have brought her out to this godforsaken place," he said every evening, after a long day's work. "But we've still got the land, Annie. We've still got the land. That's the only thing a man can hold on to in this world."

She looked up from the cooling loaves of bread and out the open window. Now the only things left of Pa and Mama's dreams were a few worn buildings, a section of land slowly blowing away as dust —and two graves up on the hill behind the house.

And herself, Annie amended. Well, that would have to be enough. She'd promised to hang on to the land and to make the ranch productive. The greater the odds grew, the more important it became to succeed. No matter what the Seth Begleys of the world did, she would fight for this land. It meant everything to her.

The bread was still too warm to slice, so Annie tore off a corner of one loaf and daubed it generously with cool butter. It melted on the tongue, crusty outside, light as air inside and fragrant with yeast. She smiled with pride. This was her one small vanity: She might not be much to look at but, by God, she could cook and bake. It just wasn't much fun to do it just for herself. Maybe she'd take the buggy over to the Whistlers' place, with a few loaves and some of that quince jam.

She was still trying to make up her mind when she heard squawking from the hen house. Some varmint in there after the chickens. Annie hurried there, pushed the door open and stamped her feet. "Shoo! Get out. Shoo!"

She didn't see the blood until she stepped in it, just inside the door. It was sticky and already darkening, but she knew blood when she saw it. She'd done enough nursing and birthing in her twenty-four years: Always a midwife, never a wife.

The hens were all safe and settled their feathers, complaining sharply among themselves. Most likely an animal predator, yet Annie didn't discount Seth's story of a wounded Comanche. The Potterville massacre of '48 was still very much alive in people's minds. Annie's Mama had told her she would be better off taking her own life than to be captured by the evil Comanche. The things they did to captives were told only in whispers. The things they did to women were never spoken of at all.

Annie checked things out and breathed a relieved sigh. Whatever—or whoever—was injured had not tarried here. She went outside and peered around. There was a spatter of bloody droplets and another splotch farther on, leading to an empty shed. After a moment's hesitation she went back to the house and fetched the rifle, and slipped her father's old Army Colt into her belt. These were unsettled times. Best to be prepared for anything.

She stood aside and threw open the shed door. "Come on out, you varmint."

There was no response. She waited. The wind blew softly, insistently, as it always did this time of year. A low sound, like a muffled groan, made the hairs on the back of her neck stand up. The marmalade cat that had littered in the shed came prancing out of the shadows and sat in the sun outside the doorway, washing her pink paws.

Annie relaxed. Ginger wouldn't have been so calm if there was anything dangerous lurking inside. Propping the rifle against the wall, she entered the shed. Rays of golden light sifted through the chinks in the dry wood and dust motes danced as Annie made her way past the jumble of odds and ends and gardening tools. She stepped around the wheelbarrow—and almost tripped on a body lying just beyond it.

She gasped and froze in place. An Indian was sprawled flat on his back on a pile of sacking, arms outflung as if he were crucified. There was dried blood down his chest and beneath it his ribs stuck out gaunt as the hoops of a broken barrel.

So this was one of the dreaded Comanche. This poor starving creature, matted with blood and dirt. But she slid the gun from her belt and held it ready. A wounded animal could prove the deadliest.

Beneath the filth and pallor the lines of his face were young. Why, he's not more than a boy, she thought, with a swift stab of pity. Then his eyelids flew up and she saw that she was wrong. No boy had eyes like this, bleak with knowledge of life's impartial cruelties. It pained her to look into them, yet she was unable to look away.

She was compelled to move closer. Annie knelt down beside him, forgetting that she held the gun. His right hand shot out and clamped around her wrist. It was strong and hard and had the heat of iron fresh from the forge. Fear constricted her throat but she knew she mustn't let him see it.

She laid her other hand firmly on his arm. "You needn't be afraid," she said, defiant of her fright. "I won't hurt you." She was pleased to hear her voice so brisk and steady. "You need help. You are injured and feverish. Let me see where you are hurt."

He stared back at her, understanding the tone, if not the words.

Weighing, judging. Then he released his grip, surprising them both.

Annie put the Colt out of reach and examined him with cool efficiency. Her calm tones and slow, deliberate actions soothed him, or perhaps he had merely resigned himself to the inevitable. She found a superficial wound some six inches long over the left shoulder. That had caused most of the bleeding. His other wound, on the outside of his right thigh, hadn't bled much because the shot was still lodged in it. The flesh was purple and puffy.

She prodded the edges. He tried to roll away and was stopped by a wall of solid pain. "This will have to come out, you know."

He didn't hear her. He'd passed out cold. Annie sat back on her heels and tried to think of what to do. First she'd have to remove the bullet and clean the wounds. She'd worry about the healing later. And she'd have to conceal him. With Seth Begley poking about, that was a prime necessity. Annie had no doubt of what he'd do to a Comanche. And she felt strangely protective of this one. After all, it had been her shed where he'd sought refuge.

The shed had very special ties for her. In the early days when Mama and Papa had first brought her to the ranch, this homely structure had been their first house. Then it had been her refuge from a hostile world, shielding the family from heat and cold, from rain and wind and hail. There was a partition at the back where her parents had slept. It would be a safer place for her uninvited guest. She stood and regarded the problem a moment, then bent and grabbed her patient by the ankles and began pulling.

What she lacked in strength she made up in determination. She didn't look up until he was completely hidden behind the flimsy wall. If he'd awakened and passed out again during the effort, she couldn't tell, and she didn't need to know. She felt a strange kinship with him. They were both alone.

Wiping her soiled hands on her apron, she retrieved the Colt and went back to the house, making a mental list of required supplies. Cloth for bandages, shears to cut it, ointment and alcohol. Canvas needle and waxed thread and Papa's knife with the thin steel blade and carved bone handle. And blankets and quilts, of course.

Without realizing it, Annie began humming a jaunty little tune under her breath.

□ □ □ □

When Buffalo Heart regained consciousness, the barn was shadowy as a cave and it took a moment to remember. If he strained his eyes, he could make out strips of dim lavender sky through chinks in the roof and walls. Someone had covered him with a woolen blanket. A white-eyes blanket.

He looked around. His left shoulder was bound with tight strips of torn sheeting, his leg with flowered calico, and his throat was as parched and cracked as a dry riverbed. A creak of wood came from beyond the inside wall and he lay still, preparing to fight for his life with all his remaining strength. There was no time to subdue his pain.

He smelled the woman before he saw or heard the rustling of her skirts. It was a pleasant scent, flowery and light, but alien. A moment later she rounded the partition with a shuttered lantern in one hand and a lidded basket in the other. She knelt beside him and opened the lantern. Her face was thin and bony and speckled like an owl's breast. There was nothing rounded or womanly about it. He wondered if all white women were so ugly.

But when she re-dressed his wounds, he forgot about her ugliness and knew only that her hands were strong and gentle. By the time she finished, he was weak, his flesh chill and clammy, and all the while Buffalo Heart wondered why she did this for him. He'd heard of white women who lived together and spent all their days aiding the ill and wounded, or kneeling in prayer before their little wooden gods. Perhaps it was their punishment for getting no husbands to provide for them.

Annie propped his head on her arm and gave him a spoonful of syrup so bitter that he spit it out immediately. "Pah!"

She was not pleased. "Don't do that again. It is very hard to come by." She poured out another and held the spoon to his mouth.

He swallowed it. Surely she would not bandage his wounds earlier, only to poison him now. But logic told him she had some ulterior reason for her aid. Perhaps she meant to keep him as a slave. It had happened to a Kiowa brave he'd known. His face was fierce as his namesake creature. No one would ever make a slave of him. He would die first. By his own hand, if necessary.

Annie stood up. Her patient was bathed, bandaged, fed, and dosed with poppy syrup. There was only one thing she'd forgotten. Until now. She rummaged through the shed and returned with a wide-mouthed brown bottle. Buffalo Heart watched her every move but his lids were drooping. When she set the bottle down within arm's reach, he picked it up and peered inside. It was empty. He flung it away. Annie retrieved it and hesitated, cheeks hot with embarrassment in the lantern light. Finally she held it somewhere in the region of her hips, then pointed at his loins.

Buffalo Heart understood and laughed aloud. Sliding his hand behind the flap in his breeches he sent a glittering stream of water arcing against the shed wall. Annie went stumbling back in dismay, but recovered herself quickly.

"Heathen!" She picked up the bottle and plunked it down beside him again. "You are to use the bottle from now on!"

He grinned at her discomfiture. When she turned and stormed out, he was still chuckling.

The next morning he had a raging fever and Annie had no time for further etiquette lessons. By the third day he was much improved, although she had to cauterize the edges of his leg wound once more. Her life took on a new rhythm. Now Annie's days were filled with purpose, and so busy she fell into bed and slept like a baby. She added extra meat to her beef broth, and when she stewed a chicken, she found herself checking and adjusting the taste: Did it need more salt? Parsley? Perhaps an extra bit of carrot? She realized how lonely she had been, and then forgot about her loneliness in this strange new life she was leading.

And on the sixth day Seth Begley came again. Annie had just opened the door of the shed.

"Afternoon, Miss Parmenter."

She let the door swing shut and started back toward the house. "I said I won't have you sneaking around here, Seth Begley. You've got no call to trespass on my property."

"That's no way to treat a visitor, now." Begley followed her onto the porch. "Right unfriendly for a woman living alone with no man to protect her." He stepped closer. "I think it's time you and me got to be friends. Good friends."

"What . . . !" Before Annie knew what he was about, Begley grabbed her by the shoulders and pushed her through the door. He backed her against the table and pawed at her and Annie walloped Begley along side of the head. He yelped, then cuffed her so soundly he split her lip. Annie's head struck the support table, dazing her. In an instant he had her down on the floor and her skirts up over her waist, tugging at her undergarments.

She realized he meant to rape her and fought as strongly as she could. The front of her dress was torn open with one swipe of Begley's big hand as Buffalo Heart burst through the door brandishing a hoe. There was a hollow smacking sound, like a pumpkin smashed against the ground, and Begley went limp atop her. Buffalo Heart took another solid swipe with the rusted hoe and then pulled the corpse off Annie. She scrambled out of the way while he kicked Begley's body over on its back. The hoe came down again, obliterating the face, then chopped at the torso. He was swift and methodical, like a hawk killing a rattler, and Annie watched unblinkingly.

When he was through, Buffalo Heart threw the hoe down and smiled at Annie. She should have been horrified. She wasn't in the least. But reaction made her sway dizzily. Buffalo Heart caught her before she hit the floor. When Annie came to, she was lying on her bed with the Comanche hovering anxiously over her. She tried to sit up but he pushed her back, quite gently. She was shaking violently.

"Stay," he commanded, as she had to him so many times.

She complied, finding it both novel and comforting to have someone else look out for her interests. He covered her with the blanket, then stretched out beside her so close she thought she could hear the beating of his heart. But maybe it was only her own, after all. She drifted into an uneasy slumber, and when she awakened, both Buffalo Heart and the body were gone.

She sat up. There was not so much as a bloodstain to tell what had happened earlier. The soft clanging that had awakened her was only the lid on the stew pot, bubbling away on the hearth. Annie rose and swung the pot off the fire, then went outside.

The Comanche was just coming up on the porch. He looked exhausted. His face was all hollows and sharp planes and the skin beneath his eyes looked bruised. She checked his bandages, but there was no fresh bleeding. How strong he was. How courageous. Later she'd ask what he did with the body. But not now.

"I set some stew to simmer earlier. I'll bring some out here for us."

They sat side by side on the porch, not talking. Neither knew the other's language. A fresh wind blew up from the northwest and cloud schooners scudded across the dark sky, fleeing the coming fury. A massive storm was brewing and the air crackled with its aura. Annie could feel the hairs prickle along the back of her arms and neck.

She jumped at the first flash of lightning and its echoing rumble of thunder. No rain followed the threat but ragged red and orange lights flared about the edges of the clouds until they seemed to be on fire. It was an awesome display, a wild celebration of the forces of life.

Annie rose. Buffalo Heart came to stand nearby. She felt small and insignificant beneath the flaming sky yet oddly exhilarated, and very glad of his protective bulk beside her. He searched the sky, wondering if this was a sign.

They watched together while the breeze picked up, blowing curtains of dust across the plains, like fine Spanish veils. The wind whipped Annie's hair loose from her neat bun until it twisted like satin ribbons behind her. Crimson flames licked the edges of the clouds. Buffalo Heart's fingers brushed her arm lightly and she turned. He gestured toward the sky.

"What is it?" she said. "I'm not sure."

He shook his head. *He* knew what it was. There was nothing in all of nature that his people did not know. It was the white-eyes name he wanted to learn. He pointed to himself and said his name in Comanche, then pointed at her and said her name, as she'd told it to him. "Ahnnie Parmenter."

The light flashed overhead and this time he spoke the Comanche word for the phenomenon and pointed from Annie back to the sky.

"Oh! What is it called? I'm not sure of the actual name. Wildfire. My papa called it wildfire."

"Wildfire." The word sounded strange but felt good on his tongue. Almost absently he caught a strand of Annie's hair and wound it through his strong fingers. "Wildfire," he murmured again. Their eyes met and held. Simultaneously they looked away. Neither of them spoke.

Annie was tense and uncomfortable. The air was charged with the coming storm. The fire-show ended abruptly and the rains came howling down. Buffalo Heart held the edge of his blanket out to shelter Annie. She shook herself free and ran into the house. He pulled the blanket up to keep the rain from his eyes and went back to the shed slowly.

Annie huddled in her rocker, with Mama's shawl around her shoulders. Thunder rattled the rafters and lightning lit the room for the next hour, seeming to race around the walls with every flash. When it ended, the sky was clear and cool starlight iced the landscape. She undressed and went to bed, but didn't sleep for some time. Hazy, half-formed plans floated through her mind. She tried not to think of "the Indian" but his image haunted her.

There was no avoiding it, so she tried to work around it. Perhaps he would stay on, help her work the ranch. After all, she had found him—a poor, half-starved, wounded creature—and saved his life. Even a Comanche could show gratitude. And the arrangement would be to his benefit as well. She could offer him good home-cooked meals, shelter from the elements. Even companionship of a sort. Why, with some decent clothing he wouldn't look so uncivilized. She could take in some of her father's old things. But try as she might, Annie couldn't picture him in a pair of trousers and lace-up boots.

She wondered what he thought of her . . . if he thought of her at all. It was nice having him around. Funny, she hadn't even realized that she was lonely until . . .

Annie let her hands fall idle, bemused. The one person she'd begun to count on, the one person whose company she enjoyed, was a Comanche. Mama would have been appalled.

She snuggled beneath the down comforter. A short time ago life had looked bleak. Now her entire outlook had changed. Irrelevantly, she wondered what the Comanche thought of her hair.

Wildfire.

Eventually her thoughts tangled up with one another and she fell into a deep, confused sleep where the night sky was filled with the strong face of a Comanche warrior and his eyes shone like dark stars. Like wildfire.

When she woke in the morning, he was gone, taking her brindle horse with him.

Annie was outraged at the Comanche's ingratitude. She felt hurt. Abandoned. She told herself she was glad to be rid of him and the extra work he entailed. But to steal her horse! And after all she'd done for him!

She worked at her chores by day, and every night she cried herself to sleep without quite knowing why. And three weeks to the day he left, Buffalo Heart returned.

He rode up to the house early one morning on a fine gray

gelding, with her brindle and six other horses in string behind it. They were fine animals. She wondered whose ranch he had stolen them from.

He tied them to the porch rail and waited. Annie walked slowly from the hen house, noting that he seemed to be completely healed of his wounds. Only a thin scar traced the path of the bullet across his shoulder and his lean frame had filled out. Someone was feeding him well.

A wife, she thought, wondering why it hadn't occurred to her before. She bit her lip and kept on her beeline to the house.

Buffalo Heart saw the stubborn set of her shoulders. He mounted the gray and rode a short distance away with the rest, but Annie refused to look at him. She took the eggs into the house and made herself an omelet with three of them and the last of the winter onions. She realized that she didn't even know his name.

When she came out of the house an hour later, the horses were still there but the Comanche was gone. Were the horses a gift? Or payment for her care of him? Annie put her hands on her hipbones and stared at them. She had neither the time nor the energy to care for them. The land came first, would always come first.

And she wanted nothing from him, nothing at all.

She filled the trough and watered the horses, her hair sticking to the back of her sweaty neck. Hot as a stovelid, and not a hint of breeze to fan her cheeks. She went inside and stubbornly closed the door. The place was like an oven.

Near sundown he returned, remaining at a distance. Each time Annie looked out the window, he was still there. Watching. Waiting. For what? The sun set in an angry puddle of light, promising a fine day on the morrow. It was hot in the little house. Annie paced the room several times then stomped over to the door, red with anger and the heat. When she opened it, he was gone. No trace. Not even a puff of dust on the horizon.

Maybe she had imagined it. Didn't the heat cause hallucinations? But the horses were real enough. Annie tended to them and went to bed early.

She spent the night tossing and turning. A dozen times she got up to look out between the crack in the shutters, thinking she heard the pad of unshod hooves, the whisper of moccasined feet over the coarse ground. Her gown clung to her shoulders and breasts and thighs. It would be more sensible to sleep naked but she could not make herself strip down.

She fell into a disturbed slumber some time before dawn and dreamed she was withering away like a dried plum, all her vital juices evaporating in the deadly heat.

She should have been happy. No one had thought of a skinny spinster in regard to Seth Begley's mysterious disappearance. Mrs. Whistler blamed it on the Comanche, although someone suggested he'd been killed by a jealous rancher. He'd had a wandering eye, had Seth Begley.

With her enemy dead, Annie thought she might sell Mama's brooch and wedding ring. Hire some hands from town to help with the planting. Maybe get some cattle. But she was too restless to make plans. She knew what it was: that Comanche, coming around again. Well, he was gone now, and good riddance.

The next morning he was there again, waiting. And the morning after that. She continued to feed and water the horses, but refused to put them in her barn. On the fourth morning she almost tripped over a pack of pelts sitting just outside her door.

Buffalo Heart sat his patient gray a few yards away. Annie was exasperated beyond bearing. "What do you want? Leave me alone, damn you. Leave me alone!"

He held out his hand to her commandingly. Annie went back inside, slamming the door behind her. She leaned against it, shaking as if she had the ague. She knew what he wanted, had known from the beginning, in the shadowed recesses of her heart. It terrified her.

"I can't do it." Her voice echoed in the small house and she brushed away the tears that streaked her face. She had worked hard all her life, asking nothing in return; but carrying the deeply buried hope that some man would see beyond her plain features and freckled skin, so she might have a home, children. A simple measure of love and respect.

Two of those dreams had withered with the passing seasons. She did have a home of her own, though. This was her ranch now. Hers! Everything her parents had worked and died for belonged to her and it was her duty to somehow see that their hopes and dreams of a flourishing ranch were realized.

Wasn't it?

Buffalo Heart waited patiently. He had learned to wait silently

as his quarry came into sight, then into the range of his arrows. A
man who rushed out at the wrong time would send the shy doe
bounding away in terror. This woman was no different. He sat his
pony as the sun arced down the great bowl of sky to its western
home.

On the tenth morning, just after sunrise, the cabin door opened
suddenly. When she came out on the porch, Buffalo Heart saw that
she'd been weeping. She stared at him for a long while, then went
back inside. He heard the bolt slide shut. He waited.

It was almost sunset when she finally came out. She was dressed
for traveling and her arms were filled with a wealth of nested pots
and pans and thick wool blankets over her arm. She didn't look his
way as she went to the henhouse and propped the door open, then
went to the stable and opened the stall doors. Annie returned to the
cabin and went inside.

A moment later she returned with a rifle in one hand and the
Army Colt revolver in the other. A leather bag of cartridges was
slung over her shoulder and a sheathed knife was tucked into the
waistband of her divided skirt. She handed him the guns and
waited for his reaction.

Buffalo Heart nodded in satisfaction. Ah, the other braves would
envy him! A strong woman and practical, too. One whose heart
was full of courage, yet as gentle as her hands had been, tending his
wounds. His own seemed filled with light and warmth. He jumped
down and secured the other horses, then strode back to Annie. He
didn't touch her until her rapid breathing slowed.

Gently he untied the yellow ribbon that held her hair in its
smooth plait, and shook the shiny tresses out so they covered her
shoulders like a tawny shawl. He stared at her until she had to look
away from the light in his eyes. Buffalo Heart wondered how had
he ever thought her ugly. She was so beautiful, with her strange,
pale eyes like a still lake, and her glorious, fiery hair. He caught a
swath of it across his palm and carried it to his cheek. Soft as the
inside of a milkweed pod.

"Wildfire," he said, and smiled.

She had never really seen him smile before. Her answering one
was tremulous and brave.

Buffalo Heart wanted to claim her then and there, to make her
truly his, but something held him back. The shadow of the house
and outbuildings, of the two neat graves with their simple crosses.

This was the past and must be left behind them both. The future lay ahead of them, west toward the setting sun.

He caught Annie by the waist and set her upon his horse, then leaped up in front of her. She wrapped her arms loosely about his waist, then more tightly as he nudged his gray into a trot. She was trembling but it eased as the heat of his strong young body radiated through hers. As they rode away from the little house with its shabby outbuildings and worn soil, its forlorn hopes and memories, she did not look back, even once.

The sun sank lower, turning the dry earth to copper and umber and gilding the bellies of the high, vaporous clouds. Buffalo Heart rode proudly, his heart bursting with the fullness of life. Joyously the bridegroom sang aloud, as they rode across the open plain toward his distant lodge.

Annie smiled and rested her cheek against his naked back. He was young and brave and strong. He was life.

As they rode away, her unbound hair streamed out behind them, shimmering in the dying light like wildfire.

The Death(s)
of Billy the Kid

Arthur Winfield Knight

BILLY: HOME

FRIENDS TELL ME I ought to leave the territory. But what
would I do in Mexico with no money? I can stay here awhile and
get some money, then go to Mexico.

Fort Sumner's home. I love this country: the Valley of Fires, the
Pecos River.

I'm not going to let Garrett scare me away.

Friends think I don't know what I'm doing when I ride around
the country in circles, tracking myself; I know where I'm going
because I've been there. I've been to Alamogordo, Tularosa, too.

I like the purple light on the mountains at twilight and the
sound of guitars coming from the cantinas along with the laughter
of the señoritas. Once, I fucked the earth, I loved it so.

I want *this* soil in my face when I die.

I know times are changing. There's a new law each day of the
week. Men like Pat call it progress. I call it loss.

This is my home. Nobody's going to make me go.

GARRETT: APPLES

The Kid was eating an apple minutes before I shot him.

He and Paulita were in bed together, naked. She'd take a bite of
the apple, then give it to Billy. They were laughing in the moon-

light, passing the apple back and forth, the moon in their eyes, licking each other's lips. Some of the juice dribbled onto Paulita's dark breasts.

Billy kissed them and said, "I love apples," then he went into the kitchen. He was silhouetted against the light when I pulled the trigger. The juice was still running down his chin when he fell.

BILLY: THE PREMONITION

"Can you feel the baby moving?" Paulita asks, placing my hand on her stomach. I hold it there a long time, too tired to move, too tired to talk. But I feel the life within her.

We lie on the double bed. The windows are open, but it's July. The heat is trapped like a fly in the barrel of a pistol, and the moon seems blue.

"The baby should be here by the first frost," she says. "I know it will be a boy."

Sometimes my groin is numb, as if a cold wind blew across my body, but there is no wind.

When I shiver, Paulita puts her arms around me. "What are you thinking?" she asks.

I think Garrett must be getting close by now; I can almost imagine him coming through the peach orchard with some men, coming to kill me, but I don't tell Paulita that.

The baby kicks like a .45 beneath my hand. "See, see," she says, laughing.

Suddenly, I'm sad.

I won't be here to see our son.

PAULITA MAXWELL: PEACHES

He brought me a peach the first time he came. It was the Fourth of July, dusk, and some children were playing with fireworks.

Billy and I sat on my father's porch, sharing the peach he'd plucked from the orchard behind our house. He seemed embarrassed when I put his left hand on my breast, holding it there. The juice from the peach ran between my breasts and my breath came faster.

A rocket exploded, showering us with blue and green sparks, and Billy's eyes were blue and green.

I was surprised at how thin his wrist was. I looked at his right palm in the light from the doorway and knew he was going to die soon.

I said, "A dark woman will love you."

PETE MAXWELL: APPLE BRANDY

I come into the house and find them—Billy and Paulita—naked. I tell her she's disgraced herself, but she just laughs. "You're my brother, not my keeper."

(When we were small, I played with Paulita in the tub.)

It's tornado weather, hot and still, and the sky's electric.

Paulita grabs Billy's black sombrero, covering her breasts, her eyes huge in the soft light.

Billy's pud's tumescent.

Paulita says, "Billy brought me brandy so the afternoon wouldn't seem so long," and I can smell apples on her breath and death on his.

BILLY: HYMNS

I'm tired of singing. It seems like that's all we ever do on Sundays.

I want to dance, want to get drunk, and I'm tired of dressing like a country Jake. But Mr. Tunstall says it's good to get some religion, so we go to McSween's house every Sunday afternoon. When we're not singing, we listen to Dr. Ealy preach about Paul and Silas at Philippi, but I'd rather be at the Wortley Hotel. They have a nice bar and the beer's cold.

I don't even know where Philippi is and I don't want to know if I can't get there on my horse. Do they serve beer?

I want to sing "Turkey in the Straw" or "Sewanee River," something I can stomp my foot to.

Why do I have to listen to all these damn hymns?

I'm not going to heaven.

CELSA GUTIERREZ: ADULTERESS

Sometimes Billy comes to me when my husband's gone.

I know Billy has another woman and it hurts when I see Paulita. She's younger. Prettier.

I know what they call women like me: Whore. *Puta*. Adulteress. They are just words. When Billy touches me, they have no meaning.

Now I hear distant fiddles as I lie next to my sleeping husband. I imagine Billy whirling around and around, dizzy, in Paulita's arms, imagine his lips touching her cheek.

I know the things he says: Oh my love.

I touch the inside of my husband's thigh, touch his sex, rubbing it, until he awakens, hard. I keep my eyes shut. I say, "Make love to me."

GARRETT: MARRIAGE

When my wife died, I married her sister. I needed someone and she always cared for me. Even the priest approved. It was a church wedding. Most of my friends came for the reception.

When Billy arrived he asked, "How does it feel to fuck your dead wife's sister?" He was holding a bottle, drunk, but that didn't make it right. I hated him all that hot afternoon.

My wife asked, "How come you sweat so much?" My white suit turned dark under the arms.

A lot of people wondered how I could shoot Billy. We'd ridden together. We'd been friends. How could I do it? They thought I must have needed the money or that I was ambitious, but it's simple: Billy ruined my wedding.

ZAVAL GUTIERREZ: CUCKOLD

The men in Fort Sumner make clucking sounds when I walk past them, and I no longer go to the cantina. I drink alone.

I watch my wife hang the laundry, watch her breasts stretch against her blouse, and I want her even though I know she has a lover.

Once, I watched from a window as Billy and Celsa undressed each other. They were laughing and did not know I was there with a pistol. I aimed at Billy, my finger tightening on the trigger at the moment he came. I wanted to say, "I hope that fuck was worth dying for," but I ran clucking into the apple orchard.

I'm not even man enough to kill my wife's lover.

BILLY: THE WASP

One of the boys caught a wasp and brought it inside, trapped in a bottle. He said, "It's going to die anyway."

It was almost fall, but the days were still hot.

The boys began to bet how long the wasp would last.

It made it through the morning and the afternoon. By dusk it was barely moving, but it was still alive when we blew out the lantern. I thought I could hear it hitting the sides of the bottle.

The heat seemed suffocating.

There was a five-hundred-dollar reward for me, dead or alive.

In the moonlight I could see beads of sweat on my arm, could see the bottle with the wasp in it on the table.

As I got up, I felt my lungs constrict. By the time I got to the table, I was panting.

Outside, I let the wasp go.

GARRETT: THE JOB

They say I never gave the Kid a chance that night in Fort Sumner. They say he came toward me naked, unarmed, and they wonder how I could shoot a friend.

Let me tell you, Billy had a six-shooter in his right hand and a butcher knife in his left. I was just defending myself, doing a job; I had a warrant for his arrest, dead or alive.

I let the Mexican women carry his body across the yard to the carpenter shop, where they laid him out on a workbench and lit candles around his body, conducting a wake. You'd have thought he was Jesus the way they were all crying when I went to look at his body.

Some of the women spit at me and swore although I told them, "He was a dangerous man, a killer. I shot him mercifully through the heart, a clean shot. Look! I'm the sheriff. I was just doing my job." But they still spit at me and called me names.

BILLY: WHORES

They're always glad to see me when I go to the Doll House. Becky and Soap Suds Sal run toward me, Sal with her hands wet; she used to be a laundress and still loves hot water.

They both ask, "What did you bring us?" and I give them dried flowers and chocolate hearts because it's nice to be wanted for something besides the price on my head.

They tug at me, both wanting me to go upstairs.

Here, I'm not a killer. I'm kind. I give them money and they say, "Billy, you're such a man." Here, things are simple. There's no bickering. No jealousy. Just an exchange: love for money.

I shiver when Sal puts a wet hand into my pants. She says, "Come with me."

GARRETT: PISS-POT

They butchered a yearling the morning they knew Billy would be back because he'd want beefsteak and beer and Billy always got what Billy wanted.

When I saw the Kid, he was silhouetted against the light from Maxwell's kitchen, licking his fingers. I wondered why so many women loved him, then I pulled the trigger.

I heard his body hitting the table, heard dishes breaking as I ran outside. An Indian woman cursed me: "Sonofabitch. Piss-pot."

I think she'd imagined Billy a prodigal son come home. After he ate the fatted calf, he wasn't supposed to die.

BILLY: SHACKLED

They bring me in chains to the house of my girlfriend so we can say goodbye.

"It's a hell of a Christmas," I say, trying to smile.

It must be ten below outside and the snow's deep enough to hide the chains on my legs.

Paulita's mother asks my guard if he'll unlock the irons so Paulita and I can go into the bedroom for an "affectionate farewell," but he tells her, "I ain't Santa Claus," and laughs when I stumble toward Paulita, my chains clanking. They put them on me when I was captured at Stinking Springs yesterday.

Paulita's face is soft in the light from the candles.

She cries, hugging me, and says, "Merry Christmas."

BOB OLINGER: DEPUTY

"You little bastard. You twerp. I'm goin' to enjoy watchin' you hang. The great Billy the Kid will kick his feet and crap in his pants just like anyone else at the end of a rope.

"You better get straight with Jesus, boy. Get straight now.

"One prisoner they hung had his head ripped off. It was bruised, kind of purple lookin'. Someone put it in a bottle of alcohol and charged people to see it.

"Maybe I could pickle your head if it rips off. Huh? Or if it don't, maybe some other part.

"They say you get a hell of a hard-on when that rope tightens around your neck. It sends all your blood rushin' down below, boy. You'll have the biggest boner of your life."

BILLY: REVENGE

They hung me by my thumbs when I tried to escape from the jail in Santa Fe. The jailer would jab me in the stomach with his shotgun and hum, "Rock-a-bye, Billy," as he watched me swing.

"This'll prepare you for the hangin'," he said and laughed until he shook.

I spit in his face, but he put his weight on me, hard, and I thought my thumbs would rip off.

When they cut me down, I couldn't move my hands or legs for hours. All I could think was, I'll get you, I'll get you.

Later, I stuck my pistol into his mouth and said, "Suck on this, you bastard." I could hear his teeth chattering on the barrel and his eyes were bloodshot between my sights.

I pulled the hammer back and asked, "How come you're not laughing now?"

SISTER BLANDINA: NAILS

When I heard they brought Billy to town, I went to see him.

The shackles around his hands and feet were nailed to the floor so he couldn't sit or stand.

He said, "I wish I could offer you a chair, Sister." That was all.

I wanted to say, "Forgive us," but I just stood there. He must have thought I was dumb.

Then I ran out of the room into the dark streets. A March wind blew.

In my dreams that night I kept seeing our Lord, His hands and feet bloody, nailed to the Cross, but He had the Kid's face and He kept saying, "I'll kill them before I let them take me again."

BILLY: SNOW BIRDS

"Suppose Pat Garrett was a pretty little bird and suppose that pretty little bird in the street was him," I say, pointing at a snow bird in front of the saloon. "If I was to shoot that little bird and hit him anywhere except in the head, it would be murder."

We've been drinking all morning.

I shoot from the hip and a headless snow bird floats in the bloody air.

I say, "No murder," then fire again and another bird runs in a bloody circle, its head missing.

Acquitted again.

The boys laugh and cheer.

The third time I fire feathers fly and the bird has a red bib where its breast used to be.

"Boys," I say, "I've murdered Pat."

GARRETT: NEW YEAR'S EVE 1900

Men shy away from me since I shot the Kid. I even had to hire an attorney to get the five hundred dollars I'd been promised for killing him.

I had a wife and seven kids to support, but no one cared about that.

When I go into a bar, the conversation stops and, these days, I always drink alone.

When the Kid was alive, we'd ride out into the country together, playing cards, drinking, dancing. Even my kids ask why I did it. I've tried to explain; I even wrote a book about me and the Kid.

Since I shot him, I've tried ranching in Roswell and Fort Stanton. Tried breeding horses in Uvalde.

I failed.

Then I rode with the Home Rangers. Worked as a cattle boss. Failed again.

Ran for sheriff in Chaves County.

Failed.

Now it's a new century, but everything ended the night I shot the Kid.

BILLY: LAST WORDS

In the other room, the girl I made love to is sleeping now.

I love these hot nights in New Mexico, love the desert air on my naked body. I'll never leave Fort Sumner.

Paulita says I can't stop laughing when I start. It's true I like to laugh and I've done it while I'm dancing or drinking or whoring, even when I've killed men. (They all deserved it.)

After I shot Deputy Olinger with his own shotgun, I danced on the balcony of the Lincoln jail for an hour, laughing.

Some of the boys asked why I didn't just ride away, but you don't get many moments like that.

Somebody's coming toward me, silhouetted against the moon. He has a familiar walk, but it's so dark I can't focus my eyes.

"*¿Quién es?* Garrett?"

I ask again, louder: "Who's that?"

SALLIE CHISUM: CANDY HEARTS

They say he was a bad man, that it was a good thing Garrett shot him, but that's a lie.

Billy brought me two candy hearts one hot afternoon in August. I remember how soft his hands seemed. It was like being touched by a cloud.

I was new at my uncle's ranch, lonely. Billy smiled and said, "Don't believe everything you hear about me."

I was thirteen and had never been kissed and the chocolate melted on my lips.

GARRETT: PALS

We drank double shots of bourbon back to back with beer. I told Billy's older brother it had to be the way it was, the Kid would never surrender, and Joe said he understood. Billy was always wild.

I told Joe that the Kid and I rode together, played cards together, drank together, slept with the same women; we were pals.

Joe said, "Now we're pals," slurring his words, his arm on my unsteady shoulder, but it wasn't the same as when Billy touched me.

The Burial
of Letty Strayhorn

Elmer Kelton

GREENLEAF STRAYHORN frowned as he rode beyond the dense liveoak motte and got his first clear look at Prosperity. The dry west wind, which had been blowing almost unbroken for a week, picked up dust from the silent streets and lifted it over the frame buildings to lose it against a cloudless blue sky. He turned toward the brown packhorse that trailed the young sorrel he was riding. His feeling of distaste deepened the wrinkles which had resulted from long years of labor in the sun.

"Wasn't much of a town when we left here, Letty, and I can't see that it's got any better. But you wanted to come back."

Prosperity had a courthouse square but no courthouse. Even after voting some of its horses and dogs, it had lost the county-seat election to rival Paradise Forks, a larger town which could rustle up more horses and dogs. Greenleaf hoped the dramshop was still operating. He had paused in Paradise Forks only long enough to buy a meal cooked by someone other than himself, and that had been yesterday. He was pleased to see the front door open. If the sign out front had been repainted during his twelve-year absence, he could not tell it.

"Finest in liquors, wines and bitters," he read aloud. *"Cold beer and billiards.* Our kind of a place. Mine, anyway. You never was one for self-indulgence."

The sorrel's ears poked forward distrustfully as a yellow dog sauntered out to inspect the procession. Greenleaf tightened his knee grip, for the young horse was still prone to regard with great suspicion such things as dogs, chickens and flying scraps of paper. It had pitched him off once already on this trip. Greenleaf was getting to an age when rodeoing was meant to be a spectator sport, not for personal participation. The dog quickly lost interest in rider and horses and angled off toward the liveoak motte to try and worry a rabbit or two.

Greenleaf tied up the horses in front of the saloon, loosening the girth so his saddlehorse could breathe easier. He checked the pack on the brown horse and found it still snug. Seeing no others tied nearby, he knew the saloon was enjoying another in a long succession of slow days.

He stepped up onto the board sidewalk, taking an extralong stride to skip over a spot where two planks had been removed. Somebody had evidently fallen through in the relatively distant past. The rest of the boards were badly weathered, splintered and worn. It was only a matter of time until they, too, caused someone embarrassment, and probably skinned shins.

The whole place looked like the tag end of a hot, dry summer. Whoever had named this town Prosperity was a terrible prophet or had a wicked sense of humor, he thought.

A black cat lay curled in the shade near the front door. It opened one eye in response to Greenleaf's approach, then closed the eye with minimum compromise to its rest.

The bartender sat on a stool, his head upon his arms atop the bar. He stirred to the jingling of spurs and looked up sleepy-eyed.

"Beer," Greenleaf said. "A cold one if you've got it."

The man delivered it to him in a mug and gave him a squinting appraisal. "Ain't your name Greenleaf Shoehorn?"

"Strayhorn."

"A name like Greenleaf ain't easily forgot. The rest of it . . ." He shrugged. "Didn't you used to work on Old Man Hopkins' place?"

"And married his daughter Letty."

Memory made the bartender smile. "Anybody who ever met Letty would remember her. A mighty strong-willed woman. Where's she at?"

"Outside, on a horse."

The bartender frowned. "You'd leave her in the hot sun while you come in here for a cool drink?" He walked to the door. "All I see is two horses."

"She's under the tarp on the packhorse, in a lard can. Her ashes, I mean."

The bartender's face fell. "She's dead?"

"Took by a fever two weeks ago. Last thing she asked me was to bring her back here and bury her on the homeplace alongside her mama and papa. It was so far, the only way I could do it was to bring her ashes."

Soberly the bartender refilled the mug Greenleaf had drained. "Sorry about Letty. Everybody liked her. Everybody except Luther Quinton. He hated all the Hopkinses, and everybody that neighbored them."

"It always makes it easier when you hate the people you set out to rob. Less troublin' on the conscience."

"He still owns the old Hopkins place. He may not take it kindly, you buryin' Letty there. Asked him yet?"

"Wasn't figurin' on askin' him. Just figured on doin' it."

The bartender's attention was drawn to the front window. "If you *was* thinkin' about askin' him, this'd be the time. That's him comin' yonder."

Greenleaf carried his beer to the door, where he watched as the black cat raised up from its nap, stretched itself luxuriously, and meandered out into the windy street, crossing Quinton's path. Quinton stopped abruptly, turning back and taking a path that led him far around the cat. It stopped in the middle of the deserted street to lick itself.

The bartender remarked, "Superstitious, Luther is. Won't buy anything by the dozen because he's afraid they may throw in an extra one on him. They say he won't even keep a mirror in his house because he's afraid he might break it."

"He probably just doesn't like to look at himself. I never liked lookin' at him either." Quinton had long legs and a short neck. He had always reminded Greenleaf of a frog.

Quinton came to the door, looking back to be sure the cat had not moved. He demanded of the bartender, "How many more lives has that tomcat got? I've been hopin' a wagon might run over him in the street."

"She ain't a tomcat, and there ain't enough traffic. She's liable to live for twenty years."

"I'd haul her off and dump her, but I know she'd come back."

Quinton's attention shifted to Greenleaf, and his eyes narrowed with recognition. "Speakin' of comin' back . . ." He pointed a thick, hairy finger. "Ain't you the hired hand that married the Hopkins girl?"

"Letty. Yep, I'm the one."

"There's no accountin' for some people's judgment. Wonder she ain't killed and scalped you before now. Has Indian blood in her, don't she?"

"Her mama was half Choctaw."

"Probably some kind of a medicine woman. That Letty laid a curse on me the day I took over the Hopkins place. Cow market went to hell. Calf crop dropped to half. Rain quit and the springs dried up. I had nothin' but bad luck for over a year."

"Only a year? She must not've put her whole heart into it."

Dread was in Quinton's eyes. "She back to cause me more misery?"

"She died."

Relief washed over Quinton's round, furrowed face like sunshine breaking through a dark cloud. He was not one to smile easily, but he ventured dangerously near. "I'm mighty sorry to hear it." He gulped down a glass of whiskey in one long swallow. "Mighty sorry."

Greenleaf grunted. "I can see that." He turned to the bartender. "Old Brother Ratliff still doin' the preachin'?"

The bartender nodded. "You'll find him at the parsonage over by the church. My sympathies about Letty."

Greenleaf thanked him and walked out. He had not expected this to be a pleasant homecoming, and running into Luther Quinton had helped it live down to his expectations. Untying the two horses, he looked a moment at the pack on the second animal, and a catch came in his throat. He had worked his way through the darkest of his grief, but a lingering sadness still shadowed him. He wanted to fulfill his promise to Letty, then put this place behind him for once and all. His and Letty's leavetaking from here had created a residue of memories bitter to the taste.

Not all the fault had been Quinton's. Letty's father should have known he was dealing himself a busted flush when he tried farming on land where the average rainfall was only about fifteen inches a year, and half of that tended to come in one night if it came at all.

Letty's stubborn nature was a natural heritage from both sides of her family. She had tried to keep on farming even though her father had accomplished four crop failures in a row. He had died of a seizure in the middle of a diatribe against the bank for letting him borrow himself so deeply into the hole and refusing to let him dig the hole any deeper.

All Quinton had done, really, was to buy the notes from the frustrated banker and foreclose on Letty. Quinton had acquired several other properties the same way. He was not a hawk that kills its prey but rather a buzzard which feeds on whatever has died a natural death.

Greenleaf had not considered Brother Ratliff an old man when he had lived here, but like the town, the minister had aged a lot in a dozen years. Greenleaf had to knock on the door a third time before it swung inward and a tall, slightly stooped gentleman peered down at him, cocking his head a little to one side to present his best ear. From Ratliff's gaunt appearance, Greenleaf judged that the Sunday offering plate had been coming back but little heavier than it went out.

"May I be of service to you, friend?"

"I'm Greenleaf Strayhorn. You may not remember, but you tied the knot for me and Letty Hopkins a long time ago."

The minister smiled broadly and made a gesture that invited him into the spare little house. "I do remember. Quite a beautiful bride, she was. Have you brought her with you?"

"In a manner of speakin', yes sir. I was wonderin' if you'd be kind enough to say some fittin' words over her so I can put her ashes in the ground?"

The minister's smile died. "The Lord calls all of us home eventually, but it would seem He has called her much too early. I hope she had a good life to compensate for its shortness."

"We did tolerable well. Got us a nice little ranch up north, though we wasn't blessed with kids. She just never could shake loose from her old family homeplace. The memory of it was always there, itchin' like a wool shirt. She wanted me to bring her back."

"It's a sad thing to preach a funeral, but part of my calling is to comfort the bereaved and commend the soul to a better land. When would you want me to perform the service?"

"Right now, if that's not too soon."

The minister put on his black coat and walked with Greenleaf to the church next door. "Would you mind pulling the bell rope for me, son? The devil has afflicted my shoulder with rheumatism."

Afterward, Greenleaf unwrapped the pack and fetched the lard can containing all that was left in the world of Letty Strayhorn. He placed it in front of the altar. A dozen or so citizens came, curious about the reason for the bell to ring in the middle of the week. Among them was the bartender, who knew. He had removed his apron and put on a coat, though the church was oppressively warm. Its doors and windows had been kept shut because the wind would have brought in too much dust.

The sermon was brief, for Brother Ratliff did not know all that much to say about Letty's past, just that she had been a hard-working, God-fearing woman who held strong opinions about right and wrong and did not easily abide compromise.

At the end of the closing prayer he said, "Now, if any of you would like to accompany the deceased to her final resting place, you are welcome to go with us to the old Hopkins farm."

A loud voice boomed from the rear of the church. "No you ain't! The place is mine, and that woman ain't fixin' to be buried in any ground that belongs to me!"

The minister was first surprised, then dismayed. "Brother Quinton, surely you would not deny that good soul the right to be buried amongst her own."

"Good soul? A witch, I'd call her. A medicine woman, somethin' from the Indian blood in her."

"She has passed on to another life. She can do you no harm now."

"I'm takin' no chances. You want her buried, bury her here in town. You ain't bringin' her out to my place."

Apologetically the minister looked back to Greenleaf. "I am sorry, Brother Strayhorn. I may argue with Brother Quinton's logic, but I cannot argue with his legal rights."

Greenleaf stood up and studied Quinton's physical stature. He decided he could probably whip the man, if it came to a contest. But he would no doubt end up in jail, and he still would not be able to carry out Letty's final wish.

"She's goin' to be disappointed," he said.

The town cemetery was a depressing place, the site picked for convenience rather than for beauty. His sleeves rolled up, Greenleaf worked with a pair of posthole diggers that belonged to the minister. Brother Ratliff, looking too frail to help in this kind of labor, sat on a marble gravestone and watched as the hole approached three feet in depth. The length of the handles would limit Greenleaf's digging. The bartender had come to the cemetery but had left after a few minutes to reopen the saloon lest he miss out on any thirsty customers. Or perhaps he had feared he might be called upon to lend a hand with the diggers.

Ratliff said, "It matters not where the body lies."

"So the old song says," Greenleaf responded, turning into the wind. Though its breath was warm, it felt cool against his sweaty face and passing through his partially soaked shirt. "But I feel like I'm breakin' a promise. I never got to do everything I wanted to for Letty while she was livin', but at least I never broke a promise to her."

"You made your promise in good faith. Now for reasons beyond your control you cannot fulfill it. She would understand that. Anyway, you brought her back to her hometown. That's close."

"I remember a couple of times my stomach was growlin' awful loud at me, and I bore down on a whitetail deer for meat but missed. Close wasn't good enough. I was still hungry."

"You've done the best you could."

"No, I ain't." Greenleaf brought the diggers up out of the hole and leaned on their handles while he pondered. "Mind lendin' me these diggers a little longer, Preacher?"

Ratliff studied him quizzically. "You'd be welcome to keep them. Should I ask you what for?"

"A man in your profession ain't supposed to lie. If I don't tell you, you won't have to lie to anybody that might ask you."

Greenleaf used the diggers to rake dirt back into the hole and tamp it down. The lard can still sat where he had placed it beside a nearby gravestone. "We had a full moon last night. It ought to be just as bright tonight."

The minister looked up at the cloudless sky. "Unless it rains. I would say our chance for rain is about as remote as the chance of Luther Quinton donating money for a new church. Would you like for me to go with you?"

"You've got to live here afterward, Preacher. I don't." Greenleaf finished filling the hole. "If I was to leave you the money, would you see to it that a proper headstone is put up for her?"

"I would consider it a privilege."

"Thanks." Greenleaf extended his hand. "You don't just know the words, Preacher. You know the *Lord*."

Even if the moon had not been bright, Greenleaf could have found the old Hopkins place without difficulty. He had ridden the road a hundred times in daylight and in darkness. Nothing had changed in the dozen years since he had last traveled this way. He rode by the deserted house where the Hopkins family had lived while they struggled futilely to extract a good living from a soil that seemed always thirsty. He stopped a moment to study the frame structure. The porch roof was sagging, one of its posts buckled out of place. He suspected the rest of the house looked as desolate. The wind, which had abated but little with moonrise, moaned through broken windows.

"Probably just as well we've come at night, Letty. I doubt you'd like the looks of the place in the daytime."

Memories flooded his mind, memories of coming to work here as hired help, of first meeting Letty, of gradually falling in love with her. A tune ran through his brain, a tune she had taught him when they had first known one another and that they had often sung together. He dwelled at length upon the night he had brought her back here after their wedding in town. Life had seemed golden then . . . for a while. But reality had soon intruded. It always did, after so long. It intruded now.

"I'd best be gettin' about the business, Letty, just in case Luther Quinton is smarter than I think he is."

The small family cemetery lay halfway up a gentle hillside some three hundred yards above the house. Rocks which the plow had turned up in the field had been hauled to the site to build a small protective fence. Greenleaf dismounted beside the gate and tied the saddlehorse to the latchpost. He let the packhorse's rein drop. The brown would not stray away from the sorrel. He untied the rope that bound the diggers to the pack, then unwrapped the pack.

Carefully he lifted down the lard can. He had been amazed at how little it weighed. Letty had never been a large woman, but it had seemed to him that her ashes should represent more weight than this. Carrying the can under one arm and the diggers under the other, he started through the gate.

He had never been of a superstitious nature, but his heart almost stopped when he saw three dark figures rise up from behind the gravestones that marked the resting places of Letty's mother and father. He gasped for breath.

The voice was not that of a ghost. It belonged to Luther Quinton. "Ain't it strange how you can tell some people *no* and they don't put up an argument? Tell others and it seems like they can't even hear you."

The shock lingered, and Greenleaf had trouble getting his voice back. "I guess it's because *no* doesn't always make much sense."

"It don't have to. All that counts is that this place belongs to me, and I don't want you on it, you or that woman of yours either. Lucky for me I set a man to watchin' you in town. He seen you fill that hole back up without puttin' anything in it but dirt."

"Look, Luther, you hurt her enough when she was livin'. At least you could let her rest in peace now. Like the preacher said, she's in no shape to do you any harm. She just wanted to be buried next to her folks. That don't seem like much to ask."

"But it is. You heard her when she laid that curse on me after I took this place. She named a dozen awful things that was fixin' to happen to me, and most of them did. Anybody that strong ain't goin' to quit just because they're dead." Quinton shook his head violently. "I'm tellin' you, she's some kind of an Indian medicine woman. If I was to let you bury her here, I'd never be shed of her. She'd be risin' up out of that grave and hauntin' my every move."

"That's a crazy notion. She never was a medicine woman or anything like that. She wasn't but a quarter Indian in the first place. The rest was white."

"All I know is what she done to me before. I don't aim to let her put a hex on me again."

"You can't watch this place all the time. I can wait. Once she's in the ground, you wouldn't have the guts to dig her up."

"I could find twenty men who'd do it for whiskey money. I'd have them carry her over into the next county and throw her in the river, can and all."

Frustration began to gnaw at Greenleaf. Quinton had him blocked.

Quinton's voice brightened with a sense of victory. "So take her back to town, where you ought to've buried her in the first place. Since you seem to enjoy funerals, you can have another one for her."

"I hope they let me know when *your* funeral takes place, Luther. I'd ride bareback two hundred miles to be here."

Quinton spoke to the two men beside him. "I want you to ride to town with him and be sure he doesn't do anything with that can of ashes. I want him to carry it where you can watch it all the way."

One of the men tied up Greenleaf's pack and lashed the diggers down tightly against it. The other held the can while Greenleaf mounted the sorrel horse, then handed it up to him.

Quinton said, "If I ever see you on my place again, I'm liable to mistake you for a coyote and shoot you. Now git!"

To underscore his order, he drew his pistol and fired a shot under the young sorrel's feet.

That was a bad mistake. The horse bawled in fright and jumped straight up, then alternated between a wild runaway and fits of frenzied pitching in a semicircle around the little cemetery. Greenleaf lost the reins at the second jump and grabbed at the saddlehorn with his left hand. He was handicapped by the lard can, which he tried to hold tightly under his right arm. He did not want to lose Letty.

It was a forlorn hope. The lid popped from the can, and the ashes began streaming out as the horse ran a few strides, then whipped about, pitched a few jumps and ran again. The west wind caught them and carried them away. At last Greenleaf felt himself losing his seat and his hold on the horn. He bumped the rim of the cantle and kicked his feet clear of the stirrups to keep from hanging up. He had the sensation of being suspended in midair for a second or two, then came down. His feet landed hard on the bare ground but did not stay beneath him. His rump hit next, and he went rolling, the can bending under his weight.

It took him a minute to regain his breath. In the moonlight he saw one of Quinton's men chasing after the sorrel horse. The packhorse stood where it had been all along, watching the show with only mild interest.

Quinton's second man came, finally, and helped Greenleaf to his feet. "You hurt?"

"Nothin' seems to be broke except my feelin's." Greenleaf bent down and picked up the can. Most of the ashes had spilled from it. He waited until Quinton approached, then poured out what remained. The wind carried part of them into Quinton's face.

The man sputtered and raged and tried desperately to brush away the ashes.

"Well, Luther," Greenleaf said, "you really done it now. If I'd buried her here, you'd've always known where she was. The way it is, you'll never know where she's at. The wind has scattered her all over the place."

Quinton seemed about to cry, still brushing wildly at his clothing. Greenleaf thrust the bent can into his hands. Quinton made some vague shrieking sound and hurled it away as if it were full of snakes.

The first Quinton man brought Greenleaf his horse. Greenleaf's hip hurt where he had fallen, and he knew it would be giving him unshirted hell tomorrow. But tonight it was almost a good pain. He felt strangely elated as he swung up into the saddle. He reached down for the packhorse's rein.

"This isn't what Letty asked for, but I have a feelin' she wouldn't mind. She'd've liked knowin' that no matter where you go on this place, she'll be there ahead of you. And she won't let you forget it, not for a minute."

Riding away, he remembered the old tune Letty had taught him a long time ago. Oddly, he felt like whistling it, so he did.

The Day of the Rain

Teddy Keller

DAVE KRAMER shouldered through the saloon's swinging doors and halted inside. The rain dripping off his slicker made little splashes at his feet. The usual sour saloon smells mingled with the scents of wet leather and soaked linsey-woolsey, of mud tracked in and warmth tracked out.

Of the half-dozen cowpokes bellied up to the bar, only Billy Holt didn't turn to eye the newcomer. But there was a tremor in Billy's raised hand, a tightening of slender shoulders beneath a faded jumper.

"There's only one gent that stomps in here like he owned the town," Billy said. "Mr. Dave Kramer came to tell me my cows ate a whole handful of his grass."

Beside Billy a puncher chuckled, another grinned. Dave's hard gaze swept the men. The chuckle choked; the grin collapsed.

"Very funny." Dave jammed fists against hips, not bothering to flip his slicker clear of his gun. "You were warned for the last time a month ago, Billy. Your stock's fat off my grass. I figure half that meat is mine, and I aim to sell those critters and keep my share."

"You can't . . ." Billy wobbled when he turned.

"If you haven't sold your horse for booze, you'd better saddle up and ride clean outa this country."

"You can't do that." Billy's legs got tangled and he sloshed whiskey out of his glass. His eyes needed time and effort to focus. "That's stealing."

"You've been stealing my grass for a year," Dave said, "and I'm tired of it. You can pay up or clear out. If you want to make a fight of it, I'll still be in town come sundown."

"Big talk," Billy muttered. "Who's gonna know sundown on a day like this?" His feet shuffled and got him turned back to the bar.

Dave growled, "We can call it sundown right now."

"Oh, listen to the big, brave rancher." Doc Avery sat at a corner table, his half-eaten steak and beans before him. He was about as big as a banty rooster with a temper to match. His thin gray hair was mussed and his wet suit coat hung over the back of his chair.

Dave nodded and said, "This isn't your business, Doc."

"Of course it's my business. I couldn't patch up Billy's brother good enough. Remember? This town doesn't need any more cripples."

"I warned him, just like I warned Billy."

"Is a little bit of grass that important to you?"

Dave half turned, and a small splash of water cascaded off his hat brim. "We've got laws about that."

"Damn the laws," Doc shouted. He slapped the table and his plate and cup jumped. "Dave Kramer, I remember when you weren't much more'n a yearling and you started to show that ornery streak. Folks thought it was kinda cute, then. Now you're an overgrown bully with a streak of cussedness and—"

"You heard me, Doc." Dave faced the bar. "And so did you, Billy. You can fight or run, but you're done stealing my grass."

Dave spun on his heel and marched out of the saloon. Ann Maitland stood on the covered boardwalk directly in front of him.

Dave halted, startled, his mind shifting from the mild turmoil of the saloon to a totally pleasant mood. "Well." He smiled and moved to her. "This is nice."

"Not very," Ann snapped. The soft rain had woven a sparkling tiara in her black hair. But her dark eyes flashed and a frown slashed furrows between her brows. Her wide, full lips clamped in a grim line. "I was on my way to . . . well, I couldn't help hearing what you said to Billy and Doc."

"That was business."

"Dave, you promised to leave your neighbors alone."

He wanted to shout his dominance, but he took his time and said, "I leave them alone until they start pushing me."

"You've got square miles of pasture. Do Billy's cows eat that much?"

"They got fat on my grass."

"You're his neighbor." She removed her dark shawl and shook the rain out of it. "Neighbors help one another."

"Good neighbors don't take advantage of each other."

She flipped the shawl over her shoulders again. She sighed, but her jaw line could've been forged. "I'm sorry, Dave."

"What does that mean?"

"It means I'm seeing a side of you I thought was gone. It means you didn't keep your word to me. It means . . ."

"What?" Dave swallowed against a rage for Billy Holt and a fear of what Ann was thinking.

"It means . . . I have some things to think about."

"What things?"

"The plans we've made."

Just then a sodden, mongrel dog limped past Ann and sagged against Dave's leg. Dave kicked sideways. The dog tumbled away, whimpering.

"Dave!" Ann cried. There was hurt in her dark eyes.

He glared at the wretched, knee-high dog, and he boiled over. "Do you expect me to back down on what I said to Billy?"

"Yes."

"I can't. I won't."

Ann made a choking sound. "Then maybe I can't." She tugged the end of the shawl over her face and turned away.

Dave wheeled around and his boot bumped against the mongrel dog. He lurched, fought for balance, and staggered for two steps. Now all his anger focused on the miserable dog. He spun around and cocked his right leg.

Too late he saw Ann plunge in front of the dog. His kick grazed her arm and his spur raked across the sleeve of her dress. She tumbled to the boards beside the soggy animal and she threw a protective arm across the dog. The dog's stub tail twitched wearily. He licked Ann's face.

Dave stepped around the dog. He bent and gripped Ann's shoulder. She shook him off and shoved to her feet. The dog, holding high its right front leg, limped to Dave.

"If you want to help somebody," Ann said, "help this poor dog."

Dave shook his head. "His leg's broken. I'll put him out of his misery."

Ann hunkered down beside the dog and put her arms around him. "You're not going to hurt anybody else."

Now the dog represented all of Dave's rage and frustration. He whirled away and stepped off the boardwalk and out from under the wooden awning. The rain settled upon his hat. Three days of heavy drizzle had turned the street into a squishy mass that would mire a wagon to its hubs. His boots were clots of mud when he swung into the saddle.

"No, no, doggie," Ann called. "Come back. Here, boy."

Dave hipped around and saw Ann, arm extended, as if reaching a helping hand. The dog limped along the boardwalk. With something like hope in its eyes, the dog peered at Dave. But it kept going.

"Dave," Ann called, "he wants you to follow him."

At the end of the boardwalk, the dog plunged into the street. He seemed to find the best footing, but even so he labored through the muck. The rain washed the matted hair of the brown back, and one shoulder was red where blood oozed from a wound at the neck. There was more blood on the short nose. A bullet was the merciful answer for the miserable animal.

Dave cursed under his breath, flicked back his slicker, and jerked the Colt from its holster. He flapped the reins. The horse came around sluggishly. Dave squeezed the trigger at the same moment the horse slipped in the mud. Dave's bullet kicked up a geyser of mud ten feet short of the dog.

"Dave Kramer!" Ann screamed. She tucked up her skirt and jumped from the boardwalk. Instantly her shoes knifed through the mud and she sank past her ankles. She called, "Here, boy," and struggled to take a step.

Doc Avery, his napkin in one hand, pushed the swinging doors and surveyed the street. "You shooting at people already?"

"All right, Ann," Dave said. "Get back to dry land. I'll follow the dog."

He left Ann and Doc to talk things over, and he wheeled his horse into the track made by three small feet. The dog was headed out of town, into a thickening curtain of rain. Dave wouldn't have to follow far before the sound of a gunshot would be muffled, and the death of a stray dog would go unnoticed.

Past the upper edge of town, the dog angled onto thick buffalo grass and found better footing. He quickened to a weary, three-legged trot. The road became more solid where it bent into the rocky earth of the canyon. But now the dog slowed. Its crippled leg dragged uselessly.

Dave touched rowels and the horse closed on the dog. The swaying brown back made an easy target. Dave pulled his gun again. He took casual aim.

The dog looked back and up into the rain, checking on Dave, and its good front leg stumbled over a small rock. The dog sprawled on its chest and uttered one small cry. Immediately he scrambled gamely to his feet and seemed more determined to guide Dave into the canyon.

The dog stumbled again. Dave holstered his gun. He swung to the ground, scooped up the dog and climbed aboard. With a small whimper, the dog clamped his teeth onto Dave's wrist.

Dave cocked his free hand to hit the dog. Then he shrugged and said, "Hurts, doesn't it, boy?"

The dog scraped a rough tongue across the wrist he had bitten. Dave grinned and urged the horse into motion. But the maneuver to retrieve the dog had shifted Dave's slicker. Cold rain began to dribble down inside his shirt.

The canyon walls squeezed closer and the road clung precariously to the near vertical cliff. The usually docile stream, gorged by rain and dirt, thundered through the gulch. The horse shied. A ragged rock, the size of a kitchen stove, slithered from above and pitched across the road to tumble down, down into the river.

Dave scanned the cliffs ahead. Three days of rain had washed Nature's mortar from around great boulders. They hung there now, ready at any moment to drop a landslide upon horse, dog and man.

Suddenly the dog squirmed from Dave's arm. He hit the ground on his feet and let out a howl. He stood a moment, swaying, then plunged down the steep slope toward the river. Only now did Dave see the wrecked wagon far below.

Dismounting, he knelt at the edge of the road for a quick survey. Through the rain he could see that a chunk of cliff had broken off and had dumped wagon and mules into the gulch. The wagon lay twisted and splintered upon the rocks. One mule hung dead in the traces. Another, cut and limping, grazed upstream from the wreckage.

The dog had reached the wagon. He paced beside it for a moment. Then he turned his face up into the rain and barked urgently.

Dave spoke words of quiet assurance to his horse while he stuffed his gunbelt into the saddlebag and tied his rope to the saddle horn. Wondering at his own intelligence, he gripped the rope and stood for a moment at the brink. Then, boots slipping at every move, he let himself down the steep slope a foot at a time. Each step threatened to dislodge a new landslide. And with each step the flooding river roared louder.

At the foot of the cliff Dave slipped and slid, found precarious footing and turned loose of the rope. The dog hobbled close, his tail wagging furiously. And Dave saw a man's body twisted across the shattered wagon seat.

Dave stepped into the lapping reaches of the brown water and dragged the man off the seat and onto the rocks. He was not past his mid-thirties, only a few years older than Dave. Now he was a pathetic rag doll, his neck and legs broken in the horrible plunge.

Dave's stomach knotted and he turned away. He found the woman lodged against a wheel, her head and shoulders under water. He pulled her out and gently placed her body beside her husband.

An unfamiliar lump wedged in Dave's throat. Hot tears mingled with the rain on his face. He bent over the couple and straightened the man's head. Then he locked the man's arm through his wife's. Even in death, the man's courage seemed plain in his face. The woman had been almost pretty. Care had etched the beginnings of maturity around her eyes, but hers was a face that had laughed a lot.

The yipping of the dog brought Dave around. Above the roar of the river, he heard a thudding sound overhead. He glanced up to see an anvil-size boulder bounding down the slope. He leaped aside. The boulder smashed down close to the bodies, then bounced high over the wagon and splashed into the booming stream.

Dave moved toward the dangling end of his rope and called to the dog. This time his guide ignored him. The dog turned an imploring gaze to the man, then whined and pawed at the water's edge where the wagon's tailgate was just out of reach. Dave watched, puzzled, for a moment. Then he hurried to the dog.

It took him one more moment to discover the small hand protruding from under the wagon's torn canvas. He stepped into the water and floundered in a knee-deep flood. Another boulder plunged down the cliff and smashed into the river twenty yards upstream.

Grabbing the tailgate, Dave hauled himself close to the wagon. He flung ripped canvas aside. A small boy blinked at him.

Dave couldn't allow himself even seconds for shock or surprise, not with more rocks rattling down the cliff. He clambered aboard the tilted, pitching wagon box. The boy sat in shallow water, with spray breaking over him. He had a foot wedged under water, beneath a clutter of heavy boxes.

Dave wrestled one box aside. As he struggled with another, he caught the deep thudding sound. He threw himself across the boy and waited. There was another heavy thud and an eternity of waiting. Then the boulder plunged into the river directly beside the wagon.

Spray drenched Dave and the boy. The wave sent up by the boulder shook the wagon. Its shattered bulk shifted, and the riverbank seemed to lurch away.

Frantically, Dave flung boxes and crates aside, and the small foot came free. Dave cradled the boy in his arms. The wagon creaked, then groaned in its death throes and floated into the wild current. Dave leaped as far as he could and plunged into the water.

The current snatched at his billowing slicker and slapped his feet from under him. He drove his boots down and felt a rock. He kicked hard. Again the swirling water yanked his feet from under him. Again he stomped down onto a solid rock and drove himself toward shore. His free hand grasped a tree root.

He set the boy on the muddy bank, then heaved himself up. For a moment he lay there, sucking in great breaths of air. Then the dog licked his face. Downstream a section of rocks and mud thundered into the river.

Dave scrambled to his feet and glanced up. A small rock sang past him. Already the wrecked wagon had been swept out of sight. He remembered the dead mule that had gone with the wagon. The other mule had wandered upstream.

Another rock splashed into the river a few yards away. Dave

didn't waste more time scanning the cliff. He bent the boy over his shoulder and floundered across to his rope. He checked the boy's balance, then gripped the rope and went up hand over hand.

Arms leaden, lungs bursting, Dave dragged himself onto the road. He pushed to his feet and placed the boy in the saddle. The horse shied as more rocks hurtled past. Dave quickly coiled his rope and climbed up behind the saddle. The horse twitched at the double load and peered back inquiringly. Apparently satisfied, he got into motion.

The boy stirred. His head twisted and his lips moved. At last he cried, "Toby! Where's Toby?"

"Whoa," Dave shouted.

He slid over the horse's rump and stepped to the edge of the road. Far below, the dog pawed weakly at the canyon wall. Then, tail drawn under, he turned and dragged himself to the bodies of the man and woman. He collapsed between them.

Small rocks clattered across the road and down to the river. Dave hesitated, staring at the dead couple, the valiant dog. He heard the boy choke out another cry.

Dave backed the horse to a point directly above the dead folks. Again he tied his rope to the saddlehorn and stepped to the cliff's edge. Plunging down the slope again, he burned his hands on the rope and banged every part of him against the slick, jagged rocks.

The end of the rope sawed through his hands. He tumbled across more rocks and mud and slammed against a boulder. The wind gushed out of him.

Gasping for air, he rolled to his hands and knees. The dog stared at him through eyes that seemed half dead. The tail managed one feeble wag. Dave crawled to the man's body, reached across and picked up the dog. Toby only groaned, apparently too weak to cry with pain.

Dave fought to get himself upright. His feet heavy with fatigue, he stumbled and staggered to the end of the rope. Now he ducked his head and arched the dog across the back of his neck, as he might have carried a deer.

He ripped a strip from his torn slicker, tied the dog's back legs together and lashed them to the good front leg. With hands raw and bleeding, he grasped the rope and sucked in a deep breath.

Through the rope he felt the horse shy again, too near the cliff's edge. Rocks plummeted down. A small boulder hurtled past, inches from man and dog.

His hands were raw, his lungs bursting. His boots slipped on the wet rocks, the rope burned in his hands. Halfway up, he bumped over a protruding rock and paused to catch his breath. He glanced up through the rain to gauge the distance and his sapped strength.

At the very rim of the canyon, far above both horse and boy on the road, a torrent of mud flushed around a giant boulder. The huge rock oozed an inch, then another.

"Giddyap, boy!" Dave shouted. He twisted the rope around his wrist. "Hey! Run for home!"

The line snapped taut. The horse peered down the cliff. The big boulder sloughed on its ancient foundation.

"Giddyap, dammit!" Dave yelled.

The horse lunged. The rope cut into Dave's wrist and dragged him off his perch. He kicked against the cliff, swinging like a crazy pendulum. The boulder crashed onto the road where horse and boy had been, then plunged on down the cliff. It flung mud into Dave's face as it hurtled past.

"Whoa!" Dave called. "Whoa, boy. Steady now."

The horse halted obediently. Toby made a sound that might've been pain or relief. Dave hauled himself up, hand over trembling hand. He knew he was too exhausted to reach the road again, but he made one more effort. He wanted to cry out his hopelessness, but he clamped his mind around the image of boy and dog, and he clutched the rope with bleeding hands.

And then he was at the brink, then onto the road. He crawled a few feet and collapsed, the dog still across his neck. After a long moment, he raised his head and peered to horse and boy. Close by a towering rock tipped and plunged and tore away a section of the road.

Dave unlashed the dog. Then he turned and peered through the rain to the raging water below. The last landslide had buried the bodies of the man and woman.

"Mama?" the boy asked. "Papa?"

Dave coiled his rope. He carefully took the dog in his arms and heaved himself up behind the saddle. When he touched heels to the horse's belly, he realized that his spurs were gone. The horse moved ahead slowly. Dave reached around dog and boy to grip the saddlehorn. He knew that he'd never been so wet and cold. But he was conscious only of the rain and his burning hands and the gentle sway of the horse.

When he opened his eyes, the rain-soaked false fronts and the ooze of the street looked like the Promised Land. Nobody stirred along the boardwalk. Dave guided his horse past the livery stable and beckoned to old Charlie there. Then he rode to directly in front of Doc Avery's office.

"Hey, Doc," he shouted. "Come on out here."

Old Charlie, head down and slicker flapping, plowed through mud to the boardwalk. He made grumbling noises.

Dave said, "Wait'll we unload. Then this guy deserves a good rubbing and plenty of oats."

Doc Avery jerked his door open and stomped onto the walk. "Dave Kramer, what in blazes are you hollering . . ." He broke off when he got a look at the horse and its burdens. "What in the world?"

"Take the boy," Dave said. "Gently. No telling what may be busted."

"Yeah," Doc growled. "I've handled hurt kids before."

Doc eased the boy from the saddle and cradled him with professional ease. Charlie offered a hand as Dave slid onto the boardwalk with the dog in his arms. Doc gave Dave and the dog a long look. Then he hurried into his office. Charlie got the horse turned. Dave patted the horse's rump as Charlie led him toward the stable.

Inside the office, Dave felt a sense of ease. A potbellied stove radiated warmth, and Doc, secure in his sanctuary, exuded skill and knowledge. The low cots, the operating table, the cabinet of instruments and bottles, all were testimony to the medical miracles performed here. The doctor was already peeling off the boy's clothing, wrapping him in blankets, placing him carefully on a cot.

Dave watched for only a moment, then put the dog down on another cot. Over a washstand he found a stack of neatly folded towels. He grabbed an armload and began working over the dog. Mud, dirt and blood stained towel after towel. Many minutes later Dave had the long brown hair dry. He wrapped Toby in a blanket and petted the frowzy face. When Dave straightened, he met Doc's outraged gaze.

"What the hell do you think you're doing?" Doc demanded. "This is no dog hospital and I'm no damn' dog doctor. Now get that fleabag out of here."

"Toby?" the boy breathed. His eyes fluttered. "Where's Toby?"

Doc glanced to Dave and then to the dog. He leaned over the boy and murmured, "Everything's fine, son. Toby's right here."

The boy smiled weakly, and his eyes closed. Doc frowned at Dave, then bent over the boy, probing, feeling, listening. Dave slumped into a chair near the stove. He pulled off his boots and related all that had happened.

After long minutes, Doc straightened beside the boy's cot. He was thoughtful as he crossed the room and placed Dave's boots closer to the stove.

"It's a miracle," Doc said, "but there're no broken bones. The boy's had a terrible shock and he's suffering from exposure. But with luck, he'll be throwing conniption fits if we try to keep him in bed after tomorrow."

"Good," Dave said. He spread his hands to the stove. "Now how about Toby?"

"I thought his leg was broken."

"Looked like it to me."

"Then he'll have to be shot."

Dave shoved upright in the chair. "Like hell."

"Maybe amputation."

"That'd be worse."

Doc shuffled to his rolltop desk, opened a drawer and took out a revolver. Jamming it into his belt, he strode to Toby's cot. He gently lifted the dog. Without a glance to Dave, he headed for the back door.

Dave leaped past Doc to block the door. Doc halted in his tracks. Underneath the blanket, Toby's tail wiggled.

"That dog went through hell to save the boy." Dave hooked his thumbs in his gunbelt. "He deserves to live, and by gadfrey, Doc, you'll see that he makes it."

Doc calmly regarded Dave for long seconds. "Your socks are making wet spots on my floor. You've already got this office smelling like a Chinese laundry."

"What about Toby?" Dave demanded.

Doc carried the dog to the cot. He stood for more long seconds and shook his head. "I don't know what to do."

"If a man breaks his leg, do you shoot him?"

"No."

Dave peeled out of his soaked vest and shirt and hung them over the back of the chair. "Of course you don't. You set the bone and you rig a splint to hold the leg and you fix him up as good as new."

"Somehow I seem to remember that."

"Well, treat Toby like a man." Dave sat in the chair and pulled off his pants. "He's done a man's job today."

"There're dry long johns in that cupboard. I can't have my surgical assistant dripping on the patient."

"Assistant?"

"You're going to help. And that get-up of yours looks purty ridiculous."

Dave found the clean things. He got behind a curtained frame and changed into dry underwear and socks and pants and a rag-gedy shirt. Nothing fit, but it was all dry. By the time he came out, Doc had transferred Toby to the operating table.

Now both men hunched over the table. Doc touched the broken leg, and Toby cringed. Dave began petting Toby, talking to him. Toby looked at Dave and an understanding seemed to cross his face. He nuzzled Dave's hands. That's when Doc seized Dave's wrists and turned his hands over.

"What in blazes did you do to your hands?" When Dave winced, Doc released the wrists and inspected the rope burns. "I'll put something on those cuts."

"After Toby's in the clear," Dave said.

Doc shrugged and turned his attention back to Toby. His stetho-scope probed across the small, brown chest and he peered into the sad, brown eyes. Then he straightened and looked long at the dog.

"Our friend's about done in. He's been going on heart too long." Doc shook his head. "Ether may kill him, but I don't think he could stand the pain without it. Can a dog take ether?"

"How would I know?" Dave grunted.

"How would anybody know?" Doc turned away to collect some instruments, then returned to the table. "Hold him."

Dave bent low over Toby again and began petting him, scratch-ing his ears, murmuring to him. Doc's face was grim. His slender hands moved quickly and gently. When Toby whimpered, Doc muttered under his breath. Perspiration glistened on his forehead. Then, after long minutes, the leg was straight. From somewhere Doc produced two rulers and fashioned a splint.

Toby exhaled slowly.

"I think he knows it's over," Dave said.

"He's a tough little guy." Doc had his stethoscope out again, and he checked Toby's heart beat. "He's a fighter, but he's got maybe one tail wag left."

Dave helped tuck the blanket around Toby, and then the boy stirred and groaned. The two men crowded over the cot. The boy blinked bright blue eyes. His white face against the dark blanket was ghost-like.

"What's the matter with Toby?" the boy asked.

"He has a broken leg," Doc said, "but he's going to be okay."

"Honest?"

Dave glanced to Doc and said, "Honest."

"What's your name, son?" Doc asked.

"Matt. Matthew Lonnergen."

"Can you tell us what happened?"

The boy's gaze flicked between the two men. Then his eyes clouded as he began to remember. "We were headed for . . . Papa told us about land that grows corn higher than you can see. Mama wanted to stop, but Papa said there was a town not very far. We needed hot food, he said. We needed a dry bed. And then . . . then the mountain fell on us."

"Do you know what happened after that?" Doc asked.

"It was awful dark." The boy's eyes brimmed. "I heard Mama crying, but I couldn't move my foot. She said Papa was . . . she said he didn't make it. And she said she couldn't move and the water was getting deeper." He choked on a sob and took a deep breath. "Pretty soon she didn't say anything more. That . . . that's when Toby went for help." He swallowed hard and his eyes were agonized. "Will Toby really be all right?"

"Sure," Doc said, his assurance sounding forced. He cleared his throat. "Sure, Matt."

Matt's solemn gaze fixed on Doc, then on Dave. Doubt clouded the blue eyes. The lids closed. He began to cry softly.

Doc's eyes filled and he muttered, "Damn."

"A child of the frontier." Dave dabbed at his own eyes. "He's seen death before." Now he turned and glanced at Toby. "You didn't convince the boy."

"It's out of our hands," Doc said with quiet resignation. He moved away from the table. "Toby's still alive, but I wouldn't say for how long."

Doc shambled to his desk and lighted another lamp. Somehow

the illumination failed to drive out the deathly gloom that filled the office.

Dave stared at the lamp, then at the dog, then at the boy. He recalled what he had seen and what the boy had told, and he knew what Toby and Matt had been through.

Hot tears spilled down his cheeks. He spun around to face the wall. In the stillness he listened for the boy's breathing and the dog's. And suddenly he knew what was wrong.

For the first time he could remember, Dave Kramer wasn't in charge. He wasn't telling people what to do. He didn't command the town and half the county.

Right now he felt helpless. He couldn't remember ever feeling helpless before. He thought of the valiant dog and the brave boy, and there was nothing he could do to help. He had seen the dead couple in the canyon, and there was nothing he could do for them. The mighty Dave Kramer was powerless.

Doc made notes at his desk and checked on both his patients. Dave slumped into the hard chair and stared at the glowing stove. In a moment, Doc came to stand over Dave.

"Let's get some salve on those hands."

Dave barely heard. His mind spun like a cyclone and he fought against the pictures that were taking shape. Half aloud, he muttered, "Is that the way Billy Holt feels?"

"Huh?" Doc grunted. "Billy doesn't have a broken leg."

Helpless. Was that why Billy clung to the bottle? Did he feel helpless and futile and frustrated? Dave remembered Ann's words, and he wondered if he really had become such an unpleasant person. Or maybe he always had been a bully.

How many times had he promised to control his foul moods? Today he had lashed out at Billy Holt. And he had kicked at Toby and at Ann. He had failed the boy by not following the dog soon enough. And now Toby was dying and there wasn't a thing Dave could do about it. In a little while the last of the boy's entire world would be taken from him.

Dave lurched up from the chair and grabbed for his ripped slicker. He jammed his feet into his wet boots. He had to get out of this place of his impotence.

The door swung open and Ann stood there, the rain still drumming down behind her, the droplets in her hair catching the lamplight. She glanced to Doc, to the two cots, to Dave, and she stepped into the room.

"Dave, what happened?" she asked. She halted, a fresh shawl wet, the hem of her skirt showing traces of mud. Again she looked at the boy, the dog, the doctor. Then her gaze held on Dave, appraising his ill-fitting clothing, his sodden boots.

"Hello, Ann," Doc said.

"It's all over town about Dave riding in with . . ." She peered at the boy. "Dave, what's wrong?" She studied him more closely. "What did you do to your hands?"

How could he explain anything to her that he couldn't explain to himself? He knew only that he couldn't stand to listen to Toby's final breaths. He muttered, "Doc'll tell you," and he rushed past her and out the door.

He halted at the edge of the boardwalk and steadied against an awning post. He barely knew where he was, and he had no idea where he was going. Surely when he lost his power, he lost his mind, maybe even his soul.

Dave stepped off the boardwalk into the mud. His legs moved him without volition. The rain curtain closed in around him, drowning his immediate memories, engulfing the town and the whole world. Sound scarcely penetrated the curtain. Then from far off he heard his name shouted. The call seemed to come from behind in a woman's voice, from ahead in a man's. Still he slogged on through the mud.

Then a voice hot with anger knifed through the rain curtain. Dave halted and stared at the boardwalk beside him. Billy Holt stood just outside the saloon's batwings.

"It's sundown, Dave," Billy shouted. "This's your idea."

"Billy?" Dave murmured.

"Let's get it over with." Billy reached for his gun.

"Dave!" Ann shouted from behind.

Dave pivoted sharply. His boots mired. He slipped and sprawled into the mud. Billy's gun roared. The bullet sprayed mud into Dave's face. From hands and knees, Dave peered around to Ann, to Billy. Doc ran along the boardwalk.

"Put your gun away, Billy," Dave said. He shoved to his feet. "I'm done fighting."

Billy stared through the rain, uncertain for a moment. Then he holstered his gun. Doc halted almost beside him.

"Dave," Doc called. "Toby's okay. He's going to pull through."

That's when Ann jumped off the boardwalk and plowed her dainty way toward Dave. Doc slapped Billy's shoulder. Ann's skirts dragged through mud as she rushed into Dave's arms. She was laughing and crying at the same time. She didn't seem to notice that Dave smeared more mud on her.

Doc helped tug the two of them up onto the boardwalk. He led them back to his office and opened the door. Matt was propped up on one elbow. There was color in his face now, and his eyes had the sparkle of a boy who had just found his strayed pup.

Toby's eyes rolled groggily. When his gaze caught Dave, the stump of a tail thumped the cot.

Ann slid an arm around Dave's muddy waist and snuggled against him. She said, "Matt can stay with me until . . . and Toby needs the run of a ranch. And the judge can draw up the adoption papers when . . ." Her face flamed, but her smile was loving and maternal.

And now Dave was warm where the cold rain would never reach. Everyone, he thought, needed to feel helpless once in a while.

"Make it soon," Doc pleaded. "If I keep this dog as a patient, folks'll start bringing me their sick cows."

Dave grinned. "I know where there's a mule that may be hurt."

"I'll refer that case," Doc said, "to my expert surgical assistant."

Sweet Revenge

Judy Alter

THE WOMAN in the bed next to me lies curled in a ball all day, moaning for her lost baby. The child, as I understand it, died at birth, and the mother went mad with grief. On the other side of me is a woman who calls out stridently, "Release me this minute! I do not belong here! If my daughter knew how you were treating me . . ." In truth, it was her daughter, unable to care for her any longer, who put her here, saw to it that she was tied each day in a rocking chair, untied only to take care of personal needs and, sometimes, for a brief walk around.

I've been here six months, and during that long tedious time, I have made it a point to be very quiet, so I am neither tied nor confined. Not that I am free to come and go. No, indeed. I sit here each day, staring out the window at the Kansas prairie, plotting my quiet revenge against the husband who put me in the county poor farm, the only place able to care for the "dangerously insane."

That was what the judge said of me at the hearing, "dangerously insane." Howard Smith stood there with all his might and influence—the town's banker who holds the mortgages on every home and business for ten counties—and swore that I'd come after him with a butcher knife when he was sleeping. "Only the grace of God that I'm alive today, your honor," he said humbly. "The woman's dangerous. I tried, Lord knows, I tried to care for her, keep her at home"—here his voice broke a little with emotion—"keep the world from knowing my shame. . . ."

In spite of good old Brother Bacon, the preacher who protested strongly and who is still my champion, the judge ruled that I should be confined in the poor farm where, as he put it, "they have the facilities to care for someone like her."

I did take after him with a butcher knife once, but the story was different than he told it. I never wanted to marry Howard Smith. When I was seventeen, he was a widower of forty, wealthy beyond measure because he was mean as sin to those that owed his bank money. He approached my parents with a marriage proposal which they leapt to accept without consulting me.

Father was a farmer in southwestern Kansas and, it pains me to admit, a weak man, bent on doing the Lord's work but never sure which way the Lord wanted him to jump. He was a great deal surer which way my mother wanted him to jump, for she made it perfectly clear. She also made it perfectly clear that the Lord had not meant her to live the poverty-stricken life of a sod farmer's wife, and she blamed my father for not providing for her in a more fitting manner. That he was a farmer when she married him never seemed to occur to her.

"A perfect marriage," she had crowed, when she told me of Howard's proposal. "You will live a life of comfort, and perhaps your poor dear father and I will not have to scrimp so—"

"Did he offer a marriage settlement?" I asked coldly.

"Oh, now, dear Callie . . . how can you think such. . . ." She was off in a flutter of denials, but I had my answer.

I never pleaded nor cried hysterically, neither being my style, but I made it plain that I did not want to go through with this marriage, that I would do almost anything to avoid it. I considered, seriously, running away but reasoned that Mr. Smith, with his wealth and connections, would no doubt find me, even in Topeka. My logical arguments to him had met with bland confidence, "Once we are married, it will all work out."

Work out, my foot! We were married in the church at Liberal, with Brother Bacon performing the ceremony and me a reluctant bride in white, Howard a beaming groom in his best black suit, though I thought the knees and seat shiny from wear. For me, a kind of hell began with that ceremony. Howard was a randy old man, always pawing at me, sometimes waking me in the middle of the night with his insatiable passion. I learned to lie perfectly still, close my eyes, and take my mind to a faraway place during his rutting. When he rolled over, sated, and began to snore, I rose to clean myself, praying each time that no child had been conceived, for I don't know what I would have done to avoid bringing a child into that household.

Days, I was a servant, though he could well have afforded household help for me. He preferred, he said, to think that his own little wife was taking care of him. So I ran the house, fed him the hearty meals he expected three times a day, made my own clothes and most of his, and worked like a dog from dawn to dark. Howard was as demanding upright as he was in bed, expecting meals on time, whisky when he called for it, my undivided attention when he wanted to recount his latest triumph.

His temper, when aroused, was fearful, and he had his hates and his dislikes. In spite of the fact they had made him wealthy, he hated farmers, swore that they were out to cheat him, that the only honest men he'd ever met were those who refused to toil on the land—just the opposite of what most men believed. And he hated schools, thought young people should be put to work at the age of twelve instead of filling their heads with the foolishness called "higher education." When he'd yell and carry on about how the universities were ruining people, I cringed, for I wanted nothing more than to attend the state university in Wichita and become a teacher. "No school will ever get a penny of my money," he would rage, shaking his mighty fist in the air. He was the epitome of the man who would, as they say, take his fortune with him to the grave if he could.

By the time I'd been married five years, I was twenty-two years old, thin and gaunt, with dark circles under my eyes and, occasionally, a bruise on my cheekbone, a black eye, and once or twice, cracked ribs. Good Brother Bacon asked often how I was feeling, but I brushed his concern aside. What could he do?

I began to refuse Howard in the night, and then I took to sleeping in a separate bedroom. Twice, he kicked open a locked door to drag me back to his bed, and on those occasions he was rougher than usual. "I'll teach you," he'd mutter between clenched teeth.

The night I took the butcher knife after him, he was drunker than usual and more violent. He'd throttled me until I nearly lost consciousness, and then had forced me to the parlor floor, where he raped me and then fell asleep. I left him on the floor and would have left him all night, but he roused, and I could see from the murderous look in his eye that he was coming for me again. Hoarse and unable to cry out—as though anyone would have helped me— I ran for the kitchen and grabbed the first thing handy, the butcher knife.

He thought I was bluffing, that I was too soft to cut someone, even him, but when he got close enough I sliced at his ribs, opening a long wide cut that bled so hard I was reminded of the proverbial stuck pig, an analogy that fit in more ways than one. Scared, he retreated to his bedroom, and I went to mine, building a barricade of furniture and sleeping with my hand on the knife handle.

Next morning, he was gone. Curious but unconcerned, I set about straightening the house and, unfortunately, had it all tidy and repaired—no sign of a struggle—by the time Howard arrived with the sheriff.

That was how I ended up in the poor farm. Howard said only one thing to me in private and that was, "A lot of women would love to have your chances. I'll find one won't come after me with a knife."

My only revenge is that it is against state law to divorce an insane person. Howard is saddled with me, and the next ladies in his life are condemned to illegitimacy. But that's cold comfort as I sit here, rocking away the endless days.

"Brother Bacon!" I fight the impulse to grin, to let my eyes light with happiness—bland is safer in this place—but I am glad beyond belief to see the old man.

"Callie, dear," he says, leaning to touch me on the shoulder, "come with me. You're leaving here."

It is almost too much to believe, too much to bear. "Leaving?" I echo.

"Take me away from here this instant!" the woman next to me demands. "I know you came to get me!"

Brother Bacon ignores her, speaking softly to me. "You're leaving. I've just gotten a court order."

"How. . . ." I am almost unable to speak, and when I rise, my knees threaten to buckle under me.

"Finally had a traveling judge come through," he says, "one that didn't know Howard. I convinced him you weren't dangerous . . . said I'd take responsibility for you myself. Now we must go."

"Howard?"

"He doesn't know."

We go through the formalities, with a disapproving matron frowning all the while she signs the necessary papers, but Brother Bacon is his usual kind and patient self. I stifle the urge to scream at the woman. When we finally are in the buggy and driving away, I demand, "Take me to Howard."

"Now, Callie . . ."

"I want to see Howard," I say with steel in my voice, though I am not sure what I will say once I am in front of the devil who has engineered my misery.

He protests but finally agrees, and we ride in silence for a long time.

"You can't just go in there," he warns as we approach the house. "It . . . well, it might be dangerous for you."

"It might be dangerous for Howard," I reply, and see in his face the first sign of doubt. Maybe, he is thinking, she did go after him with a butcher knife for no reason, and maybe I've done the wrong thing. By then we are in front of the house, and he has stopped the horse.

"It will be all right," I tell him, heading boldly up the steps of the front stoop.

The door is locked, but I knock loudly, wait a minute, and then knock again. There is no answer, no sound within. After a long wait, I return down the steps, march around the house, and enter through the kitchen door. The kitchen is a mess—dirty dishes, food crumbs, all the signs that no one has been taking care. Howard has been too cheap to hire someone to replace me.

I walk through the dining room, parlor, up the stairs to the bedroom, and there is Howard, dead in his bed, his face beginning to mottle. For a moment, I am furious enough with him to go again for the butcher knife, furious that he has had the final laugh, robbed me of whatever revenge I sought. His empty eyes stare glassily at me, and I turn slowly and with deliberate, measured tread return to Brother Bacon.

"You best come," I say. "He's dead."

"Dead?" He is alarmed. How, he wonders, could I have killed him so soon.

"I didn't do it," I assure him. "I think his own cooking killed him. You should see the kitchen."

When Brother Bacon examines Howard, he suggests it was probably a heart attack. I long instead to see a butcher knife sticking out of his chest, but it's a longing I don't even whisper.

Brother Bacon goes for the sheriff, and I wait. To pass the time, I clean the kitchen, remembering ruefully that cleaning has once before gotten me into trouble. But this is now my house, I reason, and I cannot bear for anyone to see it so ill-kept.

The sheriff is not kind. "I won't offer you sympathy, Mrs. Smith," he says. "I 'spect you're rejoicin'."

"Not quite, Sheriff," I say, "I've been robbed."

He is puzzled but won't admit it. "If I could prove you did this. . . ." His threat dangles.

"Sheriff!" Brother Bacon is angry. "Mrs. Smith was at the home and then with me. There is no way she could have any involvement in her husband's death. Ate and drank himself to death, if you ask me."

"I didn't ask," the sheriff says rudely. He used to drink with Howard of a night, and they were friends, which means he has always been my enemy.

I am the nearest relation and so in charge of arrangements. Howard is buried in the town cemetery, with bank employees and a few townspeople in attendance—he was not popular—and Brother Bacon says a few words over the grave. The good man speaks nervously as he commends Howard's soul to God, and I throw a handful of dirt on the coffin and turn away. The sheriff, who has come uninvited, opines that it's a crime not to give a man a proper church burial.

"Not," I say, "a crime for which one can be tried."

Within a week, I have made the house my own, given away every trace of Howard's clothing and personal effects, opened the windows to sunshine and air, beaten the old dust out of the rugs, and put flowers in every room, even the cubicle Howard called his office. His papers have been packed and sent to the lawyer.

Said lawyer comes to call a week later. "Mrs. Smith, you're a wealthy woman," he says and proceeds to outline my wealth.

My instructions are direct: a certain amount to my parents, not generous but enough to ensure that I won't have to worry with them daily; another, larger amount to the county poor farm, with the stipulation that it be used for treatment of the "dangerously insane."

"That barely makes a dent," the lawyer says. "Any further plans?"

"Yes. I plan to attend the university in Wichita and get an education. And I'll build them . . . let's see, a library. Yes, a library. Howard hated books. We'll call it the Howard Smith Memorial Library." I envision Howard, spinning in frustration for all eternity.

The lawyer's face is blank.

After he leaves, I go to the kitchen for the butcher knife. Now it hangs framed, in a place of honor, over my desk in the private library I have built for myself. No one ever asks about the knife, but I find it a great comfort.

Yearlings

Jim Marion Etter

IT WAS the most important cattle drive of J.T. McCoy's life. That was partly because he knew in his heart it would be his last, but mainly because his son, Jed, had come with him and this was his last chance to make the boy into what he ought to be.

McCoy, a weathered, stout man in his late fifties, felt a strange contentment as he rode apart from the others, aware of the smell of the sagebrush and the long shadows of the yucca shoots in the freshness of early morning, a hawk floating against the blue sky, the squeak of saddle leather and the soft clop of his horse and the scuffle of the cattle ahead, raising just shy of enough dust to spoil the whole pretty picture.

Funny, he thought with a pang, how a man starts noticing life all around him when he's near the end of it.

That fact also was making him think—or worry—more about Jed.

Just then another horse galloped up and slowed beside his, and he glanced over to see his son, a skinny but friendly and somewhat handsome youth of twenty-one who was holding awkwardly onto the saddle horn until his pony came down out of its rough trot.

He flashed a boyish grin. "Pretty morning, isn't it? I'm sure glad I came with you, Papa."

J.T. felt a surge of warmth, but showed it with only a thin smile. "I am, too, Son." Then he turned his eyes straight ahead: "You gotta remember, though, it'll be hot before the day's over, and you can't let that keep you from stayin' close behind these calves. We can't let any get scattered and lost before we get 'em loaded.

"The way times are now, as dry as it's been and with some extra expenses I've had lately, we can't afford to lose a single one. Most of these are just yearlin' steers and heifers that I'd like to keep and graze out this summer, and use some of the females for breedin' stock, but right now we need every pound we can take to the market.

"And by heavens," he added, "despite all the hard luck I've had, I'm going to do whatever I have to do to keep ranchin' and not go to farmin'. Our land's always goin' to raise cattle, not crops—as long as I'm alive, anyway."

Not that this little drive was anything a ten-year-old boy couldn't handle by himself, J.T. thought. Here it was around the start of the twentieth century, and western Oklahoma Territory was not only seeing more cussed fences and farms but had gotten so civilized that he and Jed and their neighbor, Woodrow Cline, and his sons had to drive the two families' combined herd of about two-hundred mixed cattle for only three or four days to the railroad at Woodward.

It was nothing like the big drives from Texas to Kansas that as recent as five years or so ago were still coming right through this part of the country—and which took his father's life less than thirty years ago, he recalled in an instant, wishing again he could blot out the nightmarish picture he saw over and over of his father's drowning.

J.T. was one of the hands on the drive that was crossing the rain-swollen Red River, and he had watched in horror from a few yards away as his father, who was trail boss, was swept from his saddle by the currents and swallowed by the nasty-red swirls. J.T. had jumped from his horse to grab him, but failed—and himself had gotten his lungs nearly full of water and had to be dragged out by the others.

But it never had been easy for J.T. to keep his son's mind on business, and this little drive was his last chance to make the boy responsible enough to become a cowman—something J.T. was hoping very hard was even possible.

"Don't worry, Papa, we'll get all of them to market," the young man was saying, then he pointed to one of several bare, red hills up ahead. "See that big mound over there? When we're in camp tonight I'm gonna draw a picture of it and put you and your horse right on top of it. And have a few clouds overhead and . . ."

J.T. breathed out in a tired gesture. "Son, we just don't have time for scratchin' on paper and such as that. What you need to be doin' is keepin' count of these calves; we gotta make sure every now and then that we still have the eighty-five head that we started with.

"And there's no time to waste. I figure the sooner we get there, the better chance we'll have of gettin' a decent price. By heavens, I aim to cross the Canadian with 'em today and have 'em at the railroad by day after tomorrow.

"Besides," he added, "if we get as far as we oughta get today, you'll be too tired tonight to do any drawin', I'll guarantee ya that."

J.T.'s father had ranched in South Texas long before he began taking his herds north over the Great Western Trail, and had fought everything from renegade Indians and gun-toting cattle and horse thieves to spells so dry the cows choked on dust and lived on mesquite beans and prickly pear cactus.

Following his father's death, J.T. had begun making arrangements to graze cattle up in the usually lush grasslands of the Indian country. And finally, eight years ago, he and his small family had made the run and homesteaded in the Cheyenne and Arapaho lands—but to raise cattle, not farm like many settlers did.

It was fine country, overall, and after living in a dugout for a while he had built a decent house.

But during a hard winter a few years later, his wife, Edna Mae, the prettiest and kindest woman he had ever known, had died of pneumonia. It made life both lonely and difficult for him and Jed, neither of whom was good at housekeeping or cooking.

Then a few years after that came the dry spell, over much of Texas and the territory, too, and many cattlemen started reducing their herds, bringing down the price of beef.

Then about six months ago, J.T. got up one morning with an odd tightness in his lower back that came and went, making him feel like he had a cottonwood pole strapped to his backbone and was walking downhill and about to fall on his face.

He finally had seen a doctor in Cheyenne—the first physician he had ever gone to—who looked him over then referred him to another doctor over in Canadian in the Texas Panhandle, who in turn sent him to another doctor out in Amarillo. He was finally

told the trouble was with some kind of male gland and was what
the medical men called a "terminal" condition. In short, they said,
it would continue to worsen until the end—which could come
within a year, maybe a little later.

J.T., who had always considered himself tough enough to handle
about any kind of trouble, finally accepted the idea, but hadn't seen
any reason to tell Jed until he had to.

And now, since ranching had always been his life as his father's
before him, his sole aim was to do a good job of passing his land,
cattle, and all his knowledge down to his son—who was all he had.

But as another bit of hard luck, he had seen years ago that
making the boy into a rancher wouldn't be easy. Jed, while always a
decent, well-mannered boy who was eager to please, couldn't seem
to do anything right. He couldn't stand to see calves burned with a
branding iron and couldn't handle the best lariat rope without it
twisting. And a horse fast enough to catch a calf, he usually
couldn't stay on.

When he was little, he was always running off to go swimming
in the Washita River when it had enough water, and when it
didn't, in the first stock tank he came to.

And when he was older, he usually wasn't around for ranch
work because he was off by himself reading books, or just wandering around looking at the country and drawing pictures.

Also, the boy had talked him into letting him go away to a school
in Missouri. Even though Jed worked at some odd jobs to help out,
the expense on J.T. was an extra burden—and then Jed came home
a few weeks ago with the crazy idea that he could be a professional
artist. He also had let on like he had met a girl, too, but talked
more about his drawing.

And while J.T. didn't mind looking at the impressive images of
events such as the Battle of the Washita, trail drives and roundups
and the nearby red hills and his own cattle and horses hanging all
over the house, he couldn't seem to convince the boy that he
couldn't run a ranch, or feed the family that he'd have someday, by
drawing pictures like a schoolboy.

Woodrow Cline trotted up on his horse, grinning in his big
happy, bucktoothed way. J.T. and Jed had known him and his two
fun-loving boys, Jeff and Andrew, both a little younger than Jed,
ever since they had come to the territory, and often partnered with

them when working their cattle and taking the animals to market. They were fine neighbors.

At that moment, one of the larger animals in the herd, a part longhorn steer owned by the Clines that had been balking and acting cantankerous in general since they started, stopped and slung his head, then bolted, heading off to the right toward the thick cover of some shinnery bushes.

"That ol' steer's the orneriest thing you ever saw when you try to drive 'im out of brush," Cline said. "One of these boys might oughta go rope 'im."

Jeff and Andrew both were bringing back a few strays to the left of the herd and were barely out of earshot—and it was obvious Jed felt the glances of the two men on him.

He hesitated a moment, then began shaking out his coiled rope as he spurred his pony into a lope.

Soon he was closing in on the steer with his loop swinging, and apparently was feeling and looking somewhat like a top hand.

"Git 'im, Jed!" Cline hollered, grinning bigger than ever.

J.T. stood up in his stirrups as he watched his son, feeling some pride but praying that it wasn't for nothing.

The steer wheeled just before reaching the shinnery, and about a second before Jed threw the lasso. Jed's loop dropped neatly over an idle tumbleweed about the time the long-legged critter was several jumps away and heading straight for a brushy canyon.

Jed's horse, meanwhile, had slid to a stop the moment Jed swung the rope, and thrown Jed plumb over the saddle's tall pommel and left him hanging by one arm around the pony's neck.

A chorus of laughter and good-natured shouts of derision arose from the Cline boys—who now were on their way over to get into the action—and even Jed, though red-faced as he eased himself to the ground, joined in with a joking excuse about how the steer was too dumb to know he was supposed to stick his head in the loop.

But J.T. wasn't having fun. He fixed Jed with a cold stare he had often given him over the years, then reined his horse off in the other direction, knowing it was like a slap in his son's face.

"Sorry, Papa," Jed said, his face flushed in a different way this time and his eyes cast downward.

"I'll go drive him back," he then said quickly, picking up his hat and climbing back on his horse.

"Let 'im go," J.T. said tiredly, rolling his eyes toward the sky.

Then he called out to the Cline brothers. "Jeff! Andrew! You boys better go bring that wild hombre in. This ol' pony Jed's ridin' has got a bad leg"—the excuse, he knew, hurting Jed even worse than his earlier insult of silence.

"Sorry, Papa," Jed said again.

The Cline brothers then took off together, both their ropes whirring impressively and their horses in an eager gallop. They went out of sight over a rise and in moments returned, their ponies in a hard run and both only a few yards behind the steer.

"Yah-hooooo!" yelled Woodrow. "They're puttin' on a regular ropin' show, ain't they?"

Andrew then threw his loop, which grazed but failed to catch one of the horns as the cagey steer slung its head.

Jeff's loop shot out like a striking rattlesnake and tightened around the base of the steer's horns, and it seemed in the same instant his stocky dun jerked the animal around and to a twisting, snorting standstill.

"Ya see, Andrew, that's how ya do it. Want me to do it again so you can watch and learn how?" the youth hollered, grinning widely.

"Lucky, ain't ya? Too bad you're so bashful about talkin' about yourself, too," answered his brother, slightly ruffled.

"Remember now, Andrew," the senior Cline said, his bucktoothed grin at its best, "like they say over in Texas, 'If you can do it, it ain't braggin'.' "

"Let's turn 'im loose and try again," Andrew said to Jeff, gathering his rope. "I'll bet ya two bits I'll beat ya this time."

But Cline, while still laughing, called an end to the fun. "That's enough, boys. No use runnin' any more fat off these hides than we have to."

"They're right smart good hands, Woodrow," J.T. said with a smile, trying to keep the bitter disappointment in his own son out of his voice for Cline's benefit—and not caring much whether he failed to for Jed's benefit.

"Yeah, but I gotta keep a tight rein on 'em," Cline said, still grinning. "Them boys of mine are just yearlin's—that's what I call 'em. They don't know much, but maybe they'll grow up and learn somethin' one of these days."

The drive during most of the afternoon was slow, dull, hot, and dry—and the drought, which was beginning to seem as bad as those he had seen in South Texas, was more and more on J.T.'s mind and in what little conversation went on between him and Woodrow.

Big, fluffy clouds with dark undersides kept building to their west over the Texas Panhandle and gave the herders a little refreshing diversion—but little hope for rain, as such cloud banks this time of year didn't always mean moisture.

J.T. noticed Jed looking in his dreamy way at the heavenly display that J.T. had to admit was truly pretty—starkly white, billowy masses suspended against the clear blue sky—knowing his son was trying to memorize every detail of the wondrous sight to put in one of his paintings.

But to J.T. and the others, the clouds only meant what likely were false promises. And they were reminded of this when, as one of the clouds moved past the sun, its wide, blessed shadow spread over them—then in a moment or so, flowed across the prairie and was gone.

The hot afternoon dragged on, the time passing as slowly as the herd and the herders trudged.

Then, at nearly sundown, the cattle and horses smelled the Canadian River.

As the cattle revived and began moving a little faster, J.T., Jed and Woodrow Cline rode around the herd in order to get a look at the river and find a good crossing before the cattle got there. Jeff and Andrew stayed back and on either side of the cattle to keep them from scattering before they hit the stream.

"I might even take me a bath," said Cline as all three horsemen went at a long trot. J.T. and Jed both laughed. All three were excited about what was ahead.

But then they heard the roar—such an odd sound that at first they couldn't believe what they knew it was.

"Now don't tell me the river's rollin'!" said Cline, wearing one of his few serious looks. "If it is, it had to've rained a bunch out in the Panhandle in the last day or two."

Then all three men lifted their horses into a lope.

Sure enough, the river, while only slightly above normal level, was visibly rising, meaning that, like the clouds had indicated and Cline had said, it had rained upstream—but the roaring, now much louder, was coming from up the river.

Jed indicated he had heard stories about people actually hearing a river flood coming down the channel before it got there, but had never thought it possible. He obviously was amazed to witness such a thing.

J.T., though, wasn't entertained. He had been in a bruising saloon fistfight once, been thrown from a few bad horses, been bitten just below the knee by a rattler, and even had a tooth pulled without benefit of liquor—but had forgotten how he feared and hated the nasty, stinking, muddy river water with its horrifying whirlpools and scummy edges that often turned up bodies of drowned varmints and occasionally even calves.

Not only was he from a dry country and had never learned to swim, having always crossed streams when the water was no higher than his stirrups, but there was the terrifying memory of his father's river drowning that had long haunted him.

Maybe he had spouted off too soon when he promised Jed they'd cross the river this same day, he thought. He hadn't given a thought to the possibility of high water—rare in this country, especially during dry periods.

But he and the others didn't have much time to ponder, as the thirsty cattle were now circling them on their way to the water, some of the animals drinking from the edge of the muddy stream while others plunged into deeper holes of the swift, swirling waters.

"Think we can push 'em across before it gets too high?" asked Cline, his face even more serious than before.

For one of the few times in his life, J.T. didn't have a quick and definite answer. "Well, I don't know much about rivers. Do you . . . You don't think it's too high already to swim the cattle over, do you?"

"I think we can do it, Papa," Jed put in, to his father's surprise. "We'd have to hurry, though, since it's nearly sundown, and while the cattle are still thirsty and won't stop to think about it."

Cline agreed. "That's right, Jed. That way, we can git 'em across before dark and before the river's any higher. Come on, fellers, let's put 'em in." He gave a loud whoop and waved his coiled lariat.

J.T.'s tightness in his lower back suddenly worsened and he also felt his heart skip a beat or two, and for a moment he was certain he would die in the middle of the muddy torrent as his father had done—but he lifted his reins and spurred his horse, shutting his eyes as he felt the cool water rush above his boot tops.

Then, despite his will, his body actually revolted, and before realizing he was doing it, he was wheeling his horse around and plunging it through the water back toward the bank.

"I can't do it!" he said before he knew what he was saying, then as he slid from his saddle to the ground, said in lower tones, and in a shamefaced manner, to whoever was listening, "I don't know what happened—it was just like I couldn't help it."

It was Jed who spoke. "Well, the river *is* rising fast, and it's nearly dark. We might have a better chance in the morning, when it might be dropping by that time."

J.T. felt grateful to his son, and that made him feel odd.

They ate their beef jerky, raisins and other few items and drank coffee made from their canteen water, then rolled out their bedding and went quickly to sleep on the ground—except for J.T.

Here he was, he thought as he looked up at the stars and listened with dread to the rushing water. He had ridden herd on his son for years because of his weaknesses, and now he himself was as scared as a trapped coyote.

He knew already what he'd do when he entered the river again, since in his brief contact with it today he hadn't been able to keep from growing as crazy as a wild cow in a thunderstorm.

And even though he hated the prospect of dying a lingering death in bed, he knew he wanted to go any other way but drowning.

But his biggest predicament now was, he didn't know which would be worse—drowning in the muddy water or seeing his son embarrassed by his father.

Funny, he thought, for the first time since he learned of his illness, that didn't seem near as big a worry as this.

It was also funny, he thought—this time he gave himself a twisted smile—this was one time he wasn't worried about how *Jed* was going to perform.

Morning came quickly—J.T. wasn't sure if he dozed any or not —and in moments all were up, drinking the coffee Woodrow Cline had boiled over a fire, eating jerky and otherwise preparing for a big day.

And J.T. looked at the river, which was roaring like he had never seen one, rushing by dizzily in filthy, reddish foam that carried occasional floating logs and tree branches.

"We might as well try it, fellers," said Cline.

J.T. wondered how anyone so silly-looking could be so cussed brave.

While it was clear no one had his heart in it, no one wanted to back down, so in a few moments J.T. and Jed, who, since they had taken the lead yesterday and were expected to today, took the lead, wading their horses gently out into the water. If they crossed, the others would drive the herd behind them, then all would gather the cattle after they scattered some on the other bank.

J.T., determined not to turn back as he did the day before, even if it meant drowning, clinched his teeth and shut his eyes as he again felt the cold water, more chilling this time, rise to his knees—then in a breathtaking instant rush to his armpits as he sensed his horse's feet leave the bottom of the river and felt both himself and the animal floating. He then nearly passed out as the water rose to his chin and he felt his body float up off the saddle. He could see only the animal's head above the water and a few inches in front of his own.

"Jed! Where are you? Help me!" He wasn't sure those were his words, but he knew they had to be, as the river now was a speeding, dizzying monster that swept him in a blur past the trees and everything else he could see on the far bank. He bent his neck backward to keep his nose out of the water and prayed.

Then suddenly, apparently as the river's main current hit him, he felt his horse go sideways to the right and, as he thought he heard Jed yell for him to hold to his horse, felt the horse's reins and mane slip from his hand in spite of himself—and he lost sight of daylight and felt himself sink and become lost in the blurry, choking world below the water's surface.

In a spasm of panic and gagging and coughing, he was fighting and clawing at the water with all his might, feeling his head bob above the surface only for a second or two at a time, and he believed he was drowning—until his right hand caught a rope that jerked him half out of the water.

"Papa! Hang on to the rope. Keep your nose out of the water when you can—and remember, stay calm." It was Jed's voice. He was off his horse, too, but was in the water a few yards ahead of him, and was holding the other end of the lariat rope. The whole thing was confusing.

"Now, Papa, keep your nose up, and kick your feet, and breathe in every time your nose is out of the water—but when your face goes under, hold your breath," Jed was saying, and every time J.T. started sinking again, jerking the rope again to make him raise his nose out of the water.

"And try to stay calm—that's the most important thing in water," Jed was saying. "Water's nothing to be afraid of, unless you fight it. Nobody knows, but maybe that's what happened to my grandpa that time in the Red River."

The water seemed less terrifying now, maybe because J.T.'s eyes were less blurry, and because he could see the bank a little ways on the other side of Jed. Then, after they had reached a little bend where the current no longer hit them full blast, he felt his feet touch the muddy bottom. It was a miracle, J.T. told himself. Thank God!

"Son, I thought I was a goner," he said to Jed as soon as he could stop coughing and found his voice. "But it'd been just as well, I reckon. You see, I'm dyin'—chances are, I don't have many months left."

"I figured that, Papa. I knew something was funny when I heard you went to three doctors, and never before had been to one in your whole life. That's why I came home to help with the drive. But let's don't worry about that till we have to. In the meantime, I'm here with you."

Then, in another moment or two, J.T. slopped out of the water, still holding to the rope that Jed was holding several feet in front of him as they climbed up the grassy bank to safety and where Woodrow Cline and his two sons were standing.

The three Clines cheered. "You made it, fellers—and both of ya'll was way out in the middle!" yelled Woodrow, his bucktoothed grin now a welcome sight for J.T.

"Wait a minute!" J.T. said, still coughing a little and spitting out river water. "What are you and the horses all doing on this side? I thought we swam across."

"No, it was too swift, Papa," said Jed. "Our horses couldn't buck the worst part of the current. When I saw you come off your horse, I let mine go, too, and swam a little ahead of you. And I threw you my rope—if I'd let you grab my hand, you might have pulled me under and drowned us both."

"Soon as we hit the main current," he added, "I knew that even if we made it, chances are most of those yearling calves wouldn't."

"Besides," he said, "I figure this side of the river's the best place for us now, anyway."

J.T. wasn't sure what he meant, but was cut off by his son when he tried to ask.

"You did good, Papa. If you hadn't stayed calm and done exactly like I told you, I couldn't have pulled you out, as strong as that current was, and chances are you'd have drowned. You did good."

"That's right," said Woodrow, still grinning. "You two swum over halfway across, then back. Next high river we have to cross, I know which two fellers are goin' in first."

"No, that ain't right, by heavens," said J.T. "I wasn't worth two cents in that water—I'd be a drowned rat if it hadn't been for my son, Jed."

He looked down as he walked slowly, his boots squishing, toward where his horse was now grazing. Even if Jed did learn what he knew about water by running off and playing when he was a kid, he had shown he was a real man when he had to be, J.T. thought. And maybe his being a grown-up man, whether he was a cattleman or anything else, was all that was important.

Maybe, J.T. thought, the boy was a lot more grown up than his old papa—who, like Woodrow might say, was the one who was still a yearling, judging by the way he had acted.

"In fact, Jed," J.T. said, forcing the words out, "I done a lot of thinkin' last night and today. I've been a cussed fool. I guess you're man enough to be an artist or whatever you wanna be. I guess . . . I guess there's things I just didn't understand."

He turned away from Jed like he had done many times before, but this time it was because he didn't want his son to see the tears that were burning his eyes. He wanted to say more, but couldn't.

"Ah, say, now, Papa, you're getting way out ahead of yourself. I'm going to be an artist, all right, because that's what I'm good at. I didn't tell you, but I've sold some of my paintings already—that's been one of my part-time 'jobs' I told you about. So I'll always be drawing pictures. After all, ranching isn't going to take *all* my time."

"What's that? You mean you're—"

"That's right, Papa. I never said I wasn't going to help you run the ranch. In fact, I'd like to talk to you about planting some alfalfa, and winter wheat, too—that's something cows can eat like grass right in the middle of wintertime. Cattle can eat other things besides buffalo grass. You don't have to give up ranching, Papa, but it doesn't hurt to steal a few ideas from the farmers."

"And as for now," he added, turning and looking at the grazing cattle. "That river's not going to go down as soon as we thought, and maybe that's just as well. We haven't come but about a third of the way to the railroad anyway, so—providing Mister Cline agrees with this—why don't we drive the herd back? Maybe we all can sit down together and figure out a way to keep from selling right now.

"For one thing, I'd like to see some of these yearling steers get some more weight on them first, and some of these females kept as replacement heifers."

J.T. used his sleeve to wipe the mud and mucus from his face, then stood agape. "How do you know about things like that?"

"I studied a few things besides art in school, Papa," Jed said, smiling patiently, then went on. "Now, I know times are hard, but I believe that if we don't get in a hurry to sell and all get our heads together, both our outfits can survive. Since we've always worked together, maybe we can combine into one big outfit, under one brand, and do better. With what I've learned in school—and with your experience, Papa—and with expert cowmen like Mister Cline and Jeff and Andrew, I'll bet we can make it."

"I got a feelin' Jed's right, J.T.," Cline said, grinning bigger than he had during the whole trip.

"And look," Jed added, nodding toward the river, then the western sky, "it's raining in the Panhandle, and that should mean the drought's about to end for us, too—so the buffalo grass should be greening up good even before we plant the alfalfa and wheat."

"Could be, Son," J.T. said thoughtfully. "Maybe you can make the ranch last longer than I will, anyway."

"That's another thing, Papa. None of us knows for sure what will happen tomorrow. And as strong as you look, I'll bet you live to see the first of your grandkids."

"Grandkids?"

Jed went on. "You see, it's probably a good thing the river was too high to cross. That'll make us all go back and do something better than sell all our cattle when the price is down. Like Amy Lee always tells me, things sometime work out for the best."

"I don't know about all this, Jed. Besides, I . . . 'Amy Lee'? Who, by heavens, are you talking about?"

"Amy Lee's a girl I met at school, Papa. I've been planning to tell you about her when I caught you in a good mood, which is why I haven't done it until now. Amy and I were married two weeks ago. I was going to send for her after this drive, but now that we're postponing that, I'll send for her right away. She's up in Kansas with her folks.

"She grew up there, by the way, and she knows about as much about cattle and alfalfa and wheat—especially wheat—as I do. She's looking forward to living on the ranch. She can cook, too."

J.T. was overwhelmed. It was the craziest cattle drive he'd ever been on—but maybe the best, come to think of it, even if the cattle weren't going anywhere this time except back home.

That thought caused him to look again at the river, which was still roaring—but it didn't seem as loud as it did, and he didn't think he was so afraid of it anymore.

All of a sudden there wasn't even a hint of stiffness in his lower back, and he felt better than he had in years. But even if he died tomorrow, he thought, he couldn't complain too much.

But he didn't plan on it, because this whole thing had given him a new aim.

During these two days he had learned that his son had grown up without his really getting to know the boy. And by heavens, he was going to live long enough to do something about that.

Bloody Badge,
Bloody Gun

Robert Gleason

THE GRIZZLED OLD MAN stood in the thoroughfare of New York's Coney Island Amusement Park. One hundred feet overhead towered the ever-turning Ferris Wheel. The steam calliope oom-pahed "Stars and Stripes Forever," while the carousel down the strip rotated in time to the music, its horses and unicorns, inundated with children, pumping up and down, up and down.

But the old man was oblivious to it all—the screaming kids, the pounding music, mechanical marvels. Instead he stood still as a statue in the middle of the thoroughfare, his brooding eyes fixed on the cracking rifles and chiming bells of the Coney Island shooting gallery.

He was a strange old man. His deeply lined face was burned brown as a hide from too many years of staring into desert sun and wind and High Plains snowstorms. His was a face set hard as concrete, bitter as gall, a face that neither asked nor gave.

He wore a black Plainsman's hat, and on the lapel of his frock coat shone a U.S. Marshal's badge. His suit was black as any undertaker's, and from the looks of the sawed-edged notches on the ivory-handled butt of the Navy Colt protruding from his half-breed shoulder-holster, he had arranged a few cheap funerals.

Reaching into his inside coat pocket, he removed a hammered-silver whiskey flask with the initials *BM* lavishly engraved in Gothic script. He poured a large draught into the two-jigger cap and tossed it off.

His eyes remained fixed on the shooting gallery. Steel horse-borne Indians, mounted on brass hinges, trotted across the target range, where young boys in short pants shot them with pellet guns.

His thoughts drifted back to another place, another time, another horse-borne horde. . . .

There were a thousand Indians this time, charging the hide-hunters' camp out of the blazing dawn sun. The hunters' Sharps rifles were scoped-in, and they were having a field day. The grizzled old ramrod was nineteen, and dropping Comanche as fast as he could slam the trigger guard forward, eject a spent shell and shove another round into the smoking breech.

Toward the end, the man beside him—twenty-four-year-old Billy Dixon—let out a fair imitation of a Cheyenne war whoop.

"I smoked that one proper—at 1600 yards," he roared.

The young man later paced the distance off himself and confirmed the kill.

"I smoked him proper," he could still hear young Billy Dixon roar, "at 1600 yards."

The cocky young vender in corduroys and a sailor's cap, running the shooting gallery, caught his eye.

"Hey, mister, come and try your luck. Bet my take against your Navy Colt and that shiny badge you can't hit 'em all."

"Save your money," another man shouted from up the thoroughfare.

It was that new young sports writer, Damon Runyon.

"Don't you know who you're challenging?" Runyon said, falling in beside the old man. "This is Marshal Masterson."

"Bat Masterson?" the young man said. "Jesus, mister, I didn't recognize you. Please don't put me out of business. Here, I'll let you shoot for free. I know you can knock them down."

A murmur spread through the fairground. "Bat Masterson?" one man muttered. "No kidding. He killed more men than Bill Hickok and Coleman Younger put together."

He was twenty-four then and marshaling in Dodge. It was late at night and he was heading home after rounds. He almost made it when his brother Ed came stumbling out of the Lady Gay Saloon, clutching his gut, his mouth flooding with blood.

Badge, Bloody Gun*

"Bat . . . Bat . . ." were his last words.

Jack Wagner and Alf Walker following him, their guns smoking, turning toward him.

But his Colt was already out, arm extended, gun hand steady.

Two more scallops were carved on his gun.

Kids crowded around him now, waving Dime Dreadfuls by Ned Buntline in his face. Many of the covers bore his own picture. The boys pleaded for autographs and begged to touch his badge, the butt of his gun.

He brushed them off and headed up the thoroughfare, away from the shouting kids. Runyon, the young reporter in a tweed suit and black bowler, fell beside him.

"Can *I* touch your gun-butt?" the reporter mocked.

"Fuck you," Masterson said.

"Bitter words," said Runyon, "from a man who's holed as many as you."

"I still say, fuck you."

He talked tough, but his bloody past was catching up with him.

"Jesus, honey," Diamond Lil had told him in Denver, before the good folks had run him out of that town too, "do you look old."

"Can't sleep," he explained.

She pulled her pink chemise tight around her shoulders and flung her long hennaed hair down over her back. Shuffling the cards, she recommenced dealing stud to him and his six associates seated at the octagonal, baize-covered poker table in the Light of Love Parlor House that November night, 1888.

"It's your conscience," Lil explained. "It's bothered by the ghosts of them you planted."

A tinhorn snickered.

"What's so funny?" Lil asked.

"Never heard no one suggest Bat had a conscience before."

"You planted as many men as him," Lil said, "yours'd ache too."

"Ease off, Lil," Bat said quietly.

"It ain't gonna get no better," Lil said. "This here's your third bottle of Sour Mash tonight, your fourth Soiled Dove, and you still can't shut your eyes."

"It's watching you deal seconds. Keeps me on edge."

"You ain't spotted me yet, honey. You'd've done something, you had."

"But I can hear you. I can hear that second tick."

"You ain't heard nuthin', Bat, 'cept the rattle of dead men's bones," Lil said.

"And the sound of that hacksaw carving scallops on your gun," the tinhorn said.

"I can still hear this," Masterson said.

The crack! *was the sound of his gun barrel laid across the man's head.*

"Jesus, honey, you do need some rest" was Lil's only remark.

"Bat," Runyon was saying as they strode cross the fairground. "You look like hell. You ought to head home, get some sleep."

"Heard that before from a lady in Denver."

"Probably ran a whorehouse, knowing you."

"That she did."

"It was good advice. You should try it."

"Maybe I will."

"Don't sound likely. Hear Theodore Roosevelt wants you for a third term. Says he won't take no for an answer. Says the Bowery is filled with desperate men. Wants you strapping on that gun and parading your badge. Gonna accept?"

He took out his notepad, indicating that his answer was for the record.

Masterson shook his head, no.

"What you going to do? You sure aren't planning on honest work."

"Thought maybe I'd take up sports-writing like yourself."

Runyon sneered. "At least, it ain't honest."

Masterson turned toward the gate.

"Where you going?" the reporter asked, putting down his pad, taking his arm. "Thought I might let you buy me a drink."

"Never happen. I'm heading home. Gonna get some rest."

"You know how?"

"Yeah, I know how. It's easy."

He unpinned his badge and unholstered his blued-steel Navy Colt. He laid them both in the reporter's hands.

"Let someone else keep the world safe for democracy. I'm done."

Runyon studied the hardware and let out an appreciative whistle. "I don't know, Bat. These are worth a lot of money. You know what you're doing?"

"I purely hope so."

"Tell you what: I'll hold them for you, 'case you want them back."

The old man fixed Runyon with a hard stare.

"You keep 'em, boy. There's blood enough on them already."

Head down, he turned and walked out the Coney Island gate without looking back.

Half a Day from Water

Gordon D. Shirreffs

There's gold, and it's haunting and haunting;
It's luring me on as of old;
Yet it isn't the gold that I'm wanting
So much as just finding the gold. . . .
—ROBERT SERVICE
"The Spell of the Yukon"

THE SOLITARIO DESERT was a hell's delight, a great sink bottomed by a vast and barren *playa*. It was rimmed by low hills and the more distant mountains with their gunsight notches and silent, hidden canyons, veiled during the summer months in a perpetually shifting haze which gave the viewer the impression that the lead-colored mountains were moving slowly up and down and sideways in a clumsy rhythmic elephantine rigadoon. The terrain was quiet as a vacuum. It was barren of life and growths. It was a lonely and brooding land, harsh and inviolate with an intense solitude that was heavy enough to break the heart. It was a vast and deadly area, merciless and sunbeaten, broiling in the summer months with an average temperature of 120 degrees. It was hell with the hide burnt off.

There was no live water in the hills to the east. At times there was water in the western hills located in the *tinajas,* so called, which were hollows eroded in the granite over many centuries by the raging, pounding "male" rains which burst across that arid country during the summer months. *Tinaja* translated from the Spanish into "large earthen jar or pot." The gringos simply called them "tanks." It did one no good to depend upon water being in the tanks very long. There was, however, one set of tanks called Solitario Tanks which could usually be depended upon for a store of water most times but like everything else in that deadly country it was always a gamble, a long shot to depend upon them at all, especially in the summer months.

There was always an eerie, frightening quality about the Solitario Desert. The absolute minimum of water required to travel on it was at least one gallon a day. The Mexicans said: "Even the ghosts of the Solitario Desert stay underground during the summer."

It was midday on the Solitario Desert.

Something moved, almost imperceptibly on the vast dun-colored surface of the *playa*. It was as though a mite was slowly crawling westward through the hazy, shimmering waves of heat.

Azro Sutro was afoot crossing the very core of the Solitario Desert—the *playa*. Once, millenniums past, the *playa* had been a miles wide primeval lake shimmering and sparkling beneath the hot sun. Now it was bone dry and billiard table flat, an expanse composed of irregularly shaped pieces of mud like a great natural jigsaw puzzle. Underfoot it was stove-top hot. The country to the east was malpais country, "bad underfoot." Boot soles could be macerated and shredded within an hour's passage on it.

Azro winced now and again as the burning heat of the mud seared his bare calloused soles. There were drying bloody footprints stretching back all the way he had traveled since before daylight. When he opened his mouth to breathe in the hot, dry air, his swollen lips would crack anew. The cloth-covered canteen hanging at his right hip was empty—dry empty. It had been that way since the day before. Azro kept his head down shading his sun-reddened eyes with the wide brim of his sweat-darkened hat. He already had a hellroarer of a headache from the sun.

Azro glanced up now and again. Somewhere in the low hills ahead of him was water. He had filled his canteens there five or six days past. He wasn't quite sure. He wasn't quite sure about *any- thing*. "My name is Azro Samuel Sutro," he grunted. *"Ass. . . ."* he added softly.

Azro wasn't too bright; he *was* determined. As a boy and teenager he had lived on his step-grandfather's farm in New Hampshire. The old man had inherited Azro when he had been orphaned. The old man had grinned. Here was a sturdy lad who would work for his keep alone. Azro had never known his parents. He had no sisters or brothers. "Not even a damned cousin," he thought. His step-grandfather was a good man; a deacon of the church he was. He was fairly good to Azro but his hand was quick and downright heavy.

The Rebels fired on Fort Sumter. Azro was almost seventeen and big for his age. He wanted to enlist. His step-grandfather tried to beat some sense into Azro. Azro hit him once and floored him. He thought he had killed the old man. He got out of the county that night and later enlisted in the Fifth New Hampshire Volunteer Infantry. Later he learned that his step-grandfather had survived and was now proud of his grandson serving his country. "Daniel Webster, a native son of New Hampshire, said New Hampshire breeds men," so Grandpa Sutro had proudly said when he had heard about Azro enlisting.

Azro grinned at the thought. "And all New Hampshire women are double-breasted," he snorted.

As he limped on he thought of Carrie Smith, his first and *only* love. She was of the bovine type: broad of beam and big of breast. Of course Azro had truly enlisted because the Flag had been fired upon by those damned Rebels. Another reason had been that Carrie had told him she was pregnant and three months on the way. She hadn't said by *whom* but she wasn't particular and she did like Azro. The state motto of New Hampshire as quoted by John Stark, a New Hampshire man of the Revolution was: *"Live free or die."* Azro had elected to live *free,* so he had enlisted.

Azro was a little more than five feet, eight inches in height. He was thick of chest, wide of shoulder and lean muscled. His hair was reddish as was his graying beard. His sun-tightened eyes were a steady gray and dark like a stormy sea. His face skin was a saddle brown, dry burnished and toughened by the winds and the sun of the Southwest. His large ears stood out from his hard block of a head like the handles on a jug. His big nose had been bent askew by a fist blow in his past. He never could quite remember where and in what barroom brawl he had taken that blow.

Azro had a rock of a jaw. It jutted out, granite-like and similar to that of The Old Man of the Mountains, the epitome of New

Hampshire. A phenomenon of Nature's whim, it jutted out from a sheer cliff 1,400 feet high up the side of Cannon Mountain in Franconia Notch, a forty-foot-high depiction of a venerable human face. It was a real Yankee face, a resolute face with the jaw firmly set, while looking south. It embodied a spirit expressed in the words of Daniel Webster, orator and statesman: "Men hang out their signs indicative of their respective trades: Shoemakers hang out a gigantic shoe; jewelers, a monster watch and the dentist hangs out a gold tooth but up in the mountains of New Hampshire, God Almighty has hung out a sign to show where He makes men."

Azro closed his burning eyes. "Amen," he murmured.

Azro's limp had been caused by a spent Rebel minie ball at bloody Antietam which had struck him just above the left knee. His regiment, the Fifth New Hampshire, had fought there across the blood-soaked Sunken Road.

The waning sun struck like a mailed fist at his eyes. Sweat ran down his burning face. On the righthand side of his skull was a lump encrusted with dried blood. He wasn't quite sure how he had acquired it. Perhaps he had fallen in the dark and struck his head on rock. Perhaps (and here it was a disconcerting and eerie thought), someone, or *something* perhaps not of this earth had struck him from behind. He had heard nothing nor seen nothing and yet the persistent thought ranged through his weary mind— perhaps he *had* been struck from behind. . . .

There was burro blood dried in his mustache. He had gone into the malpais country with three burros. One of them had been loaded with small kegs of water which Azro had filled at Solitario Tanks. The burro had fallen over a low cliff and died in a welter of its own blood and water from the smashed kegs. *All* of the water. . . . One of the other burros had strayed and he had not seen it again. There was not quite enough water for the last remaining burro and Azro to get back to Solitario Tanks. "God help me," he had murmured as he cut the burro's throat. He had drunk all of the blood he could.

The left sleeve was missing from his flannel shirt. He had filled it and tied the ends together to keep that with which he had filled the sleeve contained therein. He could feel the weight of the sleeve within his shirt pressing against his lean belly.

"How much farther?" Azro queried aloud.

"Mas alla. On beyond . . . ," the soft voice seemed to whisper into Azro's right ear.

Azro whirled, dropping his right hand to draw and cock his Colt.

There was no one there. . . .

"I've been out here far too long," croaked Azro.

He plodded on. His thirst was a living torment. He was in the first stages of deep thirst. He had experienced it before. It was a thirst more of the bones that of the flesh. At least that is what it felt like. It was a common dryness—a cottony feeling in the mouth and throat accompanied by great thirst, a deep craving for water that could only be assuaged by drinking water, *lots* of water.

Azro had stretched out his limited supply of water by gargling it without swallowing it and then spitting it back into his canteen. He had added his dwindling supply of urine to the water. All that was now gone. . . .

He was beginning to experience the second stage of great thirst —functional derangement and the onset of pathological disturbances. His tongue clung to his teeth; his ears drummed annoyingly. The hallucinations were soon to come, followed by delirium.

"Before God," murmured Azro.

"Curse man and trust God," the voice seemed to say.

This time Azro did not look back. The voice was an illusion; a chimera of the mind and memory.

Supposing there was someone, or something, behind him dogging his faltering footsteps, moving quickly and silently out of sight when Azro turned, perhaps to vanish entirely, only to return when least expected to goad him again and again?

He felt he was in the first stages of delirium.

The sun was low over the western hills. It was dying in an exquisite agony of gold, salmon and tints of yellow.

His saliva would stop flowing altogether. His mucus would dry. His lips would retract and his eyelids would stiffen. He would not be able to articulate clearly. He grinned a little. Who was out there to whom he *could* articulate? There was nothing but that damned haunting, insinuating mind voice or *whatever* the hell it was.

The sun was suddenly gone as though a vast curtain had been drawn down. Soon the wind would creep down the heights toward the cooling desert. The furnace winds would then sweep across the *playa,* burning against the flesh almost as hot as the sun had been doing.

Numbness would come next to Azro, creeping over the face, the hands and finally under the clothing against the skin, imparting a dry husklike sensation so nerve-trying that few, if any, suffering from it could resist the temptation to cast off their clothing in an automatic effort for relief.

His heart beat erratically, thumping and pounding within his chest. The desire to lie down came almost overwhelmingly. To lie down was to die. . . . He must keep on. . . . He closed his eyes as he limped on.

Azro opened his eyes. The sun was fully gone. Darkness enveloped the land. It was then he saw it, or *thought* he saw it—a quick, infinitesimal speck of light, coming and going so swiftly he could hardly believe he had seen it. It was dark again but he had noticed there was a notch in the dark mass of the hills and that he remembered the light had shown somewhere far below that notch. It was little enough to go on but he had nothing else. He plodded on through the darkness.

Azro kept on. After a long time he thought he felt loose sand beneath his blistered soles. He leaned backward, could not save himself from falling, and had an intense whirling sensation in his brain and then his thoughts left him and he knew no more.

Azro dreamt he was back lying on the snow-covered ground of the December Battle of Fredericksburg. It was night. His regiment had been one of those who had gotten close to the stone wall behind which the Rebels had mowed down like falling leaves many of the Yankee attackers. He was lying naked amid many of his dead comrades, all of whom, including himself, had been stripped of their warm uniforms during darkness by the Rebels, who lacked such clothing. During the attack the white, snow-covered ground had been fully colored blue with the bodies of the uniformed fallen. Now the ground was covered with the cold, freezing bluish bodies of the dead. Evidently Azro had been stripped while he was still unconscious.

The hands were rough and harsh against his skin. "For Christ's sake!" he croaked. "Take it easy!"

The rubbing stopped.

Azro opened his eyes. The sky to the east was faint with the coming of the gibbous moon. He was lying naked beside one of the tanks of Solitario Tanks. His thirst was still paramount. He leaned to one side to scoop water into his swollen mouth.

"*Cuidado!* Take care!" the dry voice warned in Spanish.

Azro slowly turned his head and looked up.

A small, gray-bearded old man sat on an *aparejo,* a packsaddle, about fifteen feet away. His craggy face had a wisp of gray beard. He wore a thin, ragged shirt and baggy white pantaloons. Dusty huaraches were on his brown feet. A threadbare serape hung from his right shoulder. A faint thread of tobacco smoke leaked from his nostrils. A firepit covered with a layer of ashes was at his feet. The wind swept the ashes aside to reveal glowing red embers like secretive eyes studying Azro. The sudden flareup of firelight illuminated the brown and wrinkled face of the old man like a hide left too long in the sun. His eyes were clear and dark brown; the eyes of a man old in years and in body but perhaps quite young in mind.

Azro looked about for his clothing. It was heaped to one side. His holster was empty. The loaded shirtsleeve was not visible. He got unsteadily to his feet and looked about himself.

The old man reached behind himself and brought forward the sleeve for which Azro was looking. "Here, hombre," he said quietly. He tossed it toward Azro. Azro missed it. It fell into the water. Azro plunged in after it and fell face downward in the water. He groped for the sleeve with his hands.

Azro's head was lifted from the water. He looked sideways and up into the wizened face of the old man. "Take care," warned the old man. "You've had too much water already."

"Let me alone," croaked Azro.

The old man shook his head. "No more water," he cautioned.

"I wasn't after the water," rasped Azro.

The dry sounding click, clicking of a pistol being full cocked, sounded inordinately loud in the stillness.

Azro found himself looking into the muzzle of his own pistol. "Would you shoot me, you old bastard?" he demanded.

"Try me," replied the old man. "That damned stuff in your shirtsleeve has already almost caused your death. Would you die for it now? Can you eat it? Can you drink it?"

"*¿Quién sabe?*" asked Azro. "Shoot, you old sonofabitch!"

The old man shrugged. He let down the hammer of the pistol.

He threw it into the pool. "Go get your damned treasure," he grunted. "After all, hombre, you already owe me your life."

"What do you want in return? That which is in the shirtsleeve?"

The old man shook his head. "You owe me nothing."

It was quiet except for the Aeolian hum of the night wind through the trees and brush of the *bosquecillo* on the reverse slope beyond the tanks. The desert lay like a great calm sea under the beautifully subdued illumination of the rising moon. Shadows moved gently in the wind. It was the ethereal quality of a moonlit night; a ghostly barren landscape frozen in silence.

"Beautiful, is it not, Azro Sutro? But a lizard would do well to live out there."

Azro turned. "How do you know my name?"

The old man handed Azro's wallet to him. "You name is in here."

Azro nodded. "How are you called?"

The old man bowed a little. "Gregorio Sanchez, at your service. *Arriero* and woodcutter. Now retired."

Azro smiled. "A mule packer? A woodcutter? *Here? * On the Solitario?"

Gregorio shrugged. "I *said* I was retired."

"Why are you here?"

There was no answer from Gregorio.

Azro dressed with the exception of his soleless boots. He swung his pistol belt about his waist and buckled it with practiced ease. He settled the belt about his lean waist and hips.

Gregorio eyed him. "I could have let you die or kept your shirtsleeve and killed you with your own *pistola*." He paused. "Do you wonder why I did not?"

"How much do you want?" asked Azro shortly.

"I said: You owe me nothing."

Azro waded into the pool and retrieved the shirtsleeve and his Colt. He removed the cylinder of the sixgun. There were no cartridges in the six chambers. He looked back at Gregorio. "You said: Try me. You bastard!"

Gregorio shrugged. "Why should I kill a man whose life I had just saved?"

Azro looked away. There was much about this strange and eerie old man he did not understand. An old man living in a place, where as he had said: "A lizard would do well to live out there."

Gregorio lifted the lid from an olla buried in the embers and ashes. A delicious smell emanated from the olla. "Frijoles," he said. "The beans that have made Mexico the greatest country in the world."

Azro nodded. *"Verdad.* You have been across the Solitario yourself?"

"Long ago. Long, long ago. . . ." replied Gregorio.

"Why?"

Azro looked at the bulging shirtsleeve. "The same reason you were there."

"You found no gold?"

Gregorio spread out his hands, palms upward. "I found nothing. I lost everything. I saved my life by coming back here."

"A coward's way?" suggested Azro.

Gregorio shrugged. "Perhaps. But *I* am still alive. . . ."

Azro looked about himself at the barrenness. "Still with nothing. . . ."

"It is enough that I am still alive," Gregorio said quietly. "And hombre, that is all I ask of God. And if I had not been alive, and experienced in saving men who were about to die of thirst out on that desert of Hell itself, you would not still be alive."

"I could have made it," growled Azro.

"Of course," Gregorio agreed dryly. He paused. "You have been a soldier, perhaps?"

Azro nodded. "How did you know?"

"When I stripped you to the skin, I saw the scar above your left knee and the long scar along your right ribs. Where did you get them?"

"At the Battle of Antietam in our War Between the States. And in Mexico."

Gregorio was puzzled. *"Mexico?* You fought with the French to keep Maximilian on the throne of Mexico?"

Azro shook his head. "I fought with the Juaristas. The wound along my ribs was from a French Zouave in battle." He shrugged. "It was almost a death wound. I killed the Zouave. I lived."

There was respect in Gregorio's eyes. "Why did you take up the cause and fight for the liberty of the Juaristas?"

"I was in many battles in the War Between the States. I returned home after the war. I knew no one. I had no friends and no relatives. I had grown used to war and killing. Perhaps I was beginning to like it. I knew no other trade. You see, hombre, soldiering for some men is like whoring for some women. What else can they do? So, I looked for a war and found one in Mexico. So, I joined the Juaristas."

"But why Juarez and his cause?"

"I believed in his cause. The French had no business being there in Mexico. After that, I was still homeless. I had nothing. So, I looked for gold."

"That is all? You do not seem to know your own destiny."

Azro shrugged. "Who does?"

"Verdad. But some know more about it than others."

"And some, like myself, know nothing about it at all."

"I find that hard to believe in you."

"Believe what you will."

Gregorio studied him. "And what *do* you believe in?"

Azro picked up the plump shirtsleeve. He cut loose the thong that bound one end and poured the contents down on the ground. The firelight flickered on and reflected from the material lying there. "Strawberry quartz. Matted together with gold wire and coarse gold. *This* is what I believe in. . . ." he said quietly.

Gregorio stepped fearfully back from the quartz as though it was a venomous snake lying there ready to strike and kill. "Where did you find it?" he quietly asked, never taking his eyes from it.

"Easily removed from the loose earth on the side of a sloping hill. The side of the hill and the ground below it were covered with blow sand. I dug this out with my bare hands. There seems to be a vein of it rich with natural gold coursing up the hill and perhaps down the other side as well." He paused. "Rich, rich, *very* rich, hombre," he murmured.

"Why did you leave it?" Gregorio already knew the answer.

"I was almost out of water. In fact, I was looking for water when I found the gold. No matter how rich the strike was, it could not buy me one drop of water out there. Without water, there is no life. . . ."

Gregorio studied him. "Can you find your way back there?"

Azro slowly shook his head. "I don't know. Why are you so interested?" He looked suspiciously at Gregorio. "Do you plan to look for it yourself?"

Gregorio shook his head. "Satan himself and a horde of his

demons could not drag me across that damned desert and the accursed hills beyond it."

"But why?" queried Azro.

Gregorio pointed down the rocky slope to where the blow sand merged with the flat surface of the *playa*. "What do you see?" he asked.

"Nothing but that damned desert," grunted Azro.

"Look closer. *There*. . . ."

Azro saw it then. It was a gray wooden weatherbeaten cross leaning away from the usual course of the wind. He looked at Gregorio.

Gregorio nodded. "My young wife, Lupita." His voice broke. "She died out there on the *playa*," he continued. "Many years ago. I was young and strong then as you are now. I was mad with gold fever as you are now. I could have left that place of hell but I stayed on in my lust for gold. Lupita was as fragile as smoke. She would not leave me. Where could she go? Only *I* knew that damned country or *thought* I did. I was wrong, as you are wrong. . . ." His voice died away.

"Did you find any trace of gold?" asked Azro.

"I did not," replied Gregorio.

"But you knew about the gold being somewhere in there?"

"All I knew about it or thought about it was that it was a legend, no more, hombre."

"Legends almost always have some basis in truth."

Gregorio shrugged but he did not speak.

Azro eyed Gregorio. "Tell me about your wife, Lupita."

"She was dying in those damned hills. I carried her in my arms across the *playa* to reach the water here. She died somewhere out on the *playa*. I did not know that she had died. I buried her here in the blow sand."

"Where the cross is now?"

Gregorio shook his head. Tears welled from his sad eyes. "I buried her and did not mark the grave. I was near death myself, you know, even as you had been. I left here and did not return for some years. When I did return, I could find no sign of her grave. The blowing sand, you know. All I knew was that she *was* buried somewhere in there. I carved the cross and placed it down there. You see, the whole area must be considered as her grave. I come here from time to time and try to find where she is buried. I have not been successful. But perhaps, someday. . . .”

"Why did you bring a woman out here with you?" asked Azro.

Gregorio did not reply. "The beans will be ready," he said. "Let us eat."

The beans did not last long. The two men sat on opposite sides of the dying fire, smoking two of the lean and crooked black Lobo Negro cigarillos.

"How did you get that lump on the side of your head?" Gregorio asked suddenly after a time.

"I must have fallen," replied Azro. "I have little recollection of what happened. Some of the events maybe occurred only in my imagination. I must have fallen." He paused and looked oddly at Gregorio. "I *might* have fallen," he continued quietly. "The lump might have come from the fall, or *perhaps someone I did not see struck me from behind.* The lump might have come from the fall, or the blow, or perhaps both. As I said, I have little recollection of what happened. The first thing I can truly recall was finding myself walking west on the *playa* after killing my last burro for its blood to drink. I do not clearly recall how I got hurt. I do not recall where I found the gold. All I know is that I had walked half a day from water, here at the Solitario Tanks, to the east and across the *playa* into the hills and canyons. The gold was in one of those canyons, but there are many canyons thereabouts and they all look alike."

"Verdad," agreed Gregorio.

"Why did you bring a woman with you into that place of hell?" repeated Azro.

Gregorio shrugged. "I had not been married long. I could not leave her behind for fear of losing her. I wanted the gold for her, not so much for myself. I did not find the gold and lost her."

Azro studied him. *"Verdad?"* he quietly asked.

Gregorio nodded. "Why do you ask?"

"Because if you had not brought her with you, she might still be alive all these past years. In seeking that treasure you lost the one true treasure of your life, that which you already had—your young wife."

Gregorio was quiet. Whatever he was thinking he was keeping to himself.

"How did she die, Gregorio?" asked Azro. "Was it lack of water? Exposure? Perhaps she was injured in a fall?"

"Why do you want to know? It is enough that she died."

"There is something you are not telling me," Azro suggested.

Gregorio looked away from Azro's penetrating gaze. "What are you trying to say?" he asked.

"How did she die, Gregorio?" Azro persisted.

"I was not with her when she was injured. I was absorbed in my senseless search for gold. She was alone at our camp. I got back after nightfall. She was unconscious, lying on the ground, bleeding from a scalp wound on the back of her head. She had lost much blood. She was fragile." His voice died away.

"Go on," urged Azro.

"I went loco," continued Gregorio. "The burros were gone. There was no time to look for them. I carried her across the *playa* throughout the night. She had been still alive when I picked her up. She was dead when I got here. . . ."

"Who did it?" demanded Azro. "Indians? Mexicans? Gringos?"

"No Indian would go into those canyons. To them it is haunted. Mexicans mostly avoid that country. Gringos sometimes go in there. Usually they are never seen again. I found no tracks. No signs of anyone other than Lupita being at the camp. Nothing. . . ." He paused. He looked out across the *playa* frozen in bluish moonlight and utter silence. "The place is accursed. It is haunted by *something;* something that does not want men hunting in there for gold. There are old tales about such things. I was a fool to go in there. I was double a fool to bring her with me. She did not want to go, you understand?"

"But *you* have survived."

Gregorio's eyes were bright with tears as he turned to face Azro. "You say I have survived? I should have died instead of her. I lost the one thing for which I lived back then. I did not truly know it at the time; I know it now! I know that she lies somewhere down there in the blow sand but I do not know exactly where she is. Is that not punishment worse than death?"

There was nothing Azro could say.

"What will you do now?" asked Gregorio to change the subject. He could not talk longer about it, so painful it was to him.

Azro replaced the pile of strawberry quartz into the sleeve and tied the open end of the sleeve to close it.

"You will return to those accursed canyons," stated Gregorio.

"That is so," agreed Azro.

"You know how dangerous it is. Why will you go back?"

"I have nothing else. I have no one left to return to. No family, wife, children or friends."

Gregorio nodded. "If that is true, why do you want the gold? What good will it do you? What can you buy with it that will bring you happiness? There are men who will kill you for it. Dark-minded men. Killers . . ." warned Gregorio.

Azro looked at him. "Why, amigo, *I* can kill too. . . ."

"You are a blind fool!"

Azro shook his head. "It is you who is blind, sitting here on this damned hill mooning over the lost grave of a wife who died years ago!" He instantly regretted what he had just said. After all, the old fool had saved Azro's life.

"This is the life I have chosen," said Gregorio. "At that, hombre, it is a better life than you have chosen for yourself, a life that will likely lead to your death in some remote canyon where no one will bury you and weep over your grave. At least, I have my memories and dreams. What do you plan to do now?"

Azro shrugged. "The only thing I can do—go into Yuma and cash in my gold to buy me supplies, a rifle and some burros unless you will sell me yours."

Gregorio shook his head. "They are my family," he said quietly. "The instant you show up in Yuma, looking as you do with a shirtsleeve full of high-assay gold quartz, you will be recognized for what you are. You must come back here for your water. Men in Yuma will know that. You will be followed. They will follow you through the gates of Hell itself for gold such as your quartz indicates and much less for that matter."

"What do you suggest?" asked Azro.

"If you like, I will take your gold into Yuma. I have friends there. I will trade in the gold and buy your supplies and a pair of burros, perhaps. I will bring it all back here with me although I do not want to see you go back into those lost canyons."

"How do I know that you will return?"

"This is my home most of the time. I hope to die here someday. Perhaps some kind passerby will bury me and say a few words over my grave."

"What will you want from me if you go into Yuma for me with my gold?"

Gregorio smiled. "Only your friendship."

"How long will it take you to go to Yuma and return here?"

"Perhaps a week. What will you need?"

"Food. You will know what to get. A rifle. Caliber forty-four. Cartridges. Tobacco. Liquor."

"It is dangerous to drink on your quest. You will make mistakes."

Azro grinned. "For medicinal purposes only. Maybe snakebite."

"That doesn't work."

Azro nodded. "I know. But it is a comfort to know that it might. How will you get to Yuma?"

Gregorio placed two fingers in his mouth and whistled sharply.

There was a distant clattering of something on the rocky slope behind the *tinaja*. A moment later a burro poked its head beyond some scrub brush and eyed the two men with big, soft-looking eyes.

Gregorio smiled. "That's Theresa. She is the bold one."

Theresa trotted up to Gregorio. He stroked her head and fondled her big ears.

Another burro poked its head through the brush and eyed Azro suspiciously.

"That's Filomena," explained Gregorio. "She's the shy and cautious one. It's unusual for her to show up at all when a stranger is around here."

"When does a stranger ever show up around here?" asked Azro.

Gregorio shrugged. "You did."

"Will you ride one of the burros to Yuma?"

Gregorio shook his head. "Follow me." He walked down the slope toward a thick *bosquecillo* of scrub trees and brush followed by a wondering Azro and the two little burros.

A small iron-gray California mule trotted through the *bosquecillo* toward Gregorio.

"That is Solomon, my riding mule," explained Gregorio. "I will ride him into Yuma."

Gregorio led the way through part of the *bosquecillo* toward a sheer wall of rock rising above the top level of the trees. He approached the wall and pulled aside brush piled thickly against the base of it to reveal the narrow mouth of what appeared to be a cavern opening into the solid rock.

Gregorio led the way into the cavern and lighted a lantern. "My house is your house," he said with a broad smile.

A pallet lay on the floor. Stacked wooden boxes held cans and containers of food and condiments and a few cooking utensils. A miner's spade hung from a wall peg. Several packsaddles lay against one wall. There were small oval wooden kegs which were used to carry water on burro or mule backs. A saddle, bridle, saddle blanket and other horse furniture were lying on the floor. A heavy wooden box looked familiar to Azro. It was labeled in black ink: ARMY BREAD. UNION MECHANICAL BAKING COMPANY. BALTIMORE MD. It was a container for hardtack, the flinty square biscuits, usually aswarm with weevils, which had been standard army fare during the Civil War.

Azro looked about. "You have a rifle? A carbine?" he asked.

Gregorio handed Azro a carbine. Azro recognized it as one he had carried in Mexico for some time after the war. It was the Winchester Model 1866 saddle ring carbine with a brass frame nicknamed The Yellow Boy. It fired the .44 caliber rimfire cartridge with a 200-grain bullet using a 28-grain powder propelling charge. The firing pin was double-pronged, thus striking both sides of the cartridge rim. The tubular magazine beneath the barrel carried ten cartridges.

"You won't take it to Yuma with you?" asked Azro.

Gregorio shook his head. "I have no need of it. It is yours to use, amigo."

Azro nodded. *"Gracias.* You have cartridges for it?"

"The magazine is full. Ten cartridges. That is all I have."

Gregorio left that night after moonset.

After Gregorio was gone, Azro scouted around the *tinaja* area and removed all traces of Gregorio's and his own presence there. He returned to the cavern and cleaned the Winchester inside and out. He made coffee over the firepit within the cavern. While it was brewing, he poked about in the far reaches of the cavern and found a pair of what he recognized as Apache thigh-length moccasins, the *n'deh b'keh.* He wondered how the old man had come by them. It was something to think about. Maybe the old bastard was part Apache, or perhaps had been raised by them. It was not uncommon. Azro had known a few such men. They had been captured when children by the Apaches. They rarely kept adult men captives, considering them too dangerous. Their own numbers of warriors was always low owing to almost incessant warfare with Mexicans and gringos. A very young male Mexican could easily be raised and trained as an Apache warrior. Some of them liked the Apache way of life and would remain with the band rather than returning to their own people.

The moccasins were in good shape. Azro pulled them on and drew the tops of them high around his thighs then folded them neatly below his kneecaps and tied them in place. Apaches usually used the folds to carry small personal articles. The leg parts of the moccasins were made of soft deerskin while the soles were made of tough rawhide. There was no better mode of footwear for use in the desert and rough mountains. Azro grunted in satisfaction as he stomped about the cavern getting the feel of the moccasins.

The coffee boiled. Azro opened the case of hardtack and removed some of the biscuits from it. He poured some of the coffee into a big tin mug. He looked at one of the pieces of hardtack. It brought back memories to him. During the war he and his messmates used to soak their hardtack in water and then fry it in deep bacon grease. A little sprinkling of brown sugar atop the hardtack made it almost as palatable as pastry. He grinned. "Skiligalee," he murmured. That was what they had called it—*skiligalee.* There were many memories. One night his squad had been on outpost duty along the Rappahannock River with the Rebels on the other side of the river. Azro and his squad mates had been foolish enough to sit around a roaring campfire eating skiligalee. A Rebel musket across the river cracked once like a shingle being snapped over one's knee. Joe Calder had been hit in the head. He had fallen back from the fire. Azro and the others had sprinted for cover. Azro had glanced back. Joe lay on his back. His eyes were wide open staring sightlessly at the night sky. The piece of hardtack was still held in his mouth.

Azro dipped a piece of hardtack into the steaming coffee. Weevils came scrambling out of it and swam frantically about until they died. Azro casually skimmed them from the surface of the coffee and flicked them off. He ate the coffee-soaked hardtack. Some said the weevils had a distinctive taste, somewhat like weak vinegar. Azro had never noticed it. War was war and hardtack was hardtack. One endured both or one did not survive. It was as simple as that.

Azro finished eating and let the fire die down. He put out the lantern, took the Winchester and left the cavern. The moon was almost gone. It was tomb-quiet and windless. He worked his way through the *bosquecillo.* The two burros came to him. He stroked

their ears and heads and spoke quietly to them. They looked up at
him with their big soft eyes. He knew how they must feel. Gregorio, their beloved master, was gone.

Azro softfooted up to the *tinaja* area. The desert was dark but
there was still enough of the fading moonlight for him to be able to
see fairly far out onto the *playa*. The darkness had softened the
harsh effect of the ancient lake bed but it did not soften the effect
that it had upon Azro.

"Why go back?" the mind voice said, or seemed to say out of the
stillness.

Azro whirled, full cocking the Winchester as he did so.

As before, *there was no one there.*

"I've been out here too long," murmured Azro. He knew well
enough that a gun shot would have no effect on whoever or *whatever* it was that was speaking to him, providing he *could* see it.

What was *he* really looking for? He thought of the strange and
lonely old man who had saved his life and who was now risking his
own life to help Azro. He seemed happy enough at the prospect of
spending the rest of his waning life here at Solitario Tanks in
memory of the young wife whose grave he had not been able to
locate, although he could never be very far from it. What was it he
had said to Azro? *"Why do you want the gold? What good will it do
you? What can you buy with it that will bring you happiness?"*

Azro shrugged. *"Nada,"* he murmured.

He must go back into those lost canyons to seek the gold. *He
must go.* . . .

Azro limped down the reverse slope of the area behind the
tanks. A faint wind had risen. It moaned through the *bosquecillo.*

Azro halted. He had heard something in the wind. It was not the
bodiless voice, or possible presence, he had heard before or *thought*
he had heard. He raised his head like a night-hunting wolf trying
to detect by sight, sound or smell where his prey might be.

Nothing. . . .

He waited, straining to hear the sound again.

Nothing. . . .

He went on to the cavern. He paused again to listen. The burros
were quiet. If there *had* been someone or anything alive hiding in
the *bosquecillo,* the burros would have known about it. They would
have warned Azro about it. That is, unless they were too frightened

to bray. Perhaps they had not detected anything; anything *alive,* that is.

He entered the cavern and leaned the carbine against the rear wall. A faint musical sound came as the metal buttplate struck something. Azro lighted the lantern. He looked down at the butt of the Winchester. A quart bottle with a blue and white paper label lay sideways on the rock floor.

Azro picked up the bottle and read the label aloud: "The Abyssinian Desert Companion. Good for Wind Colic, Flatulent Colic, Botts, Diarhhea, Scouring, Dysentery, Inflammation of the Bowels, Bladder and Kidney trouble, Colds in the Head, Congestion, Fits, Mad Staggers, Looseness of the Bowels and Inflammation of the Brain. For Botts it has no equal."

Azro shook the bottle and watched the deep amber contents swirl seductively about. He twisted the cork out of the bottle. He sniffed the contents. He instantly jerked back his head. His eyes watered. "Jeeesuss Kerist!" he blurted. He suspiciously studied the contents.

Azro shrugged. "What the hell," he murmured. "Maybe I've got botts." He drank about three fingers of the powerful distillation. He jerked back. He could not get his breath. His eyes watered again. His face tightened as though enclosed in a huge and powerful hand. His teeth felt as though they'd suddenly been sharpened. Then came the silent implosion in his lean gut. After a few moments of thoughtful silence Azro nodded. "Wahoo," he murmured hoarsely. "Forty rod, at least," he added.

He lowered the lantern and lay down on the pallet with the Winchester on one side of him and his Colt on the other. He closed his eyes.

He heard the voice, calling softly, but he could not distinguish the words. He shook his head and rolled over.

The sound of the voice came again. It seemed as though it was a woman.

Azro sat up suddenly and closed his hand on his Colt. He sat there, breathing quietly, listening for the voice. After a time he got up, sheathed his Colt and took up the Winchester. He waited at the mouth of the cavern. It was quiet again. He waited. Minutes ticked past. The sound of the voice, if that was what it was, did not come again. Perhaps it had been the night wind. There *was* no wind.

Azro shrugged. "This damned place *is* haunted," he murmured.

He grinned faintly. "Perhaps it was The Abyssinian Desert Companion." He lay down to sleep. He did not waken again.

It was just before dawn of the tenth day after Gregorio had left for Yuma. Azro awoke with an uneasy feeling growing within himself. The faintest of gray light showed at the cavern entrance. He stood up and took his Winchester and slung his field glasses case strap about his neck.

One of the burros brayed softly.

Azro walked softly to the cavern entrance and stood still just within it. He tilted his head forward, then turned it first to one side and then the other peering narrow-eyed into the grayness, sniffing the morning air and listening intently.

Nothing. . . .

The burro brayed again.

Azro catfooted through the *bosquecillo*. He stopped short when he saw a motionless and hatless mounted man seated on a mule just at the edge of the trees. It could be Gregorio mounted on Solomon. Why hadn't he called out? Perhaps he could not see the motionless shadowy figure of Azro within the *bosquecillo*.

A burro brayed again. There was an answering bray from the mule.

The mule entered the *bosquecillo* and moved toward Azro. The graying light struck the face of the mounted man. He was Gregorio, or at least there was some resemblance to Gregorio. Somehow the features were different. There was no doubt in Azro's mind that the mule was indeed Solomon.

Azro took a chance. He raised his carbine. "Gregorio?" he softly called out.

There was no answer to Azro's call.

The mule moved closer at the sound of Azro's voice. Gregorio's features became plainer to see in the growing light. His mouth gaped open. His eyes were wide and unblinking and they seemed to stare sightlessly toward Azro. Gregorio was obviously as dead as last night's liquor bottle. Gregorio had been lashed into his saddle. His left hand still held the reins in the cold grip of *rigor mortis*. The mule turned aside and Azro saw the haft of a knife sticking out between Gregorio's shoulder blades.

Azro moved swiftly, running softly through the *bosquecillo* until he could look out with his field glasses toward the faint trail to

Yuma and the north that traversed the long slope of the land that lay stretching below the *bosquecillo.* The area was a static landscape. Nothing moved under the light of the rising sun. There was no sign of moving men and wreathing dust.

What was it Gregorio had said? *"The instant you show up in Yuma, looking as you do with a shirtsleeve full of high-assay quartz, you will be recognized for what you are. You must come back here for your water. Men in Yuma will know that. You will be followed. They will follow you through the gates of Hell itself for gold such as your quartz indicates and much less for that matter."*

Azro went back to Gregorio. He cut loose the lashings and pulled the knife from the old man's back. The old man had not been dead too long. Whoever had murdered him was likely somewhere along the trail waiting for their chance to deal with Azro.

Azro carried the body to the *tinaja.* He got the miner's spade and an old blanket from the cavern and returned to the old man. He carried the body down to the blow sand and dug a grave near the cross Gregorio had placed there in memory of Lupita. He closed Gregorio's eyelids and then wrapped Gregorio in the blanket. He lowered him into the grave and shoveled the loose sand back into the hole. He did not mound the grave but rather smoothed out the sand so that there was no indication that a grave was there. The cross would be marker enough.

Azro took off his hat and with bowed head recited the Twenty-third Psalm. He replaced his hat and looked down at the grave. *"Vaya con Dios, amigo,"* he murmured. "Go with God." He paused then spoke again: *"Vaya con Dios, amigo . . . acaso. . . .* Go with God, friend . . . perhaps. . . ."

Azro went back to observe the trail. It was the same as it had been before, with no sign of mounted men. He was sure they were out there, perhaps hidden in an arroyo waiting for their chance to surprise him, probably under cover of darkness.

To run would be against every fighting fiber in Azro's body.

"Run or fight? Which is it to be?" the mind voice seemed to say.

To fight on this ground would serve no purpose. His best course would be to leave the area as soon as possible and strike back across the *playa,* hoping to possibly evade whoever was out there and get into the hills and canyons beyond the *playa.* He'd need to carry as much water with himself as possible. He had the two burros to carry the water kegs and supplies. He could ride Solomon, if need be.

Azro went back to Solomon and instantly realized the mule was about done. He'd never last out on the *playa* and in the hills beyond. He looked through the saddlebags on the mule. There was no trace of his sleeve filled with strawberry quartz. He hadn't expected any. He did find two full bottles of Abyssinian Desert Companion, a supply of Lobo Negro cigarillos and some loose tobacco and a small sack of beans.

He hefted the bottles of Abyssinian Desert Companion. "Better than nothing." He grinned. "Maybe a helluva lot better."

Azro went to the cavern. He dumped what food he could find into a sack. The small oval water kegs seemed to be in fair shape. They had not thoroughly dried yet. He carried eight of them to the *tinaja* and immersed them, to soak them and swell the seams, weighting them down with rocks. They'd hardly carry enough water to get him beyond the canyons to the east. Yuma would be the closest and safest source of water within striking distance of Solitario Tanks, but of course he could not go there. In the other directions, south and east, there might be *some* water in a few isolated *tinajas* but he did not know quite where they were and most, if not all, of them were seasonal and it was now the driest part of the year. He would not have enough water in the kegs to support himself and the two burros for very long and perhaps not long enough to find any other water to the southeast, if there was any to be found. He *might* make it alone. . . .

It was midmorning. The sun blazed down. Azro checked the trail to Yuma. As before, there was no sign of life. The only movement he could see was that of a *zopilote,* the great buzzard of the Sonoran type of desert seemingly hanging almost motionless high in the sky like a scrap of charred paper carried highly upward from the draft of a bonfire. Azro *thought* he saw it. . . . It might be a portent of death lurking somewhere in the area. *Whose* death, he thought.

Solomon was still alive, but barely. There was no hope for him. "Sorry, Solomon," murmured Azro as he pulled the mule's head to one side and cut its throat. He let the blood drain onto the ground. Azro had spent some time with the Apaches, *friendly* ones, that is. Their usual canteen was the long gut or intestine of a horse or mule, sketchily cleaned, tied at one end and filled with water, then tied at the open end and looped about the neck of their horse. It was greasy, as was the water contained therein with an indescribable taste of its own, but it *was* water. Azro cut free the intestine and hung it from a tree branch while he cut some cooking meat including the mule's upper lip from the body. Apaches liked the sweeter mule meat better than beef.

Azro carried the intestine to the *tinaja* and placed it in the water. He returned to the cavern and cooked the mule meat. The long, hot afternoon began. The dry hot wind picked up. Wind devils appeared on the flat dusty surface of the *playa*. Heat waves endlessly shimmered and postured: Distant objects were magnified while seemingly rising from the superheated ground into the shimmering heat waves.

Now and again Azro checked the Yuma trail. If there was anyone out there, they would likely be squatting in the hot shade of their horses waiting for nightfall. "Sweat, you bastards," he grunted. He grinned.

He'd have to leave the *tinaja* area before dusk. He'd have little chance against them if they closed in on him during the premoon darkness. He didn't know how many of them there might be. He was used to having the odds against him. He knew one thing for sure—he'd fight to the death before he let them take him alive. They would not try to kill, at first anyway. They would want to know the site of the gold lode. He grinned wryly. "I don't even know myself," he murmured.

He turned the mule intestine inside out and cleaned it as well as he could. He turned it inside out again, tied one end and filled the intestine by means of his coffee cup. When the intestine was full and bulging, he tied the open end closed. He took out the kegs he had placed in the water to soak. He got the packsaddles from the cavern and placed them on the two burros. He made sure the kegs were full and then placed the stoppers in them. He loaded each of the burros with four of the dripping kegs. He shook his head. Would they keep dripping? He hoped the seams would swell enough to hold the water within the kegs. If not . . . ? He shook his head. It was not good to think about it. He coiled the mule intestine and looped it about Filomena's neck.

The wind had increased. The wind devils traveled with the wind, appearing suddenly only to reappear again somewhere else to whirl and spiral, rising higher and higher as they moved along and then disappeared again. It would be sheer hell to cross the *playa* that day. Azro had no choice whatsoever. Cross the *playa* or die. It was that simple. Cross the *playa* and *then* die, he thought.

They would not be able to wring out of him the site of the gold lode. He didn't know himself so how could he tell them? In reality he could not show them the location of the lode. They would not believe him. Either way he would be certain to die, either by their hands or by crossing the *playa* at the worst possible time of the year into a burning, waterless wasteland. He would be damned if he stayed and would be damned if he left.

He still planned to move at dusk, if they allowed him to do so. He stood at the *tinaja* and looked down at the lone cross there. He could still see the faint outline of the grave of Gregorio. In time the wind would level it off. The wind was shifting and fanning itself along the line of the blow sand, neatly sweeping up the higher levels of sand and then redistributing them to the lower levels to fill in the lower levels in its constant and never-ending task of tidying up the desert floor.

Both burros brayed loud and clear.

Azro whirled in the direction of the braying. A man was running crouched toward Azro, with a sixshooter in his right hand and a Winchester from his left hand. Azro fired his Winchester twice from his hip. The pair of slugs caught the man in the belly and slammed him backward. He fired his pistol into the air as he staggered sideways to the edge of the pool and then fell flat on his back, dropping the pistol into the water.

Something warned Azro to turn. As he did so he saw a man standing not far from himself with his clubbed rifle ready to strike. He evidently wanted Azro *alive*. He slammed the rifle down across the barrel of Azro's Winchester in an effort to turn it aside, then brought the butt upward to strike at Azro's jaw. Azro turned his head aside and caught the blow alongside his skull above his right ear. He staggered but he did not go down. He stood there swaying back and forth. It was a blow that might have felled an ox. Azro's attacker jumped back open-mouthed in astonishment that Azro had not gone down from such a blow.

Azro moved in swiftly with a crooked grin on his face. "That's New Hampshire granite you're hitting, you sonofabitch!" he rasped out. His hamlike left fist caught his attacker in the lower part of his belly. The man bent forward from the waist. His chin met Azro's upward driving right knee. He raised his head with the impact. Azro gave him the old one-two, a left to the belly and a hard right to the jaw. He staggered backward to the edge of the pool. Azro charged, butting the man in the chest with his hard head, and driving him flat on his back into the water. Azro was on top of him in an instant. His big hands closed about the man's throat. He forced his head under the water and squeezed his throat with all his strength. The man forced his body upward. Azro forced it back down. A reddish haze seemed to appear before Azro's eyes. Vivid memories of the violent and bloody hand-to-hand fighting at Antietam and Spotsylvania Court House poured through his tired mind. He squeezed his hands tighter and tighter.

Azro found himself standing on the edge of the pool looking down at the contorted face of the man he had just killed. It was just distinguishable under the water's surface. A few bubbles rose from his gaping mouth and burst on the surface.

It was very quiet. The air was dry and hot. The vagrant wind was beginning to beat its wings. Out on the surface of the *playa* there arose, here and there the many ubiquitous wind devils, appearing and disappearing only to reappear again in the distance, whirling and spiraling upward.

Azro did not want to move. A lethargy had overcome him. He had had the same feeling after many of the battles during the Civil War and later while fighting in Mexico. It was difficult to shake off. Even the debauches with cheap liquor and drunken two-bit whores had never been able to erase the bloodshed from his tired mind. Still, he had always gone back into other battles when ordered to do so.

Azro picked up the Winchester '73 dropped by the second man he had killed. The magazine was full. He went to the first man he had killed. He removed all of the .44-40 cartridges from the man's pistol belt and fed as many as he could into the empty loops on his own pistol belt and then placed the remaining cartridges into his shirt pockets. He entered the pool next to the body of the second man he had killed and removed the pistol belt heavy with cartridges, holstered Colt and sheathed knife. He got out of the pool and emptied the cylinder chambers of the revolver and then shook it to get rid of the surplus water and then wiped it as dry as he could. He reloaded the cylinder and thrust the Colt under his belt.

Azro picketed Filomena and Theresa near the *tinaja*. "Stay here, you pretty little bitches," he said. "I'll be needing you soon."

Azro took up his station near the rock formation overlooking the Yuma Trail. He focused his field glasses on it. A thin thread of dust hung in the air but he did not see anyone on the trail itself. The dust was no wandering wind devil. It was moving slowly *against* the wind, instead of traveling with it as a wind devil was bound to do. Likely those who had been traveling toward Solitario Tanks had sent the two men he had killed to get Azro under control.

Azro scratched at his crotch. "Get *me* under control? The bastards!" He levered a round into the chamber of his Winchester. He grinned crookedly. "I'm a mean sonofabitch," he added quietly. "I'm a real cocked pistol man. I'm mean enough to hunt grizzly bears with a willow switch."

The trail wound up close to where Azro had stationed himself. He knew now they were too close for him to get safely away from the *tinaja* area. He'd have to make a stand where he was.

The dust thickened and then suddenly, as though like marionettes controlled by the strings of a master, five horsemen appeared on a rise in the trail seemingly coming up out of nowhere from the depths. They rode steadily onward with ready rifles across their thighs. The fine clear lenses of Azro's field glasses picked out their faces; hard faces with jaws set like closed wolf traps. They neared the bottom of the slope. They halted their mounts about 150 yards downslope from where Azro waited for them. The leader rode his dun horse closer, perhaps 100 yards from Azro.

Azro stepped out into the open. "That's far enough!" he shouted. His voice rolled echoing along the slopes: *"That's far enough. . . . That's far. . . . That's. . . ."* The sound slowly died away in the distance. It was quiet again except for the dry moaning of the wind through the *bosquecillo*.

The lead horseman reined in. "You're Sutro, eh!" he called out.

They must have gotten his name from Gregorio. That is, before they had murdered him.

"What do you want?" demanded Azro.

"Didn't Jim and Harry tell you?"

"They didn't have time."

"Where are they?"

"Dead," replied Azro. I killed them."

"Why?"

Azro shrugged. "They tried to kill me."

"That wasn't my orders."

"I didn't know that," said Azro. "When armed men attack me, I figure they kill *me* or *I* kill *them.*" He paused. "I killed them."

The leader was quiet for a short time, as though he was sizing up the situation.

"What do you want?" asked Azro.

"I want to talk with you."

Azro shrugged again. "Talk," he said.

"We know you know where that strawberry quartz came from. You show us where you found it. We'll cut you in on the deal. Fair enough?"

"And if I don't?"

There was a pause. "You'll die," said the leader.

Azro grinned. "So, I show you where the quartz was found. You cut me in on the deal. What's my guarantee?"

"My word."

Azro laughed. "Is that the same deal you offered old Gregorio?"

"The old fool wouldn't talk."

"Because he himself didn't know where I found it. Did he tell you as well that I really didn't know?"

The leader shifted about in his saddle. "We need water," he said. "Let us come and get it. We can talk later."

"That so? You'll have to wait."

One of the men waiting behind the leader turned his horse as if to ride toward the far edge of the *bosquecillo.* Azro's Winchester cracked flatly. The horseman's hat was lifted from his head as if by magic. A second slug whined just over his head. He turned his mount and took cover in an arroyo. The double report echoed along the ridge into the distance. The powdersmoke drifted upward from Azro's position but he was no longer there. He had moved instantly after the second shot.

The leader had not moved. "You can't keep us much longer," he warned.

"I can try," said Azro. He moved again.

"We'll come after dusk."

Azro grinned. "You'll be damned thirsty by then."

It was quiet again.

"Damn you!" shouted the leader. He raised his Winchester and spurred his dun into a run toward Azro's position.

Azro fired. The dun went down with a .44-40 slug through its head. It was dead before it hit the ground. The horseman hit the ground running. A slug whispered just past his ear. He ran back toward his companions. One of them took him up behind himself on his horse and galloped his mount back toward the arroyo.

Azro trotted back to the *tinaja* area. He led the two burros down the slope to the blow sand. He took off his hat as he passed the lone cross. He struck off at a steady mile-eating pace across the *playa*. A half mile or so outward he looked back toward the *tinaja* site. He could see them walking about near the water. They would water up and start right out after him, he figured. He could put up a fight and maybe hold them off for a time but odds were they'd get him in the end. He'd die before he would tell them anything. He grinned. What *could* he tell them? *"Nada,"* he said and turned to lead on the burros.

He was three miles out on the *playa* before he looked back again. He could see them on the edge of the *playa* moving toward himself. They would be walking their horses.

The wind picked up. Here and there rose swirling, spiraling wind devils rising higher and higher hundreds of feet as the wind increased in velocity. Now and again one of them would pass between the line of vision of Azro and his pursuers, temporarily blotting them out from each other's sight. It would be a deadly game of hide-and-go-seek between them. Then, at irregular intervals the air between them would be clear again until the arrival of one or more of the sight-blocking wind devils.

Azro plodded on. He did not look back again. The drops of water leaking from the water kegs would vanish almost instantly as they fell and struck the hard dry surface of the insatiable *playa*.

As the afternoon wore on, the wind velocity increased so that at times the masses of heated air within the wind devils was whirled spirally into a rising column of dust. There was nothing on the hot dry surface of the *playa* to impede or obstruct the progress of the columns as they continued on hour after hour as the day wore on so that it became almost impossible to see beyond them across the miles wide surface of the *playa*. Sometimes the columns would remain almost stationary for hours at a time. The distant hills and the faraway mountains were almost completely lost to the sight of anyone on the surface of the *playa*. It had become a no-man's-land of hellfire heat and burning dust. In time nothing could be distinguished other than the wind devils themselves. After all, was it not their undisputed territory? Into this superheated nothingness plodded Azro Sutro leading his two burros. In time his pursuers turned back, realizing it was a hopeless chase into the deadly unknown after a man, who in reality, was probably not a man at all but rather a fleeting phantom.

EPILOGUE

Azro Samuel Sutro was never seen again, at least by anyone who could tell the tale about it. There were tales told by some who claimed to have seen him in the long following years after his disappearance—a dim figure seen through the dust and haze of the windswept *playa*—but it was never close enough to distinguish any true and particular features. Some claimed the phantom, or whatever it was, was that of a chunky, ragged-beard figure of a man with haunted eyes walking with a slight limp and always leading his two burros, but he was always traveling in the opposite direction from where he was first seen and always moving toward and into the remote hills and canyons east of the vast *playa*. The Apaches and Mexicans claimed he had turned into one of the wind devils which periodically swept clean the surface of the *playa*. The gringos said nothing. No true trace of Azro Sutro was ever found.

Somewhere in the tangled and isolated canyons and hills east of the Solitario Desert and its ominous *playa* there may yet be traces of Azro Sutro. Perhaps there is an empty sun-tinted bottle with a long faded blue and white label of The Abyssinian Desert Companion. There may be only one distinguishable printed line left to identify its long-gone contents: "For Botts it has no equal." The delicate sun-bleached bones of a burro or two might be found as well. Perhaps there might be a grinning skull nearby. None of these relics have ever been reported. One *might* also find a vein of strawberry quartz of great potential value but who will dare enter that haunted land to find it?

Perhaps Azro Sutro *did* find the lost vein of strawberry quartz. *¿Quién sabe?*

We'll Kill
the Old Red Rooster
When She Comes

R. C. House

TIGER AND I just about always stop in the bar at Reno's in Mojave and have a couple of what we call ditchwater highballs in celebration on our way home from Bakersfield and share a little bullshit with the boys who hang around there. We've come to know most of them by name or by sight. Kind of keeps us in touch with our fellow man, you might say. We live pretty far off the beaten track out in the Mojave Desert and don't see other people that often. We only get to Reno's about every couple of months.

After a while we go into the coffee shop and load up on a citified meal. The coffee shop of an evening is usually full of escapees from L.A., if it's around a weekend. They roar in there on their motor-sickles or crunch in with their four-wheelers, or vans pull in with trailers loaded with those dirt bikes and such. Or they'll be retired folks passing through in their motor homes stopping off for burgers or grilled cheeses or a bowl of chili.

Wintertime, the place is a regular stop-off for L.A. skiers headed up to Mammoth or some such in the Sierra in their spiffy snowsuits and fancy brand-new sweaters and fashionable little sports cars outside with racks for his-and-hers skis. Lord, the number of times they must have to change clothes in a day to suit the occasion in those places, it's a wonder to me where they stow their duffle in those little motorized roller skates.

Stopping off at Reno's gets to be a tradition with just about anybody who goes through Mojave with any frequency. Being flush for a change after our occasional runs to Bakersfield, Tiger and I stoke up on steak and eggs, hashbrowns, good sourdough toast and a mess of coffee-shop coffee before heading on home. Home is a two-room cement-block shack up on the slopes of the El Paso Mountains near Garlock, of which there isn't much left these days, and a hop, skip and jump from Randsburg, perched up there over across the way on the slopes of the Rand Mountains.

Everything else is forty miles from nowhere, just the unending sprawl of rock and gravel and chaparral sweeping away to no place in particular. Randsburg's fabulous Yellow Aster Mine played out years ago, so there isn't much left around Randsburg and its neighbor town, Johannesburg, either, except over in Randsburg there's Olga Guyette's "The Joint," where Tiger and I pass the time when we go to town, the general store and soda fountain next to the post office, and a bunch of bottle shops. And all around are a few modest little houses and shacks and kind of dilapidated old house trailers scattered random as raindrops.

And up the hill above town the great mounds of jumbled tailings from the old Yellow Aster.

Tiger and I—they call me Ten High—have been partners out here for a lot of years. Both divorced, both living on Army retirement pensions; that's about all it took for us to become pals. We discovered that there's quite a bit of gold and a little silver in the El Pasos above our place, at least enough to whet a man's appetite. Oh, I had a hunch that a good-sized strike waited up there, but Tiger and I found enough on our claim to get by. For the hell of it, we took to calling it the Red Rooster Mine; never quite got around to filing any legal papers.

We spied the place about a mile above our shack; a long, high and steep crumbling granite wall of a wash where here and there a few flecks or a cluster of small bits of flake gold in a sort of vein showed themselves. Tiger and I got pretty good at spotting them quickly and breaking them out with our little pick-hammers.

In a couple of days of poking and pecking around up there, we can come down with all the small rocks we can carry in our knapsacks that'll run maybe three, four hundred dollars. Both of us were twenty-year Army men and we're getting small pension checks. So, between the two, we don't want for much. Beans and bacon and some ground beef and fresh eggs once in a while. A quart of Ten High bourbon does us for about a week. Well, sometimes maybe less; get a chilly evening with a fire glowing in the stove and the philosophy ricochetting like bullets off the walls, and the level in that Ten High quart will go down like the tank of a gas-guzzling Cadillac.

A man finds he doesn't need much more than that in this kind of country. Oh, there are times in the late summer when it burns like it's a hundred miles from water and only six inches from hell and lots of the time the wind'll rare up on its hind legs and paw the air fierce enough to sandblast the skin off a man's back and rattle his bones. Other times, it can get colder than the bejeebers a few winter weeks of the year.

But mostly the old Mojave Desert is kind to us, and that's all that matters. We've both about had our bellies full of women—been married, each of us, and badly—and our fellow man. Not that we're antisocial. It's just that conventional ways don't suit us much anymore.

If we get caught short of funds before the checks come in, we hike up to the Red Rooster and fill our knapsacks with promising rocks. Then we pile into Tiger's old International truck—we call it "The Binder"; with its worn and fading paint and its butterfly collection on the radiator—and head out of Mojave on 58 for Bakersfield. We know a fellow there, a shifty kind of gent, if you ask me, who'll pay us fifty cents or so on the dollar for the gold in our rocks. We leave it up to him to deal with the proper authorities and go through the bureaucratic rigmarole and the dull baloney of officially selling it off into the gold market. He's a pretty good judge of what's in those rocks, and besides, Tiger and I aren't all that particular. Just looking to get by.

Tiger's a little whip of a fellow I got to know in and around Randsburg and Johannesburg—the place we call Joburg—after my wife and I called it quits and I was left with not much more than a pot to piss in and a pitifully small Army pension. We were still wearing parts of our old uniforms in those days and that got us talking around a nightfire of guys like us out on the desert and we've been partners ever since.

Tiger's lean and tough as jerky and not many shades lighter than the same color. Could be part Indian for all I know; black, straight hair without a hint of white at his age. In his room at the shack, he still keeps a mess of medals and engraved loving cups from his days of match shooting on Army teams and individual relays at the old

Camp Perry shoots in Ohio. He keeps his trophies tucked away; that is to say, Tiger doesn't brag on them, though he was a crack shot with an issue .45 Colt automatic and an M1 Garand, or an oh-three Springfield for that matter.

Still, neither of us keeps guns around. We've had enough of meanness and spite in our lives. If it comes to defense, and in this country it might, Tiger has an old pitchfork with the tines kept shiny and filed to points next to his bed. I've got a big old Bowie with a ten-inch blade in a scabbard that I keep handy and honed to a razor's edge and needle-tipped. I believe it's pretty old and came to this country with the first prospectors. Matter of fact, I traded an old guy out of it for about a half-quart of Ten High one night around a fire when we were drinking around camp and batting the breeze up there in the mining hills above Randsburg.

I spent my Army tour mostly as a company clerk and have my own share of trophies. But they are for what the Army considered whiz-bang typing skills. I guess I maybe still hold the Army record for error-free words-per-minute. Trouble is, these old knotty fingers probably couldn't so much as hunt-and-peck anymore.

Tiger and I drained the last drops of our ditchwater highballs in Reno's bar that night here sometime back. I looked at him and asked, "What say?" figuring it was time to get into the coffee shop for our steak and eggs before pointing The Binder for home. My stomach grumbled agreeably with the notion. It was a cold November night outside and our couple of jiggers apiece of well bourbon, light on the ditchwater, had kind of taken the chill-sting out of our toes and fingers. The heater in The Binder has been on the fritz for years, and neither of us really cares a damn. Minor annoyances we kind of take as a fact of life.

It was later so only a few of the L.A. escapees were there—you can spot these characters a mile away—and only one old retired couple in for a late snack. I imagined they had a Win-a-Bagel motorhome outside with their Good Sam Club sticker in the back window and "Min and Bill" or some such in glittery letters under the racked collapsible aluminum chairs on the chromed rear bumper.

A pretty good looking woman at the counter warmed herself with a cup of coffee, nothing more. She kind of looked Tiger and me up and down as we came in from the bar, but then went back to staring into her java. She was bundled up for the road, but not all that fancy bundled up either; hiker's boots, faded, stained Levi's and a thin, old windbreaker probably liberated from a Salvation Army store in L.A., over one or two sweatshirts. A thick wool scarf was tucked around the windbreaker's upturned collar, and wool knit gloves the same color as a Navy watch cap jammed over long blond hair that hadn't seen shampoo in a while. There was a strange kind of haunted hunger in her eyes. She had one of those pear-shaped blue knapsacks that are all the rage with the hikers and skiers bulging on the floor beside the stool. Probably everything she owned was in it. Tiger and I aren't strangers to down-and-out; there are earmarks and telltale signs. Tiger and I looked at each other as we walked past her and I'm sure we had the same thought. We would have bet she didn't have wheels out in the parking lot, and for one reason or another was bumming her way east out of L.A.

She was gone from the counter by the time we anted up for our grub. When Tiger fired up The Binder, backed out of the slot and The Binder's headlights swung on the highway, there she was at the curb watching the traffic outbound from L.A. on 14 through Mojave. There were precious few headlights eastbound, and practically none westbound but for a semi or two.

"That's the one, isn't it?" Tiger asked. "She's headed east all right."

"Or north to Bakersfield," I said. The junction is about a half-mile away where 58 splits away north and 14 continues sort of east by north.

It was Tiger's turn. "What say, Ten? Want to find out where's she's headed?"

"Don't get any big ideas, Tiger. Lord knows what she's carrying."

"Aw, hell, Ten, that wasn't on my mind at all. It's colder than a stepmother's breath out there, and she looks like she's pickin' in mighty poor cotton."

"Dammit, Tiger, we ain't taking her to Bakersfield, and that's final. I'm gettin' weary. If she's going out 14, that's fine. We can take her as far as the Randsburg cutoff."

"That'd be even a worse place to drop her, Ten." Tiger let The Binder idle in the lot while we debated.

"We ain't taking her up to the cabin," I protested. "Unless you want to give her your bed and you can sleep on the floor. The way you've been bitching about your bursitis lately, I wouldn't recommend it." I didn't approve of any of this.

"I ain't even thought that far ahead. Hell, Ten, you been down on your luck like that before. How many times have you stood out someplace like that in cold like this? And she's a woman. A pretty one at that. She's gonna be fair game for some perverted bastard or a carload."

I grunted. "I get your point."

"Last thing in the world I'd do is take advantage of her weakness."

I consented, but I didn't like it. "Okay, pull on out there. I'll ask her where she's going." Tiger eased The Binder along the curb next to her and I rolled down the window a crack to keep in what warmth we'd generated sitting there and banging our gums. "Which way you headed?" The wind had a hiss to it; a skosh this side of freezing.

She looked up at me, her pretty face scrunched up with the cold, and she had a tough time making her lips work. "Wherever the road's going, I guess." Her voice had the clear, tinkly quality of pieces of fine crystal clinking together—like the nice set my wife and I had before she hocked it for the hootch; between her and her binges, she went through my life savings and our nice things like a dose of salts.

"We're headed out 14 toward Ridgecrest. Want a lift that way?"

"Better'n standin' here."

I looked at Tiger. "Okay?"

"Yeah."

I opened the door and got out to let her in between us. "Believe I'd rather sit against the door," she said, and I caught a testy tone in her voice. I reacted.

"Look, you want a ride or don't ya'? Don't read the cards wrong, little lady," I said. "Me and Tiger been in the same tight fixes a few times that you are in right this minute and we got no more notions about you than to help you out. Besides, we're both old enough to be your daddy and aren't likely to forget it."

Her face softened. "Okay," she said, and pushed past me to her place alongside Tiger. I hopped in and Tiger eased The Binder out into the road. We bounced over the Santa Fe spur track and past a couple more gas stations and hung a right on 14 where 58 swings up north past Tehachapi and then the long haul into Bakersfield.

We were quickly headed out 14 across open desert as dense and as black as the inside of a boot. The only light was The Binder's yellow beams tracing the dips and occasional curves of the two-lane road that's mostly straight as a string.

Just the warmth of our three bodies took some of the chill out of the cab. We drove quite a while without saying a word. "You comin' from L.A.?" Tiger asked, breaking the silence. She'd been quiet, probably out of unfamiliarity with us two bozos.

"Yeah," she responded. "Had enough of that place and that's for sure."

"What'd you do there?"

"Huh!" she grunted. She mulled over an answer. "Nice girls don't say, but I haven't been what you'd call a nice girl and I guess that answers your question."

"Huh!" I grunted, astonished by her frankness, but I always respect people who don't beat around the bush.

She got a little talkative. "Maybe I'm older than you think. I've operated in L.A. about ten years. Came here from Omaha when I was twenty-three. That ought to give you an idea. What do you fellas do?"

"Not much," Tiger said. "We got a little place up in the hills on out here a ways. We're what you might call retarded."

"You mean retired," she said.

"He was making a joke," I said over the roar of The Binder's engine and transmission. "We're what they call desert rats."

"Married?" she asked.

"Used to be," Tiger answered. "Both of us."

"I get it. Taken to the cleaners. Like me, you're living pretty close to the bone these days."

"That's a polite way to put it," I said. "We don't want for much and we don't ask for much. Where you bound?"

"Any place but L.A. Nothing left for me there. And I couldn't hold my head up in Omaha, so that's out."

"You got any particular line of work? I mean other than . . ." I knew right there I'd put my foot in it. It didn't faze her.

She laughed a little and it was a nice kind of laugh; one that you'd like to hear more of. "Nope. Don't worry. I ain't sensitive about it. Was doing some little theater work before in Omaha. That's about all."

"I suppose that's what got you to L.A.," Tiger said.

"That and Crazy Charlie. Saw me in a show in Omaha and said he'd be my agent in Hollywood and get me into the movies. Stars in my eyes and all that good stuff, and I bit. Man, did I bite! Next thing I knew I was working American Legion conventions but from flat on my back. The bucks began rolling in, Crazy Charlie was getting fat off me, and from there it was downhill all the way. I was out of there yesterday morning about two jumps ahead of Skid Row."

"It seems to me I've heard that song before . . ." I sang.

She laughed again and then I knew I wanted to hear more of that laughter and sensed that in recent times it hadn't come often. I wanted to do something to bring more of that laughter back into her life. I didn't really have a fatherly interest in her, but at the same time, I didn't feel any urges about getting into her knickers.

"Look at it this way," she said. "At first they sent limousines around to my door. I finally wound up taking the bus to my dates. You figure it out. A few days ago, Crazy Charlie found a way into my bank account, him being my business manager and such, and looted it without my knowing it. When I was away, he came over to my place and stole everything worth hocking. To top it off, so I'd have no place to turn, he moved out of his apartment with no forwarding address. Probably found some younger chick to feed off of. I cried for two days and I came out of it saying, well, the same to you, L.A. and C.C."

"C.C.?" I asked.

"Crazy Charlie."

"Only C.C. I ever heard about," I said, "was the nickname for the compound cathartic we got from the Army medics on sick call when we were bound up."

She was damned quick on the uptake. "Same thing," she said. "Crazy Charlie could give you the shits, too." The Binder's lights picked up the road sign announcing the Randsburg cutoff coming up in two miles.

"This is it, Tiger," I said. "It's one o'clock in the gawdam morning and about 40 degrees in a raw wind out there, and it's halfway between nothin' and no place."

"Uh-huh," Tiger grunted. "What did you say your name was, lady?"

"Didn't. But it's Ann. Not my real name but the one I went under in L.A. That's still good enough. I'm used to it."

"Gentle Annie," Tiger said.

"What's that mean?" I asked.

"Gentle Annie. Something my mother used to say in place of swear words when I was a kid."

"Well, Gentle Annie," I said to her, "I figure about now I speak for Tiger and me. Ain't nothing out of the ordinary going to happen, but we'll take you on to our place for tonight. We'll get you back to the road here in the morning. We ain't got much but for now what we got is yours."

"I accept with gratitude, kind sir," she said with a Shakespearian theatrical tone. "He's Tiger. What's your handle?"

"Ten High. I've got another name, too. For now Ten High's good enough."

"Tell her, Ten. Tell her how you got your name!"

I tried to affect a Shakespearian theatrical tone. "I'll fight any ten men in the Tenth Battalion at ten o'clock tonight for ten quarts of Ten High and a ten-dollar bill!"

"He was drunk as a Lord one night when a gang of us lived at a place called Ballarat—ghost town—up around the Panamint Mountains. I heard him say that and I hung the name Ten High on him," Tiger said.

I heard Gentle Annie's delightfully tinkly laughter again. "So how'd you get the name 'Tiger'?"

I spoke up. "He used to be quite the man with the ladies."

"Used to be," Tiger said, and let it go at that as he swung The Binder into the long, rolling ribbon of asphalt that was the way to Garlock and the road running over to Randsburg. Our place is about three miles this side of where the Randsburg road splits off, partway up on the slopes of the El Pasos.

"I've got a confession to make," she said. "Remember I was in the business for ten years. You didn't scare me back there. If you were to get pushy, I know ways to put both of you out of action. It's just that I didn't want to have to do it in a car. A girl stands to get herself killed that way."

"Well then, you ain't got a lot to worry about," Tiger said dryly. "Pain and me ain't on the best of terms."

We built a fire in the stove when we got home and fixed her something to eat. We brewed up some coffee and added a dollop of Ten High in our cups and sat up the rest of the night talking. At daylight, we put Gentle Annie up in Tiger's room. I let Tiger have my bed because of his bursitis. I pumped up an old air mattress, and with what blankets there were left over, I had myself a pretty good day's sleep. We talked a lot more that next evening before it was too late to drop Annie off up at the highway.

We took her up to the Red Rooster the next day, figuring we didn't have too many worries about her as a claim jumper; even let her peck out some rocks with a few flakes of color in them. She got quite a kick out of it.

"Red Rooster?" she asked. "You guys sure come up with some quaint names. How'd you come by that one?"

I sang from "She'll Be Comin' 'Round the Mountain": "We'll kill the old red rooster when she comes . . ."

Gentle Annie's openness surfaced again. "I guess I did quite a lot of that in my time."

"How's that?" Tiger asked.

"Killed a few red roosters."

Tiger and I looked at each other with raised eyebrows; we'd caught her drift.

"Only when I got through with them, they had the reverse of rigor mortis," she added with kind of a philosophical tone. Tiger and I stayed silent. "It wasn't really all that bad a life, in spite of what the sob-sisters and the do-gooders try to make it out to be. You learn how to handle the pushy ones and the sadists. After what I've been through I believe that, if it came to a knock-down-drag-out, I could hold my own with any man. On the other hand, you get to meet some really nice people who treat you right, feed you in swell places, take you to shows once in a while, things like that. Been to Vegas any number of times, never gambled, but always came home money ahead. About all that's missing is that you don't have much of a place to anchor your emotions, your true feelings. To get over that one, you've got to get yourself strong—no, tough —inside. If you don't, you're dead. That's what's been so nice about getting to know you two characters. You've let me be myself. No passes. And I'm here to tell you, I appreciate it."

Tiger and I looked at each other. In a lot of ways, she was also talking about him and me when it came to our feelings toward our "fellow man." At that moment, she became one of us; cut from the same leather. We both knew that, as long as Annie wanted to stay with us, she'd have a place. In our shack, and in our hearts.

The next day we three went over to Randsburg and had a few

drinks and a couple of hilarious games of three-way rotation on the beat-up pool table at "The Joint." We also took in the little Kern County Museum about Randsburg across the alley from "The Joint." Gentle Annie appeared to enjoy every minute of her visit and soaked up the information like a sponge.

Another day, we rode into Ridgecrest and got a cheap cut of meat and some beef heart and chili fixin's. Back at the shack, Gentle Annie used my old dutch oven to whomp up one of the finest chilis I ever sat down to. Lord, that woman can cook!

Annie stayed on and did everything she could to justify her keep.

Next thing we knew, a month had gone by and Tiger and I were low on funds again. We made another hike up to the Red Rooster for some serious pecking. In the morning, we all rode in The Binder to Bakersfield.

When we left old Sam Tolliver's place—the guy we have our gold dealings with—we drove Annie over to one of the better thrift stores and turned her loose with fifteen bucks. While Tiger and I had a couple of ditchwater highballs in a place across the street, she managed to fill up two grocery sacks with the kind of duds she'd need for the desert or the road, and a few things to get herself dolled up once in a while.

Both of us got a peck on the cheek by way of gratitude. Tiger and I registered proper embarrassment over her show of affection. Naturally we stopped off at Reno's on the way back for a couple more bourbons-and-branchwater before wrapping ourselves around heaping portions of our beloved steak and eggs.

Over the next few days, we got to playing Hearts with an old deck Tiger had in his duffle. When we got tired of cards, we sat around relaxing and philosophized and talked about our views about God and the Congress into the early hours. Annie took over most of the cooking and tidied up a bit here and there, but not so much as to get on the nerves of two old jaspers who didn't care much about having things too fancy.

We got to accepting her as part of our routine and she made no moves about leaving. Tiger and I were just as happy with her being around and becoming damned important to our lives.

I got to thinking how rough it was going to be again when Annie decided she had to go. I knew I would miss her—to beat hell. With three mouths to feed now, our gold takes and our pension checks didn't go as far as before. Our hikes up to the Red

Rooster and cranking up The Binder—its windows specked with bug guts and smelling inside of crankcase oil—for the Bakersfield run became more frequent.

Tiger and I didn't care; the woman had brought a new dimension and a fresh attitude and new outlooks to our lives. We were content to have her stay as long as that was what made her happy. Spring in the desert had burst forth in all its glory when we hit the big strike at the Red Rooster. Rather Gentle Annie hit the big strike. We'd gotten her a pick-hammer in Bakersfield and that day she was far up at the head end of the wash bank filling her little blue haversack with chunks of rock that showed plenty of good color.

It had rained pretty heavy—a common spring occurrence in the desert—for about three days and we'd stayed inside with the stove glowing and playing cards and drinking our coffee laced with Ten High. All that rain had loosened the crumbly rock along the bank. When we pecked out promising chunks of fractured granite, a lot of stuff around it would shear off and tumble to our feet.

Tiger and I worked midway along the bank. We heard Gentle Annie scream and we looked quick to see a big chunk of the bank —about a wheelbarrow load—break loose and cascade around her. Still shrieking in surprise, she jumped back and narrowly missed being hit by the slide.

She fell and Tiger and I sprinted to help her. She was sitting up when we got there, staring at the bank like she was in a trance. I thought maybe she'd got walloped in the head. "You okay, Annie?" I yelled.

She just sat there, eyes upturned at the bank above her. "Yeah. Yeah. I'm all right. But, Sweet Jesus, would you look at that!"

Tiger and I tore our eyes from her to the bank and what held her attention; the slide had exposed a vein of almost pure gold running several yards long and a half to three-quarters of an inch thick and imbedded in the crumbly granite probably deeper than we could imagine. It was the strike I had a hunch was there all along. It looked like we could liberate chunks worth tens of thousands. My breath jammed in my throat. That pure gold would come out of there like slabs of peanut brittle.

Tiger and I stared at the rich strike, incapable of words. Tiger looked at me, and from that look, I knew his words before he said them. "We got to talk this over." You could build a lot of meanings into the way he said it.

"We're rich, Tiger!" I yelled. "Look at that! That's just the start! That vein probably goes back into that hill to where hell wouldn't have it." It seemed to be the thickest where it disappeared into the hillside.

"We got to talk this over," Tiger repeated, now with more emphasis. "Down at the camp."

"We can't leave it just like that, Tiger, all open and everything! What if somebody comes by? We'll be shit out of luck."

"Who's going to come by here, Ten? The only easy way in here is past our shack. Last Chance Canyon is miles west with the old road washed out, and the Mesquite Canyon road is about as far the other way. Nobody's going to come up here, Ten."

Annie stood by and listened, favoring one leg as she looked at the fabulous vein. "Think I pulled something," she said. "Like a cramp. I'll be all right. Don't you fellas have a claim or something on this?"

"Annie," Tiger said. "Ten and me don't own title to doodly-squat. We're just occupying our shack till somebody comes along with the right papers and tells us to get the hell out."

"Can't you file a claim?"

"Could," Tiger said, "but Ten and me figure we had enough of that bureaucracy bullshit. Let's get on down the hill. This stuff'll keep."

We were silent on the hike down, each busy with his own thoughts. You'd have thought we'd be screaming and shouting and running in circles. But there was more at stake here than just gold, an undercurrent of pretty serious things to think about, something Tiger and I hadn't done much of in recent times.

Tiger didn't speak again until we were back in the shack. "Annie, brew us up a pot of coffee. Ten, break out your bottle. Let's loosen up a little. I'm tighter than a violin string."

I could easily see why Tiger was discharged as a master sergeant and I never made it past buck sergeant; he knew how to take command. When the coffee was ready, he poured a stiff dollop of booze into his and downed it pretty fast and went to the stove for a refill. On the way back to his chair, he laced it stout with Ten High.

"Okay, folks," he said. "Let's lay it out. All the cards face up. Annie, this afternoon you went from being a guest in this place to full partner. You've got a say in this now, just as much as Ten and I have."

"But I don't—" she started.

"Put a lid on it, sister," Tiger said with emphasis. "Your say is asked, and it's needed. You been around long enough now. Like us, you been over life's road. Your vote counts."

"What's to vote on?" I asked. I was never gifted with seeing the forest for the trees.

Tiger's look bore straight into me. "You ready to turn your life around, Ten? You got any idea what's involved?"

"All I know is we're rich!"

"Think past the end of your nose, friend. With this stuff, there'll be no more pussyfootin' around with Sam Tolliver. We've hit the big time, and from here on out, we'll deal with the big guys by ourselves. Besides, old Tolliver's mixed up in a lot more sleazy stuff that just laundering our ill-gotten gains. All this could get a little sticky trying to deal with Sam Tolliver."

"Damned if you don't talk like a college perfesser, Tiger," I said.

"Okay. Let's look at both sides of the coin. One side is all bright and shiny; what we see right now, today, after Annie's discovery. The other side is darkened and dull; that represents the days ahead."

Gentle Annie intruded. "I don't see anything dark, Tiger. With what you've probably got up there, you and Ten could buy your own mountain to live on."

"We," Tiger said, emphasizing that she was part of the action. "I don't deny that, Annie. That might be part of the bright side. Again, it might be the dark side. But for now, leave it on the bright side. Money to do about what we please."

"What do you think it's worth, Tiger?" Annie asked.

"Who can say? But for figuring purposes, let's say we file a claim and then take the easy route and get an assay and get some engineers or geologists up here to look at it. Then let's say we offer the claim for sale and after everybody takes his cut—and there'll be a dozen or so show up with proper papers and their hands out—we clear a half million. I'm only guessing at that. I got no real idea what's at stake here."

Annie gasped. "That's a lot of money. Almost scary."

"Yeah. Scary for certain," Tiger went on. "I guess that's what I'm getting at. That's about all that's left on the bright side. Oh, you could do a lot of thinking about how and where to spend it. Me and Ten buy that mountain you talked about, Annie, and go live on it. You could take your share and go back to Omaha with your head high and open your own gawdam theater, to hell with the Crazy Charlies of this world."

"But I don't deserve—" she started.

Again Tiger cut her short. "We're just talkin' here. Speculatin'. But about a hundred and seventy thousand apiece sure begins to sound good in this place." Tiger looked wistfully around at our digs.

"Sounds mighty good, Tiger," I said.

Tiger looked at both of us a long time, thinking. "Yeah," he said finally. "But how is it going to change us? A couple of booze-ridden, broken-down old bums and a has-been whore!"

The shock of Tiger's outburst spread around us like a sullen gray cloud. Annie and I looked at each other with our mouths open; there was no denying in the looks that passed between us that we both knew that Tiger spoke the truth.

Before anybody said anything, Tiger got up and refilled his cup and went for his splash of Ten High to reinforce it. He came back and sat down. "I'm sorry," he said. "Didn't mean that to sound unkindly. It just struck me up there on the hill that we got to face facts, who we are, and what that stuff up there will make of us. By civilized standards we're losers, society's rubbish, all three of us."

Annie and I let him ramble; didn't say a word.

"If we go ahead and try to make something of that find, we'll have to start dealing with the big shots, get thick with the government, go through lots of red-tape bullshit, filling out forms, going for interviews. We'll have to hire accountants and high-priced attorneys and financial consultants and all such as that. In the process —and mark my words—it'll destroy who we are and what we've got here." He tapped his chest. "In our hearts and in our heads. In this shack, between us, together. Us three. That's what will be destroyed. How long do you think it would be before we'd be at one another's throats?"

"Never," I said.

"Come on, Ten. Grow up. Put it this way: Are you willing to stake your third of the Red Rooster against the chance that six months from now we won't be speaking to each other? I wouldn't."

"Since you put it that way, Tiger," I said, "I see why you said what you said up at the Red Rooster. You saw it clearer than me or Annie."

"What's that?"

"That we had to talk about it. You saw the reality right away."

"Yeah," Tiger said, watching my eyes. "Let me ask you something, Ten."

"Uh-huh."

"These last eleven, twelve years. Most of that time we've been pardners. Haven't they been rich enough for you? They sure as hell have been for me. Like you told Annie the night we drove her out from Mojave. We don't want for much."

Annie piped up. "And I don't really want to go back to Omaha —or anyplace else—with or without money." Somehow she was talking to Tiger. "You and Ten have been decent with me, even beyond decent. I've come to think of us as a little family. You've made me feel that way and to feel wanted. All my life, the only things about me anybody wanted was my body and my twat. But not you guys. As long as you want me, I'll stay. When I've worn out my welcome, well, I'll be on my way . . . and happily. And I hope you'll both be man enough to tell me when."

"That'll never happen, Annie," I assured her. "I guess it's time for a vote. Me, I don't want any more gawdam gold than we're able to pick out of the hillside up there like before and pass along to Sam Tolliver. The way we've been doing all along. I don't want to change a thing."

"Annie?" Tiger asked.

"I already spoke my piece. I vote with Ten."

"Agreed," Tiger said. "I got an idea what we can do. We'll take enough of the gold to hammer out some little lumps that we can put on chains to wear around our necks. That'll always remind us of this day and our decision. And what we mean to each other. Be our talismans. And that way we'll none of us ever be totally broke again."

Annie laughed that delightfully tinkly laugh. "You sure know how to put things in their proper perspective, Tiger."

Tiger went on with his thoughts. "We'll set a dynamite charge in the hill above that vein. That should drop enough real estate over it to hide it for good and all. We'll always know that it's there, but tough as hell to get at and go on as though it wasn't there. Agreed?"

"Agreed," I said.

Annie looked at both of us. "Uh-huh," she said without a shred of regret or reluctance in her tone.

Tiger straightened in his chair. "Annie, we need something to eat. But I'm going to have another of Ten's 'coffee royales' to celebrate three people, including my two best friends in this world, coming to their senses."

He walked over to the coffeepot, still spouting a little vapor on the stove.

"I like cooking for you two birds," Annie said happily, heading for the stove behind him. "Even though you ain't got a pot to piss in."

Tiger stepped back with his filled cup, looked at the two of us and grinned. "Gentle Annie," he said. "God love ya."

"Who's for a game of Hearts after supper?" I asked, getting up to root around for the cards. As I did, something deep inside made me want to whistle. It came out as the tune of "She'll Be Comin' 'Round the Mountain." Annie started to sing as she banged around with the pots and pans. Tiger and I joined in.

". . . We'll kill the old red rooster when she comes; oh, we'll kill the old red rooster when she comes; yes, we'll kill the old red rooster; we will kill the old red rooster; we will kill the old red rooster when she comes!"

Suddenly Annie stopped and Tiger and I stopped too.

"Great idea," she said. "What say on Sunday I whomp us up a big mess of chicken and dumplings?"

"Now I vote in favor of that one," Tiger said.

"Me, too," I said. "Like everything around here, it's unanimous. Tiger, is there any of that coffee left? Tomorrow, we'd better crank up The Binder and hike over to Ridgecrest and get us a fresh jug of Ten High!"

From Our Special Correspondent

Dale L. Walker

[New York Herald, July 4, 1877]:

IN CAMP, ABOVE THE LITTLE BIG HORN RIVER, MONTANA TERR.

—One year and nine days have passed since Lt. Col. G. A. Custer and over 200 officers and men of the Seventh U.S. Cavalry perished here and the artifacts of that appalling fight are still everywhere in evidence.

I arrived here yesterday with Capt. Michael V. Sheridan, U.S.A., commanding a detail of soldiers, Crow and Arikara scouts, civilian guides, and teamsters with four ox-wagons. My party journeyed from Bismarck, Dakota Terr., on the steamer *John Fletcher* to Cantonment Tongue River and thence to the mouth of the Little Big Horn River. There we rendezvoused on 28 June with Company I, Seventh Cavalry, consisting of eighty-eight men and two officers (Capt. Nowlan and Lt. Scott), which had traveled overland from Bismarck.

During our bivouac at the mouth of the Little Big Horn on the 29th, a dozen pine coffins were knocked together by a civilian carpenter in Capt. Nowlan's party and placed on the ox-wagons.

The mission of this forlorn force is to reclaim the remains of Col. Custer and the fifteen other officers who fell here.

□ □ □ □

LONDON DAILY NEWS, JULY 14, 1879

IN CAMP, FIELD OF ISANDHLWANA, ZULULAND

—It was the Portuguese under Bartholomew Diaz who sailed around Cape Horn in February, 1488, landing at Mossel Bay to fill their water casks, who first encountered the black denizens of this savage country. When the Hottentots showered the white interlopers with stones, Diaz, or so legend has it, aimed a crossbow and drove a shaft through the heart of the nearest native.

No doubt it is too much to say, but to one schooled in history, and steeped in the ironies of history, that first white incursion in South Africa may be said to have come full circle here on this brutal and eerie field where we have now come to pick among the bones.

On this rock-strewn plain on 22 January last, a mere six months save thirteen days ago, a Zulu "impi," a fighting force of perhaps 20,000 warriors, poured across the veldt from their kraals around Ulundi in a pitiless black tidal wave and onto this camp beneath the shadow of an ugly spur of the Nqutu range called Isandhlwana. By mid-day Europe had paid fifteen hundred-fold for Diaz's quarrel four centuries ago. King Cetshwayo's Zulus, armed only with spears and clubs, annihilated fifty-eight British officers, eight hundred British soldiers and an estimated six hundred native levies.

Six companies of an illustrious British regiment, the 24th Foot, died here, and at least a thousand Zulus, a free people who the British High Commissioner of South Africa said were little more than "drunkards and wild beasts," and whose presence in their own lands was termed "an incubus" to imperial designs, died here.

CAMP, LITTLE BIG HORN RIVER, JULY 4

. . . When Col. Custer and five companies of the Seventh U.S. Cavalry died here last summer, this valley was a vast carpet of dust. So says Tom LeForge, one of Capt. Nowlan's scouts, who has visited this field several times. Now the noisome breath of death, which a Sioux warrior named Pretty Shield said endured the whole of last summer, has dissipated, replaced by the glorious perfume of wild flowers and the sweet scent of grass, which is as high as our stirrups as we pick our way from one cairn of bones to another.

God's creatures and His elements have done their work. In a year of wind, rain and snow, the vultures, ravens and wolves have come foraging, gnawing the human and horse remains, and even the identifying stakes on the pitiful graves scratched in this sanguinary hillside by Capt. Frederick Benteen's men.

There is too little remaining here to really depict this unthinkable debacle. Most of the horror of it, in any event, has been reported in the months since it occurred from testimony of those in Col. John Gibbon's Montana Column (who relieved Capt. Marcus Reno's surviving force), and from the members of Capt. Benteen's detachment who, on 27 June last year, were the first to see this place after the battle.

We know that the corpse of Col. Custer was not mutilated. We know that Capt. Tom Custer had to be identified by a tattoo on his arm: his head was smashed flat to the ground by the war clubs of the Red savages; he was scalped and disemboweled. We know that Mark Kellogg, correspondent of the Bismarck Tribune and New York Herald, a colleague I never met, was scalped and his ears cut off. His oilskin satchel, found later among the abandoned Indian lodges, contained but a pathetic diary, a sack of tobacco and a shirt. We know there were atrocities that begger description: all the wounded were killed and all the dead were stripped of their clothing. There were beheadings, limbs hacked off, disembowelings, blindings, scalpings, and other, unspeakable, mutilations.

The Indian attacking force, said to number upwards of three thousand warriors, killed all the horses save one, Capt. Keogh's buckskin, which was found with many wounds wandering the battlefield, and in their frenzy even punched holes with their axes and knives in all the tinware, ration and supply boxes that were strewn about the field, by then a vile porridge of dirt, blood, human and horse intestines.

All this and a multitude of other details we know as this fatigue detail, in which I am assisting under a remorseless Montana sun, works to rebury the enlisted dead and to collect what remains of the officers who died here.

CAMP, FIELD OF ISANDHLWANA, ZULULAND, JULY 14

. . . Every living thing here was killed: oxen, horses, mules, even pet dogs. Officers and men, and two drummer boys (who were hung by their chins on butcher's hooks), died hideously. They died singly, in clumps of two or three, in last-stand groups of fifty and more trying feebly to form the square, and a few died as far as two miles distant from the camp proper. They died largely in the open, but some died in their tents and in or under the waggons. They died when they ran out of bullets, died with hunting knives clasped in their fists, died shoulder-to-shoulder and back-to-back. They were stabbed to death by Zulu assegais, those short-hafted spears with an iron head honed and pointed to razor sharpness, then were cut open from sternum to groin, their bowels spilled on the ground. They were scalped, their noses, lower jaws, and private parts excised. Some were beheaded. They were stripped of their clothing, their red tunics an especial prize, it seems. The camp was looted and everything not carried off was punctured by assegai, including small tins of meat and sardines.

At least a thousand Zulus fell here, victims of the Martini-Henry rifle and its long bayonet, but there are few Zulu remains to count as most of the black corpses were carried off by their comrades, the wounded as well.

King Cetshwayo's nation of warriors has now, of course, been destroyed, his kraal and all the others in the vicinity of it burned to the ground. The King himself has fled to the north and his capture is imminent.

There will be mass graves dug here at the camp of Isandhlwana to cover over this dreadful massacre and in a few years all that will remain will be a scattering of stone cairns, each doubtlessly decorated with a bronze plaque presented in Her Majesty's name, markers which will fail utterly to say what happened here on 22 January last.

CAMP, LITTLE BIG HORN RIVER, JULY 4

. . . What happened here? How came this stupefying defeat of our Arms? Even crediting the highest estimate of three thousand Red savages, and their undoubted collective courage, how could this rabble, armed with bows and arrows, war clubs and a miscellany of old, stolen weapons, which they knew not how to use, defeat and kill to a man over two hundred of one of the keenest, best-trained fighting forces in the civilized world, a force armed with, and skilled in the use of, the Springfield breech-loader, the finest and deadliest weapon of the day?

The essentials of the making of this massacre are by now generally known though they will be debated for many years to come. Col. Custer's advent into this valley was but an extension of the Army's policy, since the close of the late War, to wage unceasing war against the recalcitrant Sioux Nation and its neighboring and like-minded tribes. It is known that Col. Custer's command of twelve companies of the Seventh U.S. Cavalry, something over six hundred officers and men in all, together with a contingent of Indian scouts, marched off from the mouth of the Rosebud on 22 June. It is known that Col. Custer refused the offer of an additional battalion of the Second Cavalry, and also the offer of three Gatling guns. (These, he said, would impede his progress over the rough terrain between the Rosebud and the Little Big Horn.) It is known that Col. Custer and his command arrived here on 25 June after a grueling four days' march.

It is also known that Col. Custer defied a principle of war by dividing his command. He sent Capts. Benteen and Reno out with three companies each; left Capt. McDougall with over a hundred men in care of the pack train in the rear; and himself, with about two hundred men, occupied this bald and untenable position.

CAMP, FIELD OF ISANDHLWANA, ZULULAND, JULY 14

. . . The officers and men killed here were part of what is being called Lt. Gen. Lord Chelmsford's "middle invasion force," which means there was another force to the north and another to the south, a three-pronged invasion, as it were, of Zululand. The middle force crossed the Buffalo River at Rorke's Drift on 11 January and, it being the rainy season, bogged down its supply train, getting no further than Isandhlwana, ten miles to the west of Rorke's Drift, on 22 January, in its march toward Ulundi.

There is a maxim of the great scourge of Europe, Napoleon I, fully seconded by his nemesis, our immortal Duke of Wellington, which says, "Nothing is so important in war as an undivided com-

mand." This tenet, a truth never assailed by any thinking com-
mander in war, somehow escaped the notice of Lord Chelmsford in
the preparations for this ill-fated expedition into this Godforsaken
land. He not only split his command into three at the outset, but,
taking command of the doomed "middle invasion column," split
even that, on 22 January, by taking a sizable force away from
Isandhlwana on reconnaissance, leaving behind only six hundred
Imperial troops, reinforced by a contingent under command of Col.
Anthony Durnford. That gallant officer's brutalized corpse is
among those many being buried here today.

CAMP, LITTLE BIG HORN RIVER, JULY 4

. . . It might be said, perhaps ought to be said, that this blood-
soaked ground is a dividend collected by our Red Brethren for the
infamous Treaty of 1868 at Fort Laramie in which our White
Brethren consigned to the Sioux the Black Hills "for as long as the
grass was green and the sky was blue." This field of death might
also be thought of as a second Red response to the late Capt.
William T. Fetterman of the Eighteenth U.S. Cavalry who liked to
boast that he could "take eighty men and ride through the whole
Sioux Nation." The first answer to the valiant but wrongheaded
Capt. Fetterman was delivered eleven years ago, on 21 December, if
memory serves, when he and eighty of his men were killed by the
Sioux at Fort Kearney.

And, of course, some have already viewed this abbatoir of a
battlefield as a demonstration of the veracity of what Col. Custer
wrote in his book just three short years ago. In that extraordinary
work, Col. Custer expressed his belief that the Indian must give
way to "civilizing influence" but that they would not do this on
their own accord and would have to be forced by a "stern, arbitrary
power." And in his book, Col. Custer "stripped the beautiful ro-
mance" from the Indians of Fenimore Cooper's novels and said the
Red Man is anything but noble; is, in fact, "a savage in every sense
of the word . . . one whose cruel and ferocious nature far exceeds
that of any wild beast of the desert."

CAMP, FIELD OF ISANDHLWANA, ZULULAND, JULY 14

. . . The astounding debacle that occurred here on 22 January last is already being called "Durnford's Disaster," a calumny against a courageous officer with a splendid record of fighting in the Kaffir wars. If blame is to be apportioned, let a fair share be assigned to the High Commissioner, Sir Bartle Frere, whose misjudgment of the strength and resolve of the Zulu army infected all who came to fight it, Lord Chelmsford chief among them. It was the High Commissioner who assured all and sundry that the Zulus were scarcely more than drunkards and wild beasts who, "once cowed would not rally." It was the High Commissioner who viewed English suzerainty over Zululand as the only answer to the "black threats and resistence" these people allegedly posed to Natal and its neighbors.

The Zulus have faced white encroachment in their land since the 1830s when the first Boers trekked here from Cape Colony. The Boers, no friends of England or its Empire, have great respect for the might and resolve, if not for the territory, of their Zulu antagonists and tried to warn the British commanders that a march into Zululand would be no promenade.

If what happened here in the shadow of Isandhlwana is Durnford's Disaster, it is in equal parts Chelmsford's Catastrophe, and Frere's Folly.

CAMP, LITTLE BIG HORN RIVER, JULY 4

. . . Our work here is nearly done and we will soon be moving on to Capt. Reno's battle ground to exhume the remains buried there, and after that will return to the mouth of the Little Big Horn to rendezvous with the *John Fletcher* to remove these pathetic pine boxes and their grisly contents to places more convenient, if less hallowed, than this ground.

Here, as the day closes, I can almost hear the notes of the "Gary Owen," that merry yet melancholy, sad yet triumphant, old Irish drinking song which the Seventh played on the march and claimed as its own. And, I'm wondering if we will remember this place, two years, a decade, a hundred years and more from now, and, if we do remember it, how we will remember it.

Will we remember this place and what happened here as, to date at least, the only complete extermination of a United States military force in the field of battle? Or will we remember it as Col. Custer's Massacre, an unfortunate, minor and momentary embarrassment in the spectacle of the white American's eternal efforts to "civilize" his non-white, and therefore savage, brothers?

Or will we ask ourselves what we were doing here? Will we remember this place for the lessons it teaches about that march of civilization if we will only read the bones that are strewn in the line of march?

CAMP, FIELD OF ISANDHLWANA, ZULULAND, JULY 14

. . . History will no doubt place Isandhlwana beside such inglorious incidents of our glorious military past as the tragic retreat from Afghanistan in 1842, and the splendid blunder that cost our Light Brigade at Balaklava in the Crimea. But Isandhlwana is more than these. The Afghan catastrophe was not a battle but a slaughter, in the main, of civilian innocents, and Balaklava would never have found a paragraph in history were it not for Lord Tennyson's bombastic poem.

Isandhlwana is much more than these. This field ought to give all of England pause, from Our Gracious Majesty down to the lowliest subject in our far-flung Empire.

But Englishmen have a short memory, I fear. Who today remembers such bloody fields of our own century as Ciudad Rodrigo, Badajoz, and Salamanca in Spain; Mudki, Aliwal, Delhi, and Lucknow in India; the Alma, Inkermann, and Sebastopol, in the Crimea?

Who will remember this pathetic battleground?

If Isandhlwana is remembered at all a decade or century from now, I hope the future historians of our Empire will remember it by answering this simple question: Why were we here?

The Wedding Dress

Win Blevins

HE CAME the day after the Nariya dance. Running Water was ready. Excited. She could hardly keep a decent demeanor. She kept wanting to look straight into his eyes, or even touch him.

Since she first saw Morgan, she had hoped for today.

He gave her father six good horses, which was a splendid gift for a second daughter. All her life she'd expected to end up married to Horn, her sister's husband, in the manner of her Shoshone people. That would have been all right, she guessed. That was until she saw Morgan and her thoughts said what her heart felt.

The world was changing. The old way was good. On it the people prospered, and she revered it. But there was new way now, since the Tibos, the white people, came. Your rabbit might run a different path, she thought.

The Shoshones told a story. When you were born, the spirit of a rabbit came ahead of you and took off running. It ran some particular path on the earth, a path you would never know. But whatever path it ran, you would follow that.

Her grandmother had told her the rabbit path might twist and turn crazily, might double back on itself, might seem to make no sense, but you must follow it. It's your path. Even if you didn't want to, her grandmother said, even if you rebelled against the path, you would follow it.

Because of the Tibos, Running Water thought, the rabbit might run new paths now.

When her grandmother was young, the people had never seen a white man. Just before her mother was born, the fur trappers built Fort Wyeth, right in the middle of their homeland. In another ten winters the Mormons came and thousands of them built houses down by the big salty water. Another fifteen winters and the whites built a road straight through her people's country and all the way to the gold mines in the faraway place called Montana. You could trade for white-man things, pots and knives and guns and cloth, at trading posts right on that road.

Things were changing, and something in her dreams, she couldn't have said what, said she must change with them. Not change everything. She might learn about God and wear a cross, but remember what the blackrobes said to forget, Duma Apa, and the people's dances and prayers. She might learn to live in a cabin but not prefer it. She might start sitting in chairs. According to her sisters, she would have to learn to let Morgan act improperly with her. White men acted nasty when it came to sex, Shoshone women said. Sometimes they giggled about it, and sometimes they were serious. Either way, Running Water would have to get used to it.

Morgan instead of her sister's husband—that was the commitment to the new way, maybe her rabbit ran that way. It was what her heart wanted, if that was a clue. A new path.

Morgan did more than she hoped for, took her straight to the mission and made their marriage official, as he called it, in the eyes of the Tibo. The blackrobe said the sacred words and wrote their names in the book. Morgan Roberts Morgan (she found out then he had these three names) said that made them really married. She knew that Tibos often took Shoshone women and later abandoned them. None she knew of had made the marriage "official."

When the blackrobe was finished with the words, Morgan did something incredible. He took out a piece of *nappaus,* one of the gold pieces the Tibos were so crazy about, one hammered into a ring. He put it on the fourth finger of her left hand and said it made them really married.

She blinked back the tears. Now she was sure.

She asked the blackrobe to write her name in his book as Marian, the name Morgan called her. Her people's name for her was Running Water, but Marian was special to him, his grandmother's name, and now it was special to her.

Yes, this was the path her rabbit ran.

□ □ □ □

Morgan Roberts Morgan could have conked himself for what he let
happen next.

He could see the real marriage ceremony thrilled her, and the
ring. Her feeling touched his old heart. (He was twenty-nine, but
had been in the mountains ten years, and so was known to com-
padres as "old Morgan.") Then they went down the Tibo road to
Anderson Station to pick up the other horses he'd traded for, and
his mail. Marian thought the mail was peculiar, all those books and
magazines, but she said naught but to ask if there were letters from
Wales. He told her kindly that there would be no letters ever from
Wales. He had no family over there anymore, only memories of the
slate quarries he never wanted to see again, and he would never
ever go back. He saw on her face that she thought that was terrible,
and determined to make it up to him.

Cor, but that was as he wanted it. When he first laid eyes on this
girl, he fancied her, he did. Said to himself that very day in his
native Welsh, *"Dwi am Broidi'r eneth ma cwtches."* I'm going to
marry that girl and have love and hugs and such like.

He wondered if her mind was on giving him the relatives he
didn't have, her entire family. He wasn't so keen on that part of it.
He'd run across an ocean and a continent to get away from relatives.

While he wasn't paying attention, Mrs. Anderson spoiled things.
She showed Marian her wedding dress.

The Andersons were Mormons. Morgan brought Marian here to
trade because Mormons treated Indians decently. For some reason
Mrs. Anderson couldn't stick to flour and boots (neither of which
would impress Marian a bit) or the wood stove that warmed the
cabin and you could even cook on the top of it. All the grand stuff
that came up the Salt Lake road headed for the Montana mining
camps.

Morgan was proud of himself. He'd trapped enough fur over the
winter not only to trade for horses for her father, but another,
bigger string of horses, and all this flour and bacon and coffee and
sugar and blankets and tobacco, enough to make Marian think she
was marrying a rich man.

When Mrs. Anderson put her foot into it by mentioning the
wedding dress, Marian begged to see it. Mrs. Anderson got it out of
a box. She herself had gotten married in it five years ago, she

explained. It was boughten goods, she said, from a catalog, and wasn't it a beauty? She showed Marian the bodice, which was beaded with seed pearls. The skirts were full, very full, and resplendent—the material was satin, said Mrs. Anderson. "See, the sleeves are belled," meaning tight on the arms with huge puffs around the shoulders. "And look at this lace!" Even Morgan had to admit the color was fine, what Mrs. Anderson called "candlelight," creamy, the color of a gorgeously tanned sheepskin with a special luster.

Marian was big-eyed as if she'd been struck by lightning. Morgan watched the changes in her face, and the thoughts behind them. She'd never seen anything so beautiful in her whole life. They were buying so much . . . She didn't dare ask . . . But they were so rich . . . Well, it was her wedding day.

But Morgan, still thinking like a white man, was taken blind side by what she said next. "Morgan, will you buy me this wedding dress?"

Cor, she would ask, for wasn't it her wedding day? She didn't know the offense.

"Oh!" cried Mrs. Anderson, and turned away to hide her face.

Morgan knew what would be on the face, that expression of a respectable white woman when the way you acted was just too, too sodding awful. Marian knew it too, from a different angle. Morgan saw the hot blood of humiliation rise in her, and she went outside so the white woman wouldn't see her embarrassment.

Morgan cursed himself and followed.

She felt drenched in shame. She'd resolved to learn the Tibo way, as she'd been learning the Tibo language, and make a good Tibo life for Morgan. On her very wedding day she'd made a blunder.

The worst of it was, she still yearned for the wedding dress. She had to bite back words. Why couldn't she have it?

They left the trading post in a hurry, which was the way Tibos behaved when they were embarrassed, to run away, and started home. As they rode east, the three Tetons in front of them for pilot knobs, her husband patiently explained her mistake. It was not for sale. It was Mrs. Anderson's wedding dress, and you never wore it but once, that was the rule, or maybe a second time to celebrate being married twenty-five winters, or maybe you gave it to your daughter to get married in. It would be bad medicine, he said, terrible medicine, he said, to sell it.

Besides, Marian couldn't wear it anymore. The wedding ceremony was over. If only Morgan had known, he would have bought her a wedding dress for the ceremony, but . . .

Her poor husband looked truly distraught.

Marian told herself she would make many mistakes following this new Tibo way, and she would just have to be forgiving of herself and others until she understood better how to act. But she didn't feel that way. Her blood was thick with shame, and she wanted to get back at Mrs. Anderson. She forced herself to tell Morgan it was fine, she didn't need a wedding dress, she was excited with all the wonderful *things* they had (half of which she couldn't guess the use of), and she was really looking forward to getting to her new home.

She touched her new yellow-metal ring, rotated it gently on her finger. It was wonderful. Morgan was wonderful.

She couldn't help thinking, as they rode, that she could wear such a dress at the shuffling dance next summer, and the Nariya dance, and her sisters would ooh and ah over it.

That night she felt better. The cabin was good, their place good. She fixed up the cabin and made supper outside, while he was setting up the stove. They spent their first night in the blankets together on the wood floor, on the pallet of dry grass and buffalo hides, and she thought this husband was everything she wanted. She hoped she could please him, with his funny Tibo ways. He didn't seem nasty in the blankets to her. Just the opposite.

When Morgan first rode up to her village, four years ago, on a big American horse with his red hair and red beard flying (why were Tibos so hairy?), she had the strangest feeling of her life. It was like she knew him from that other world, the world where you went at night and the spirits came to you, and you knew things more deeply and truly than in the waking world. She watched him that day half-frightened, not knowing whether he was demon or angel.

All she knew, then or now, was that she washed with feelings for him, feelings powerful as the suck of a swift river. Last summer he began to court her, and she felt the true downhill-water-flowing force of her life.

Wherever these feelings took her, wherever this new rabbit path with Morgan went, she would gladly go.

Marian looked out the window at the blue shadows on the snow. The sun was almost gone and the wind was running through the coulees and rattling the cottonwood limbs and she was scared and she was lonely.

What she wanted was for Morgan to get home. Now.

She shivered, either from the cold or the lonesomeness, both terrible.

Home. Funny word in the English she was still learning. He had a strong feeling about home. He used that word a lot about this place. And home, or that feeling of his, home was part of the trouble.

So she thought sometimes.

Where was he?

She got up and threw two chunks of wood into the stove, but the heat wouldn't really help. The cabin wasn't well enough chinked, and the wind blew through the cracks between the logs. If you stood near the stove, you blistered on one side and froze on the other. If you didn't, you just froze.

The stove, the precious stove that he had freighted clear up from Salt Lake. It was a big deal to him, not only because it cost so many of the important dollars, but because it was her wedding present, as he called it, and because this thing *home* was a big deal.

Where was he? Why didn't he come to her?

She remembered his pride when he showed her the cabin he'd built, one room of stout cottonwood timbers. His pride in the wood stove, which you cooked on top of. But his real feeling, she could see, wasn't for the little structure there in the cottonwood bottom between the creek and the river. It was for what he called their place, the meadows along the creek bottom that had good grass, the little lake that drew winged creatures, the good water in the creek, and the beaver and fish there. Their place.

Place meant something different to Marian, something wider. She'd lived in this country all her seventeen years, most of them before the reservation. Her Shoshone people, whom the whites mistakenly called the Snakes, had lived on this land since before the memories of the grandfathers of the oldest grandfathers. She loved the four-leggeds, the rooteds, all the wingeds, all the swimmers—

all that lives, all the relatives of human beings. It was the same as loving the earth and life and yourself.

It was home, all of it. The people moved around the whole big place—up to the mountains, out onto the lava, over to the hot springs, down into the grassy, sheltered bottoms along the river, west to the falls. One place they got the best grass for the horses, another place beaver and otter skins, another salmon to eat, another good lodgepoles, another the camas. On the lava flow they trapped rockchucks to cook in a pit.

This man her new husband saw home differently. To him their place was this land you could walk around in less than a day, their home this cabin. A glory of a place, as he called it, yes. But small. And not the family's place, or the clan's, or the people's, but his personally, theirs personally.

She saw he loved it, and was glad. A Welshman from so far away, with a language and ways born of another place, come to her homeland and in love with it.

But it was a little strange to her, this cramped notion of home. At night, when he read to her out of all the books he had, especially that Shakespeare, she listened for that word "home" and tried to feel what it meant.

She hadn't told him on their wedding day that she didn't like the cabin. She'd heard that a cabin let in more winter wind than a lodge, and she could see it was darker. It was the wrong shape, for there was something in the circle of a lodge that was like the earth when a square wasn't. But mainly it didn't move. The cabin was stuck in one place, so you couldn't go to the camas easily, or out onto the lava to find the ice that stayed hidden in the caves all summer, or go high with the elk in the summer and low in the winter. She didn't tell him because she knew the cabin was home to him, and she had a special, heart-held feeling, itself like a dream.

Besides, she had to keep in mind, this was the new Tibo path.

He banged the door back hard and loud, without intending to. He dropped the armload of firewood behind the stove, and saw from her face that he had his dark look on. Again. Everything was sour, yes, he was truly making a cock of his marriage. He was in a fug about it.

Yes, she was lonely, yes, she was cold, yes, she missed her family. But what could he sodding do about it? Didn't she see?

In silence he took off his blanket coat and sat on a box. She dipped from the stew pot on the stove and handed him a full bowl, and some bread.

He traded for the horses because they could make a living from them. He'd guided that government outfit around the Jackson Hole country. He'd taken a dude party into the Yellowstone country, and they'd liked his work, he said. There would be more guiding in the future. Yellowstone was a sodding national park now, whatever that meant. Well, it meant lots of white folks would come to see it, and need his horses.

If they didn't lose the horses. Some of her people burned the nearby hills off in the fall, sod them, and he wouldn't have good grass for another spring or two. That burning made Morgan curse. It was a demon of a winter—deep snow, more than a month of unbroken cold, sharp winds. Here it was the beginning of March, and Marian said she couldn't remember a winter colder or with deeper snow.

Yes, sod all, he had to be out all day feeding the horses bark of the sweet cottonwood, or driving them a few miles away onto better grass, grass they could paw down to. When he moved the herd onto better graze, he would be gone for several days, even a week, yes. Couldn't she see?

The other day he saw fear on her face. She was afraid of his dark looks, he knew, afraid of her own husband.

She said the other night that at home, among her people, she would have her mother and aunts and sisters to talk to. They would have projects to do together—not only cooking but making winter moccasins, sewing blankets into warm coats and hats, making parfleches to store their belongings, beading and quilling special dresses for the dances next summer. While they worked, they would talk and laugh and be a family. But bugger all, wasn't this her home now? Wasn't he her family?

Maybe not. She wouldn't give herself to him in the blankets anymore. He knew the Shoshones thought whites were odd in bed. Maybe she was disgusted by him. Not that he had any peculiar tastes, but you never knew what she might not like. Why did she shut him out? It was driving him bedlam for a truth, not so much the lack of sex as the wondering.

And she kept talking about home, meaning the village near Fort

Wyeth. Home. Bloody hell, did anybody have a home anymore? Weren't they creating a home?

Maybe new paths were always scary, she told herself. Or maybe, if the new path meant being alone all the time, it wasn't for her.

"The Appaloosas are gone," he finally said. "North."

Meaning the two mares in foal. Meaning that their tracks went toward the hills, where the wind had blown some of the ridges nearly clear of snow and the animals had hope of grass. Meaning that he would go after them, for otherwise anyone might drop a rope on them, or they might wander farther away and simply disappear, or they would not find enough grass and would spend their spirit hunting for it and come spring Morgan would find the skeletons.

When he went after them, he might be gone for days and days.

She sat next to him and touched his hand. "Come to bed," she said. Bed where she could get him to hold her, where she could feel close to him.

She knew he wasn't so keen on bed anymore. She was pregnant, and she couldn't make love with him—decent people didn't do that. She wondered, and then decided even Tibos knew that. She'd told him plain as could be: I can't eat meat with fat for a while. She wouldn't mention it, act like she thought he was stupid. *Everybody* knew you didn't have sex when you were pregnant.

So he must know she was making life grow within. But he said nothing about it. Why not? Wasn't he glad?

Tibos were very strange. She would wait patiently.

And he was nasty about sex sometimes. Until she pushed him away one day, he actually touched her out of doors. Took her hand, touched her hip with his hand, even tried to touch her breasts.

When she pushed him away, he looked hurt and mumbled something about no one being within ten miles. She supposed that made some difference, and tried to make it up to him, but right out in the sun was still right out in the sun.

Also, once he wanted to make love with the candle lantern burning. Said he wanted to see her.

She wouldn't even giggle with her sisters about that. That was *too* nasty.

"Come to bed," she said again. She wanted his closeness.

"Got to get started before they get too far," he answered, and stood up.

She grabbed him and put her head on his chest. He was very tall, this man of her new path, and her head didn't come to his chin. She put her arms around him. Though she couldn't see his face, she knew he had a hard look, a faraway look, the look of a man who was fighting and losing and despised himself for it.

Before she thought the words, they were out. "Let me come with you." She heard the pathos in her own voice, but she went on, "I can help. Please let me come with you."

He held her a little away and looked into her eyes, at least he did that much, truly look at her, and she wondered what was inside his head. Then he turned off and said in a remote way, "I've got to move fast."

And with his blanket coat and gloves and wolfskin hat was out the door into the dark, howling night.

She didn't say a word, that would have been improper, but it hurt, hurt in a big lump behind her breastbone. She had offered to help, she wanted to help, she could help. She had said so and he hadn't answered. Instead he drove them farther apart, made them both more alone, he in the fierce weather, she in the blankets that were not as thick and warm as buffalo robes.

She touched her belly. Yes, the child sometime next summer. But would she still have a man? New path or old? Which way had her rabbit run?

Right now she would give anything for her mother, her sisters, her father and brothers and nephews and nieces, the warm lodge, the talk, the sense of family.

She went to bed and shivered. She was pretty sure these Tibos didn't know how to live.

In the middle of the night she heard it, the wind. She went to the door and looked out. It was whipping even here in the bottom by the creek. She looked up toward the ridges of the hills.

It was mad, she knew. She also knew she was going to do it. Quickly she got into Morgan's funny long underwear, an elkskin dress, knee leggings, winter moccasins, her blanket coat, and rabbit mittens. As an afterthought she took a blanket to wrap over her head and around her chest.

It was mad. Why was she going?

Out the door, into the driving wind. Its force took her breath away. It was like the current of a fast river—you didn't realize until you were in it. She leaned into the wind and started for the hills to the north. She would pick up his tracks on the way.

Probably she had in mind standing on top of the first hill, or the bigger one beyond, and saying a prayer for him. A moment of vigil, a wife's devotion.

It wasn't like that. As soon as she cleared the trees, she saw that his tracks were drifting in. Before long the blowing snow would fill them, and even the tracks she herself was leaving. As she rose above the creek bottom, the wind picked up. It arrowed at her, whipped, blustered, and slashed. It buffeted her, and near the top of the first hill it clubbed her. She staggered and turned her back. Though she shouldn't have been surprised, she gasped. And sucked in cold that hurt her chest.

This was a full-scale ground blizzard, howling, flinging ice crystals in your face, blinding you, whipping away your body's heat like driven leaves. She wondered if Morgan had a chance in this blizzard.

"Hear me, Father," she murmured softly in her own language— *Numee Nahgai Ook, Duma Apa.* She realized she hadn't heard her own voice. She said it again, *"Numee Nahgai Ook, Duma Apa,"* belting it out this time, almost in anger, not a way to speak to the spirits. Then she whispered, *"Numee shone deah,"* Have mercy on us.

She turned her back to the wind and ran down the hillside in big, clumsy steps, sinking to her knees on every step.

Halfway down she had a thought like an icicle shafting into her chest: She was running to her death. Or was it Morgan's death she felt inside?

She smothered the thought and kept running. Her tracks were not quite filled in, still dimples on the snow. She didn't slow down till she got to the trees, or even until she saw the dark shape of the cabin.

She stoked the stove and undressed fast by its heat. She was shivering so hard her fingers fumbled at her clothes. She slid the pallet and blankets next to the stove, through all the clothes on top, and got in. Morgan would be all right, she told herself. He would know what to do. He would get himself and the pony into the lee of some rock and build a fire. Wouldn't he?

□ □ □ □

Before dawn she heard the change. Or felt it. Or somehow . . .

She burst out the door. She knew . . .

Yes, the wind was still blowing, a stiff breeze now instead of a howling monster, and it was warm. Warm. A black wind. The whites called it a chinook.

Black winds were gifts. Even in the middle of winter they would melt the snow, and it would be balmy for a few days, and all the four-leggeds could graze and get better. Then maybe winter again. But now, so near spring, the horses would survive.

And surely Morgan was alive, and he would come in sometime today. And his dark look would be gone, and he would hold her again, and love her.

She was so confident she made the batter for the flapjacks he liked for breakfast.

He banged the door again. He saw on her face again that she hated the noise, and the dark look was still on his face. Oh, a fine cock-up, this marriage. Well, maybe she was cocking it up. Wasn't she the one who wouldn't give herself?

"Didn't catch up with them Appaloosas," he said. "Have a look at my cheeks, will you? Fingers too."

She checked the frosted places, and said it was not serious.

He ate like a bear in the spring, devouring the flapjacks. Bears would eat carrion that time of year. He smiled sardonically. Like them, he was dangerous now.

"I've got to go after the horses," he said when he finished the third plateful. "They went off toward Sanders's. Look here, though." He got one of his books from the stack in the corner.

Morgan was crazy for these books. Sometimes Marian hated them, and sometimes she wanted to get him to teach her to read.

This was one of the books they called a catalog, full of Tibo things to buy. It was slow. You gave Mr. Anderson some hides and he wrote them down as dollars, and he sent papers in the important Tibo mail, and months later from the Mormon village at the big salt water, the village the people called Many Houses Close Together, whatever you ordered would come. She could make everything they needed, and that was her job, but the Tibos acted like these things that came in the mail were very special, like they had a feeling of . . . well, surely it wasn't a sacred feeling . . . about them.

"You want to go over to Anderson's next month?" he asked. "Do some trading? Get the mail?"

She nodded. She'd never be pleased to see Mrs. Anderson again, not after the embarrassment over the wedding dress, but she liked to trade for a few things, and seeing someone, anyone, would feel good after being cooped up for the winter. Well, the truth was, she was afraid to be away from Morgan.

He opened the book to the page he had marked. Pictures of panniers. He'd made new pack saddles during the fall, not as nice as the ready-made ones, he admitted, but sturdy. She'd made him panniers of rawhide, like big parfleches that her people stored their belongings in. He said he liked them, though they weren't as good as canvas panniers because they were stiff and didn't really fit the mules.

"We've got a pack of beaver," he said, "and the others. I think we can afford these." The panniers on the page were ones of heavy canvas like he wanted. The dudes would like them, he always said. "Dudes" was a new word, according to Morgan, and he pronounced it with a certain relish. Dudes were Tibos who didn't know how to live in this country, he said, who only could get along in cities like his books showed. Marian was shocked to think that there were Tibos even more helpless than most of those who came through here, who couldn't find game to eat or water to drink most of the time, and would get lost without a road.

The panniers were important to him. So was the glass he wanted, to replace the thin-scraped hide that covered their window. With glass this cabin wouldn't be so dark, and she'd like that.

"You want to order some clothes?" He showed her cloth dresses. She loved cloth, loved the soft feel of it, the way it clung to your skin. But it cost so many of the dollars, while deerskin cost just one ball of lead and some time. It would be irresponsible of her to order cloth for a dress.

"We need panniers more, and the glass," she said. "We could trade for more blankets." He nodded and turned the catalog pages.

One day she would have a cloth dress, though, and she would wear it in the shuffling dance.

He just gave her a look and a hint of lop-sided smile on the way out. She wanted him to touch her, but he didn't.

□ □ □ □

In a fury she threw her awl against a wall. She was supposed to get to go!

Sanders had stopped by and brought the Appaloosas. He was on his way to the mountains, he said, he was starved for meat. She didn't ask him in because she didn't like him and Morgan told her not to invite anyone in when she was alone. Sanders's cabin was on Henry's Fork, one sleep west and north, and she hoped he stayed over there. He always called her "the squaw woman," and Shoshones hated that word.

Now he said Morgan was gone to Anderson's to get the mail and asked Sanders to tell Marian he would be back in a few days.

It wasn't true! Not a few days! A week, seven sleeps he would be gone! And he'd promised her she could go!

The precious mail, those goddamn books. "Goddamn" was a Tibo word she was really getting used to. Morgan said it was a bad-medicine curse, but the Tibos didn't seem to take that seriously and just said it about anything they didn't like. There was plenty she didn't like.

Later that night, when she thought about it, she understood. It was wrong, everything was wrong. One winter, that's all it took for her and Morgan to discover they weren't for each other. He had grown to dislike her, that was obvious—he preferred being away from her. Even now, when the grass would be coming green in a couple of weeks, when all the rooted and four-legged and winged and all creatures were coming back to life, he didn't want to be near her. He avoided touching her, but kept his back to her under the blankets.

And he didn't understand about her being with child but fretted because she wouldn't make love to him. And he made them live far away from her family. And, and, and!

She'd wondered once or twice if he knew she was with child. She'd let him know in all the little ways, changing her customs, and he must have felt the changes in her belly even if they didn't show. She thought about bringing it straight up to him, but that would be rude. Rude to say the obvious, and rude to talk openly about what must be unspoken.

Besides, if he didn't know, if he was that careless, that ignorant, maybe she didn't want to tell him. Maybe . . .

She slept fitfully and had strange dreams. In the morning she couldn't remember what the dreams were, but was left only with a feeling, the sense of them, like the sense of what a song says even when you don't hear the words. This meaning was clear. Go home. You are not a Tibo. The Tibo way is not for you, is not your rabbit path. Go home.

She felt a gush of relief. How could she ever have thought otherwise? What a strange way the Tibos lived, out alone, far from each other. No village, no family close, no company. No ceremonies either, as if Duma Apa didn't deserve honor. No lodge for the women's moon house. No sweat lodge, no medicine dreams, no prayers or dances to invoke the blessings of the spirits. It was a bad way, not for her, probably not for any Shoshone. A new way, yes, maybe the way of the future, but a bad way.

The future. It would be hard. Maybe her father could help, maybe she wouldn't have to become the wife of Horn, her older sister's husband. Three Bucks Dancing was an influential man, and could help his daughter. It would be worse for her child, to be half Tibo. *Numa-Tibo,* the people would call her child, half Shoshone, half Tibo. Bad. No one liked *Numa-Tibos,* and some people shunned them. The child would have no family on the father's side. But she couldn't help that, and there would still be family, always. Somehow she would make things work.

In an hour she had caught two horses, packed one and saddled the other. Her heart twisted a little. It wanted to stay with Morgan. But maybe her heart was wayward. Her mother always told her it was wayward.

She clucked at her mount and was on the way to her village, her real home.

Morgan came to the village after only two days. He must have gotten home early from Anderson's with the mail, or maybe he saw Sanders on the way and his friend told him the cabin was empty, the "squaw woman" was gone. Also, she heard, Morgan wore out his horses getting here fast.

She refused to see him. Her father talked to him. All Morgan would say to Three Bucks Dancing was, "I want to talk to Marian."

"I told him I have no daughter by that name," her father reported to her, "only one named Running Water who doesn't want to talk to him." He smiled at his daughter. "I also told him he's not welcome in our lodge right now, or with any of our people living here." Her father gave one of his satisfied looks.

Good. Morgan would know the village wasn't safe for him, and would go home. To his home, not hers. She felt relieved.

"Marian."

The word was soft, but she jumped.

Morgan, standing next to the willow he must have hidden behind. She was surprised. She was carrying a shiny brass bucket to the river for water because she was sure he'd left. It had been four days since he found out his scalp was in danger here.

What a fool he was, skulking around! He must have been sleeping in that dirty horse blanket he had over his shoulders.

She sat near him on a boulder by the bank, with a decent space between. She felt jittery. She was afraid to say someone from the village might see them, maybe her father, or worse, Horn. But she had to tell him the truth.

She took a deep breath. "Tomorrow I will to move into Horn's lodge," she said. "I'm lucky he'll take me."

She watched the pain wash across his face, and regretted there was nothing she could do about it.

"Lucky because of the child?"

So he did know.

"I'm sorry," he said. "I didn't know until Sanders asked me are you . . ." He touched his own belly. "I'm sorry."

What was he sorry about? That she was making life within? That he hadn't known? That it was her duty to refuse him? That he didn't know how to act like a human being?

He reached out and took her hand. It felt good. Instead of pulling it away, she turned hers on top, and looked at the two colors, her dark brown-red and his pale, underside-of-the-arm white. She looked into his face and saw that he understood what she was showing him. Too different. Impossible.

True, we have conceived a child. True, no Shoshone wants to be father to a *Numa-Tibo*. What difference did that make?

She felt tremulous, but she reminded herself, My rabbit path is not his.

"I been to Anderson's," he said.

Yes, you ran off to Anderson's to get mail and left me alone.

"I'm sorry I went by myself," he said. "I wanted to sort things out . . . about you and me. I done it." He let the words sit there, which was his way. "Things came real clear."

He reached inside his blanket coat and pulled out something, a deerskin hide folded around something, and handed it to her.

She unfolded the hide, quaking, telling herself it didn't matter what was in it.

She held some cloth and let it fall out full length.

Mrs. Anderson's wedding dress.

"I sent a note to Anderson's last fall," he said simply.

Oh, Marian would bet Mrs. Anderson had acted miffed about this order. She laughed.

Then she hugged the dress to herself, and felt the silky smoothness. It was so beautiful.

"It's just like Mrs. Anderson's," he said, "only new.

"I want you to wear it at the round dance this summer," he went on. "I wrote my dudes not to come till after that. Said I couldn't guide before then. Baby in the moon when the rivers are full," he plunged on, "then the Nariya dance. Us together."

He looked at her, and she saw the understanding in his eye.

"Thought you might like to stay with your folks after that, while I'm gone to Yellowstone. That way you'd have all summer with them. You could wear that dress out."

She couldn't speak. There was a hot stone in her throat. Besides, she was looking down the new path, and it was still scary.

He put an arm around her shoulders and drew her to him. She actually started to kiss him before she realized. They were out in plain daylight!

She pulled away but smiled at him with her eyes and her lips. Would he understand now?

He hesitated. Then he held out his blanket stretched across his shoulders and one arm, an invitation.

She stepped in. He closed it around both of them.

Where no one could see, she did a brazen thing, took his hand and squeezed it.

They walked back toward the tipis together. She looked around the lodges, the circle of lodges, and saw her people looking back.

Morgan's eyes were happy. So he knew this was her declaration in front of everyone.

Rabbit paths are funny things, she thought happily. They twist around and go off at crazy angles and double back and don't seem to make sense, but they take you where you need to go.

More Silent than the Male

Riley Froh

The female of the species is more deadly than the male.
—RUDYARD KIPLING

SHE LOOKED AWAY from the May 1953 page of the Ace Reid calendar advertising the local cattleman's bank where they kept their tiny checking account a dollar or two above the red. As usual, Ace made her think of herself and her husband, for the comic illustrations of cowboys and their hard-used wives were all too painfully accurate for many Texas ranch couples. These marginal families lived out Reid's cartoons by taking as part of their pay living quarters on the ranch where they worked the long hours required to keep a place going for the owner.

"We don't look that bad yet," she thought as she turned to the window. "Another day like today and I will though," she added. In fact, at the Saturday night dance at Watterson they would soon attend as their only social life other than church, she knew that she and her husband would cut one of the handsomest figures on the floor. He still kept the reckless boyish good looks he had sported in high school, and the strenuous ranch work over the years had only served to keep her figure trim. If you didn't look too closely at the lines in their faces, they didn't look much different from the same two seventeen-year-olds who married right out of high school twenty years earlier in the first half of the Great Depression.

With these thoughts in her mind he rode into the picture the window framed, and by the way he sat his horse with a casual ease after such a long day in the saddle she sensed he had some ropin' 'n' ridin' tale to tell while they got the dirt off for the dance. When he sauntered in as tired as his horse, she always knew that he had doctored screw worm cases all day with no excitement. Then she saw he'd picked up a pretty good scratch on his face.

She lit the butane flame under the coffeepot while he unsaddled and turned his mare into the small horse pasture with his gelding, threw his chaps over the saddle tree back of his horse blanket, and clomped and jangled toward the back door, talking to the dogs that squirmed in the excitement of someone to communicate with. (He said he wore only one spur because if one side of the horse went at the speed he wanted he was sure that the other side would go along.) He kicked off his boots right inside the kitchen before easing himself into his place behind the table.

She saw that the scratch was worse than she thought but not as bad as she feared. She went on over it as though it were a grave matter as she had for two decades to keep the little boy in her precious husband happy. Mainly she saw his eye was all right as the gash went up the cheek and across the eyebrow into the forehead. The black screw worm medicine he had dabbed on would kill the infection, although she doubted any doctor would recommend it for humans.

"You know that ol' half-bramer cow that's so big and always looking for a fight," he explained. "Well, she'd hid her calf in the weeds over by the river and had grazed up out of the bottom. I caught the calf and sure enough the screw worms had plum eat his navel out but I no more'n got the medicine on then here she come like a freight train. Tried to hook my head off as I fell backards and she just went right over me with my hat on her horn. Time she turned around I was on Penny and you know how she can dodge them horns while I was having to get the calf rope off my saddle horn and grab my other rope from behind me. I couldn't see out of one eye 'cause of the blood and I done good to catch that old bramer by the hind legs on the third try. Penny busted 'er good and kept backin' and trippin' her up while I got back off Penny and turned that blamed calf loose. I let the old killer step out of the loop and she still made one more run at me and Penny 'fore she went back to her calf. I ought to have tied her down and hauled her off and sold her while I had her."

She nodded approval, but she knew full well that the last thing her husband would do would be to sell the old renegade. She provided too much fun and excitement for her wild husband. And besides, she fought coyotes the same way she fought men and probably saved enough calves to make her worth keeping. Mother cows were all bad when their calves were small and the danger went with doctoring them. She was married to a cowboy known by old-time cowmen as the best man with a horse, a dog, or a cow in the county. He was just like her father, and she knew it when she married him.

Her husband's reputation and her capacity for hard work had got them this good job. Their small house had indoor plumbing the day they had moved in a decade earlier. She got the pick of the feed sacks with the best prints for sewing his shirts and her dresses. The ranch owner's wife had taken a liking to her and now and then gave her a piece of expensive furniture or a stylish dress from Neiman-Marcus she was going to discard. At their own lovely ranch house closer to town the old couple sometimes invited them to their parties, particularly when local politicians were entertained. Every two years the land owner bought a new Chevrolet pickup and passed the old one on to them for ranch work, but it was understood that they could drive it for personal use on their free time. They were allowed to run up to ten of their own cows with the rancher's herd as an added fringe benefit and the ranch bull worked for nothing, making no distinction as to brands. What chickens she wanted to keep and the garden space were her own business. Even with their tiny monthly salary they made do, and more importantly her husband was happy.

Her own father and mother still made their living the same way on a neighboring ranch and it was all she had ever known before marrying. But as a girl she had been exposed to the cutting blasts of Texas northers, driving a team of mules while her mother and father threw the hay out to the cold and surging cattle from the back of a wagon. Now she sat in the comfort of a nice heated pickup cab while her husband tossed out the regular winter feed. She knew her mother now drove a pickup for her father's feeding chores, and she realized deep-down that her own ways would never change, but she was also content with her life. Their hours were their own. She never tired of watching the fascinating habits of wild and domesticated birds and animals. She could keep all the

pets she ever wanted, and her husband was always bringing her a
baby squirrel that fell from a nest or an orphan fawn to cuddle
until it grew up and ran back to the wild. She never penned any of
her pets up, not even the brown thrasher that was her favorite.
Brownie had flitted and hopped about her home for a year before
flashing away to his own kind one spring, never to return. There
was a quiet and a peace and a contentment in ranch life that could
only be theirs with the job they did. Her own happiness exceeded
that of her husband's, although his boyish exuberance reflected it
much more openly.

But he was finishing his deer sausage and purple hull peas and
fried potatoes and she knew from his dancing eyes that he was
about to share another experience from his day's adventures. She
got him another cup of coffee and pretended to give him full
attention while she did the dishes.

"You know that ol' sharp drop off by the high ridge over by the
river bend," he started. "That old crazy muley cow hides her calf
out there every year and I figured that's where she was at this
mornin'. But Penny wouldn't go up the cattle trail even with me
spurrin' her good and when I finally seen what was botherin' her I
understood what she smelled when I started up the ridge. There,
right at the top, coiled an' waitin' to bite the first cotton tail to come
by was the biggest rattlesnake in the state. I know he's the one bit
that old Hereford bull last year that barely made it back up here to
the house, you remember."

Indeed, she did remember. They had found the fang marks in
the neck where the swelling was already getting out of control. The
bull lay out under the oldest mesquite tree on the place behind the
barn and heaved and wheezed and whistled all night long trying to
suck air through his constricted wind pipe. Finally she had got the
deer rifle to put him out of his misery, but he had stopped her,
saying the bull had as much right to try to live as anyone else. And
survive he did, no worse for the experience. Her father had come
over to see him right before dark and had said only an uncommonly big snake could have pumped that much poison into the
bull's brisket to cause such a swelling.

Her husband fished around under a battered package of Camel
cigarettes in his shirt pocket, extracted the lengthy string of rattles,
and shook them ever so tantalizingly over his empty coffee cup. She
took them, and after mussing around the clutter of her sewing

machine, she dropped them into a faded cigar box with the other smaller rattles and the growing collection of Indian arrowheads they found together in their Sunday afternoon prowlings of the ranch property. She planned to frame them all and hang them up one of these days.

"Well, I got off Penny and tied her to a elm tree," her husband continued. "And you know how it is when you find a snake needs killin' an' you can't find no big rocks layin' around to chunk always seems like. But there was this piece of cedar fence post that had broke off but hadn't rotted much and I grabbed it and waded into that snake. He shore wasn't fixing to run. Just stood his ground, coiled up weavin' that head back an' forth tryin' to get a shot at me. I throwed him over that high bob war fence over by the gulley yonder an' he drags the ground on both sides."

Her husband was content to smoke over his third cup of coffee while she quickly finished up the kitchen. She was in a hurry, for she wanted to get a good table around the dance floor before every one was taken. Here their group would settle in, her husband would repeat his stories while she caught up on the news from the same friends she had been talking to in the Watterson dance hall since high school. She felt thankful to be going to the dance after the battles she had fought that day.

First had been her fight with the water moccasin. Now that the drought had thinned out the frogs down at the creek, she had been seeing moccasins ever closer to the house, and this one had entered the barn in search of a meal where she was hunting the ever elusive hen eggs. The snake had hit her thigh, burying and catching its curved fangs deep in the folds of her pleated denim skirt, shooting a spew of venom between her skirt and slip. Instinctively she had thrown up her hands, whirling automatically like a ballerina while the snake flopped and writhed sickeningly against her shuddering form.

"Get him," she shouted at the nervous terrier who had been busy ratting around the feedsacks. "Snake, snake, sic him," she rasped. With the timing of the best circus dog in a juggling act, Fibber, in one graceful leap, ripped the thick, black horror from her clothes by its neck, hitting the ground already shaking his prize with a fury long bred into the breed. Gasping for breath, she waited until her own legs quit their trembling before throwing the battered remains of Fibber's kill over the fence with a hoe.

She sat on the edge of the horse trough, bathing her face with her hands and thanking the Lord for deliverance from harm. Her goldfish rose from the green depths and peered at her with goggle eyes, waiting for the oatmeal she sometimes threw them before going back to nibbling the thick algae when no handout was forthcoming. Watching them calmed her and she remembered to call Fibber from his busy search of other dragons to slay and rub his ears and praise him highly, especially mentioning his high intelligence. Fibber seemed to nod his head in agreement and took on his look and pose of importance that such comments always brought out in him. Old Dorothy, the pit-bull and cur-dog cross, trained to get bad cattle out of thick brush, nosed her way in, jealous for a share of the attention.

A red-tailed hawk sailed the fence line in the distance, eventually resting on a corner post. Barn yard sounds began to reach her ears again as she got her complacency back. Snorts and grunts from a nearby pen told her the shoats needed their feed. She stepped into the pen with her half sack of Purina hog chow, tripping over the end of the hog trough as the five animals crowded around. Suddenly, the boar went for her ankle, got a mouthful of blue jean skirt and slip which he rent with a passion as he moved up her prostrate form for her face, gnashing and rooting horribly. All the gruesome but true stories of hogs eating children surged in her brain. Screaming for Dorothy she kicked at the filthy beast between her legs, a mouthful of denim under his snout with his little intelligent pig's eyes piercing hers from his grotesque position. Dorothy hit the swine with her usual ferocity, ripping the right ear before bloodying the hog's nostrils. As the pig's left ear was being shredded, the attacker released the skirt to run to the far end of the pen to squeal in pain and disillusionment as Dorothy kept up the vicious assault, nipping pieces of tender hide from leg and tail. In the meantime, Fibber had entered the fray with much noise and yapping and some more tooth work on the enemy's battered ears.

It was all she could do to call Dorothy off, who would stop and raise a foreleg, growling deep in her throat and threatening to return to battle as she reluctantly left the pen. The boar sulled in the corner, its face a bloody mess but its little malignant eyes shining with the thought of a new menu.

She cleaned her face in the horse trough, while Fibber looked on quizzically, head turned sideways at such theatrics. Now it was

Fibber's turn to try to horn in on the kind words and caresses aimed at old Dorothy.

Clearly it was time to go to the house, but a casual glance through the bars of the horse corral showed her a guinea egg, lying in the sand by the snubbing post. She ought not to go home without anything for her troubles, she reasoned, and absentmindedly she slipped the latch and passed through the gate. As she bent over and grasped the egg, the stallion went for her, seizing her belt, skirt waist, and slip from behind in its powerful teeth. She instinctively realized that she had been too addled to think. Ranch raised and the daughter of a noted bronc stomper, she knew better than to go around a stud horse during her period. She had helped her father with the horses all her early life, but he had always kept her away from the stallions at certain times of the month after she reached puberty. Menstruating women sometimes drove them to do strange things.

Now in spite of her training she was being spun in a circle, unable to breathe but certainly able to pray. She was about to promise never to attend a Saturday night dance again when her belt broke off in the teeth of the horse and her skirt and slip ripped off with it. The force of the release rolled her under the bottom bar of the pen where she lay for a while. When she became conscious that the guinea egg was clutched unbroken in her hand, she began to laugh. As the tears of laughter and release coursed her face, old Dorothy whimpered for some sort of consolation. Trained since a pup to leave horses and deer alone, she had been torn between loyalty and guidance during the final episode, and the old dog knew somehow that she should have helped. "It's all right, baby," she crooned to the ugly face as Dorothy's powerful halitosis almost overwhelmed her.

She started for the house in her panties and blouse. A bath and a cold Coca-Cola were in order even if the rest of the chores never got done. Too late she heard the crunch of tires as the local Watkins' Products salesman and the oldest Baptist deacon in their church coaxed his ancient, creaking Plymouth around his usual U-turn by the horse pens. This time both his window and his whole face were hanging open, though he was speechless as he gaped in startled amazement.

"I don't need nothing today, Deacon," she said with uncharacteristic coldness as she passed the car looking straight ahead.

"You may not want nothing but you sure need something," the Deacon said to himself as he shook his head in wonder and risked one eye for a last glimpse at the receding firm cheeks of a half-nude ascending a staircase.

As she put the day's workload out of her mind with the last dish she was washing, the scrape of her husband's chair brought her back to the present. "You don't want no more pie?" she asked as he started to leave.

"I don't reckon," he answered. "Let's go dancin'."

"Say," he said, "you think after we get bathed off and 'fore we get ready we could—"

"You know we can't now," she interrupted tenderly. "Maybe tomorrow."

"Oh, yeah," he said, reminded. And he added as an afterthought, "What went on around here today?"

"Oh, nothing much," she answered. "Just the usual."

The Leave-taking

Ruth Willett Lanza

BENNETTIE stood on the hill, a short distance from their tent, alone. She felt more alone than she'd felt in all her fifteen years, as the hot prairie breeze blew the bluestem grasses around her ankles, catching her cotton stockings and bunching the hem of her calico skirt.

She stood, leaning her spare body into the wind, and held her hand to the brim of her sunbonnet to shade her eyes; eyes that were an unforgettable gray-blue.

Heaving a deep sigh, she stood motionless, gazing across the endless plain of knee-high grasses swaying in the wind, at the western horizon of Oklahoma Territory, and a lump constricted her throat.

Holding back tears, she strained after the wagon train snaking across the flat expanse that yawned before her. It carried with it all she'd known of love and security—her mamma and papa, and her two younger sisters, Sophia and Sephrina.

When the wagons had first started out on the trail to California that morning, she'd heard the creaking and grinding of the massive wooden wheels, and above the clamor, she'd taken comfort in the sound of her father's voice calling out to the six-span of oxen. Then from their wagon, which was the last in the line of white-canvassed prairie schooners, she'd heard the voices of Sophie and Sephrina drifting across the waving sea of grass as they called out to her.

"Bye, Bennie, bye," they'd called over and over again, their sweet voices sounding like a meadowlark on the wing, until she could no longer hear them, and could see only the faint outline of the two children as they waved from the back of the wagon. Soon they, too, faded from view, as the wagons lumbered along, tilting from side to side, gradually growing smaller and dimmer, like a line of white ants.

Even so, her ears strained for one more sound, only to hear the sighing of the wind. Finally, as she gazed across the open space, unblotched by tree or cloud, the wagons disappeared over the edge of the earth.

"Oh, Mamma," she whispered under her breath, as she brushed away a hot tear with the back of her hand, "how could you have left me here, all alone?" Alone in this wild, unsettled land they'd all just come to. Alone, amid the roaming bands of Chickasaw Indians, those fearful, redskinned savages, whose land they'd confiscated in the Run and where she and Henry would make their home?

Alone—except for Henry. *Why did you have to go? When will I ever see your dear faces again? Probably not in my lifetime.* All these thoughts swirled through her brain, and she felt the hot winds closing in around her until she couldn't breathe. Then the tears she'd been holding back for the last several days squeezed out from behind her tightly closed lids, burning the fair, freckled skin of her cheeks.

Furiously, she wiped them away with the hem of her skirt, streaking her sunburned face with the red dust of the Oklahoma plain. Impatiently, she tore off the sunbonnet to wipe the perspiration from her forehead as the noontime sun beat down relentlessly, and setting her chin, she promised herself she'd not cry again.

Henry had said, "Your eyes are like the evening light, shot through with stars." She smiled, for she knew she was plain-looking—except for her eyes.

Mamma had told her she was strong, and smarter than most. That should be enough, thought Bennettie. But how she longed to be pretty, like the small-waisted, buxom girls with hair the color of goldenrod whom she envied.

"Whoa, whoa there, now." His voice rose deep and strong, breaking the silence that surrounded her. She turned to see him yanking the team of horses to a standstill, his sturdy body straining against their pull; watched as he hopped down lightly and secured the reins, tying them to the handle of the plow.

Then, raising his arm, he waved to her, a smile creasing his broad face, which was the color of a walnut. *Almost as dark as the braves who belong to this land,* she thought.

His black curly locks—inherited from his little French mother, back in Missouri—fell across his forehead, and his shoulders strained against the muslin of his shirt.

The sight of him made a warm, mushy feeling rise up inside her. Gulping back her grief, she waved at him. Then she tied on her bonnet, even though the hot winds felt good as they dried the strands of hair dampened by sweat. For she remembered her Gram's words: "Always keep your hat on, Ben, to protect your skin from freckling." She laughed when she remembered, for her skin was freckled like nutmeg on a cup of eggnog.

She watched as Henry strode across the field with his boots sinking in the earth, his stocky, compact frame bent into the wind. He strode up the slope to where she stood so straight and still, with her small, high bosom heaving with emotion, and perspiration trickling down her neck onto the edge of her dimity collar.

Henry reached out his arms, tanned and muscular, covered with fine black hairs, as he said, "Come, Bennie, you can't stand here all day. You'll get sunstroke for sure, and all the watching won't bring them back. You'll just make yourself sick, strainin' to see what isn't there."

She nodded that she knew he was right, but no words came.

"They've gone now, darlin' Bennie, for sure. They're well on their way to California by now, but you'll see them again someday. I *promise* you that!"

He wiped her tearstained face with his fingers, calloused by the plow handles, ax, and saw—tools of settling in this "Promised Land"—and wrapped his arms around her slender waist.

She, who stood nearly as tall as he, *hard and straight, like a tree,* she thought, leaned her head onto his shoulder, and her voice trembled when she finally spoke.

"Oh, Henry. What will I do without Mamma and Phenie and little Sophie? Without Papa?" She sighed, brushing a wisp of sparrow-brown hair back under the edge of her sunbonnet brim, and remembered.

□ □ □ □

"Have to go West," Papa had said to Mamma. She could still see the big white house with its peeling paint, and the airy rooms of her grandmother's plantation, the sleek race horses, and the rolling green hills of Kentucky.

"It's been a shambles since the Rebellion. It'll never come back, Melinda," he'd said. "Our only chance is out West."

"With Indians and *desperados?* Oh . . . Benjamin," Melinda had wailed.

Bennettie had never forgotten the look of terror in her mamma's eyes. *Mamma was brave,* she thought. But it was her father who'd suffered most, seeing himself as a Kentucky gentleman, he'd never been able to adjust to life as a pioneer. *Poor Papa,* she thought. And now her parents were off again, following another of her father's dreams.

When he'd heard that the government planned to open up the Indian Territory to settlement, in the spring of 1889, he decided to make the "Run" for free land.

"Oklahoma! I've heard that that means land of the redman," said Melinda, her voice trembling at the thought of going into that strange, wild country.

But when Bennettie looked at her father, new hope surged in her. His eyes were bright with anticipation at the thought of a new beginning. Benjamin loved beginnings. It was the staying and finishing of things he couldn't face. She knew that, now.

Bennettie guessed her father didn't see the look of fear in her mother's eyes, because he just laughed.

"It'll be an adventure, Melinda," he'd said. "And it's our chance to get a piece of the Promised Land."

So they'd set out in their wagon for Indian Territory.

Benjamin rode alongside on his Kentucky mare, which was his most cherished possession, the only thing of value they'd brought from the plantation. Except, of course, the silver castor set, with its cut glass condiment bottles, that Melinda had wrapped carefully in an old blanket to keep from breaking.

As their wagon rolled along behind the wagon train with Melinda driving the oxen, Bennettie sat up on the seat beside her, since she was the oldest. Sophie and Phenie rode in the back of the wagon, hanging their legs over the edge, watching Kentucky, Illinois, and finally Missouri, disappear from sight.

The first day on the open prairie seemed endless, with the sun beating down like a trip-hammer and the wind blowing against their faces like a blast from a hot oven. But at the sight of a dark, undulating mass of brown monsters grazing some distance away and hundreds of wild horses streaking across the prairie, Bennettie felt goosebumps rise on her arms, and she shivered with excitement.

She'd never seen buffalo, and she wished with all her might she could lasso a wild pony to have for her very own, for like her father, she loved horses.

She decided that she must have inherited a little of his spirit of adventure, too. After all, she was his namesake, even though she hated her name, given to her because she was supposed to be a boy. *How could anyone ever like a girl called Ben?* she asked herself, *and one as plain as me?*

When the western sky turned a rosy pink with shades of lavender, they looked for a place to camp. Benjamin rode up ahead to consult with the wagon master. Then, pointing to a fringe of green, he'd called back to Melinda.

"Over there, by those trees. That means there's water, they say, first we've seen and most we're likely to. We'll pull up there for the night."

Melinda heaved a sigh of relief, and stretching her neck and twisting her back, she turned the oxen toward the small clump of trees, pulling the wagon to a halt by the tallest cottonwood.

The children were down and out of the wagon in an instant, running to the river, splashing water on each other and squealing with delight. Bennettie wanted to join them, but before she could move, her father started giving directions.

"Ben, you gather some buffalo chips, should be plenty around here, so we can make a fire. And go get Flossie's bucket, so your mamma can get started makin' the corn bread."

Bennettie untied the bucket from behind the wagon, where Flossie's cream had jiggled all day until it had turned into butter. Her mouth watered as she thought of Mamma's hot cornbread spread thick with butter and sorghum molasses, and she was thankful that Papa hadn't asked her to milk Flossie, too.

That night she slept out under the stars on her bedroll, glad to give the wagon over to the little ones, because she liked to be alone to look up at the spreading canopy of stars that blinked overhead, to listen to the coyotes yipping, and to hear the soft hooting of the great-horned owl she'd noticed sitting on the limb of a cottonwood tree.

She thought of Kentucky, with the rolling blue-green hills, her grandmother's white-pillared house, and for an instant, she wished to be back there, safe and secure. But there was something about the wildness and freedom of this land they were crossing, something that put joy in her heart.

In the days that followed, she could tell they were approaching an Indian village by the spotted ponies grazing on a hill. Then the white, deerskin tipis loomed on the horizon, with curls of smoke rising from the smoke-holes and campfires. She felt worried when the barking dogs warned the Indians of their approaching wagons.

One day, three warriors, with their bare, coppery-skinned chests glistening in the sun, holding their lances high, rode out to meet them.

Bennettie drew in her breath with anticipation and a tinge of fear, but when the Indians held up their arms, muscular and ringed with silver, to greet them in peace, she let out a sigh of relief and looked over at her mother.

Melinda, green eyes filled with apprehension, smiled a tight little smile. Then she grasped Bennettie's hand and glanced in the back of the wagon at the children.

"Hush, Phenie, keep Sophie quiet . . . Indians!"

But it turned out that they were friendlies. When the wagons drew to a stop, Indian women wrapped in blankets and brown-skinned children, half-naked, came out to mill around the wagons and peer inside, pointing to the copper pots and lamps and other treasures hanging from the side of the wagons.

The men traded whiskey and tools to the warriors for fox and bear furs. Melinda bargained with a sober-faced Indian woman, trading her a blue glass oil lamp for a willow basket.

Bennettie accepted a pair of soft, beaded moccasins from an Indian maiden, named Morning Star, in exchange for *Little Women* (one of her favorite books, since she'd always imagined herself as Jo).

"Can you read?" Bennettie asked, surprised.

Morning Star looked at Bennettie, her black eyes sparkling with humor, and nodded, somberly.

"Go to Mission School," she said, "Nuns teach me to read good."

Bennettie admired Morning Star's smooth brown skin and large dark eyes. She was so lovely to look at. And she had such a pretty name. *Even Indian girls are beautiful,* she thought. *Oh, how I wish I was pretty, too.* And she wished that she and Morning Star could truly be friends. As they rode away from the village, she waved at the Indian maiden and Morning Star waved back. *Maybe someday we'll meet again,* thought Bennettie.

Benjamin explained to the children that the tribes were all different and that they were divided into nations.

"The Cherokees, the ones we just passed, are the most educated ones. But the Pawnees, they say, are wild and fierce."

So, they all hugged close together when they drew near the Pawnee nation. Bennettie noticed that her mamma clenched the reins so tightly she wore blisters on her hand and bit her lower lip until the blood came. She didn't look to right or left, as though she was fearful of what she might see. But if the Pawnees saw them, they let them be.

After weeks of traveling, they finally made camp by the South Canadian River, smack in the middle of the Chickasaw Nation, and there they waited for the big day—to make the Run.

Tents dotted the prairie as far as they could see, for hundreds of people from everywhere had gotten there before them. They'd come in wagons, buckboards, buggies, and even on the train. Gamblers had set up fortune wheels, so that the men could bet on which day the Run would be held and on who had the fastest horse to carry them to their free 160 acres.

Melinda wouldn't let Benjamin gamble on the fortune wheels, so to keep peace, he spent his days playing cards or pitching horseshoes with the other men. At night he sat in the tent and poured over his maps by the light of an oil lamp, trying select the best site for their homestead.

The women washed clothes in the river, cooked meals over the open campfires, and tried to keep track of the children.

Bennettie wandered down to the river when her chores were done, and sitting on the riverbank, she unlaced her high-top shoes and dipped her bare feet in the cool water.

She took a tablet and stub of pencil out of her apron pocket, and as she watched a hawk soar across the blue sky, she tried to think of a poem. Licking the lead point, she wrote a few words:

Far away from Kentucky
I sit on a table of grass
Wondering and waiting
For my tomorrow . . .

Will I ever get more schooling? she wondered. How would she ever get more learning out here in this new country? There weren't any schools, or churches, not even roads or anything. She envied Morning Star, who was not only pretty as a newborn colt—with her glossy black braids—but was able to attend a Mission School.

Glancing back toward the camp, she saw her mother and noticed how frazzled she looked. *Gram should see her daughter now,* thought Bennettie. *Mamma's boots all caked with red mud, and her beautiful auburn hair,* so *dull and sticky with dust and sweat.*

And although Mamma kept wearing her sunbonnet most days to keep the sun off her skin, the sunbonnet was all limp and bedraggled and her skin was burnt red as a tomato.

Bennettie had heard her crying some nights after Papa was asleep, and it made her feel sad and confused. *Mamma's just tired of movin', I guess,* she thought. *It ain't been easy for her.*

The rains began just before the big day. At first everybody all along the river let out a yell of elation, because rain in this dry country was a blessing, for sure. It would cool down everything, making it all easier to bear.

Bennettie watched the little kids run through the rain, splashing in the puddles, letting it soak through to their skins, because it felt so good. She wished she was little enough to do it, too. But she stood by to help her mamma clean them up when they came back to the tent, dripping wet and grinning.

The rain didn't stop, but poured down in buckets, drenching them for three days. Everybody finally hunkered down in their tents and wagons to wait it out. Then the river began to rise, and they all forgot about getting wet and just stood around watching with horror as the river rose to the edge of the bank.

The menfolk stood all night, holding their lanterns high, watching the river and talking about what would happen if "she" overflowed the banks.

Benjamin stalked into the tent, his boots caked with sticky red mud, and throwing off his slicker, he spoke to Melinda softly, so the kids wouldn't hear. But Bennettie heard.

"Better, say some prayers, Melinda. If that river doesn't stop rising soon, don't know how we'll get across on the Big Day to make the Run."

Melinda nodded her head, numb-like, and grasped Benjamin's hand, squeezing it. Bennettie knew her mother had been praying all along.

The rain must have stopped in the middle of the night, because Bennettie was awakened one morning with everybody hollering and yelling bloody murder.

"She's goin' back! The river's goin' back! Praise the Lord!"

She and Phenie ran out in their nightclothes to see what all the excitement was about. The men were already pulling their rafts close to the riverbank to get across for the Run. People were taking down their tents and loading their wagons, making ready to take off when the gun was shot, giving them the signal. For the Big Day was here.

At noon—suntime—the government men stood on the line across the river, holding their guns in readiness and checking their watches. Then slowly they raised their arms, as a great silence spread over the camp and up and down the riverbank. The creaking of the wagons, and the pawing of horses hoofs against the muddy bank and an occasional whinny, were the only sounds.

Men on horseback and in buggies, buckboards, covered wagons, even men on foot, stood in readiness, holding their breath, waiting to hear the shot.

Her father would ride *alone* on Prancer, his chestnut mare, " 'Cause a man alone can ride faster and go further," he said. "You and the youngins can wait here in camp until I stake my claim and come back for you," he told Melinda.

So, her mamma and the children sat breathlessly in the wagon, waiting to hear the shot that would signal the start of the race.

Bennettie stood, so she could see her father take off. He looked so handsome, dressed in his best Prince Albert coat, his wide-brimmed white hat, and his new string tie.

Finally, the government men fired the shots into the air! Everyone took off with whoops and hollers, splashing across the river and up the other bank.

Benjamin was one of the first to reach the other side, and Bennettie watched him and Prancer race across the prairie, until they faded from sight.

For the next week, they waited and watched in the nearly abandoned camp for Benjamin's return.

Bennettie spent hours standing on a high rise a ways down the river, looking through field glasses, straining for sight of her father.

Had he met up with uncouth people?

"There's lots of rough characters, jumpin' claims and stealin' horses, what'd just a soon shoot you as look at you," she confided to Phenie. "Then there's them Sooners what crept into the territory before the gun was shot—some long before—taking their piece of land before it was time." And they both wondered if Papa, with his Southern gentlemanly ways, could stand up to the likes of them.

One day, they saw dust whorls spinning over the plain, like a tumbleweed. As the horse and rider drew closer, they could see that it was Prancer. Her glossy body glistened with sweat, and Benjamin was grinning and waving his big white hat.

"Praise the Lord!" she heard Melinda whisper under her breath. And they all let out a yell, "It's Papa. Look, he's coming. Papa's coming."

Her mamma hugged her and little Sophie to her breast in thankfulness. And Phenie ran up and down the riverbank, jumping up and down with joy.

When her papa got across the river, Melinda hugged him, and Phenie and Sophie clung to the tails of his Prince Albert coat.

"It's done," he said. "We're land owners. Got a dandy claim, just ten miles south of Edmond Station on Bluff Creek."

They all hollered with joy, and Bennettie saw her mother wipe her eyes with the hem of her apron.

"We've got to get goin'," said Benjamin, "because I left a friend guarding my claim, until we get back."

Once again they set out across the prairie, and on the third evening they crossed Bluff Creek with the aid of lanterns, and an air of apprehension settled over them.

Was their claim safe? Bennettie saw the strained look on her mamma's face, and she held her breath while her papa fired three shots into the air with his rifle.

After an endless moment of silence, they heard from way over a hill an answering shot.

"Thank God," said Benjamin, "our claim is safe."

The next morning, when they reached their land, Bennettie walked away from the tent to see what they'd come to.

It is so beautiful, she thought, as she stood in the waist-high grass and marveled at the wildflowers spread across the prairie like a patchwork quilt of purple, white, and yellow. A majestic eagle sailed and dipped overhead, its wings spread wide, and a flock of prairie chickens strutted nearby, puffing orange ruffs all around their little faces.

I know Mamma hates it, she thought, *but I love it all: the wide open space, the soft, hot wind in my face, the sky arching overhead till it touches the edge of the earth, like a pale blue tent. I love the newness of it all. It's like a piece of blank paper, still to be wrote on. Papa says it's a young land, settled by young people. It's my land, for sure.*

And then she met Henry. She smiled when she remembered how Henry had ridden across the prairie on his fine black stallion from his own claim to greet them, since they were neighbors. He owned a team of horses, and Papa said that horses were more valuable than gold in this new land—horses and a wife.

Bennettie liked Henry from the very first; the way his brown eyes sparkled with fun-lovin' and the softness that shone in them when he looked at her.

Then one day he came striding up the hill, his black boots newly polished, carrying a bouquet of wildflowers: blue larkspur, wild roses, and black-eyed Susans. He tipped his hat to her and asked if she'd like to ride into town with him the next day for a sarsaparilla.

She couldn't speak, but just nodded, as she felt the blush creep up her neck and onto her face, while her heart did somersaults.

Later, he talked of his dreams.

"I can see a town with churches and schools and a white house on a hill. We'll be leaders in this new land, because we're young and strong, and because we both love this prairie with its waving sea of grasses that grow as high as a horse's belly."

That night when she lay out under the stars, beneath the pale light of the moon, away from the others, wide awake, listening to the distant howl of a wolf, Bennettie thought of Henry.

Slowly, she smoothed her flannel gown with her hand, down the length of her long body, feeling the flatness of her stomach, the sharpness of her hipbones, then back up again until her hand cupped the small mound of her breast. She was no longer a child, she knew. But was she woman enough for a man like Henry? she wondered. She shivered with the thought of it.

□ □ □ □

The wagon train carrying her loved ones had disappeared over the edge of the horizon, and as Bennettie and Henry stood together on their hill, he tilted her chin up to make her look at him.

"Darlin' Bennie, my precious wife, you have *me*. I'll always take care of you, just as I promised. Have you forgotten all our plans and dreams? It's you and me for it, Bennie."

Suddenly, forgetting Mamma and Papa, Sophie and Phenie, she ripped off her bonnet, and with a smile creasing her face and a twinkle in her eyes, she said, "I'll race you to the tent." Then, lifting her calico skirt and her petticoats, so she wouldn't trip, she dashed with long-legged strides down the hill, laughing and panting for breath.

When he finally caught up with her, he grabbed her around the waist, whirling her to a stop, and they both fell to the ground, their laughter riding the wind across the prairie. Encircled in each other's arms, they rolled together in the tall grasses, which closed over and above them.

Henry placed a kiss on her freckled nose and said softly, "I love you, Bennie. I love you, my darlin' girl."

Bennettie closed her eyes and sighed, with a deep feeling of contentment, as she told herself, *Henry likes my name. He thinks I'm beautiful, and that my eyes are like an evening star. And someday I'll get more learning. I know for sure—that for me and Henry—this Oklahoma Territory is truly the Promised Land.*

A Two-Gun Man

Joyce Roach

THE WAY Fudge had it figured, he was about ready and himself was the only obstacle standing in his way. "A man's got to do what's right"—that's what his daddy said and Fudge had never known his daddy to lie or to shirk his job as a cowboy on the great Crosswinds ranch, so named because the wind blew across the ranch nearly all of the time. Buck, his daddy's friend, said only the wind knew the way across so many acres but that wherever they were the wind found them. Buck was not a man to tell a lie, but he laughed a lot when he told the truth. Fudge aimed to be a cowboy himself, and that's why he had to do what he had to do which was to become a crack shot with a pistola in either hand, a two-gun man.

For several reasons, an uneasiness, a tightness, was building in Fudge, and he was thinking about guns morning, noon and night. Not that Fudge had ever seen his daddy shoot with both hands, but he had seen it done with one hand, and at a rattlesnake at that when he nearly put his own little hand right on the rattler. His daddy had put a bullet in that old snake's head not inches away from where he reached down to pick up a rock. His daddy fired, was off his big Cinnamon horse with his arms around him, and laughing before Fudge had time to be scared. Daddy pulled out a knife from his belt, handed it to Fudge and showed him how to whack the rattler off the snake. Then he scooped him up into the big saddle on Cinnamon and rode for the bunk house hollering,

"Look here what my Fudge done. He ain't afraid of no rattler. No, sir. He whacked off his tale, and I'm proud of 'im." And the men cheered. But the boss man's wife came running out from the house, gathered Fudge up in her arms, squeezed him nearly to death and yelled at his daddy all in the same breath about how snakes, or horns or careless men were going to be the death of Fudge before he was six years old. The gun was the fault of all the hullabaloo, he thought. And he had seen the other men, his daddy's friends and his, target practice for fun at old tin cans that Mr. Richards' wife let them have. They joked about tin cans instead of the real thing. Fudge knew the real thing to be game for the table—turkey, quail, antelope, deer and sometimes a beef. The men seemed to imply more in their teasing with one another, and sometimes they drew their guns on each other, but they just made bang, bang noises with their mouths. Fudge knew they were playing a game of some kind. He used his finger and thumb for such games, and then the men put their guns away and played finger-thumb guns back with him.

Sometimes the cowboys would take their ease about the bunkhouse late in the evenings when they returned from chores done for Mr. Richards, things such as building fence or moving cattle from one place to another, or doctoring stock. After supper around the big table in Mrs. Richards' backyard, the men would take their plates and utensils to a big washtub of soapy water, wash them out in one bucket, rinse them in another and stack them in yet another. Then they were free to lollygag—that's what Mrs. Richards called it—but she laughed and Fudge knew that what they did was approved. Fudge did the same, sharing the good food, observing the table manners of the men practiced under Mrs. Richards' watchful eye, only he had to empty the water buckets and tidy up, as Mrs. Richards called it, after the men finished. It was the one time of the day they were under the stern hand of a high-toned woman, but to be able to get such eats on a ranch, to have canned peaches at every meal and a feast on Sunday was worth enduring prayer, napkins, two utensils, table etiquette and dish washing. That's what the boys all said, although Fudge had never known life to be any other way. Seldom were all of the men together at one time anyway since at any given day many were scattered clear to the Mexican border or camping and working in pastures twenty miles from the home place. They kept to a schedule, however, and rotation to the big house place was an event to be looked forward to rather than dreaded, except for Fudge, who rotated only from the hen house where the rooster chased him, to the barn where the peacocks acted like they were going to, to the bunk house where the cowboys razzed him, to the big white house where Ma'am worried him, to the table where nobody noticed him and where he got his name, Fudge—roly, poly, brown and sweet—that's what the cowboys said.

About the farthermost he got away from the ranch grounds was to the outhouse situated a far distance out from everything else. That, he guessed, was why they called it an outhouse, but then Fudge had to guess about a lot of things. Trips out there beyond the chicken yard might turn up snakes, horned toads, scorpions and grandaddy longlegs spiders. Yes, Fudge's days were filled with tension and sometimes terror, although nobody guessed it. Too much time, he thought, was spent pouring the dishwater on the garden, checking for eggs in the henhouse or reporting the theft of eggs by animals too terrible to imagine, even planting and hoeing and gathering. "There sure is a lot of farming to be done on this ranch," Mrs. Richards said at least once a day as she worked beside Fudge or directed his chores. "They damn sure is," Fudge had replied once, but only once. Damn and guns were two items denied the youngest cowboy at Crosswinds.

Until recently when Fudge decided to become a two-gun man just as quick as he mastered being a one-gun man, the outhouse held no interest. Now, the place was beginning to look like just the right spot to do a little practicing. Fudge, however, had some hard times coming and difficult days ahead just to figure out how to get his hands on a gun of any kind let alone shoot it. Now, with roundup and driving and shipping to be done, there wouldn't hardly be time to go to the outhouse for any reason, let alone to study on how to be a two-gun man.

Fudge knew a secret about guns at Crosswinds that nobody else knew. At least he thought no one knew but him. Mrs. Richards sometimes carried a gun, a rifle, and she could use it. She could do a lot of things that the men did such as ride a horse and even throw a rope, but the gun business surprised him some. The boy knew nothing of women except what he saw, and he once saw Mrs. Richards, whom he called Ma'am as did everyone else, away off from the house emptying cartridges into a target of some kind. It must have been okay since Mr. Richards was standing behind her pointing and motioning this way and that.

What really had Fudge determined to handle and shoot guns, however, was a recent event, one that burned in his memory during the day and brought him awake at night. One morning Ma'am called him from the bunkhouse before he started chores and said that he was going to town with her, maybe. She didn't explain why he was going since he had never in all his six years gone to a town, whatever and wherever that was. Never. Ma'am was upset, kind of mad like. His daddy was off down close to the border, so there was no way he could ask him. The other men were off doing what they always did and he couldn't ask them. Nobody was at the big house or on the grounds that morning except him and Mr. Richards and Ma'am. After Ma'am left the bunkhouse, Fudge became aware that not all was right at the big house. He could hear strong words, loud words, and then crying. Fudge was startled only by the crying. Sometimes he used to cry when he was a baby, but Ma'am or his daddy or Mr. Richards talked to him about it and said he shouldn't. He had to be a man, they said. And Fudge wanted more than anything to be a man and do such things as ride and rope and shoot a gun, two guns. So he cried as little as he could. Never in his life had he heard anyone else cry. He was in the loft of the barn trying to escape the rooster who was below flashing his spurs and flying up as far as he could when he heard the sound. It was Ma'am crying and she had to be carrying on loudly for Fudge to have heard. Her piercing sobs struck a chord deep inside Fudge. He knew not to bother Mr. Richards and Ma'am, but he ran as fast as his fat legs could carry him as far as the front porch steps, then up to the front window. They were in the hallway, which ran the whole width of the house. Mr. Richards was the one doing the talking now. "Ruth, the boy's not yours. You can't just up and take him and be gone two weeks What's got the bit in your teeth? Have I done something to you? Have any of the men hurt your feelings or been disrespectful?"

"Cater, you stop that! You know that isn't so. You're just wishing it was something you could do something about. I just want to go to town. It's been two years. I want to go to church, find out what the women are wearing, buy some, some . . . things, do-dads."

None of what she was saying made any sense at all. Town?

Fudge had been to a line camp or two, but not town. Church he knew. He went up to the big house along with any cowboy who was about to hear the pump organ play and sing "Shall We Gather at the River." That would be the Pecos. Then Mr. Richards would say, "Shall we pray?" Nobody ever really decided whether to or not, so Mr. Richards did. "Dear Lord, hold us in the palm of your mighty hand. Give us what we need and a little of what we want. Amen." It was always the same prayer. It was just something to say to somebody named Lord, but Fudge liked the part about giving a little of what he wanted. He wanted a gun, two guns, and he had been filling in with words of his own lately and telling more than asking Lord because he was getting more and more worried. Then Ma'am read from the Bible. He surely knew about that book. He had to read from it himself every day in front of her. He even liked the time he spent in the house since it gave him a little relief from roosters, peacocks, spiders and rattlers. He read just from the first part and there were stories about men who moved their cattle here and there and got into arguments about land and who was going to get it. Ma'am explained a lot of what he didn't understand. The words were so funny and hard, but life sounded pretty much the same in the book as it did where he lived. Camels, asses and sheep were in some of the stories, but nothing about guns. David whipped a lion pretty bad with the jaw bone of an ass and killed a giant with a rock, but none of the folks in the book seemed to be able to get hold of a pistola either.

All these thoughts flashed through Fudge's head as he listened to the pair in the hall. What were do-dads? Mr. Richards was saying, "Now, Ruth. . . . I can't do without you this time of year and I can't let you go alone knowing you'd be two hard days riding before you could meet up with the train to get you to Toad. And what good would Fudge be to you? He's got a good father and he's better off here away from people for a while. Darrell Lee Barclay is the best man in the world and he's my best man here at Cross-winds. I don't know what I'd do without him. And Fudge is better off here with him now."

Ma'am's voice was low in the beginning, "Cater, you know we must do something for Fudge. I'm raising him and there are things he needs even if he sleeps in the bunkhouse with his daddy and the men. For starters, he needs clothes and boots. . . ." Fudge lost a lot of other things Ma'am said at the mention of boots. He looked down at his feet on which were sandals like the Mexicans wore. He got a new pair every few months when Old Manuel came through in his peddler's wagon. Manuel wore guns and ammunition strapped crisscross on his chest, two guns. That's how Fudge knew about some who carried two guns all the time. The cowboys at Crosswinds wore only one gun most of the time. In Manuel's wagon were more things, pots and pans and cloth, but Fudge knew Manuel carried shells for the cowboys in the wagon because he had seen. And Manuel had The News; that's what the men said, "Manuel, amigo, what's The News?" Even Ma'am wanted to know, but he never got to hear what it was that was The News.

". . . and I'm thirty-five years old and you know we aren't ever going to have . . . a . . ." Ma'am never finished the sentence but began to cry so badly she couldn't talk. Mr. Richards reached out his hand and touched Ma'am, patted her on the shoulder just like he did the men now and then, only softer. So, Ma'am was a real old woman, and there were some things she wanted and going to town would get part of them. And what was she doing to him, this raising word? Whatever it was, he liked most of it, but if she cried so then maybe she was going to quit. Would the do-dads fix everything? Another whispy thought crossed Fudge's mind, but it was gone too before he could make it take form. Were there other people, other Ma'ams somewhere out there who? Who what?

Fudge had no way to ask the whole questions in his mind and part of the trouble in thinking was that he had always to keep his mind on whatever was after him. From the corner of his eye, he caught the movement of the rooster moving in. If the rooster got up on the porch and came after Fudge, then the Mister and Ma'am would know he was there listening.

". . . think what will happen to Fudge, Ruth. Everyone in town will ask questions, questions we have never asked of his daddy when he rode up here four years ago with that baby boy. We just took 'em in and never been sorry. Nobody in town will understand." Mr. Richards said more and so did Ma'am, but Fudge never heard more because he had to do something about El Gallo, another of his daddy's words for rooster.

Fudge climbed over the porch rail and fell to the ground just as El Gallo jumped up the last step and came after him. What the boy did was an act of courage. Instead of retreating from the rooster, the child charged back up the steps after the bird, hollering at the same time. "Git out of Ma'am's yard. Git!" The noise brought the couple outside immediately and in time to see the rooster fly in Fudge's face, spurs up, and a spurt of blood appear near the boy's right eye. It was Mr. Richards who grabbed Fudge, separating him from the bird. It was Ma'am who grabbed a broom and, with both hands on the stick, swung at the rooster. Fudge looked on out of his one good eye at the bird as he arched high in the air and landed far from the porch, flopping around and around on the ground. Fudge looked clearly for the first time in his life at Ma'am. He saw that she was tall, noticeably taller than Mr. Richards. Before the rooster could gain his feet, Ma'am ran to the flopping desperado. He could see the soles of her boots as she hiked her skirts and gathered the apron she always wore. A broad-brimmed sombrero such as old Manuel wore bounced on a leather string behind her back. When she got to the object of her anger, she began to kick the bird. Then she kicked him again. Step, kick. Step, kick and crying, sobbing, with every kick. Ma'am kicked the bird until she was a long way off. Then she stopped, took one hand to fuss with her blond hair, which had come undone in the midst of battle, and with the other reached into her apron pocket, took out something small and began to shoot at the rooster as he ran crazily away. Almost all of the scene flashed before Fudge's eyes like the pictures he saw in the stereoptican he looked at in the front room of the big house, but the detail of what Ma'am held in her hand lodged in Fudge's mind while everything was forgotten. Ma'am looked like she was playing thumb-and-finger guns, but the rooster was running from the noise in her hand.

When she finally returned, Fudge was still beside Mr. Richards as he squatted down by the boy, blood running all over both of them, and both still immobile at the scene they had just witnessed. "Cater, can't you see the boy is hurt, maybe blind. And I could have killed the monster, but then what would we do without a rooster?" Even in his pain and fright, the thought flashed through Fudge's mind that the bird wasn't going to be in any shape to help her much for a while. Ma'am kept on talking without stopping for breath, "and he may have blinded Fudge," as she wrenched him from inside Mr. Richards' protective arm and marched into the house, still talking. "You see . . . see . . . don't you, what life is like. I'm lonesome and I'm scared and I just hate you, Cater, and I'm going to town because Fudge needs to real bad and . . . and you get me some more ammunition for the little gun because I shot it all up . . . and yes, some for the rifle, for the shotgun . . . and some for your pistolas too . . . and make sure the men's guns have plenty . . . 'cause I'm going to town and all of you will need every cartridge you can get your hands on while I'm gone. Yes, I know I've got this fine woodboard house, and trees growing and flowers too, and a windmill and I even got a Sears catalog to order the rest of the things I need, but now I want a little of what I want, not what I got, and I'm going to town and that's that!"

Of all the words Ma'am had spoken, only one word, ammunition, stuck in Fudge's feverish mind the next few days and nothing else of what Ma'am had said. She was talking big people's talk and he didn't understand much of anything he overheard that wasn't said directly to him. The rooster's spurs had indeed come almost too close to the little boy's right eye. Ma'am had washed his face, gently but over and over. She poured something on the rag which made his cheek burn, but not nearly as much as when she covered up his left eye too and began to push the skin under his right eye. Then he felt every prick of the needle as she sewed the skin in place. Fudge knew without being told what she was doing. Not more than a few months ago, he watched her do the same thing to one of Buck's horses. Buck had come to the back door of the house, called "Ma'am, Ma'am? Could you come to the corral and look at Jack? Mr. Richards says I was to ast you first before I put a bullet in 'im. Jack's cut hisself awful bad, Ma'am." Ma'am put down the Sears and Roebuck catalog, which was the other book Fudge read from, and went to see to Jack, taking with her the sewing basket and talking as she went out the back door, "Oh yes, I'll come, Buck, and sew up your horse, Buck, that has a man's name while you, Buck, have a horse's name." And sew she did, a great gaping tear on Jack's shoulder.

Ma'am said stuff all the time that didn't make any sense, but the hands seemed to think a lot of it was funny and a lot of it didn't make any sense to them either, so they said in the bunkhouse when Fudge asked for explanations.

Now, Fudge stayed as still as Jack when Ma'am stitched up the big horse. After the woman sewed up Fudge's cheek, she made him swallow something bitter. Then he went to sleep, and when he woke up, his face was throbbing and burning and he dreamed between the waking and hurting about guns and bullets, roosters,

rattlers, scorpions, and phantoms with no names to call them and
Ma'am taking something from her pocket that made a rooster get
up and run.

Ma'am woke Fudge up when he didn't want to wake up and
spooned warm liquid down him. He tried to swallow it, but most
of it ran down his chin. Fever raged along with the infection and
swelling on the right side of his face. His daddy and Buck, Rowdy,
Skeeter, Fuzz and all the rest drifted dimly above him from time to
time. Ma'am he knew by cool touch and her singing "Shall we
gather at the river that flows by the throne of God."

Fudge had no idea how long he'd been coming and going from
shadow to light mainly because of what Ma'am made him swallow,
but one morning before daylight, he knew that he was waking up
all the way. Pain like a thousand sharp knives was in his eye. He
felt gently near the spot where the rooster got him and the skin was
fat and puffy and he couldn't see at all on the right side of him. He
lay awhile looking around out of the left eye. Shapes became objects
in those moments just before dawn, and he recognized parts of his
own body, then the bed and the covers of quilts, a chest of wood at
the end of the bed, the slop jar, a chair with rockers on it and
something shiny on the wall along with pictures of some people.
Fudge was drawn to the shiny thing. He had seen items like those
in the room before in other places in the house or bunkhouse, but
never anything so bright and getting brighter as the sun was on the
verge of rising. Fudge got up quietly and battled the pain in his
face and eye. It was only a few steps to the shining on the wall, but
when he got there, he was below the framed light, and his whole
head throbbed with every beat of his heart. Seeing the chair as a
solution, although a moving one, Fudge quietly moved the piece
underneath the wall and climbed up. After he steadied the swaying
motion, Fudge peered into a mirror and saw reflected back a
brown face, black hair and one blue eye. The other he guessed was
buried in the folds and puffs of blue-brown skin on the right side of
his face. The reflection was not a sight to make a body feel all right
about itself, especially if the body had never known that such an
apparatus as a mirror existed in the world. Since the face heretofore
had nothing with which to compare itself, however, the shock was
not as bad as it might have been. And after Fudge had taken the
measure of himself, both face and upper body, and after his heart
had quieted some and along with it his face, the boy caught the

glimpse of something behind him hanging on the right side of his bed. Draped over the high post was a holster and two guns, pisto-las! The guns were smaller than the ones Old Manuel and the cowboys carried.

Fudge got down out of the chair and replaced it. Then he climbed back in bed and stood up beside the belt full of ammuni-tion with the double holsters. Then he took out one of the guns, but only one, and without a minute's hesitation went back to the rock-ing chair, replaced it in front of the mirror, all the while holding the gun in his right hand. Then he climbed up on the swaying chair and, between coming closer and farther away, looked at himself as he held the gun in the front of him. Then he heard Ma'am coming.

By the time Ma'am entered the door, everything was exactly where she'd left it the night before except that the rocking chair was moving a little and Fudge was awake. "Why, Fudge, you're awake and you've even been up to the rocking chair. How do you feel?" and by the time she said it, the woman was touching and probing Fudge's distended cheek. "It does look better this morning, and I'll just bet in a few more days you can maybe even see. I'll get the stitches out. Oh, I hope you can see as good as new," but she didn't dwell on the words and went right on chatting about how some of the men were coming in from near and far . . . would be at Crosswinds for a week or more . . . were bringing a new bull, one without horns . . . talk, talk, talk . . . new kind of cattle soon . . . folks using some kind of wire they called bob war, which was really barbed wire, to fence places so they wouldn't have to ride so far. Manuel came by and brought her some plants from the border country called Spanish Dagger to put with the Prickly Pear Cactus and the thorny Ocotillo called Devil's Whip. She laughed shrilly, not at all like Ma'am, and finished with, "Every-thing goes armed here, Fudge. Even the rooster and the plants. Now the fences got points, spurs and thorns." Then she said some more things and added right before she left the room that they'd be going to town for sure in just a few days, at the most.

Fudge had never heard Ma'am talk so much. It amounted to jabbering, like they said Manuel did. But Fudge liked Manuel's jabbering. He did not like Ma'am's. Maybe it was because he did not understand much of anything she said. She even told him once he was like the little slate she used to teach him letters and figures. He was just being written on. Then everything was erased and something new put on it. All he had to do, she said, was let himself be written on. Ma'am was jabbering again when she said those words. He knew it wasn't supposed to make sense.

After Ma'am left, Fudge knew he wasn't going to be a slate to be written on any longer. He was going to do something, something good, something right, something that would make the whole ranch proud of him, especially Ma'am. Every man on the place including Mr. Richards and Ma'am told him all the time they were proud of him. "Fudge," they'd say at roundup, "I'm proud you brought me the iron." Or, "I'd be proud if you'd hand me a dipper of water." Or, "Stand up there proud, Fudge." Well, he was fixing to make them all prouder because he was going to learn to use two guns and he was going to do it in private and surprise them all. He didn't know if the secret part would make them proud, but they'd forget it just as soon as they saw what he could do. He knew if he could shoot the guns, then everything would come right for Ma'am and everyone else.

Then Fudge heard the rooster crow and it sent a shiver through him.

Once a thing is decided on, sometimes life just helps out. Fudge thought such a thought during the next few days after he made the decision to actively become a two-gun man. The men did gather from all directions. For a while every time Fudge looked for Ma'am, he found her standing on the perimeters of the ranch, one hand on her waist and one hand shading her eyes against the sun looking for something or someone. She counted everyone who came and spoke with sincere concern about the yellow-haired boy, Pete, or the black man, Mose, who hadn't shown up yet. Two men, she said, lived with their families on places nearer the border. She hoped they would bring their folks, but they didn't. Seldom had he seen them all together at one time even at roundup, but now they came in to Crosswinds by twos and threes and sometimes alone. Their coming had something to do with the new bull and bob war and stringing it out and something to do with getting ready for trouble ahead. As the men came in, they were doing a lot of talking. Some were in the bunkhouse and some camped close by, but all came to Ma'am's table in the backyard to eat in two shifts of ten. Ma'am was busy laughing, cooking and having Fudge tote and fetch for her the things she needed in the house, but she wouldn't let him go back to his place in the bunkhouse. Somebody else was in his bed anyhow, and anyhow, he had business in the house in front of the mirror, anyhow. That's the way Fudge looked at it. The men paid little attention to Fudge, not even his daddy. Old Manuel rolled in and at the sight of him the men cheered, and the man stood up, drew back on the reins of the mules, threw back his head and hollered "Ay-yi-yi-yi-yi" at the top of his lungs. Fudge had never seen the peddler act in such a way before. Everybody was sure glad to see everybody else, probably. However they were behaving left Fudge time to do what he had to do.

Three times a day, before daylight, in the afternoon and after dark, Fudge went upstairs, took off his leather sandals, climbed up on the bed and got a pistola out of the holster, moved the rocking chair in front of the mirror and, swaying back and forth, put his finger on the trigger and aimed. "Bang, bang," he whispered. Then he would perform the ritual backward and scoot for downstairs. Nobody missed him even once.

After two days of practice, Fudge grew tired of what he was doing upstairs. Nothing was coming of it anyway. It was, he thought, time to make a bold move. Since nobody paid any attention to him at all, morning, noon or night, because they were all wrapped up in wire and the stuff Manuel had in the wagon, Fudge grew bolder. He was going to take the mirror and the guns outside. That's what he would do—in the dark, of course, but by all means, outside. Outside, that's where guns belonged and that's where Fudge belonged too.

The lay of the ranch consisted of a group of buildings with the house in the center front; then miles and miles of open country in every direction. Fudge studied the layout from the inside out and realized that the place was perfect for his plan. If you were riding in from the south, that's what a person saw first, the house. A big corral and smaller pens, a barn, garden plot, chicken yard, home of El Gallo and henhouse where the *gallinas* laid their eggs, were behind the big house and fanned out on either side. The outhouse was beyond the chicken yard, and as he knew well, a person had to go around or through the chicken yard to get to it. The outhouse was really for Ma'am. He couldn't tell that anybody else made much use of it. And that, Fudge knew, was the perfect place to take the guns and the mirror.

After dark, but before the men turned in, they gathered around a big fire pit drinking coffee, told wild tales and made Ma'am laugh. "Angus, why didn't you bring Margaret Nell and the girls? We could have done some sewing or something," Ma'am was saying to one of the men. He answered, "Now, Mrs. Richards, I took her to a funeral in town not two years ago." From the sound of it Fudge knew Angus had cracked a funny by the way they all laughed, but he knew too that there was an uneasiness, a tension, in everyone, but he didn't have time to understand why. He was strung tighter than a wire himself.

It was during the campfire time that the gunman made his move. Fudge scooted for the house. On the way he heard the chickens squawking softly in the henhouse, knew the rooster was likewise settled in. Everything was bedding down, and he could tell not by the silence but by the noises everything made—the horses snuffling and stomping, the night birds asking, the chirping of crickets, the scratching of mice, even the soft meowing of Ma'am's beloved and pampered cat, as if they were all signaling their presence to each other in the dark. The noises were as comforting to Fudge at night as many of them were terrifying by day.

The child entered the dark house by the front door since everyone else was out back. He lighted no lamps, but rather felt his way upstairs. Fudge went immediately to the bed, climbed up, but this time he took not just one gun but removed the entire belt holding the cartridges, holsters and guns. The items were much heavier than Fudge had imagined, and try as he did, the boy couldn't carry the load without dragging the guns on the ground. When he got to the stairs, he moved with the confidence of one who knows he is not being watched and who is so scared that caution is thrown to the winds. He forged ahead and dragged the weapons behind him, bouncing them down the stairs. The term "gun slinger" took on new dimensions under Fudge's command. He continued the dragging procedure out the front door and down the porch steps, past the corral, the barn, the chicken yard and finally behind the outhouse. His destination reached with nothing but open land ahead, Fudge collapsed in a terrified heap behind the building at the same time he wet his pants. It was a problem he had not counted on when he thought he had calculated every other single detail. Fudge cried then. He may as well, he concluded, since he'd done everything else wrong. In the midst of the tears it dawned on him that he had forgotten to bring the mirror.

After a few minutes of crying, Fudge realized that what he'd come to do was ruined, his first practice with two guns ruined. Nobody heard anything at all, except for the creatures at Crosswinds. The cat heard the dragging in the dirt and thought it might be mice. One of the horses nickered to another to ask whether or not to nicker again. The chickens were always alert for whatever might invade the hen house and clucking was coming close to squawking.

Fudge got up at the noises which he himself had caused, but he didn't know that. He started to get gathered up and start back for the house, but listening. His heart was beginning to pound again. Talk at the campfire stopped and one of the men said, "What's that?" Another said, "Nothing but the horses moving, I think. Buck, you're mighty jumpy." The group returned to their talk, but with one ear to the world outside their safe circle.

Fudge had just turned the corner from behind the outhouse when he saw it, saw something. Something was moving through the chicken yard. The boy felt his cheek sting and his eye begin to burn at the same instant he guessed at what the shape was. It might be El Gallo and making straight for him, he reasoned. Fudge returned to his hiding place behind the outhouse dragging the guns with him. At the same instant he knew that he was not hidden from the monster which, no doubt, was coming around the corner any minute. What to do? He would get in the outhouse. That was it! But too late. The phantom form rounded one corner just as Fudge went around the other.

Quicker than greased lightning, the child dropped the gun belt on the ground and pulled one of the guns free. While in the very act of saying bang, bang, his finger went to the trigger and pulled. Ma'am's calico cat which had come to hunt for mice yowled. Whatever Fudge had done was not stopping the creature. He closed his eyes and pulled the trigger again. Then again and again aiming high and low, deep and wide, and in whatever direction the gun, with a will of its own, wanted to fire.

While Fudge was putting down one gun and pulling out the other, the men around the fire were running toward the noise in an instant. Buck grabbed the rifle, went down on his belly, slid through the chicken yard and opened fire on the hen house. Not knowing the source of the gunfire, but only the direction, other cowboys pulled guns and fired too. Like good men and true, their guns were aimed mostly in the air until they divined the source and shape of the trouble. Fudge just kept pulling the trigger on the other gun until it clicked as Fudge continued to say, "bang, bang."

Horses were running in the corral. The force of their weight knocked down one rail and the whole bunch broke for Mexico. The new bull in the barn began to bellow. He had been hit. The chickens moved from their roosts and fell squawking as they were shot. Glass shattered.

No one knew how long the battle raged before someone realized that only the cowboys of Crosswinds ranch were doing the shooting. Fudge's daddy was the first one who said, "Hey, hold up. Hey!" Buck was next: "Hold off. Stop. Darrell, is that you? You okay?" Fudge's daddy yelled, "Yeah. I'm okay." With the action over, the other men came up from behind troughs and from behind buildings. Before anybody had time to determine what had happened, Ma'am screamed, "Oh my Lord! Where is Fudge?" And with her own rifle spent in her hands, she ran toward the outhouse.

Finding out where Fudge was and just what had happened took some time, angry words, a whipping with the back of Darrell's hand, more tears, hysterics from Ma'am and decisions about Fudge's future which included a horse, boots and a trip to town. Gathering back the horses, digging bullets out of the bull, mending the corral, scalding dead chickens for plucking and cooking, repairing Manuel's wagon, cleaning the chicken yard off of Buck, ordering more glass for the house windows and scraping what was left of the cat off the outhouse wall took even more time.

Only one issue was clear and that was that Fudge was not going to pursue a career as a two-gun man. His daddy started him on a big old shotgun which knocked him down every time he fired it. "When the gun don't knock you down no more, Fudge, then Ma'am says you can get on with the rifle, and then the pistola business," his daddy said grimly. "And Mrs. Richards says we ain't gonna' call you Fudge no more. We're gonna' call you by your right name, which is Darrell Lee Barclay. But we'll call you Lee for short."

Lee's daddy was good to his word, every last word. And Old Manuel and the rooster in the chicken yard who lost not a feather heard it all.

News travels slowly, not fast, in the vast expanses of the West. An event might be translated, rearranged and filtered through the eyes and minds of many. So it was with the reputation of Lee Barclay, alias Fudge.

The law travels slowly in the West, too. When Marshal Barclay was sworn in as one of the first along the Rio Grande border, he wore two guns and carried a rifle in the boot of his saddle, plain for all to see. As to his appearance, a deep scar on his right cheek close to his eye was visible. Any who cared to look closely noticed the clear blue eyes, the dark hair under a broad-brimmed Mexican-style hat which was secured with a leather string, and the bronzed skin from more than just a lifetime in the sun. For twenty years, the man dispensed justice fairly. *Mexicano y Tejano* claimed him, and called him friend. After all, they said, he carries two guns, one for each side of the border.

A newspaper reporter roaming the border country collecting fabulous stories to send back East once asked the marshal where he learned to shoot two guns.

"From a woman," the marshal replied without the slightest trace of a smile. The newspaperman responded with a sarcastic "Yeah, yeah, I'll bet," as he folded up his notebook and put it in his shirt pocket. Some stories were too preposterous to repeat, even for a newspaperman.

Reunion

Lenore Carroll

NOTES TO TOURISTS.—The uniform railroad fare in the Territory averages ten cents per mile. Stage routes run all through the mountains, fare from ten to twenty cents per mile. The uniform rate of board is four dollars per day, and almost every-where can be found excellent living; the nicest of beef steak, bread and biscuit. In many of the mountain resorts plenty of good fishing can be found, and delicate trout are common viands of the hotel tables. The best season of the year for a visit to Colorado is in July and August. As then the snow has nearly disappeared from the mountains, and all the beautiful parks and valleys are easily approachable.

—WILLIAMS, *The Pacific Tourist and guide across the continent,* 1878

KATE'S KNEES ached when she stepped down out of the stage-coach. The slope of the mountain tipped the seats forward and she had been standing on the brake, it seemed, since Leadville. The road dust penetrated all the layers of fabric, all the folds of her skin. She felt pounded sore from days of riding, not like the old days when they left town on a moment's notice and never counted the effort. At least the air was cool here in Glenwood Springs and the high-altitude sun bright and the clouds soft.

She looked down the main street from the hotel to the steaming hot springs trickling into the foaming Colorado River. She would have to take the ferry across the river for a hot soak, get the stiffness out. She was only thirty-five, but she felt time's touch in

the joints of her sturdy hands, and while her homely Hungarian
face was still smooth, silver hairs twined in the knot on top of her
head.

Later, she lay immersed in a concrete tub, the chemical-smelling
water steaming. The sound of running water made her feel she
were floating in a warm river. Was this what an unborn child felt
floating in the sac of the womb, what her child had felt? Was this
some internal refuge in the Earth, where she could draw strength?

She couldn't face him yet.

He had sent for her once again. The letter came the day they
were breaking horses, when she heard the men's cries from the
corral, and the dust hung thick in the air around the ranch house
kitchen. She sat at the table in her room, the shade pulled against
the heat, and held the letter, written in his perfect hand, for a long
time, waiting for her heart to slow its ricochet around her chest.
She'd have sworn her feeling for him was as dried and forgotten as
a flower pressed in a book, but the envelope trembled in her hand.
Memories came back, as real as the Arizona heat. She propped the
envelope on her dresser and left it for four days.

When she read it, she packed and got on a train, then rode the
stages over the mountains. She always came when he asked.

"Where may I find Mr. Holliday?" she asked the desk clerk.

She knew the man saw a stout, middle-aged woman, probably
never pretty, the week's travel in her face. He checked her signa-
ture on the register.

"Are you a friend of his?" asked the clerk.

"He sent word he wanted to see me," she answered. "If you'll
tell him I'm here."

She waited in her room. Her traveling outfit went to be cleaned
and she changed into fresh clothes. She sat with her feet up and
watched out the tall, narrow window as a late afternoon shower
moved down the mountain through the sun, and she felt the breeze
stir the curtains. Fragments from the old days came back—the wild
times. Drinking. His gambling. Loving. Scarred-over places she
had ignored for years ached.

Did her arms remember his delicate touch or only the bruises?
Did her eyes swell shut or did they remember his lips tasting her
tears? Could she feel his fevered body in her arms? Did her blood

race inside skin that burned from caresses, skin that took the print of his rage? Did the hate he spoke bruise the heart inside sore ribs?

Eventually, a man knocked and asked would she please to follow.

She hesitated outside the door, afraid to look at the once-familiar face, feel something give way inside, launch herself again into his sphere.

"You look mighty bad, Doc," she said. The servant, who seemed to be something between a valet and a nurse, pushed a chair near the bed where the wasted man with TB lay propped on pillows. She sat and took his white hand. She wanted his scent, individual, like his voice, but the stuffy, sickroom smell was all she could catch.

"It was good of you to come," he said. His blue eyes were too bright. Morphine? The spotless nightshirt was buttoned. His thin, graying hair had been brushed straight back, obviously by someone else. His mustache needed trimming. Someone had cut his nails, but not filed them smooth.

"I always came," she said.

"But it has been a long time. I wasn't sure."

The cough she remembered took him and he pulled his hand away from hers to hold a blue handkerchief to his mouth. It came away streaked with red. She took a glass of water from the table and held his head while he drank a little. It made her shaky to touch him, remember the soft hair, the fine skull beneath, the warm flesh she met.

"Why now?" she asked. He always had such nice manners, like all Southern men, when they chose, and she was always too abrupt.

"I've been dying for years," he said with a glint of humor. "This time I think I shall succeed."

"You're too mean." She tried to sound jolly but failed.

"You're the one who's tough. You look mighty fat and sassy," he countered. "What are you doing these days?"

She thought of her days cooking for the ranch hands. That wouldn't sound good enough. "Last time I got a stake, I bought a cattle ranch instead of another whorehouse. I thought the cows would be smarter than the girls."

"Are they?"

"No, but they make me a living." It was like walking a razor to talk as though nothing were the matter.

"You survive, Kate." He made it a benediction.

She bowed her head. A headache drummed behind her eyes. She never cried in front of him, not when he beat her, swore at her, forced her to lie for him. She never gave him the satisfaction.

"I treated you badly," he whispered.

"What's a few broken ribs between friends?" she said, false and hearty.

"I wanted to say I was sorry, before I'm gone."

"I didn't have to come here for that. I knew you were sorry. Afterward."

"I could have sent another letter, I suppose."

"You were always a great one for letters."

The writing desk in his room held only medicine bottles and glass tumblers. Brush and comb on the dresser, handkerchiefs and water glass on the nightstand. Where were the sheets of spidery copperplate, finger-smudged rough drafts and flawless fair copies, that she remembered?

"Do you still write to your cousin?" she asked.

"She died."

"I'm sorry. Her prayers probably kept you alive all these years." And Kate was sorry she said that.

His hands shook and he coughed again. After the spasm passed, he closed his eyes. She waited for him to look at her again so she could apologize for what she said, but he slept, exhausted.

She got up and turned to the manservant who stood near the door. "I want to talk to him again."

The man shook his head.

She grabbed his arm above the elbow and steered him into the hall.

"I have traveled a week to get here." She spoke softly, but with force. "Don't shake your head at me."

The man looked mulish.

"How does he pay you?" she asked.

"I won't tell you."

"He doesn't pay you, is that it?"

The man looked startled.

"How long are you going to look after him? What do you live on?"

"People in town pay his bill, pay me a little. Sometimes."

"Is he alert when he is awake?"

"Pretty much."

"He doped up to talk to me."

The man shrugged.

"I want to talk to him again." She chewed her thumb a moment. "I'm going to the dining room for supper, then I will be in my room. If he wakes up within a few hours, fetch me."

The man's eyebrows went up.

She ignored him. "Tomorrow I will be available after ten." She thought again. "If I don't see him within twenty-four hours, I'll assume he died and hire an undertaker. Does a doctor see him?"

The man said yes.

"I want to talk to him, too." She studied the servant, who looked too stubborn to take orders from her. "If you want to get paid, you'll do as I say."

She walked down the steps to the lobby, across the wide plank floor and into the dining room, golden in lamplight as summer night settled in.

"He came for the vapors," said the banker. "One-way ticket. And the sulfur ate what was left of his lungs." The banker's watch fob gleamed against his waistcoat. "He is well liked. He tried to practice dentistry at first, but he was too ill to stand for hours. Don't know how he drank all night and kept a clear head for cards."

He could always keep a clear head, she thought, and remember the cards.

"Of course, everyone expected him to use his sidearm, but as far as I know he never drew it."

Only if some yahoo challenged his honor. Only if he intended to kill. Kate told the banker what she wanted. "If he needs more, let me know. Telegraph. I want a complete accounting when it's over. Tell him you took up a collection."

She signed some papers and walked back to the hotel.

Glenwood Springs looked prosperous. New buildings lined the streets that tilted down the mountainside, houses with gingerbread and fences, stores with wide windows. She noted the number of saloons and wondered how many miners' silver dollars Doc had won playing cards. He'd chosen a beautiful place to die. She looked up from the storefronts and drank in the valley of the Colorado, the green and golden mountains, perfect, picturesque—ready for the stereopticon.

□ □ □ □

"I fell asleep," he said. He had again been brushed and propped up. She sat beside the bed.

"Don't overdo," she said and felt stupid.

"I wanted to beg your forgiveness," he said.

"You have it."

"I saw a priest."

"Cousin Mattie's deathbed request?"

"Don't mock me."

"I hated her," Kate said. She pressed her palms into the bunched fabric over her heavy thighs. "You would write to her—long letters. Educated letters. She wrote you back. We'd stay together for a while, high times. You were reckless because you knew you were dying. I was wild because I didn't have anything more to lose. Men liked that. You'd take me down, and when you were satisfied, you'd knock me around and throw me out."

"How many times?"

"Ten? A dozen? I don't remember. I'd leave. Then you'd take sick and write to me. I just always came back."

"Forgive me."

"I was the same person I'd been the day before you beat me. You knew what I was when we started together."

"When was that?"

"Fort Griffin, maybe. Texas, then Kansas? I liked you because you were clean and you treated me nice, at first. My husband was a dentist, too, in Atlanta."

"He died."

"And my little boy."

"Poor Kate."

"Nobody pities me."

"Of course." His bloodless hands plucked at the blanket. Only his eyes were alive. "We had some times, didn't we?"

"Always."

She must say it, make him hear it before he faded away again. "It took me all these years before I understood it all. Why we came together. Why you hated me, treated me bad. Why I always came back."

"I couldn't help it."

"I thought about it a lot, nursing split lips and black eyes. One time I had headaches for a month. Then I remembered it always happened after one of her letters. Your cousin Mattie, your first cousin who became Sister Melanie in the convent. I bet they wouldn't let you get married."

He started and one waxen hand lifted from the blanket for a moment. "No!"

"You got in some trouble, and came West. She went into the convent in Savannah. But she was the one you loved and she was pure, and when you couldn't have her, you took the lowest, dirtiest, wildest woman you could find."

The pale hand trembled and he frowned. "No," he said. "I loved you."

"Like a dog." She rubbed her thick nose with a linen handkerchief. "You wanted her and couldn't have her, so you took me and we did the wild things. And you hated yourself and you hated me. Because I loved that wicked part of you."

His delicate hand scratched the blanket. "Forgive me," he said again. "Kate." His voice faded to dry husks whispering.

"Yes." She leaned closer. She smelled death on him.

"I had to see you one more time."

And finally, after all those years, stinging like a slap, sharp as cheap whiskey, came her tears.

Spring Comes to the Widow

John D. Nesbitt

SAM FONTAINE was riding south when he found the death camp. The breeze was blowing north from a small stand of junipers, and he caught his first whiff nearly a quarter of a mile away.

He had ridden north all spring and summer, eating dust and fighting flies, to deliver a trail herd in Montana. When the boss paid them off, Sam bought his favorite horse out of the remuda before the string was sold. Rather than go on a spree with the boys, Sam turned the good horse Sandy straight back south and rode alone, a season's wages in his pocket, a lightness in his heart, and a song on his lips.

The lightness and the song ended when he smelled death. It was never a good smell, but if a fellow saw what it was before he smelled it, things went a little easier. When the smell came first, the thing to do was to give it a wide flank, come at it upwind, and get the story before moving on.

Sam was nearly even with the trees when he heard a cry, the small cry of a small thing, like a lamb, but it wasn't a lamb. It was a baby. He touched his spurs to Sandy and got to the trees on a lope.

Four buzzards lifted from the camp as Sandy settled to a halt and Sam slid from the saddle, fighting the heaves that pounded in his stomach. He yanked on the reins to keep the horse from backstepping, and then he looked at the camp.

It was a camp of Mexican folk who had come to the end of their luck. Two oxen slumped dead in the harness of a wooden-wheeled cart. Next to a mounded grave with a wooden cross lay the body of a man with its mouth open. Sam looked away. The baby's cry came again from the off side of the cart, where the last of the morning shade still lingered. Tugging on the reins, he stepped around the end of the cart. There was a young woman sitting blank-eyed against the wheel, rocking the baby vacantly. She didn't seem to have the strength or the focus to care for the baby beyond that automatic movement.

Sam knelt by the woman. *"¿Qué pasó?"* he asked. What happened?

She licked her lips. *"Muertos. Todos muertos."* Dead. All dead.

Sam nodded. *"Sí. Hombre muerto. Vacas muerto. ¿Qué pasó?"* Yes. Dead man. Dead cows. What happened?

The woman rolled her eyes. *"Agua."* Water.

"¿Quiere agua?" You want water?

"No. No agua. Agua mala." No. No water. Bad water.

"¿Mala?" Bad?

"Veneno." Poison.

"¿Quiere agua? ¿Agua buena, fresca?" Do you want water? Good water? Fresh?

The woman nodded. Sam unslung one of his canteens and held it to her lips. She drank and nodded again. *"Gracias."*

He dribbled a little water on the baby's mouth, but the baby just sputtered and coughed and cried. Sam settled onto his heels, still squatting, and asked again what had happened.

The woman spoke rapidly in a voice somewhere between crying and heavy sighing, a voice full of agony and sadness, a voice that seemed far too old for a young mother. From her rambling, Sam pieced together the story. They had all drunk from a poisoned spring, all but the baby. Her husband and son had died first, and then her brother-in-law, who presumably had lived long enough to bury the other two in a common grave. The woman seemed certain that she, too, was going to die.

Sam offered her more water and she took it, but it oozed out of her mouth and down her chin, sprinkling a few drops on the baby. She moved her mouth as if trying to speak, but no words came. Relaxing her hold on the baby to let it lie on her lap, she closed her eyes and leaned her head back against the hub of the wheel. She was on the way out, he could see that. He patted her hand and said the only thing he could think of, *"Vaya con Dios."* God be with you. The hand fluttered, and that was it.

In less than an hour, Sam had buried the brother-in-law, cut loose the oxen, and with Sandy straining, dragged the dead animals a hundred yards distant. All the while, the baby cried. When Sam returned to the cart, where he had stretched the woman out in the shade, the baby had crawled onto the mother's abdomen and was kneading at the dead left breast. That was the hardest moment, and it stayed with him through the burying, the mumbled words to God and the dead mother, and the long ride through daylight and darkness until he reached the town of Socorro.

La señora Ramos ground the dry oatmeal to a finer grain in her stone *metate* before cooking it for the baby. Fontaine sat at the table by candlelight, rolling a cigarette and then smoking it as the woman went about her work. When the gruel was cooked, she set it aside to cool, then went about the task of changing the baby's diapers. Sam looked away, studying a crucifix that seemed to move on the wall as the candle flickered.

La señora Ramos spoke good English. "I cannot keep this baby, you know, not forever," she said as she spooned mush into the infant. She looked at Sam, and he nodded. "When I was younger and my house was full of children, I never counted them. Everybody's children went to everybody's house. What was one more? I had eight myself. And four dead ones." She crossed herself. Then she resumed feeding the baby. "But my children are gone now, to their own families, and I am an old widow. I have to wash clothes and clean houses. The time is past for me." She shook her head and then smiled as she looked into the baby's eyes.

Sam took out the makings and rolled another cigarette. He lit it with the candle and blew out a cloud of smoke. "What do you think we should do? Could we ask around and maybe find a home for it?"

She shrugged. "We could."

"You don't seem to like that idea."

"There are two problems. A family might take the baby in a sense of obligation. Or a family could get jealous who did not get the baby."

"Uh-huh." Fontaine ashed his cigarette in his palm and rubbed the ashes into his pant leg. "You must have another idea."

She raised her eyebrows. "We could offer the baby through the Church."

"What's the problem there?"

"There is a couple, the Reyes, who have money but no children."

"And you wouldn't want them to get the baby."

"I would not prefer it."

Sam looked at the ceiling and then back at the woman. He shook his head. "What do we do, then?"

"You could keep the baby. You found the baby and saved its life. It would not be wrong. Perhaps it is God's gift to you."

Sam nodded. The thought of keeping it had occurred to him as he had cradled the baby in his right arm on the long ride into Socorro. "I can think on it," he said. "But I don't know how I could take care of it. I've got to work, too."

La señora Ramos had apparently been doing some thinking herself. "Get yourself a young widow," she said.

Having told the señora he would study on it, and having gotten her to agree to keep the baby for a week, Sam rode to Albuquerque with no more definite plan than to study on it.

Always before, when he had thought about marriage, Sam Fontaine had imagined a blue-eyed girl with light-colored hair, an innocent, untouched girl who, through his guidance, would step into adult life. There would be marriage and then children.

Now, life presented a different possible order. He had a child if he wanted it. The memory of the baby pushing against the dead mother's breast, together with the memory of it squirming against his own body as he cradled it on horseback, gave rise to a strong feeling he could not brush aside. Yes, he had a child if he wanted it, and he could find a marriage to match.

There was plenty for Sam to study in Albuquerque. He saw the blue-eyed girls, apparently untouched, and he saw their dark-eyed, dark-haired counterparts. He saw young mothers with their children, older mothers with older children, women without children but with the look of motherhood about them. As he studied, the girls moved him less and less, while the women interested him more and more. He did not covet these women, but in the mature presence of a woman who had had a child, there was a definite power or pull.

It was absurd to think of shopping for a woman as a man might look for a cow pony or a draft horse, but he did need to form a clear idea of what he was looking for. The señora, in her practical wisdom, had started him thinking that way. A young widow would not be rushed from girlhood into motherhood. She would have matured some, and she might already have a child or two. At any rate she would have her own baggage, as Sam would have his. There would be an equality of sorts. And a young widow, Sam thought for the first time, with a widening smile, would be fit to have more. That would be a nice mix, he thought—mine, hers, and ours.

The young widow began to take on a definite image. She was a woman, not a girl—a young mother with one or possibly two at her side. She had dark eyes, dark hair, and skin the color of dark honey. Working backward, from child to marriage, had defined that for him—the baby should be raised in the language and customs of its mother.

"*Señora*," he said as he laid his hat on the table, "I have decided to keep the baby." Then he winked. "But I have one question."

"Yes?"

"Is it a boy or a girl?"

La señora Ramos smiled. "He's a little boy. And we don't know his name, or whether he's been baptized, or—"

"Hold on," Sam interjected. "I've got to find the young widow first, and then we'll take care of the rest."

When he had sketched out the lines of his recent thinking, the señora nodded in agreement. "Well, we can look around," she said. "I know of one woman, in my town of Palomas."

"Down on the border?"

"Yes." At Sam's hesitation she added, "You could go take a look. You don't have to take the first one you see."

"It's a start," he said. Then, thinking, he asked, "What's the word for widow?"

"*Viuda.*"

"Beeyutha."

"That's close."

"Will she be dressed in black?"

"I think he has more than one year dead."

"How do you say, 'What does that mean?' "

"You'll need that one. *¿Qué quiere decir?*"

He practiced it a few times.

"And how do you say 'it doesn't matter'?"

"No le hace."

"Nolayossay."

"That's close. What doesn't matter?"

"Whether it was a boy or a girl. And there'll be other things." He thought for another minute and then said, "I think I'd feel funny ridin' down there and knockin' on her door."

"It would be her father's door. She lives at his house."

"All the more reason. Hmmm. Does she have children?"

"I think she has one girl."

"Do you think you could get her to come here for a visit? Do you know her that well?"

"I barely know her, but I know her family. I can try."

The young widow María and the niña Ramona came to Socorro for a stay. Mother and daughter were dark, darker than the niño (who still went by the name of Niño) or his late mother, darker than the dark honey of Sam's imagination. Not that the darkness mattered—*no le hace*—but he had to adjust the qualifications he had projected. He admired the woman's fine features and shapely body, but more than that, he felt readily comfortable with her presence. She seemed to take a liking to him—probably would not have come if she had not been prepared to.

María was twenty-one and Sam was twenty-eight. Ramona was three and Niño was not yet a year old, the women agreed. María took a mother's interest in Niño, and Sam was instantly fond of Ramona, who, in turn, took a liking to both Sam and Sandy, as well as a natural interest in the baby. It looked to Sam as if every-thing was going to fit together.

After a month of round-robin acquaintance, Sam asked María to marry him, and she said *"Sí."*

They did not marry in the church or from her father's house, but with the justice of the peace in Socorro. Theirs was not a boisterous celebration, and María seemed pleased. That night, when she took him to her, she said, *"Te quiero mucho, Sem."*

He repeated the pledge in English. "I love you, María."

In the morning sunlight he sat on the edge of the bed and held her at arm's length, standing before him, his hands on her hips. It was a beautiful being he had joined himself with, this even-toned, full-bodied woman who in her presence meant togetherness and family. That was where it began, for them, the fitting together of a family, and now they could fill in with the daily confidences and agreements that had already begun to develop. He pulled her toward him and kissed her on the stomach. "My wife. *Mi mujer.*"

She held his head against her, the fingers of her left hand in his hair, the palm of her right hand against his cheek. *"Mi hombre."*

As the cool weather set in, Sam looked around for work to help them through the winter. There wasn't much work, but he did find two horses to break and train for pleasure riding. He spent the afternoons at that, and so he brought in a few dollars in November.

One evening la señora Ramos came to visit. After the preliminaries she made it clear she had come with a purpose. She spoke in the pattern she had developed for speaking with María and Sam: first in Spanish, then backing up to repeat or clarify in English, as Sam's expressions made the need clear. And so she launched into this evening's business.

This was a beautiful thing, this life and this love between two people, the joining of a family, a full life for them all, a life of pride for Ramona and Roberto (as Niño had come to be called). Everybody could see it. But you know how people can be. Some people can have everything yet wish to have something that belonged to someone else. There was no need to tell names, but there was a couple in the town who thought that perhaps not enough care had been taken to discover Roberto's true family. These people thought perhaps Roberto's future had been determined too quickly, perhaps the matter needed reconsideration.

These people had spoken with the priest and with the judge, and it was hoped by this couple that Roberto might be placed with a family who had no interest in the matter, until a satisfactory inquiry could be made. It was thought that if Roberto proved to be indeed without a family, then he could be eligible for legal adoption, with lawyers and the court and all of that.

Sam and María sat side by side in their chairs, their hand grip growing tighter. But Roberto has a family, María said.

Yes, and nobody can deny that. But his place is not secure. It is clear that there are some people who want a baby enough to take it.

Sam and María looked at each other. He said, in broken Spanish, this is not a good town for us. There is not much work. I don't like to run, but this is not a good town for us.

I think you are right, resumed la señora Ramos. You do not have

relatives here, or a business. You are my friends, and I do not like to
see my friends leave, especially at my age, but I agree with you.

Sam took María's hand in both of his. We could go south, he
said.

She shook her head, not violently, but to show there was no
strain in that direction.

We could go north. To a place I saw on the cow trip. It is cold
there, very cold in the winter.

At what distance does it lie? asked María.

In good weather, three weeks. In bad weather, who knows?
Maybe not until spring.

Three weeks in good weather, said la señora Ramos. That seems
to me to be a good place.

Sam looked at María. It is a good place, she said, even if it should
be cold. What is it called?

Wyoming. On the other side of Colorado. Much wind and very
cold. Nobody wants to go there. A good place.

They all laughed. It was seeming easier already.

Every night on the trip north, when they were bedded down in the
wagon, María cried. Sometimes they made love when the children
were asleep and sometimes they didn't, but every night she cried.
Sam held her and hugged her and patted her, brushed the damp
strands of hair from her face and kissed her. He came to understand that it was the distance from home, growing longer each day,
that weighed on her. Even though her family seemed agreeable to
letting her go from the very first, and even though she showed no
strong desire to make a home near them, the separation was being
felt sharply.

Sam wondered if it was anything else. Your friends?

No. My father and my mother.

Your country?

No. Just my parents.

Your brothers and your sisters?

Yes, them, too.

Sam took a skate on thin ice. Your dead husband?

No, no. My father and my mother.

"Te quiero mucho, María." I love you very much, María.

"Te quiero, Sem. Para siempre." I love you, Sam. Forever.

□ □ □ □

They rested a week in Denver and another four days in Cheyenne. It was an open winter so far, as folks said in Cheyenne. Trails were open north; trains were running east and west. There was plenty of time yet to get snowed in, but it was an open winter so far.

In mid-January the Fontaines filed on a quarter section of land, rolling plains country a few miles off the Platte. They rented a small house in town, a drafty clapboard shack that had been vacated by a Texas family who went back south for the weather. Sam and María patched cracks, kept a fire going in the sheet-iron stove, and waited for the thaw.

The family lived on deer meat all that winter. María, who'd been raised on tough beef, took to it fine, as did the children. Sam liked all food.

Will we be able to grow chiles here?

I think so. The summers are hot. They grow wheat. And I've seen apple trees.

This is good meat, but I will want to cook it with chiles.

We'll see. I think we can grow chiles.

María did not cry every night now, just once in a while. Things had come together again. For a while it had seemed as if they were four people, from different places, not living in any of them, speaking a mish-mash. Now it was seeming to flow together again, the ebb and flow of their common life, the melting of boundaries, the mingling of selves, the overflow and overlap of words. Sam could look back and hope that the worst was behind them, strung out in the cold trek north, left on the frozen plains, part of the wasteland between the place they left and the place they came to.

Spring came on slowly, starting in late March with the first green shoots of grass in the snowmelt, then freezing up solid again before the gradual teasing of warmer weather. In early May they took the wagon to their parcel, to camp out and get a view of things.

They set camp at a clump of chokecherry trees, where two draws came together. Sam and María spread a canvas for the children and then went to look at the greening branches.

A close look at the branches startled him. The branches were bristling with the furry green tips of leaves, and the smooth bark was freckled with white dots. The trees seemed to be bursting with life, eager for the new season.

"*Una fruta,*" he said. A fruit.

"¿*Buena?*" Good?

"*Sí. No muy dulce. Chica.*" Yes. Not very sweet. Small. He pressed his left thumbnail against the tip of the little finger. "*Así de grande.*" This big.

She nodded. "*Está bueno.*" That's good.

They walked, hand in hand, to a rise in the ground where they could see their land slope away to the north.

"¿*Te gusta?*" he asked. It was important that she like the place.

"*Sí, me gusta.*" Yes, I like it.

"¿*Te gusta casa aquí?*" You like the house here? He pointed down at the place where he thought to build a house.

"*Sí.*"

Still, that night, she cried again, after they made love in the wagon.

Maybe it's the wagon, he thought.

In the morning she was sick, and when she returned from beyond the chokecherry trees, he looked up from the fire he was fanning with his hat. "¿*Estás enferma?*" Are you sick?

She took his hand, and he stood up.

"¿*Qué pasa?*" What's going on?

She looked at the wagon, where the children still slept. "*Estoy embarazada.*"

He looked at her questioningly. "¿*Qué quiere decir?*" What does that mean?

She placed his hand on her stomach. "*Bebé. Voy a tener un bebé.*" Child. I'm going to have a child.

Sam looked at his wife through watery eyes. "¿*Niño?*" Then his joy faded as he saw she was crying. "¿*Qué pasa?*"

"I sorry," she said. "I lie."

Her speaking in English alarmed him. She was confessing a lie and was coming over halfway to tell him. "Lie? ¿*Mentira?* ¿*No niño?*"

"*Sí, niño,*" she said, using his word and smiling through her tears.

"¿*Qué mentira?*" What lie?

She looked downward. "*Yo no era viuda.*" I wasn't a widow.

"¿*No viuda, tú?*" No widow, you?

"*No, no viuda.*" No, no widow.

"¿*No esposo, no hombre?* ¿*No hombre muerto?*" No husband, no man? No dead man?

"*No, no esposo. Nunca.*" No, no husband. Never.

Sam smiled at her and kissed her on the forehead. He knelt and kissed her on the stomach, then stood up and held her hands as he looked her in the eyes. "*No le hace. No importa.*" It doesn't matter. It's not important.

"*¿Está bien?*" It's all right?

"*Sí. Tú eres mi mujer. Te quiero.*" Yes. You are my wife. I love you.

"*Yo te quiero a ti, Sem. Para siempre. ¿Está bien, yo no viuda?*" I love you, Sam. Forever. It's all right, I'm no widow?

"*Está bien.*" It's all right. He loosened his right hand and made a triangular, circular motion to take in her, the baby that would be, and himself. Then he made a wider motion to take in themselves and the two children sleeping in the wagon. "*Familia.*"

"*Sí. Familia.*"

Iron Heart's Story

Loren D. Estleman

PORCUPINE WOMAN and Sees Water were concerned about Iron Heart.

"He speaks of nothing but things dead," Sees Water declared. "He is a great hero of our people, but he grows older with each story."

Porcupine Woman, mother to Sees Water and Iron Heart's mate these past forty winters, continued to drag the strip of hide in her hands back and forth across the stone resting in her lap. Those hands now were as coarse as the stone was smooth, worn so from long use, as if the two surfaces had traded places. "It is the way of the People to say these things many times to our young, that they will remember and speak of them to their children, and they to theirs. In this way the deeds of our heroes do not drift away like the dry snow that comes in the Moon of Dead Trees."

"I understand this. Still, my father has lost interest in everything but the old stories. I think that he is waiting to die."

Porcupine Woman considered. It was a custom of her people, called the Cut Arms by their friends the Sioux, and the Cheyenne by the white long knives such as those who had followed the Yellow Hair chief to attack the People at the Washita the winter before, to listen betimes to the counsel of the young, who saw things differently and sometimes more clearly than their wiser elders. And Sees Water, whose breasts were high and whose face knew no creases, was uncommonly grave and thoughtful for one of her small years.

"Iron Heart is a great warrior," Porcupine Woman said. "He has stolen many horses from our enemies the Crow and counted many coup, and so has earned the right to speak of these things. It is just as true that he remembers the color of the feathers in the headdress of Spotted Calf, dead these twenty summers, at the cost of forgetting whether he broke his own fast this morning. This is bad, for he is not as old as old Broken Lodge, who has seen seventy winters and rides and shoots as well as a brave half his age. Yet he seems older."

"What shall we do, Mother?"

"In old times I would suggest that he go to the buffalo, or steal horses from the Crow. But the buffalo grow smaller in numbers each winter, and we have given our word to the great white chief of the long knives that we will live in peace with the Crow if they will do the same with us."

"Then he will die surely. The Wise One Above does not grant the gift of life to those who are not thankful."

During Porcupine Woman's silence the sun moved. The hide grew softer with each motion across the stone. At length she spoke.

"Be of good heart, child. Your mother is old, but she has not forgotten those things that set a man's heart afire. We shall go to Iron Heart and ask him to tell us one of the old stories."

The face of Sees Water fell. "Mother, you have not heard me. It is the old stories that are killing him."

"This one will save him."

They went to Iron Heart, who sat cross-legged in a patch of sun holding up a tooth that had fallen from his head, staring at it as if it contained some great truth. His long hair had gone as gray as his name and the skin had begun to hang from his bones, but in the old face Porcupine Woman always saw the handsome brave who had taken her to his lodge when her summers were but sixteen. They sat facing him.

"The Powder River will freeze this winter," said he without greeting. "The beaver plew will be as thick as the grass that comes after the planting rain."

Porcupine Woman said, "The beaver are gone, my husband. The last one left before Sees Water first saw the sun."

"Sam Tyree said he will trade two bolts of gingham for each good plew."

The women exchanged glances.

"Sam Tyree was killed by the Pawnee the year the snow forgot to fall," Porcupine Woman said.

"I think I shall ask for three bolts. Sam Tyree will cheat us if we let him."

"Speak not of him. Tell us of the time you and I and Mounts-His-Horse-Funny tried to skin the grandfather elk."

Iron Heart turned the tooth between his fingers. "Why must I speak of this thing? You were there."

"No one tells it as well as you, and Sees Water wishes to hear it." She prodded her daughter with her elbow.

"Yes, Father," said Sees Water, with a start. "Tell of the time you and Mother and Mounts-His-Horse-Funny tried to skin the grandfather elk."

"It is a long story. My belly is empty."

"Your bowl is still warm from your last meal, my husband. Tell the story."

He filled and emptied his lungs with great resignation. But his eyes glittered. He deposited the tooth in the medicine bag tied around his neck, forgetting in his eagerness that the tooth was his own and as such carried no medicine for him.

"It was in the Summer That Should Have Been Autumn," he said. "Mounts-His-Horse-Funny and I had been in the high country for eight suns, shooting birds and rabbits and looking for larger game to feed the camp."

Porcupine Woman touched his knee. "My husband, the Summer That Should Have Been Autumn was not the time. It was in the Spring That Stayed Dead, when the snow refused to melt."

"It was the hot autumn. Old Standing Hawk fell dead of the heat."

"No, you are thinking of the time his wife gave birth to a dead son. Standing Hawk died the next autumn."

After a moment he nodded. "You are right. The hunt was the first time I wore the robe you made from the white buffalo. The air was cold."

"Tell the story, my husband."

"I am telling it. The camp was starving because of the cold. The buffalo did not come that time and we were heading for the mountains to look for the long-legged kind. Porcupine Woman came along to hold the horses when we climbed. You were not born yet, Daughter."

"It was her first spring," Porcupine Woman corrected. "I left her with White Water Woman, the sister of your mother."

His glitter faded. "What is that to the story?"

"You have always spoken of the importance of telling these tales the same way every time if they are to be remembered as they happened."

"This is so." Nodding absently, he looked far off, past the broken peaks of the tall rocks the white long knives called the Tetons; for there, in the silvery mists beyond the edge of the world, resided the people and things he found and brought back for his listeners. With each winter he saw them more clearly than those he walked among on this side. The day would come, he knew, when he would decide to stay with them rather than return to this place of fading shadows.

"Mounts-His-Horse-Funny had a blue roan which he stole from a Crow chief. Only Mounts could ride it, for it stamped its forefeet and showed its teeth to anyone else who approached. It pulled up lame and Mounts got off to see what was the matter."

"It was a pinto, and everyone could ride it who wished to except Mounts, whom it threw off at every opportunity. That was why he was afoot to see the grandfather elk."

Sees Water glanced annoyedly at her mother, who seemed determined not to let Iron Heart continue the story which she said would pull him back from the land of mists. But Porcupine Woman had eyes only for her husband.

"It was a roan. Mounts traded it to Standing Hawk for his daughter Crab Woman and a breastplate made from the bones of one hundred and forty field mice. Hawk gave it back when he found he could not ride it."

"You are thinking of Black Bull. Mounts was married to Wool Woman, who came to him after the death of her husband Runs-in-the-Rain."

"I remember this unimportant thing. Mounts fell off the pinto and tore his legging. When he bent to look at it, he saw the elk's track at his feet. He thought it was buffalo and we began to follow it. Two suns and two sleeps we followed, high into the mountains where the air is hard to breathe. By then we had seen its droppings and knew they were not those of the buffalo, though its hoofprint was larger than any elk's known to us, or to our fathers, or to their fathers. A spread hand would not cover it.

"The third sun was barely clear of the earth when we broke camp and saw it against the sky. We thought at first it was a trick of the mist, which fools the eye and makes a thing seem larger than it is. Bigger than any buffalo it was, the points upon its antlers as many as the wild ponies that ran in the land before the first long knives came. Its hide was as red as blood."

"Brown," Porcupine Woman said. "Brown like hickory, and it was not so big as that, though it weighed as much as a buffalo cow."

Iron Heart's glare was black. "Does my wife prefer this story to come from her lips?"

"No one tells it as well as you, my husband."

"It is so. I was carrying the musket that cost me twelve plew and a blanket at Bent's Fort, and I fired at the same time Mounts released a shaft from his bow. I do not know even now which of us delivered the fatal injury. The elk ran the length of a lance thrust and fell. We removed the entrails and fashioned a travois from the boughs of the lodgepole pine to drag the carcass back to camp, for neither of our horses would bear its weight. Then came the difficult business of removing the hide.

"No knife would penetrate its thick skin," he continued. "No axe would part its fibers. I myself broke a clovis point fashioned by my great-grandfather in the time of the white king, trying to make the first notch. We had first to place the tools in a fire until they glowed as red as the lifting sun that they would burn through the hide and hair. Still it would not surrender its hold upon the flesh. At last we hitched both our horses to the burned edge and slapped their rumps, that they would bolt and tear it away from the carcass. The turtle that carries the sun upon its back crossed the sky in the time it took to skin the grandfather elk."

Porcupine Woman cleared her throat. The face Iron Heart turned upon her was a stone slab. Yet he said nothing, allowing her to speak.

"It was not a clovis point you broke, but a bone knife. You always did insist upon using a fleshing tool for cutting. And we hitched one horse to the hide, not two. The turtle that carries the sun had half its journey still ahead of it when we finished. You traded six plew, not twelve, for the musket you bought at Bent's Fort. Even then you were cheated. It misfired that day, and so it was Mounts-His-Horse-Funny's arrow that killed the elk, which fell where it stood and did not run. But for those small things you told the story perfectly."

"Bah!" He scrambled to his feet and strode in the direction of the horses.

"Where are you going, my husband?"

"To the tall rocks, who will listen to my stories without interruption."

Moments later the women heard the rataplan of hoofs fading from camp.

"I have not seen Father so angry in many moons," Sees Water declared. "Why did you upset him so?"

Rising, Porcupine Woman shook the dust from the hem of her doeskin. "The story of the time we skinned the grandfather elk is one of the few he never tells right. Whenever I correct him, the blood comes into his face and the fire into his eyes and he is as he was the day I gave him my heart. He will be like this for a long while."

"And when he is over it?"

"Then I shall ask him to tell us of the time he and Otter Belt swam across the Canadian to steal horses from the Kiowa. He never tells that one right either." She touched one of her daughter's braids. "Come, child. Your father will bring back game to prepare and we must have our work done."

Frontier Birds

Linda Sparks

ICY WIND swirled around Cat Burnum and her cowhand as they forked hay off the beavertail stack in a rhythmic counterpoint. Below, cows jostled for position. At the jingle of sleigh bells, Cat paused. "Gotta go be a lady, Hank," she said, before spearing the fork into a snow drift and dropping lightly from the stack. The angle of her Uncle Matt's brows reminded her that riding the train in worn Levi's and battered Stetson wasn't the image she should be striving to attain. She climbed into the cutter.

"Humph!" he snorted.

Poking him playfully with an elbow, she leaned close. "I'll hide in the trainyard and sneak in after dark."

"Not likely. That husband of yours may's well kiss any hope of a political career good-bye the same time he kisses you hello."

Cat sighed. Raised amid cows and cowboys, she was secure in her role as managing partner of the Ax T ranch. Playing the lady in Cheyenne made her feel like a cow pony at one of those fancy Eastern fox hunts Matt storied about. But the thought of enduring an entire winter separated from Harry by the snow-choked Laramie Mountains created an aching hole in her center.

Harrison Burnum wiped excess ink from the nib and leaned across his mahogany desk, extending the pen to Crayton Winsley. "Sign here, and here," he said, pointing to a manicured finger.

Sliding the document to the second man, the lawyer caught a

flicker of movement. Good Lord! he thought, seeing the slender Stetson-topped form lounging in his doorway.

"You fellas ain't buying land, is ya? This polecat sold me a piece was nothin' but scrub! Pisser of a crick was alkali."

"Never mind, gentlemen, this is a joke," Burnum said, rising and striding across the room. Looming over the denim-clad intruder, he glowered. "This is *not* the time or the place!"

"You fellas git any cows in the deal, best check 'em close. Prob'ly tick 'fested."

The two dandified businessmen sidled through the doorway, one sucking hard at his portly stomach to avoid brushing against the cow-stenched denim as he escaped.

"Catherine! You are outrageous!" Harry growled.

"They're just Britishers. Prob'ly don't know steer from bull," she said, laughing as she slid her arms around his neck.

"They're clients—" His words were cut off as her lips searched under his luxuriant mustaches.

"I'll reform," she promised, as her kisses traveled to his chin.

Remembering Winsley's face as he squeezed through the doorway, Harry stifled a chuckle and grumbled, "In a pig's eye!"

Cat's stilted, high-button-shoe walk swished fine wool over pyramided petticoats as she strolled the afternoon boardwalks. From a shop window the pheasant wing perched in her chestnut hair reflected back at her. Harry claimed it was a hat. Wriggling inside the prison of her stays, she giggled, remembering it had taken his help to get her rigged out in this getup. A whole month of being prim for her husband's la-di-da friends; images of formal dinners and the *the-a-ter* were daunting.

Cheyenne was interesting to visit, but she wondered how Harry endured living here. Wagon and carriage wheels churned dust and dung together, then gusts flung it in her eyes, nose, and mouth; even the snowbanks lurking in the shadows were brown-furred. Coal and wood smoke grayed the air. Restaurant kitchens belched, mingling their reeking breath with laundry steam. The thuds and creaks of the wagons, the clanging of metal on metal as cars shifted in the railyards, and the ground-shaking rumble of the one-thirty train pulling into the station two blocks away deafened Cat's ears. And people, people, people: So many, her every breath smelled used. Eleven years of ranch life had purged cities from Cat's blood.

Stepping into the doorway of Waugh's Laundry, she gave way to a broad-beamed woman, her cape and skirts flapping, dragging three stair-step children down the boardwalk. A frigate, sails unfurled, Cat thought, towing dingies in her wake. She chuckled to herself. *Least I can talk like a book when I want to—all Matt's teaching isn't wasted.* These days her uncle was torn between pride and consternation at her proficiency in handling cowpunchers and stock. He was hoping Harry would ladyfy her.

Resuming her stroll, Cat was nearly knocked into the street when a girl was forcibly ejected from the drugstore. She lay sniffling in the street, and Cat's temper flared.

"What happened? Didn't you have enough money?" Cat asked, brushing dust from the girl's satin skirt, its shimmery blue sure to blind men to the old stains and fraying hem.

"Throwed me out, but I got the cash. I need the medicine for my sister. She's bad sick." Tears eroded her store complexion as she smoothed a crumpled scrap of paper.

"My name's Cat. Give me your list and quit crying. My rig's five doors down. One with the gray horse. Get in. I'll get your list."

Cat strode into the drugstore, piercing the weedy-looking fellow behind the counter with her silver eyes. "Excuse me, but did you just refuse a young girl service?"

"We don't do business with soiled doves, ma'am."

"I assume you will do business with me?" She watched his eyes sweep over her expensive cedar green coat, dyed-to-match deerskin gloves, and fancy hat, knowing she looked the lady despite the fact she was barely twenty.

The druggist nodded.

"Then fill the child's list and be quick about it." Cat slapped the paper on the counter. The druggist's expression said he would like to have seen her flying out the door on the heels of the other one, but the command in her voice and the sparks in her steely eyes sent his pale hands scurrying among the bottles and jars.

Minutes later, still seething, Cat returned to her husband's spider phaeton. "Get in, girl."

"Oh, ma'am, I can't ride in your buggy. The townfolk, they'd stone you." The girl's whine became a wail as tears again coursed through paint and powder.

Cat stared at the round-faced child: her mousy hair thin, her pale eyes already haunted. *Uppity damn town!* At least in Baltimore Cat remembered the whores as being adults; or so they'd seemed to her ten-year-old eyes. She softened her voice and corralled the girl's slumped shoulders with an arm. "Would you please get in the buggy? And stop crying. You have to tell me where your sister is, and I can't understand you when you're crying." Cat hoped that sounded like Matt; that kind of treacle worked for him. "No one's going to stone *this* buggy!"

Sniffling, the girl gathered her skirt and scrambled in, pointing south. She scrubbed her drippy nose on a cuff, pulled the thin wrap tight around her shoulders, and said her name was Alice. With more encouragement, she admitted to thirteen and said her sister, Maude, was sixteen. By the time Cat had learned that much, they'd reached the shack south of the tracks where the girls lived and worked. The inside was swept and neat and so cold Cat's breath formed damp clouds. The hovel smelled of piss and men, and the metallic odor of blood.

Maude was crumpled in the only bed. On the floor below, a pool of blood increased, one splat at a time, as the soaked mattress yielded droplets. Cat knew the pharmaceuticals were useless.

"What happened, Alice? Tell me quickly!"

"She got knocked up."

"And she lost it?"

"Doc got rid a it."

"Christ! Goddamn butcher! All right, we're going to try to save your sister. No more crying, no more hand-wringing!"

Sniffing, the girl helped Cat wrap Maude in the skimpy blanket and carry her to Harry's gleaming buggy. Clutching her sister, Alice's fingers crept reverently across the button-tufted Morocco to touch a soft fold of Cat's coat as she stood spraddle-legged, reins in hand, easing the horse into the street.

"Where's there a decent doctor?"

"Eddy 'bove Eighteenth. But, ma'am, he won't see Maude."

"He most certainly will!" Cat said. Cheyenne citizenry's concern for appearances was one of Matt's frequent lectures, but to let a girl die out of snobbery . . .

"Oh, no, ma'am, he only sees the swells. The only doctor what'll see us girls is the one left Maudie like this." Cat set her teeth, imagining the legal havoc her lawyer-husband would wreak on the doctor for refusing a patient.

And Cat wasn't taking Maude back to the butcher. She pulled

up in front of the doctor's office and dashed inside. Ruched and bustled women, some with children, crowded the waiting room. She strode to the inner door and pounded a gloved fist. The scrape of a chair sounded, then heavy heels on bare floor, before a man in a Prince Albert coat opened the door. Gray winged back from his temples and dirt-lined creases sprouted above his nose. "Yes, what is it?"

The smell of sweat, old blood, and pus wafted from him, and Cat found herself staring at filthy fingernails embedded in the ends of his stubby fingers. Bile rose in her throat. "I've got an emergency. I'm looking for the doctor, is he here?"

"I'm Dr. Moresby, miss. What's the problem?"

Cat recoiled. *My God, I wouldn't deliver a calf with hands that filthy. 'Wash the hands and the heifer's posterior areas thoroughly with chloride of lime'—that's what Robert Jennings' book said. Hell, the veterinary surgeons were twenty years more advanced than this doctor!* Matt's friendship with Ben Craddick, M.D. of Laramie, had exposed her to only one doctor—he washed. She fled, tottery in the unfamiliar shoes. In the buggy, her mind raced. "Think, Alice, there must be more than two doctors in this town!"

"Nope, 'ceptin' the Army doctor down at the fort. And that little fat fella. Folks says he's touched in the head."

"How? I mean, why do they say that?"

"Don't want folks usin' ditch water. Always sweepin' and boilin'."

Hopeful, Cat thought. She pried the location of the fat fella out of Alice and touched the gray gelding with the whip.

Minutes later, barging though the fat doctor's door, she found a spotless, empty waiting room and the door to the office ajar. Carbolic fumes tickled her nose. Peering through the door, she saw a moon-faced man reading a journal at the desk, his prematurely balding head shiny in a ray of winter sun. With little time left, Cat marched across the room and snatched a hand from the journal. The nails were short and clean.

"You the doc? Got an emergency in the buggy. Need help carrying her."

Apparently amazed to see this striking young woman bull into his office and examine his hand, the rotund little man trotted along like a hound on fresh trail.

After carrying Maude to his table, the doctor examined her while

Cat shed her coat, rolled her sleeves, and scrubbed. "I'll help, just tell me what to do." The doctor gave instructions, and in less than ten minutes they had cleaned up the girl and packed her to stop the bleeding. After moving Maude to a bed and assigning Alice to watch her, Cat and the doctor washed again and walked into the waiting room.

Extending a work-roughened hand, she said, "Thanks, Doc. My name's Catherine Burnum." *Catherine!* she snickered to herself; she hated the name, but Harry called her nothing else. "My husband's Harrison Burnum."

"My pleasure, ma'am. Everyone's heard of your husband. I'm Wilhelm Abramson. My friends, when I used to have them, called me Wil. How did you come to bring me a . . . a girl with a botched abortion? It's incongruous. And why me? I've been here four months but nobody uses my services."

"Incongruous?" Cat mused, suddenly remembering it was anything but. "The why is easy. Of the sons-of-bitches that call themselves doctors, one did the butchery and the other one . . . well, he and his office smell like the hind end of a fresh cut and branded calf!" *Whoops, not very ladified.*

"Doctor Moresby's very popular. And my dirt fanaticism has scared off the rest of the town," Wil said. "But how—"

The ticking grandfather clock, its moon at half-phase, drew a gasp from Cat. "Damn! If that clock's right, I gotta go. My husband's expecting me." *Oh hell, I did it again.* She reached into her reticule and plucked out several scrunched bills, pressing them into the doctor's hand.

"Mrs. Burnum, this is too much money!"

"Depends on your point of view, Doc. S'long."

She hurried across the narrow walkway connecting the little house with the street, imagining Mrs. Frobisher, or whoever, smiling over her sherry and simpering: "What did you do on your first day in town, dear? Did you enjoy yourself?" "Yes, thanks. A stinking hovel, a revolting doctor, and a bleeding whore. A perfect afternoon." She giggled. Then she remembered her promise to behave.

Just before alighting on the buggy seat, her hand slid on the bloody smears. *Shit! Harry will have a conniption.* She drove off standing up.

□ □ □ □

When Burnum led his horse into the carriage shed, Catherine was scrubbing the phaeton's seat. All the signs said she was in a cougar mood, but something was missing. Putting up his horse, he studied her, remembering her bravado in his office. That was it, he thought, the cockiness is missing.

He removed overcoat and suit coat, rolled up his shirt sleeves, and picking up a rag, walked to the other side of the buggy. The first wipe identified the offending substance. "This is blood!" Scrutinizing her, he discovered a large blotch, rusty against the mint of her skirt. His heart thudded. "And there's blood on your skirt! Catherine, are you all right?"

"I wouldn't be scrubbing this seat if I weren't."

Harry didn't mind the growling, but he was a dismal failure at mind reading. Stepping over the shafts, he took the rag from her. "Tell me why you're angry, Catherine. I can't help if I don't know what the problem is."

"The problem is getting the damn blood off the seat!" She groaned, then leaned her forehead against his shoulder in apology. "I'm sorry. You didn't deserve that. After this mess is cleaned up, I . . . I have something to tell you."

A slave to Southern propriety from babyhood, he secretly envied his wife's devil-take-the-hindmost audacity. Now, suddenly it was gone, replaced by a hunted look. That look, that loss, didn't go with her brusque tone and he wondered if she knew she was frightened. He doubted it; he thought fear was as foreign to her as a parasol. Its familiar cold fingers crept around his throat.

In the parlor, Cat paced from his rolltop to the window and back while Harry waited, silent between the arms of his wing chair. When she began, her voice rang with anger as she told him about Maude.

"May I ask some questions?" he said when she'd finished. At her nod, he began. "I know about your penchant for rescues, but what set off this one? Cheyenne ladies give the, uh, *filles de joie* a wide berth."

"They're whores, Harry. My cowhands call 'em whores. I'm not lace and ruffles, I don't faint." She turned, stalking to the window. It was dark outside and the ebony panes reflected the lamp-lit interior of his cozy parlor: the fire burning cheerily, the bentwood rocker, the books stacked on the table. They evoked in her memo-

ries from a childhood spent peering into the windows of real homes
back in Baltimore. The illusion rubbed the same scar that had
itched when she saw Alice pitched into the street.

The glass was cool against her forehead. *My God, how will I tell
him? Why didn't I tell him before?* That answer was easy: She'd been
afraid it would scare him off. Maybe if he understood—if she could
bring herself to tell him—her behavior wouldn't be so reprehensi-
ble.

Prowling the parlor, she fought back the prickle of tears. When
she was sure her voice was steady, she said, "I hardly ever see them.
Even on my occasional trips to Laramie, I just visit my friends. The
few days I'm ever in Cheyenne, we see your friends."

"Catherine," Harry's Texas drawl reached out, caressing her, "no
one can hurt you here. Tell me what's frightened you."

She gulped a breath. "When that girl came flying out of that
store, when I saw her lying in the dust . . . she was me."

When nothing more followed, Harry prodded, "Go on, dear."

"You don't know. You had parents."

"And you have me. Tell me."

She fixed her eyes, now stone gray, on his blue ones. "I lived in a
bawdy house in Baltimore with my mama. If she hadn't shipped
me off to her brother before she died, if Uncle Matt hadn't been
. . . Uncle Matt . . . I'd be a whore." Tears gathered but she
refused to let them spill.

"Good Lord, girl," Harry said, crossing the room in four long
strides, "it's me you're afraid of!" He pulled her rigid body into his
arms, laying his cheek atop her head. "You don't think I care about
that? You were only ten."

"Your mother would! Your Cheyenne friends will," she said,
pushing away. "I'm no better than Alice and Maude, or any of the
rest of them south of the tracks, just luckier."

Harry had already come to grips with her history; Matt had
shared that confidence before the wedding. It was Harry's deal and
he knew Catherine needed a winning hand.

"That's ancient history. Catherine, you and Wyoming busted
some of the puffery out of me. I was a jackass when you married
me. Too much Southern upbringing and too much Harvard. I'm
still not sure why you bothered with me." He chuckled, recalling
why, two years earlier, he'd bothered with her: She'd had the sin-
ewy grace and beauty of a panther on the dance floor at the Stock

Growers' social. And one kiss had scorched him to a cinder. He also recalled his mental anguish when he discovered he'd fallen in love with a whiskey-drinking, pants-wearing cattle rancher. Marrying her had taken all the courage he could muster. But ah, the rewards he'd reaped for that mustering, he thought, feeling his desire for her stir. Harry cupped her chin in his palm and grinned. "Pa'd call you a cactus wren. Know why?"

Cat shook her head.

"Because the cactus wren is a tough bit of feathers that carves a hole in a big, spiny cactus and tucks her nest in it. She's a survivor. From all that thorny armor, she darts into the world to take what she wants." He kissed the tip of his wife's nose. "Do you know what else?"

"What?" she asked, her eyes slowly returning to silver.

"You need to spend more time with me. Get to know the man you married."

The hall clock bonged and Catherine's eyes widened. "Your dinner plans! I rushed home and now—"

"The toffs at the Cheyenne Club will have to do without you on the dance floor tonight. We're righting wrongs!" he said, pulling on his lawyer face and injecting his voice with a brisk, efficient tone. A hawk in Cheyenne's business and legal community, Harry was a swift and agile wheeler-dealer. "What do you want to do about the, uh, soiled doves and the doctors?"

Cat's lips thinned at his euphemism. "I can't do anything about them. I can't get that doctor arrested. I'm not that naive."

"Darlin', there's always something that can be done about an unjust situation. It just takes studying on." Lord, he thought, Matt had taught her the principles of business, ranching and political maneuvering, but he'd failed to teach her how to manipulate the real world. Harry pulled her down on his lap. "Now then, since your Dr. Abramson doesn't have any patients anyway, see if he'll treat the . . . the whores. We should be able to find some place decent on the other side of the tracks for him to set up an office." That, he thought, might even pay future dividends—handled correctly it could draw votes from both sides of the tracks.

"Do you mean that?"

"Of course, I mean it."

Cat kissed him soundly. "Do you think he'd do it?"

"Probably."

"He would if you asked him. Oh Harry, it's perfect."

Then Harry actually felt her elation trickle away.

"Everybody saw Alice and Maude in your buggy. I ruined your reputation!"

"There'll be talk. Nothing I can't handle." Especially, he thought, after I make you out as another Florence Nightingale. "I do wish you'd learn to tell me when you have a problem. We could work on it together. That's what marriage is about, and you aren't getting any practice living out there in the wilderness. Move to town. Let your foreman run the ranch."

Lightning in her eyes flashed a denial before she nestled down, rubbing her cheek invitingly against his silk-clad shoulder.

The next morning the Burnums visited Wil Abramson. Despite his relative youth, Harry radiated self-assurance, but he deliberately kept his manner easy. "I hear Catherine recruited you in one of her rescues. We have a proposition for you. Interested in the particulars?"

"I'm always willing to listen. Please come into the parlor. Good morning, Mrs. Burnum. I've coffee hot, can I get you a cup?"

"If you'll call me Catherine. How's Maude? Do you mind if I see her?"

"Maude's weak, but she'll recover, Mrs. . . . . Catherine. They were asleep when I checked on her earlier, but you're welcome to look in."

She did. When she returned, Harry and Wil were chatting like old friends.

"Did you ask him, Harry? Will you do it, Doctor?"

Questions bloomed in the doctor's eyes.

Harry chuckled. "This is your project. I'm just providing guidance and moral support. You ask him."

She bit her lip, a wordless appeal shining in her eyes.

"Just tell him what you have in mind, dear," Harry said gently. He knew she'd spent a rare sleepless night worrying over it; this went beyond cows and cowboys, but the enterprise might involve her deeply enough to keep her in the city. He wanted her with him, wanted her scent in his nostrils while he slept.

Cat perched on the edge of the horsehair settee and outlined the plan. She hadn't gotten very far into the explanation before delight shone on the doctor's rosy face. "You'll do it, won't you?" she said.

"Oh, I'm so glad. I'll help with everything. We have to find a place, and get your supplies, and don't worry about the money. There's so much to do. We'll have to get started right away. Maybe we can find a place today."

Catching her hand, Harry halted the tumbling words. "Catherine, the man's still trying to catch his breath. Drop me at my office and you can have the buggy. By the time you return, the doctor will have had time to collect his thoughts."

Harry rose, smiling at Abramson. "Lord help you, Doctor. Don't let her stampede you into doing something you don't want to do. She's like the Wyoming wind."

Wil Abramson walked out with them. As he drove off, Burnum saw bewilderment still decorating the round boyish face.

Cat and the doctor had found a likely building and the following day Harry met them at noon to look over their choice. Located several blocks south of the railroad roundhouse, it had been a carriage repair shop. From the leather scraps scattered about, the three good-sized rooms in the front had been used for harness-working. The large, floored room in the rear, where carriage parts had been milled, would serve as a ward. And Wil planned to live upstairs. Harry poked at walls, corners, and into the underside of the roof with his silver-headed cane, pleased to find that the building was in good condition and appeared to be weatherproof throughout.

Much of Harry's legal work was in real estate investment and leasing. The richest city of its size, Cheyenne teemed with offices and businesses. Harry bought, renovated, managed, and sold buildings, and agented for other investors. Less subject to the vagaries of Wyoming weather than the cattle barons' stock, Harry's properties were making him a rich man.

"Looks like you two made an excellent choice. I'll have my clerk find the owner and get you a good lease." Harry slid a hand under the tendrils of hair curling over his wife's collar. "Once that's done, I'll send my crew to fix up this place. And," he said to his wife, his hand firm on her neck, "they don't need a ramrod. They're quite professional."

Outside, Harry surveyed the neighborhood. On the way down, he'd ridden by a strip of bawdy houses, cheap saloons, billiard parlors, and one place—less than two blocks away—that leaked the

sweet odor of opium. The building they'd selected stood among
seedy businesses that catered to the laborers, railroad men, and
independent whores living south of the tracks. While it was a good
spot for the clinic, he didn't relish the thought of Catherine passing
daily through these streets. She might not always think of herself as
womanly, but no man made that mistake.

"You may as well order your equipment and supplies, Doc,"
Harry said. "By the time they get here, this place should be ready to
go. You'll need to come to the bank while we open an account for
the clinic. Know what you're going to call it?"

Doctor Abramson shook his head, his moon face shining. "I can't
convince myself this is real. You two are overwhelming! Two days
ago, I didn't know where next month's rent was coming from and
now you're telling me I have a whole building, can order whatever
I want, and not worry about money. I can't begin to thank you."

Harry laughed. "If you're as good at doctoring as Catherine says,
you'll be doing the whole town a service. And you're right, Catherine and I are pushy. I suppose that's because she's the finest ranch
manager in Wyoming, and I'm the best business lawyer in the
Territories. We're used to doing things our way."

By month's end, the clinic building had been renovated and stocked
with medical equipment, supplies, and furniture. Its two paid assis-
tants, also scrubbed-up and clad in shirtwaists and skirts, looked
quite proper. Maude, who could read and write, would help with
the books and patients. Alice was going back to school, but she
would help with laundry and cleaning. These two had spread the
word that the clinic would be open the first of the following month.
Folks could stop in for medical care or just to say hello and look
around.

Maude would never be pretty, but health, regular hours, and
good food had given her hair shine and bounce, and her smile put
points of light in hazel eyes. She'd appointed herself Wil's cook and
housekeeper, and Catherine suspected the girls ate with the doctor.

Harry had purchased an ivory-handled derringer and insisted
Catherine carry it. The piece was as elegant and refined as her
husband, but to her a gun meant the .44 thumb-buster that fit
snugly against her hip when she was riding line, doctoring cows, or
working roundup. Catherine thought the toy gun silly, but Harry
refused to debate with her. He'd simply said she was not, under any

circumstance, to go to the clinic without the pocket pistol. Some mornings he checked, as if she were a recalcitrant child. A month of teas and champagne socials in Cheyenne's mansions, of soirees, concerts, and theater had conditioned Catherine to ladies' ways: Ladies didn't have guns dragging down the pockets of their day dresses. Nevertheless, with each step, the derringer thumped against her leg.

On opening day, Catherine arrived at the clinic at nine to find the doctor all aflutter. "No one will come, Catherine, I know it. You'll have spent all this money and no one will come."

"Oh pooh, Wil, the doves all sleep 'til past noon."

The first patient arrived at two, hovering by the door until encouraged to enter. By four o'clock, laces, satins, and rough woolens scented the waiting room with flowers, musk, and tobacco. They weren't all patients; some came to gawk and others to quiz the sick ones as they left. But they came, and they would come back and bring others.

Harry stopped by after he closed the law office, his black cashmere overcoat swinging open as he crossed to where Catherine sat behind the waiting room desk. The chairs and benches still overflowed with the ruffles of the doves' shimmery plumage, while a few men leaned against the walls. "It looks like your enterprise is a huge success, darlin'," he whispered, propping his well-tailored rear on the edge of the desk and leaning close. He wound a vagrant tendril of her chestnut hair around one finger. "Have I lost you forever to social reform? Will you come home with me?"

"It should be cleared out by eight o'clock. The girls have to work." Laughter percolated through Catherine. Old and young, the whores in the waiting room were whispering and poking each other, the men eyeing Harry with a mixture of awe and distaste. In his charcoal suit, silver-belly Stetson, and gleaming black boots, her handsome husband was quite the swell.

"I'll come back for you. Wait inside."

"That's not necessary," she hissed. As if Harry had to protect her! she thought. He never even carried a gun.

"I won't have you on these streets alone at night. Would you rather I wait here?"

"No!" she whispered, standing. "You're out of place. They all think you're my first client for the evening."

Harry glanced around the room, where expressions confirmed

her words. Slipping a hand behind her neck, he pulled her into a searing kiss. When he released her, he ordered, "Eight o'clock, woman. I won't wait a minute past." Rising from the desk, he sauntered out, swinging his silver-headed ebony cane and touching his hat to the ladies. Catherine's face flamed, and giggles ate through her composure, threatening to erupt. *So much for the Harvard blue-nose with his oh-so-proper airs! His mother would expire!* And even if north of the tracks Harry's Victorian propriety remained impeccable, she was tickled he'd loosened up a little. In private, he wasn't the least bit stuffy.

Several days later, Catherine was manning the waiting room desk when a man in a rusty-black Prince Albert coat stomped through the front door. Veins spider-webbed his nose and ruddy cheeks. A scraggly beard bushed around his mouth, trapping fragments from some recent meal. He exuded alcohol with each breath, but the underlying stench was worse. His wild eyes started nervous clawings in Catherine's innards. "Sir, if you'll have a seat, the doctor will be with you shortly. Or was there something—" she asked.

"Yeah, I want to see the doctor. I want to see the sneaky little bastard who's stealin' my patients. Get out here, Jew-boy!" the man bellowed, his words slurring. The disturbance brought Wil from the back room, allowing Catherine to move from behind the desk and sidle out of the man's line of vision. The last two women in the waiting room bolted.

Catherine's stomach knotted; her hands sought her pockets and the reassuring solidity of the little Colt with its two-and-a-half-inch barrel. It suddenly didn't seem silly; the .41 slug would stop anything on two legs at under twelve feet. This had to be the doctor who'd botched the abortion on Maude, and he sounded completely swacked. When he pulled a Colt Navy revolver from under his coat and pointed it at Wil, time snailed.

Catherine's brain registered two facts: that the piece was still uncocked; and if he cocked it, she would kill him.

The gun waved and danced in drunken hands, but continued to point in Wil's direction. Catherine dared not take her eyes from the weapon, but she was sure all the blood had drained from Wil's face and he was quaking; violence terrified the little man. Catherine began talking—a continuous, calm, low-pitched monotone. "Put the gun down, mister. You don't want to hurt anyone. If you're a doctor, you're sworn to save lives, not take them. Please, put the gun down. You kill him, you'll hang for sure. What will your wife and family do if you're dead?"

The muzzle of his gun wandered sideways toward her as the drunken doctor's eyes shifted. "Shut up, bitch! Wife died years ago."

Staring into the barrel of the Navy dried the spit in Catherine's mouth. Her eyes burned—she dared not blink. She must not miss the cocking of the hammer; only then could the gun be fired. She pulled the derringer from her pocket, then stuffed it back; the drunk would never take it seriously. Anger burned in Catherine, reverting her to ranch boss and ramrod. Command rang in her voice. "Doctor, put it down! If you don't, you'll force me to kill you. I won't let you hurt my friends. Goddammit, man, put the gun down!"

The drunk's left hand groped the air, searching for the hand already holding the revolver. When his left hand found the pistol grip, both thumbs pulled at the hammer.

She never heard the crack of her derringer, nor felt the powder burn her thigh. The big slug bore into the man's right side beneath his raised arm.

The Navy's report thundered in the closed room. Its bullet splintered the door frame next to Wil, and the rotund little doctor sank to his knees, sobbing. Wide-eyed in the doorway, Maude and Alice clung to one another.

Crossing the room through a haze of eye-burning gunsmoke, Catherine raised the doctor to his feet and turned him toward the amazed sisters. "Here," she ordered. "Take him back in the office. Get him a drink."

Catherine squared her shoulders and returned to the man on the floor. Bright froth pumped from his nose and mouth. Blood pooled under his arm. "You stupid son-of-a-bitch, it was your fault we started this clinic. If you hadn't nearly killed Maude, none of this would have happened." *Lord, at home killing you'd just be varmit extermination. Here, they'll try me for murder.*

Pushing open the front door, Catherine found a half-dozen over-all- and denim-clad men and boys clumped in the street. "Will someone please get the sheriff?" she asked, hearing her own voice coming from far away. "I also need a boy who can run fast. It's worth fifty cents."

A little tow-headed fellow of about ten scurried up the steps. Catherine returned to the desk and wrote two notes. The first she asked the boy to read aloud.

He read: "Burnum and Thorndike, Eighteenth Street and Ferguson."

"Good boy. Keep that, that's where you're going. Do you know where it is?" He nodded. Catherine continued, "Please take this second note to Mr. Burnum, it's very important, so make sure he gets it. Here's two bits, and tell him he's to give you another quarter. And please, run as fast as you can."

The boy raced off. Although his legs seemed to move in long leisurely bounds, something inside her told Catherine he only looked slow. Sinking to the sagging step, she shut out the world. *Oh God, Harry, I'm sorry. I'll never be civilized. I should never have stayed in town.*

Harry heard his name and rose. Through mullion-paned windows he saw his clerk waving gartered, paper-cuffed arms, trying to hush and shoo a youngster, but the boy ducked, rushing past. Harry hurried from his glass-enclosed office.

"You Mr. Burnum? She said to give it just to Mr. Burnum. She said you'd give me two bits."

Harry unfolded the crumpled note. The fingers of one hand searched a pocket, finding a silver dollar and pressing it absently into the boy's palm. There were only two lines on the slip of paper:

I needed the derringer.
Now I need you. C.

"Damnation!" Harry exclaimed, whirling to race out the back to his horse. He reached the clinic within fifteen minutes of the shooting to find his wife still sitting—coatless—on the front step, stiff with cold. Pulling off his suit coat and wrapping it around her, Harry lifted her to her feet and turned her toward the door.

She balked, her foot braced against the step, resisting the hands propelling her. "No. I don't want to go in there."

"Darlin', you're chilled to the bone. I'm right here, everything will be all right. You need to be inside where it's warm. Come dear, let's go inside."

Still she resisted. "I ruined everything," she mumbled dispiritedly.

"Catherine!" he said sharply, turning her toward him. "Look at me! Do you know who I am?"

Lead gray eyes blinked, focusing on his face, and she nodded. "I'll go back to the ranch. I won't embarrass you anymore. I promise I won't."

"Nonsense," Harry said. "We're going inside. Whatever happened, it's over." He could fix it, he knew. Whatever it was. Whatever it cost.

She sagged against him as he guided her around the body of the doctor and into Wil's office. Harry took a quick look to see if anyone else had been hurt and found the girls still trying to stop Wil's blubbering. "Sit here, Catherine," he said, helping her to a chair.

He went to Wil and stood the little man up, shaking him. "Get a grip on yourself, man! This is no time to fall apart." When the doctor continued to cry, Harry slapped him twice, hard across the face. Wil gasped and stopped, sobering.

Harry heard a halloo from the outer office and stepped through the door. One of Sheriff Potter's deputies was prodding the body with a boot toe. "Wanna tell me what happened here?" The officious voice worked its way around the cud of chaw in the deputy's cheek.

"My wife apparently shot this man. Why, I don't know. Maybe the girls who work here can tell you what happened. When I got here—not more than three, four minutes ago—Doc Abramson was hysterical. My wife's in shock. Everybody is back here, Deputy." Harry led the way into the office.

The deputy took one look at the sisters and turned to Harry. "These girls is hoores, counselor, what makes ya think they work here?" The back of his hand wiped at a bit of brown drool and he glanced around for a place to spit.

"Because, Deputy, the doctor hired them. I would appreciate you addressing them accordingly. I'm sure you can handle things here. I'm taking my wife home."

The deputy swallowed his spit with a grimace and an audible gulp. "Hold on there, Mr. Burnum. Ain't nobody leavin' here tills I question 'em. Then I decide who leaves."

"I'll talk to him, Harry. I'm fine," Catherine said, rising and starting toward her husband. Her knees buckled on the second step and Harry snaked an arm around her waist as she went down.

Cradling his wife on the floor, Harry ground his teeth, betraying an urge to rip the deputy limb from limb.

Catherine's collapse was enough to restore Wil's professional manner. He hurried to her, a bottle of smelling salts in hand. "Leave her alone, Officer, she saved our lives," Wil snapped. "It's no wonder she fainted. She tried to talk that mad man out of shooting us, but he wouldn't listen." Wil passed the smelling salts under Catherine's nostrils. She coughed, twisting away from him, but he caught her chin firmly, waving the bottle under her nose again.

Her eyes flew open. "Damn, get that stuff away from me! Why are we on the floor?" Then the smelling salts and her position made the circumstances clear. Color flooded her cheeks and she struggled against Harry's arms.

Abramson said, "Lie still, Catherine. You've had a severe shock and fainting's only normal."

"Sheriff knows my house, Deputy," Harry said, smoothing back the tendrils of hair that had escaped Catherine's chignon. "He can speak with her tomorrow. She's in no condition now."

Rising and pressing the salts on Harry, the doctor said, "Absolutely right! Take these with you, in case she has more spells. She should be in bed."

Alice hurried to retrieve Catherine's coat and help her on with it, as Harry steadied her. Then he pulled on his own coat and swept her up in his arms. She struggled and Harry's arms tightened. "Shhh . . . be still, darlin', I'll have you home in a few minutes." Carrying her out to his horse, he set her sidesaddle, swinging up behind her and turning the horse toward home.

Not the least surprised by her action, Harry was concerned about her reactions. Most of all, he was mystified over why she thought he'd be embarrassed. When the word got around, he'd be married to a heroine.

"Spells, indeed! I don't have spells! I was just dizzy. I don't faint! Dammit, Harry, let me go back there and tell that man what happened." *Good Lord, a month in skirts and fripperies, surrounded by ladies, and I've taken to having the vapors! It's contagious!* She shivered in disgust.

"Take it easy, girl, you're all right now, but you were *non compos mentis* when I arrived. And you make no statements to the law until we talk." When the horse walked into the carriage house, Harry stepped down, lifting Catherine off. "Can you walk, darlin'?"

"Of course I can walk!" *By God if I'll let him treat me like some hanky-waver.*

In the parlor, he poured a whiskey and held it for her to sip.

"Stop treating me like an invalid," she growled, taking the bourbon.

"Now, now, killing a man at close range is hard on anyone. I'm told it gives many a strong man the shakes, and sleepless nights as well." He sat next to her, taking her hand. "When you're able, start at the beginning and tell me everything, exactly the way it happened."

She drank the bourbon in four swallows and started at the beginning. When she finished, Harry nodded. "You're all right: there probably won't even be a trial. Now let's get you a nice hot bath and into bed. The sheriff will need the dress and the gun." Catherine no longer protested as he shepherded her up the stairs.

When she was in bed, he pulled up a chair, prepared to sit with her until she fell asleep.

"He didn't give me a choice, Harry."

"I know, darlin'. Close your eyes. I'll be right here."

Her hand gripped Harry's, but behind closed lids her mind replayed the events. *I unloaded the whole problem on Harry! And he took over. Like I was a Miss Pitapat. And fainting! Good grief! That's the price of skirts, silly high-button shoes, and refined ladyism. All those buttons, stays, and laces must keep blood from getting to the brain. I'm going back to the ranch.* In boots, pants, and a Stetson, she knew who she was and trusted her instincts. The clinic didn't need her anymore and Harry . . . well . . . Harry's reputation and aspirations would be better off without her suddenness. She sighed, slipping toward sleep. Dear Harry, he surely must wish he'd married a refined lady—a gentlewoman, she thought, as her grip on his hand softened.

He felt her let go, saw the tension melt from the line of her lips. She'd have no sleepless nights! He wondered how it felt to know what was right. Not to weigh the politics, profitability, or social correctness of an action—to just know it was right. And have the courage to act. By God, he admired courage!

Long Ride Back

Ed Gorman

SOON AS I SNUCK into his campsite, and kicked him in the leg so he'd jerk up from his blanket, I brought down the stock of my single-shot .40-90 Sharps and did some real damage to his teeth.

He was swearing and crying all the time I got him in handcuffs, spraying blood that looked black in the dawn flames of the fading campfire.

In the dewy grass, in the hard frosty cold of the September morning, the white birches just now starting to gleam in the early sunlight, I got the Kid's roan saddled and then went back for the Kid himself.

"I ain't scared of you," he said, talking around his busted teeth and bloody tongue.

"Well, that makes us even. I ain't scared of you, either."

I dragged him over to the horse, got him in the saddle, then took a two-foot piece of rawhide and lashed him to the horn.

"You sonofabitch," the Kid said. He said that a lot.

Then I was up in my own saddle and we headed back to town. It was a long day's ride.

"They'll be braggin' about ya, I suppose, over to the saloon, I mean," the Kid said a little later, as we moved steadily along the stage road.

"I don't pay attention to stuff like that."

"How the big brave sheriff went out and captured the Kid all by his lonesome."

"Why don't you be quiet for a while?"

"Yessir. All by his lonesome. And you know how many murder counts are on the Kid's head? Why, three of them in Nebraska alone. And two more right here in Kansas. Why, even the James Boys walked wide of the Kid—and then here's this hick sheriff capturin' him all by hisself. What a hero."

This time I didn't ask him.

I leaned over and backhanded him so hard, he started to slide off his saddle. Through his pain and blood, he started calling me names again.

It went like that most of the morning, him starting up with his ugly tongue and me quieting him down with the back of my hand.

At least the countryside was pretty, autumn blazing in the hills surrounding this dusty valley, chickenhawks arcing against the soft blue sky.

Then he said, "You goin' to be there when they hang me?"

I shrugged.

"When they put the rope around my neck and the hood over my face and give the nod to the hangman?"

I said nothing. I rode. Nice and steady. Nice and easy.

"Oh, you're a fine one, you are," the Kid said. "A fine one."

Around noon, the sun very high and hot, I stopped at a fast blue creek and gave the horses water and me and the Kid some jerky.

I ate mine. The Kid spit his out. Right in my face.

Then we were up and riding again.

"You sonofabitch," the Kid said. There was so much anger in him, it never seemed to wane at all.

I sighed. "There's nothing to say, Kid."

"There's plenty to say and you know it."

"In three years you killed six people, two of them women, and all so you could get yourself some easy money from banks. There's not one goddamned thing to add to that. Not one goddamned thing." Now it was me who was angry.

"You sonofabitch," he said, "I'm your son. Don't that mean any-thing?"

"Yeah, Karl, it means plenty. It means I had to watch your mother die a slow death of shame and heartbreak. And it means you put me in a position I didn't ask for—you shot a man in cold blood in my jurisdiction. So I had to come after you. I didn't want to—I prayed you'd be smart enough to get out of my territory before I found you. But you weren't smart at all. You figured I'd let you go." I looked down at the silver star on my leather vest. "But I couldn't, Karl. I just couldn't."

He started crying, then, and I wanted to say something or do something to comfort him but I didn't know what.

I just listened to the owls in the woods, and rode on, with my own son next to me in handcuffs, toward the town that a hanging judge named Coughlin visited seven times a year, a town where the citizens turned hangings into civic events, complete with parades and picnics after.

"You really gonna let 'em hang me, Pa?" Karl said after a while, still crying, and sounding young and scared now. "You really gonna let 'em hang me?"

I didn't say anything. There was just the soughing wind.

"Ma woulda let me go if she was here. You know she would."

I just rode on, closer, ever closer to town. Three more hours. To make my mind up. To be sure.

"Pa, you can't let 'em hang me, you can't." He was crying again.

And then I realized that I was crying, too, as we rode on closer and closer and closer to where men with singing saws and blunt hard hammers and silver shining nails waited for another life to place on the altar of the scaffold.

"You gotta let me go, Pa, you just gotta," Karl said.

Three more hours and one way or another, it would all be over. Maybe I would change my mind, maybe not.

We rode on toward the dusty autumn hills.

Making History

Sally Zanjani

INSIDE the black tape recorder, tiny wheels turned busily. Satisfied that the tape was still running, the interviewer leaned toward Henry once more, fixed her intent gray-green eyes on his face, and asked, "Why did you go?"

Henry shifted uncomfortably on the plaid couch. The boy he was more than seventy years ago would have squirmed and ducked his head. The young man who had left for Goldfield in 1906 might have averted his eyes and turned sullen. The eighty-two-year-old that Henry had become in 1969, his blue eyes faded, his hair a white shock falling over the brow of a leonine head, his once powerful body a big shell, gave little sign that the question had struck home, except that his gnarled fingers gripped the cane more tightly.

"Went to make my fortune," he said. "Same as everybody else." That was the usual answer, the one that nobody questioned.

The interviewer sensed that there was more to be said. She was good that way. A little too good. "It must have been a big change for a nineteen-year-old boy who'd been clerking in a dry goods store in Iowa to go dashing off to Goldfield," she said helpfully, trying to bring him along with her.

"It was," said Henry, clamping his wide mouth shut. He did not want to be brought. In fact, just now he was sorry he had agreed to be interviewed. She'd started asking questions he didn't want to answer.

"What did your parents say when you told them you were join-ing a gold rush?" she asked, coming toward him from another angle.

Henry coughed and looked away from the intent gray-green eyes. There was something hypnotic about those eyes. They could draw the words right out of you if you weren't careful. You'd find yourself saying things you never meant to say. And there they would stay, in the little machine with the turning wheels, where you couldn't get them back.

"Said I was a young fool. They were right." There was more, of course. The sign ALTMAN & SON, DRY GOODS & SUNDRIES painted only a year earlier and hung proudly over the store. His father's anger and hurt, his mother's sobs, almost as though she had known, in spite of all his promises, that she would never see his face again.

"Did you ever go back to Iowa?"

"No, I never did. My parents came down with pneumonia that winter—the winter of 1906—while I was in Goldfield. By the time I heard they were sick, they were dead and buried. My uncle took over the dry goods business. There wasn't much to go back for after my folks were gone."

The guilt still wrenched him after more than sixty years. Not taking the time to stand for an hour or two in the mail line at the post office. Not even hiring a boy to do it for him because he'd been spending all his money at Jake's. Allowing the letter that told him of his parents' illness to wait there uncollected for weeks. Not being with them when they needed him.

She seemed to sense his pain and decently turned away. Henry liked her for that. Sometimes he had a feeling that she'd been working him over pretty smart, asking the ordinary questions she knew would start an old gaffer talking and then sliding in with the ones that cut to the bone. All the same, she'd taken the trouble to read up on Goldfield in the old newspapers, which was more than you could say for most of the young folks with tape recorders and notepads who came down to Tonopah to poke and prod at the last of the old gold rushers left alive. Nowadays that came down to Henry and his friend Chester, who lived next door in the tumble-down shack beside Henry's neat cabin.

"By the way, you said you went to make a fortune. Did you make one?"

"Guess not. Wouldn't be here if I did." Henry smiled grimly. It was a damn silly question, in his opinion. If he'd made a fortune, he wouldn't be sitting in a tiny cabin on a hillside in Tonopah. He'd be taking his ease in a mansion by the sea in Long Beach or San Francisco, where the nabobs went after they'd made a killing in the mines. Maybe she knew that and just kept circling back, by different ways, to the thing he didn't want to talk about. Couldn't talk about. It would have felt like taking his clothes off on Main Street.

"Did many people make fortunes in those gold rushes?"

"Very few. And even those who made money—well, mostly it went back into the ground."

She liked this phrase. "Went back into the ground," she repeated, cocking her head, with the straight brown hair clipped almost as short as a boy. "Now what does that mean?"

"Means you couldn't stay satisfied. Kept thinking you'd strike it rich again. Sank all the money you made into worthless mines."

She nodded. "Before I leave, I'd like to ask you a few follow-up questions about Goldfield in the boom days around 1906. You mentioned a dance hall called Jake's. What was it like in there?"

Henry relaxed. Now she was moving into safer territory.

"Jake's was noisy," he said. "People drinking and talking and laughing. Little band sawing away. And crowded. They had a fine maple wood floor down at Jake's, but we were squeezed in so tight we couldn't hardly get around. Of course, there were the girls, lots of pretty girls. That's what we came for."

He smiled at her and knew he didn't have the words to make her understand the way it was, the eerie desert stillness of the Malapai outside, with the ghostly shapes of joshua trees in the dim starlight, and the glowing warmth, the gay music, and the laughing voices that tugged you into Jake's. Tugged like a magnet to the iron nail that was you. You might have thought you'd be going somewhere else after coming in from the mines, having a wash, and starting out from your tent cabin of an evening, but you always ended up at Jake's. He remembered it still, the burn of whiskey in his throat, the stubbled faces of the miners and prospectors around him, the sweet curved body of a girl nestling in his arms for a dance. Gus in a green silk dress.

"About how often would you go to Jake's?"

"Pretty often." Actually, it was damn near every night.

"What kind of names did the girls have? I'm assuming they didn't use their real names."

Henry nodded. "None of them used their real names. Men's names were the fashion in those days—and boxers. Names like Jimmie Britt and Bat Nelson and Gus and Ray and Fighting Bill. Others too, Klondike Kitty and Maizie and Swivel Hips Sue."

He watched carefully to see if she would react to Gus's name. He had noticed during their interviews over the last three days that when she was hot on the trail of something she'd lean a fraction closer toward him, as though listening with her whole body, not just her ears, and the large gray-green eyes would widen and then narrow just a little. But she showed none of these signs. Maybe she wasn't on to Gus.

"How long did a dance last?" the interviewer continued.

"Not near long enough if you had one of the dance hall queens in your arms," said Henry, still remembering Gus. Some of the girls had their glasses filled with colored water when you bought them drinks, but not Gus. She could drink you under the table with the real stuff, dance all night, and then, if you were lucky, lead you by the hand to her cabin out back and love you till noon. "Jake kept the dances pretty short to make more money," he added.

"How much did those dance hall queens make? I've heard they made as much as five hundred dollars a night."

"I believe that's an exaggeration. But they did pretty well."

How well would *you* have done back in Jake's, thought Henry to himself, letting his eyes skate skeptically over the interviewer. First you'd have to grow you some hair, enough so it takes a good ten minutes to take all the hairpins out and a man can bury his face in it like a hog in a wallow, hair like Gus's long dark brown mane. And you'd have to put some meat on, so you'd be more than an armful of bones. You'd have to move altogether different. He thought of the smooth kind of wiggle, like a fish twitching its tail in a stream, that was Gus moving toward him across the crowded dance floor and the way her body seemed to flow around a man.

"How did the girls dress?"

"Bright colors. Pretty skimpy. They didn't wear overly much."

That's another thing you'd have to change, he thought, eyeing the woman's jeans with disapproval. You'd have had to dress like a female, in something like the green silk outfit that had clung to Gus's waist and switched from her hips. Henry hadn't minded when he woke up in the twenties to find a lot of female knees staring him in the face, as Will Rogers put it, and again in the sixties. Skirts could go up or down for all he cared, and best of all over a woman's head, but pants did nothing for the female form.

"Did any romances develop?"

"Might have. Can't rightly say." Henry knew himself for a bare-faced liar.

"I've wondered if some of these girls might have had an appeal that a respectable woman, say a school teacher, didn't have?"

"They were pretty, some of them," said Henry, dodging the question.

"Do you know what happened to the girls after Goldfield went into decline and Jake's closed down?"

She was leaning forward now, eyes a little narrowed.

"I really can't say," said Henry, on guard.

"I've been told that some of the dance hall queens, as you call them, made good marriages and moved away and turned into pillars of society. Can you tell me any more about that?"

"I don't believe I can," said Henry, looking vague.

Somebody must have told her something. Maybe that fool Chester, who didn't know when to stop talking. But not Gus's married name, not where she lived, if she was still living, and Henry didn't want to imagine Gus any other way. He'd learned to live with how Goldfield was now, since the big fire of '23 left the better part of it a blackened smoking ruin, but he liked to picture Gus as the toast of high society, as once she'd been the toast of Jake's. Necessarily an older Gus, with a few streaks of gray in the dark brown mass of her hair, but still very much the same. He'd seen her photograph a few times in the society pages of a big-city newspaper, and that was how he wanted to think of her, laden with jewels at a charity ball, skimming over sunny seas in a yacht, sashaying down the aisle at the opera with just a touch of the old fish tail wiggle. When she married the tycoon who carried her off on the same kind of sudden whim that made her throw everything she had on the roulette wheel when she felt lucky or spur her horse to a thundering gallop when she fancied a ride at dawn, Henry had wished her well. He knew she'd favored him, but Gus was never just his girl. Only the best he ever had.

"I could turn off the tape recorder if there's anything you'd like to tell me in confidence, Mr. Altman," coaxed the interviewer.

"Think I've told you just about everything I know." Just about.

Never Gus. And not the other, which was kind of mixed up with Gus, in a way.

"I guess I haven't asked you if you found what you were looking for in Goldfield?"

She had asked him, several different ways, and they both knew it. He wondered briefly if she had figured out the answer and only wanted him to say she was right. The intent eyes had softened. Henry sensed that she would press him no further.

"Told you I never made much," he muttered, sticking to his story.

"I guess that about wraps it up then," she said. She snapped off the tape recorder and put it carefully in her carrying bag. Noticing that Henry was working to gather his strength, she added, "Please don't bother to get up."

She stepped quickly over to him, gripped his hand, and said shyly, in a sudden rush, "Thank you so much for talking with me, Mr. Altman. You know, you guys were making history down there in Goldfield, and you've helped me understand how it was. I'll let you know when the book comes out."

Henry shook her hand, feeling subtly rebuked. Making history. That was why he talked to these people who came down from the University up north in Reno. When he read some of the fool nonsense they were writing these days about the great rush to Goldfield, it made him so mad he'd cracked his cane on the doorpost. So when these writers came around wanting to see him, he tried to set them right about how the union got busted and how Goldfield was in the wild days before the mine owners turned it into a company town.

But if he was trying to set them right, why had he pointed her wrong with that easy answer about making his fortune? She hadn't believed it either. He wondered if he should have tried to explain. Looking out the window, he watched her dark green car making its way slowly down the hill toward Main Street and wondered if he should ask her to come back. Maybe phone her at the motel. She would doubtless be gone, though, speeding along the highway north to Reno. That was the trouble with these writers. They never stayed long enough to find out what it was really like in Tonopah, or thirty miles down the highway in Goldfield. And if you lived here long enough to learn how the mirages shimmered across the white sands of the Clayton Playa, how the wind blew when a storm was coming in, or how the hills turned into melting strawberry ice cream in the late afternoon light, then you probably didn't know how to write books.

With more effort than it had once taken him to demolish a hard rock ledge in the mines with his drill, Henry hoisted himself to his feet, leaning heavily on his cane. Every movement seemed like such an effort today that Henry was inclined to think he might not be around to see this latest book come out. Sometimes these writers took years to squeeze out a skimpy little book you could read in less time than it took to play a decent game of poker. Other times no book showed up at all. Maybe somebody ought to interview them and make them explain why this writing business took so long. Slowly, with faltering steps, he made his way to the door. It was almost three o'clock, the time of day when he always sat outside for a while with Chester, and Henry did not like to have his routine interrupted.

After he had negotiated the door, Henry saw Chester already waiting for him in an old kitchen chair on the porch in front of the cabin next door. The well-nailed tightly set boards and trim railing of Henry's porch, kept in good repair by the young man down the street, were decidedly better than the cracked uneven boards with widening gaps, set just a foot or so above the ground, that Chester called a porch, but Chester liked to sit on his own porch because two years ago he had seen a rattler slither under the boards. Ever since, he had been waiting to decapitate it with his shovel. Lean and wizened, his thin chest caved in like an old barrel, his bald head mottled, and his shapeless nose reddened by years of hard drinking, Chester sat out on the porch, coughing, smoking the cigarettes long forbidden to him by the doctor, stubbing them out in an empty can, and tapping on the boards now and then with the shovel he kept by his side. "I can hear him. He's still rustling around under there," he would say to Henry, and Henry humored him. Waiting for the snake lent a certain excitement to their afternoons.

Henry lowered himself with difficulty into the sagging seat of the dilapidated rocking chair beside Chester and sat looking silently over the rooftops and the abandoned mines of Tonopah below them. New places had gone up here and there, but some of the old buildings like the Mizpah Hotel still stood on Main Street. To Henry's way of thinking, that meant that Tonopah had grown old in the right way, like a person losing his hair and wrinkling up but still recognizably himself. Not like Reno and Las Vegas, so changed now that a man could walk down the street and feel he'd never been there before.

Henry turned his glance to Chester, seeing in the mottled ancient beside him a shade of the wild and wiry youngster, dark hair pasted to his skull like shoe polish and cigarette pasted to his lip, who used to pour drinks at Jake's over sixty years ago. "She been to see you?" he inquired.

"Came and went this morning," said Chester. "Told her all about me and Wyatt Earp. I even drew her a picture. Said I was standing here"—he tapped with the shovel—"and old Wyatt was over there, cool as you please, and them claim jumpers busted into the mine right there with guns a-blazin'. You got to draw 'em a picture, Henry. It gets 'em every time."

"She was just too polite to tell you what an old liar you are," said Henry. "She probably knows Wyatt Earp was long gone for California before you ever got here."

Chester chuckled. "I'm tellin' you, Henry, I had her goin'. And the fella with the big concha belt and the little bitty mustache that come by last year—he swallered it whole. All you got to do is draw 'em a picture. Now here's ole Wyatt . . ." His chuckles hoarsened into a prolonged fit of coughing.

"Did she ask about Gus?" asked Henry when the coughs had subsided.

"She asked about them dance hall queens. Told her some of 'em married nabobs and moved away and turned into society queens. A course I didn't point to no places, and I didn't name no names." He looked at Henry with a teasing twinkle in his bleary eyes.

"You sure you didn't let that mouth of yours run away with you?" demanded Henry, eyeing him severely.

"I wouldn't tell on your girlfriend, Henry. Don't I know you'd split my head wide open with that cane of yours if I did?"

Henry leaned back in the rocking chair, feeling easier in his mind. Gus was safe from the black tape recorders and the prying eyes of history. None of the old crowd who used to watch her shimmy across the floor at Jake's was left to tell but him and Chester. She'd go to her grave a fine lady, with no one any the wiser.

He watched the shadows move down the slope over Tonopah, washing over the pale hillocks of tailings across the highway. Down below a rancher's pickup rattled noisily up the street, loaded with supplies. That was part of what had drawn Henry back to To- nopah, after he'd finally "played his string out," as the old Com- stockers used to say in Goldfield. If Tonopah wasn't clotted with burros and prospectors and freight wagons the way he'd first seen it, at least it was still a real place, not fancied up for tourists like Virginia City. No strangers with maps and cameras cluttering up the sidewalks and pointing at things. Most everybody you met on Main Street had business there, which was the way Henry liked it to be. Tonopah was still a working town, done with silver mining maybe, but a supply center for ranches and mines in the country all around and a main stop on the highway south from Reno. The kind of place where Henry could keep his bearings, without feeling as if he was turning into the display in a lighted glass case in a museum.

"She ask why you went to Goldfield?" he said to Chester after a while. It was a question he had never put to Chester in all these years. To Henry's way of thinking, your reasons—your real reasons —were as much a part of you as your arm. Maybe that was why he didn't like this writer probing at him any better than he liked the doctor pressing and testing the hurtful places in his naked flesh. And why he never thought about his reasons any more than he thought about his other parts until something started aching. Like now.

"She asked why we come right enough," said Chester. "Told her Pap said we was goin', so we just up'n went."

"Did your dad figure on striking it rich there?"

"Don't know if he thought so big as all that. Don't b'lieve he hardly gave no thought to it at all. It come on him more like an itch. Everybody in Cripple Creek was goin' to Goldfield, and so was we. We was like geese flyin' south, or grasshoppers, or them ratty little creeturs that runs into the sea all in a bunch. We was just goin'. When folks was movin', Pap couldn't stay put."

A sudden thought struck him. "I should've thought quicker," he said, chuckling. "When she asked why we come, I should've said it was Wyatt. Now Wyatt wrote me this letter, see. He says, 'Chester, I'm in a tight spot, and I need your help real bad . . .'"

Henry wasn't listening. He was thinking about going to the gold rushes to make your fortune. That had made sense to people, when he told them the stories he'd read about the nabobs who made millions in the mining booms. John Mackay, who was nothing but a poor Irish miner when he started and came out of the Comstock with money to burn. Or Al Myers, so poor he had to hock his trunk before Goldfield turned him into a millionaire.

Mining booms were risky, of course. He'd admitted that, sitting at the kitchen table back in Iowa with the newspaper stories about Goldfield spread out in front of him. His father had listened, hurt darkening his eyes, while his mother sat with her handkerchief to her face. But when he explained how with no capital and a lot of hard work you stood a good chance of making a fortune in a gold rush, it sounded like a dollars-and-cents decision. A way to make money that they could understand if not approve. Almost logical.

What he couldn't tell his father, or the interviewer, or anyone else, was the yearning that had curled in the heart of a young man and left him wide-awake at night, staring at the forked shadows cast on his bedroom window by the old elm tree and thinking of the world out beyond the elm tree that he would never see. Not unless he cut himself loose from Altman & Son and all that was safe and familiar in the little town where he had grown up. He had spoken to his father of mining millionaires and dollars and cents because he couldn't talk about the truth, the secret wishes and the pictures in his head that couldn't come out in words. Pacing in his room at night, he had imagined himself riding through vast deserts and pitching his tent on the empty plain like the first explorers. The sun glittered on the icy peaks of the far Sierra. Hawks wheeled overhead. Herds of mustangs, sorrel, black, and white galloped through the canyons of purple mountain ranges. The spicy smell of sagebrush filled the air. The moon rose over silver sands by night as coyotes howled eerily in the distance, and mirages of impossible castles and gardens trembled over the horizon by day.

He would pause in his pacing to read the newspaper clippings he already knew by heart and look at the books about the West that stood stacked in the same spot on his bedside table where his mother had kept the Bible. The dream grew stronger by the day. He saw himself with his pants tucked into his boot tops in the miner's way striding into the saloons of an evening. He would listen to the stories the grizzled prospectors told, drink raw whiskey that smoldered like live coals in his belly, and throw his dice at a green table with adventurers from all the four corners of the world. He wouldn't care if he won or lost, and neither would anyone else. No trickle of whispers running through the neighborhood about what he did and what time he came home. No watchful eyes peeping out from behind the curtains. No more evenings spent in a parlor on a stiff little chair not half his size trying to make small talk and wondering if later on he might have the chance to hold a woman's hand.

The women in that saloon flickered through his daydreams, a bevy of beauties dressed in brilliant colors. They'd never worry about what was nice and proper or what folks might say, not if they had the grit to follow a gold rush. These would be the wild and wanton ones he could never meet at a church social in Iowa. He saw their gleaming naked shoulders. They had a way of moving to make a man stare and met the stares with bold eyes. Women whose touch could make a man's blood sing.

Gus, long before he knew her name.

Manitow and Ironhand

A Tale of the Stony Mountains

John Jakes

Dedicated to the memory of Karl May.

THE FREE TRAPPER, a strapping shaggy white man of indeterminate age, waded into his secret stream about a quarter mile above the wide beaver dam. His darting glance revealed no dangers; nor did he truly expect any, this far into the wilderness.

His buckskin shirt was wet, and soiled by many hasty meals. His buckskin leggings were stagged at the knees, where he'd sewn on pieces of fine English blanket, which wouldn't shrink. Leggings and his wool-lined moccasins were last year's tipi of a Crow chief of his acquaintance.

Shadows of quaking aspens and bending willows were growing longer. It was nearing the twilight hour, the ideal time for setting out traps. He would set this one, his fifth of the afternoon, then one more before returning to his campsite, there to rest until he rose before daybreak to clear the traps. He shifted his campsite nightly; a professional precaution of those who worked alone. Also, he now had eighty plews to protect—a valuable mixed bale of beaver, marten, and otter, weighing nearly a hundred pounds. So far the spring trapping season had been bountiful.

The late afternoon air was light and warm, but the water was still icy from the melted snows. The soft-burbling stream froze his bones and set his hands to aching, the good right one and the mangled left one he concealed with a filthy mitten except when he was at his trade, as now. He went by the name "Old Ironhand," though he really wasn't old, except in spirit. The snowy white streaks in his long hair were premature. There was a bitter cynicism in his eyes, the oldest part of him.

Once his name had been Ewing. Ewing Something. It was a name he no longer used, and struggled to remember. Ever since he'd split with the Four Flags outfit, and Mr. Alexander Jaggers— ever since they'd crippled his left hand, causing him to compensate with exercises that strengthened the other one, welding five digits into a weapon—to the free trappers and those who still gave allegiance to the large outfits, he was Old Ironhand.

He waded along, carrying the seven-pound trap and chain in his left hand, the pin pole in his right. He moved carefully, the small sounds of his passage undetectable because of the water's purl. This was a fine stream; he'd been working it for a year. It yielded fat mature beaver, fifty to sixty pounds each, with choice tails he charred, skinned, then boiled as a mealtime delicacy. Hip deep in his secret stream, he felt good as he approached a natural beaver slide worn into the bank at the water's edge. The shadowed air was sweet. The trees were a-bud, the mountain peaks pristine as a new wedding dress, the sky a pale pink, like a scene from a book about fairyland. He saw a mockingbird singing alertly on a bush. It was 1833, in the Stony Mountains, far from the civilized perfidy of other white men.

He laid the pin pole on the bank. He crouched in the water and lowered the trap to the bottom, drawing out the chain with its ring at the end. By now he was bent like a bow, half his beard immersed. The water smelled icy and clean.

He pushed the pin pole through the ring on the chain. Then he grasped the pole with both hands and began to twist it into the marly bottom. He leaned and pushed and twisted with his great right hand bloodless-white around the pole. If the trapped beaver didn't gnaw his paw off and escape—if he died as he should, by drowning—the pole would site his carcass.

In order to leave as little man-scent as possible, Ironhand worked obliquely backward toward the bank, to a willowy branch he'd already selected for its pronounced droop. He unstoppered his horn of medicine, which he compounded from secret ingredients added to the musky secretions of beaver glands, and with this he coated the end of the drooping branch. The strongly scented end of the branch hung near the pin pole.

Hands on his hips, he inspected his work. Though by now his teeth were chattering—the spring warmth was leaching from the plum-colored shadows—he was satisfied. Felt better than he had in a long spell. One more trap to place, then he'd have his supper, and a pipe.

He was turning to move on to the next location when the rifle shot rang out. The bullet hit him high in the back. Toppling, he thought not of the awful hot pain but instead of his failure to hear the rifleman stealing up for the cowardly ambush. *Careless damn fool! Should of kept your eyes skinned!* He was reasonably sure of his attacker's identity, but that wasn't much damn satisfaction as the muddy bank hurled up to strike him.

And that was all there was.

Someone had dragged him to level ground.

Someone had rolled him on his back.

Someone had built a fire whose comforting heat played along the left side of his seamed face, and the back of his ruined hand. The fire was vivid, shooting off sparks as brilliant as the mountain stars. A curtain of smoke blew away on a puff of breeze.

He elbowed himself to a raised position, clenching his teeth against the pain. The Samaritan was squatting on the other side of the fire. A young Indian, with a well-sculpted nose, firm mouth, light brown skin that shimmered bronze in the firelight. His glowing dark eyes were not unfriendly, only carefully, unemotionally observant.

Bluish-black hair hung like a veil down his back, to his waist. His costume consisted of moccasins ornamented with porcupine quills and bright trade beads, fringed leggings, a hunting coat of elk leather. Around his neck hung a small medicine bag that nestled inside his coat against his bare chest. Outside the coat, ornamentation was a three-strand necklace of bear claws. A double-barrel rifle rested within his reach.

"I put medicine on you. The ball is still there. It must come out. Do you understand?"

"Delaware," Ironhand grunted, not as a question. He understood perfectly.

"Yes." The Indian nodded. "I am Manitow."

"My pardner, the one they killed at the rendezvous two year ago, he was Delaware. Named after the great old chief Tammany. Fine man." So were most of the members of the tribe who roved the Stony Mountains. The Delaware had been driven from Eastern hunting grounds eighty to ninety years ago; had migrated over the Mississippi and successfully taken up farming on the plains. A few, more restless and independent, had pushed farther on to the mountains. Enemies of the Delaware, including ignorant whites, sneered at them as Petticoat Indians. That was not only stupid but dangerous. Ironhand knew the Delaware to be keen shots, excellent horsemen, superb trackers and readers of sign. They were honest; quick to learn; resourceful in the wilderness. You could depend on them unless for some reason they hated you.

The Delaware could find the remotest beaver streams as handily as a magnet snapped bits of iron to itself. Thus they were prized pardners of the free trappers, or prized employees of the outfits such as Four Flags.

The white man licked his dry lips, then said, "I'm called Old Ironhand."

"I have heard of you. Who shot you?"

"I think it was the Frenchman, *Petit Josep. Petit Josep Clair de Lune.* Little Joe Moonlight."

"Works for Jaggers."

"I worked for Jaggers . . ."

"I know that. Don't talk anymore. The ball must come out." In a calm, almost stately way, Manitow rose from his crouch. His hair shimmered, black as the seepage of one of the oil springs that produced the tar trappers like Ironhand rubbed on their arthritic joints.

Without being told, Ironhand rolled over to his belly. It hurt hellishly. In the firelight a long rustfree knife sparkled in Manitow's hand; an authentic Green River—Ironhand glimpsed the GR, *George Rex,* stamped into the blade in England. It was a knife as good as Ironhand's own, which he'd left with his possibles bag, his bale of plews, and his carbine, in what he'd presumed was a safe clearing upstream.

Manitow laid the knife on the ground. From a pocket in his coat he took the all-purpose awl most Delaware carried. He placed this beside the knife. One or the other, or maybe both, would mine for lead in Ironhand's back. The trapper stared at the implements with bleary eyes and made a heavy swallowing sound.

Manitow knelt beside him. With a gentle touch he lifted Ironhand's bloody shirt high enough to expose the wound glistening with smelly salve. With the fingers of his left hand Manitow spread the dark brown edges of the wound. A swift, sharp inhale from Ironhand was the only sound.

"Be sure you get it out," he said. "I don't want to go down with the sun. That bastard Jaggers has to pay. Little Joe Moonlight will pay. Go ahead, dig."

"I don't have whiskey," Manitow said.

"I don't need any whiskey," Ironhand said. "Dig."

A night bird trilled in the darkness. Old Ironhand listened drowsily. He was coming awake; hadn't died under Manitow's ministrations, which had hurt infernally. He had, however, fainted at the moment the Indian worked the rifle ball out of the wound with bloody fingers, ending the ordeal.

Ironhand's eyes fluttered open. Against a morning sky the color of lemons, Manitow crouched by the fire as he had the night before; a small dented pot, blue enamelware, sat in the embers.

A white mist floated on the high peaks. The air nipped; Manitow had found a colorful trade blanket as a coverlet for the trapper. Ironhand heard a nickering; tried to rise up.

"Your horses are safe, with mine," Manitow said. "Your gun and plews also." Small comfort, now that Ironhand realized the outfit was still after him.

Manitow stretched out his hand, offering a strip of *charqui,* the smoked buffalo meat that was a staple of frontiersmen. The trapper caught the meat between his teeth. He lay back, gazing at the sky, and chewed.

The enamel pot lid clinked when Manitow lifted it. "Coffee is boiling. Ready soon."

Ironhand grunted and kept chewing. A hawk sailed in heaven, then plunged and vanished in the mists. The cold ground smelled of damp and made him think of death, not springtime. On his back under his shirt, where the Indian had prospected for lead, a thick pad of some kind told him Manitow had improvised a dressing.

"You have been a trapper for many years," the Indian said in a reflective way.

Old Ironhand pushed the jerky into his cheek, like a cud, while he answered. "Twenty years next summer."

"All that time. And a man stalks you and you don't see any sign?"

"I wasn't looking for none."

"You didn't hear him?"

His anger was sudden, overriding his pain. "I was in the stream. It makes noise. I was thinking about my traps. I thought the outfit was done with me. Christ, they did me enough damage—why not?"

Manitow's grunt seemed to scorn that naive conclusion. The damn Indian made Ironhand uneasy with his quiet, unruffled manner. His air of wisdom annoyed and puzzled the trapper, because of Manitow's relative youth.

"Done with you?" Manitow repeated. "Not when the fur trade is sickly and you steal profits from the company by working for yourself and selling to others."

"You sure"—a gasp of pain punctuated the sentence—"seem to know a devil of a lot about me. How come?"

Ironhand's head was rolled to the side now; his old reddened eyes stared. Almost shyly, Manitow dropped his own gaze to the smoldering fire, from which he pulled the dented pot. He poured steaming coffee into Ironhand's own drinking cup.

"Help me sit up. Then answer my damn question."

There followed a slow and elaborate ritual of raising him, Manitow gently pulling on his forearms rather than pushing at his back. Resting on his elbows worsened Ironhand's pain again, but his position enabled him to suck some of the bitter hot coffee out of the cup Manitow held to his lips. At length the Indian said:

"The people in the Stony Mountains know Old Ironhand. They know the evil ways of Four Flags, too. For five winters and summers I have been north, Canada, hunting and trapping. Even so far away, we heard of the crimes of Four Flags. No more talk. Rest awhile now."

"I've got to go," the trapper protested, wriggling on his elbows and accidentally falling back, a terrific jolt that made him cry out. "Got to go," he repeated in a hoarse voice. "Catch that Little Joe . . ."

"In a day or two. No sooner."

The Indian's flat declaration angered the trapper again. Then a bolt of guilt struck him; he was being an ungrateful bastard. After licking a drop of coffee from his droopy mustache, he said, "I didn't thank you proper yet. For taking care of my wound and all. For coming along when you did. That was a piece of luck."

Manitow silently watched the ethereal mist drifting over the hidden peaks.

"Anyway—it's a debt I owe."

Manitow's eyes, black and opaque, met his again. "I am sorry I did not come in time to stop the assassin. Fortunately he was a bad shot."

"Little Joe has a big opinion of himself. I 'spect he thought he couldn't miss."

"And I was coming close, so he couldn't wait to find out. I was not far behind him, though approaching from a different direction. That's why I didn't see his sign, only heard his rifle. Until then I did not know there were two hunting you."

Confusion was followed by a stab of fear. "Two? Who else . . . ?"

Manitow stared.

"You? Why?"

"To see what kind of man you were. Are. I hold you responsible."

"For what?"

"The death of my brother. The one who was your partner."

Ah, Christ, Christ, Ironhand cried silently, stunned harder than he was when the rifle ball struck him. *He's no friend. He saved me for the pleasure of killing me himself.*

But there was no apparent hostility in the Indian's speech or demeanor. He merely asked the trapper to give him a brief history of the quarrel that had led to his brother's death, and the cowardly attack by the lackey of Four Flags.

"I'd have to go back a few years," Old Ironhand said. "The summer rendezvous of 'twenty-eight. I had quit as a brigade leader for the outfit a year before, but on good terms with Jaggers—we had an agreement that Four Flags would take all my plews and I'd work for no other." Four Flags was a fur company as big and powerful as Astor's. English, French, Russian, and American interests had pooled money to establish it. The boss west of St. Louis was Alexander Jaggers, who headquartered at Kirk's Fort.

The annual summer rendezvous was a combination trade mart and revel; a great gathering where spring plews were sold, and trappers bought new equipment pack-trained out from St. Louis, all in the midst of much drinking and horse racing and woman swapping and other familiar entertainments of the frontier. Manitow said that before he went to Canada he had come down from the Wind Rivers several times, to the barren and unlovely Upper Valley of the Green, there to take part in the rendezvous himself. Ironhand didn't remember meeting him, or hearing his name.

Speaking slowly, taking occasional sips of the cooling coffee, the trapper explained that it was at the summer rendezvous of 'twenty-eight that he saw his first black silk topper. A disreputable German merchant of traps, cutlery, and other metalware was wearing it. The hat was already hard-used, soiled by filthy stains and pierced by a bullet front and back. Ironhand had quickly understood it was the enemy when the peddler said:

"These they are wearing on the Continent now. Gents in the East are taking up the fashion. It's the modern style, beaver hats will go out, you mark me. Also my cousin in Köln writes me to say inventors are perfecting machines to manufacture fine felting cheaply from all kinds of materials, even paper. This trade will die. Is dying now."

The following two years confirmed it. In the great days, the high days of the trade, when Ironhand was still a brigade leader, the company paid as much as $9 a plew to certain free trappers to keep them working exclusively for Four Flags. By 1830 all was changed; average plews selling for $4 at St. Louis slipped to $3.75, no matter who trapped the animals. Then buyers at the summer rendezvous refused to go above $3.50. Ironhand was haunted by memories of the silk topper.

Alexander Jaggers was a short, prim Scot; a Glaswegian. A bachelor, his two passions were Four Flags and his religion. When he first came out to Kirk's Fort in 1822, he had transported a compact gleaming Philadelphia-made pump organ on which he played and sang Christian hymns in a stentorian voice.

In 1831 Jaggers spoke to Ironhand about the price of plews. They were still dropping. Every free trapper working for Four

Flags would have to accept $3, St. Louis, or further business was impossible. Ironhand refused.

Alexander Jaggers showed no visible anger, merely turned his back, swished up his coattails, sat at the organ, and began to play and sing "Saviour, Like a Shepherd Lead Us." But to bring Ironhand in line, discipline him, show him his error, Jaggers's henchman, Little Joe Moonlight, set on Ironhand's pardner at the summer rendezvous.

Little Joe, a mustachioed weasel-chinned fellow, turned up with a couple of the bravos who frequently backed his most brutal plays. They cornered Ironhand's pardner while the trapper was occupied with a comely Snake woman, the Snake women being universally conceded as the most attractive, and the most generous with their favors, of all the women of the many tribes.

Little Joe and his cronies pretended they were merely sporting with Tammany, hazing him, before the accident happened. As Ironhand learned afterward, Little Joe and his bravos seized the Indian's wrist and swung him round and round in circles, cracking his arm like a whip. Tammany tried to fight them but the odds were wrong; he was soon reeling.

One of the bravos knocked the bung from a small whiskey keg and poured the contents over the Delaware. The bravos and Little Joe roared. But they swore ever afterward that the dousing was supposed to be the end of it. How the stray ember from a nearby cook fire accidentally fell on Tammany, igniting the spirits, was a mystery. Damn shame, but a mystery. Little Joe and his bravos fled the rendezvous before Ironhand could catch up to them. Ironhand's pardner lived a day and a night, in broiled black agony, before the mercy of death.

Ironhand, who at the time still went by his old name, left the encampment at once. He rode night and day for Kirk's Fort, there to confront Alexander Jaggers, who never personally went to the rendezvous. Little Joe Moonlight had beaten Ironhand to the fort and was hovering in Jaggers's quarters when Ironhand, full of drink, kicked the door down and leaped on the Scot to strangle him.

"Little Joe whistled up his bravos," Ironhand said to Manitow. "They swarmed on me. Looking pious as a deacon, Mr. Jaggers said that in a spirit of Christian forgiveness, Little Joe would only break the hand I used least."

He held up the twisted crooked fingers; Manitow had removed the dirty mitten while he slept.

The misshapen claw was sufficient to suggest the scene: Little Joe's helpers knocking Ironhand to the floor, stomping him into a stupor. Little Joe slapping Ironhand's outstretched arm over a table while the bravos held fast to the groggy trapper's shoulders; the bravos had flung him to a kneeling position.

Gleefully, Little Joe raised a trade hatchet and smashed the blunt end of the blade on the outstretched hand. At the organ, his back turned to the mayhem, Mr. Jaggers pumped and sang.

> "We've a story to tell to the nations
> That shall turn their hearts to the right!
> A story of truth and mercy!
> A story of peace and light!"

Little Joe Moonlight grasped Ironhand's index finger, bent it and broke it. Then he broke the middle finger. Next the ring finger. After a few more blows with the now-bloody hatchet, he broke the little finger. To Ironhand's everlasting disgust, when Little Joe bent the thumb backward and that snapped, he screamed. More than once. Sweaty-cheeked, Mr. Jaggers pumped faster, and sang to drown the noise:

> "We've a song to be sung to the nations
> That shall lift their hearts to the Lord!
> A song that shall conquer evil
> And shatter the spear and sword!
> For the darkness shall turn to dawning . . ."

He remembered his hand lying on the table like a bloody red piece of buffalo hump. He remembered starting to swoon.

> "And the dawning to noonday bright!
> And Christ's great kingdom shall come on earth,
> The kingdom of Love and Light!"

Then Ironhand heard Little Joe, his voice very distant, as though he were shouting in a windy cave. "You don't need to play no more, Mr. Jaggers, he's all done screaming."

Little Joe lifted his head by the hair and let it fall, thump . . .

Out of some perverse piety that governed him, Mr. Jaggers

rushed Ironhand to a comfortable bunk in the fort barracks, and saw to it that he was given excellent treatment until he recovered his senses.

His hand, of course, was permanently maimed. This Mr. Jaggers totally ignored when he and Ironhand parted. Jaggers shook the trapper's right hand—the left was already concealed by the first of many mittens. "The account book is closed, laddie." It was not, but Ironhand was too enraged to do anything except glare. "We part as competitors, but eternal friends. Christ counsels forgiveness above all."

"Forgiveness," Ironhand muttered, waving his mitten in an obvious way. Mr. Jaggers merely beamed and pumped the other hand . . .

"That was two years back," Ironhand explained to Manitow in a weary voice. "After a while I came to believe his crazy cant about forgiving and forgetting. I wanted to mend my life, so I didn't take after him as I could have. I sold my plews to Astor, though they say he's tired of falling prices too and will get out . . . what a fool I was, wouldn't you say? Trying to get on with keeping alive, forgetting Jaggers?"

The spring sun had burned off the spectral mist; the snow peaks were brilliant against hazy lavender sky. Ironhand was exhausted from speaking. Manitow chewed on a strip of *charqui* and considered what he'd heard. At last he said:

"Many traps are set in this wilderness. You were caught in the cruelest of all. Trust."

And do I dare trust you, you ring-tailed savage? Not so far's as I could throw you. I daren't turn my back.

Still, there were necessities:

"Will you help me up? I have to pee."

"Clasp my arm with both hands."

Ironhand braced his boot heels and was slowly, painfully raised to standing position. His eyes were close to Manitow's a moment but he could read nothing there, except what he imagined was there—an intent to murder. The trap of trust, was it? Well, not a second time . . .

As he hobbled toward a grove of white birch trees, he bit out, "This time I won't turn my cheek. I'm going after that pissant who does the dirty work for Jaggers."

"I will go with you."

Ironhand twisted around, causing a hell-hot pain in his bandaged back. "Why? So's you can pass judgment?"

His face a smooth bronze mask, Manitow said, "It may be so."

I won't turn my back, you red devil . . .

But he hobbled on, grasping Manitow's arm for support; for the present he was at the mercy of the unavoidable necessities.

They rode southeast, the direction of Kirk's Fort. The fort stood sixty miles beyond the foothills of the Stony Mountains, at the confluence of two shallow muddy streams. It was the jumping-off place for St. Louis. Ironhand presumed it was also the destination of the quarry whose sign they were following. He was in constant pain, but it was bearable. Hate was a stronger painkiller than opium.

He trailed his three pack mules behind his old roan. Manitow could have sped ahead because he had a better horse, which he rode with only a scrap of blanket and his moccasined heels. The Indian's horse was small, with spots like swollen inkblots on his white rump. The trapper enviously compared his faithful but sorry saddle animal, Brownie, with the other horse, which the Cayuse tribe had bred and sold to the Indian. Cayuse and Nez Perce horses were the best a man could find. Ironhand had evidence of it the first morning. He woke in his odorous blankets to find Manitow gone. A distant drumming stilled his sudden alarm. Somewhere in the foothills Manitow was galloping his spotted horse.

Another thing bred envy, in the same dark inner place as Ironhand's suspicion of murder being planned: Manitow's skill with sign. The second noon, examining horse dung, Ironhand said, "He's near a day in front of us."

Manitow shook his head. "Less than half a day. Moving slowly. Not fearful he will be caught."

Ironhand's cheeks turned red above his beard that still held crumbs of ship's biscuit from breakfast. "Why'n hell not? He knows he didn't put me down for good."

"That may be so, it may not. I will show you why he doesn't worry." Manitow led him to a clump of stunted shrubbery, stepped around it, pointed. Ironhand saw more droppings. "There are three now. Your assassin and two more."

"Since when in hell—?"

"Sunset, yesterday."

"You damn well should of told me."

Manitow smiled. "It would have spoiled our supper. If I had told you then, would you have stopped this chase?"

"Not likely."

The Indian bobbed his head, vindicated.

They talked intermittently as they tracked Little Joe Moonlight and his companions moving southeast ahead of them. Manitow expressed no surprise at the treatment the trapper had received from Four Flags. "Theft, ambush, murder—it is the way of the strong companies against the single weak rebel. It is the way of those white men who are evil."

Which should have soothed Ironhand's suspicion a little, since it was clear from Manitow's voice and expression which side he favored. But Ironhand wasn't soothed. He continued to insist that Manitow ride ahead of him; they had sorted that out before they started. Ironhand still believed Manitow would try to murder him at the first opportunity.

They exchanged stories of their trials in the wilderness. Manitow pushed up the sleeve of his hunting coat to reveal a snake-like scar on his left forearm. Ironhand, who had seen plenty of horrors in his time, was nevertheless a little sick at the sight of the healed tissue, because of what had made it. Manitow had survived the bites of a rabid wolf, in the land of the Apaches, far south. He didn't explain why he had been in the land of the Apaches.

Ironhand told of nearly starving to death several times during his career. "I slew my mules and drank their blood once. I ate my moccasins twice. Another time, all I could find to feed on after five days was ants from an anthill." Manitow seemed to find these exploits unremarkable; almost to be expected.

He did express admiration for Ironhand's carbine. The trapper explained that it was a custom creation from the armory of the legendary Wyatt Henry of St. Louis. The revolving magazine, Henry's unique design, held five rounds.

Manitow asked to handle the piece. Ironhand said no. Manitow looked at him, and seemed to sneer just before he trotted his spotted horse ahead again.

As the mountains fell behind, the twisted gullies straightened; the shale ridges sank; the spring prairie rose up to greet them. They saw a migratory herd of buffalo passing southward in a dust cloud that boiled nearly to the apex of the sky. "Thousands upon thousands of shaggy brothers," Manitow said. Ironhand growled something under his breath; he already knew the herd was huge, they had been watching it the best part of an hour. The upstart savage was beginning to anger as well as worry him.

Or was it the sign they'd read—two unknown bravos and a third smug killer lolling their way toward Kirk's Fort without concern? Manitow insisted the trio was only a couple of hours ahead now.

A sunlit dust seemed to float above the silent plain surrounding them. The sky was tawny, like the earth, only a few cottonwoods with twisted shapes breaking the horizon. The vista had the serene quality of a landscape painting, but the diffuse light and dust gave it a touch of the unreal, like a picture from one of those fables of old Greek gods Ironhand dimly remembered reading from a hornbook when he was a child, in a civilized place somewhere.

At sunset they stopped to camp and eat. The trapper took some kindling from a parfleche strapped to a mule. Manitow watched him build a small pyramid of sticks, then said, "If you cook they will see the smoke."

"Hardly matters, does it? We'll find each other one way or another. That's the idea."

Late next day they approached a wide turgid stream Ironhand identified as Paint River, though the only artist's color represented in its flow was dirty brown. Natural features surrounding Kirk's Fort had been named by the fur men passing through.

While they watered and rested their animals, Ironhand advised the Indian that one more day would bring them to the headquarters of Four Flags. "I have to speed up. Leave the mules. Catch them before they're safe inside the fort."

"Even with three against you?"

Ironhand answered with a nod.

Manitow sighted ahead. "I will go on a little way."

He didn't ask permission, hitting his spotted horse with his heels and splashing on across Paint River. Ironhand hunkered down on the long narrow hump of an island in the middle of the water, where they'd pulled up. What the hell was the upstart savage about?

Manitow galloped away till he was a speck, then galloped back. He threw himself off his spotted horse, looking unhappy.

"One has gone on ahead, leaving two. Their tracks turn north. I think they saw the smoke and are circling back."

Ironhand's gaze crawled to stunted trees on the northern horizon. Nothing moved there, nor anyplace. Manitow said, "We should camp. I do not think you need to chase your enemy anymore. He will find you. He knows you are hurt. But he will think you are alone."

Ironhand scowled, gripping his Henry rifle with his powerful right hand. "I am. Isn't your fight."

"I am here, so it will be. There is no reason not to cook again. Have you any sticks left in the saddlebag?"

Ironhand slept badly, rolling around with his carbine clutched against his middle, the way he'd slept with it nightly since he met the prowling Indian. A new moon shed pale light on the plain, which was flat for miles in every direction save north, where a pronounced tilt raised the horizon. Along that horizon the crooked trees stood out. If there were a fight on this barren hump of island, would he have to look out for Manitow and Little Joe Moonlight at the same time? A threat of death from two directions . . . ?

He wished he could sleep but it was impossible. Manitow lay to his left, hands crossed on his shirt bosom, profile sharp in the pale moonshine. The Indian breathed softly, steadily, like a small boy sleeping without care.

He must have dozed. He woke to Manitow barking his name. Ironhand floundered to his knees, saw Manitow standing beyond the mules and pointing to the stunted trees. Two riders were pounding down the inclined plain, riding with their knees and reins in their teeth. Each held a brace of revolvers. Four guns against his one.

"Protect yourself," Manitow cried, diving under the belly of a snorting bucking mule. Seizing Ironhand, he tried to throw him to the ground. Little Joe Moonlight and his burly pardner were riding hell-bent for the hump island, but Ironhand refused to cower. He shook off the Indian and took his fighting stance with his carbine at his shoulder. His blood was up; he didn't care that he presented a perfect target.

The riders were closer. He distinctly saw Little Joe's mean white triangular face, his long Chinese-style mustaches, his leering smirk. Still short of the river bank, Little Joe and his pardner opened up with all four barrels. Ironhand stood his ground and squeezed his trigger. Manitow tackled him. Yelling, Ironhand toppled. Only the fall prevented one of the flying bullets from finding him.

He didn't realize this; all his anger was directed against the damned Indian. He screamed oaths, trying to get up as Little Joe Moonlight galloped into the stream, closely followed by his henchman. Manitow snatched his double-barrel rifle from its saddle loop. The blued metal flashed.

The charging horses tossed up fans of moonlit water. Little Joe passed to the left of Ironhand and the Indian, the henchman to the right. They were firing continuously. One of their bullets hit Manitow's rifle, a lucky shot that blew apart the breech. Manitow leaped back, momentarily blinded. A bullet hit Ironhand's left thigh just as he stood up. With a cry he fell a second time. The back of his head struck the earth. Stars danced.

The mules bucked and bellowed. Two of them tore their picket pins out and ran into the stream, braying. Ironhand heard the attackers splash to the bank of Paint River behind him and there wheel for another charge. His back wound, cruelly bruised by his fall, hurt nearly as much as the thigh wound bleeding into the leg of his hide trousers. He had to get up . . . *had* to. Tried it and, with a howl of despair and fury, fell back again. He heard the attacking horses coming on, in the river.

Standing over the wounded trapper, Manitow said, "Give me the rifle."

He'll use it to kill me . . .

"The rifle!"

Don't dare, I can't trust . . .

"White man, if you don't, we'll die."

There was a halo of hoof-driven dust around Manitow's head. He looked like some ghost of one of his primitive ancestors. His outstretched brown hand opened, demanding. "White man—*obey me!*"

The hoofs were thunderous. Risking all, the supreme act of trust, Ironhand flung the carbine upward and Manitow snatched it and put it to his shoulder. Bullets were flying again but Manitow stood firm and fired and kept firing. As the horse of Little Joe's henchman passed within Ironhand's field of vision, the trapper saw the nameless bravo lift in his saddle as if being jerked to heaven. The bravo's horse ran out from under him and he crashed and rolled into the brown water, staining it with blood from his open belly.

Ironhand was shouting without realizing it. "Stop firing, there are only five—"

Too late; some part of his brain had already counted five shots. Manitow had exhausted the magazine in one volley.

And Little Joe Moonlight, his long thin mustaches whipping against his cheeks, was unhurt.

He wheeled his horse in the water, making him dance to the island, then stand still while Little Joe raised his revolver with his shooting hand, clasped it with his other hand and pointed it at Manitow's head at close range.

It all happened quickly. Ironhand acted from instinct, coming upright, dizzy and tortured by pain but willing it not to matter. He leaped at Little Joe Moonlight and his prancing horse. Little Joe was angrily heeling the animal while trying to steady himself for the shot. Manitow crouched and pulled his knife to throw it but Little Joe would fire first. There was no cover to keep the Indian from death.

The horse sidestepped again; Little Joe screamed a filthy oath. He realized too late that his mount had sidestepped *toward* Ironhand . . .

Ironhand's face contorted into a bestial parody of a grin. His filthy mitten closed on Little Joe's right arm. Little Joe understood his peril and shrieked girlishly. Ironhand brought his huge right hand upward from his hip at great speed while pulling his enemy out of the saddle. The angle was right; the edge of the trapper's hand struck Little Joe's windpipe with speed and force.

Paralyzed, Little Joe dropped his revolver. Two streams of blood spurted from his nostrils. Ironhand threw Little Joe on the sere ground and knelt on his chest with one knee. He snatched his knife from the thong at his waist. Poised to cut Little Joe's throat, Ironhand started at a touch on his shoulder.

"Wait. Look at him. His spirit is gone. It flew before he touched the earth."

Ironhand changed position so that he could press an ear to his enemy's chest. He hunched that way for a long space, then raised his head, starting to shake from shock. Manitow was right again. The heart of Little Joe Moonlight had stopped.

Ironhand lurched up. His wounded leg would barely support him. His back was screaming with pain. He poked his knife at the thong loop on his belt and missed. He missed a second time.

Manitow took the knife from him and put it in place, giving the thong an extra twist to secure the hilt.

Ironhand raked a trembling hand through his dirty beard. "I—didn't want to give you the rifle."

"Why?"

"I knew you'd kill me after you saved yourself."

"Why?"

"Your brother—"

"The white man's mind," Manitow said with enormous disgust. "Don't you think I had a hundred opportunities to kill you before this?"

"But you said I was responsible—"

"That was before I met you. I wanted to learn what sort you are. I learned. You learned nothing, you were full of the poison bile of fear. You're like all the rest of the whites, even though not as bad as some. It's lucky you broke down and gave me the rifle or the story would end differently."

He stepped forward suddenly—it seemed menacing until Ironhand realized the true import. Then he felt a fool. Manitow supported his back and forearm gently. "Now you had better lie down before you fall down, white man." He no longer sounded scornful.

Stiff and sore in heavy bandages, Ironhand rode alone up the dirt track to the gate of Kirk's Fort. Draped in a U over the neck of his horse Brownie was the smelly corpse of Little Joe Moonlight.

Kirk's Fort was old and famous on the plains. It was a large rectangular stockade with a blockhouse at every corner. Cabins and warehouse buildings formed two of its walls. Ironhand passed through the palisade by the main gate, which opened on a long dirt corridor of sheds and shops. A second inner gate led to the quadrangle, where Indians were never admitted; all trading was done in the corridor, though even here there were precautions. Bars on the shop windows; iron shutters on the windows of the store-house that held trade goods.

A toothless fort Indian sat against the wall, looking sadly displaced in a white man's knitted cap and a white soldier's discarded blouse. He popped his eyes at Ironhand, whom he recognized. The trapper rode on through the second gate and straight across the trampled soil of the quadrangle to the Four Flags headquarters building. Company employees appeared around corners or from doorways of the accounting office, the strongbox room, the powder house, staring at Ironhand in a bewildered way. Someone called a greeting he didn't acknowledge. No one stopped him as he kicked the office door open and lumbered through, Little Joe's stiffening body folded over his shoulder, his Henry carbine tucked under his arm.

Alexander Jaggers was occupied with familiar things: his quill, his account books. Seeing the looming figure, he exclaimed, "Ewing! Laddie—what's this? Ye dinna hae the courtesy to knock or announce yersel—"

He was stopped by Ironhand slipping the Henry onto the seat of a chair, then laying the body of Little Joe Moonlight on top of the wide wooden desk. It disarranged the account books and overturned the ink pot, which dripped its contents on the old floor.

"He met with an accident. It happens often in the mountains," Ironhand said with a meaningful look at the master of Four Flags.

Jaggers reddened, puffing out his cheeks. He darted a hand to a drawer of the desk but Ironhand was quicker. He leaped on the desk, over Little Joe's corpse, and pushed Jaggers, toppling him and his chair at the same time. Jaggers flailed, kicking his legs in the air and yelling decidedly un-Christian oaths.

Ironhand jumped down and retrieved his Henry rifle from the chair. He took aim and emptied the revolving magazine, five rounds, into Mr. Jaggers's pump organ in the corner. After the roar of the volley, the organ exhaled once, loudly, like a man with pierced lungs gasping his last.

The trapper stepped to the pump organ and attacked its wood cabinet with his right hand. The hand beat and smashed like a hammer; a mace; a sledge. Thin veneers cracked and snapped. Jaggers was screaming and vainly trying to rise, but his fall had sprung some leg muscle, and each attempt was more futile than the last; he continued to wail on his back, heels in the air.

Ironhand locked his two hands together, the good with the ruined, and brought this huge hammer-head of flesh and bone down on the frame of the organ, breaking it in two as if it were a man's spine.

Jaggers screamed misery and rage.

Ironhand picked up his Henry and walked out without a backward look.

□ □ □ □

The daylight was waning too soon. Sunset was many hours away. But the sky and the prairie were dark, and the air was damp. Away in the north, thunder was bumping.

The dew and damp produced a ground mist that congealed and spread rapidly. As Ironhand rode to the cottonwood grove two miles west of the fort, he craned around in his saddle—at no small cost in pain—and saw the corner blockhouses floating above murky gray mist-clouds, like ogres' castles in the sky in a fairytale.

When he reached the grove, Manitow woke up, scratched his back, stood, asked:

"Where for you now?"

"Back to the mountains. Back to the beaver. It's the only trade I know. They aren't all wearing silk toppers in New York town yet, I wager."

Manitow paused before saying, "I know secret streams, Old Ironhand. Three or four, locked so far in the Stony Mountains you would never find them alone."

"Hmm. Well. Let's see. I'd like a pardner again. A free trapper needs a pardner. But I never paid your brother any sort of fee, like many do. We split what the plews brought in."

"That would be agreeable."

"If you think you can trust me not to cost you your life?" Ironhand asked, a sudden flash of sourness.

Manitow took it calmly; seriously. "The old Scot will trouble you no more, I think. But can you trust me?"

Ironhand's wreck of a face seemed to relax. "We crossed that river a while back."

Slowly, with graceful ceremonious moves, Manitow the Delaware drew from his waist his splendid long Green River knife. He held it out, handle first.

With equal ceremony, Ironhand took his equally fine knife from its thong. He held it out the same way. Among the men of the mountains, white and red, there was no more significant gesture of trust.

"Pardner."

"Pardner."

They exchanged knives. Manitow kissed the fingers of his right hand and raised them over his head in a mystical gesture. Ironhand laughed, deep and rumbling. They mounted up and rode away together into the storm.

AFTERWORD

The western writer Karl May probably did more to promote the splendor and excitement of the West to non-Americans than anyone except Buffalo Bill Cody, king of the scouts, the arena show and the dime novel. Yet not many fans of the genre, perhaps excluding specialist scholars, know of him.

Surely this is because Karl May was born in Saxony in 1842, wrote only in German, and visited America just once—four years before his death in 1912. By that time he had written seventy-four volumes, forty of them set in "the American Wild West."

May was decidedly an odd bird for this sort of missionary work. He knew about the West only through reading—some of which was done in prison. May was jailed four times in his early life, for assorted thefts and swindles. During his longest sentence, four years, he ran a prison library.

May's youth was hard. He was afflicted with spells of near-blindness. He came from what we would call a dysfunctional family. Of thirteen brothers and sisters, nine died.

When old enough, he entered a preparatory school for teachers. He was expelled for stealing. It didn't seem to teach him a lesson; other crimes—other incarcerations—followed.

But reading somehow turned him around, much as it turns around quite a few convict-writers. In 1875 Karl May published the first of his westerns.

His white hero had different names in different stories: Old Surehand; Old Firehand; Old Shatterhand. He was a *Westmänner* (Westman)—not a native frontiersman but a strong, suave, cultured European who quickly adapted to the rigors and perils of the West by means of intelligence and physical strength. Old Shatterhand possessed a "mighty fist" useful for dispatch of villains. But he also carried firepower, in the form of a fantastic repeating rifle custom-crafted by the "legendary" gunsmith, Mr. Henry of St. Louis. This *Henrystutzen* (Henry carbine) with its revolving chamber holding twenty-five rounds is not to be confused with the more familiar Henrys; there is no connection beyond the name.

Partnered with May's Surehand/Shatterhand character was a

young Indian, first introduced to readers around 1892. Winnetou is a consistently brave and brainy Apache chief educated by a Christian tutor, hence receptive to the "civilized" ways of Europe, and the white man with whom he adventures.

The two heroes wandered all over the map of the West, meeting again and again by remarkable coincidence, and removing an untold number of malefactors. In one historical quarterly, a scholar did a body count of four representative May novels totaling 2,300 pages. The number of persons going to their rewards was 2,012. They were dispatched by shooting, scalping, knifing, drowning, poisoning—and sixty-one were put down by the "mighty fist" previously cited.

May had a fair grasp of Western geography, except in one respect. In addition to familiar settings of mountains and deserts, he repeatedly used "an impenetrable cactus forest"—exact location unspecified.

May's works have been translated into many languages but seldom, if at all, into English. Yet they've sold upwards of fifty million copies, and continue to sell. You find long shelves of May in almost every bookshop in Germany, just as you find long shelves of L'Amour throughout the United States.

At least thirty films have been made from May's novels. An entire publishing house devoted to them was founded in 1913. At summer encampments similar to those of American Civil War reenactors, mild-mannered fans gather in costume to act out the exploits of their two heroes. Now doctoral dissertations are being written about Karl May.

So it seemed fitting, and an enjoyable challenge, to pay respects to him with a story about a couple of Westerners who battle a decidedly rotten crew from a fur trust. The story takes place in what May sometimes called the Stony Mountains.

I have used variations of the names of his two leading characters, and kept the marvelous repeating Henry (reduced to an arbitrary five shots). Those are the only resemblances. Ironhand is not a "blond Teutonic superman who speaks a dozen languages fluently and lards his conversations with little sermons about God and Christianity." Manitow is neither a chief nor an Apache. My intent was to create *un hommage* to an important figure in the literature of the West, not to write a pastiche of May's work, which I can't translate very well anyway with my rudimentary German. I

wanted a story bathed in a diffuse pastel-colored mist, like a legend.
A story not overly realistic. In short, the kind of western story
someone might have written from afar.

One other note: The hymn Mr. Jaggers sings is reverse anachro-
nism; it was composed years after the period of the story. But in
context, the lyrics proved irresistible.

—J.J.

About the Authors

Presently Director of Texas Christian University Press, JUDY ALTER, is the author of several novels, including the recently published *Libbie,* based on the life of Mrs. George Armstrong Custer. *Luke and the Van Zandt County War* (TCU Press) won the 1984 prize for juvenile literature from the Texas Institute of Letters, and *Mattie* (Doubleday, 1988) was named Best Western Novel of the Year by Western Writers of America, Inc. Her short story "Fool Girl" won a Western Heritage (Wrangler) Award from the National Cowboy Hall of Fame in 1993. She is a past president of Western Writers of America and currently secretary-treasurer of the Texas Institute of Letters. A native of Chicago, she holds an undergraduate degree from the University of Chicago and a Ph.D. in English, with a special interest in the literature of the American West, from Texas Christian University. A single parent of four now-grown children, she lists reading and cooking among her hobbies and likes to travel throughout the American West.

WIN BLEVINS brings authentic western flavor and style to his books and tales of America's last century. There's a laconic quality to his best work that reflects the times he writes about. Blevins has the same feel for his characters, who are always real, always individual, and always compelling. In the past few years, he has begun to build himself a real following among critics and readers alike. His books include *Give Your Heart to the Hawks* and *The High Missouri.*

ALBERT BUTLER has been a newspaper reporter, radio and TV copywriter, and has written two books for teenagers and five western/historical novels. He and his wife, Joan, live in Boise, Idaho, where he is presently at work on a long historical novel, *No Lion in the Path.* His books include *Get Judge Parker, Lockhart's Trail,* and *Three Rivers to Run.*

LENORE CARROLL's fiction is painted in many colors, some gentle, some not gentle at all. She has a particularly good sense of how people get along—or don't get along—in stressful moments, when the truth of them tends to come out. Her stories show us that there are many ways to recreate the old West—and the contemporary West, too. Lenore's is a provocative and singular literary voice.

LOREN D. ESTLEMAN may well be the best western novelist of his generation. Whether it is his masterpiece *Bloody Season* or his hardboiled and evocative Page Murdock series, Estleman is a formidable writer and stylist who accomplished more by age thirty-five than most writers accomplish in a lifetime. His growing number of fans will be happy to learn that, after an absence of nearly ten years, Page Murdock is returning to action. And Estleman hints that even larger historical western novels are also in the works.

JIM MARION ETTER, now of Oklahoma City, grew up during the 1930s and 1940s in the small eastern Oklahoma community of Oktaha, and since boyhood has loved storytelling flavored with the Old West and regional folklore. As a rural feature writer, he has roamed Oklahoma, mainly as a staff member of *The Oklahoman* newspaper, and some of Texas, where he has also lived. Books he has authored or co-authored include *Between Me & You & the Gatepost—Rural Expressions of Oklahoma, Duaghters of the Land, The Salt of the Earth,* and *Oktaha, a Track in the Sand.* His articles have appeared in such magazines as *Persimmon Hill, Western Horseman, Cowboy, The Ketch Pen, Frontier Times, True West,* and *Oklahoma Today.* He rides his own horse regularly, and claims to have done "a little amateur rodeoin'."

RILEY FROH was born in Luling, Texas, where he grew up in the 1950s around ranch people very similar to the characters in his short story. He is descended from original settlers of the town. His great-grandfather drove cattle up the trails and his great-great-grandfather was a noted Texas Ranger. He holds a Bachelor's and a Master's degree from Southwest Texas State University and a Ph.D. from Texas A&M University, and presently teaches Texas history at San Jacinto College. He is the author of *Wildcatter Extraordinary, Edgar B. Davis and Sequences in Business Capitalism,* and several scholarly articles on Texas themes. He is married to Mary Binz of San Antonio, Texas, whose father was well known in the Alamo City as a horse trainer and trick rider. Their son, Noble King Froh, continues the cowboy tradition of both families.

ROBERT GLEASON is presently Editor-in-Chief of Tor/Forge Books in New York. And he is also an important writer of serious fiction both in and out of the western genre, as his forthcoming major novel, *The Wrath of God,* will amply demonstrate. In western fiction, Gleason created the Jackson Cain cycle of novels, which take a balladic approach to the Old West of both myth and fact. Hopefully, these novels will be reissued soon. They fall on the ear like music, and are damned good reads besides. There is nothing else like them in all of western fiction.

Bill Pronzini said of ED GORMAN's Leo Guild westerns, "[They] have a haunting, almost mystical quality that lifts them to the brink of allegory." In addition to the five novels about bounty hunter Guild, Gorman has also written four other westerns, notably *Wolf Moon*, about which *Reflections* said, "If Jim Thompson had ever written a pure western, this would have been it." When Gorman submitted this story, he noted that he'd always wanted to write something for the 1940s pulp *Dime Western* and that this story would have been perfect for them.

MARTIN H. GREENBERG is a veteran anthologist who has edited or coedited over five hundred books—more than fifty of them in the western field, including *The Western Hall of Fame, The Arbor House Treasury of Great Western Stories,* and *In the Big Country*. He resides in Green Bay, Wisconsin.

After forty-five years in journalism, mostly as corporate communications specialist with such firms as Ford Motor Company in Ohio and Michigan and the NASA/Caltech Jet Propulsion Lab (JPL) in Pasadena, California, R. C. HOUSE "retired" at sixty-five to write westerns full-time. He has eleven novels and an Old West collectibles book published or in production, as well as an estimated two hundred magazine credits in short western fiction, book reviews, essays, columns, and articles on western history, collecting, and shooting muzzleloaders, and the hobby of "buckskinning." A member of Western Writers of America since 1976, he has been WWA president and editor of the association magazine, *Roundup*. An asteroid has been named for him, the tribute of its discoverer, a JPL astronomer and close friend, for his JPL contributions. The House family makes its home on acreage in rural Fallbrook, North San Diego County, California.

Americans love success stories, and few success stories—rags to riches, as it were—match that of JOHN JAKES. Following a long career in advertising, during which he wrote innumerable novels and short stories, Jakes found his literary fortunes waning. He was reduced to writing a movie novelization for very modest money. Then, in the mid-1970s, he was commissioned to write The American Bicentennial Series and very quickly became one of the world's bestselling authors. Jakes has written virtually every kind of fiction, and excelled at all of them, but the western seems to bring out his best work and most passionate feelings. He is particularly good with the characters common to the American frontier.

The transition may or may not have been inevitable, but TEDDY KELLER, who was born and raised in Kansas and lived for years in Colorado and New Mexico, gravitated naturally to the lives and legends of the West. His stories have appeared in many publications and have been anthologized and reprinted from Australia to Germany. He still feuds with editors who are certain that the Old West was unrelentingly earnest.

ELMER KELTON has brought realism, scope, depth, and almost operatic feeling to the serious novel of the West. He has chronicled the vagaries of his beloved Texas with a passion and fondness that imbue his work with humor, heart, and hard prairie wisdom. Among his many succesful novels are *The Time It Never Rained, The Day the Cowboys Quit, The Wolf and the Buffalo, The Good Old Boys,* and *The Man Who Rode Midnight.* He is a seminal figure in western fiction.

ARTHUR WINFIELD KNIGHT has worked in a number of genres, veins, and styles, doing especially notable work with his reminiscences of significant people in the Beat literary movement of the late fifties and early sixties. He has a true sense of the Old West, and is able to convey it in prose that is always a pleasure to read.

RUTH WILLETT LANZA, born and raised in Oklahoma, has lived with her husband in Colorado since 1947. She attended Lindenwood College and Oklahoma University, and began writing seriously after raising six children. Specializing in southwestern history, her articles have appeared in regional and national magazines. Her short fiction placed first in a recent NLAPW State Contest and has been published in *American Humane Magazine* and *The Rampant Guinea Pig.* She's now at work on a novel, *A Vision in the Wind,* about the Ute Indians of Colorado. "The Leave-taking" was inspired by her maternal grandmother, who was an Oklahoma 89'er.

ELMORE LEONARD spent many years writing books that only a small audience was aware of. From his beginning in the pulps of the early 1950s, it was clear that Leonard had his own literary voice, and planned on doing things his own way. While he has become a worldwide bestseller known for his blackly comedic hardboiled crime stories, a number of critics feel that his best work has been done in the western genre—and such novels as *Hombre, Valdez Is Coming,* and *Gunsights* make it hard to dispute. The majority of readers seem to think he's a master of both genres, and that's probably a truer assessment.

JOHN D. NESBITT lives in the plains country of Wyoming. He teaches English and Spanish at Eastern Wyoming College in Torrington. His western stories have appeared in *Far West, Just Pulp,* and others; his modern West stories have appeared in *West Wind Review, American Literary Review,* and others. His fiction, nonfiction, poetry, and literary articles have appeared in numerous literary magazines. He has won many prizes and awards for his work, including a Wyoming Arts Council literary fellowship for his fiction writing. A western novel, *One-Eyed Cowboy Wild*, is forthcoming from Walker and Company.

JOYCE ROACH is a three-time Spur Award Winner from Western Writers of America: nonfiction book, *The Cowgirls*; short nonfiction, "A High Toned Woman;" and short fiction, "Just as I Am," and was the recipient of the Texas Institute of Letters $5000 nonfiction book prize for *Eats: A Folk History of Texas Foods*. She has served as chairman of both the WWA Spur Awards and the Owen Wister Award.

GORDON D. SHIRREFFS is one of the grand old names of traditional (and not-so-traditional) western fiction. A particular favorite of paperback original readers, Shirreffs has spent many decades bringing resolute historical truth to the novel of the West, and doing so with high and colorful style. His many novels include *The Untamed Breed*, considered by many to be his masterpiece—and one of the true masterpieces of mountain man literature—*Showdown in Sonora, Gunswift* (as Stewart Gordon), and *Rio Desperado*.

"Frontier Birds" marks LINDA SPARKS's debut into the realm of fiction. After twenty-five years of service with the federal government, she followed her heart to the West. More than a hundred of her articles about dogs have appeared in specialized magazines, and in 1991 she was published in *Western Horseman*. That same year she decided to try her hand at fiction. Linda currently lives with her husband and five dogs in a log house in the Rockies. Her current project is a four-volume fictional history of the Ax T ranch and the four generations of Thorndikes and Burnums, who look back fondly on Cat and Harry Burnum.

DALE L. WALKER has distinguished himself both as a critic and a creator of serious and innovative western fiction. When the dust settles on our particular era of western stories, the reviews and criticism of Dale Walker will be among the work passed on to succeeding generations. His fiction will likely accompany his reviews because he applies his rigid critical standards to his own stories as well, as his story here demonstrates.

Bestselling author and lecturer MARIANNE WILLMAN has won both popular and critical acclaim for her work. She has published both fiction and nonfiction, including guest columns and book reviews for the *Detroit Free Press*, and her twelve historical novels have been sold in twenty-six countries around the globe. Her first western novel, *Pieces of Sky*, received the Reviewer's Choice Award and was named as one of the ten all-time best western historical romances by *Rave Reviews*.

Yesterday's Shadows was also honored by the Reviewer's Choice Award, and Marianne was a contributor to the WWA anthology, *The West That Was*. She co-authored three screenplays currently in preproduction, and her newest novel, *The Court of Three Sisters*, was published by HarperCollins in April 1994.

An adjunct professor of political science at the University of Nevada in Reno, SALLY ZANJANI has published numerous articles on Nevada history and four nonfiction books. *The Ignoble Conspiracy: Radicalism on Trial in Nevada*, with Guy L. Rocha (1986), was largely responsible for posthumous pardons granted to Goldfield union radicals Morrie Preston and Joseph Smith in 1987, eighty years after their conviction. Her most recent book, *Goldfield: The Last Gold Rush on the Western Frontier* (1992), won the Westerners International Award.

Acknowledgments